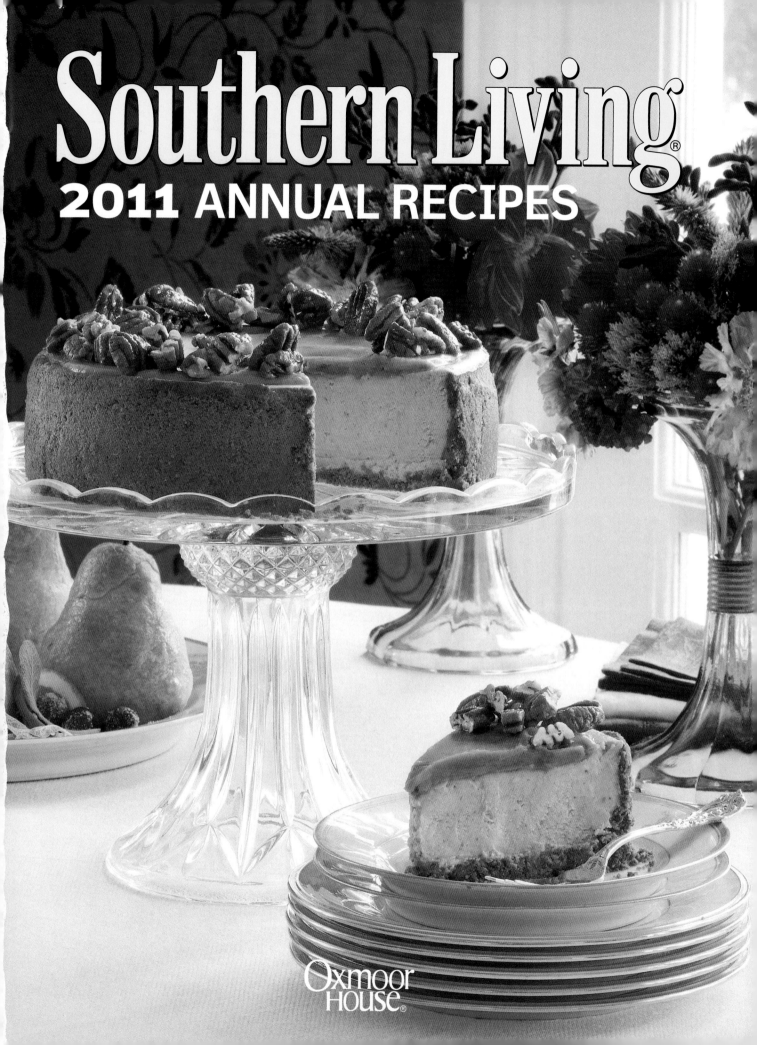

Southern Living®
2011 ANNUAL RECIPES

Oxmoor House®

Best Recipes of 2011

Not all recipes are created equal. At *Southern Living,* only those that have passed muster with our Test Kitchen staff and Food Editors—not an easy crowd to please—make it onto the pages of our magazine. Members of our Food staff gather almost every day to taste-test recipes to ensure not only that they're reliable, but also that they taste as good as they possibly can. Here we share this year's favorites.

Muffuletta Dip ▶ *(page 40)* Olive salad and Parmesan cheese serve as the base for this versatile dip that pairs well with crostini or tossed with a Caesar salad.

Nashville-Style Hot Catfish
(page 43) Habanero hot sauce adds a dash of heat to this crispy fried catfish.

▲ **Baked Smokin' Macaroni and Cheese** *(page 32)*
A sprinkling of ground red pepper and smoked ham adds a
new take on this traditional comfort food. With four cheesy
variations, you're sure to say, "More mac and cheese, please!"

Luscious Orange Panna Cotta *(page 28)*, not pictured,
A bright dose of citrus livens up this rich, silky custard.

Orange Mimosa Marmalade *(page 30)*, not pictured,
Oranges and sparkling white wine combine in this deliciously
sweet marmalade, perfect for spooning over hot biscuits.

Lime-Cornmeal Cookies *(page 31)*, not pictured,
Cornmeal lends a crisp, crunchy texture to these
distinctively Southern cookies.

Cappuccino-Walnut Toffee *(page 56)* Instant espresso, walnuts, and chocolate team up in this irresistible candy creation.

Blue Cheese "Hot Wing" Dip *(page 38)*, not pictured, Paired with fried chicken tenders, celery sticks, or radishes, this creamy dip is the perfect snack for game day.

Warm Artichoke-Shrimp Dip *(page 40)*, not pictured, Canned artichokes and cooked shrimp make for a quick-and-easy crowd-pleasing appetizer.

Lemon Aïoli *(page 46)*, not pictured, Much better than ordinary mayonnaise, Chef Mike Lata's recipe is a perfect dipping sauce for roasted oysters, vegetables, or other seafood.

The Fat Elvis and Peanut Butter Spread *(page 116)*, not pictured, This luscious peanut butter-banana-bacon ode to the King won a blue ribbon at Knoxville's International Biscuit Festival.

New Orleans Beignets *(page 60)* These light and tender pastries deliver a taste of the "Big Easy" to your own kitchen.

Amaretto-Almond Pound Cake and Amaretto Glaze *(page 73)* Glazing this cake while still hot makes for a decadent, moist treat sure to satisfy your sweet tooth.

▲ **Key Lime Pound Cake** *(page 75)* This sweet-tart cake combines the flavors of two classic desserts into one new favorite.

Peach Melba Shortbread Bars *(page 81)*, not pictured, Be the hit of the bake sale with these bars that boast an ideal balance of chewy-gooeyness and crunch thanks to a sprinkle of almonds.

Buttermilk Custard Sauce *(page 72)*, not pictured, A drizzle of this delectable sauce elevates traditional pound cake to a new level.

Sweet Tea Tiramisù *(page 102)*, not pictured, Substituting sweet tea in place of coffee makes for a distinctively Southern take on this Italian classic.

Peach-Pecan Muffins *(page 69)*
Pecans and peaches dress up a
truly Southern muffin that's
perfect any time of the day.

Bing Cherry Salad *(page 69)*
This traditional gelatin salad is sure to evoke
a sense of nostalgia with its tasty simplicity.

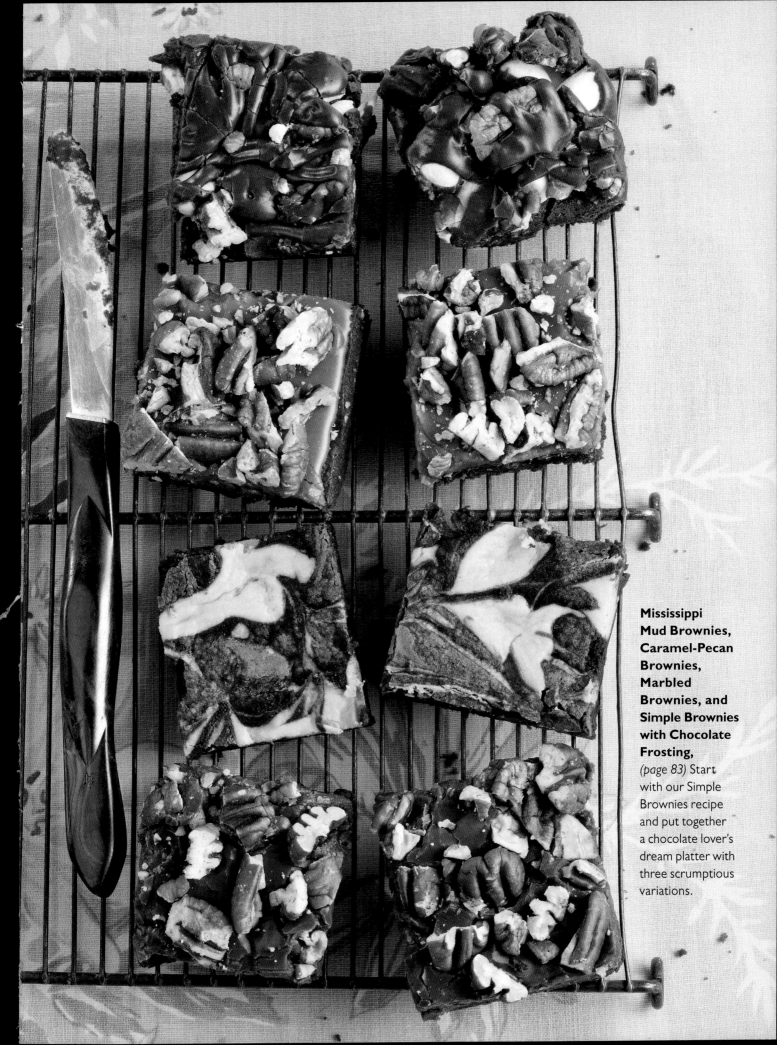

Mississippi Mud Brownies, Caramel-Pecan Brownies, Marbled Brownies, and Simple Brownies with Chocolate Frosting, *(page 83)* Start with our Simple Brownies recipe and put together a chocolate lover's dream platter with three scrumptious variations.

▲ **Classic Parmesan Scalloped Potatoes** (page 92) Buttery Yukon gold potatoes and Parmesan cheese combine in this heartwarming casserole.

Lemon Meringue Ice-Cream Pie (page 194), not pictured, Bursting with bright citrus flavor, this pie is a cool and refreshing treat on a hot summer afternoon.

Balsamic-Plum Preserves (page 206), not pictured, Sweet plums and balsamic vinegar create a mouthwatering topping for turkey, pork, or Brie cheese that you can make in the microwave.

Mocha Ganache (page 193), not pictured, Get your chocolate fix with this quick-and-easy three-ingredient topping.

Roasted Turkey with Béarnaise Butter (page 250), not pictured, Instead of traditional gravy this Thanksgiving, try serving this buttery variation of Béarnaise sauce that will have your family asking for turkey year-round.

Caramelized Pear Cannoli with Praline Sauce (page 236), not pictured, Roasted pears and a warm sauce make this delicious twist on traditional cannoli an ideal make-ahead fall treat.

Sweet Tea-Brined Chicken *(page 101)* The guests at your next barbecue will never guess that the secret ingredient in this delectable chicken is the South's signature beverage—sweet tea.

Grilled Shrimp Salad with Sweet Tea Vinaigrette *(page 100)* Shrimp, grilled sweet peaches, and a dressing made with—you guessed it—sweet tea combine to make this quintessential summer salad.

Chicken-and-Tortellini Salad
(page 125) Thirty minutes is all it takes to whip up this bright and refreshing pasta dinner.

Kentucky Benedictine Tea Sandwiches
(page 124) Be a star hostess with these easy, breezy finger sandwiches.

▲ **Bacon-Parmesan Tassies and Gorgonzola-Grilled Pear Crostini** *(pages 124-125)* Perfect for a backyard summer party, these no-fuss appetizers are sure to impress.

Apple-Pear Salad with Maple-Pecan Bacon *(page 233)*, not pictured, Bacon has a sweet side thanks to a coating of maple syrup in this salad rich with fall's bounty.

Pecan Clusters *(page 232)*, not pictured, The combination of pecans, chocolate, and caramel will have you coming back for seconds (or thirds) of these irresistible candies.

Hot Cider Nog *(page 274)*, not pictured, Welcome guests with this creamy combination of two favorite holiday drinks.

Fried Confetti Corn *(page 255)*, not pictured, Crispy, crunchy bacon is the perfect topping for this colorful and creamy corn sensation.

Mama's German Chocolate Cake *(page 230)*, not pictured, One taste of this luscious chocolate cake topped with rich Coconut-Pecan Frosting and you'll see why this recipe has been a favorite for generations.

▲ **Lowcountry Shrimp-and-Okra Pilau** *(page 211)*
Pronounced "perl-loo," this rich, savory Charleston favorite inspires a taste of the Lowcountry.

Pear Dumplings *(page 259)*, not pictured, Ginger is the secret ingredient in the zesty sauce that tops these darling dumplings that are just as tasty as they are pretty.

Blackberry-Apple Pie and Cranberry-Apple Pie *(page 258)*, not pictured, These two variations of the all-American apple pie will bring to mind old memories as well as inspiring new ones.

Pumpkin-Pecan Cheesecake and Sweet Potato-Pecan Cheesecake *(page 258)*, not pictured, Three holiday classics converge in these delectable desserts sure to please everyone at your table.

Chocolate-Pecan Chess Pie *(page 257)*, not pictured, Dark and rich, this intensely chocolaty pie is one of the best we've ever tasted.

Sour Cream Pocketbook Rolls *(page 256)*, not pictured, Take two of these light and feathery favorites before they disappear.

Okra-Shrimp Beignets *(page 212)*
Studded with okra, peppers, and shrimp,
these beignets are anything but ordinary.

▲ **Apple-Cream Cheese Bundt Cake** *(page 214)* A rich cream cheese filling and praline frosting make this cake an indulgent delight to welcome autumn.

Fresh Applesauce *(page 217)*, not pictured, A variety of fresh apples highlights this healthy fall harvest treat.

Lemon Curd Pound Cake and Lime Curd Pound Cake *(page 260-261)*, not pictured, Perfect for entertaining, this quintessential Southern cake gets a zesty zing from the addition of citrus.

Mocha-Apple Cake with Browned Butter Frosting *(page 216)*, not pictured, This melt-in-your-mouth showstopper gets a boost of richness from a dose of creamy, buttery frosting.

Coffee-Chocolate Ice Cream *(page 136)*, not pictured, Ice cream lovers rejoice with this low-calorie concoction that's sure to have you coming back for more.

Tiny Tomato Tarts *(page 264)*, not pictured, These miniature versions of the traditional recipe are the ultimate party fare for nibbling while mingling.

Our Year at
Southern Living®

Dear Food Friends,

Much like a family, our *Southern Living* staff gathers at the table every day to enjoy new recipes from cooks across the South. Our purpose: to taste, review, and thoughtfully select each dish to bring you delicious ideas for everyday cooking, casual entertaining, and special occasions. Though a tough (but tasty!) job, we remain committed to giving you kitchen-tested recipes that reflect today's Southern palate, while at the same time honoring the traditions that have been passed down through generations of fabulous cooks.

Our Food Staff has been hard at work, creating recipes, photographs, and stories that fill these pages and embody the soul of the South. Our column "Mama's Way or Your Way?" continues to pass down time-honored dishes from mothers and daughters across the region, offering recipes that appeal to beginners and pros. For busy families, our column "Quick-Fix Suppers" makes weeknight cooking a breeze with fast prep, smart tips, and our best supermarket shortcuts. And because "Southern" doesn't always have to mean a pound of butter or cup of bacon grease, we continue to bring you healthier, just-as-delicious versions of your down-home favorites in "Lighten Up!" for a healthy balance.

> *"Our purpose: to taste, review, and thoughtfully select each dish..."*

Southern Living turned forty-five this year, and, as we celebrate this milestone, we hope you enjoy this delicious collection from our kitchen to yours. Join us as we pay tribute to the traditions and the recipes born from the pride of place we hold so dear. Thanks for inviting us into your homes, and I look forward to hearing from you and seeing more of your recipes soon.

Sincerely,

Shannon

Shannon Sliter Satterwhite
Food Director

ISBN-13: 978-0-8487-3487-9
ISBN-10: 0-8487-3487-4
ISSN: 0272-2003

Printed in the United States of America
First printing 2011

To order additional publications, call 1-800-765-6400.

For more books to enrich your life, visit **oxmoorhouse.com**

To search, savor, and share thousands of recipes, visit
myrecipes.com

Cover: Chocolate Velvet Cake with Cream Cheese Frosting,
page 330
Page 1: Pumpkin-Pecan Cheesecake, page 258; Pear Dumplings,
page 259

Southern Living®

Editor: M. Lindsay Bierman
Managing Editor: Candace Higginbotham
Art Director: Chris Hoke
Executive Editor: Rachel Hardage
Food Director: Shannon Sliter Satterwhite
Test Kitchen Director: Rebecca Kracke Gordon
Senior Writer: Donna Florio
Senior Food Editors: Shirley Harrington, Mary Allen Perry
Recipe Editor: JoAnn Weatherly
Assistant Recipe Editor: Ashley Arthur
Test Kitchen Specialists/Food Styling: Marian Cooper Cairns,
    Vanessa McNeil Rocchio
Test Kitchen Professionals: Norman King, Pam Lolley,
    Angela Sellers
Editorial Assistant: Pat York
Senior Photographers: Ralph Anderson, Jennifer Davick,
Senior Photo Stylist: Buffy Hargett
Assistant Photo Stylist: Amy Burke
Copy Chief: Susan Emack Alison
Assistant Copy Chief: Katie Bowlby
Copy Editor: Ashley Leath
Production Manager: Mary Elizabeth McGinn
Assistant Production Manager: Christy Coleman
Production Coordinator: Paula Dennis
Photo Research Coordinator: Ginny P. Allen

Oxmoor House

VP, Publishing Director: Jim Childs
Editorial Director: Susan Payne Dobbs
Creative Director: Felicity Keane
Brand Manager: Daniel Fagan
Senior Editor: Rebecca Brennan
Managing Editor: Laurie S. Herr

Southern Living® *2011 Annual Recipes*

Editor: Susan Hernandez Ray
Photography Director: Jim Bathie
Senior Photo Stylist: Kay Clarke
Test Kitchen Director: Elizabeth Tyler Austin
Test Kitchen Professional: Catherine Steele
Senior Production Manager: Greg A. Amason

Contributors

Designer: Nancy Johnson
Copy Editor: Donna Baldone
Proofreaders: Adrienne Davis, Barry Smith
Indexer: Mary Ann Laurens
Index Copy Editors: Catherine Fowler, Dolores Hydock
Editorial Interns: Jessica Cox, Laura Hoxworth,
    Alison Loughman

Contents

Favorite Columns

Each month, we focus on topics that are important to our readers—
from delicious menus to healthy options to handy tips for almost anything.

LIGHTEN UP!

♥ Gooey macaroni and cheese satisfies as a side dish but can wreak havoc on your waistline. These lightened recipes use less butter and cheese but still provide the comfort-food creaminess that you crave. Plus, twists like smoked ham and gouda or sweet peas and prosciutto take this dinnertime staple to the next level (page 32).

♥ Love lasagna? Then you'll be quick to add this lighter version to your go-to recipes. Chock-full of zucchini, mushrooms, and peppers, this entrée will fill up the family on a Meatless Monday without weighing you down with extra calories (page 59).

♥ Take the Big Easy home with this low-fat version of Red Beans and Rice, complete with smoky andouille chicken sausage. Plus, work some more fiber and protein into your diet with inexpensive red beans (page 70).

♥ Despite the carrots in carrot cake, this dessert favorite tends toward the unhealthy side. With our healthier Layered Carrot Cake recipe, you still get the tender cake chock-full of grated carrots and crushed pineapple and delectable cream cheese frosting—you just don't get the guilt (page 87).

♥ Satisfy your sweet tooth with a healthier Lightened Vanilla Bean Ice Cream perfect for the summer months ahead. Plus, we've tried out some stellar flavor variations, including Cherry-Bourbon and Key Lime Pie, that will have your homemade ice cream rivaling the big names in the freezer aisle (page 136).

♥ Summer's fresh yellow squash doesn't need to be smothered in cream and butter to make a top-notch side dish—just try our Lightened Squash Casserole and enjoy the covered-dish classic sans regret. Also, learn to use squash in other tasty, interesting ways like Fresh Squash Chips (page 156).

♥ In this special section, we show the health-conscious cook how to revamp Southern favorites without sacrificing the traditional tastes you know and love. From hearty Turnip Greens Stew and Oven-Fried Chicken to creamy, dreamy Key "Light" Pie, you will be able to show off your Southern heritage and your figure with ease (page 218).

MAMA'S WAY OR YOUR WAY?

♥ Keep Super Bowl party guests warm with a steaming bowl of chili. Cater to carnivores with Mama's rich, beer-infused Game Day Chili or feed a flock of vegetarians with bold Big-Batch Veggie Chili. Cook and serve it in a heavy-bottomed Dutch oven for both style and convenience (page 34).

♥ A perennial favorite, Chicken Pot Pie hits the spot with its classic combination of chicken, veggies, and savory sauce. The Double-Crust Chicken Pot Pie provides an impressive presentation at a dinner party and a scrumptious from-scratch cream sauce. On a weeknight, serve up Stovetop Chicken Pie over a base of biscuits, cornbread waffles, or wild rice (page 54).

♥ No dinner party spread could be complete without a delicious, starchy side. For a buttery casserole, try Classic Parmesan Scalloped Potatoes rich with cheese and flavored with garlic. Scalloped Sweet Potato Stacks bring together modern presentation and the unique combination of sweet potatoes, mozzarella, and thyme for a knockout result. Either recipe will be sure to earn you praise from around the table (page 92).

♥ Rejoice in the sweet, succulent summer tomato harvest with these two recipes that are bursting with seasonal flavor. Mama's Tomato Pie features a homemade Sour Cream Pastry for a traditional pie that looks right at home on a gingham tablecloth. The easy-to-serve Herbed Tomato Tart works great as an appetizer, sure to lure guests with its delectable herbal aroma and get gobbled up quickly (page 204).

♥ For this mother-daughter duo, grilled chicken is anything but ordinary. Mama's Chicken Under a Skillet bursts with juiciness and flavor flecked with fresh herbs. Tangy, tasty Spicy Honey-Lime Grilled Drumsticks use sharp lime and cilantro to full effect for an update on this classic (page 238).

♥ Serve up some retro-chic appetizers like Marinated Shrimp-and-Artichokes and Cheese Ring with Strawberry Preserves at your big holiday bash (page 262).

SOUTHERN HOSPITALITY

♥ Need to throw a showstopping shower in less than an hour? These recipes work for a bridal brunch, baby shower, or ladies luncheon: the winning combination of fragrant Tomato-Herb Mini Frittatas and luscious Gouda Grits suits all of these soirees. (page 84).

♥ South meets Southwest in our Cinco de Mayo celebration. Pork in tostadas, beer in margaritas, and bourbon in our spicy Iced Mexican Chocolate Sipper are just some of the creative surprises sure to guarantee a fun and festive party (page 106).

♥ Fourth of July promises fireworks, fun, and, most important, food! Serve our stress-free menu for a surefire combination of great taste and good times. All-American Smoky Chicken Barbecue Kabobs, heat-infused Grilled Jalapeño-Lime Corn on the Cob, and creamy, fruity Ice-Cream Floats cover the picnic table that we have also helped you decorate (page 148).

♥ Savor this seasonal menu bursting with a cornucopia of fall's best flavors. Guests can sip on Sparkling Autumn Chianti and nibble on artful Cheddar-Pecan Shortbread Leaves. Serve an impressive Smoked Paprika Pork Roast with Sticky Stout Barbecue Sauce and desserts rich with autumn's harvest of figs and pears (page 234).

♥ Try all of these extra special versions of Company-Ready Cider: spiked with bourbon for just-arrived out-of-town guests and sparkling for a pre-party treat (page 274).

♥ Host a holiday open house complete with an array of delicious appetizers, festive beverages, and some tasty sweets (page 283).

QUICK-FIX MEALS

♥ Whether dinner calls for warm, hearty Cheesy Chili Hash Brown Bake or fresh Mediterranean Chicken Salad, you can get it onto the table in a jiffy with these recipes (page 52).

♥ Find perfect pairs of main dishes and sides with these super-simple recipes that combine meat, veggies, and starches with delicious success. Serve Tangy Turkey Burgers alongside sweet potato fries, Grilled Steak and Vegetable Kabobs with zucchini sticks, and fusion-style Roasted Sesame Pork Tenderloin with Asian Slaw (page 66).

♥ Use refrigerator staples for extraordinary meals: Dijon mustard goes into Grilled Pork Tenderloin with Squash Medley, mayonnaise binds the Pickled Okra and Shrimp Salad, and chipotle hot sauce adds heat to Grilled Chicken Tacos. Plus, our test kitchen professional lists more of these winning combinations to jazz up your meals while emptying out the pantry (page 93).

♥ Get the grill going with our easy, tasty recipes that take classic cookout fare to the next level. Juicy Cilantro Flank Steak, hot-and-sour Chipotle-Orange Chicken Legs and Mediterranean-inspired Lamb Burgers take your weeknight routine from lukewarm to hot, especially when you use our tested grilling tips (page 110).

♥ Make your seaside daydreams even more vivid with the bright beach flavors in these simple suppers. Keep it homestyle by frying Crunchy Crab Cakes, baking Barbecue Shrimp, or searing Grilled Grouper with Watermelon Salsa. For international flavor, try the kickin' Poblano Fish tacos with queso fresco or the Asian-inspired Spicy Shrimp Noodle Bowl (page 128).

♥ Next time you come home from the farmers' market with a basket full of summer's bountiful beans, corn, and tomatoes, put them to work in these quick-fix meals that are bright with fresh veggie tastes. Serve up a nutritious appetizer with Pepper and Chicken Nachos and try the main-and-side combination of Caribbean Pork with Butter Pea Toss (page 152).

♥ Hearty, savory dishes are the secret to a successful meatless meal, and here we offer five options that require minimal effort for maximum flavor. Go farmers'-market fab with Zucchini-and-Spinach Lasagna or Southern-style with Black eyed Pea Cakes with Heirloom Tomatoes and Slaw (page 196).

♥ Revamp your favorite Italian flavors: swap in some fish with Crispy Oven-Baked Tilapia with Lemon-Tomato Fettuccine, serve steak alongside ravioli, or try a continental-meets-country blend with Pesto-Crusted Pork Chops with Sweet-and-Sour Collards (page 227).

♥ Simple and satisfying, casseroles offer that creamy richness you crave. Yet the same old casserole soon gets groans around the dinner table. Solution? Suggestions like Chicken Enchiladas, topped with a cheesy sauce, and grown-up Shrimp Casserole with a hint of Cajun spice (page 245).

♥ Nothing could be cozier this time of year than a dinner of soups and sandwiches. Try some of our quick and easy favorites that are sure to please (page 286).

Cook's Chat

Our readers chat online about what they think of our recipes and how they use them. Here, they brag about some of their favorites.

APPETIZERS

Loaded Baked Potato Dip, page 40—Very easy to make and pretty tasty. I made this for a bunch of teenage boys watching the Super Bowl and they all loved it. It's best to serve it at room temperature because it's pretty thick. The longer it sits, the better the flavors meld. I would definitely make this again!

Warm Artichoke-Shrimp Dip, page 40—Anything *Southern Living* is great. Made this as appetizer at Christmas. Had to make more because everyone gobbled it up, even the kids. Every single person left with this recipe. Easy to make when friends and family drop by.

Muffuletta Dip, page 40—This really reminded me of a muffuletta. I served it at a Mardi Gras party and everyone loved it. I served it with plain bagel chips and it went great!

Beer-Cheese Fondue with Baby Cauliflower, page 65—This was outstanding. I love the beer/cheeses combination but think Swiss would work just as well and be a bit easier on the budget.

Gorgonzola-Grilled Pear Crostini, page 125—Wow! Easy and delicious! Some quick assembly and you have a delicious, out-of-the-ordinary crowd-pleaser!

Crunchy Crab Cakes, page 128—I made these for Father's Day and dad said they were the best he'd ever had. The key to getting them to stay together is to make sure the crabmeat is well shredded (I started with jumbo lump and shredded it with my fingers).

BREAKFAST

Praline-Pecan French Toast, page 49—As I take the last bite from my plate of this delicious casserole, all I can say is Mmmm...SO delicious! This recipe is a definite keeper. Would make a nice brunch recipe for family or when you want something to serve for a special occasion. I served with bacon and my family loved it. Thank you *Southern Living* for yet another awesome recipe!

Spicy Ham-and-Greens Quiche, page 37—The best use of greens that I've seen. Very good for people that don't even like greens. Will keep this recipe in my recipe box. Excellent!

New Orleans Beignets, page 60—I found these beignets to be tender and delicious. They are not too sweet and remind me exactly of Café Du Monde. They do need to be eaten shortly after being cooked but the uncooked dough keeps in the fridge for a day or two. Extremely happy with this recipe.

Tomato-Herb Mini Frittatas, page 84—I used a 13- x 9-inch baking dish since I didn't have the individual dishes. The flavor was fresh with the herbs–and had a fluffy texture since the eggs and half-and-half are blended in a blender. It was a big hit at the brunch I gave, especially with the Gouda Grits!

BREADS

Spiced Peach-Carrot Bread, page 143—Nice surprise with the diced peaches. We love carrot cake and the peaches added a summer-fresh taste. Gave away loaves to friends who loved it as well!

SALADS

Panzanella Salad with Cornbread Croutons, page 51—I made this, but used Roma tomatoes, sliced and quartered. I served it warm (the dressing is warmed from the cooked onions and peppers). It was excellent.

Mango-Spinach Salad with Warm Bacon Vinaigrette, page 63—Yummy! Easy to prepare. My kids loved it. My oldest asked for seconds. I used feta cheese instead of the crumbled queso fresco because that is what I had in the fridge. Would be a good salad for company because it is colorful and tasty. We enjoyed it with salmon patties.

Cathedral Chicken Salad, page 69—There's a reason why this recipe has been served year after year to church members during Lent. It's outstanding.

Grilled Green Tomatoes Caprese, page 133—These were a great hit at a dinner party tonight with the adults—and even my toddlers! Fantastic balance of flavor and extremely quick and easy!

Veggie Potato Salad, page 135—Love it. I made it for a big summer party and it was a hit. Great twist to the original, lighter and very nice presentation!

Insalata con Peche, page 141—As a Southerner living in New England (who can get her hands on decent Southern peaches only a few precious weeks of summer) I loved this recipe! As it happened, our local raspberries were in season so I added those for more color and flavor. And with the fresh thyme right out of the garden, this is a great recipe. I brought the unassembled but prepped ingredients to Tanglewood and it was a perfect summer lunch. Thank you!

Tortellini-and-Tomato Salad, page 155—Served it for company and it was great, I did not have any Worcestershire and used balsamic vinegar as a suggestion from a friend. It was fantastic! Fresh tomatoes and basil and corn were the kicker!

SOUPS/SANDWICHES

Game Day Chili, page 34—I have been looking for a good, classic, simple chili receipe! This fit the bill. It was simple to make and my family loved it! I made "northern style" cornbread to go along with it. Yum! Yum! I substituted MorningStar Farms Grillers in place of beef and two boxes of Swanson's Vegetable Broth in place of the beef broth and dark beer.

"Big Easy" Gumbo, page 36—This was wonderful!!! I will be making this again. Everyone loved it…even my 3 y.o. It was even better as leftovers! Loved the Hoppin' John with it, but will double the recipe next time and serve with cornbread. Perfect dish on a cold, snowy day.

BLT Benedict with Avocado-Tomato Relish, page 62—Made this for dinner, and it was wonderful. Didn't have grape tomatoes, so diced a vine-ripened one instead, probably added a little extra juice to the relish. Did the egg over-easy, rather than poached. This was a great blend of salty, sweet crunch. Will definitely make it again!

Chicken, Mushroom, and Wild Rice Soup, page 68—We have soup for lunch just about every day when the weather is cold, and this goes into the top two or three in my soup recipe collection. A real winner, as good as it gets. Very flavorful and reheats well.

Goat Cheese and Strawberry Grilled Cheese, page 71—I thought this sandwich was delicious! I used a local soft goat cheese that was very mild and creamy and used the watercress with the strawberries and basil. The red pepper jelly gave it just a bit of a zip. Can't wait to make this again.

SIDES

Baked Smokin' Macaroni and Cheese, page 32—We really liked this. Good family dinner for my husband and three kids. The cheese didn't get "gloppy" like some homemade mac and cheese.

Creole-Roasted Black-eyed Peas, page 36—I thought these were a great healthy alternative to nuts. Brought to work and have given the recipe out to several people. I increased the Creole and had to double the recipe because they shrink up so much. Don't cook too long or they will taste burnt.

Classic Parmesan Scalloped Potatoes, page 92—These were outstanding and took just minutes to throw together. My husband—who's a real potato lover—said these were the best scalloped potatoes he's ever eaten. I didn't have any fresh parsley on hand, so I used finely chopped fresh basil leaves instead, which tasted fresh and flat-out wonderful. The leftover potatoes were just as good (and maybe even better) reheated the next day.

Lightened Squash Casserole, page 156—Yummy! We loved it. This could also easily be a main course—rich and satisfying.

ENTRÉES

Bourbon-Brown Sugar Pork Tenderloin, page 49—Served entrée to guests who were excellent chefs in their own right. This recipe got rave reviews.

Spicy Mango Shrimp, page 51—We have a special Valentine's Day dinner with 12 other people. This year's recipe was the Spicy Mango Shrimp and it was a huge hit. The chef said that he prepared it exactly as stated in the recipe. Each bite was a mix of wonderful tastes. One of the guests usually doesn't eat rice and she finished every morsel. Kudos!

ENTRÉES *(continued)*

Double-Crust Chicken Pot Pie, page 54—I made this recipe for my mother-in-law after bringing her home from the hospital. She cannot quit raving about how good it was!!! This is a keeper! Not too hard to prepare and it tastes GREAT.

Springtime Pasta with Bacon, page 63—This is a flavorful kid-friendly recipe. Very simple and wholesome ingredients. I have made substitutions and it is still delicious so it is very flexible as well. My usual is use fresh green beans instead of the peas and extra lemon juice. My little one always helps herself to seconds.

Stovetop Red Beans and Rice, page 70—Great authentic flavor! Had never used chicken andouille before and don't think I will ever buy the pork variety again! Served it to company and kids and adults alike went back for seconds!! Definitely a keeper!

Rosemary Roast Lamb, page 79—I made this dish for Easter and everyone loved it. I served it with a potato, onion and tomato gratin and asparagus-and-green onion risotto. I will definitely serve this dish again!

Brown Sugar-Bourbon-Glazed Ham, page 96—We served the ham at a family gathering on Sunday. A big hit! It will now be our regular Easter Sunday dinner for years to come. Served it with twice-baked potatoes and grilled red peppers, asparagus, carrots, and zucchini. The only change to the ham was we used Southern Comfort instead of regular bourbon. Yum!

Sweet Tea-Brined Chicken, page 101—Awesome, outstanding. The very best BBQ chicken I have ever had. Easy to do. The whole family loved it. Don't hesitate—just do it! You will be amazed!

Kentucky Hot Brown Tart, page 109—I made this for company on the day of the Kentucky Derby. Everyone loved it. The recipe is a little involved, but well worth it! It is definitely a keeper.

Tomato Pie, page 204—I made this for dinner last night using tomatoes from my garden. It was one of the best dishes I've ever tasted! It was incredible, easy and fast! I will most certainly make it again!!!

DESSERTS

Bacon-Peanut Truffles, page 64—These were awesome! I made them exactly as the recipe listed and served them to several guests. Everyone said they were the best combination of sweet and salty. Yum.

Amaretto-Almond Pound Cake, page 73—Decadent, rich, moist pound cake. Using a hot glaze on a hot cake is a terrific idea. I like the idea of saving some of the glaze to drizzle over the cake after it's removed from the pan. Will try that next time just for appearance!

Key Lime Pound Cake, page 75—Decadent! Extremely moist. The Key lime flavor adds a new dimension. I made this in a square tube pan, and it was beautiful. This will now be in my "go-to" favorite pound cake recipes!

Peach Melba Shortbread Bars, page 81—I received these fabulous cookies as a gift this weekend. Couldn't believe how wonderful they are. Am making them right now for my neighbor. I particularly love the browned crust around the edges. Try this fantastic recipe.

Peanut Butter-Chocolate-Oatmeal Cereal Bars, page 81—Took this as a dessert to an Easter party. None left and everyone was asking for the recipe.

Strawberry-Lemon Shortbread Bars, page 82—Super easy and very tasty! Makes lots of yummy bars so may be best for a small get-together or you may find yourself eating lots! Top with the garnish for looks but really good without the extra cream and strawberry.

Peach Brûlée with Honey Crème Anglaise, page 143—This recipe is incredibly delicious and easy to make! I have an awesome creme brûlée recipe, which is a two-day process in the making. My family begs me to make it, but it takes so long. I added a tablespoon of vanilla to this recipe and look forward to adding a real vanilla bean next time I make it. This recipe received rave reviews from the entire family! It will be a staple in our house. Thanks for sharing this treasure, *Southern Living*!

Brown Sugar-Cinnamon Peach Pie, page 144—I made this pie this evening and my 4 year olds told me that it made their "mouth happy"! It is a great recipe.

January

Sweet on Citrus

Call on the incomparable sassy tartness and vibrant good looks of citrus to brighten the season's sweet dishes.

Elegant Citrus Tart

make-ahead • party perfect

MAKES: 8 servings
HANDS-ON TIME: 20 min.
TOTAL TIME: 10 hr., 5 min., including curd

Topping our tart are Florida-grown Ruby Red grapefruit and navel oranges and the brightest red grapefruit you can buy—the Rio Star from Texas.

- ⅓ cup sweetened flaked coconut
- 2 cups all-purpose flour
- ⅔ cup powdered sugar
- ¾ cup cold butter, cut into pieces
- ¼ tsp. coconut extract
   Buttery Orange Curd (next page)
- 9 assorted citrus fruits, peeled and sectioned

1. Preheat oven to 350°. Bake coconut in a single layer in a shallow pan 4 to 5 minutes or until toasted and fragrant, stirring halfway through; cool completely (about 15 minutes).

2. Pulse coconut, flour, and powdered sugar in a food processor 3 to 4 times or until combined. Add butter and coconut extract, and pulse 5 to 6 times or until crumbly. With processor running, gradually add 3 Tbsp. water, and process until dough forms a ball and leaves sides of bowl.

3. Roll dough into a 12½- x 8-inch rectangle (about ¼ inch thick) on a lightly floured surface; press on bottom and up sides of a 12- x 9-inch tart pan with removable bottom. Trim excess dough, and discard.

4. Bake at 350° for 30 minutes. Cool completely on a wire rack (about 40 minutes).

5. Spread Buttery Orange Curd over crust. Top with citrus sections. (See the following page to learn how to cut pretty sections.)

NOTE: To make a round tart, roll dough into a 10-inch circle (about ¼ inch thick) on a lightly floured surface; press on bottom and up sides of a 9-inch round tart pan with removable bottom. Trim excess dough, and discard. Bake as directed.

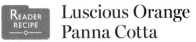

Luscious Orange Panna Cotta

make-ahead • party perfect

MAKES: 6 servings
HANDS-ON TIME: 20 min.
TOTAL TIME: 8 hr., 25 min.

Panna cotta is a silky custard made without eggs that's often topped with a sauce. Tossing orange sections with turbinado sugar adds a rich flavor you won't get using granulated sugar.

- 1 (¼-oz.) envelope unflavored gelatin
- 1 cup cold milk, divided
- 3 navel oranges, divided
- 1¾ cups heavy cream
- ¼ cup granulated sugar
- ½ tsp. vanilla extract
- ¾ cup turbinado sugar
- 1 cup Buttery Orange Curd (next page)
   Garnishes: sweetened whipped cream, fresh mint sprigs

1. Sprinkle gelatin over ¼ cup milk in a small bowl; stir until moistened. Let stand 5 minutes. (Mixture will be lumpy.)

2. Meanwhile, carefully remove 3 (2- x 1-inch) strips of zest from 1 navel orange using a vegetable peeler. Reserve orange for another use.

3. Cook heavy cream, granulated sugar, and orange zest strips in a saucepan over medium-low heat, stirring occasionally, 4 minutes or until sugar is dissolved. Remove from heat, and add gelatin mixture, stirring until mixture is dissolved. Stir in vanilla and remaining ¾ cup milk. Discard orange zest strips.

4. Pour mixture into 6 (4-oz.) dessert glasses or wineglasses. Cover and chill 8 hours.

Pretty Pieces

It's a delicious experience to peel citrus by hand, break apart segments, and enjoy in minutes. But when you want beautiful sections, as seen on our tart, you need a very sharp paring knife and a little patience.

{1}
STEADY IT

Cut ¼-inch-thick slices from each end of citrus (we're using a navel orange) using a sharp, thin-bladed knife. Stand fruit, cut side down, on a cutting board.

{2}
PEEL AWAY

Remove peel and bitter white pith by cutting down curvature of fruit in a sawing motion. If you miss any white pith, simply go back and trim it away.

{3}
RELEASE SECTIONS

Slice between membranes, and gently remove whole segments. (Hold fruit over a bowl to collect juices, if desired.) Discard membrane and seeds.

---

5. Peel and section remaining 2 navel oranges. (See above.) Roll orange sections in turbinado sugar. Top panna cotta with Buttery Orange Curd and sugared oranges. Garnish, if desired. Store leftover panna cotta in refrigerator up to 3 days.

NOTE: We tested with HAIN Pure Foods Natural Turbinado Sugar.

RECIPE INSPIRED BY JINA BREAZEALE
GUYTON, GEORGIA

Buttery Orange Curd

quick prep • make-ahead • party perfect

MAKES: about 2 cups
HANDS-ON TIME: 15 min.
TOTAL TIME: 8 hr., 15 min.

⅔ **cup sugar**
2½ **Tbsp. cornstarch**
1⅓ **cups orange juice**
1 **large egg, lightly beaten**
3 **Tbsp. butter**
2 **tsp. orange zest**
  Pinch of salt

1. Combine sugar and cornstarch in a 3-qt. saucepan; gradually whisk in orange juice. Whisk in egg. Bring to a boil; boil, whisking constantly, 3 to 4 minutes.

2. Remove from heat; whisk in butter, zest, and salt. Place heavy-duty plastic wrap directly on curd (to prevent a film from forming), and chill 8 hours. Store leftovers in refrigerator up to 3 days.

NOTE: We tested with Simply Orange 100% Pure Squeezed Orange Juice.

Sweet Citrus Marmalade

make-ahead • party perfect

MAKES: about 2 cups
HANDS-ON TIME: 20 min.
TOTAL TIME: 2 hr., 15 min., plus
1 day for chilling

This recipe produces a sweeter, less bitter marmalade than what's commonly sold.

- **2 large Valencia or navel oranges**
- **2 medium-size red grapefruit**
- **1 lemon**
- **2 cups sugar**
- **⅛ tsp. kosher salt**

1. Grate zest from oranges to equal 1 Tbsp. Repeat with grapefruit. Grate zest from lemon to equal 1 tsp.

2. Peel and section oranges, grapefruit, and lemon, holding fruit over a bowl to collect juices (see page 29).

3. Stir together zest, fruit segments, sugar, kosher salt, ⅓ cup fruit juices, and 1¾ cups water in a large saucepan; bring to a boil. Reduce heat, and simmer, stirring occasionally, 50 minutes or until a candy thermometer registers 225° and mixture is slightly thickened. Cool completely (about 1 hour; mixture will thicken as it cools). Pour into 2 (8-oz.) jars or airtight containers, and chill 24 hours. Store marmalade in refrigerator up to 3 weeks.

Try These Twists!

Our delicate marmalade flavors are soft enough to spoon over—and soak deliciously into—hot biscuits.

{1}

ORANGE MIMOSA MARMALADE

Prepare recipe as directed, substituting 2 Valencia or navel oranges for grapefruit and 1¾ cups sparkling rosé or sparkling white wine for water.

{2}

CITRUS-VANILLA BEAN MARMALADE

Split 1 vanilla bean lengthwise, and scrape out seeds. Prepare recipe as directed, stirring vanilla bean and seeds into fruit mixture with zest in Step 3. Discard vanilla bean before pouring mixture into jars.

{3}

GINGER-CITRUS MARMALADE

Prepare recipe as directed, stirring in 1 Tbsp. minced fresh ginger with zest in Step 3.

Test Kitchen Essentials

OXO Good Grips Citrus Juicer #34781, about $14, *oxo.com*

Use the small reamer for smaller citrus; then flip over to larger reamer for bigger fruit. Seeds catch in the top, while juice flows into a measuring cup below. The juicer comes apart and is dishwasher safe.
TIP: Juices will release more easily from citrus if you roll the fruit gently on the counter first.

Microplane Classic Series Zester/Grater, about $13, *microplane.com*

This tool has tiny, sharp, surgical steel holes that make zesting simple.
TIP: Scrape fruit swiftly across the holes a couple of times; then turn fruit to a new area and repeat. This should help you avoid scraping into the bitter white pith.

Lime-Cornmeal Cookies

make-ahead • party perfect

MAKES: about 2½ dozen
HANDS-ON TIME: 20 min.
TOTAL TIME: 10 hr.

Don't skip the chill time after mixing or the dough will be too soft to shape into a log.

- 1¼ cups all-purpose flour
- ½ cup plain yellow cornmeal
- ½ cup butter, softened
- ½ cup sugar
- 1 large egg
- 1 Tbsp. lime zest
- 1 Tbsp. fresh lime juice
- ½ tsp. vanilla extract
  Wax paper

1. Combine flour and cornmeal. Beat butter and sugar at medium speed with an electric mixer until light and fluffy. Add egg and next 3 ingredients, beating until blended. Gradually add flour mixture, beating just until blended after each addition. Cover and chill dough 1 hour.

2. Shape dough into a 12-inch log using wax paper. Wrap tightly in plastic wrap, and chill 8 hours.

3. Preheat oven to 375°. Cut log into ¼-inch-thick slices. Place 1 inch apart on ungreased baking sheets. Bake 12 minutes or until set. Transfer to wire racks; cool completely (about 15 minutes).

RECIPE FROM LANNY P. LANCARTE II, CHEF/OWNER
LANNY'S ALTA COCINA MEXICANA
FORT WORTH, TEXAS

TRY THIS TWIST!

Chocolate-Orange Cornmeal Cookies: Substitute orange zest and fresh orange juice for lime zest and juice. Drizzle ¼ cup melted semisweet chocolate morsels over cooled cookies.

Test Kitchen Notebook

You can also freeze blackberries in the summer to have all winter long. It's best not to wash the blackberries before you freeze them so that they do not become too mushy. To freeze, line blackberries on a baking sheet and freeze for a few hours. Once the blackberries are completely frozen, place them in an airtight container to store in the freezer.

Lemon-Poppy Seed Belgian Waffles with Blackberry Maple Syrup

party perfect

MAKES: 4 servings
HANDS-ON TIME: 25 min.
TOTAL TIME: 30 min., including syrup

- 2 cups all-purpose baking mix
- 1 to 2 Tbsp. poppy seeds
- 1 Tbsp. lemon zest
- 1¼ cups cold club soda
- 1 large egg, lightly beaten
- ¼ cup butter, melted
  Blackberry Maple Syrup (at right)
  Crème fraîche (optional)
  Garnish: fresh mint sprigs

1. Stir together baking mix, poppy seeds, and lemon zest. Whisk together club soda, egg, and butter in a small bowl; gently whisk egg mixture into poppy seed mixture. (Mixture will be lumpy.) Let stand 3 minutes.

2. Cook batter in a preheated, oiled Belgian-style waffle iron until golden (about ¾ to 1 cup batter each). Serve with Blackberry Maple Syrup and, if desired, crème fraîche. Garnish, if desired.

NOTE: If you don't have a Belgian-style waffle iron, use ½ cup batter for each waffle in a traditional waffle iron.

RECIPE INSPIRED BY LILANN HUNTER TAYLOR
SAVANNAH, GEORGIA

TRY THIS TWIST!

Lemon-Poppy Seed Pancakes: Prepare batter as directed. Pour about ¼ cup batter for each pancake onto a hot, lightly greased griddle or large nonstick skillet. Cook pancakes 3 to 4 minutes or until tops are covered with bubbles and edges look dry and cooked; turn and cook other side.

Blackberry Maple Syrup

quick prep • make-ahead • party perfect

MAKES: 2 cups
HANDS-ON TIME: 5 min.
TOTAL TIME: 5 min.

- ½ cup maple syrup
- 1 (12-oz.) package frozen blackberries, thawed*
- 1 tsp. lemon zest
- 2 tsp. lemon juice

1. Combine all ingredients in a medium bowl.

*Frozen mixed berries, thawed, may be substituted.

Mac and Cheese

Give up the guilt trip and resolve to enjoy your favorite comfort food. These delicious recipes are light on the butter and cheese yet still melt in your mouth.

Creamy Macaroni and Cheese

Test Kitchen Favorite

MAKES: about 6 servings
HANDS-ON TIME: 25 min.
TOTAL TIME: 50 min.

½ (16-oz.) package multigrain penne pasta
1 Tbsp. butter
3 Tbsp. all-purpose flour
3 cups fat-free milk
½ tsp. salt
½ tsp. dry mustard
1 (8-oz.) block 2% reduced-fat sharp Cheddar cheese, shredded and divided
Vegetable cooking spray

1. Preheat oven to 375°. Cook pasta according to package directions; drain.
2. Melt butter in a large saucepan over medium heat. Whisk in flour, and cook, whisking constantly, 2 minutes. Gradually whisk in milk, salt, and dry mustard; cook, whisking constantly, 5 minutes or until slightly thickened. Remove from heat.
3. Add 1½ cups cheese, stirring until cheese melts and mixture is smooth. Stir in pasta until well combined.
4. Spoon mixture into an 8-inch square baking dish coated with cooking spray. Sprinkle with remaining ½ cup cheese.
5. Bake at 375° for 20 minutes or until golden and bubbly. Let stand 5 minutes before serving.

PER SERVING: CALORIES 332; **FAT** 10.7G (SAT 6.6G, MONO 0.6G, POLY 0.3G); **PROTEIN** 21.1G; **CARB** 36.5G; **FIBER:** 2.8G; **CHOL** 33MG; **IRON** 1.4MG; **SODIUM** 609MG; **CALC** 407MG

Baked Smokin' Macaroni and Cheese

party perfect

MAKES: 8 servings
HANDS-ON TIME: 25 min.
TOTAL TIME: 1 hr.
(Pictured on page 3)

1 lb. uncooked cellentani (corkscrew) pasta
2 Tbsp. butter
¼ cup all-purpose flour
3 cups fat-free milk
1 (12-oz.) can fat-free evaporated milk
1 cup (4 oz.) shredded smoked Gouda cheese
½ cup (2 oz.) shredded 1.5% reduced-fat sharp Cheddar cheese
3 oz. fat-free cream cheese, softened
½ tsp. salt
¼ tsp. ground red pepper, divided
1 (8-oz.) package chopped smoked ham
Vegetable cooking spray
1¼ cups cornflakes cereal, crushed
1 Tbsp. butter, melted

1. Preheat oven to 350°. Prepare cellentani pasta according to package directions.
2. Meanwhile, melt 2 Tbsp. butter in a Dutch oven over medium heat. Gradually whisk in flour; cook, whisking constantly, 1 minute. Gradually whisk in milk and evaporated milk until smooth; cook, whisking constantly, 8 to 10 minutes or until slightly thickened. Whisk in Gouda cheese, next 3 ingredients, and ⅛ tsp. ground red pepper until smooth. Remove from heat, and stir in ham and pasta.
3. Pour pasta mixture into a 13- x 9-inch baking dish coated with cooking spray. Stir together crushed cereal, 1 Tbsp. melted butter, and remaining ⅛ tsp. ground red pepper; sprinkle over pasta mixture.
4. Bake at 350° for 30 minutes or until golden and bubbly. Let stand 5 minutes before serving.

NOTE: We tested with Barilla Cellentani pasta and Cabot 1.5% Reduced-Fat Sharp Cheddar Cheese.

PER SERVING: CALORIES 453; **FAT** 12.1G (SAT 6.8G, MONO 2.3G, POLY 0.3G); **PROTEIN** 26.8G; **CARB** 59.9G; **FIBER** 2.1G; **CHOL** 48MG; **IRON** 3MG; **SODIUM** 846MG; **CALC** 398MG

TRY THIS TWIST!

Stove-Top Smokin' Macaroni and Cheese: Omit cornflakes cereal and 1 Tbsp. melted butter. Reduce ground red pepper to ⅛ tsp. Substitute 3 oz. ⅓-less-fat cream cheese for fat-free cream cheese. Prepare recipe as directed through Step 2. Serve immediately. Hands-on time: 25 min., Total time: 25 min.

PER SERVING: CALORIES 441; **FAT** 12.8G (SAT 7.4G, MONO 1.9G, POLY 0.2G); **PROTEIN** 26.1G; **CARB** 55.9G; **FIBER** 1.9G; **CHOL** 51.2MG; **IRON** 2.2MG; **SODIUM** 784MG; **CALC** 386MG

More Mac and Cheese, Please!

Change the flavor profile of our recipes with any of these delicious substitutions and additions.

{1}

PEPPER JACK MACARONI AND CHEESE

Substitute 1½ cups 1.5% reduced-fat pepper Jack cheese for Gouda and Cheddar cheeses. Omit ground red pepper, if desired. Stir 1 (4.5-oz.) can chopped green chiles into pasta mixture.

PER SERVING (BAKED WITH TOPPING): **CALORIES** 456; **FAT** 11.7G (SAT 6.6G, MONO 1.2G, POLY 0.2G); **PROTEIN** 26.6G; **CARB** 59.9G; **FIBER** 2.6G; **CHOL** 44MG; **IRON** 3MG; **SODIUM** 883MG; **CALC** 270MG

{2}

SWEET PEA-AND-PROSCIUTTO MACARONI AND CHEESE

Omit ham. Sauté 2 oz. thin prosciutto slices, cut into thin strips, in a small skillet over medium-high heat 2 minutes or until slightly browned. Stir prosciutto and 1 cup frozen sweet peas, thawed, into pasta mixture.

PER SERVING (BAKED WITH TOPPING): **CALORIES** 449; **FAT** 11.2G (SAT 6.6G, MONO 2.3G, POLY 0.3G); **PROTEIN** 24.9G; **CARB** 62.6G; **FIBER** 2.9G; **CHOL** 39MG; **IRON** 3.3MG; **SODIUM** 688MG; **CALC** 402MG

{3}

PIMIENTO MACARONI AND CHEESE

Substitute 1½ cups 2% reduced-fat sharp Cheddar cheese for Gouda and Cheddar cheeses. Stir 1 (4-oz.) jar diced pimiento, drained, into pasta mixture.

PER SERVING (BAKED WITH TOPPING): **CALORIES** 440; **FAT** 10.5G (SAT 5.8G, MONO 1.2G, POLY 0.2G); **PROTEIN** 27.4G; **CARB** 60.8G; **FIBER** 2.4G; **CHOL** 40MG; **IRON** 3.2MG; **SODIUM** 817MG; **CALC** 400MG

{4}

HAM-AND-BROCCOLI MACARONI AND CHEESE

Stir 1½ cups frozen broccoli florets, thawed and coarsely chopped, into pasta mixture.

PER SERVING (BAKED WITH TOPPING): **CALORIES** 459; **FAT** 12.1G (SAT 6.8G, MONO 2.3G, POLY 0.3G); **PROTEIN** 27G; **CARB** 60.7G; **FIBER** 2.5G; **CHOL** 48MG; **IRON** 3MG; **SODIUM** 850MG; **CALC** 402MG

Chili for a Crowd

One is a meaty favorite, perfect for a football party. The other is hearty, meatless, and even better the next day. Both versions freeze beautifully.

WHY WE LOVE
Your Way
- Bold chili flavor
- Makes enough for a crowd
- Packed with heart-healthy beans

WHY WE LOVE
Mama's Way
- A cold-weather classic
- Rich flavor from the beer
- Easy, on-hand ingredients

MAMA'S WAY
Game Day Chili
make-ahead • party perfect

MAKES: 8 to 10 servings
HANDS-ON TIME: 25 min.
TOTAL TIME: 2 hr., 30 min.

- 2 **lb. ground chuck**
- 1 **medium onion, chopped**
- 3 **to 4 garlic cloves, minced**
- 2 **Tbsp. chili powder**
- 2 **tsp. ground cumin**
- 1 **to 2 tsp. ground red pepper**
- 1 **tsp. paprika**
- 1 **(6-oz.) can tomato paste**
- 1 **(14.5-oz.) can beef broth**
- 1 **(12-oz.) bottle dark beer**
- 3 **(8-oz.) cans tomato sauce**
- 2 **(15-oz.) cans pinto beans, drained and rinsed**
- 1 **(4.5-oz.) can chopped green chiles, undrained**
- 1 **Tbsp. Worcestershire sauce**

1. Cook first 3 ingredients in a 5- to 6-qt. Dutch oven over medium heat, stirring occasionally, 8 to 10 minutes or until meat crumbles and is no longer pink. Drain well, and return to Dutch oven. Add chili powder and next 3 ingredients; cook 1 minute. Add tomato paste, and cook 1 minute. Add remaining ingredients. Bring to a boil. Cover, reduce heat to low, and simmer 2 hours.

CHANGE IT UP!
Try these substitutions: another can of beef broth for the bottle of beer and black beans instead of pintos.

YOUR WAY
Big-Batch Veggie Chili
good for you • make-ahead • party perfect

MAKES: 12 to 15 servings
HANDS-ON TIME: 20 min.
TOTAL TIME: 55 min.
(Pictured on page 164)

- 2 **large carrots, diced**
- 1 **medium onion, diced**
- 1 **Tbsp. vegetable oil**
- 1 **(3.625-oz.) package chili seasoning kit**
- 1 **(8-oz.) can tomato sauce**
- 3 **cups tomato juice**
- 2 **(14.5-oz.) cans diced tomatoes, undrained**
- 2 **(15-oz.) cans black beans, drained and rinsed**
- 2 **(15-oz.) cans great Northern beans, drained and rinsed**
- 1 **large zucchini, chopped**
- 1 **yellow squash, chopped**
- 1 **cup frozen whole kernel corn**
  Toppings: chopped fresh cilantro, sour cream, chopped green onions, shredded sharp Cheddar cheese, chopped tomatoes

1. Sauté carrots and onion in hot oil in a 5- to 6-qt. Dutch oven over medium heat 7 minutes or until onions are translucent. Stir in half of red pepper packet from chili kit; stir in all of remaining packets. Sauté mixture 2 minutes. Stir in tomato sauce and next 7 ingredients.
2. Bring to a boil; cover, reduce heat to medium low, and simmer, stirring occasionally, 30 minutes or until vegetables are tender. Serve with desired toppings.
NOTE: We tested with Wick Fowler's 2 Alarm Chili Kit.

Pick Your Pot!

A good pot should have a heavy bottom and sides for even cooking with no scorching. Choose one that's also handsome, so you can serve from it at casual gatherings.

Lodge Enamel Dutch Oven
6-quart in Apple Green,
$129.95, *lodgemfg.com*

Tramontina 5-Qt. 18/10 Stainless Steel Dutch Oven
$59.97, *walmart.com*

Simply Calphalon Enamel Nonstick 5-Qt. Chili Pot
$49.95, *calphalon.com*

Giada De Laurentiis for Target 6-Qt. Cast-iron Dutch Oven
$89.99, *target.com*

Tradition with a Twist

Take a fresh look at New Year's black-eyed peas and greens—from a hearty Creole gumbo to a simple ham quiche.

"Big Easy" Gumbo

make-ahead • party perfect

MAKES: 8 to 10 servings
HANDS-ON TIME: 18 min.
TOTAL TIME: 48 min.

Adding flour to hot oil creates a fast and flavorful roux. Serve this party favorite with scoops of Hoppin' John and a fresh green salad tossed with your favorite vinaigrette. (Pictured on page 165)

½ cup peanut oil
½ cup all-purpose flour
1 cup chopped sweet onion
1 cup chopped green bell pepper
1 cup chopped celery
2 tsp. Creole seasoning
2 tsp. minced garlic
3 (14-oz.) cans low-sodium chicken broth
4 cups shredded cooked chicken
½ lb. andouille sausage, cut into ¼-inch-thick slices
1½ cups frozen black-eyed peas, thawed
1 lb. peeled, large raw shrimp (16/20 count)

1. Heat oil in a large Dutch oven over medium-high heat; gradually whisk in flour, and cook, whisking constantly, 5 to 7 minutes or until flour is chocolate colored. (Do not burn mixture.)
2. Reduce heat to medium. Stir in onion and next 4 ingredients, and cook, stirring constantly, 3 minutes. Gradually stir in chicken broth; add chicken and next 2 ingredients. Increase heat to medium-high, and bring to a boil. Reduce heat to low, and simmer, stirring occasionally, 20 minutes. Add shrimp, and cook 5 minutes or just until shrimp turn pink.
NOTE: We tested with Zatarain's Creole Seasoning and Savoie's Andouille Sausage.

Creole-Roasted Black-eyed Peas

quick prep • good for you • make-ahead • party perfect

MAKES: 2 cups
HANDS-ON TIME: 10 min.
TOTAL TIME: 1 hr., 25 min.

Eat these extra-crunchy peas by the handful like nuts, or sprinkle over a leafy green salad.

Preheat oven to 425°. Gently toss 2 (15.8-oz.) cans black-eyed peas, drained and rinsed, with 3 Tbsp. olive oil and 1½ tsp. Creole seasoning. Transfer mixture to a lightly greased 17- x 12-inch jelly-roll pan. Bake at 425° for 55 to 60 minutes or until crispy and dry, stirring every 10 minutes. Let cool 20 minutes.
NOTE: We tested with Bush's Best Blackeye Peas.

Hoppin' John

good for you • make-ahead • party perfect

MAKES: 3 cups
HANDS-ON TIME: 15 min.
TOTAL TIME: 15 min.

1. Sauté 1 cup diced sweet onion in 2 Tbsp. bacon drippings in a large skillet over medium-high heat 5 minutes or until golden. Stir in 1 (8.5-oz.) package ready-to-serve jasmine rice and 2 cups cooked and drained black-eyed peas; cook, stirring gently, 5 minutes or until thoroughly heated. Add salt and pepper to taste.

Spicy Ham-and-Greens Quiche

party perfect

MAKES: 6 to 8 servings
HANDS-ON TIME: 25 min.
TOTAL TIME: 1 hr.

- 1 cup chopped baked ham
- 1½ tsp. olive oil
- ½ (16-oz.) package frozen chopped collard greens, thawed and drained
- ½ cup diced onion
- 1½ cups (6 oz.) shredded pepper Jack cheese
- 1 cup milk
- 2 large eggs
- ½ cup all-purpose baking mix
- ¼ tsp. salt

1. Preheat oven to 400°. Sauté ham in hot oil in a large skillet over medium-high heat 5 minutes or until browned. Stir in collards and onion, and sauté 5 minutes or until onion is tender and liquid evaporates. Layer half of collard mixture in a lightly greased 9-inch pie plate; top with ¾ cup cheese. Repeat layers once.

2. Whisk together milk and remaining ingredients until smooth; pour over collard-and-cheese mixture in pie plate.

3. Bake at 400° for 25 to 35 minutes or until a knife inserted in center comes out clean. Let stand 10 minutes before serving.

NOTE: We tested with Bisquick Original Pancake and Baking Mix.

Lucky Black-eyed Pea Salad

good for you • make-ahead • party perfect

MAKES: 6 servings
HANDS-ON TIME: 20 min.
TOTAL TIME: 10 hr., 5 min.

Peppery watercress fills in for traditional greens. January is peak season for fresh Chilean peaches—ripen at room temp in a brown paper bag until fragrant and juicy.

- 1 (16-oz.) package frozen black-eyed peas
- ¼ cup chopped fresh cilantro
- ¼ cup red pepper jelly
- ¼ cup red wine vinegar
- 2 Tbsp. olive oil
- 1 jalapeño pepper, seeded and minced
- ¾ tsp. salt
- ¼ tsp. freshly ground pepper
- 1 cup diced red bell pepper
- ⅓ cup diced red onion
- 2 large fresh peaches, peeled and diced
- 2 cups torn watercress

1. Prepare peas according to package directions, simmering only until al dente; drain and let cool 1 hour.

2. Whisk together cilantro and next 6 ingredients in a large bowl. Add cooked black-eyed peas, bell pepper, and onion, tossing to coat; cover and chill 8 hours. Stir peaches and watercress into pea mixture just before serving.

Super Dips for Bowl Games

The women 'round here nicknamed these "man cave appetizers." But they're not for guys only—we girls sank our share of chips into these dips!

Test Kitchen Tip

Don't have a chip-and-dip set? Top a serving tray with a bowl and call it done.

Blue Cheese "Hot Wing" Dip

Blue Cheese "Hot Wing" Dip

quick prep • make-ahead • party perfect

MAKES: about 3 cups
HANDS-ON TIME: 10 min.
TOTAL TIME: 1 hr., 10 min.

Try this spicy dip on burgers or tomatoes. We do not recommend fat-free products in this recipe. (Pictured on page 163)

Serve with: *fried chicken breast tenders, celery sticks, radishes, hot wing sauce*

- 1 (8-oz.) package ⅓-less-fat cream cheese, softened and cut into pieces
- ½ cup loosely packed fresh flat-leaf parsley leaves
- ¼ cup chopped green onions
- ¼ cup reduced-fat mayonnaise
- ¼ cup reduced-fat sour cream
- 2 Tbsp. white wine vinegar
- 1 garlic clove, minced
- 1 tsp. hot sauce
- 1 tsp. lemon zest
- ½ tsp. coarsely ground pepper
- 1 (4-oz.) package crumbled blue cheese
- 1 to 2 Tbsp. milk (optional)
  Garnishes: crumbled blue cheese, chopped green onions, freshly cracked pepper

1. Pulse first 10 ingredients in a food processor 4 times or just until blended. Transfer mixture to a serving bowl, and gently stir in blue cheese. If desired, stir in 1 to 2 Tbsp. milk, 1 tsp. at a time, for desired consistency. Cover and chill 1 to 2 hours before serving. Garnish, if desired. Serve with chicken tenders, celery sticks, radishes, and hot wing sauce. Store leftovers in refrigerator up to 7 days.

Southwest Salsa

quick prep • make-ahead • party perfect

MAKES: about 2 cups
HANDS-ON TIME: 10 min.
TOTAL TIME: 1 hr., 10 min.

Double the jalapeños and red pepper, if desired. (Pictured on page 162)

Serve with: *tortilla chips*

- 1 (14½-oz.) can diced tomatoes and zesty green chiles
- 5 pickled jalapeño pepper slices
- ¼ cup firmly packed fresh cilantro leaves
- ¼ cup chopped red onion
- 1 Tbsp. fresh lime juice
- ¼ tsp. ground cumin
- ¼ tsp. garlic powder
- ¼ tsp. dried crushed red pepper
- ¼ tsp. salt
- Garnishes: fresh cilantro sprigs, pickled jalapeño pepper slices

1. Drain liquid from tomatoes, reserving 1 Tbsp. liquid; discard remaining liquid. Place reserved liquid, tomatoes, and next 8 ingredients in a food processor or blender. Pulse 5 to 6 times or until finely chopped. Cover and chill 1 to 24 hours before serving. Garnish, if desired. Serve with tortilla chips. Store leftovers in refrigerator up to 7 days.

NOTE: We tested with DelMonte Diced Tomatoes with Zesty Mild Green Chilies.

RECIPE FROM ROXIE HARRIS
SCOTTSDALE, ARIZONA

Sausage, Bean, and Spinach Dip

party perfect

MAKES: about 6 cups
HANDS-ON TIME: 25 min.
TOTAL TIME: 45 min.

Serve with: *Corn chip scoops, red bell pepper strips, pretzel rods*

- 1 sweet onion, diced
- 1 red bell pepper, diced
- 1 (1-lb.) package hot ground pork sausage
- 2 garlic cloves, minced
- 1 tsp. chopped fresh thyme
- ½ cup dry white wine
- 1 (8-oz.) package cream cheese, softened
- 1 (6-oz.) package fresh baby spinach, coarsely chopped
- ¼ tsp. salt
- 1 (15-oz.) can pinto beans, drained and rinsed
- ½ cup (2 oz.) shredded Parmesan cheese

1. Preheat oven to 375°. Cook diced onion and next 2 ingredients in a large skillet over medium-high heat, stirring often, 8 to 10 minutes or until meat crumbles and is no longer pink. Drain. Stir in garlic and thyme; cook 1 minute. Stir in wine; cook 2 minutes or until liquid has almost completely evaporated.
2. Add cream cheese, and cook, stirring constantly, 2 minutes or until cream cheese is melted. Stir in spinach and salt, and cook, stirring constantly, 2 minutes or until spinach is wilted. Gently stir in beans. Pour mixture into a 2-qt. baking dish; sprinkle with Parmesan cheese.
3. Bake at 375° for 18 to 20 minutes or until golden brown. Serve with corn chip scoops, bell pepper strips, and pretzel rods.

RECIPE FROM BRENT GRAINGER
BIRMINGHAM, ALABAMA

Baked Tex-Mex Pimiento Cheese Dip

quick prep • party perfect

MAKES: about 4 cups
HANDS-ON TIME: 15 min.
TOTAL TIME: 35 min.

You can also bake the mixture in two (1-qt.) baking dishes. (Pictured on page 162)

Serve with: *French bread cubes*

- 1½ cups mayonnaise
- ½ (12-oz.) jar roasted red bell peppers, drained and chopped
- ¼ cup chopped green onions
- 1 jalapeño pepper, seeded and minced
- 1 (8-oz.) block extra-sharp Cheddar cheese, shredded
- 1 (8-oz.) block pepper Jack cheese, shredded
- Garnish: fresh cilantro leaves

1. Preheat oven to 350°. Stir together first 4 ingredients in a large bowl; stir in cheeses. Spoon mixture into a lightly greased 2-qt. baking dish.
2. Bake at 350° for 20 to 25 minutes or until dip is golden and bubbly. Garnish, if desired. Serve with French bread cubes.

Warm Artichoke-Shrimp Dip

Muffuletta Dip

quick prep • make-ahead • party perfect

MAKES: about 4 cups
HANDS-ON TIME: 10 min.
TOTAL TIME: 1 hr., 10 min.

We could call this Saints Dip for the 2010 Super Bowl winners! Parmesan cheese helps hold ingredients together. You can also serve this versatile recipe with crackers over a block of cream cheese or toss leftovers in a Caesar salad. (Pictured on page 2)

Serve with: *French bread crostini*

- 1 cup Italian olive salad, drained
- 1 cup diced salami (about 4 oz.)
- ¼ cup grated Parmesan cheese
- ¼ cup chopped pepperoncini salad peppers
- 1 (2¼-oz.) can sliced black olives, drained
- 4 oz. provolone cheese, diced
- 1 celery rib, finely chopped
- ½ red bell pepper, chopped
- 1 Tbsp. olive oil
- ¼ cup chopped fresh parsley

1. Stir together first 9 ingredients. Cover and chill 1 to 24 hours before serving. Stir in parsley just before serving. Serve with French bread crostini. Store leftovers in refrigerator up to 5 days.

NOTE: We tested with Boscoli Italian Olive Salad. **RECIPE INSPIRED BY KELLI TUTTLE** DRUMMOND, WISCONSIN

Warm Artichoke-Shrimp Dip

quick prep • party perfect

MAKES: about 4 cups
HANDS-ON TIME: 15 min.
TOTAL TIME: 15 min.

Serve half of dip first, keeping remaining half warm in saucepan.

Serve with: *pita crackers, breadsticks*

- 2 (14-oz.) cans artichoke hearts, drained and chopped
- 1 cup freshly grated Parmesan cheese
- ¾ cup mayonnaise
- ½ cup fine, dry breadcrumbs
- 2 garlic cloves, minced
- 2 Tbsp. lemon juice
- ½ lb. peeled, cooked shrimp, chopped
  Garnishes: lemon zest; peeled, cooked shrimp

1. Combine artichoke hearts and next 5 ingredients in a large saucepan. Cook over medium heat, stirring often, 4 to 5 minutes or until thoroughly heated. Stir in shrimp. Transfer to a serving bowl. Garnish, if desired. Serve with pita crackers and breadsticks.

Loaded Baked Potato Dip

quick prep • make-ahead • party perfect

MAKES: about 4 cups
HANDS-ON TIME: 15 min.
TOTAL TIME: 1 hr., 25 min.

We baked frozen waffle fries extra-crispy for our dippers.

Serve with: *waffle fries*

- 1 (2.1-oz.) package fully cooked bacon slices
- 1 (16-oz.) container sour cream
- 2 cups (8 oz.) freshly shredded sharp Cheddar cheese
- ⅓ cup sliced fresh chives
- 2 tsp. hot sauce
  Garnishes: cooked, crumbled bacon; sliced fresh chives; freshly cracked pepper

1. Microwave bacon according to package directions until crisp; drain on paper towels. Cool 10 minutes; crumble. Stir together bacon and next 4 ingredients. Cover and chill 1 to 24 hours before serving. Garnish, if desired. Serve with crispy, warm waffle fries. Store leftovers in refrigerator up to 7 days.

NOTE: We tested with Oscar Mayer Fully Cooked Bacon.

February

Some Like It *Hot!*

Fiery hot sauce moves from a supporting role as condiment to the star of the show, adding a flavorful kick to this delicious mix of Southern favorites.

You see it on tables all across the South—usually crusty-topped with the cap half on—from country meat 'n' threes to coastal seafood shacks. Hot sauce, in all its many styles, is our region's ultimate condiment. It gives spicy tang to a bowlful of shrimp and grits, a pop of heat to a mess of greens or field peas, and a finishing touch to fried catfish. These days, hot sauce is so much more than a fiery spark for bland food. Hundreds of small producers have turned their passion for peppers into successful cottage industries, and their products crowd supermarket shelves alongside traditional Caribbean, Hispanic, and Asian sauces.

Some of the more fervent pepperheads crave the most incendiary, brow-sopping concoctions, the hotter the better. But those of us who still have taste buds think of hot sauce as more than just liquid heat. The flavor subtleties from brand to brand are practically endless. In fact, while testing these delicious recipes (developed by our own Marian Cooper Cairns), Food staffers used such adjectives as tropical, smoky, fruity, and sweet to describe our impressive lineup of commercial offerings. Bottom line: The best sauces have a balance of heat and flavor, rather than full-throttle fire.

When considering the importance of hot sauce in her own kitchen, Marcia McQuaig, owner of Minorcan Datil Pepper Products, LLC in St. Augustine, Florida, passionately declares, "I can't imagine a day without it." Her family's been making sauces with the fiery, slightly sweet datil pepper for almost 20 years. "A dash or two takes ordinary deviled eggs or potato salad, for instance, to a whole new level," explains McQuaig. That's exactly what Test Kitchen Pro Marian Cooper Cairns was thinking when she developed these zesty recipes. Question is, are they hot enough for you?

Sweet Heat Hot Dogs
party perfect

MAKES: 8 servings
HANDS-ON TIME: 30 min.
TOTAL TIME: 30 min.

- ¾ cup mayonnaise
- 1 Tbsp. whole grain mustard
- 1 green onion, minced
- 2 Tbsp. Asian sriracha hot chili sauce
- 8 hot dogs
- 8 hot dog buns, toasted
- 1 cup chopped sweet-hot pickles
- 2 cups shredded red cabbage

1. Preheat grill to 350° to 400° (medium-high) heat.
2. Combine first 3 ingredients and 1 Tbsp. chili sauce in a small bowl. Brush hot dogs with remaining 1 Tbsp. chili sauce.
3. Grill hot dogs, covered with grill lid, 4 to 6 minutes or until thoroughly heated. Place hot dogs in buns, and top with mayonnaise mixture. Sprinkle with chopped pickles and shredded cabbage.
NOTE: We tested with Wickles Pickles and Huy Fong Sriracha Hot Chili Sauce.

> *"The best sauces have a balance of heat and flavor, rather than full-throttle fire."*
>
> **SCOTT JONES**
> FORMER EXECUTIVE FOOD EDITOR

Hot Spiced Boiled Peanuts

Nashville-Style Hot Catfish
party perfect

MAKES: 6 to 8 servings
HANDS-ON TIME: 45 min.
TOTAL TIME: 45 min., plus 24 hr. for chilling
(Pictured on page 2)

- ½ cup buttermilk
- 1 (5-oz.) bottle habanero hot sauce
- 3 lb. small catfish fillets
- 2 cups all-purpose flour
- 2 tsp. salt
- ¾ tsp. pepper
- ¾ tsp. onion powder
  Vegetable oil

1. Whisk together buttermilk and hot sauce in a large bowl. Add catfish. Cover and chill 24 hours.
2. Combine flour and next 3 ingredients. Remove catfish from buttermilk mixture, discarding mixture. Dredge catfish in flour mixture, shaking off excess.
3. Pour oil to depth of 1½ inches into a large, deep skillet; heat to 325°. Fry catfish, in batches, 4 to 5 minutes on each side or until golden brown and fish flakes with a fork. Drain on a wire rack over paper towels. Sprinkle with salt to taste. Serve with additional hot sauce, if desired.
NOTE: We tested with Tabasco Habanero Sauce.

TRY THIS TWIST!
Nashville-Style Hot Chicken:
Substitute 3 lb. chicken drumsticks for catfish. Proceed with recipe as directed through Step 2. Preheat oven to 350°. Pour oil to depth of 1 inch into a large, deep skillet; heat to 325°. Fry drumsticks, in batches, 6 to 8 minutes or until lightly browned, turning occasionally. Transfer to a wire rack in a jelly-roll pan. Bake 15 minutes or until done. Hands-on time: 40 min.; Total time: 55 min., plus 24 hr. for chilling.

Hot Spiced Boiled Peanuts
quick prep • make-ahead • party perfect

MAKES: about 4 cups
HANDS-ON TIME: 10 min.
TOTAL TIME: 5 hr., 20 min.

- 2 lb. raw peanuts in the shell
- ⅓ cup salt
- ¾ cup hot sauce
- 1 (3-inch) piece fresh ginger, sliced
- 1 Tbsp. black peppercorns
- 2 tsp. coriander seeds
- 2 bay leaves

1. Bring all ingredients and 1 gal. water to a boil in a stockpot over high heat. Cover, reduce heat to medium-low, and cook, stirring occasionally, 4 hours or until peanuts are tender. Add water as needed to keep peanuts covered.
2. Remove from heat; let stand, covered, 1 hour.
NOTE: We tested with Texas Pete Original Hot Sauce.

Boiled Peanut Hummus
quick prep • good for you • make-ahead • party perfect

MAKES: 1 cup
HANDS-ON TIME: 25 min.
TOTAL TIME: 25 min.

- 1 cup shelled boiled peanuts
- 2 Tbsp. chopped fresh cilantro
- 2 Tbsp. fresh lime juice
- 2 Tbsp. peanut butter
- 1½ tsp. hot sauce
- 1 tsp. minced fresh garlic
- ¼ tsp. ground cumin
- 2 Tbsp. olive oil
- 1 Tbsp. toasted sesame seeds
  Rice crackers, cucumber slices, bell pepper strips

1. Process first 7 ingredients in a food processor until coarsely chopped, stopping to scrape down sides. With processor running, pour olive oil through food chute in a slow, steady stream, processing until mixture is smooth. Stir in up to 5 Tbsp. water, 1 Tbsp. at a time, for desired consistency. Stir in sesame seeds. Serve with rice crackers and vegetables.

Sweet and Spicy Barbecue Slaw Wrap

MAKES: 6 servings
HANDS-ON TIME: 25 min.
TOTAL TIME: 35 min.

- 1 (3-oz.) package ramen noodle soup mix
- ½ cup slivered almonds
- 3 Tbsp. cider vinegar
- 2 Tbsp. olive oil
- 2 Tbsp. spice sauce*
- 2 Tbsp. honey
- 1 (12-oz.) package broccoli slaw
- 1 Tbsp. toasted sesame seeds
- 1 lb. shredded barbecued pork without sauce (about 3 cups), warmed
- 6 (10-inch) burrito-size flour tortillas

1. Reserve flavor packet from soup mix for another use. Crumble noodles.

2. Heat crumbled noodles and almonds in a small nonstick skillet over medium-low heat, stirring often, 3 to 5 minutes or until toasted and fragrant.

3. Whisk together vinegar and next 3 ingredients in a large bowl. Add noodle mixture, broccoli slaw, and sesame seeds; toss to combine. Let stand 10 minutes.

4. Spoon about ½ cup barbecue pork just below center of each tortilla. Top each with ¾ cup noodle mixture and, if desired, additional spice sauce. Fold opposite side of tortilla over filling, and roll up.

*We tested with Original Cackalacky Spice Sauce. Tiger Sauce The Original may be substituted.

RECIPE FROM H. PAGE SKELTON, SR.
CHAPEL HILL, NORTH CAROLINA

Green Tomato Bloody Mary

Green Tomato Bloody Mary

make-ahead • party perfect

MAKES: about 5 cups
HANDS-ON TIME: 30 min.
TOTAL TIME: 30 min.

We used an assortment of fresh herbs, such as basil, parsley, dill, and cilantro. We suggest making this a day ahead to allow the flavors to fully develop. Store in the refrigerator; stir before serving.

- 4 medium-size green tomatoes (about 1½ lb.), cored and quartered
- 10 fresh tomatillos (about 15 oz.), husks removed and cored
- 2 green onions
- ¾ cup vodka*
- ½ cup loosely packed assorted fresh herbs
- 3 Tbsp. lime juice
- 3 Tbsp. green hot sauce
- 1 garlic clove, minced
- 1 tsp. celery salt
- ½ tsp. salt
  Garnishes: halved pickled okra, lemon wedges

1. Cook first 2 ingredients in boiling salted water to cover 3 minutes; drain. Plunge into ice water to stop the cooking process; drain.

2. Process tomatoes, tomatillos, green onions, and next 7 ingredients in a blender until smooth. Pour mixture through a fine wire-mesh strainer into a pitcher, discarding solids. Serve over ice. Garnish, if desired.

*Tequila may be substituted.

NOTE: We tested with Tabasco Green Pepper Sauce.

"There's this cool connection between hot sauce and the South," says Page Skelton, owner of Cackalacky Condiment Company. "Both are a wonderful blend of flavors and cultures."

Tasting Notes

With heat ranging from mild to meltdown, check out our Food staff's picks and comments.

FRANK'S REDHOT ORIGINAL
Instant heat, vinegary

TABASCO GARLIC
Assertive garlic flavor, good used in cooking, mixed with butter

CHOLULA ORIGINAL
Medium heat, balanced

EL YUCATECO (JALAPEÑO)
Editors' pick for green, full-bodied flavor

HUY FONG SRIRACHA
Pureed HOT peppers

TABASCO CHIPOTLE
Thick and smoky, vinegar kick, hint of tobacco

DAVE'S GOURMET HURTIN' HABANERO
Medium heat, great for chili

TAPATIO SALSA PICANTE
Raw chili flavor, hint of garlic

LA VICTORIA SALSA BRAVA
Mild flavor, perfect for dipping

TIGER SAUCE
Mild, sweet, and fruity

TABASCO GREEN
Sweet-hot vinegar

CACKALACKY SPICE SAUCE
Chow-chow flavor, great for black-eyed peas

CRYSTAL
Vinegary and HOT

TABASCO HABANERO
Sweet and HOT, fruity palate

TEXAS PETE
Vinegary, medium heat, ultimate for wings, workhorse in the kitchen

GENUINE ONE DROP MILD
Great with sliced fruit

EL YUCATECO (RED)
Chili powder burn

GOYA SALSA PICANTE
Perfect for wings

DEL PRIMO (GREEN)
Smooth and mild, great for tacos, editors' pick for mild

GENUINE ONE DROP BLAZZING
Fiery HOT and very sweet

TRAPPEY'S
Sweet and salty, perfect for fried foods and greens

LOUISIANA
Like HOT pickle juice

PAPAW TOM'S
Headin' to the Creek Spicy and robust

TABASCO PEPPER SAUCE
More vinegar than spice, great for cooking

CAJUN SUNSHINE
Good for wings

NOT YO' MAMA'S
Very smoky and HOT— serve with a warning!

ALAGA
Bloody Mary-esque flavor

PAIN IS GOOD JAMAICAN STYLE BATCH #114 HOT SAUCE
Spicy-sweet barbecue flavor

VALENTINA
Raw chili flavor, great for tacos

LEE KUM KEE SRIRACHA
Medium heat, versatile tomato flavor

Bushel of Fun in the Lowcountry

Award-winning Charleston chef Mike Lata proves it's never too chilly for a party, especially with oysters at their peak. We'll tell you everything you need to know—from roasting to recipes—to host your own.

Oyster Roast

SERVES 5

Oysters
(see box on opposite page)

Mike's Cocktail Sauce

Lemon Aïoli

Shoo-fly Punch

A winter breeze blows over the Bohicket Creek on Wadmalaw Island, rustling the amber marsh grasses, tall pines, and moss-covered oaks. The breeze also carries the unmistakable aroma of a campfire along the creek's bank on Rosebank Plantation, where a good ol' Lowcountry party is in full swing.

"There's nothing like an oyster roast in the winter to warm you up inside and out," declares Charleston chef Mike Lata, as he adds another layer of clustered bivalves onto the hot, metal-topped roasting rig. A soaking burlap sack hisses as gentle heat from the steam coaxes open the shells. The hot coals from the fire impart a subtle smokiness that transcends both the classic raw and steamed oyster experiences.

"It doesn't get any better than this," says Mike, whose notable restaurant FIG is one of our region's top eateries. He looks forward to this time of year when he can kick back with friends. Together, they'll fortify themselves with the warm oysters and Shoo-Fly Punch, Mike's potent bourbon-based toddy.

Join the fun by creating your own neighborhood roast. Follow our simple instructions for building a pit and cooking the oysters. (Or, if you'd rather, fire up your grill.) We've also included two of Mike's favorite dipping sauces. Even if you're landlocked, this festive idea gives you an authentic taste of the Lowcountry in your own backyard.

Mike's Cocktail Sauce
quick prep • make-ahead • party perfect

MAKES: about 2 cups
HANDS-ON TIME: 10 min.
TOTAL TIME: 40 min.

- 1½ cups ketchup
- 5 Tbsp. fresh lemon juice
- 2½ Tbsp. extra-hot horseradish
- 1 Tbsp. Worcestershire sauce
- ½ tsp. pepper
- ¼ tsp. salt
- ¼ tsp. hot sauce

1. Stir together all ingredients until blended. Cover and chill 30 minutes before serving. Store leftovers in an airtight container in refrigerator up to 5 days.
NOTE: We tested with Tabasco hot sauce.

Lemon Aïoli
quick prep • make-ahead • party perfect

MAKES: 2 cups
HANDS-ON TIME: 10 min.
TOTAL TIME: 2 hr., 10 min.

- ½ cup heavy cream
- 1 cup mayonnaise
- 3 Tbsp. olive oil
- 2 tsp. lemon zest
- 1 Tbsp. fresh lemon juice
- 1 garlic clove, finely grated
- ¼ tsp. salt

1. Beat heavy cream at medium-high speed with an electric mixer until stiff peaks form. Beat in remaining ingredients at low speed until blended. Cover mixture, and chill 2 hours before serving. Store leftovers in an airtight container in refrigerator up to 3 days.

Test Kitchen Notebook

THE SHELL GAME: Whether they are Virginia's Chincoteagues; plump Apalachicola singles; or small, tangy Texas clusters, native oysters are the same species—*Crassostrea virginica*, the Eastern oyster. Where they live and what they eat determines whether the oysters will be salty or mild, large or small, and they run the gamut.

—DONNA FLORIO

Host Your Own Roast

The term "roasting" is a bit of a misnomer: While the oysters are definitely roasting as they sit directly on the hot sheet metal, the process actually involves a lot more steaming. For planning, figure a bushel (about 50 pounds) for every 5 people. You'll also need oyster knives (thick paring knives will do), some heavy gloves (thick, cotton-lined rubber gloves are best), and a trash can lined with a heavy-duty plastic trash bag.

HERE'S HOW IT'S DONE

{1}

WASH UP

If you're lucky enough to harvest your own oysters, give them a good rinse with a water hose to remove any mud. Oysters from a purveyor or seafood shack most likely have already been washed.

{2}

BUILD A PIT

You basically need a large piece of sheet metal (we prefer one that's about 3½ feet square and ⅛ to ¼ inch thick) and four standard-size masonry blocks. Build a fire appropriate to the size of your sheet metal, and position one masonry block vertically at each corner. (Some folks prefer a burner and propane tank in lieu of a wood fire.) Place the sheet metal on top of the masonry blocks just as the flames begin to die down. Sprinkle a few drops of water on the metal—if the water sizzles, you're ready to go. Add oysters in a single layer.

{3}

CREATE THE STEAM

Cover oysters with a soaking-wet burlap sack or thick beach towel. Cook oysters 8 to 10 minutes. (The shells will open about ¼ to ½ inch.) If you prefer lightly steamed oysters, stick to the lower end of the time range. Transfer the oysters with a clean shovel or large metal dustpan to a newspaper-lined table. Allow the metal to reheat; then repeat the procedure with more oysters, adding more wood as needed.

{4}

DIG IN

Pry open oysters using an oyster knife, discarding the empty half shells. Run the knife under the oyster meat to release it. Serve with dipping sauce.

OTHER COOKING METHODS

GRILL: Preheat grill to 350° to 400° (medium-high) heat. Grill oysters without grill lid 8 to 10 minutes or until shells open (about ¼ to ½ inch). Remove from grill. Pry open oysters using an oyster knife, discarding the empty half shells. Run the knife under the oyster meat to release it .

OVEN: Preheat oven to 450°. Place oysters in a single layer in a jelly-roll pan. Bake 8 to 10 minutes or until shells open (about ¼ to ½ inch). Remove from oven. Pry open oysters using an oyster knife, discarding the empty half shells. Run the knife under the oyster meat to release it.

Shoo-Fly
Punch

Shoo-Fly Punch

quick prep • party perfect

MAKES: 1 serving
HANDS-ON TIME: 5 min.
TOTAL TIME: 1 hr., 15 min., including
Simple Syrup

*Ginger beer is a nonalcoholic fizzy beverage
with a pop of spicy ginger. It's the flavor
secret in this spicy but refreshing cocktail.*

  5 **Tbsp. bourbon**
  2 **Tbsp. ginger liqueur**
  1 **Tbsp. fresh lemon juice**
  1 **Tbsp. Simple Syrup**
  ¼ **tsp. bitters**
     Crushed ice
     Nonalcoholic ginger beer, chilled
     Garnishes: orange slices, fresh
     mint sprigs

1. Stir together first 5 ingredients.
Fill 1 (16-oz.) glass or mason jar with
crushed ice. Pour bourbon mixture over
ice; top with ginger beer (about ⅓ cup).
Garnish, if desired. Serve immediately.
NOTE: We tested with Maker's Mark Bourbon, Domaine de Canton ginger liqueur,
and Reed's Extra Ginger Brew and Goya
Jamaican Style Ginger Beer.

Simple Syrup

quick prep • make-ahead • party perfect

MAKES: 1½ cups
HANDS-ON TIME: 5 min.
TOTAL TIME: 1 hr., 10 min.

1. Bring 1 cup sugar and 1 cup water to a
boil in a medium saucepan. Boil, stirring
often, 1 minute or until sugar is dissolved.
Remove syrup from heat, and let cool
completely (about 1 hour).

Update from the Gulf: Keep on Shucking!

After the oil spill in the Gulf of
Mexico in 2010, the obvious question, in the eyes of most consumers,
remains: Are Gulf oysters safe to
eat? The answer is yes! "Very little of
the Gulf oyster grounds ever saw oil.
Ninety percent of the closures were
precautionary," says Mike Voisin,
owner of Motivatit Seafood in
Houma, Louisiana, and a member of
the Louisiana Wildlife and Fisheries
Commission. "There have been no
signs of oysters, specifically, and
seafood, in general, taking up PAHs
due to the oil spill." (PAHs, polycyclic
aromatic hydrocarbons, are naturally
found in crude oil and are the most
common contaminants associated
with seafood.)

Still this has been one of the
biggest PR battles growers and
retailers on the Gulf have had to
tackle. The industry is working
overtime to restore consumer
confidence in one of the South's
most iconic foods. In fact, Mike goes
one step further when explaining
the U.S. government's rigorous
testing of Gulf oysters and seafood.
"Not only is our seafood (including
oysters) safe to eat, but it's also the
most carefully tested, looked-at
seafood on the planet—and that's a
good thing." For more info visit the
Gulf Oyster Industry Council Web
site at gulfoysters.org.

Add a New Southern Twist!

Simple changes in cooking techniques and an updated list of lightened ingredients offer fresh takes on comfort food classics.

Praline-Pecan
French Toast with fresh berries

Praline-Pecan French Toast

quick prep • make-ahead • party perfect

MAKES: 8 to 10 servings
HANDS-ON TIME: 20 min.
TOTAL TIME: 8 hr., 55 min.

The twist: A short-order breakfast special gets an easy hands-off finish in the oven.

- 1 (16-oz.) French bread loaf
- 1 cup firmly packed light brown sugar
- ⅓ cup butter, melted
- 2 Tbsp. maple syrup
- ¾ cup chopped pecans
- 4 large eggs, lightly beaten
- 1 cup 2% reduced-fat milk
- 2 Tbsp. granulated sugar
- 1 tsp. ground cinnamon
- 1 tsp. vanilla extract

1. Cut 10 (1-inch-thick) slices of bread. Reserve remaining bread for another use.
2. Stir together brown sugar and next 2 ingredients; pour into a lightly greased 13- x 9-inch baking dish. Sprinkle with chopped pecans.
3. Whisk together eggs and next 4 ingredients. Arrange bread slices over pecans; pour egg mixture over bread. Cover and chill 8 hours.
4. Preheat oven to 350°. Bake bread 35 to 37 minutes or until golden brown. Serve immediately.

Bourbon-Brown Sugar Pork Tenderloin

party perfect

MAKES: 6 to 8 servings
HANDS-ON TIME: 30 min.
TOTAL TIME: 8 hr., 30 min.
(Pictured on page 166)

The twist: It's a fresh, weeknight-easy spin on Sunday pork roast with gravy. A quick reduction transforms the flavorful marinade into an indulgent sauce.

- 2 (1-lb.) pork tenderloins*
- ¼ cup firmly packed dark brown sugar
- ¼ cup minced green onions
- ¼ cup bourbon
- ¼ cup soy sauce
- ¼ cup Dijon mustard
- ½ tsp. freshly ground pepper
- ½ tsp. cornstarch

1. Remove silver skin from tenderloins, leaving a thin layer of fat. Combine brown sugar and next 5 ingredients in a large zip-top plastic freezer bag; add pork. Seal bag, and chill 8 to 18 hours, turning bag occasionally. Remove pork from marinade, reserving marinade.
2. Preheat grill to 350° to 400° (medium-high) heat. Grill pork, covered with grill lid, 8 minutes on each side or until a meat thermometer inserted into thickest portion registers 155°. Remove from grill, and let stand 10 minutes.
3. Meanwhile, combine reserved marinade and cornstarch in a saucepan. Bring to a boil over medium heat; cook, stirring constantly, 1 minute. Cut pork diagonally into thin slices, and arrange on a serving platter; drizzle with warm sauce.
* 1½ lb. flank steak may be substituted. Reduce grill time to 6 to 8 minutes on each side or to desired degree of doneness.

Garlic-Chive Mashed Potatoes

quick prep • good for you • party perfect

MAKES: 6 servings
HANDS-ON TIME: 10 min.
TOTAL TIME: 20 min.
(Pictured on page 166)

The twist: *A swirl of fat-free cream cheese turns hot cooked mashed potatoes into a deceptively rich side dish.*

1. Microwave 1 (24-oz.) package frozen steam-and-mash potatoes according to package directions. Meanwhile, melt 1 Tbsp. butter in a small skillet over medium heat; add 4 minced garlic cloves, and sauté 1 minute. Transfer cooked potatoes to a large bowl. Add garlic mixture, 4 oz. fat-free cream cheese, ⅔ cup fat-free milk, ⅓ cup chopped fresh chives, and salt and freshly ground pepper to taste; mash to desired consistency.
NOTE: We tested with Ore-Ida Steam 'n' Mash Cut Russet Potatoes.

Skillet Cornbread

quick prep • good for you • make-ahead • party perfect

MAKES: 8 servings
HANDS-ON TIME: 10 min.
TOTAL TIME: 40 min.

The twist: *It's a dead ringer for the cast-iron classic—minus the traditional skilletful of bacon drippings.*

1. Preheat oven to 425°. Coat bottom and sides of a 10-inch cast-iron skillet with 2 tsp. canola oil; heat in oven 5 minutes. Meanwhile, whisk together 1¾ cups self-rising white cornmeal mix; 2 cups nonfat buttermilk; ¼ cup all-purpose flour; 1 large egg, lightly beaten; 2 Tbsp. melted butter; and 1 Tbsp. sugar. Pour batter into hot skillet. Bake 25 to 30 minutes until golden.

Grits and Grillades

good for you • party perfect

MAKES: 6 servings
HANDS-ON TIME: 30 min.
TOTAL TIME: 3 hr., 30 min., including grits

The twist: *Lean round steak browns in a reduced amount of oil, then simmers to fork-tender perfection in a slow cooker.*

- 1½ lb. top round steak (½ inch thick), trimmed
- 3 Tbsp. all-purpose flour
- 2 tsp. Creole seasoning
- 2 Tbsp. vegetable oil
- 1 (14½-oz.) can fire-roasted diced tomatoes
- 1 (10-oz.) package frozen diced onion, red and green bell pepper, and celery, thawed
- 3 garlic cloves, pressed
  Asiago Cheese Grits

1. Place steak between 2 sheets of heavy-duty plastic wrap, and flatten to ¼-inch thickness using a rolling pin or flat side of a meat mallet; cut into 2-inch squares.
2. Combine flour and Creole seasoning in a large zip-top plastic freezer bag. Add steak; seal bag, and shake to coat.
3. Heat 1 Tbsp. oil in a large skillet over medium-high heat. Add half of steak, and cook 2 to 3 minutes on each side or until browned; transfer steak to a 4- or 5-qt. lightly greased slow cooker. Repeat procedure with remaining oil and steak. Add tomatoes and next 2 ingredients to slow cooker, and stir.
4. Cover and cook on HIGH 3 hours or until steak is tender. Meanwhile, prepare Asiago Cheese Grits. Serve steak mixture over grits.

Southern Revival

If you've never experienced the fresh corn taste of stone-ground grits, the first intoxicating forkful will make you a believer. Thanks to the whole food movement, they can now be delivered to your door with the click of a mouse: Visit Anson Mills (anson-mills.com) or McEwen and Sons (mcewenandsons.com). Natural oils in the germ deteriorate rapidly at room temperature, so store in the freezer.

Asiago Cheese Grits

quick prep • party perfect

MAKES: 6 servings
HANDS-ON TIME: 5 min.
TOTAL TIME: 3 hr., 5 min.

The twist: *The slow cooker's steady moist heat releases the starch in stone-ground grits with minimal stirring, creating a naturally rich, creamy texture with little or no added dairy products.*

- 1 cup uncooked stone-ground grits
- ½ cup (2 oz.) shredded Asiago cheese
- 1 Tbsp. butter
- ½ tsp. salt
- ½ tsp. freshly ground pepper

1. Stir together grits and 3 cups water in a 3-qt. slow cooker. Let stand 1 to 2 minutes, allowing grits to settle to bottom; tilt slow cooker slightly, and skim off solids using a fine wire-mesh strainer. Cover and cook on HIGH 2½ to 3 hours or until grits are creamy and tender, stirring every 45 minutes.
2. Stir in cheese and next 3 ingredients.

Panzanella Salad with Cornbread Croutons

quick prep • good for you • party perfect

MAKES: 6 to 8 servings
HANDS-ON TIME: 25 min.
TOTAL TIME: 1 hr., 30 min., including cornbread
(Pictured on page 167)

The twist: Think cornbread salad with an Italian accent. A light, lemony vinaigrette replaces the traditional sour cream-and-mayo dressing.

**Skillet Cornbread, cooled com-
pletely (recipe at left)**
1 **yellow bell pepper, diced**
1 **small red onion, diced**
½ **cup olive oil, divided**
2 **tsp. lemon zest**
¼ **cup fresh lemon juice**
½ **tsp. honey**
**Salt and freshly ground
pepper to taste**
1 **pt. grape tomatoes, halved**
½ **English cucumber,
quartered and sliced**
½ **cup pitted kalamata olives, halved**
½ **cup torn fresh basil leaves**

1. Preheat oven to 400°. Cut cornbread into 1-inch cubes. Bake in a single layer on a lightly greased jelly-roll pan 15 minutes or until edges are golden, stirring halfway through.
2. Meanwhile, sauté bell pepper and onion in 1 Tbsp. hot olive oil in a small skillet over medium-high heat 5 minutes or until crisp-tender.
3. Whisk together lemon zest, lemon juice, honey, remaining 7 Tbsp. olive oil, and salt and pepper to taste in a large bowl; stir in onion mixture, tomatoes, and next 3 ingredients. Add toasted cornbread cubes, and toss to coat. Serve immediately.

Pantry Panache

In the trendy culinary world of faux-real favorites, hickory-smoked salt tops our list. Add instant depth to soups, stews, and speckled butterbeans. You can even trick out a big fat burger on an indoor grill. The color and texture of the salt crystals vary by brand, as does the intensity of flavor. The best are slowly smoked over a natural wood fire— skip those with any hint of artificial ingredients.

Spicy Mango Shrimp

quick prep • good for you • party perfect

MAKES: 6 to 8 servings
HANDS-ON TIME: 35 min.
TOTAL TIME: 35 min., including rice
(Pictured on page 167)

The twist: A quick and colorful skillet sauté topped with toasted coconut offers a light, innovative take on the sweet-hot flavor of fried coconut shrimp with honey mustard sauce.

Coconut-Lime Rice
1½ **lb. peeled, large raw shrimp
(16/20 count)**
3 **Tbsp. olive oil, divided**
1 **cup chopped green onions**
1 **cup diced red bell pepper**
2 **garlic cloves, minced**
1 **Tbsp. grated fresh ginger**
½ **to 1 tsp. dried crushed red pepper**
1 **cup chopped fresh mango**
¼ **cup chopped fresh
cilantro**
¼ **cup soy sauce**
2 **Tbsp. fresh lime juice**
**Topping: toasted sweetened flaked
coconut**

1. Prepare Coconut-Lime Rice.
2. Meanwhile, sauté half of shrimp in 1 Tbsp. hot oil in a large skillet over medium-high heat 2 to 3 minutes or just until shrimp turn pink. Remove shrimp from skillet. Repeat procedure with 1 Tbsp. hot oil and remaining shrimp.
3. Sauté onions and next 4 ingredients in remaining 1 Tbsp. hot oil over medium-high heat 1 minute. Stir in mango and next 3 ingredients, and cook 1 minute; stir in shrimp. Serve over hot cooked Coconut-Lime Rice; top with toasted coconut.

Coconut-Lime Rice

quick prep • good for you • party perfect

MAKES: 6 servings
HANDS-ON TIME: 10 min.
TOTAL TIME: 35 min.
(Pictured on page 167)

The twist: Light coconut milk and a splash of fresh citrus add a sunny tropical edge to jasmine rice.

1 **cup light coconut milk**
½ **tsp. salt**
1½ **cups uncooked jasmine rice**
1 **tsp. lime zest**
1½ **Tbsp. fresh lime juice**

1. Bring coconut milk, salt, and 2 cups water to a boil in a saucepan over medium heat. Stir in rice; cover, reduce heat to low, and simmer, stirring occasionally to prevent scorching, 20 to 25 minutes or until liquid is absorbed and rice is tender. Stir in lime zest and juice.

Cutting-Edge Collards

good for you • make-ahead

MAKES: 8 servings
HANDS-ON TIME: 30 min.
TOTAL TIME: 55 min.

The twist: *Hickory-smoked salt adds a sizzling hit of pork-rich flavor (and zero fat grams) to thinly cut ribbons of greens.*

 2 **bunches fresh collard greens (about 3 lb.)**
 1 **large red onion, finely chopped**
 2 **Tbsp. vegetable oil**
2½ **cups vegetable broth**
 ¼ **cup cider vinegar**
 2 **Tbsp. dark brown sugar**
1½ **tsp. hickory-smoked salt**
 ½ **tsp. dried crushed red pepper**

1. Separate collard bunches into leaves. Trim and discard tough stalk from center of leaves; stack leaves, and roll up, starting at 1 long side. Cut roll into ⅛-inch-thick slices. Rinse slices under cold running water. Drain well.
2. Sauté onion in hot oil in a Dutch oven over medium-high heat 5 to 7 minutes or until tender. Add broth and next 4 ingredients. Bring to a boil.
3. Gradually add collards to Dutch oven, and cook, stirring occasionally, 6 to 8 minutes or just until wilted. Reduce heat to medium, and cook, stirring occasionally, 20 minutes or until tender.

What's for Supper?

Grab a plate and pull up a chair. Five easy meals (plus a few quick tricks) take the pressure off weeknight cooking.

Cheesy Chili Hash Brown Bake

quick prep • party perfect

MAKES: 8 servings
HANDS-ON TIME: 12 min.
TOTAL TIME: 57 min.
(Pictured on page 169)

Easy side: *Cook 1 (10-oz.) package frozen broccoli spears in butter sauce according to package directions. Sprinkle with ½ tsp. lemon pepper.*

1½ **lb. lean ground beef or turkey**
 1 **(15.5-oz.) can original sloppy joe sauce**
 1 **(15-oz.) can chili with beans**
 ½ **(30-oz.) package frozen country-style shredded hash browns (about 4 cups)**
 2 **cups (8 oz.) shredded Cheddar cheese**

1. Preheat oven to 425°. Brown ground beef in a large skillet over medium-high heat, stirring often, 7 to 10 minutes or until meat crumbles and is no longer pink. Stir in sloppy joe sauce and chili.
2. Spoon chili mixture into 8 lightly greased 10-oz. ramekins. Top with frozen hash browns.
3. Bake, covered, at 425° for 30 minutes; uncover and bake 10 more minutes or until browned and crisp. Sprinkle with cheese, and bake 5 more minutes or until cheese is melted.
NOTE: We tested with Manwich Original Sloppy Joe Sauce and Hormel Chili with Beans. Chili mixture can be baked in a lightly greased 13- x 9-inch baking dish as directed.

Sweet-and-Hot Pork Stir-fry

quick prep • party perfect

MAKES: 6 servings
HANDS-ON TIME: 30 min.
TOTAL TIME: 30 min.

 1 **lb. pork tenderloin**
 3 **Tbsp. peanut oil, divided**
 6 **green onions, cut into 1-inch pieces**
 3 **cups chopped fresh broccoli**
 1 **Tbsp. minced fresh or 1 tsp. ground ginger**
 2 **garlic cloves, minced**
 1 **(8-oz.) can pineapple tidbits in juice**
 ¾ **cup chicken broth**
 2 **Tbsp. soy sauce**
 2 **tsp. cornstarch**
    Hot cooked rice

1. Cut pork into 1-inch pieces.
2. Stir-fry half of pork in 1 Tbsp. hot oil in a large skillet or wok over high heat 4 to 5 minutes or until browned. Remove from skillet. Repeat procedure with 1 Tbsp. oil and remaining pork.
3. Stir-fry green onions and next 3 ingredients in remaining 1 Tbsp. hot oil 3 to 4 minutes. Return pork to skillet; stir-fry 2 minutes.
4. Stir together pineapple and next 3 ingredients until smooth; add to pork mixture, and stir-fry 3 to 4 minutes or until thickened. Serve over hot cooked rice.

Steak Salad with Roasted Sweet Potatoes

quick prep • party perfect

MAKES: 8 servings
HANDS-ON TIME: 30 min.
TOTAL TIME: 30 min.

- ½ lb. fresh green beans
- 1 (20-oz.) package frozen sweet potato fries
- 1 medium-size sweet onion, cut into wedges
  Vegetable cooking spray
- 2 Tbsp. olive oil, divided
- 1½ tsp. salt, divided
- ¾ tsp. pepper, divided
- 2 rib-eye steaks (about 1¼ lb.)
- 2 garlic cloves, pressed
- 1 large head romaine lettuce, torn
- 4 plum tomatoes, chopped
- ½ cup smoked almonds, coarsely chopped
- ½ cup bottled peppercorn Ranch dressing

1. Preheat oven to 425°. Cook beans in boiling salted water to cover 5 minutes or until crisp-tender; drain. Plunge into ice water to stop the cooking process; drain.
2. Place sweet potatoes and onion in a large aluminum foil-lined jelly-roll pan coated with cooking spray. Drizzle potato mixture with 1 Tbsp. oil, and sprinkle with ½ tsp. salt and ¼ tsp. pepper. Toss to coat.
3. Bake at 425° for 25 to 30 minutes or until potatoes and onions are tender and golden, stirring occasionally.
4. Meanwhile, rub steaks with garlic and remaining 1 Tbsp. oil, 1 tsp. salt, and ½ tsp. pepper.
5. Heat a grill pan over medium-high heat; cook steaks in pan 4 to 5 minutes on each side or to desired degree of doneness. Let stand 10 minutes.
6. Toss together lettuce, tomatoes, almonds, and green beans. Thinly slice steak, and place on salad. Serve with potato mixture and dressing.

Mediterranean Chicken Salad

quick prep • make-ahead • party perfect

MAKES: 6 servings
HANDS-ON TIME: 15 min.
TOTAL TIME: 35 min.

- 2 cups boiling water
- 1 cup uncooked bulgur wheat
- 1½ tsp. salt, divided
- 3 cups chopped cooked chicken
- 1 cup grape tomatoes, halved
- 2 garlic cloves, pressed
- ¾ cup chopped fresh parsley
- ½ cup bottled Caesar dressing
- ¼ cup finely chopped red onion
- 1 (4-oz.) package crumbled feta
- 1 medium cucumber, peeled and chopped
- 1 head Bibb lettuce

1. Combine boiling water, bulgur wheat, and 1 tsp. salt. Cover and let stand 20 minutes or until tender. Drain and rinse with cold water.
2. Combine bulgur wheat, chicken, next 7 ingredients, and remaining ½ tsp. salt. Serve over Bibb lettuce leaves.

Try This Twist!

MEDITERRANEAN CHICKEN SALAD WITH RICE: Reduce salt to ½ tsp. Omit boiling water. Substitute 1 (6-oz.) package long-grain and wild rice mix for bulgur wheat. Prepare rice according to package directions. Proceed with recipe as directed in Step 2.

Chicken Cutlets with Pecan Sauce

quick prep • party perfect

MAKES: 4 servings
HANDS-ON TIME: 23 min.
TOTAL TIME: 23 min.
(Pictured on page 169)

Easy side: *Cook 1 (11-oz.) package frozen steam-in-bag baby mixed vegetables according to package directions. Toss with 1 tsp. freshly ground garlic-pepper seasoning. We tested with Green Giant Valley Fresh Steamers Market Blend and McCormick seasoning.*

- ½ cup pecans
- ¼ cup butter, divided
- 4 chicken cutlets (about 1¼ lb.)
- 1 tsp. salt
- ½ tsp. pepper
- 3 Tbsp. all-purpose flour
- 3 Tbsp. olive oil
- ½ cup chicken broth
- 1 Tbsp. brown sugar
- 2 Tbsp. cider vinegar
- ½ tsp. dried thyme

1. Heat pecans and 2 Tbsp. butter in a large nonstick skillet over medium-low heat, stirring often, 2 to 3 minutes or until toasted and fragrant. Remove from skillet.
2. Sprinkle chicken with salt and pepper. Dredge in flour, shaking off excess.
3. Cook chicken in hot oil in skillet over medium heat 3 to 4 minutes on each side or until golden brown and done. Transfer to a serving platter. Top with pecans.
4. Add chicken broth to skillet, and cook 2 minutes, stirring to loosen particles from bottom of skillet. Add brown sugar, vinegar, and thyme, and cook 3 to 4 minutes or until sugar is melted and sauce is slightly thickened. Whisk in remaining 2 Tbsp. butter. Serve sauce over chicken.

MAMA'S WAY OR YOUR WAY?

Chicken Pot Pie

Rediscover an old-fashioned favorite baked with a rich puff pastry crust, or spoon a deliciously quick stovetop twist over buttermilk biscuits.

Double-Crust Chicken Pot Pie

> **WHY WE LOVE**
> *Mama's Way*
> - Made-from-scratch cream sauce
> - Deluxe double crust
> - Sautéed leeks and seasoned potatoes

MAMA'S WAY

Double-Crust Chicken Pot Pie
make-ahead • party perfect

MAKES: 6 to 8 servings
HANDS-ON TIME: 31 min.
TOTAL TIME: 1 hr., 41 min.
(Pictured on page 161)

- ½ cup butter
- 2 medium leeks, sliced
- ½ cup all-purpose flour
- 1 (14.5-oz.) can chicken broth
- 3 cups chopped cooked chicken
- 1½ cups frozen cubed hash browns with onions and peppers
- 1 cup matchstick carrots
- ⅓ cup chopped fresh flat-leaf parsley
- ½ tsp. salt
- ½ tsp. freshly ground pepper
- 1 (17.3-oz.) package frozen puff pastry sheets, thawed
- 1 large egg

1. Preheat oven to 375°. Melt butter in a large skillet over medium heat; add leeks, and sauté 3 minutes. Sprinkle with flour; cook, stirring constantly, 3 minutes. Whisk in chicken broth; bring to a boil, whisking constantly. Remove from heat; stir in chicken and next 5 ingredients.

2. Roll each pastry sheet into a 12- x 10-inch rectangle on a lightly floured surface. Fit 1 sheet into a 9-inch deep-dish pie plate; spoon chicken mixture into pastry. Place remaining pastry sheet over filling in opposite direction of bottom sheet; fold edges under, and press with tines of a fork, sealing to bottom crust. Whisk together egg and 1 Tbsp. water, and brush over top of pie.

3. Bake at 375° on lower oven rack 55 to 60 minutes or until browned. Let stand 15 minutes.

YOUR WAY

Stovetop Chicken Pie

party perfect

MAKES: 6 to 8 servings
HANDS-ON TIME: 35 min.
TOTAL TIME: 35 min.

A family-size rotisserie chicken yields the perfect amount of chopped cooked chicken for this recipe.

- 8 **frozen buttermilk biscuits**
- 1 **small sweet onion, diced**
- 1 **Tbsp. canola oil**
- 1 **(8-oz.) package sliced fresh mushrooms**
- 4 **cups chopped cooked chicken**
- 1 **(10¾-oz.) can reduced-fat cream of mushroom soup**
- 1 **cup low-sodium chicken broth**
- ½ **cup dry white wine**
- ½ **(8-oz.) package ⅓-less-fat cream cheese, cubed**
- ½ **(0.7-oz.) envelope Italian dressing mix (about 2 tsp.)**
- 1 **cup frozen baby peas, thawed**

1. Bake biscuits according to package directions.

2. Meanwhile, sauté onion in hot oil in a large skillet over medium-high heat 5 minutes or until golden. Add mushrooms, and sauté 5 minutes or until tender. Stir in chicken and next 5 ingredients; cook, stirring frequently, 5 minutes or until cheese is melted and mixture is thoroughly heated. Stir in peas, and cook 2 minutes. Spoon chicken mixture over hot split biscuits.

Short Order Gourmet

Skip the biscuits, and serve Stovetop Chicken Pie over something a bit more unpredictable.

{1}

CORNBREAD WAFFLES
Prepare cornbread mix according to package directions; cook batter, in batches, in a hot, oiled waffle iron until done.

{2}

HOT COOKED PASTA
Choose a sturdy penne, fusilli, or bow-tie pasta. Toss with a drizzle of olive oil and freshly grated Parmesan cheese.

{3}

BAKED POTATOES
Prepare frozen seasoned potato wedges according to package directions; toss with chopped fresh parsley.

{4}

PECAN WILD RICE
Stir chopped fresh parsley, sweetened dried cranberries, and toasted pecans into hot cooked long-grain and wild rice mix.

Little Love Bites

Charm your sweeties this Valentine's Day with confections such as our ultra-easy truffles, caramels, sparkly cookies, and chocolaty cherries.

Indulgent Cherries

make-ahead • party perfect

MAKES: about 2 dozen
HANDS-ON TIME: 30 min.
TOTAL TIME: 9 hr.

Soaked cherries can be left in the freezer for up to 2 days before you dip them into the chocolate. Drizzle the leftover cherry-flavored Southern Comfort over vanilla ice cream.

1 **(10-oz.) jar maraschino cherries (with stems)**
½ **cup Southern Comfort***
1½ **cups semisweet chocolate morsels**
1 **Tbsp. shortening**
Wax paper

1. Drain maraschino cherries, and return to jar. Pour Southern Comfort into jar; cover with lid, and freeze 8 hours. Drain cherries, and pat very dry, reserving Southern Comfort for another use.
2. Microwave chocolate morsels and shortening in a small microwave-safe bowl at HIGH 1 to 1½ minutes or until melted and smooth, stirring at 30-second intervals.
3. Dip cherries quickly into melted chocolate, coating well. Place cherries on wax paper, stem sides up, and let stand until chocolate is firm (about 30 minutes). Serve immediately. Store leftovers in an airtight container in refrigerator up to 2 days.
*Brandy may be substituted.

Cappuccino-Walnut Toffee

make-ahead • party perfect

MAKES: about 2 lb.
HANDS-ON TIME: 35 min.
TOTAL TIME: 2 hr., 18 min.

Some brands of butter have slightly higher water content than others. We preferred Land O'Lakes butter. (Pictured on page 4)

2 **cups chopped walnuts**
1¼ **cups butter**
1 **cup granulated sugar**
⅓ **cup firmly packed light brown sugar**
1 **Tbsp. dark unsulphured molasses**
2 **tsp. instant espresso**
½ **tsp. ground cinnamon**
¼ **tsp. salt**
1 **cup milk chocolate morsels**
1 **cup white chocolate morsels**

1. Preheat oven to 350°. Butter a 15- x 10-inch jelly-roll pan.
2. Bake walnuts at 350° in a single layer in a shallow pan 8 to 10 minutes or until toasted and fragrant, stirring halfway through. Let cool 30 minutes.
3. Melt 1¼ cups butter in a 3½-qt. heavy saucepan over medium heat; stir in granulated sugar, next 5 ingredients, and ⅓ cup water. Cook, stirring constantly, until a candy thermometer registers 290° (soft crack stage), about 20 minutes. Remove pan from heat, and stir in walnuts.
4. Quickly pour mixture into prepared pan, and spread into an even layer. Immediately sprinkle milk chocolate and white chocolate morsels over top; let stand 5 minutes. Swirl chocolate using an off-set spatula. Cover and chill until firm (about 1 hour). Break toffee into pieces. Store in an airtight container in refrigerator up to 7 days. Serve cold or at room temperature.

RECIPE FROM GRETA CARLILE
SCOTTSBORO, ALABAMA

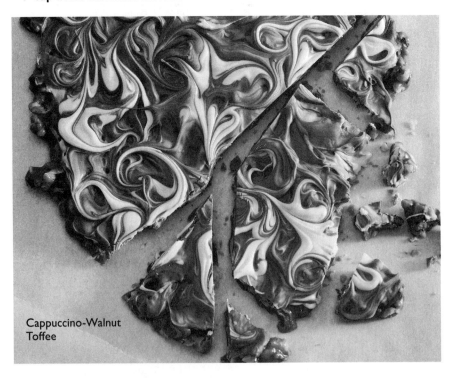

Cappuccino-Walnut Toffee

Homemade Chocolate-Dipped Caramels

make-ahead • party perfect

MAKES: 5 dozen
HANDS-ON TIME: 50 min.
TOTAL TIME: 10 hr., 35 min.

The hot caramel mixture needs to be poured immediately after stirring in vanilla, so be sure to butter your pan ahead of time.

- 1 cup sugar
- 1 cup dark corn syrup
- 1 cup butter
- 1 (14-oz.) can sweetened condensed milk
- 1 tsp. vanilla extract
- 1 (12-oz.) package semisweet chocolate morsels
- 2 Tbsp. shortening
  Wax paper
  Chopped crystallized ginger (optional)
  Coarse sea salt (optional)

1. Bring first 3 ingredients to a boil in a 3-qt. saucepan over medium heat; cook, without stirring, 7 minutes.
2. Stir in condensed milk, and bring to a boil over medium heat; cook, stirring constantly, until a candy thermometer registers 238° to 240° (soft ball stage), about 20 to 25 minutes.
3. Remove from heat, and stir in vanilla. Pour into a buttered 8-inch square pan. Let stand at room temperature 8 hours.
4. Invert caramel onto a cutting board; cut into 1-inch squares using a bench scraper or knife.
5. Cook chocolate and shortening in a saucepan over medium heat 3 to 5 minutes until melted and smooth. Remove from heat. Toss caramels in chocolate mixture, in batches, until thoroughly coated, using a fork. Transfer to wax paper. Sprinkle with crystallized ginger or coarse sea salt, if desired. Chill 1 hour. Let stand at room temperature 30 to 45 minutes before serving. Store leftovers in refrigerator up to 5 days.

Test Kitchen Secret

It can be intimidating to make candy. But keep your eye on the prize—a delicious treat—and go for it. Start with an accurate candy thermometer, and use these tips to make your caramels look candy-shop perfect.

{1}
CUT SQUARES THE EASY WAY
Grasp a bench scraper by the handle, place sharp edge on caramel, and press down to cut. This tool, sometimes called a dough scraper or pastry scraper, sells for about $6.

{2}
CREATE A FLAWLESS COATING
Drop squares into chocolate mixture; then lift out with a fork. Drag the fork against the lip of the pan to remove excess chocolate as you transfer each candy to wax paper.

Peanut Butter Truffles

quick prep • make-ahead • party perfect

MAKES: about 2 dozen
HANDS-ON TIME: 20 min.
TOTAL TIME: 3 hr., 30 min.

If you overbeat the chocolate mixture in Step 2, beat in 2 to 3 Tbsp. more whipping cream to return mixture to a smooth consistency.

- 1 (12-oz.) package semisweet chocolate morsels
- ½ cup whipping cream
- 3 Tbsp. creamy peanut butter
- ¾ cup finely chopped, lightly salted roasted peanuts
  Wax paper

1. Microwave first 3 ingredients in a medium-size microwave-safe bowl at HIGH 1 to 1½ minutes or until melted and smooth, stirring at 30-second intervals. Let cool 10 minutes.
2. Beat chocolate mixture at medium speed with an electric mixer 1 to 2 minutes or until whipped and smooth. Cover and chill 2 hours or until firm.
3. Shape chocolate mixture into 1-inch balls, using a small ice-cream scoop. Roll in chopped peanuts. (If chocolate mixture becomes too soft to shape, refrigerate until firm.) Place on wax paper-lined baking sheets. Chill 1 hour before serving. Store truffles in an airtight container in refrigerator up to 5 days.

Sweetheart Sugar Cookies

make-ahead • party perfect

MAKES: about 3 dozen
HANDS-ON TIME: 30 min.
TOTAL TIME: I hr., 45 min.

You may need to prepare additional meringue powder-and-water mixture as you decorate cookies. Sanding sugar may also be called "fine" sugar.

I	**cup butter, softened**
I	**cup granulated sugar**
I	**tsp. vanilla extract**
I	**large egg**
2¼	**cups all-purpose flour**
¼	**tsp. salt**
2	**tsp. meringue powder**
	Pink sanding sugar

1. Preheat oven to 350°. Beat butter, granulated sugar, and vanilla at medium speed with an electric mixer until fluffy. Add egg, beating until blended.

2. Combine flour and salt; gradually add to butter mixture, beating just until blended.

3. Divide dough into 2 equal portions; flatten each portion into a disk. Cover and chill 10 minutes.

4. Place I dough disk on a heavily floured surface, and roll to ⅛-inch thickness. Cut with a 3-inch heart-shaped cutter. Place 2 inches apart on lightly greased baking sheets. Repeat procedure with remaining dough disk.

5. Bake at 350° for 10 to 12 minutes or until edges are lightly browned. Let cool on baking sheets 5 minutes; transfer to wire racks, and let cool completely (about 30 minutes).

6. Whisk together meringue powder and 2 Tbsp. water. Brush cookies with mixture, or dip cookies in mixture, and sprinkle with sanding sugar.

Make Big and Little Cookies Too!

FOR JUMBO COOKIES:
Cut rolled-out dough with a 4½-inch heart-shaped cutter. Bake at 350° for 15 to 17 minutes or until edges are lightly browned. Makes: about I dozen

FOR BITE-SIZE COOKIES:
Cut rolled-out dough with a I-inch heart-shaped cutter. Bake at 350° for 8 to II minutes or until edges are lightly browned. Makes: about 20 dozen

Tipsy Pecan Clusters

make-ahead • party perfect

MAKES: I dozen
HANDS-ON TIME: 30 min.
TOTAL TIME: 2 hr., 40 min.

This recipe makes just enough to satisfy without having a lot of leftover temptations on hand. Recipe can easily be doubled.

60	**pecan halves**
6	**Tbsp. bourbon, divided**
½	**tsp. kosher salt**
	Wax paper
26	**caramels (about ½ [14-oz.] package caramels)**
2	**Tbsp. butter, divided**
I	**(4-oz.) bittersweet chocolate baking bar, chopped**
	Garnish: kosher salt

1. Preheat oven to 350°. Toss pecans with 4 Tbsp. bourbon in a small bowl, and let stand 30 minutes, stirring occasionally. Drain pecans, and toss with kosher salt. Bake pecans in a single layer in a jelly-roll pan 10 to 12 minutes or until toasted and fragrant, stirring halfway through. Cool in pan completely (about 30 minutes).

2. Remove pecans from pan; line pan with wax paper. Lightly grease wax paper. Return pecans to pan, and divide into 12 clusters (5 pecans per cluster).

3. Cook caramels, I Tbsp. butter, and remaining 2 Tbsp. bourbon in a heavy saucepan over low heat, stirring constantly, 12 to 14 minutes or until caramels melt and mixture is smooth.

4. Top each pecan cluster with about I Tbsp. caramel mixture. Freeze 30 minutes.

5. Microwave chocolate and remaining I Tbsp. butter in a glass measuring cup at HIGH I to 1½ minutes or until melted and smooth, stirring at 30-second intervals. Drizzle over clusters. Let stand 30 minutes before serving. Garnish, if desired. Candies may be stored in an airtight container in refrigerator up to 5 days.

Lasagna

This family favorite has less fat and calories than traditional versions, and it's a delicious way to sneak veggies onto the plate.

Fresh Vegetable Lasagna

quick prep • good for you • make-ahead • party perfect

MAKES: 8 servings
HANDS-ON TIME: 30 min.
TOTAL TIME: 3 hr., 14 min., including sauce

If you're in a hurry, use your favorite store-bought low-sodium marinara sauce. (Pictured on page 168)

- 4 medium zucchini, halved lengthwise and thinly sliced (about 1½ lb.)
- 1 (8-oz.) package sliced fresh mushrooms
- 2 garlic cloves, minced
  Vegetable cooking spray
- 1 medium-size red bell pepper, chopped
- 1 medium-size yellow bell pepper, chopped
- 1 yellow onion, chopped
- ½ tsp. salt
- 1½ cups fat-free ricotta cheese
- 1 large egg
- 2 cups (8 oz.) shredded part-skim mozzarella cheese, divided
- ½ cup freshly grated Parmesan cheese, divided
- 5 cups Basic Marinara Sauce
- 1 (8-oz.) package no-boil lasagna noodles

1. Preheat oven to 450°. Bake zucchini, mushrooms, and garlic in a jelly-roll pan coated with cooking spray 12 to 14 minutes or until vegetables are crisp-tender, stirring halfway through. Repeat procedure with bell peppers and onion. Reduce oven temperature to 350°. Toss together vegetables and salt in a bowl.

2. Stir together ricotta, egg, 1½ cups shredded mozzarella cheese, and ¼ cup grated Parmesan cheese.

3. Spread 1 cup Basic Marinara Sauce in a 13- x 9-inch baking dish coated with cooking spray. Top with 3 noodles, 1 cup sauce, one-third of ricotta mixture, and one-third of vegetable mixture; repeat layers twice, beginning with 3 noodles. Top with remaining noodles and 1 cup sauce. Sprinkle with remaining ½ cup shredded mozzarella and ¼ cup grated Parmesan.

4. Bake, covered, at 350° for 45 minutes. Uncover and bake 10 to 15 more minutes or until cheese is melted and golden. Let stand 10 minutes.

NOTE: We tested with Ronzoni Oven Ready Lasagna.

PER SERVING: **CALORIES** 282; **FAT** 9.8G (SAT 4.9G, MONO 2.5G, POLY 0.6G); **PROTEIN** 19.9G; **CARB** 28.8G; **FIBER** 4.1G; **CHOL** 50MG; **IRON** 2.6MG; **SODIUM** 837MG; **CALC** 456MG

Basic Marinara Sauce

quick prep • good for you • make-ahead

MAKES: 11 cups
HANDS-ON TIME: 17 min.
TOTAL TIME: 1 hr., 15 min.

This recipe makes a big batch. Make it ahead, and store it in the refrigerator up to 5 days, or freeze it in smaller batches up to 3 months.

- 3 cups chopped yellow onions (about 3 medium)
- 1 Tbsp. olive oil
- 1 Tbsp. sugar
- 3 garlic cloves, minced
- 5 tsp. freshly ground Italian seasoning
- 2 tsp. salt
- 2 Tbsp. balsamic vinegar
- 2 cups low-sodium fat-free vegetable broth
- 3 (28-oz.) cans no-salt-added crushed tomatoes

1. Sauté onions in hot oil in a large Dutch oven over medium-high heat 5 minutes or until tender. Add sugar and next 3 ingredients; sauté 1 minute. Stir in vinegar; cook 30 seconds. Add broth and tomatoes. Bring to a boil; reduce heat to low, and simmer, stirring occasionally, 55 minutes or until sauce thickens.

NOTE: We tested with McCormick Italian Herb Seasoning Grinder (set on medium) and Dei Fratelli Crushed Tomatoes.

PER CUP: **CALORIES** 71; **FAT** 1.6G (SAT 0.2G, MONO 1G, POLY 0.2G); **PROTEIN** 2.1G; **CARB** 13.9G; **FIBER** 2.7G; **CHOL** 0MG; **IRON** 2.2MG; **SODIUM** 557MG; **CALC** 77MG

New Orleans Beignets

Fry up these golden gems just like they do in the French Quarter. We show you how in just four easy steps.

New Orleans Beignets

party perfect

MAKES: about 6 dozen
HANDS-ON TIME: 43 min.
TOTAL TIME: 4 hr., 48 min.
(Pictured on page 5)

- 1 (¼-oz.) envelope active dry yeast
- 1½ cups warm water (105° to 115°), divided
- ½ cup granulated sugar
- 1 cup evaporated milk
- 2 large eggs, lightly beaten
- 1 tsp. salt
- ¼ cup shortening
- 6½ to 7 cups bread flour
   Vegetable oil
   Sifted powdered sugar

Test Kitchen Secret

Keep the freshly fried beignets warm in a 200° oven up to 30 minutes. To make ahead, store the dough in an airtight container in the refrigerator up to 1 week.

Four Easy Steps

{1}
MAKE THE YEAST MIXTURE

Combine yeast, ½ cup warm water, and 1 tsp. granulated sugar in bowl of a heavy-duty stand mixer; let stand 5 minutes. Add milk, eggs, salt, and remaining granulated sugar.

{2}
FORM A DOUGH

Microwave remaining 1 cup water until hot (about 115°); stir in shortening until melted. Add to yeast mixture. Beat at low speed, gradually adding 4 cups flour, until smooth. Gradually add remaining 2½ to 3 cups flour, beating until a sticky dough forms. Transfer to a lightly greased bowl; turn to grease top. Cover and chill 4 to 24 hours.

{3}
ROLL AND CUT

Turn dough out onto a floured surface; roll to ¼-inch thickness. Cut into 2½-inch squares.

{4}
FRY UNTIL GOLDEN

Pour oil to depth of 2 to 3 inches into a Dutch oven; heat to 360°. Fry dough, in batches, 2 to 3 minutes on each side or until golden brown. Drain on a wire rack. Dust immediately with powdered sugar.

March

Everything's Better with Bacon

There's a reason pork-lovers playfully refer to this crisp, mouthwatering Southern staple as "God's Bookmark." Its sweet-salty-smoky flavor lends a heavenly touch to everything from savory meals to (mark our words!) drinks and dessert.

Bacon Boot Camp

Three Foolproof Ways To Prepare It:

{1}

THE CLASSIC Cook bacon in a large cast-iron skillet over medium-low heat, turning occasionally, 30 minutes or until crisp; remove bacon, and drain on paper towels.

{2}

THE CLEANEST Preheat oven to 400°. Arrange bacon in a single layer, with sides touching, in an aluminum foil-lined broiler pan. Bake 14 to 16 minutes or until crisp; remove bacon, and drain on paper towels.

{3}

THE FASTEST Wrap six bacon slices loosely in paper towels. Microwave at HIGH 4 to 4½ minutes. Let stand 1 to 2 minutes or until crisp.

BLT Benedict with Avocado-Tomato Relish

quick prep

MAKES: 6 servings
HANDS-ON TIME: 23 min.
TOTAL TIME: 23 min.

Sunny-side up or sliced boiled eggs would work just as well as poached eggs for this dish you've got to try. (Pictured on page 170)

- 1 cup halved grape tomatoes
- 1 avocado, diced
- 1 Tbsp. chopped fresh basil
- 1 garlic clove, minced
- 2 Tbsp. extra virgin olive oil
  Salt and pepper to taste
- 1 Tbsp. red wine vinegar, divided
- 6 large eggs
- ¼ cup mayonnaise
- 6 (¾-inch-thick) bakery bread slices, toasted
- 3 cups firmly packed arugula
- 12 thick bacon slices, cooked

1. Combine tomatoes and next 5 ingredients and 2½ tsp. red wine vinegar in a small bowl.
2. Add water to depth of 3 inches in a large saucepan. Bring to a boil; reduce heat, and maintain at a light simmer. Add remaining ½ tsp. red wine vinegar. Break eggs, and slip into water, 1 at a time, as close as possible to surface. Simmer 3 to 5 minutes or to desired degree of doneness. Remove with a slotted spoon. Trim edges, if desired.
3. Spread mayonnaise on 1 side of each bread slice. Layer each with ½ cup arugula, 2 bacon slices, and 1 egg. Top with tomato mixture.

Cantaloupe-Bacon Relish

quick prep • party perfect

MAKES: about 2½ cups
HANDS-ON TIME: 20 min.
TOTAL TIME: 20 min.

Serve relish over salad greens topped with sliced grilled chicken, or try it on grilled crostini with goat cheese as an appetizer.

1½ cups finely diced cantaloupe
½ cup seeded, diced
    cucumber
5 bacon slices, cooked and crumbled
1 green onion, minced
1 Tbsp. chopped fresh mint
2 Tbsp. extra virgin olive oil
2 to 3 tsp. red wine vinegar
¼ tsp. pepper
    Pinch of salt

1. Combine all ingredients. Serve immediately.

Bacon-Infused Bourbon

party perfect

MAKES: 1 (750-milliliter) bottle
HANDS-ON TIME: 10 min.
TOTAL TIME: 4 hr., 10 min., plus 3 days for chilling

1. Remove ¼ cup bourbon from 1 (750-milliliter) bottle. Pour ¼ cup warm bacon grease into bottle. Cover and let stand 4 hours, shaking bottle occasionally. Chill 3 to 7 days. Pour bourbon through a wire-mesh strainer lined with a coffee filter into a bowl; discard filter. Clean bottle. Pour strained bourbon into bottle, and store at room temperature up to 6 months.
NOTE: We tested with Benton's Smoked Country Bacon and Woodford Reserve Bourbon.

Mango-Spinach Salad with Warm Bacon Vinaigrette

quick prep • party perfect

MAKES: 4 servings
HANDS-ON TIME: 18 min.
TOTAL TIME: 18 min.

This is a delicious partner for grilled fish. Don't forget fresh crusty bread to soak up every bit of the warm vinaigrette. (Pictured on page 171)

4 thick bacon slices, diced
½ medium-size red onion,
    thinly sliced
¼ cup red wine vinegar
1 Tbsp. lime juice
1 Tbsp. honey
1 (9-oz.) package fresh spinach
1 mango, peeled and diced
⅓ cup crumbled queso fresco
    (fresh Mexican cheese)
    Salt and pepper to taste

1. Cook bacon in a skillet over medium-high heat 6 to 8 minutes or until crisp; remove bacon, and drain on paper towels, reserving 1 Tbsp. drippings in skillet.
2. Sauté onion in hot drippings 2 to 3 minutes or until soft. Add vinegar, lime juice, and honey; cook 2 minutes, stirring to loosen particles from bottom of skillet.
3. Place spinach in a serving bowl. Add warm vinaigrette, and toss to coat. Top with mango, queso fresco, and bacon; season with salt and pepper to taste. Serve immediately.

Springtime Pasta with Bacon

quick prep • party perfect

MAKES: 6 to 8 servings
HANDS-ON TIME: 20 min.
TOTAL TIME: 30 min.

Enjoy this colorful dish warm or chilled; leftovers are perfect for a brown bag lunch the next day. Add grilled shrimp kabobs and a crisp Sauvignon Blanc for a relaxing meal with friends. (Pictured on page 171)

1 (16-oz.) package orecchiette
    pasta*
1 cup frozen sweet peas
1½ cups fresh snow peas
8 radishes, cut into wedges
2 large carrots, grated
2 green onions, thinly sliced
⅓ cup coarsely chopped
    fresh parsley
¼ cup lemon juice
¼ cup olive oil
    Salt and pepper to taste
6 thick bacon slices, cooked
    and crumbled
4 oz. crumbled goat cheese
    (optional)

1. Cook pasta according to package directions, adding sweet peas and snow peas during last minute of cook time. Drain.
2. Toss pasta mixture with radishes and next 5 ingredients; season with salt and pepper to taste. Sprinkle with bacon and, if desired, crumbled goat cheese.
*1 (16-oz.) package farfalle (bow-tie) pasta may be substituted.

Just Add Grease

That's right. Just like the recipe says, we added smoky flavor to bourbon using what sometimes gets tossed.

Bacon-Herb Cupcakes

party perfect

MAKES: about 32
HANDS-ON TIME: 25 min.
TOTAL TIME: 1 hr., 21 min.

Try these as a perfect companion to a cocktail. Test Kitchen Specialist Marian Cooper Cairns likes to use a combination of parsley, thyme, and oregano, but sage, rosemary, basil, and chives will work just as well. Using a small cookie dough scoop for the batter gives the baked cupcakes a pretty round top.

1½   cups sour cream
½   cup cooked, finely crumbled bacon
½   cup melted butter
¼   cup finely chopped assorted
     fresh herbs
2   green onions, chopped
½   tsp. pepper
2   cups self-rising flour
6   oz. cream cheese, softened
     Garnishes: assorted fresh herbs,
     cooked and crumbled bacon

1. Preheat oven to 375°. Stir together first 6 ingredients. Stir in flour until blended. (Mixture will be thick.) Spoon batter into lightly greased miniature muffin pans, filling completely full.

2. Bake at 375° for 26 to 28 minutes or until golden brown. Remove cupcakes from pans to a wire rack, and cool completely (about 30 minutes). Spread or pipe tops of cupcakes with cream cheese. Garnish, if desired.

Bacon-Peanut Truffles

make-ahead • party perfect

MAKES: about 2 dozen
HANDS-ON TIME: 30 min.
TOTAL TIME: 4 hr.

2   Tbsp. dark brown sugar
¼   tsp. salt
¾   cup honey-roasted peanuts
8   thick bacon slices, cooked
     and divided
⅓   cup creamy peanut butter
     Parchment paper
6   oz. bittersweet chocolate,
     chopped

Bacon Bits

Here's how to sprinkle smoky, salty bacon in a new way. (Step aside, ho-hum baked potato.)

BEETS AND ORANGES: Arrange sliced roasted beets, sliced oranges, and fresh parsley leaves on a platter. Sprinkle with crumbled blue cheese and cooked, crumbled bacon. Drizzle with extra virgin olive oil, and sprinkle with salt and pepper to taste.

STREET-STYLE GRILLED CORN: Brush hot grilled corn with mayonnaise. Roll in cooked, finely crumbled bacon. Sprinkle with Mexican chili powder. Serve with lime wedges.

LAYERED GUACAMOLE: Top guacamole with crumbled goat cheese; halved grape tomatoes; thinly sliced fresh basil; and cooked, crumbled bacon. Serve with pita chips.

DRESSY SALTINES: Arrange saltine crackers on a baking sheet; brush with beaten egg white. Sprinkle with cooked, finely crumbled bacon; grated Parmesan cheese; and pepper. Bake at 325° for 8 to 10 minutes or until golden.

BACON-CAKES AND BERRIES: Stir cooked, crumbled bacon into buttermilk pancake batter. Cook pancakes, in batches, in a lightly greased skillet over medium heat. Top with assorted fresh berries. Serve with warm maple syrup.

GRILLED ONION CROSTINI: Spread grilled French bread baguette rounds with softened cream cheese (or Brie or buttery garlic-and-herb spreadable cheese). Top with grilled red onions, chopped, and cooked, crumbled bacon. Sprinkle with fresh thyme leaves and pepper to taste.

ROASTED CARROTS AND PARSNIPS: Diagonally slice ¾ lb. each carrots and parsnips. Toss with 2 Tbsp. olive oil, ½ tsp. ground ginger, and salt and pepper to taste. Bake at 425° for 30 to 35 minutes or until golden. Sprinkle with cooked, crumbled bacon and chopped fresh chives.

APPETIZER PIZZA: Spread a thin layer of fig preserves onto a prebaked thin pizza crust. Sprinkle with crumbled Gorgonzola cheese; chopped pecans; and cooked, crumbled bacon. Season with pepper to taste. Bake at 450° for 8 minutes or until crisp. Top with fresh arugula.

ITALIAN BEAN SALAD: Toss drained and rinsed canned cannellini beans with chopped sun-dried tomatoes, toasted pine nuts, and balsamic vinaigrette. Spoon over thinly sliced zucchini. Sprinkle with cooked, crumbled bacon and crumbled feta cheese.

1. Process first 3 ingredients and 6 bacon slices in a food processor 20 to 30 seconds or until finely ground. Stir together bacon mixture and peanut butter in a small bowl until smooth. Cover and chill 2 hours.

2. Shape rounded teaspoonfuls of bacon mixture into ¾-inch balls. Place on a parchment paper-lined baking sheet; chill 1 hour.

3. Chop remaining 2 bacon slices. Microwave chocolate in a microwave-safe bowl at HIGH 1 to 1½ minutes or until melted and smooth, stirring at 30-second intervals. Dip chilled bacon balls into chocolate. Place on a parchment paper-lined baking sheet. Immediately sprinkle tops with bacon. Chill 30 minutes before serving. Store in an airtight container in refrigerator up to 2 weeks.

Garden-Fresh Baby Vegetables

Here's how to work these tender-sweet (and tiny!) tastes of spring into your rotation.

Beer-Cheese Fondue with Baby Cauliflower

quick prep • party perfect

MAKES: 6 servings
HANDS-ON TIME: 15 min.
TOTAL TIME: 20 min.

- 2 cups (8 oz.) shredded extra-sharp white Cheddar cheese
- 2 cups (8 oz.) shredded Jarlsberg cheese
- 1½ Tbsp. all-purpose flour
- 1 cup beer
- 3 Tbsp. chopped fresh chives
  Assorted baby cauliflower

1. Toss cheeses with flour. Bring beer to a boil in a large heavy saucepan; reduce heat to medium-low. Gradually whisk cheeses into beer, whisking constantly until melted. Stir in chives. Place cauliflower in a steamer basket over boiling water. Cover and steam 5 to 7 minutes or until fork-tender. Serve with fondue.

Glazed Baby Carrots

Glazed Baby Carrots

good for you • party perfect

MAKES: 6 servings
HANDS-ON TIME: 20 min.
TOTAL TIME: 55 min.

- 1½ lb. baby carrots with tops (about 3 bunches)
- ½ cup orange marmalade
- ½ cup fresh orange juice
- 2 Tbsp. butter
- 1 Tbsp. Dijon mustard

1. Preheat oven to 425°. Cut tops from carrots, leaving 1 inch of stems on each; gently wash and peel carrots. Bring marmalade and next 3 ingredients to a boil in a large ovenproof skillet over medium-high heat; add carrots, stirring to coat. Bake 30 minutes or until carrots are tender and lightly browned, stirring every 10 minutes.

Roasted Baby Beet Salad

good for you • party perfect

MAKES: 6 servings
HANDS-ON TIME: 20 min.
TOTAL TIME: 1 hr., 35 min., including vinaigrette

Trim the tops, but leave part of the stems to ensure the colorful pigment remains inside the beet during roasting.

- 2 lb. assorted baby beets with tops
- 1 Tbsp. olive oil
  Brown Sugar Vinaigrette
- 5 cups loosely packed baby lettuces
- 1 cup crumbled Gorgonzola cheese
- 1 cup lightly salted roasted pecan halves

1. Preheat oven to 400°. Trim beet tops to ½ inch; gently wash beets. Place beets in a single layer in a shallow baking pan; drizzle with oil, tossing gently to coat. Cover pan tightly with aluminum foil.
2. Bake at 400° for 40 minutes or until tender. Transfer to a wire rack, and let cool 30 minutes.
3. Peel beets, and cut in half. Gently toss beets with ⅓ cup Brown Sugar Vinaigrette. Arrange lettuces on a serving platter. Top with beet mixture, Gorgonzola cheese, and pecans; serve with remaining Brown Sugar Vinaigrette.

Brown Sugar Vinaigrette

quick prep

MAKES: ⅔ cup
HANDS-ON TIME: 5 min.
TOTAL TIME: 5 min.

1. Whisk together ⅓ cup white balsamic vinegar; 1 large shallot, minced; 2 Tbsp. light brown sugar; ½ tsp. freshly ground pepper; ½ tsp. vanilla extract; and ¼ tsp. salt in a small bowl. Add ⅓ cup olive oil in a slow, steady stream, whisking constantly until smooth.

Sautéed Baby Beet Greens

quick prep • good for you

MAKES: 4 servings
HANDS-ON TIME: 10 min.
TOTAL TIME: 10 min.

Similar in flavor to Swiss chard, beet greens can be prepared in the same way as turnip or collard greens or sautéed like fresh spinach.

1 **garlic clove, thinly sliced**
1 **tsp. olive oil**
8 **cups fresh beet greens**
   Salt and pepper to taste

1. Sauté garlic in hot oil in a large skillet over medium-high heat 30 seconds. Add beet greens, and sauté 2 to 3 minutes or until wilted. Season with salt and pepper to taste.

Sautéed Baby Squash and Leeks

quick prep • good for you • party perfect

MAKES: 6 servings
HANDS-ON TIME: 10 min.
TOTAL TIME: 10 min.

1½ **lb. assorted baby squash, halved**
1 **cup sliced baby leeks**
2 **Tbsp. olive oil**
   Salt and pepper to taste
½ **cup crumbled feta cheese**
2 **Tbsp. finely chopped fresh basil**

1. Sauté squash and leeks in hot oil in a large skillet over medium-high heat 5 minutes or until tender. Season with salt and pepper to taste; sprinkle with cheese and basil.

5 No-Fuss Dinners

Streamline weeknight cooking with these five delicious main-dish ideas paired with simple sides.

Tangy Turkey Burgers

quick prep • party perfect

MAKES: 6 servings
HANDS-ON TIME: 27 min.
TOTAL TIME: 27 min.

Easy side: *Toss 1 (20-oz.) package frozen sweet potato fries with 1 Tbsp. sesame seeds, 1 Tbsp. sesame oil, and 1 tsp. kosher salt. Bake according to package directions.*

1½ **lb. ground turkey**
2 **green onions, chopped**
2 **Tbsp. white wine-and-herb chicken marinade**
1 **tsp. garlic salt with parsley**
1 **tsp. pepper**
6 **French hamburger buns, toasted**
   Toppings: gourmet mixed lettuce leaves, sliced avocado, mayonnaise

1. Gently combine first 5 ingredients. Shape mixture into 6 (4-inch) patties.
2. Heat a cast-iron grill pan over medium-high heat. Cook patties in pan 6 to 8 minutes on each side or until done. Serve burgers on buns with desired toppings.
NOTE: We tested with Publix French Hamburger Buns, McCormick California Style Garlic Salt with Parsley, and Lea & Perrins Marinade for Chicken.

RECIPE INSPIRED BY MARK MOORE
SAN ANTONIO, TEXAS

Lime Chicken Tenders and Orzo Salad

quick prep • good for you

MAKES: 6 servings
HANDS-ON TIME: 20 min.
TOTAL TIME: 30 min.

Easy side: *Stir together 2 large avocadoes, thinly sliced, and 2 Tbsp. thinly sliced red onion; sprinkle with juice from 1 lime. Serve over Bibb lettuce leaves. Season with salt and pepper to taste.*

1 **lime**
1¼ **lb. chicken breast tenders**
5 **Tbsp. olive oil, divided**
2 **garlic cloves, pressed**
2 **tsp. kosher salt**
½ **tsp. pepper**
1½ **cups uncooked orzo pasta**
3 **Tbsp. red wine vinegar**
2 **tsp. country-style Dijon mustard**
1 **medium-size red bell pepper, chopped**
¾ **cup peeled and diced cucumber**
2 **Tbsp. chopped fresh dill**

1. Preheat grill to 300° to 350° (medium) heat. Grate zest from lime to equal 1 tsp. Cut lime in half; squeeze juice from lime to equal 3 Tbsp.
2. Combine chicken, lime zest, lime juice, ¼ cup olive oil, and next 3 ingredients. Let stand 10 minutes. Remove chicken from marinade, discarding marinade.
3. Grill chicken, covered with grill lid, 5 to 7 minutes on each side or until done.
4. Prepare pasta according to package directions. Combine vinegar, mustard, and remaining 1 Tbsp. olive oil. Toss orzo, bell pepper, cucumber, and dill with vinegar mixture. Season with salt and pepper to taste. Serve with grilled chicken.

Tuna Cakes with Creole Mayonnaise

quick prep • good for you

MAKES: 8 servings
HANDS-ON TIME: 36 min.
TOTAL TIME: 36 min.

Easy side: Cut 2 carrots and 2 yellow squash into very thin strips using a Y-shaped vegetable peeler. Sauté in 1 Tbsp. hot olive oil until vegetables are tender. Sprinkle with salt and pepper to taste.

- 2 (12-oz.) cans solid white tuna in spring water, drained*
- 1¼ cups Italian breadcrumbs
- 2 large eggs, lightly beaten
- 2 tsp. lemon zest
- 2 tsp. Dijon mustard
- 1 cup mayonnaise, divided
- 1¼ tsp. Creole seasoning, divided
- ¼ cup olive oil
- 1 tsp. lemon juice

1. Drain and rinse tuna. Place tuna and breadcrumbs in a large bowl; stir in eggs, lemon zest, mustard, ⅓ cup mayonnaise, and 1 tsp. Creole seasoning. Shape mixture into 8 (3-inch) patties.

2. Cook 4 patties in 2 Tbsp. hot oil in a large skillet over medium-high heat 2 to 3 minutes on each side or until golden; drain on paper towels. Repeat with remaining tuna cakes and oil.

3. Combine lemon juice and remaining ⅔ cup mayonnaise and ¼ tsp. Creole seasoning. Serve with hot tuna cakes.

*5 (5-oz.) cans solid white tuna in spring water, drained well, may be substituted.

Grilled Steak and Vegetable Kabobs

good for you • party perfect

MAKES: 4 servings
HANDS-ON TIME: 20 min.
TOTAL TIME: 55 min.

Easy side: Cut 2 large zucchini into 2-inch-long sticks. Place on an aluminum-foil lined baking sheet, and toss with 1 Tbsp. olive oil and 1 tsp. salt. Bake at 425° for 25 minutes or until browned, turning once.

- 1½ Tbsp. honey
- 1½ Tbsp. soy sauce
- 1 Tbsp. olive oil
- ¼ tsp. salt
- 1 lb. flat-iron steaks, cut into 1-inch cubes
- 8 (7- to 8-inch) wooden skewers
- 1 large sweet onion, cut into ½-inch wedges
- 1 (8-oz.) package fresh mushrooms
- 1 medium-size green bell pepper, cut into 1-inch cubes

1. Preheat grill to 350° to 400° (medium-high) heat. Whisk together first 4 ingredients in a large shallow dish or zip-top plastic freezer bag; add beef, turning to coat. Cover or seal bag, and chill 20 minutes, turning once.

2. Meanwhile, soak the wooden skewers in water 10 minutes.

3. Remove beef from marinade, discarding marinade. Thread beef onto 4 skewers, onion onto 2 skewers, and mushrooms and peppers onto remaining 2 skewers. Sprinkle kabobs with desired amount of salt and pepper.

4. Grill beef and vegetables at the same time, covered with grill lid. Grill beef 6 minutes on each side or to desired degree of doneness. Grill vegetables 10 minutes or until tender, turning occasionally.

Roasted Sesame Pork Tenderloin with Asian Slaw

good for you • party perfect

MAKES: 4 servings
HANDS-ON TIME: 15 min.
TOTAL TIME: 50 min.

For a tasty next-day lunch, wrap leftovers in a flour tortilla.

- 3 Tbsp. soy sauce
- ½ cup sesame-ginger dressing, divided
- 1 (1-lb.) pork tenderloin
- 1 head napa cabbage, shredded (about 4 cups)
- 4 green onions, sliced
- 2 large carrots, grated
- 1 cup chopped fresh cilantro
- ¼ cup chopped wasabi-and-soy sauce-flavored almonds

1. Preheat oven to 450°. Whisk together soy sauce and ¼ cup dressing in a large shallow dish or zip-top plastic freezer bag; add pork, turning to coat. Cover or seal, and chill 10 minutes, turning once.

2. Meanwhile, combine cabbage, next 3 ingredients, and remaining ¼ cup dressing. Cover and chill until ready to serve.

3. Remove pork from marinade, discarding marinade. Place pork on a lightly greased aluminum foil-lined baking sheet.

4. Bake at 450° for 20 to 25 minutes or until done. Remove from oven, and let stand 5 minutes before slicing.

5. Toss slaw with almonds; serve with pork.

NOTE: We tested with Maple Grove Farms of Vermont All Natural Sesame Ginger Dressing and Blue Diamond Bold Wasabi & Soy Sauce Almonds.

Soul Food

Lenten lunches at Birmingham's Cathedral Church of the Advent have inspired a hungry following.

More than 100 years ago, church volunteers in the Magic City wanted to find a way to encourage people to attend weekday sermons during the 40 days of Lent. Their tactic? Great food. Today, hundreds of locals show up to get fed after they, well, get fed. Here are the crowd-pleasing dishes. Some are classic Southern; all are simple and delicious.

Lenten Lunch

SERVES 6

Chicken, Mushroom, and
Wild Rice Soup

Cathedral Chicken Salad

Bing Cherry Salad

Peach-Pecan Muffins

Chicken, Mushroom, and Wild Rice Soup

party perfect

MAKES: 14 cups
HANDS-ON TIME: 40 min.
TOTAL TIME: 40 min.

Volunteers at the Cathedral Church of the Advent prepare chicken broth from scratch, making this hearty soup doubly delicious.

- 2 (6-oz.) packages long-grain and wild rice mix
- 10 cups chicken broth, divided
- 3 Tbsp. butter
- 1 cup sliced fresh mushrooms
- 1 cup chopped onion
- 1 cup chopped celery
- ¼ cup butter
- ½ cup all-purpose flour
- ½ cup half-and-half
- 2 Tbsp. dry white wine
- 2 cups shredded cooked chicken breasts
  Garnishes: fresh parsley leaves, freshly cracked pepper

1. Bring rice, 4 cups chicken broth, and 1 seasoning packet from rice mix to a boil in a saucepan over medium-high heat. Cover, reduce heat to low, and simmer 20 minutes or until liquid is absorbed and rice is tender. (Reserve remaining seasoning packet for another use.)

2. Meanwhile, melt 3 Tbsp. butter in a large skillet over medium heat; add mushrooms, onion, and celery, and cook, stirring often, 10 to 12 minutes or until tender.

3. Melt ¼ cup butter in a Dutch oven over medium heat; whisk in flour, and cook, whisking constantly, 1 minute or until thickened and bubbly. Gradually whisk in remaining 6 cups broth, and cook, stirring often, 8 to 10 minutes or until slightly thickened. Whisk in half-and-half and wine. Stir in mushroom mixture, chicken, and rice. Cook, stirring occasionally, 5 to 10 minutes or until thoroughly heated. (Do not boil.) Garnish, if desired.

Chicken, Mushroom, and
Wild Rice Soup

A Divine Tradition

Though many Southern churches serve lunches during Lent, few can boast a 100-year-plus history. Originally, the ladies of The Advent served light meals only to parishioners who came for the noon sermons. They began serving hot meals in 1980 to raise funds for outreach programs. Now team leaders Eleanor Estes, Fontaine Pope, and Marian Phillips (pictured at right) manage a crew of several hundred volunteers who make homemade soups, salads, and more. "Preparing the lunches brings church members together," says volunteer Robin Anderson. "That's been a wonderful bonus."

Cathedral Chicken Salad

good for you • make-ahead • party perfect

MAKES: about 3 ½ cups
HANDS-ON TIME: 15 min.
TOTAL TIME: 15 min.

Serve this deliciously simple recipe like they do at The Advent: on a lettuce leaf with a sprinkle of paprika.

½ cup mayonnaise
1 Tbsp. fresh lemon juice
2 tsp. Dijon mustard
½ tsp. ground white pepper
½ tsp. seasoning salt
3 cups chopped cooked chicken
½ cup chopped celery

1. Stir together first 5 ingredients until blended.
2. Place chicken and celery in a large bowl; add mayonnaise mixture, and toss to combine.
NOTE: We tested with Hellmann's Real Mayonnaise and Lawry's Seasoned Salt.

Bing Cherry Salad

good for you • make-ahead

MAKES: 8 servings
HANDS-ON TIME: 12 min.
TOTAL TIME: 9 hr., 50 min.
(Pictured on page 8)

1 (15-oz.) can Bing cherries (dark, sweet pitted cherries)
2 (8-oz.) cans crushed pineapple in juice
1 (6-oz.) package cherry-flavored gelatin
1 cup cold water
Mayonnaise (optional)
Garnishes: poppy seeds, arugula leaves

1. Drain cherries and pineapple, reserving 1½ cups juice in a saucepan. (If necessary, add water to equal 1½ cups.) Bring juice mixture to a boil over medium heat; stir in gelatin, and cook, stirring constantly, 2 minutes or until gelatin dissolves. Remove from heat, and stir in 1 cup cold water. Chill until consistency of unbeaten egg whites (about 1½ hours).
2. Gently stir in drained cherries and pineapple. Pour mixture into an 8-inch square baking dish or 8 (⅔-cup) molds. Cover and chill 8 hours or until firm. Dollop with mayonnaise, and garnish, if desired.

Peach-Pecan Muffins

quick prep • make-ahead

MAKES: 12 muffins
HANDS-ON TIME: 15 min.
TOTAL TIME: 45 min.
(Pictured on page 8)

PECAN STREUSEL

½ cup chopped pecans
⅓ cup firmly packed brown sugar
¼ cup all-purpose flour
2 Tbsp. melted butter
1 tsp. ground cinnamon

MUFFINS

1½ cups all-purpose flour
½ cup granulated sugar
2 tsp. baking powder
1 tsp. ground cinnamon
¼ tsp. salt
½ cup butter, melted
¼ cup milk
1 large egg
1 cup frozen sliced peaches, thawed and diced
12 paper baking cups
Vegetable cooking spray

1. Prepare Streusel: Stir together pecans and next 4 ingredients until crumbly.
2. Prepare Muffins: Preheat oven to 400°. Combine flour and next 4 ingredients in a large bowl; make a well in center of mixture. Stir together butter, milk, and egg; add to dry ingredients, stirring just until moistened. Gently stir in peaches.
3. Place paper baking cups in 1 (12-cup) muffin pan, and coat with cooking spray; spoon batter into cups, filling two-thirds full. Sprinkle with Pecan Streusel.
4. Bake at 400° for 20 to 25 minutes or until a wooden pick inserted in center comes out clean. Cool in pan on a wire rack 10 minutes; remove from pan, and serve warm or at room temperature.

Red Beans and Rice

Here's a low-fat spin on a Louisiana favorite, with all the classic, cue-the-trombones flavor you'd expect in this hearty dish.

Five Reasons to Eat More Beans

{1}

The fiber in beans helps you feel full faster and prevents overeating.

{2}

Beans are an excellent (and inexpensive) source of protein.

{3}

They can help lower your cholesterol and reduce the risk of heart attack.

{4}

Beans have a positive effect on blood sugar, giving you long-lasting energy.

{5}

They help protect you from some cancers.

Stovetop Red Beans and Rice

good for you • make-ahead • party perfect

MAKES: about 10 cups
HANDS-ON TIME: 15 min.
TOTAL TIME: 2 hr., 45 min.

Make a big batch for company, or freeze leftovers for later.

- 1 lb. dried red kidney beans
- ½ lb. andouille smoked chicken sausage, thinly sliced
- 3 celery ribs, chopped
- 1 green bell pepper, chopped
- 1 medium onion, chopped
- 3 garlic cloves, minced
- 1 Tbsp. Creole seasoning
- 3 cups uncooked long-grain rice
- Garnish: sliced green onions

1. Place beans in a Dutch oven; add water 2 inches above beans. Bring to a boil. Boil 1 minute; cover, remove from heat, and soak 1 hour. Drain.

2. Sauté sausage and next 3 ingredients in Dutch oven over medium-high heat 10 minutes or until sausage is browned. Add garlic; sauté 1 minute. Add beans, Creole seasoning, and 7 cups water. Bring to a boil; reduce heat to low, and simmer 1 to 1½ hours or until beans are tender.

3. Meanwhile, cook rice according to package directions. Serve with red bean mixture. Garnish, if desired.

NOTE: We tested with Aidells Organic Fully Cooked Cajun Style Andouille Smoked Chicken Sausage.

PER SERVING (ABOUT 1 CUP BEAN MIXTURE AND 1 CUP RICE): CALORIES 397; FAT 2.3G (SAT 0.8G, MONO 0.2G, POLY 0.3G); PROTEIN 18.9G; CARB 74.4G; FIBER 11.3G; CHOL 24MG; IRON 5.6MG; SODIUM 319MG; CALC 99MG

Try These Twists!

VEGETARIAN RED BEANS AND RICE: Omit chicken sausage. Prepare recipe as directed in Step 1. Coarsely chop celery, green bell pepper, onion, and 1 red bell pepper. Sauté chopped vegetables and garlic in 1 Tbsp. hot olive oil 6 to 8 minutes or until tender. Stir together vegetables, beans, Creole seasoning, 1 tsp. smoked paprika, 1 vegetable bouillon cube, and 7 cups water in Dutch oven. Bring to a boil, reduce heat to low, and simmer as directed. Season with salt to taste. Serve with rice. Makes: 10 cups.

PER SERVING (ABOUT 1 CUP BEAN MIXTURE AND 1 CUP RICE): CALORIES 373; FAT 1.1G (SAT .03G, MONO 0.2G, POLY 0.3G); PROTEIN 15.4G; CARB 74.9G; FIBER 11.6G; CHOL 0MG; IRON 5.2MG; SODIUM 377MG; CALC 81MG

QUICK RED BEANS AND RICE: Substitute 2 (16-oz.) cans light kidney beans, drained and rinsed, for dried beans. Reduce Creole seasoning to 2 tsp. Prepare recipe as directed in Step 2, substituting 2 cups low-sodium, fat-free chicken broth for 7 cups water and simmering 20 minutes. Serve with rice. Makes: about 7 cups.

PER SERVING (ABOUT 1 CUP BEAN MIXTURE AND 1 CUP RICE): CALORIES 420; FAT 3.5G (SAT 1G, MONO 0.2G, POLY 0.2G); PROTEIN 19.7G; CARB 76.3G; FIBER 13G; CHOL 35MG; IRON 1.1MG; SODIUM 490MG; CALC 65MG

SLOW-COOKER RED BEANS AND RICE: Omit Steps 1 and 2. Stir together first 7 ingredients and 7 cups water in a 4-qt. slow cooker. Cover and cook on HIGH 7 hours or until beans are tender. Serve with rice. Makes: about 10 cups.

PER SERVING (ABOUT 1 CUP BEAN MIXTURE AND 1 CUP RICE): CALORIES 397; FAT 2.3G (SAT 0.8G, MONO 0.2G, POLY 0.3G); PROTEIN 18.9G; CARB 74.4G; FIBER 11.3G; CHOL 24MG; IRON 5.6MG; SODIUM 319MG; CALC 99MG

Upgrade Your Grilled Cheese

Think this classic can't be good for you? Think again. Our sandwich packs some surprises—goat cheese and fruit. Go ahead, treat yourself!

Grilled cheese is a favorite comfort food, but you don't have to go overboard with calories to enjoy that rich taste. Shake things up by substituting flavorful goat cheese. Bonus: You even get servings of fruit and veggies!

Test Kitchen Notebook

WHY WE LOVE IT

- Goat cheese has about 80 calories and 6 grams of fat per ounce compared to cow's milk cheese, which has 100 calories and 10 grams of fat.
- It's high in calcium, which strengthens bones and can help prevent breast cancer.
- People who are lactose intolerant can often enjoy goat cheese because it's easy to digest.

Goat Cheese and Strawberry Grilled Cheese
quick prep • good for you

MAKES: 3 servings
HANDS-ON TIME: 20 min.
TOTAL TIME: 20 min.

- 1 (4-oz.) goat cheese log, softened
- 6 whole grain bread slices
- 4½ tsp. red pepper jelly
- ¾ cup sliced fresh strawberries
- 6 large fresh basil leaves
- 1½ cups fresh watercress or arugula
  Salt and pepper to taste

1. Spread goat cheese on 1 side of 3 bread slices. Spread pepper jelly on 1 side of remaining bread slices; layer with strawberries, basil leaves, and watercress. Sprinkle with salt and pepper to taste.
2. Top with remaining bread, goat cheese sides down. Cook sandwiches in a large, lightly greased nonstick skillet over medium heat 2 to 3 minutes on each side or until golden brown.

Entertain with Easy Goat Cheese Appetizers

PECAN-GOAT CHEESE TRUFFLES:
Stir together equal amounts of goat cheese and cream cheese; stir in minced sweetened dried cranberries and salt and pepper to taste. Shape by teaspoonfuls into balls; roll in chopped toasted pecans.

GRAPE CROSTINI:
Spread toasted baguette slices with goat cheese. Top with chopped seedless red grapes, thinly sliced green onions, minced fresh rosemary, and salt and pepper to taste. Drizzle with store-bought balsamic glaze.

CHERRY TARTLETS:
Fill frozen mini-phyllo pastry shells, thawed, with crumbled goat cheese. Top each with cherry preserves, cooked and crumbled bacon, freshly cracked pepper, and chopped fresh chives. Bake tartlets at 350° for 5 minutes.

BRUNCH MUFFINS:
Spread softened honey-flavored goat cheese on toasted multigrain English muffins. Top with toasted walnuts and sliced plums or pears. Drizzle with honey. Note: We tested with La Bonne Vie Honey Goat Cheese.

HERB DIP:
Process 4 oz. softened goat cheese, ½ cup plain nonfat yogurt, 3 Tbsp. assorted chopped fresh herbs, 1 minced garlic clove, and 1 Tbsp. lemon juice in a food processor until smooth. Add salt and pepper to taste. Serve with fresh cut vegetables.

7 Perfect Pound Cakes

Give your go-to pound cake recipe a breather and try one of these blessedly buttery variations.

Pair it with...

A fresh-from-the-French press café au lait for a sweet brunch.

READER RECIPE

Buttermilk Pound Cake with Custard Sauce

MAKES: 12 servings
HANDS-ON TIME: 15 min.
TOTAL TIME: 2 hr., 45 min., including sauce

We sampled this traditional pairing several different ways and loved them all, but our favorite was warm cake with chilled custard. (Pictured on page 172)

- 1⅓ cups butter, softened
- 2½ cups sugar
- 6 large eggs
- 3 cups all-purpose flour
- ½ cup buttermilk
- 1 tsp. vanilla extract
  Buttermilk Custard Sauce

1. Preheat oven to 325°. Beat butter at medium speed with a heavy-duty electric stand mixer until creamy. Gradually add sugar, beating at medium speed until light and fluffy. Add eggs, 1 at a time, beating just until blended after each addition.
2. Add flour to butter mixture alternately with buttermilk, beginning and ending with flour. Beat at low speed just until blended after each addition. Stir in vanilla. Pour batter into a greased and floured 10-inch (12-cup) tube pan.
3. Bake at 325° for 1 hour and 5 minutes to 1 hour and 10 minutes or until a long wooden pick inserted in center comes out clean. Cool in pan on a wire rack 10 to 15 minutes; remove from pan to wire rack, and cool completely (about 1 hour). Serve with Buttermilk Custard Sauce as desired.

Buttermilk Custard Sauce
quick prep • make-ahead

MAKES: about 2⅓ cups
HANDS-ON TIME: 15 min.
TOTAL TIME: 15 min.

1. Whisk together 2 cups buttermilk, ½ cup sugar, 1 Tbsp. cornstarch, and 3 egg yolks in a heavy 3-qt. saucepan. Bring to a boil over medium heat, whisking constantly, and boil 1 minute. Remove from heat, and stir in 1 tsp. vanilla extract. Serve warm or cold. Store leftovers in an airtight container in refrigerator up to 1 week.

RECIPE FROM KATHLEEN SMITH
JENNINGS, LOUISIANA

Amaretto-Almond Pound Cake

make-ahead • party perfect

MAKES: 12 servings
HANDS-ON TIME: 20 min.
TOTAL TIME: 3 hr., 5 min., including glaze
(Pictured on page 6)

1¼ cups butter, softened
1 (3-oz.) package cream cheese, softened
2½ cups sugar
3 Tbsp. almond liqueur
1 Tbsp. vanilla extract
2½ cups all-purpose flour
6 large eggs
⅓ cup sliced almonds
   Amaretto Glaze

1. Preheat oven to 325°. Beat butter and cream cheese at medium speed with a heavy-duty electric stand mixer until creamy. Gradually add sugar, beating at medium speed until light and fluffy. Add liqueur and vanilla, beating just until blended. Gradually add flour to butter mixture, beating at low speed just until blended after each addition.

2. Add eggs, 1 at a time, beating at low speed just until blended after each addition. Sprinkle almonds over bottom of a greased and floured 12-cup Bundt pan; pour batter into pan.

3. Bake at 325° for 1 hour and 5 minutes to 1 hour and 10 minutes or until a long wooden pick inserted in center comes out clean.

4. During last 10 minutes of baking, prepare Amaretto Glaze. Remove cake from oven, and gradually spoon hot Amaretto Glaze over cake in pan. (Continue to spoon glaze over cake until all of glaze is used, allowing it to soak into cake after each addition.) Cool completely in pan on a wire rack (about 1 hour and 30 minutes).

Pair them with...

Try the Amaretto-Almond Pound Cake with a cup of afternoon tea, or wash down the richly textured Sauvignon Blanc Pound Cake with a glass of rosé.

Amaretto Glaze

MAKES: about 1¼ cups
HANDS-ON TIME: 10 min.
TOTAL TIME: 10 min.

1. Bring ¾ cup sugar, 6 Tbsp. butter, ¼ cup almond liqueur, and 2 Tbsp. water to a boil in a small 1-qt. saucepan over medium heat, stirring often; reduce heat to medium-low, and boil, stirring constantly, 3 minutes. Remove from heat, and use immediately.

RECIPE FROM ETHLEEN SCARBOROUGH
AUGUSTA, GEORGIA

 ## Sauvignon Blanc Pound Cake

make-ahead • party perfect

MAKES: 12 servings
HANDS-ON TIME: 15 min.
TOTAL TIME: 2 hr., 35 min., including glaze
(Pictured on page 173)

⅔ cup milk
⅓ cup Sauvignon Blanc
1 cup butter, softened
2 cups sugar
4 large eggs
3 cups all-purpose flour
½ tsp. baking powder
½ tsp. baking soda
¼ tsp. salt
1 tsp. vanilla extract
   Sauvignon Blanc Glaze

1. Preheat oven to 325°. Stir together milk and wine; let stand 10 minutes.

2. Meanwhile, beat butter at medium speed with a heavy-duty electric stand mixer until creamy. Gradually add sugar, beating at medium speed until light and fluffy. Add eggs, 1 at a time, beating just until blended after each addition.

3. Stir together flour, baking powder, baking soda, and salt. Add to butter mixture alternately with milk mixture, beginning and ending with flour mixture. Beat at low speed just until blended after each addition. Stir in vanilla. Pour batter into a greased and floured 12-cup Bundt pan.

4. Bake at 325° for 1 hour and 5 minutes to 1 hour and 10 minutes or until a long wooden pick inserted in center comes out clean. Cool in pan on a wire rack 10 to 15 minutes; remove from pan to wire rack. Brush or drizzle Sauvignon Blanc Glaze over top and sides of cake. Cool completely (about 1 hour).

Sauvignon Blanc Glaze

quick prep

MAKES: about ⅔ cup
HANDS-ON TIME: 5 min.
TOTAL TIME: 5 min.

1. Whisk together 1½ cups powdered sugar, 2 Tbsp. Sauvignon Blanc, and 1 Tbsp. milk until smooth.

RECIPE FROM CINDY NICHOLS
MEMPHIS, TENNESSEE

Lemon-Coconut Pound Cake Loaf

Reader Recipe

make-ahead • party perfect

MAKES: 8 to 10 servings
HANDS-ON TIME: 15 min.
TOTAL TIME: 2 hr., 35 min., including glaze

Garnish with flaked coconut or, for a dressier look, curly shavings (Pictured and explained below). (Pictured on page 173)

- ½ cup butter, softened
- 1⅓ cups granulated sugar
- 3 large eggs
- 1½ cups all-purpose flour
- ½ tsp. salt
- ⅛ tsp. baking soda
- ½ cup sour cream
- 2 tsp. lemon zest
- 1 cup sweetened flaked coconut, divided
  Lemon Glaze

1. Preheat oven to 325°. Beat butter at medium speed with a heavy-duty electric stand mixer until creamy. Gradually add sugar, beating until light and fluffy. Add eggs, 1 at a time, beating just until blended after each addition.

2. Stir together flour, salt, and baking soda. Add to butter mixture alternately with sour cream, beginning and ending with flour mixture. Beat at low speed just until blended after each addition. Stir in lemon zest and ½ cup coconut. Pour batter into a greased and floured 9- x 5-inch loaf pan.

3. Bake at 325° for 1 hour and 5 minutes to 1 hour and 10 minutes or until a long wooden pick inserted in center comes out clean. Cool in pan on a wire rack 10 to 15 minutes; remove from pan to wire rack, and cool completely (about 1 hour).

4. Spoon Lemon Glaze over cake, and sprinkle with remaining ½ cup coconut.

Pair them with...

A sparkling wine, like a Prosecco, will go well with both the Lemon-Coconut Cake Loaf and the Pound Cake with Balsamic Strawberries and Basil Whipped Cream. Garnish your Champagne flute with a strawberry.

Lemon Glaze
quick prep

MAKES: about 1 cup
HANDS-ON TIME: 5 min.
TOTAL TIME: 5 min.

1. Whisk together 2 cups powdered sugar, 2 Tbsp. milk, and 2 tsp. fresh lemon juice, adding an additional 1 Tbsp. milk, 1 tsp. at a time, for desired consistency.

GET THE LOOK
Coconut Curlicues

Add a sweet tangle of fresh coconut shavings to any cake that could use an elegant, tropical note. Pierce 2 coconut eyes with an ice pick and hammer; drain liquid, and reserve for another use. Place coconut in a 9-inch cake pan. Bake at 350° for 25 minutes or until shell begins to crack; cool 10 minutes. Break open the outer shell with a hammer, and split coconut into several large pieces. Separate coconut meat from the shell using a sturdy, blunt-ended knife, and rinse in cold water. Cut thin strips from the meat using a vegetable peeler. Use immediately, or layer between damp paper towels in an airtight container, and chill up to 2 days.

Lemon-Coconut Pound Cake Loaf

Pound Cake with Balsamic Strawberries and Basil Whipped Cream

make-ahead • party perfect

MAKES: 8 servings
HANDS-ON TIME: 17 min.
TOTAL TIME: 9 hr., 17 min., not including time for cake

- 2 cups whipping cream
- 5 basil leaves, torn (about 3 Tbsp.)
- ¼ cup balsamic vinegar
- ¼ cup firmly packed light brown sugar
- ¼ tsp. freshly ground pepper
- 2 (16-oz.) packages fresh strawberries, sliced
- 6 Tbsp. powdered sugar
- 8 Buttermilk Pound Cake slices (recipe on page 72)

1. Stir together whipping cream and basil in a small bowl; cover and chill 8 to 12 hours.

2. Cook vinegar and brown sugar in a small saucepan over medium heat, stirring constantly, 2 to 3 minutes or until sugar dissolves. Remove from heat, and stir in pepper; cool completely (about 30 minutes).

3. Stir together sliced strawberries and vinegar mixture in a large bowl; cover and let stand 30 minutes.

4. Pour cream mixture through a wire-mesh strainer into a bowl, discarding basil. Beat whipping cream at high speed with an electric mixer until foamy; gradually add powdered sugar, beating until soft peaks form.

5. Serve pound cake slices with strawberry mixture and basil whipped cream.

RECIPE FROM KENDALL BLYTHE
BRIDGEWATER, NEW JERSEY

Key Lime Pound Cake

Key Lime Pound Cake

MAKES: 12 servings
HANDS-ON TIME: 15 min.
TOTAL TIME: 2 hr., 45 min., including glaze
(Pictured on page 7)

- 1 cup butter, softened
- ½ cup shortening
- 3 cups sugar
- 6 large eggs
- 3 cups all-purpose flour
- ½ tsp. baking powder
- ⅛ tsp. salt
- 1 cup milk
- 1 tsp. vanilla extract
- 1 tsp. lime zest
- ¼ cup fresh Key lime juice
  Key Lime Glaze
  Garnishes: whipped cream, Key lime slices

1. Preheat oven to 325°. Beat butter and shortening at medium speed with a heavy-duty electric stand mixer until creamy. Gradually add sugar, beating at medium speed until light and fluffy. Add eggs, 1 at a time, beating just until blended after each addition.

2. Stir together flour, baking powder, and salt. Add to butter mixture alternately with milk, beginning and ending with flour mixture. Beat at low speed just until blended after each addition. Stir in vanilla, lime zest, and lime juice. Pour batter into a greased and floured 10-inch (12-cup) tube pan.

3. Bake at 325° for 1 hour and 15 minutes to 1 hour and 20 minutes or until a long wooden pick inserted in center comes out clean. Cool in pan on a wire rack 10 to 15 minutes; remove from pan to wire rack.

4. Prepare Key Lime Glaze, and immediately brush over top and sides of cake. Cool completely (about 1 hour). Garnish, if desired.

Key Lime Glaze

quick prep

MAKES: about ½ cup
HANDS-ON TIME: 5 min.
TOTAL TIME: 5 min.

1. Whisk together 1 cup powdered sugar, 2 Tbsp. fresh Key lime juice, and ½ tsp. vanilla extract until smooth. Use immediately.

RECIPE FROM KATHLEEN BLACKMAN
PONCE INLET, FLORIDA

Test Kitchen Notebook

The charms of homemade pound cake are many. Beguilingly simple, they tumble from the pan perfectly golden and party ready. Toppings and trimmings and flirtatious strawberry swirls merely add that delightful bit of excess for which we Southerners are famous.

Shamelessly indulgent, we will serve a pound cake any time of day or night. We have even been known to butter and toast a slice or two for breakfast. Such moments of recklessness aside, we are fiercely opinionated about the particulars of pound cake. Subtle differences in crumb texture and the virtues of sad streaks (that moist sugary ribbon of deliciously underbaked batter) are no small matters.

Traditional recipes call for a pound each of butter, sugar, eggs, and flour. Over the years, accomplished hostesses have come up with countless variations, replacing a portion of the butter with cream cheese or a few of the eggs with sour cream and leavening. Each cake bears a mark of distinction as unique and lovely as the hands that make it. Enjoy our selection of highly prized favorites perfect for springtime entertaining.

MARY ALLEN PERRY
SENIOR FOOD EDITOR

Strawberry Swirl Cream Cheese Pound Cake

Strawberry Swirl Cream Cheese Pound Cake

make-ahead • party perfect

MAKES: 12 servings
HANDS-ON TIME: 25 min.
TOTAL TIME: 2 hr., 35 min.

Here the cream cheese is added after beating the butter and sugar, and the cake bakes at a slightly higher temperature than usual. (Pictured on page 172)

- 1½ cups butter, softened
- 3 cups sugar
- 1 (8-oz.) package cream cheese, softened
- 6 large eggs
- 3 cups all-purpose flour
- 1 tsp. almond extract
- ½ tsp. vanilla extract
- ⅔ cup strawberry glaze
- 1 (6-inch) wooden skewer

1. Preheat oven to 350°. Beat butter at medium speed with a heavy-duty electric stand mixer until creamy. Gradually add sugar, beating at medium speed until light and fluffy. Add cream cheese, beating until creamy. Add eggs, 1 at a time, beating just until blended after each addition.

2. Gradually add flour to butter mixture. Beat at low speed just until blended after each addition, stopping to scrape bowl as needed. Stir in almond and vanilla extracts. Pour one-third of batter into a greased and floured 10-inch (14-cup) tube pan (about 2⅔ cups batter). Dollop 8 rounded teaspoonfuls strawberry glaze over batter, and swirl with wooden skewer. Repeat procedure, and top with remaining third of batter.

3. Bake at 350° for 1 hour to 1 hour and 10 minutes or until a long wooden pick inserted in center comes out clean. Cool in pan on a wire rack 10 to 15 minutes; remove from pan to wire rack, and cool completely (about 1 hour).

NOTE: We tested with Marzetti Glaze for Strawberries.

RECIPE FROM NANCY H. TEST
WEST CHESTER, OHIO

April

An Easter Blessing

Alabama entrepreneur Tasia Malakasis's Greek and Southern roots inspire a delicious, cross-cultural menu in a refreshingly laid-back setting.

Split Pea Hummus

With a name that means "resurrection" in Greek, it's no surprise that Tasia Malakasis is a big fan of Easter. "It's is a huge deal in Greece, where my father was from. It's even bigger than Christmas," she says. "In Alabama, kids have cute little dresses, bonnets, and egg hunts, but in Greece, they're out of school for two weeks, and there are tons of events."

Tasia (ta-SHEE-uh) established her own traditions as an adult when she moved back to Huntsville after a few stints in the Northeast and became owner of Belle Chèvre goat cheese creamery. Her celebrations are based on her love of food and friends. "I have very little family here," she says, "so my friends have become my family. My son, Kelly, and I share Sunday suppers and holidays with them, and I love teaching them about my Greek Easter traditions."

Her food is easy to prepare, with many make-ahead elements. Succulent roast lamb is always at the center of her Easter table. "They serve it everywhere in Greece," she says. "It is *divine*."

Her version is equally delicious, paired with other seasonal dishes. But her new favorite four-legged animal gets pride of place in dessert. Creamy goat fromage blanc fills delicate, strawberry-topped tartlets, the perfect ending to this multicultural feast. Compliments to the chèvre.

Split Pea Hummus

quick prep • good for you •
make-ahead • party perfect

MAKES: 2 ¼ cups
HANDS-ON TIME: 25 min.
TOTAL TIME: 55 min.

This fun Southern twist on traditional hummus is inexpensive and tasty. Serve it as an appetizer with fresh vegetables and pita chips.

1 **cup dried green split peas**
1 **garlic clove**
½ **tsp. salt, divided**
¼ **cup olive oil**
1 **Tbsp. lemon juice**
¼ **tsp. ground cumin**

1. Sort and wash peas. Bring garlic and 3 cups water to a boil in medium saucepan. Add peas; return to a boil. Cover, reduce heat, and simmer 25 minutes. Stir in ¼ tsp. salt; cook 15 minutes or until tender. Drain.
2. Combine peas, olive oil, next 2 ingredients, and remaining ¼ tsp. salt in a food processor; pulse 5 to 7 times or until smooth, stopping to scrape down sides as needed. Serve at room temperature.

Rosemary Roast Lamb

party perfect

MAKES: 6 to 8 servings
HANDS-ON TIME: 20 min.
TOTAL TIME: 4 hr., 20 min.

¼ cup olive oil
2½ Tbsp. chopped fresh
   rosemary
6 garlic cloves, minced
1 Tbsp. anchovy paste
1 tsp. lemon zest
1 Tbsp. lemon juice
1 (5- to 6-lb.) bone-in
   leg of lamb
2 tsp. salt
¾ tsp. pepper

1. Combine first 6 ingredients in a small bowl.
2. Pat lamb dry, and place, fat side up, on a rack in a roasting pan. Make several 1-inch-deep slits in lamb with a paring knife; rub olive oil mixture over lamb, pressing mixture into slits. Cover loosely with foil, and let stand at room temperature 30 minutes.
3. Meanwhile, preheat oven to 400°. Uncover lamb, and sprinkle with salt and pepper.
4. Bake at 400° for 2 hours and 30 minutes or until a meat thermometer inserted into thickest portion registers 145° (medium rare). Let stand 30 minutes before slicing.

Roasted Carrots

Roasted Carrots

good for you • make-ahead • party perfect

MAKES: 6 to 8 servings
HANDS-ON TIME: 10 min.
TOTAL TIME: 45 min.

You can use bagged baby carrots, but young carrots with tops taste better.

3 lb. small carrots with tops
1 Tbsp. olive oil
¾ tsp. salt
¼ tsp. pepper

1. Preheat oven to 450°. Peel carrots, if desired. Trim tops to 1 inch.
2. Toss carrots with oil, salt, and pepper. Place on a 17- x 12-inch jelly-roll pan.
3. Bake at 450° for 20 minutes, stirring once. Reduce heat to 325°, and bake, stirring occasionally, 15 minutes or until carrots are browned and tender.

Asparagus-and-Green Onion Risotto

good for you • party perfect

MAKES: 6 servings
HANDS-ON TIME: 1 hr.
TOTAL TIME: 1 hr.

2 Tbsp. butter
¾ cup chopped green onions
½ tsp. chopped fresh thyme
1½ cups uncooked Arborio
   rice (short-grain)
5 cups low-sodium chicken broth
½ lb. fresh asparagus, cut into 1-inch
   pieces
⅓ cup freshly grated Parmesan
   cheese
   Garnish: shaved fresh Parmesan
   cheese

1. Melt butter in a large heavy saucepan over medium heat; add green onions and thyme, and sauté 1 minute or until onions are soft. Add rice, stirring to coat. Add 2½ cups broth, and bring to a boil. Reduce heat to medium-low; simmer, stirring occasionally, 15 minutes. Add ½ cup broth, and cook, stirring constantly, until liquid is absorbed. Repeat procedure with remaining broth, ½ cup at a time. (Total cooking time is about 20 minutes.)
2. Stir in asparagus. Simmer 3 to 5 more minutes or until asparagus is tender and mixture is creamy. Stir in Parmesan cheese. Serve immediately. Garnish, if desired.

HOW TO
Set Up a Cheese Plate

Tasia shares her best tips.

{1}

START SOFT.

Chèvre's Greek Kiss, which comes wrapped in grape leaves for a dramatic presentation ($7.50 for 4 ounces; *bellechevre.com*).

{2}

ADD SOMETHING CREAMY...

Belle Chèvre's Fromage Blanc ($8 for 8 ounces) spreads easily on crackers.

{3}

...AND HARD.

Tasia likes an aged goat cheese or a Manchego.

{4}

TOSS IN A CONVERSATION STARTER.

Belle Chèvre's julep-inspired Southern Belle is dressed with mint, bourbon pecans, and sugar ($7.50 for 4 ounces).

{5}

ADD EDIBLE ACCENTS.

Bread, fruit, nuts, and honey. "I like to tuck in a beautiful honeycomb for texture," Tasia says.

From left: Fromage Blanc, Southern Belle, Greek Kiss

Strawberry-Fromage Blanc Tartlets

party perfect

MAKES: 30 tartlets
HANDS-ON TIME: 30 min.
TOTAL TIME: 1 hr., 20 min.

You can make these delicious little sweets without their toppings up to a day ahead and reheat them in the oven before serving. Children may prefer them without the balsamic drizzle, so be sure to set some aside if you're having young guests. Fromage blanc is a soft, mild, fresh cream cheese.

1 (6-oz.) container fromage blanc
1 large egg
4 Tbsp. honey
1 Tbsp. orange liqueur
1 Tbsp. lemon juice
  Pinch of nutmeg
2 Tbsp. all-purpose flour
2 (1.9-oz.) packages frozen
  mini-phyllo pastry shells
1 cup balsamic vinegar
½ pt. fresh strawberries, chopped
2 Tbsp. sugar

1. Preheat oven to 350°. Process first 6 ingredients in a food processor until smooth. Slowly sift in flour; process until blended.

2. Spoon 1 heaping teaspoonful mixture into each phyllo shell. Place on a baking sheet.

3. Bake at 350° for 10 minutes or until set.

4. Meanwhile, cook balsamic vinegar in a large saucepan over medium heat 10 minutes or until reduced to ¼ cup. Cool completely (about 30 minutes).

5. Toss strawberries with sugar. Spoon strawberries over tartlets; drizzle with balsamic reduction. Serve immediately.

NOTE: We tested with Belle Chèvre fromage blanc, Grand Marnier orange liqueur, and Colavita Balsamic Vinegar.

Best-Ever Bar Cookies

Leave these chewy squares unattended and they'll disappear faster than you can say "But those were for the bake sale!"

Peach Melba Shortbread Bars

make-ahead • party perfect

MAKES: 1½ to 2 dozen bars
HANDS-ON TIME: 20 min.
TOTAL TIME: 2 hr., 20 min.

- 2 **cups all-purpose flour**
- ½ **cup granulated sugar**
- ¼ **tsp. salt**
- 1 **cup cold butter**
- 1 **cup peach preserves**
- 6 **tsp. raspberry preserves**
- ½ **cup sliced almonds**
- **Garnish: powdered sugar**

1. Preheat oven to 350°. Combine first 3 ingredients in a medium bowl. Cut in butter with a pastry blender until crumbly. Reserve 1 cup flour mixture.

2. Lightly grease an 11- x 7-inch or 9-inch square pan. Press remaining flour mixture onto bottom of prepared pan.

3. Bake at 350° for 25 to 30 minutes or until lightly browned.

4. Spread peach preserves over crust in pan. Dollop raspberry preserves by ½ teaspoonfuls over peach preserves. Sprinkle reserved 1 cup flour mixture over preserves. Sprinkle with almonds.

5. Bake at 350° for 35 to 40 minutes or until golden brown. Let cool 1 hour on a wire rack. Cut into bars. Garnish, if desired.

Test Kitchen Notebook

TIPS FOR PRETTIER BARS

{1}

Coarsely chop pecan halves with a chef's knife, instead of pulsing in the food processor.

{2}

Use a mesh tea strainer to dust desserts with powdered sugar.

{3}

Wipe the knife edge clean between cuts for tidy-looking treats.

{4}

Shop flea markets for bakeware with vintage charm.

Peanut Butter-Chocolate-Oatmeal Cereal Bars

make-ahead • party perfect

MAKES: 4 dozen
HANDS-ON TIME: 15 min.
TOTAL TIME: 1 hr., 25 min.

- 2 **cups uncooked quick-cooking oats**
- ¾ **cup firmly packed dark brown sugar**
- ¾ **cup all-purpose flour**
- ¾ **cup butter, melted**
- 1 **large egg**
- 1 **cup light corn syrup**
- 1 **cup granulated sugar**
- 1 **cup creamy peanut butter**
- 4 **cups crisp rice cereal**
- 1 **(12-oz.) package semisweet chocolate morsels**
- 1 **(10-oz.) package peanut butter morsels**
- 1 **cup chopped dry-roasted peanuts**

1. Preheat oven to 350°. Combine first 5 ingredients in a medium bowl. Press firmly onto bottom of a lightly greased 15- x 10-inch jelly-roll pan. (Mixture will be thin.) Bake 12 minutes. Let cool on a wire rack 10 minutes.

2. Microwave corn syrup, sugar, and peanut butter in a large microwave-safe glass bowl at HIGH 2 minutes or until melted and smooth, stirring at 30-second intervals. Stir in cereal. Press mixture firmly over oat mixture in pan.

3. Microwave chocolate and peanut butter morsels in a microwave-safe glass bowl at HIGH 1 to 1½ minutes or until melted and smooth, stirring at 30-second intervals. Spread over cereal mixture. Sprinkle with chopped peanuts. Cool 45 minutes. Cut into bars.

NOTE: We tested with Reese's Peanut Butter Chips and Rice Krispies cereal.

RECIPE BY DOLORES VACCARO
PUEBLO, COLORADO

Ginger-Lemon Bars with Almond Streusel

make-ahead • party perfect

MAKES: 4 dozen
HANDS-ON TIME: 20 min.
TOTAL TIME: I hr., 50 min.

- 2 cups all-purpose flour
- ½ cup powdered sugar
- ½ tsp. baking soda
- ¼ tsp. salt
- ¾ cup cold butter
- ¾ cup slivered almonds
- I (10-oz.) jar lemon curd
- 3 Tbsp. finely chopped crystallized ginger
  Garnish: powdered sugar

1. Preheat oven to 350°. Combine first 4 ingredients in a large bowl; cut in butter with a pastry blender until crumbly. Toss in almonds; reserve I cup flour mixture. Press remaining flour mixture onto bottom of a lightly greased 13- x 9-inch pan.
2. Bake at 350° for 15 to 20 minutes or until lightly browned. Spread lemon curd over crust, leaving a ¼-inch border. Sprinkle with ginger and reserved flour mixture. Bake 15 to 20 minutes or until lightly browned. Let cool I hour on a wire rack. Garnish, if desired.
NOTE: We tested with Dickinson's Lemon Curd.

> ## Test Kitchen Tip
>
> Don't worry if you don't have a pastry blender; a fork works just fine for cutting the butter into the flour mixture when making the crust.

Strawberry-Lemon Shortbread Bars

make-ahead • party perfect

MAKES: 4 dozen
HANDS-ON TIME: 20 min.
TOTAL TIME: 6 hr., 8 min.

Refrigerate leftovers. Store them in an airtight container up to 2 days.

- 2 cups all-purpose flour
- ½ cup powdered sugar
- ¾ tsp. lemon zest, divided
- ¾ cup cold butter
- 2 (8-oz.) packages cream cheese, softened
- ¾ cup granulated sugar
- 2 large eggs
- I Tbsp. fresh lemon juice
- I cup strawberry preserves
  Garnishes: sweetened whipped cream, fresh strawberry slices

1. Preheat oven to 350°. Stir together flour, powdered sugar, and ½ tsp. lemon zest in a medium bowl; cut in butter with a pastry blender until crumbly. Press mixture onto bottom of a lightly greased 13- x 9-inch pan.
2. Bake at 350° for 20 to 22 minutes or until lightly browned.
3. Meanwhile, beat cream cheese and granulated sugar with an electric mixer until smooth. Add eggs, I at a time, and beat just until blended after each addition. Stir in fresh lemon juice and remaining ¼ tsp. lemon zest, beating well.
4. Spread preserves over shortbread. Pour cream cheese mixture over preserves, spreading to edges. Bake 28 to 32 more minutes or until set. Let cool I hour on a wire rack. Cover and chill 4 to 8 hours. Cut into bars; garnish, if desired.

Tequila-Lime-Coconut Macaroon Bars

make-ahead • party perfect

MAKES: 3 dozen
HANDS-ON TIME: 20 min.
TOTAL TIME: 2 hr., 5 min.

- 2 cups all-purpose flour, divided
- 2 cups sugar, divided
- ½ cup cold butter, cut into pieces
- 4 large eggs
- I ½ cups sweetened flaked coconut
- I tsp. lime zest
- ⅓ cup fresh lime juice
- 3 Tbsp. tequila
- ½ tsp. baking powder
- ¼ tsp. salt
  Garnishes: powdered sugar, lime zest curls

1. Preheat oven to 350°. Line bottom and sides of a 13- x 9-inch pan with heavy-duty aluminum foil, allowing 2 inches to extend over sides; lightly grease foil.
2. Stir together I ¾ cups flour and ½ cup sugar. Cut in butter with a pastry blender or fork until crumbly. Press mixture onto bottom of prepared pan.
3. Bake at 350° for 20 to 23 minutes or until lightly browned.
4. Meanwhile, whisk eggs in a medium bowl until smooth; whisk in coconut, next 3 ingredients, and remaining I½ cups sugar. Stir together baking powder, salt, and remaining ¼ cup flour; whisk into egg mixture. Pour over hot crust.
5. Bake at 350° for 25 minutes or until filling is set. Let cool I hour on a wire rack. Lift from pan, using foil sides as handles. Remove foil, and cut into bars. Garnish, if desired.

READER RECIPE

Simple Brownies with Chocolate Frosting

make-ahead • party perfect

MAKES: 4 dozen
HANDS-ON TIME: 15 min.
TOTAL TIME: 1 hr., 56 min., including frosting
(Pictured on page 9)

- 1½ cups coarsely chopped pecans
- 1 (4-oz.) unsweetened chocolate baking bar, chopped
- ¾ cup butter
- 2 cups sugar
- 4 large eggs
- 1 cup all-purpose flour
- Chocolate Frosting

1. Preheat oven to 350°. Bake pecans in a single layer in a shallow pan 6 to 8 minutes or until lightly toasted and fragrant.
2. Microwave chocolate and butter in a large microwave-safe bowl at HIGH 1 to 1½ minutes or until melted and smooth, stirring at 30-second intervals. Whisk in sugar and eggs until well blended. Stir in flour. Spread batter into a greased 13- x 9-inch pan.
3. Bake at 350° for 25 to 30 minutes or until a wooden pick inserted in center comes out with a few moist crumbs.
4. Prepare Chocolate Frosting. Pour over warm brownies; spread to edges. Sprinkle with pecans. Let cool 1 hour on a wire rack. Cut into squares.

Chocolate Frosting

MAKES: 2 cups
HANDS-ON TIME: 10 min.
TOTAL TIME: 10 min.

- ½ cup butter
- ⅓ cup milk
- 6 Tbsp. unsweetened cocoa
- 1 (16-oz.) package powdered sugar
- 1 tsp. vanilla extract

1. Cook first 3 ingredients over medium heat in a large saucepan, stirring constantly, 4 to 5 minutes or until butter melts. Remove from heat, and beat in powdered sugar and vanilla at medium speed with an electric mixer until smooth.

RECIPE FROM ANNE KRACKE
BIRMINGHAM, ALABAMA

Try These Twists!

MISSISSIPPI MUD BROWNIES: Prepare recipe above as directed through Step 3. Sprinkle warm brownies with toasted pecans and 3 cups miniature marshmallows. Prepare Chocolate Frosting as directed; pour over pecans and marshmallows. Cool 1 hour on a wire rack. Cut into squares.

CARAMEL-PECAN BROWNIES: Prepare recipe above as directed through Step 3. Cool 1 hour on a wire rack. Combine 1 cup firmly packed dark brown sugar, ½ cup milk, 2 Tbsp. butter, and ¼ tsp. salt in a large saucepan; bring to a boil over medium-high heat, stirring occasionally. Reduce heat to medium-low, and simmer, stirring occasionally, 5 minutes or until slightly thickened. Remove from heat. Let stand 5 minutes. Beat in 1½ cups powdered sugar and ½ tsp. vanilla extract at medium speed with an electric mixer until smooth. Pour over brownies, spreading to edges; sprinkle with toasted pecans. Cool 30 minutes. Hands-on time: 25 min.; Total time: 2 hr., 20 min.

MARBLED BROWNIES: *(Pictured on page 9)* Omit pecans and Chocolate Frosting. Preheat oven to 325°. Prepare batter as directed; spread half of batter into greased pan. Beat 1 (8-oz.) package softened cream cheese, ¼ cup sugar, 1 egg yolk, and 1 tsp. vanilla extract at medium speed with an electric mixer until smooth. Dollop cream cheese mixture over brownie batter in pan. Dollop with remaining brownie batter, and swirl together using a paring knife. Bake 35 to 40 minutes. Cool 1 hour on a wire rack. Hands-on time: 30 min. Total time: 2 hr., 5 min.

Hello Dolly Bars

make-ahead • party perfect

MAKES: 3 dozen
HANDS-ON TIME: 15 min.
TOTAL TIME: 1 hr., 43 min.

- 2 cups graham cracker crumbs
- ⅓ cup melted butter
- 3 Tbsp. sugar
- 1 cup chopped pecans
- 1 cup semisweet chocolate morsels
- ⅔ cup sweetened flaked coconut
- 1 (14-oz.) can sweetened condensed milk

1. Preheat oven to 350°. Combine first 3 ingredients in a medium bowl. Press mixture onto bottom of a lightly greased 13- x 9-inch pan. Bake 8 minutes. Sprinkle pecans, chocolate morsels, and coconut over hot crust. Pour condensed milk over top. (Do not stir.)
2. Bake at 350° for 20 to 25 minutes or until lightly browned and edges are bubbly. Let cool 1 hour on a wire rack. Cut into bars.

Our Easiest Shower Ever

For our first installment of Southern Hospitality, we've created a menu you can use to honor a bride-to-be or expectant mom. But the real cause for celebration? Nothing takes more than 30 minutes.

Spring Celebration

SERVES 8

Tomato-Herb Mini Frittatas

Fruit Salad with Yogurt

Gouda Grits

Quick Buttermilk Biscuits with Lemon-Herb, Blackberry, or Walnut-Honey Butter

Sparkling Ginger-Orange Cocktails or Mocktails

Iced sugar cookies

"A few bud vases with bold flower stems add sophistication to the occasion without being fussy."

REBECCA KRACKE GORDON
TEST KITCHEN DIRECTOR

The Main Spread

Tomato-Herb Mini Frittatas

good for you • party perfect

MAKES: 8 servings
HANDS-ON TIME: 15 min.
TOTAL TIME: 30 min.

Transferring the bottom baking sheet to the middle rack during the last few minutes of cooking time allows the top to brown slightly. (Pictured on page 175)

- 12 **large eggs**
- 1 **cup half-and-half**
- ½ **tsp. salt**
- ¼ **tsp. freshly ground pepper**
- 2 **Tbsp. chopped fresh chives**
- 1 **Tbsp. chopped fresh parsley**
- 1 **tsp. chopped fresh oregano**
- 1 **pt. grape tomatoes, halved**
- 1½ **cups (6 oz.) shredded Italian three-cheese blend**

1. Preheat oven to 450°. Process first 4 ingredients in a blender until blended. Stir together chives and next 2 ingredients in a small bowl. Place 8 lightly greased 4-inch (6-oz.) ramekins on 2 baking sheets; layer tomatoes, 1 cup cheese, and chive mixture in ramekins. Pour egg mixture over top, and sprinkle with remaining ½ cup cheese.

2. Bake at 450° for 7 minutes, placing 1 baking sheet on middle oven rack and other on lower oven rack. Switch baking sheets, and bake 7 to 8 more minutes or until set. Remove top baking sheet from oven; transfer bottom sheet to middle rack, and bake 1 to 2 more minutes or until lightly browned.

Tomato-Herb Frittata: Prepare recipe as directed, substituting a lightly greased 13- x 9-inch baking dish for ramekins and increasing bake time to 18 to 20 minutes or until set. **NOTE:** Mixture will rise about 1 inch above rim of baking dish. Hands-on time: 10 min., Total time: 30 min.

FAST FLOURISH

Give the tarts a restaurant finish: Top them with mixed baby greens tossed with olive oil, lemon juice, salt, and pepper.

Plan Ahead

Set aside a half-hour each day to pull off your pretty party with ease.

3 DAYS BEFORE:
- Prepare biscuits and freeze according to recipe instructions.
- Set up party table and assess serving pieces.

2 DAYS BEFORE:
- Prepare butters and press linens.

1 DAY BEFORE:
- Toss together fruit in a serving bowl; cover and refrigerate.
- Prep and measure ingredients for frittatas, and refrigerate.

30 MINUTES BEFORE GUESTS ARRIVE:
- Start grits.
- Assemble and bake frittatas.
- Bake biscuits after frittatas have been removed from the oven.

JUST BEFORE GUESTS ARRIVE:
- Stir together beverage, and prepare yogurt as directed for fruit.

Style Tip

Mix and match vintage plates, cups, and saucers for a carefree and whimsical feel. Borrow from Grandma, or look for them at garage sales and flea markets.

Fruit Salad with Yogurt

quick prep • good for you • party perfect

MAKES: 8 servings
HANDS-ON TIME: 30 min.
TOTAL TIME: 30 min.
(Pictured on page 174)

- 4 cups fresh pineapple chunks
- 1 qt. strawberries, hulled and sliced in half
- 3 cups seedless green grapes
- 2 mangoes, peeled and sliced
- 2 (4-oz.) containers fresh raspberries
- 2 cups Greek yogurt
- 1 Tbsp. dark brown sugar
- 1 Tbsp. honey

1. Toss together first 5 ingredients in a large serving bowl. Spoon yogurt into a separate serving bowl; sprinkle yogurt with sugar, and drizzle with honey. Serve fruit with yogurt mixture.

Gouda Grits

quick prep • party perfect

MAKES: 8 servings
HANDS-ON TIME: 10 min.
TOTAL TIME: 30 min.

- 4 cups chicken broth
- 1 cup whipping cream
- 1 tsp. salt
- ¼ tsp. freshly ground pepper
- 2 cups uncooked quick-cooking grits
- 2 cups (8 oz.) shredded Gouda cheese
- ½ cup buttermilk
- ¼ cup butter
- 2 tsp. hot sauce

1. Bring first 4 ingredients and 4 cups water to a boil in a Dutch oven over high heat; whisk in grits, reduce heat to medium-low, and simmer, stirring occasionally, 15 minutes or until thickened. Remove from heat, and stir in Gouda and remaining ingredients.

The Drinks

Serve Ginger-Orange Mocktails for moms-to-be, or try our sparkling wine variation to toast a wedding engagement. Garnish with orange slices and fresh mint sprigs, if desired.

SPARKLING GINGER-ORANGE COCKTAILS: Place 1 Tbsp. finely grated ginger in a piece of cheesecloth, and squeeze juice from ginger into a large pitcher; discard cheesecloth and solids. Stir 2 (750-milliliter) bottles chilled sparkling wine; 1 (89-oz.) container orange juice; and 1 (46-oz.) can chilled pineapple juice into ginger juice. Serve over ice. Makes: about 23 cups. Hands-on time: 10 min. Total time: 10 min.
NOTE: We recommend Freixenet Spumante for sparkling wine.

GINGER-ORANGE MOCKTAILS: Stir together 1 (89-oz.) container orange juice, 1 (2-liter) bottle chilled ginger ale, and 1 (46-oz.) can chilled pineapple juice. Serve over ice. Makes: about 25 cups. Hands-on time: 5 min., Total time: 5 min.

The Dessert

Pick up a cookie assortment from a local bakery, or order them online. **Icing on the Cookie,** in Homewood, Alabama, specializes in custom occasion cookies for about $2.25 each. *icingonthecookie.net* or 205/871-9852.

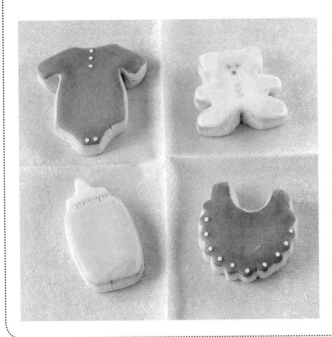

Quick Buttermilk Biscuits

quick prep • make-ahead • party perfect

MAKES: about 3 dozen
HANDS-ON TIME: 10 min.
TOTAL TIME: 22 min.

Fill biscuits with thinly sliced ham, if desired. (Pictured on page 175)

  1 **cup shortening**
  4 **cups self-rising soft-wheat flour**
  1¾ **cups buttermilk**

Test Kitchen Tip

PARTY IMPROV: Really want to simplify? Bake up a bag of Mary B's frozen tea biscuits. Serve with our special butters.

---

1. Preheat oven to 425°. Cut shortening into flour with a pastry blender until crumbly. Add buttermilk, stirring just until dry ingredients are moistened.
2. Turn dough out onto a lightly floured surface, and knead lightly 4 to 5 times. Pat or roll dough to ¾-inch thickness, cut with a 1½-inch round cutter, and place on 2 lightly greased baking sheets.
3. Bake at 425° for 12 to 14 minutes or until lightly browned.

FREEZING INSTRUCTIONS: Place unbaked biscuits on pans in freezer for 30 minutes or until frozen. Transfer frozen biscuits to zip-top plastic freezer bags, and freeze up to 3 months. Bake frozen biscuits at 425° on lightly greased baking sheets 14 to 16 minutes or until lightly browned.

Lemon-Herb Butter: Stir together ½ cup softened butter, 2 tsp. lemon zest, 1 tsp. chopped fresh chives, 1 tsp. chopped fresh oregano, and 1 tsp. chopped fresh parsley. Makes: about ½ cup. Hands-on time: 5 min., Total time: 5 min.

Blackberry Butter: Stir together ½ cup softened butter and 3 Tbsp. blackberry preserves. Makes: about ¾ cup. Hands-on time: 5 min., Total time: 5 min.

Walnut-Honey Butter: Bake ¼ cup finely chopped walnuts at 350° in a single layer in a pan 5 to 7 minutes or until lightly toasted, stirring halfway through. Cool 15 minutes. Stir together ½ cup softened butter, 2 Tbsp. honey, and walnuts. Makes: about ¾ cup. Hands-on time: 5 min., Total time: 25 min.

Carrot Cake

This healthier take comes complete with cream cheese frosting. You can thank us later, when your mouth isn't full.

Layered Carrot Cake

good for you • make-ahead • party perfect

This delicious dessert features a tender cake packed with grated carrots and crushed pineapple, and is topped with a rich cream cheese frosting, just like a traditional carrot cake.

MAKES: 16 servings
HANDS-ON TIME: 30 min.
TOTAL TIME: 2 hr.

CARROT CAKE BATTER

- 2 **cups all-purpose flour**
- ¾ **cup granulated sugar**
- 2 **tsp. baking soda**
- 1 **tsp. ground cinnamon**
- 1 **tsp. salt**
- 1 **(8-oz.) can crushed pineapple in juice, drained**
- ¼ **cup vegetable oil**
- 2 **large eggs**
- 2 **egg whites**
- 1 **Tbsp. vanilla extract**
- 3 **cups grated carrots**
   Vegetable cooking spray

CREAM CHEESE FROSTING

- ½ **(8-oz.) package ⅓-less-fat cream cheese**
- 2 **Tbsp. butter, softened**
- 1 **tsp. vanilla extract**
- 3 **cups powdered sugar**
- 1 **to 2 tsp. fat-free milk (optional)**

Try This Twist!

CARROT CAKE MUFFINS: Omit frosting. Place about 15 paper baking cups in muffin pans, and coat with cooking spray. Prepare batter, and fold in ½ cup chopped toasted pecans and ½ cup golden raisins with carrots. Spoon batter into baking cups, filling about two-thirds full.

Bake as directed. Cool in pans on a wire rack 10 minutes. Serve warm or at room temperature. Makes about 15 muffins.

PER SERVING: CALORIES 204; FAT 7.3G (SAT 1G, MONO 2.6G, POLY 3.4G); PROTEIN 3.8G; CARB 31.9G; FIBER 1.9G; CHOL 28MG; IRON 1.2MG; SODIUM 356MG; CALC 23MG

PREPARE BATTER:

1. Preheat oven to 350°. Combine first 5 ingredients in a large bowl; make a well in center of mixture. Whisk together pineapple and next 4 ingredients; add pineapple mixture to flour mixture, stirring just until dry ingredients are moistened. Fold in carrots. Pour batter into 2 (8-inch) round cake pans coated with cooking spray.

2. Bake at 350° for 22 to 25 minutes or until a wooden pick inserted in center comes out clean. Cool in pans on a wire rack 10 minutes. Remove from pans to a wire rack; cool completely (about 1 hour).

PREPARE FROSTING:

1. Beat first 3 ingredients at medium speed with an electric mixer until smooth. Gradually add powdered sugar to butter mixture; beat at low speed just until blended. (Do not overbeat.) Beat in up to 2 tsp. milk for desired consistency. Place 1 cake layer on a serving plate; spread with ⅔ cup frosting, and top with remaining cake layer. Spread remaining frosting over top and sides of cake.

PER SERVING: CALORIES 273; FAT 7.4G (SAT 2.7G, MONO 1.4G, POLY 2.5G); PROTEIN 3.9G; CARB 48.6G; FIBER 1.3G; CHOL 35MG; IRON 1MG; SODIUM 375MG; CALC 23MG

TRY THIS TWIST!

Carrot Sheet Cake: Prepare batter, and pour into a 13- x 9-inch pan coated with cooking spray. Bake as directed. Cool in pan completely on a wire rack (about 1 hour). Spread with frosting. Makes 16 servings.

PER SERVING: CALORIES 273; FAT 7.4G (SAT 2.7G, MONO 1.4G, POLY 2.5G); PROTEIN 3.9G; CARB 48.6G; FIBER 1.3G; CHOL 35.3MG; IRON 1MG; SODIUM 375MG; CALC 23MG

Cooking with Fresh-Cut Corn

Florida's supersweet corn, already ripe with summer flavor, is in stores now!

Test Kitchen Tip

MAKING THE CUT
Stand corn upright on a large cutting board. Using a sharp knife, cut straight down across the base of the kernels.

Grilled Cheesy Corn

Grilled Cheesy Corn

good for you • party perfect

1. Preheat grill to 350° to 400° (medium-high) heat. Pull back husks from ears of fresh corn; remove and discard silks. Tie husks together with kitchen string to form a handle. Soak in cold salted water to cover 10 minutes; drain. Grill corn, covered with grill lid, 15 minutes or until golden brown, turning occasionally. Remove from grill. Brush corn with melted butter; sprinkle with salt, chili powder, smoked paprika, and grated Cotija or Parmesan cheese. Serve with fresh lime wedges.

Can't get enough? Check out The Zellwood Sweet Corn Festival in Florida each May! *zellwoodcornfestival.com*

Good To Know

- Don't be fooled by color: All shades of Florida supersweet corn taste equally sweet. Unlike other varieties, the fresh flavor lasts up to a week after picking.
- Look for tight rows of plump, shiny kernels, glossy silks, and moist green husks.
- Remember: One ear yields ½ to ¾ cup kernels. Try our ideas for fresh-cut corn on the following page.

Curried Shrimp-and-Corn Chowder

good for you • party perfect

MAKES: 8 servings
HANDS-ON TIME: I hr.
TOTAL TIME: I hr., 25 min.

Put this in your favorites file for casual weekend get-togethers with friends.

- I medium-size sweet onion, diced
- 2 Tbsp. olive oil
- 2 garlic cloves, chopped
- 2 large Yukon gold potatoes (14 oz.), peeled and diced
- I large sweet potato (I lb.), peeled and diced
- 2 cups fresh corn kernels (about 5 ears)
- I (14-oz.) can chicken broth
- I (13.5-oz.) can unsweetened lite coconut milk
- 2 tsp. curry powder
- I tsp. salt
- ¼ tsp. pepper
- I lb. peeled, large raw shrimp (26/30 count)
  Toppings: toasted coconut, thinly sliced green onions, coarsely chopped roasted peanuts

1. Sauté onion in hot oil in a Dutch oven over medium heat 5 minutes or until tender; add garlic, and sauté I minute. Add Yukon gold potatoes and next 7 ingredients; bring to a boil, stirring often. Reduce heat, and simmer, stirring occasionally, 25 minutes or until potatoes are tender. Stir in shrimp; cook 4 to 5 minutes or just until shrimp turn pink. Season with salt and pepper to taste. Serve with desired toppings.

RECIPE FROM PATRICIA GLEASON
LYNCHBURG, VIRGINIA

TRY THIS TWIST!
Shrimp-and-Corn Chowder: We're big curry fans, but you can just as easily make a traditional chowder. Substitute I (12-oz.) can evaporated milk for lite coconut milk. Omit curry powder.

10 More Quick Ideas

{1}
Top off a Margherita pizza.

{2}
Brighten a fresh tomato salsa.

{3}
Stir into hot mashed potatoes with shredded smoked Gouda cheese and chopped fresh cilantro.

{4}
Add an extra layer of flavor to Mexican lasagna.

{5}
Fold into beaten eggs for a fresh corn omelet.

{6}
Tuck inside a green chile-goat cheese quesadilla.

{7}
Toss with hot pasta carbonara.

{8}
Sprinkle over a crisp green salad.

{9}
Whisk into hot grits with shredded Parmesan and chopped fresh basil.

{10}
Freshen up a can of chicken noodle soup.

Fresh Corn-and-Potato Salad

quick prep • good for you •
make-ahead • party perfect

MAKES: 6 servings
HANDS-ON TIME: 35 min.
TOTAL TIME: 35 min.

- I lb. baby red potatoes
- ¼ cup chopped fresh cilantro
- 3 Tbsp. fresh lime juice
- 2 Tbsp. olive oil
- ½ tsp. salt
- ½ tsp. freshly ground pepper
- 3 cups fresh corn kernels (about 6 ears)
- ½ large red bell pepper, diced
- I avocado, peeled and diced
- ½ cup sliced green onions

Test Kitchen Notebook

Florida supersweet corn is so deliciously crisp and tender that it can be cut fresh from the cob and added to dishes without being cooked.

1. Bring potatoes and salted cold water to cover to a boil in a large Dutch oven; boil 10 minutes or just until tender. Drain and let cool 15 minutes.
2. Whisk together cilantro and next 4 ingredients in a large bowl. Add warm potatoes, corn, and remaining 3 ingredients; toss to coat. Serve at room temperature or chilled.

Egg-cellent Idea

Set a pretty Easter table by displaying flower- and candy-filled eggs along with treasured family silver.

GATHER

I dozen eggs
Pushpins
Spoon
Bleach
Wooden skewers
Craft foam
Brush & craft paint
Assorted pieces of silver (or pewter)

{1}
CRACK
Gently tap a pushpin into the top of an egg with the bottom of a spoon. Work in a circle to create an opening the size of a quarter or bigger. To make this job easier, leave the egg in the carton.

{2}
CLEAN
Empty the contents of each egg into a bowl and discard. Mix I tablespoon bleach with a gallon of water, and use to rinse out the inside of eggs. Return eggs to carton and allow to air-dry (about I5 minutes).

{3}
PAINT
Stick wooden skewers into craft foam and set eggs atop to paint. When dry, fill with candy or flowers, like ranunculus, daffodils, hydrangeas, or viburnum. Display with silver down the center of your table.

Devilishly Good for You

Eggs aren't as sinful as you may think, deviled or not. In fact, they're low in saturated fat and a good source of calcium-friendly vitamin D. Whip up these wickedly delicious gems, and watch them disappear.

5 New Favorites

Try these innovative stir-ins to make your own signature deviled eggs. Prepare recipe as directed, stirring one of the following delicious combos into yolk mixture (Step 3).

{1}

CREOLE SHRIMP: ½ cup finely chopped cooked shrimp, 3 Tbsp. sautéed chopped green bell pepper, I minced green onion, ¼ tsp. Creole seasoning, ¼ tsp. hot sauce. Top with cooked shrimp.

{2}

TEXAS CAVIAR: 3 Tbsp. chopped roasted red bell pepper, I minced green onion, I Tbsp. minced pickled jalapeño pepper, I Tbsp. chopped fresh cilantro, I tsp. Italian dressing mix. Top with canned black-eyed peas and fresh cilantro leaves.

{3}

HIGH SOCIETY: ½ cup cooked fresh lump crabmeat, 2 tsp. fresh tarragon, ½ tsp. lemon zest, ¼ tsp. pepper. Top with cooked fresh crabmeat and watercress.

{4}

GEORGIA PEACH: 3 Tbsp. peach preserves, ¼ cup finely chopped country ham, I tsp. grated Vidalia onion, ½ tsp. apple cider vinegar, ¼ tsp. pepper. Top with sliced fresh peaches and chopped toasted pecans.

{5}

TRIPLE PICKLE: 3 Tbsp. chopped bread-and-butter pickles, 2 Tbsp. chopped capers. Top with pickled okra slices.

Simply Deviled Eggs

quick prep • good for you • make-ahead • party perfect

MAKES: 2 dozen
HANDS-ON TIME: 25 min.
TOTAL TIME: 40 min.

- I2 large eggs
- ⅓ cup fat-free Greek yogurt
- 2 oz. ⅓-less-fat cream cheese
- I Tbsp. chopped fresh parsley
- I tsp. Dijon mustard
- ⅛ tsp. salt

1. Place eggs in a single layer in a stainless steel saucepan. (Do not use nonstick.) Add water to depth of 3 inches. Bring to a rolling boil; cook I minute. Cover, remove from heat, and let stand 10 minutes. Drain.
2. Place eggs under cold running water until just cool enough to handle. Tap eggs on the counter until cracks form; peel.
3. Slice eggs in half lengthwise, and carefully remove yolks. Mash together yolks, yogurt, and next 4 ingredients until smooth using a fork. Spoon yolk mixture into egg white halves. Serve immediately, or cover and chill I hour before serving.

Scalloped Potatoes

One is a lavishly rich casserole ideal for family suppers. The other bakes sweet potatoes, cheese, and thyme in individual stacks fancy enough for company.

WHY WE LOVE
Mama's Way

- Cheesy, golden crust
- Well-seasoned, but not overpowering
- Buttery Yukon gold potatoes

Classic Parmesan
Scalloped Potatoes

MAMA'S WAY

Classic Parmesan Scalloped Potatoes

party perfect

MAKES: 8 to 10 servings
HANDS-ON TIME: 20 min.
TOTAL TIME: 1 hr., 15 min.

Gently stirring twice while baking promotes even cooking and creaminess to this dish. Pull out of the oven, stir once more, then sprinkle with cheese, and continue baking without stirring for a casserole that's golden brown on top. (Pictured on page 10)

- 2 lb. Yukon gold potatoes, peeled and thinly sliced
- 3 cups whipping cream
- ¼ cup chopped fresh flat-leaf parsley
- 2 garlic cloves, chopped
- 1½ tsp. salt
- ¼ tsp. freshly ground pepper
- ½ cup grated Parmesan cheese

1. Preheat oven to 400°. Layer potatoes in a 13- x 9-inch or 3-qt. baking dish.
2. Stir together cream and next 4 ingredients in a large bowl. Pour cream mixture over potatoes.
3. Bake at 400° for 30 minutes, stirring gently every 10 minutes. Sprinkle with cheese; bake 15 to 20 minutes or until bubbly and golden brown. Let stand on a wire rack 10 minutes before serving.

TRY THIS TWIST!

Gruyère Scalloped Potatoes: Substitute finely shredded Gruyère cheese for Parmesan. Reduce parsley to 2 Tbsp. and salt to 1 tsp. Prepare recipe as directed, stirring 1 tsp. freshly ground Italian seasoning into cream mixture in Step 2.
NOTE: We tested with McCormick Italian Herb Seasoning Grinder.

WHY WE LOVE
Your Way

- Surprisingly savory flavor
- Layers of melted mozzarella
- No special tools needed, just a muffin pan

Scalloped Sweet
Potato Stacks

YOUR WAY

Scalloped Sweet Potato Stacks

party perfect

MAKES: 12 servings
HANDS-ON TIME: 25 min.
TOTAL TIME: 1 hr., 5 min.

Each muffin cup flares slightly, so place slices from ends of potatoes in the bottom and use wider slices from the middle of the potato at the top. We also like this with Gruyère instead of mozzarella.

- 1½ lb. small sweet potatoes, peeled and thinly sliced
- 2 tsp. chopped fresh thyme, divided
- 1 cup (4 oz.) freshly shredded mozzarella cheese, divided*
- ⅔ cup heavy cream
- 1 garlic clove, pressed
- ½ to ¾ tsp. salt
- ¼ tsp. freshly ground pepper
  Garnish: fresh thyme

1. Preheat oven to 375°. Layer half of sweet potatoes in a lightly greased 12-cup muffin pan. Sprinkle with 1½ tsp. thyme and ½ cup cheese. Top with remaining sweet potatoes. (Potatoes will come slightly above the rim of each cup.)
2. Microwave cream, next 3 ingredients, and remaining ½ tsp. thyme at HIGH 1 minute. Pour cream mixture into muffin cups (about 1 Tbsp. per cup).
3. Bake at 375°, covered with aluminum foil, 30 minutes. Uncover and sprinkle with remaining ½ cup cheese. Bake 5 to 7 minutes or until cheese is melted and slightly golden.
4. Let stand 5 minutes. Run a sharp knife around rim of each cup, and lift potato stacks from cups using a spoon or thin spatula. Transfer to a serving platter. Garnish, if desired.

*Gruyère cheese may be substituted.

Quick-Fix Meals

Mayonnaise on bread. Mustard on a bun. (Yawn.) Use these ordinary condiments to whip up extraordinary things with these use-what-you've-got recipes.

Grilled Pork Tenderloin with Squash Medley

quick prep • good for you

MAKES: 4 servings
HANDS-ON TIME: 10 min.
TOTAL TIME: 50 min.

Easy side: Prepare 1 (24-oz.) package frozen steam-and-mash potatoes according to package directions. Stir in ⅓ cup whipped chive-flavored cream cheese. Add pepper to taste and 2 Tbsp. melted butter.

 1 (1-lb.) pork tenderloin
 2 tsp. salt, divided
 ¾ tsp. pepper, divided
 2 Tbsp. Dijon mustard
 1 Tbsp. chopped fresh thyme
 1 Tbsp. olive oil
 1 Tbsp. honey
 1 garlic clove, minced
 2 yellow squash
 2 zucchini
 1 tsp. olive oil
 1 tsp. fresh thyme leaves

1. Preheat grill to 350° to 400° (medium-high) heat. Remove silver skin from tenderloin, leaving a thin layer of fat.
2. Sprinkle pork with 1 tsp. salt and ½ tsp. pepper. Combine mustard and next 4 ingredients. Rub mustard mixture on pork; cover and let stand 10 minutes.
3. Preheat oven to 450°. Cut squash and zucchini into ½-inch slices; cut into half moons. Toss with 1 tsp. olive oil and remaining 1 tsp. salt and ¼ tsp. pepper. Place on an aluminum foil-lined jelly-roll pan, and bake 20 minutes or until tender.
4. Meanwhile, grill pork, covered with grill lid, 10 to 12 minutes on each side or until a meat thermometer inserted into thickest portion registers 155°. Remove from grill; cover with foil, and let stand 10 minutes. Slice pork, and serve with squash medley. Sprinkle with thyme.

Pickled Okra and Shrimp Salad

quick prep • good for you •
make-ahead • party perfect

MAKES: 6 servings
HANDS-ON TIME: 10 min.
TOTAL TIME: 40 min.

Easy side: Spread a thin layer of softened butter onto 1 side of 12 (½-inch-thick) French bread baguette slices. Bake at 425° for 4 minutes or until toasted. Combine 2 Tbsp. mayonnaise with 1 cup grated extra-sharp Cheddar cheese. Spread onto 1 side of bread. Sprinkle lightly with paprika. Bake 5 to 6 minutes or until cheese is melted.

 1 (3-oz.) package boil-in-bag shrimp-and-crab boil
 1½ lb. peeled and deveined, medium-size raw shrimp (31/40 count)
 ½ cup sliced sweet-hot pickled okra
 1 (4-oz.) jar diced pimiento, drained
 ⅓ cup mayonnaise
 3 Tbsp. minced red onion
 ½ tsp. lime zest
 3 Tbsp. fresh lime juice
 ¼ tsp. pepper
 ⅛ tsp. salt
 3 large avocados, sliced

1. Bring 8 cups water to a boil in a 3-qt. saucepan; add crab boil, and cook 5 minutes. Add shrimp; cover, remove from heat, and let stand 10 minutes or just until shrimp turn pink. Drain and cool 10 minutes.
2. Meanwhile, combine pickled okra, diced pimiento, and next 6 ingredients. Add shrimp, and serve immediately with avocado slices, or cover and chill until ready to serve.
NOTE: We tested with Wickles pickled okra.

Rosemary Chicken Kabobs

quick prep • good for you • party perfect

MAKES: 4 servings
HANDS-ON TIME: 15 min.
TOTAL TIME: 40 min.

Easy side: Toss 1 (5-oz.) head Bibb lettuce with ½ cup drained mandarin oranges. Serve with bottled ginger dressing.

⅓ cup red wine vinegar
⅓ cup olive oil
4 garlic cloves, pressed
1 Tbsp. fresh rosemary leaves
1 tsp. salt
1 tsp. Dijon mustard
1 lb. skinned and boned chicken breasts, cut into 2-inch pieces
1 large green bell pepper, cut into 2-inch pieces
1 pt. cherry tomatoes
1 (8-oz.) package fresh mushrooms
16 (6-inch) metal skewers

1. Preheat grill to 350° to 400° (medium-high) heat. Whisk together first 6 ingredients in a small bowl. Pour half of olive oil mixture into a shallow bowl or zip-top plastic freezer bag; add chicken, turning to coat. Cover or seal, and let stand 10 minutes. Pour remaining olive oil mixture into another bowl or freezer bag; add bell pepper, tomatoes, and mushrooms, and toss to coat; cover or seal, and let stand 10 minutes.

2. Remove chicken and vegetables from marinade, discarding marinade. Thread chicken onto 8 skewers. Thread vegetables alternately onto remaining 8 skewers.

3. Grill kabobs, covered with grill lid, 10 to 12 minutes or until chicken is done and vegetables are tender, turning occasionally. Remove kabobs from grill. Let stand 5 minutes before serving.

Test Kitchen Notebook

MORE IDEAS FOR CONDIMENTS!

Test Kitchen Specialist Vanessa McNeil Rocchio reveals how to get creative with staples.

- Bottled vinaigrette serves as a quick marinade for meats and veggies.

- Honey is a natural sweetener for drinks, dressings, sauces, and even pancake batter.

- Hot sauce adds just enough heat to biscuit doughs, scrambled eggs, and cheese grits.

- Jams, jellies, and preserves are sweet stir-ins for plain yogurt. Add granola for a healthy dessert.

- Ketchup mixed with mayo and capers is an easy and tasty sauce for shrimp.

- Maple syrup adds Southern sweetness to lemonade and tea.

- Mayonnaise is a healthier fat than butter; brush it on a grilled cheese for a tasty golden crust.

- Olive oil stirred with herbs and sea salt makes a heart-healthy dipping sauce for bread.

- Pickle relish is a zesty topper for chili.

- Red wine vinegar adds zing to marinades and vinaigrettes. A teaspoonful is also said to cure hiccups!

- Salsa is a veggie-loaded alternative to salad dressing.

- Soy sauce can replace salt in many dishes while adding flavor.

Roasted Salmon with Lemon and Dill

quick prep • good for you

MAKES: 4 servings
HANDS-ON TIME: 15 min.
TOTAL TIME: 30 min.

Easy side: Cook 2 (8.8-oz.) pouches ready-to-serve basmati rice according to package directions. Stir in 1 cup frozen sweet peas, thawed; ¼ cup chopped fresh parsley; 1 Tbsp. chopped fresh mint; and salt and pepper to taste.

4 (6-oz.) salmon fillets
½ tsp. salt
¼ tsp. freshly ground pepper
8 fresh dill sprigs
4 lemon slices, halved

1. Preheat oven to 425°. Place salmon fillets on a lightly greased rack on an aluminum foil-lined jelly-roll pan; sprinkle with salt and pepper. Place 2 dill sprigs and 2 lemon halves on each fillet.
2. Bake at 425° for 15 to 20 minutes or just until fish flakes with a fork.

TRY IT WITH:
Creamy Lemon Horseradish Sauce: Stir together 1 (8-oz.) container sour cream, 6 Tbsp. mayonnaise, 3 Tbsp. horseradish, 1 tsp. lemon zest, and 1 tsp. fresh lemon juice. Chill until ready to serve. Store in an airtight container in refrigerator up to 1 week. Makes: 1½ cups. Hands-on time: 5 min. Total time: 5 min.

Grilled Chicken Tacos

quick prep • good for you • party perfect

MAKES: 4 to 6 servings
HANDS-ON TIME: 20 min.
TOTAL TIME: 42 min.

Easy side: Combine 2 (20.5-oz.) cans refried black beans, ½ (8-oz.) package whipped chive-flavored cream cheese, and ½ tsp. ground cumin in a 2-qt. baking dish. Top with 2 Tbsp. finely chopped red onion and 1 cup crumbled queso fresco (fresh Mexican cheese). Bake at 450° for 20 to 30 minutes or until cheese melts.

3 Tbsp. olive oil
2 Tbsp. lime juice
4 tsp. Montreal chicken seasoning
1½ lb. chicken breast tenders
1 (8-oz.) container refrigerated fresh salsa
1 large mango, peeled and chopped
¼ cup chopped fresh cilantro
2 tsp. chipotle hot sauce
6 (6-inch) fajita-size flour tortillas, warmed
Toppings: crumbled queso fresco (fresh Mexican cheese), and shredded romaine lettuce

1. Preheat grill to 300° to 350° (medium) heat. Combine first 3 ingredients in a zip-top plastic freezer bag; add chicken, turning to coat. Seal and chill 10 minutes, turning once.
2. Meanwhile, combine salsa and next 3 ingredients. Cover and chill until ready to serve.
3. Remove chicken from marinade, discarding marinade. Grill chicken, covered with grill lid, 6 minutes on each side or until done. Serve in flour tortillas with mango salsa and desired toppings.
NOTE: We tested with McCormick Grill Mates Montreal Chicken Seasoning.

How to: Bake a Perfect Ham

Master the art of this Southern classic in three easy steps.

Brown Sugar-Bourbon-Glazed Ham

Brown Sugar-Bourbon-Glazed Ham

party perfect

MAKES: 8 to 10 servings
HANDS-ON TIME: 20 min.
TOTAL TIME: 3 hr., 10 min.

Choose a bone-in half-ham brined with natural juices. Leaving a thin layer of fat after trimming amps up the flavor and keeps the meat moist.

- 1 (6- to 8-lb.) fully cooked, bone-in ham
- 48 whole cloves
- 1 (16-oz.) package light brown sugar
- 1 cup spicy brown mustard
- 1 cup cola soft drink
- ¾ cup bourbon

1. Preheat oven to 350°. Remove skin from ham, and trim fat to ¼-inch thickness. Make shallow cuts in fat ¾ inch apart in a diamond pattern.

2. Insert cloves in centers of diamonds. Place ham in a lightly greased 13- x 9-inch pan. Stir together brown sugar and next 3 ingredients; spoon mixture over ham.
3. Bake at 350° on lowest oven rack 2 hours and 30 minutes, basting slowly with pan juices every 15 to 20 minutes. Remove ham from oven, and let stand 20 minutes before slicing, basting occasionally with pan juices.

Test Kitchen Tips

GET THE LOOK
Score the surface with shallow diamond-shape cuts. It adds a decorative edge and also ensures the outer coating of fat crisps to a rich golden brown.

SPICE IT UP
Stud the ham with festive rows of aromatic cloves. Piercing a small hole first with the sharp point of a wooden skewer makes it easy to insert the cloves.

SEAL THE DEAL
Spoon the glaze over the top and sides of the ham as it cools for a glistening finish. Allow at least 20 minutes of downtime before carving to lock in the juices.

May

Sweet as Can Be!

Break out the tumblers and fire up the grill—the secret to these summertime favorites is out of the bag! If you think the South's love affair with tea is all about the thirst-quenching charms of a tall frosty pitcher, wait until you see what we've cooked up.

Southern Sweet Tea

quick prep • make-ahead • party perfect

MAKES: 10 cups
HANDS-ON TIME: 10 min.
TOTAL TIME: 26 min.

It's known as the house wine of the South, and every family has a signature brew.

- 3 **cups water**
- 2 **family-size tea bags**
- ¾ **cup sugar**
- 7 **cups cold water**

1. Bring 3 cups water to a boil in a saucepan; add tea bags. Boil 1 minute; remove from heat. Cover and steep 10 minutes.
2. Discard tea bags. Add sugar, stirring until dissolved. Pour into a 1-gal. container, and add 7 cups cold water. Serve over ice.
NOTE: See box on next page for Sweet Tea variations.

Governor's Mansion Summer Peach Tea Punch

READER RECIPE

quick prep • make-ahead • party perfect

MAKES: about 1 gal.
HANDS-ON TIME: 10 min.
TOTAL TIME: 9 hr., 5 min., including simple syrup

- 3 **family-size tea bags**
- 2 **cups loosely packed fresh mint leaves**
- 1 **(33.8-oz.) bottle peach nectar**
- ½ **(12-oz.) can frozen lemonade concentrate, thawed**
- ½ **cup Simple Sugar Syrup**
- 1 **(1-liter) bottle ginger ale, chilled**
- 1 **(1-liter) bottle club soda, chilled**
   Garnish: fresh peach wedges

1. Bring 4 cups water to a boil in a medium saucepan; add tea bags and mint leaves. Boil 1 minute; remove from heat. Cover and steep 10 minutes.
2. Discard tea bags and mint. Pour into a 1-gal. container; add peach nectar, lemonade concentrate, and Simple Sugar Syrup. Cover and chill 8 to 24 hours.
3. Pour chilled tea mixture into a punch bowl or pitcher. Stir in ginger ale and club soda just before serving. Garnish, if desired.

RECIPE FROM *AUSTIN ENTERTAINS*
JUNIOR LEAGUE OF AUSTIN, TEXAS

Simple Sugar Syrup

MAKES: about 1¾ cups
HANDS-ON TIME: 10 min.
TOTAL TIME: 40 min.

1. Bring 2 cups sugar and 1 cup water to a boil in a medium saucepan over medium-high heat. Boil, stirring occasionally, 4 minutes or until sugar is dissolved and mixture is clear. Cool to room temperature (about 30 minutes).

Governor's Mansion
Summer Peach Tea Punch

Sweet Tea Variations

Mint Julep Sweet Tea

MAKES: 4 cups
HANDS-ON TIME: 10 min.
TOTAL TIME: 10 min.

- ½ cup loosely packed fresh mint leaves
- 1 lemon, sliced
- 2 Tbsp. sugar
- 3 cups cold sweetened tea
- 1 cup bourbon
- Crushed ice
- Garnish: fresh mint sprigs

1. Combine first 3 ingredients in a 2-qt. pitcher. Press mint leaves against sides of pitcher with back of a spoon to release flavors. Stir in tea and bourbon. Serve over crushed ice. Garnish, if desired.

Blackberry Sweet Tea

MAKES: about 7 cups
HANDS-ON TIME: 25 min.
TOTAL TIME: 2 hr., 30 min.

- 3 cups fresh or frozen blackberries, thawed
- 1¼ cups sugar
- 1 Tbsp. chopped fresh mint
- Pinch of baking soda
- 4 cups boiling water
- 2 family-size tea bags
- 2½ cups cold water
- Garnish: fresh blackberries

1. Combine blackberries and sugar in a large container, and crush with a wooden spoon; stir in mint and baking soda.
2. Pour 4 cups boiling water over tea bags; cover and steep 5 minutes. Discard tea bags.
3. Pour tea over blackberry mixture; let stand at room temperature 1 hour. Pour tea through a wire-mesh strainer into a large pitcher, discarding solids. Add 2½ cups cold water, stirring until sugar dissolves. Cover and chill 1 hour. Garnish, if desired.

Lemon-Blueberry Sweet Tea

MAKES: 5 cups
HANDS-ON TIME: 30 min.
TOTAL TIME: 1 hr., 30 min.

- 1 (12-oz.) package frozen blueberries
- ½ cup fresh lemon juice
- 3 family-size tea bags
- ¾ cup sugar
- Garnishes: fresh blueberries, lemon zest strips

1. Bring blueberries and lemon juice to a boil in a large saucepan over medium heat; cook, stirring occasionally, 5 minutes. Remove from heat; pour through a wire-mesh strainer into a bowl, using back of a spoon to squeeze out juice. Discard solids. Rinse saucepan clean.
2. Bring 4 cups water to a boil in same saucepan; add 3 tea bags; let stand 5 minutes. Discard tea bags. Stir in sugar and blueberry juice mixture. Pour into a pitcher; cover and chill 1 hour. Serve over ice. Garnish, if desired.

Lemonade Sweet Tea

MAKES: about 8 cups
HANDS-ON TIME: 25 min.
TOTAL TIME: 25 min.

- 3 cups water
- 2 family-size tea bags
- 1 cup loosely packed fresh mint leaves
- ½ cup sugar
- 4 cups cold water
- ½ (12-oz.) can frozen lemonade concentrate, thawed
- Garnishes: halved orange slices, lemon balm

1. Bring 3 cups water to a boil in a 2-qt. saucepan. Remove from heat, add tea bags, and stir in fresh mint. Cover and steep 10 minutes.

2. Discard tea bags and mint. Stir in sugar until dissolved. Pour tea into a 3-qt. container, and stir in 4 cups cold water and lemonade concentrate. Serve over ice. Garnish, if desired.

Spiked Lemonade Sweet Tea: Prepare Lemonade Sweet Tea recipe as directed. Stir in 1 cup bourbon or 1 cup spiced dark rum just before serving. Garnish with fresh sugarcane and fresh pineapple slices, if desired.

Ginger-and-Honey Sweet Tea: Prepare Southern Sweet Tea recipe as directed, omitting sugar and stirring in ½ cup honey and 1 Tbsp. grated fresh ginger. Garnish with lemon slices, if desired.

Citrus Sweet Tea

MAKES: 5 cups
HANDS-ON TIME: 15 min.
TOTAL TIME: 1 hr., 30 min.

- 2 whole cloves
- 1 family-size tea bag
- 1½ cups pineapple juice
- ½ cup orange juice
- ¼ cup fresh lemon juice
- ⅔ cup sugar
- Crushed ice
- Garnish: lemon slices

1. Bring 3 cups water and cloves to a boil in a saucepan over medium heat; reduce heat to low, and simmer 10 minutes. Remove from heat, and add tea bag; steep 10 minutes.
2. Discard tea bag and cloves. Add fruit juices and sugar, stirring until sugar dissolves. Cover and chill for 1 hour; serve over crushed ice. Garnish, if desired.

Tea, Beyond the Glass

{1}

DYE LINENS: Prop Stylist Lydia DeGaris Pursell tinted the beautiful table linens for this story by steeping them in warm tea. Depending on the type of tea, colors range from antique ivory and ecru to dusty rose and berry pink. The longer the linens soak, the darker the shade.

{2}

FEED YOUR FERNS: Substitute brewed (unsweet) tea when watering ferns and other houseplants— both indoors and out. You can also toss used tea bags into your compost pile to help acidify the soil.

{3}

THROW A GROWN-UP TEA PARTY: A tea-themed shower is a sweet idea for a bride or mom-to-be. Send an invite complete with a tea bag and note saying "Good times are brewin' in honor of [name]." Mail it in a small Mason jar. Decorate with flower-filled pitchers.

Grilled Shrimp Salad with Sweet Tea Vinaigrette

 READER RECIPE

Grilled Shrimp Salad with Sweet Tea Vinaigrette

good for you • party perfect

MAKES: 6 servings
HANDS-ON TIME: 16 min.
TOTAL TIME: 1 hr., 6 min., including vinaigrette
(Pictured on page 11)

- 1 **cup coarsely chopped pecans**
- 1 **lb. peeled, jumbo raw shrimp (16/20 count)**
- 1 **Tbsp. olive oil**
- 2 **large fresh peaches, cut into 8 wedges each**
- 1 **(6-oz.) bag mixed baby salad greens**
  Sweet Tea Vinaigrette
  Salt and pepper to taste
- 1 **cup crumbled blue cheese**

1. Preheat oven to 350°. Bake pecans in a single layer in a shallow pan 5 to 7 minutes or until lightly toasted and fragrant, stirring halfway through.

2. Preheat grill to 350° to 400° (medium-high) heat. Devein shrimp, if desired, and toss with olive oil. Grill shrimp, covered with grill lid, 2 to 3 minutes on each side or just until shrimp turn pink. Grill peach wedges 1 to 2 minutes on each side or until grill marks appear.

3. Toss salad greens with Sweet Tea Vinaigrette; season with salt and pepper to taste, and top with grilled shrimp, peaches, blue cheese, and pecans. Serve immediately.

RECIPE FROM *THE BILTMORE COMPANY*
ASHEVILLE, NORTH CAROLINA

Sweet Tea Vinaigrette

quick prep • party perfect

MAKES: about ¾ cup
HANDS-ON TIME: 10 min.
TOTAL TIME: 45 min.

1. Bring 1 cup sweetened tea to a boil in a saucepan over medium-low heat; reduce heat to low, and simmer 9 to 10 minutes or until reduced to ⅓ cup. Remove from heat; cool 20 minutes. Whisk in 2 Tbsp. cider vinegar, ¼ tsp. honey, ¼ tsp. Dijon mustard, and a pinch of salt. Whisk in 6 Tbsp. canola oil in a slow, steady stream.

Sweet Tea-Brined Chicken

make-ahead • party perfect

MAKES: 6 to 8 servings
HANDS-ON TIME: 30 min.
TOTAL TIME: 2 hr., 35 min., plus I day
for marinating
(*Pictured on page II*)

2 family-size tea bags
½ cup firmly packed light
   brown sugar
¼ cup kosher salt
I small sweet onion, thinly sliced
I lemon, thinly sliced
3 garlic cloves, halved
2 (6-inch) fresh rosemary sprigs
I Tbsp. freshly cracked pepper
2 cups ice cubes
I (3½- to 4-lb.) cut-up whole chicken

1. Bring 4 cups water to a boil in a 3-qt.
heavy saucepan; add tea bags. Remove
from heat; cover and steep 10 minutes.
2. Discard tea bags. Stir in sugar and next
6 ingredients, stirring until sugar dissolves.
Cool completely (about 45 minutes); stir
in ice. (Mixture should be cold before
adding chicken.)
3. Place tea mixture and chicken in a large
zip-top plastic freezer bag; seal. Place bag
in a shallow baking dish, and chill 24 hours.
Remove chicken from marinade, discarding
marinade; pat chicken dry with paper
towels.
4. Light one side of grill, heating to
300° to 350° (medium) heat; leave other
side unlit. Place chicken, skin side down,
over unlit side, and grill, covered
with grill lid, 20 minutes. Turn chicken,
and grill, covered with grill lid, 40 to
50 minutes or until done. Transfer chicken,
skin side down, to lit side of grill, and grill
2 to 3 minutes or until skin is crispy. Let
stand 5 minutes before serving.

Sweet Tea Dulce de Leche

make-ahead • party perfect

MAKES: 1½ cups
HANDS-ON TIME: 15 min.
TOTAL TIME: 13 hr., 5 min.

Serve over ice cream with salted nuts.

I family-size tea bag
I cup sugar
I cup heavy cream

1. Bring 2 cups water to a boil in a 3-qt.
heavy saucepan; add tea bag. Remove
from heat; cover and steep 10 minutes.
2. Discard tea bag. Add sugar, stirring
until dissolved. Bring tea mixture to a boil
over medium-high heat, and cook, stirring
occasionally, 10 more minutes or until
mixture turns amber brown and reduces
to a honeylike consistency. Gradually
add cream, and cook, stirring constantly,
I to 2 minutes or until smooth. (Mixture
will be very thin.) Cool completely
(about 30 minutes). Cover and chill
24 hours. (After chilling, mixture will
have the consistency of heavy cream.)

Sweet Tea Rice

quick prep • party perfect

MAKES: 6 servings
HANDS-ON TIME: 5 min.
TOTAL TIME: 25 min.

2 cups sweetened tea
I cup uncooked long-grain rice
½ tsp. salt

1. Bring tea to a boil in a 3-qt. saucepan
over medium-high heat; stir in rice and
salt. Cover, reduce heat to low, and simmer 20 minutes or until tea is absorbed
and rice is tender.

TRY THESE TWISTS!

**Sweet Tea Rice with Jalapeño,
Peaches, and Pecans:** Prepare recipe as
directed. Meanwhile, melt 2 Tbsp. butter in
a large skillet over medium heat; add ½ cup
chopped pecans, and cook, stirring often,
3 to 4 minutes or until toasted and fragrant.
Add I large seeded and minced jalapeño
pepper, and sauté I minute. Stir in hot
cooked rice, I large peeled and diced fresh
peach, I Tbsp. chopped fresh chives, ¼ tsp.
salt, and ¼ tsp. pepper. Hands-on time:
10 min. Total time: 25 min.

**Sweet Tea Rice with Caramelized
Onions:** Prepare recipe as directed.
Meanwhile, melt 2 Tbsp. butter in a large
skillet over medium heat; add I diced, large
sweet onion, and sauté 20 minutes or until
caramel colored. Stir in I Tbsp. balsamic
vinegar, ¼ tsp. salt, and ¼ tsp. pepper. Stir in
hot cooked rice. Hands-on time: 25 min.
Total time: 25 min.

Sweet Tea Rice Tabbouleh: Prepare
recipe as directed. Transfer rice to a large
bowl, and let cool completely (about
30 minutes). Stir in 2 seeded and diced
plum tomatoes, 3 thinly sliced green
onions, ⅓ cup chopped fresh parsley,
2 Tbsp. chopped fresh mint, 3 Tbsp. olive
oil, 2 tsp. lemon zest, ⅓ cup fresh lemon
juice, ½ tsp. salt, and ½ tsp. pepper. Cover
and chill I hour. Hands-on time: 10 min.
Total time: 2 hr.

**Sweet Tea Rice with Fresh Ginger
and Pears:** Prepare recipe as directed.
Meanwhile, melt 2 Tbsp. butter in a large
skillet over medium-high heat; add
2 minced large shallots, and sauté I minute.
Add I peeled and diced large pear,
2 tsp. grated fresh ginger, ½ tsp. pepper,
and ¼ tsp. salt, and sauté 5 minutes or until
pear is tender. Stir in hot cooked rice.
Hands-on time: 10 min. Total time: 25 min.

Sweet Tea Tiramisù

make-ahead • party perfect

MAKES: 10 to 12 servings
HANDS-ON TIME: 20 min.
TOTAL TIME: 13 hr., 30 min.

For topping: Toss sliced strawberries and pitted fresh cherries with a little sugar and almond liqueur; add shaved chocolate.

- 2 **family-size tea bags**
- 1½ **cups sugar, divided**
- 2 **(8-oz.) containers mascarpone cheese**
- 1 **Tbsp. vanilla bean paste or vanilla extract**
- 2 **cups whipping cream**
- 2 **(3-oz.) packages ladyfingers**
- 1 **to 2 tsp. unsweetened cocoa**

1. Bring 4 cups water to a boil in a 3-qt. heavy saucepan; add tea bags. Remove from heat; cover and steep 10 minutes.
2. Discard tea bags. Add 1 cup sugar, stirring until dissolved. Bring tea mixture to a boil over medium-high heat, and cook, stirring occasionally, 20 to 22 minutes or until mixture is reduced to 1 cup. Remove mixture from heat, and let cool to room temperature (about 30 minutes).
3. Stir together mascarpone cheese, vanilla bean paste, and remaining ½ cup sugar.
4. Beat whipping cream at medium speed with an electric mixer until soft peaks form; fold into cheese mixture.
5. Separate ladyfingers in half. Arrange 24 ladyfinger halves, flat sides up, in the bottom of an 11- x 7-inch baking dish. Drizzle with half of tea mixture. Top with half of cheese mixture. Repeat layers once. Cover and chill 12 hours. Sift cocoa over top just before serving.

Sweet Tea Icebox Tart

Sweet Tea Icebox Tart

make-ahead • party perfect

MAKES: 12 servings
HANDS-ON TIME: 25 min.
TOTAL TIME: 5 hr., 52 min., including Gingersnap Crust
(Pictured on page 177)

- 2 **Tbsp. unsweetened instant iced tea mix**
- 1 **(14-oz.) can sweetened condensed milk**
- ½ **tsp. orange zest**
- ½ **tsp. lime zest**
- ⅓ **cup fresh orange juice**
- ¼ **cup fresh lemon juice**
- 2 **large eggs, lightly beaten Gingersnap Crust***
- 1 **cup heavy cream**
- 3 **Tbsp. sugar**
  Garnishes: lemon slices, fresh mint sprigs

1. Preheat oven to 350°. Stir together iced tea mix and 2 Tbsp. water in a large bowl. Whisk in sweetened condensed milk and next 5 ingredients until blended. Place Gingersnap Crust on a baking sheet; pour in milk mixture.
2. Bake at 350° for 20 to 25 minutes or

just until filling is set. Cool completely on a wire rack (about 1 hour). Cover and chill 4 to 24 hours. Remove tart from pan, and place on a serving dish.
3. Beat cream and sugar at medium speed with an electric mixer until stiff peaks form. Pipe or dollop on top of tart; garnish, if desired.
*2 (4-oz.) packages ready-made mini graham cracker piecrusts may be substituted.
NOTE: You may also bake this tart in a 14- x 4-inch tart pan with removable bottom; increase bake time to 25 to 28 minutes or until filling is set.

Gingersnap Crust

quick prep • party perfect

MAKES: 1 (9-inch) crust
HANDS-ON TIME: 7 min.
TOTAL TIME: 7 min.

- 1½ **cups crushed gingersnap cookies**
- 5 **Tbsp. butter, melted**
- 2 **Tbsp. light brown sugar**
- ¼ **tsp. ground cinnamon**

1. Stir together all ingredients. Press mixture into a 9-inch tart pan with removable bottom.

Splendid in the Grass

Surprise Mom with a laid-back, let's-just-enjoy-each-other picnic. This portable menu is filled with delicious treats, including bite-size fried chicken and sweet little pies.

Plan Ahead

Set aside a half-hour each day to pull off your pretty party with ease.

2 DAYS BEFORE:
- Bake the hand pies; marinate the chicken.

THE DAY BEFORE:
- Fry the chicken (warm it in the oven, or serve cold); make the simple syrup, and squeeze the fresh juice.

3 HOURS BEFORE:
- Skewer the fruit and cheese, and make the salsa.

Spring Picnic

SERVES 4 TO 6

Lime Fizz

Fried Chicken Bites

Fruit, Cheese, and Herb Skewers

Spring Salsa

Strawberry-Rhubarb Hand Pies

Meet the Mother/Daughter

North Carolina native Elena Rosemond-Hoerr (right) discovered her passion for true Southern cooking from her grandma. Now she writes an award-winning Southern food blog (biscuitsandsuch.com), chock-full of make-you-hungry photos. Here, she and her mother, Cathy Waldron Rosemond, share a laugh over refreshing Lime Fizzes.

Lime Fizz
quick prep • party perfect

MAKES: 4¾ cups
HANDS-ON TIME: 5 min.
TOTAL TIME: 1 hr., 15 min., including simple syrup

For an adult version, stir ⅔ cup vodka in with simple syrup.

 Crushed ice
¾ to 1 cup Lime Simple Syrup
½ cup fresh lime juice
3½ cups chilled club soda

1. Fill a large pitcher with crushed ice. Pour Lime Simple Syrup and lime juice over ice. Add club soda, and stir gently to combine. Serve immediately.

Lime Simple Syrup
make-ahead • party perfect

MAKES: 1½ cups
HANDS-ON TIME: 10 min.
TOTAL TIME: 1 hr., 10 min.

Stir leftovers into unsweetened iced tea.

1 cup sugar
1 Tbsp. lime zest
½ cup fresh lime juice

1. Cook sugar and ½ cup water in a small saucepan over medium heat, stirring constantly, 3 minutes or until sugar is dissolved. Remove from heat; stir in lime zest and lime juice. Cover and chill 1 hour.

Fried Chicken Bites

make-ahead • party perfect

MAKES: 4 to 6 servings
HANDS-ON TIME: 50 min.
TOTAL TIME: 50 min., plus 1 day for marinating
(Pictured on page 176)

- 1½ tsp. to 1 Tbsp. ground red pepper
- 1½ tsp. ground chipotle chile pepper
- 1½ tsp. garlic powder
- 1½ tsp. dried crushed red pepper
- 1½ tsp. ground black pepper
- ¾ tsp. salt
- ½ tsp. paprika
- 2 lb. skinned and boned chicken breasts
- 2 cups buttermilk
- 3 bread slices, toasted
- 1 cup all-purpose flour
  Peanut oil
  Blue cheese dressing or honey mustard dressing

1. Combine first 7 ingredients in a small bowl; reserve half of spice mixture. Cut chicken into 1-inch pieces. Place chicken in a medium bowl, and toss with remaining spice mixture until coated. Stir in buttermilk; cover and chill 24 hours.

2. Tear bread into pieces, and place in a food processor with reserved spice mixture. Process until mixture resembles cornmeal. Stir in flour. Remove chicken pieces from buttermilk, discarding buttermilk. Dredge chicken in bread-crumb mixture.

3. Pour oil to depth of 2 inches into a Dutch oven; heat to 350°. Fry chicken, in batches, 6 to 7 minutes on each side or until golden brown and done. Drain on a wire rack over paper towels. Sprinkle with salt to taste. Serve warm or cold with blue cheese dressing or honey mustard dressing.

Fruit, Cheese, and Herb Skewers

Fruit, Cheese, and Herb Skewers

quick prep • good for you • make-ahead • party perfect

Thread various combinations of fruit, fresh small mozzarella cheese balls, and herbs on 6-inch wooden skewers up to three hours ahead.

Blackberry Skewers: 2 basil leaves, 2 fresh small mozzarella cheese balls, 2 to 3 blackberries

Raspberry Skewers: 2 mint leaves, 2 fresh small mozzarella cheese balls, 4 raspberries

Strawberry Skewers: 1 large basil leaf, torn in half; 2 strawberries; 1 fresh small mozzarella cheese ball

Blueberry Skewers: 1 large basil leaf, torn in half; 6 blueberries; 2 fresh small mozzarella cheese balls

---

Picnic Panache

An eclectic mix of new, modern serving pieces; hand-me-down vintage blankets; and not-so-perfect wicker baskets showcase Elena's signature charm. She recommends looking for quilts and baskets at thrift stores and antiques shops.

Spring Salsa

quick prep • good for you •
make-ahead • party perfect

MAKES: 3 ½ cups
HANDS-ON TIME: 15 min.
TOTAL TIME: 15 min.

*This colorful salsa would be equally delicious
served over salad greens or in warm tortillas
with grilled chicken.*

- 1½ **cups cherry tomatoes, seeded
  and chopped**
- 1 **cup frozen whole kernel corn,
  thawed**
- ¼ **cup chopped red onion**
- 2 **Tbsp. chopped fresh cilantro**
- 1 **garlic clove, minced**
- 1 **jalapeño pepper, seeded and
  minced**
- 2 **Tbsp. fresh lime juice**
  Salt and pepper to taste
  Tortilla chips

1. Stir together first 7 ingredients. Season
with salt and pepper to taste. Cover and
chill until ready to serve (up to 3 hours).
Serve with chips.

Spring Salsa

Strawberry-Rhubarb Hand Pies

Strawberry-Rhubarb
Hand Pies

make-ahead • party perfect

MAKES: 2 dozen
HANDS-ON TIME: 1 hr.
TOTAL TIME: 2 hr., 10 min.

*Crisp rhubarb has a tart flavor that teams
up perfectly with sweet strawberries. Both
are in season in the spring. (Pictured on
page 176)*

- ¾ **cup finely diced fresh
  strawberries**
- ¾ **cup finely diced rhubarb**
- 1 **Tbsp. cornstarch**
- 6 **Tbsp. sugar, divided**
- 3 **tsp. orange zest, divided**
- 2¼ **cups all-purpose flour**
- ¼ **tsp. salt**
- ½ **cup butter, cold**
- ¼ **cup shortening, chilled**
- 3 **Tbsp. ice-cold water**
- 3 **Tbsp. orange juice**
  Parchment paper
- 1 **egg yolk, beaten**
- 1 **Tbsp. whipping cream**
  Sugar

1. Combine strawberries, rhubarb, cornstarch, 2 Tbsp. sugar, and 1½ tsp. orange
zest in a small bowl.

2. Preheat oven to 375°. Combine flour,
salt, and remaining ¼ cup sugar in a large
bowl. Cut in butter and shortening with
a pastry blender until mixture resembles
small peas. Stir in remaining 1½ tsp. orange
zest. Drizzle with ice-cold water and
orange juice. Stir with a fork until combined. (Mixture will be crumbly and dry.)
Knead mixture lightly, and shape dough
into a disk. Divide dough in half.

3. Roll half of dough to ⅛-inch thickness
on a heavily floured surface. (Cover
remaining dough with plastic wrap.) Cut
with a 2¼-inch round cutter, rerolling
scraps as needed. Place half of dough
rounds 2 inches apart on a parchment
paper-lined baking sheets. Top with
1 rounded teaspoonful strawberry mixture. Dampen edges of dough with water,
and top with remaining dough rounds,
pressing edges to seal. Crimp edges with a
fork, and cut a slit in top of each round for
steam to escape. Repeat procedure with
remaining dough and strawberry mixture.

4. Stir together egg yolk and cream; brush
pies with egg wash. Sprinkle with sugar.
Freeze pies 10 minutes.

5. Bake at 375° for 20 to 25 minutes or
until lightly browned. Cool 10 minutes.
Serve warm or at room temperature.
Store in an airtight container up to 2 days.

Fiesta in Style

Cinco de Mayo may be a South-of-the-border holiday, but you can infuse your celebration with a few south-of-the-Mason twists. Enjoy!

Plan Ahead

3 DAYS BEFORE:
• Press linens. Pull serving pieces, glasses, silverware, and plates.

2 DAYS BEFORE:
• Cut strawberries for drink garnishes. Prepare salsa and barbecue sauce.

I DAY BEFORE:
• Prepare sour cream, slaw, and churros.

30 MINUTES BEFORE GUESTS ARRIVE:
• Make queso; place chips into serving dishes (we love to use paper bags). Blend cocktails.

Cinco de Mayo Celebration

SERVES 10

Easy Barbecue Tostadas

Spicy Queso Dip

Fresh Salsa

Strawberry Margarita Spritzers

Beer 'Garitas

Iced Mexican Chocolate Sipper

Oven-Baked Churros

Easy Barbecue Tostadas
quick prep • party perfect

MAKES: 10 servings
HANDS-ON TIME: 10 min.
TOTAL TIME: 30 min., including barbecue sauce, sour cream, and slaw

Pick up shredded pork or chicken from your favorite barbecue joint.

    10 tostada shells
     I (16-oz.) can refried beans
     2 lb. shredded barbecued pork
        or chicken without sauce
        Mole Barbecue Sauce
        Chipotle Sour Cream
        Jicama Slaw

1. Spread tostada shells with refried beans. Top with barbecued pork or chicken, Mole Barbecue Sauce, Chipotle Sour Cream, and Jicama Slaw. Serve immediately.

Mole Barbecue Sauce

1. Dissolve I Tbsp. mole sauce in ¼ cup hot water, whisking until smooth. Whisk in I cup barbecue sauce, I Tbsp. lime juice, and I Tbsp. chopped fresh cilantro. Makes: about 1½ cups. Hands-on time: 5 min., Total time: 5 min.

Chipotle Sour Cream

1. Stir together ½ cup sour cream; I chipotle pepper in adobo sauce, minced; and a pinch of salt. Makes: ½ cup. Hands-on time: 5 min., Total time: 5 min.

Jicama Slaw
quick prep • good for you • make-ahead • party perfect

MAKES: 10 servings
HANDS-ON TIME: 10 min.
TOTAL TIME: 10 min.

     2 cups shredded red cabbage (about
        ½ medium-size red cabbage)
     2 cups thinly sliced jicama (about
        ½ medium jicama)
     ¼ cup thinly sliced red onion
     ¼ cup chopped fresh cilantro
     I Tbsp. olive oil
     I Tbsp. fresh lime juice
     ½ tsp. salt
     ½ tsp. sugar

1. Toss together all ingredients.

"Create multiple pit stops—salsa here, drinks over there—to avoid a party guest pileup."

REBECCA KRACKE GORDON
TEST KITCHEN DIRECTOR

Spicy Queso Dip
quick prep • party perfect

MAKES: about 3 cups
HANDS-ON TIME: 20 min.
TOTAL TIME: 20 min.

For a milder dip, prepare with regular pasteurized cheese product. (Pictured on page 181)

- 1 small onion, diced
- 1 Tbsp. oil
- 1 garlic clove, minced
- 1 (16-oz.) package pepper Jack pasteurized prepared cheese product, cubed
- 1 (10-oz.) can diced tomatoes and green chiles
- 2 Tbsp. chopped fresh cilantro
   Tortilla chips

1. Cook onion in hot oil in a large nonstick skillet over medium-high heat 8 minutes or until tender. Add garlic, and cook 1 minute. Remove from heat.
2. Combine cheese, tomatoes, and onion mixture in a large microwave-safe glass bowl. Microwave at HIGH 5 minutes, stirring every 2½ minutes. Stir in cilantro. Serve with tortilla chips.
NOTE: We tested with Velveeta Pepper Jack.

Fresh Salsa
quick prep • good for you • make-ahead • party perfect

MAKES: about 4 cups
HANDS-ON TIME: 15 min.
TOTAL TIME: 15 min.

Serve salsa with chips to munch on before—and during—the main meal. (Pictured on page 181)

- ¼ medium-size sweet onion, coarsely chopped
- 1 small garlic clove, quartered
- 1 jalapeño pepper, seeded and quartered
- ¼ cup loosely packed fresh cilantro leaves
- 2 lb. tomatoes
- 1 lime
- 1¼ tsp. salt
   Tortilla chips

1. Pulse first 4 ingredients in a food processor until finely chopped.
2. Cut each tomato into 4 pieces. Cut core away from each piece; discard core. Add tomatoes to food processor in batches, and pulse each batch until well blended. Transfer to a large bowl. Squeeze juice from lime over salsa, and stir in salt. Serve with chips.

Strawberry Margarita Spritzers
quick prep • party perfect

MAKES: about 8 cups
HANDS-ON TIME: 10 min.
TOTAL TIME: 10 min.

- 1 (10-oz.) package frozen whole strawberries, thawed
- 1 (10-oz.) can frozen strawberry daiquiri mix, thawed
- 1 cup tequila
- ¼ cup orange liqueur
- 2 Tbsp. fresh lime juice
- 1 (1-liter) bottle club soda, chilled
   Garnishes: lime slices and quartered fresh strawberries

1. Pulse first 5 ingredients in a blender until smooth. Pour into a pitcher, and stir in club soda just before serving. Serve over ice. Garnish, if desired.
NOTE: We tested with Triple Sec.

Beer 'Garitas
quick prep • party perfect

MAKES: about 6 cups
HANDS-ON TIME: 5 min.
TOTAL TIME: 5 min.

For fast measuring, you can use the empty can of limeade concentrate to measure the tequila. One 12-oz. can is equivalent to 1½ cups. Serve in salt-rimmed glasses, if desired. (Pictured on page 181)

- 1 (12-oz.) container limeade concentrate, thawed
- 1½ cups tequila
- 2 (12-oz.) bottles beer
   Crushed ice
   Garnish: lime slices

1. Stir together first 3 ingredients in a large pitcher until blended. Serve immediately over crushed ice. Garnish, if desired.
NOTE: We tested with Yazoo Dos Perros Ale, Grolsch Premium Lager, Truck Stop Honey Brown Ale, and Bud Light beer.

Test Kitchen Notebook

SOUTHERN HOSPITALITY FIESTA IN STYLE: If short on time, use these tricks to get the party started.

{1}
Stir lime juice and chopped fresh cilantro into jarred salsa.

{2}
Toss together a mix of blue and yellow corn chips for interest.

{3}
Dress up store-bought guacamole with chopped red onion and drained jarred chunky salsa.

REBECCA KRACKE GORDON
TEST KITCHEN DIRECTOR

Iced Mexican
Chocolate Sipper and
Oven-Baked Churros

SOUTHERN CLASSIC

Kentucky Hot Browns

In need of a little comfort? Tuck into the classic knife-and-fork sandwich, or turn the hot combo into a decadent tart.

The Back Story

In the 1920s, dinner dances at Louisville's Brown Hotel drew more than 1,000 guests. During band breaks, hungry revelers refueled on chef Fred Schmidt's late-night eats. His signature? The Kentucky Hot Brown, a pillowy cushion of toasted bread topped with sliced turkey and an avalanche of Mornay sauce—all broiled until golden brown. Crisp bacon strips and tomato added the final flourish.

Iced Mexican Chocolate Sipper

quick prep • party perfect

MAKES: about 7 cups
HANDS-ON TIME: 10 min.
TOTAL TIME: 10 min.

To make garnish, pin orange zest strips around straws and leave for 15 minutes. (Pictured on page 180)

- 2 (14-oz.) containers premium chocolate ice cream
- 2 cups milk
- ¾ to 1 tsp. ground cinnamon
- ½ tsp. orange zest
- 1 cup bourbon
  Garnish: orange zest curls

1. Pulse first 4 ingredients in a blender until smooth. Stir in bourbon. Serve immediately over ice. Garnish, if desired.
NOTE: We tested with Häagen-Dazs Ice Cream.

Oven-Baked Churros

quick prep • make-ahead • party perfect

MAKES: 3 dozen
HANDS-ON TIME: 15 min.
TOTAL TIME: 30 min.
(Pictured on page 180)

- 1 (17.3-oz.) package frozen puff pastry sheets, thawed
- ¼ cup sugar
- 1 tsp. ground cinnamon
- ¼ cup melted butter

1. Preheat oven to 450°. Unfold and cut puff pastry sheets in half lengthwise, and cut each half crosswise into 1-inch-wide strips. Place strips on a lightly greased parchment paper-lined baking sheet. Bake 10 minutes or until golden brown.
2. Meanwhile, combine sugar and cinnamon. Remove pastry strips from oven, and dip in butter; roll in cinnamon-sugar mixture. Let stand on a wire rack 5 minutes or until dry.

Kentucky Hot Browns

quick prep

MAKES: 4 servings
HANDS-ON TIME: 20 min.
TOTAL TIME: 35 min., including sauce
(Pictured on page 178)

    4 thick white bread slices
    ¾ lb. sliced roasted turkey
       Mornay Sauce
    1 cup (4 oz.) shredded
       Parmesan cheese
    3 plum tomatoes, sliced
    8 bacon slices, cooked

1. Preheat broiler with oven rack 6 inches from heat. Place bread slices on a baking sheet, and broil 1 to 2 minutes on each side or until toasted.
2. Arrange bread slices in 4 lightly greased broiler-safe individual baking dishes. Top bread with turkey slices. Pour hot Mornay Sauce over turkey. Sprinkle with Parmesan cheese.
3. Broil 6 inches from heat 3 to 4 minutes or until bubbly and lightly browned; remove from oven. Top sandwiches with tomatoes and bacon. Serve immediately.

Mornay Sauce

MAKES: 4 cups
HANDS-ON TIME: 10 min.
TOTAL TIME: 10 min.

    ½ cup butter
    ⅓ cup all-purpose flour
    3½ cups milk
    ½ cup (2 oz.) shredded
       Parmesan cheese
    ¼ tsp. salt
    ¼ tsp. pepper

1. Melt butter in a 3-qt. saucepan over medium-high heat. Whisk in flour; cook, whisking constantly, 1 minute. Gradually whisk in milk. Bring to a boil, and cook, whisking constantly, 1 to 2 minutes or until thickened. Whisk in Parmesan cheese, salt, and pepper.

Kentucky Hot Browns

Kentucky Hot Brown Tart

party perfect

MAKES: 6 to 8 servings
HANDS-ON TIME: 20 min.
TOTAL TIME: 1 hr., 50 min.
(Pictured on page 179)

    1 (14.1-oz.) package
       refrigerated piecrusts
    1½ cups chopped cooked turkey
    2 cups (8 oz.) shredded white
       Cheddar cheese
    ¼ cup finely chopped
       fresh chives
    6 bacon slices, cooked
       and crumbled
    1½ cups half-and-half
    4 large eggs
    ½ tsp. salt
    ¼ tsp. freshly ground pepper
    2 plum tomatoes, cut into
       ¼-inch-thick slices
    ½ cup (2 oz.) freshly grated
       Parmesan cheese

1. Preheat oven to 425°. Unroll piecrusts; stack on a lightly greased surface. Roll stacked piecrusts into a 12-inch circle. Fit piecrust into a 10-inch deep-dish tart pan with removable bottom; press into fluted edges. Trim off excess piecrust along edges. Line piecrust with aluminum foil or parchment paper, and fill with pie weights or dried beans. Place pan on a foil-lined baking sheet. Bake 12 minutes. Remove weights and foil from piecrust, and bake 8 more minutes. Cool completely on baking sheet on a wire rack (about 15 minutes). Reduce oven temperature to 350°.
2. Layer turkey and next 3 ingredients in tart shell on baking sheet.
3. Whisk together half-and-half and next 3 ingredients; pour over turkey.
4. Bake at 350° for 30 to 40 minutes or until set.
5. Place tomatoes in a single layer on paper towels; press lightly with paper towels. Arrange over top of tart, and sprinkle with Parmesan cheese. Bake 10 to 15 minutes or until cheese is melted. Cool on baking sheet on wire rack 15 minutes.

Quick-Fix Meals

Grab your tongs, and fire up the grill. Warmer weather makes weeknight cooking a breeze.

Four Great Grilling Tips

{1}

Let meat stand 10 min. at room temp to take the chill off before grilling. Salt and pepper add simple flavor.

{2}

Use tongs instead of forks when turning meat. Piercing allows juices to escape, resulting in a dry product.

{3}

When cooking indoors, try an enameled cast-iron grill skillet, which offers good grilled flavor and easy cleanup.

{4}

Grill fruits that caramelize well (pineapple rings, peach slices, and citrus wedges) for an easy side dish.

Cilantro Flank Steak

quick prep • good for you • party perfect

MAKES: 6 servings
HANDS-ON TIME: 24 min.
TOTAL TIME: 24 min.

Easy Side: Prepare 2 (8.5-oz.) packages ready-to-serve roasted garlic whole grain rice according to package directions. Stir in 1 (8-oz.) can sweet whole kernel corn, drained, and ¼ cup chopped fresh cilantro.

- 1½ lb. flank steak
- 5 Tbsp. olive oil, divided
- 1½ tsp. Montreal steak seasoning
- 1½ cups firmly packed fresh cilantro leaves
- 2 Tbsp. fresh lime juice
- 2 garlic cloves, minced
- ½ tsp. salt

1. Brush steak with 1 Tbsp. oil; sprinkle with seasoning.
2. Heat a cast-iron grill pan over medium-high heat; cook steak in pan 7 to 9 minutes on each side or to desired degree of doneness.
3. Process cilantro, next 3 ingredients, and remaining 4 Tbsp. oil in a food processor until smooth. Cut steak diagonally across the grain into thin slices. Serve sauce with steak.

INSPIRED BY ANGELA BUCHANAN
BOULDER, COLORADO

Pineapple Grilled Pork Tenderloin

quick prep • good for you • party perfect

MAKES: 6 servings
HANDS-ON TIME: 18 min.
TOTAL TIME: 48 min.

Easy Side: Cube 2 large sweet potatoes (about 2 lb.), and toss with 2 Tbsp. olive oil. Bake at 425° for 25 minutes. Remove from oven, and toss with 1 tsp. salt and ½ tsp. pepper.

- 2 (1-lb.) pork tenderloins
- 1 tsp. salt
- ½ tsp. freshly ground pepper
- 1 (8-oz.) can pineapple slices in juice
- 2 limes
- ¼ cup orange marmalade
- 3 Tbsp. hoisin sauce
- 3 Tbsp. soy sauce
- 2 garlic cloves, pressed
- 1 tsp. Dijon mustard
- ½ tsp. ground ginger

1. Preheat grill to 350° to 400° (medium-high) heat. Remove silver skin from tenderloins, leaving a thin layer of fat. Sprinkle pork with salt and pepper.
2. Drain pineapple, reserving ⅓ cup juice. Grate zest from limes to equal 1 Tbsp.; squeeze juice from limes to equal ⅓ cup.
3. Bring reserved pineapple juice, lime juice, zest, marmalade, and next 5 ingredients to a boil in a saucepan over medium-high heat. Boil 3 to 4 minutes or until slightly thickened. Reserve half of mixture in a bowl.
4. Grill pork, covered with grill lid, 10 to 12 minutes on each side or until a meat thermometer inserted into thickest portion registers 155°, basting with remaining half of pineapple mixture. Remove from grill; cover with aluminum foil, and let stand 10 minutes.
5. Meanwhile, grill pineapple slices 1 to 2 minutes on each side. Serve grilled pineapple and reserved pineapple-marmalade mixture with grilled pork.

Lamb Burgers

Chipotle-Orange Chicken Legs
quick prep

MAKES: 4 to 6 servings
HANDS-ON TIME: 20 min.
TOTAL TIME: 50 min.

Easy Side: Combine 1 (16-oz.) package shredded coleslaw mix, 1 (8-oz.) container sour cream, 2 Tbsp. fresh lemon juice, and 1 tsp. salt. Cover and chill until ready to serve.

- 1 **cup fresh orange juice, divided**
- 5 **Tbsp. soy sauce, divided**
- 3 **Tbsp. brown sugar**
- 2 **Tbsp. olive oil**
- 6 **garlic cloves, pressed**
- 1 **Tbsp. orange zest**
- 1½ **tsp. kosher salt**
- 1 **tsp. ground chipotle chile pepper**
- 2 **lb. chicken drumsticks (about 8 drumsticks)**
- 2 **tsp. brown sugar**
- 2 **tsp. cornstarch**

1. Preheat grill to 350° to 400° (medium-high) heat. Combine ¼ cup orange juice, 3 Tbsp. soy sauce, 3 Tbsp. brown sugar, and next 5 ingredients in a shallow dish or large zip-top plastic freezer bag; add chicken. Cover or seal, and chill 10 minutes. Remove chicken from marinade, discarding marinade.
2. Grill chicken, covered with grill lid, 10 to 12 minutes on each side or until done. Remove from grill; cover with aluminum foil, and let stand 10 minutes.
3. Meanwhile, whisk together 2 tsp. brown sugar, remaining ¾ cup orange juice, and 2 Tbsp. soy sauce in a small saucepan. Whisk together cornstarch and 2 tsp. water, and whisk into orange juice mixture. Bring mixture to a boil over medium heat, and cook, whisking constantly, 1 minute or until thickened. Brush sauce over chicken.

Lamb Burgers
quick prep • good for you

MAKES: 6 servings
HANDS-ON TIME: 30 min.
TOTAL TIME: 30 min.

Easy Side: Serve this with tabbouleh salad. We tested with Near East Taboule Mix Wheat Salad.

- 1 **cup fat-free Greek yogurt**
- ½ **cup grated cucumber**
- 1 **tsp. finely chopped fresh mint**
- 3 **garlic cloves, pressed and divided**
- 1¾ **tsp. salt, divided**
- 2 **lb. ground lamb**
- ¼ **cup minced red onion**
- ¼ **cup finely chopped fresh mint**
- 1 **Tbsp. finely chopped fresh oregano**
- 1 **Tbsp. whole grain mustard**
- 4 **hamburger buns**
  Toppings: Bibb lettuce, sliced tomatoes, sliced red onion, dill pickle chips

1. Preheat grill to 350° to 400° (medium-high) heat. Stir together first 3 ingredients, 1 pressed garlic clove, and ½ tsp. salt. Cover and chill until ready to serve.
2. Gently combine lamb, next 4 ingredients, and remaining 2 pressed garlic cloves and 1¼ tsp. salt. Shape mixture into 6 (4-inch) patties.
3. Grill patties, covered with grill lid, 5 to 6 minutes on each side or to desired degree of doneness. Serve burgers on buns with yogurt sauce and desired toppings.

Tomato-Chicken Salad

quick prep • good for you • party perfect

MAKES: 4 to 6 servings
HANDS-ON TIME: 20 min.
TOTAL TIME: 30 min.

Easy Side: *Preheat grill to 400° to 450° (high) heat. Rub 6 (1-inch-thick) ciabatta or French bread baguette slices with a garlic clove; brush with extra virgin olive oil. Grill bread 1 to 2 minutes on each side or until toasted.*

- 1 **lemon**
- 2 **lb. assorted tomatoes, halved or chopped**
- 3 **cups chopped cooked chicken**
- 1 **large English cucumber, sliced**
- ½ **cup chopped fresh flat-leaf parsley**
- ¼ **cup sliced green onion**
- ¼ **cup loosely packed fresh basil leaves**
- 2 **Tbsp. olive oil**
- 1 **tsp. salt**
- ½ **tsp. freshly ground pepper**
- ½ **cup crumbled feta cheese**

1. Grate zest from lemon to equal 2 tsp.; squeeze juice from lemon to equal 2 Tbsp. Combine lemon zest, juice, tomatoes, and next 8 ingredients in a large bowl. Let stand 10 minutes. Toss with crumbled feta just before serving.

OFF THE EATEN PATH

The South's Best Road Food

In our new book, *Off the Eaten Path,* we celebrate 75 Southern dives, diners, and other out-of-the-way restaurants. Here, some favorites. (That sound? It's your stomach growling.)

When Morgan Murphy hits the road in his 1959 Eldorado, he doesn't stay hungry for long. A former travel editor for *Southern Living,* Morgan stays on the lookout for true road-food places—those unchained, one-of-a-kind restaurants where thick steaks sizzle, the tomatoes are homegrown, and macaroni and cheese is listed on the menu as a vegetable. Morgan compiled a list of locally loved eclectic eateries from Texas to Maryland, sweet-talked recipes from each, and put it all together in SOUTHERN LIVING *OFF THE EATEN PATH: FAVORITE SOUTHERN DIVES AND 150 RECIPES THAT MADE THEM FAMOUS* (Oxmoor House, 2011). Here's a peek at five of his favorite fillin' up stations.

Doe's Broiled Shrimp

quick prep • party perfect

MAKES: 2 servings
HANDS-ON TIME: 15 min.
TOTAL TIME: 15 min.

This classic Southern dish is a favorite from Doe's Eat Place located in Greenville, Mississippi.

- 24 **unpeeled, large raw shrimp (31/35 count)**
- ¼ **cup roasted garlic-flavored butter, melted**
- 2 **Tbsp. fresh lemon juice**
- ¾ **tsp. Worcestershire sauce**
- ½ **tsp. Creole seasoning**
- ½ **tsp. paprika**
- ½ **tsp. dried Italian seasoning**
  Hot cooked rice (optional)

1. Preheat broiler with oven rack 5 inches from heat. Peel shrimp; devein, if desired. Place shrimp in a lightly greased broiler pan. Combine melted garlic butter and next 5 ingredients, stirring well. Drizzle butter mixture over shrimp. Broil 4 to 5 minutes or just until shrimp turn pink. Serve over hot cooked rice, if desired.
NOTE: We tested with Land O'Lakes Roasted Garlic Butter with Oil and Tony Chachere's Original Creole Seasoning.

Five Don't-Miss Diners & Dives

{1}
DOE'S EAT PLACE:
Greenville, Mississippi;
doeseatplace.com

Dominick "Doe" and Mamie Signa opened this landmark eatery (now run by their by their sons) in 1941. They first served just Mamie's hot tamales, until friends started showing up asking Doe to grill a steak or two.

BE SURE TO TRY:
Doe's Broiled Shrimp. The steaks are to die for, but order a plate of the shrimp and you're really living.

SIDE DISH:
If you can't get to Greenville, find the Signa family-run Doe's in Paducah, Kentucky, or one of the eight franchises of the original restaurant in Arkansas, Oklahoma, Missouri, and Louisiana.

{2}
GRITS AND GROCERIES:
Belton, South Carolina;
gritsandgroceries.com

Owners Heidi and Joe Trull both worked as chefs in New Orleans (Heidi as founder and head chef of Elizabeth's Restaurant, Joe as pastry chef at Emeril Lagasse's NOLA), before returning to Heidi's home state.

BE SURE TO TRY:
Praline Bacon and Buttermilk Biscuits. The slow-roasted, thick-cut, brown sugar-and-pecan-topped bacon provides the perfect crispy companion to the biscuits' buttery crust.

SIDE DISH:
Check out the restaurant's Web site to see when Heidi is offering her once-a-month, Saturday night, whatever-she-feels-like-fixing feast. You won't want to miss it ($35/person).

{3}
LA FOGATA:
San Antonio, Texas;
lafogata.com

Owner Dwight Lieb is an old hand at creating laid-back eateries—he opened his first more than 20 years ago. Sitting in the courtyard it's easy to forget you're so close to downtown.

BE SURE TO TRY:
The Perfect Margarita. This cooling concoction is made with a special blend of premium tequila, Cointreau orange liqueur, and fresh lime juice. It's a true, fresh taste of San Antonio.

SIDE DISH:
La Fogata takes reservations, but you still may have to wait a while on weekends when things get busy. So pick up a margarita or a cold beer at the bar near the hostess stand and wait with a smile.

{4}
LYNN'S PARADISE CAFE:
Louisville, Kentucky;
lynnsparadisecafe.com

Lynn Winter fell in love with the food business while waiting tables, and opened Lynn's Paradise Cafe in 1991. Now folks come from all over to enjoy the cafe's eclectic decor and fill up on Lynn's hearty specialties.

BE SURE TO TRY:
Pan-Fried Pecan Chicken in Woodford Reserve-Mustard-Maple Cream Sauce. Made with Kentucky's own Woodford Reserve bourbon and sweetened with maple syrup, this is one fair fowl.

SIDE DISH:
After lunch, stop by Lynn's World of Swirl gift shop, filled with one-of-a-kind pottery, decorative arts, and assorted wacky knickknacks.

{5}
STINKY'S FISH CAMP:
Santa Rosa Beach, Florida;
stinkysfishcamp.com

Owner and executive chef Jim Richard worked as sous chef at Commander's Palace in New Orleans, so he knows how to handle boat-to-table fare.

BE SURE TO TRY:
Stinky's Stew. A bowl of this heaping combination of fish, mussels, shrimp, oysters, snow crab, corn, potatoes, and tomatoes in a delicious broth makes an awesome companion to a piece of Stinky's Crawfish Pie.

SIDE DISH:
Some of the best rock and blues bands in the Panhandle play original songs on a stage in the corner a few times a month. (Call for details.)

Morning Light

A healthy spin on strawberry shortcake makes an irresistible breakfast treat for Mother's Day.

English Muffin French Toast

good for you • make-ahead

MAKES: 6 servings
HANDS-ON TIME: 20 min.
TOTAL TIME: 8 hr., 20 min.

- 4 **large eggs**
- 1 **cup nonfat buttermilk**
- 2 **tsp. orange zest**
- 1 **tsp. vanilla extract**
- 6 **English muffins, split**
  Vegetable cooking spray
- 1 **cup fat-free Greek yogurt**
- 2 **Tbsp. maple syrup**
  Toppings: chopped fresh strawberries, chopped fresh nectarines

1. Whisk together first 4 ingredients in a bowl. Place English muffins in a 13- x 9-inch baking dish, overlapping edges. Pour egg mixture over muffins. Cover and chill 8 to 12 hours.
2. Remove muffins from remaining liquid, discarding liquid.
3. Cook muffins, in batches, in a large skillet coated with cooking spray over medium-high heat 2 to 3 minutes on each side or until muffins are golden. Stir together yogurt and syrup until blended; serve with muffin French toast and toppings.

PER SERVING WITH 2 TBSP. YOGURT MIXTURE (NOT INCLUDING FRUIT TOPPING): **CALORIES** 235; **FAT** 4.4G (SAT 1.2G); **PROTEIN** 13.6G; **CARB** 35G; **FIBER** 0.1G; **SODIUM** 298MG; **CALC** 201MG

"Mom-mosa"

quick prep • good for you • party perfect

1. Place 2 to 3 dashes of orange bitters in each of 6 Champagne flutes or glasses. Add 1 Tbsp. lemon liqueur to each, and stir. Top each with Champagne or sparkling wine; garnish with lemon zest twist, if desired.

TIP: If you can't find lemon liqueur, whisk together ⅓ cup fresh lemon juice and ¼ cup powdered sugar. Prepare recipe as directed, dividing lemon juice mixture among 6 Champagne flutes.

PER SERVING: CALORIES 147

5 Good-for-You Ingredients

This wholesome menu packs in powerful benefits.

{1}

MULTIGRAIN MUFFIN: Need more fiber? Swap out whole or multigrain English muffins for regular ones in this recipe. They cook the same, and some brands have up to 8 grams of fiber per serving! (That's about 30% of your daily needs.)

{2}

BUTTERMILK: This Southern staple is also a "probiotic" powerhouse. Try it in a smoothie in place of yogurt; it measures easier, is less expensive, and has the same live active cultures and richness. Plus, it tastes great.

{3}

ORANGE AND RED FRUITS: The powerful antioxidants in these colorful fruits help lower cancer risks and support the immune system. Stock up on seasonal favorites like strawberries and nectarines, and freeze some for later.

{4}

GREEK YOGURT: Also full of probiotics, Greek yogurt has many uses in the kitchen. Its rich texture makes it a perfect substitute for sour cream. Add a flavorful tang to mashed or baked potatoes. Or make a tasty dip with it.

{5}

CHAMPAGNE: Not only does it offer heart health benefits but also it's loaded with antioxidants. Please indulge yourself in this "grape juice-plus" in moderation. A glass here or there is beneficial. A whole bottle is not!

IN SEASON
Berry Picking

Summer is on its way, and so is a bounty of cobbler-sweet berries. Grab a basket, and forage the fencerows until your hands are purple!

DRESS THE PART
Blackberries' thorny canes attach more quickly than kudzu, so opt for snag-resistant long-sleeved shirts and jeans. And ditch the shades—tinted lenses disguise under-ripe fruit. (Berries don't get any sweeter after picking.)

GO ROGUE...
Look for berries in sunny areas along country roads, at the edge of clearings, and beneath power lines. Make noise when entering unfamiliar territory to avoid startling wildlife, such as bears, deer, and snakes.

...OR TRY A FARM
Timid about walking on the wild side? Click on pickyourown.org to find a berry farm near you. If the bushes are loaded, you can fill a quart bucket (just the right amount for a fresh-baked pie!) in 10 minutes.

PICK RIPE ONES
Color isn't the only indicator of ripeness. Blackberries are sweetest when their glossy sheen changes to matte. Blackberries and blueberries slip from the stem with a light touch; strawberries still need a gentle twist.

TAKE 'EM HOME
Plan to use berries within a few days of picking, or freeze right away: Spread rinsed and dried berries on a rimmed baking sheet; freeze until firm. Transfer to zip-top plastic freezer bags, and freeze up to six months.

PRIDE OF PLACE

Only in the South...

...is the biscuit so important that it merits its own three-day festival and bake-off.

Grand Prize winner Kimberly Pack

On May 26 through 28, baking aficionados tied on their aprons and gathered in Knoxville, Tennessee's Market Square for a biscuit bake-off, part of the second annual International Biscuit Festival. Categories included Basic, Sweet, Savory, and Most Creative, from which one buttery, flaky finalist took the Grand Prize. The 2010 winner was Knoxville native Kimberly Pack, who wowed the judges with The Fat Elvis, her luscious peanut butter-banana-bacon ode to the King. To her we say, "Thank ya, thank ya very much" for sharing her winning recipe.

THE WINNING BISCUIT!

The Fat Elvis

quick prep

MAKES: 10 biscuits
HANDS-ON TIME: 15 min.
TOTAL TIME: 30 min., including spread

- 5 to 6 ripe bananas
- 2 cups all-purpose flour
- 1½ cups powdered sugar
- 2 tsp. baking powder
- ½ tsp. baking soda
- ½ tsp. salt
- ½ cup honey-roasted peanuts, chopped
- ⅓ cup frozen butter
- ½ cup buttermilk
  Peanut Butter Spread
- 10 cooked bacon slices, halved

1. Preheat oven to 450°. Cut 4 bananas into 2-inch pieces; halve each piece lengthwise. Mash remaining bananas to equal ½ cup. Sift together flour and next 4 ingredients in a large bowl; add mashed bananas and peanuts. Grate butter over flour mixture, using large holes of a box grater. Cut butter into flour mixture with a pastry blender or fork until crumbly. Add buttermilk, stirring just until mixture is slightly moistened.
2. Turn dough out onto a heavily floured surface; shape into a ball. Pat into a ½-inch-thick circle.
3. Cut with a floured, 3-inch round cutter, and place biscuits 1 inch apart on a lightly greased baking sheet.
4. Bake at 450° for 10 to 12 minutes or until golden. Split warm biscuits; spread bottom halves of biscuits with Peanut Butter Spread. Top each with 2 bacon pieces and 2 banana slices. Cover with biscuit tops.

Join the Festival!

WHERE: Market Square in downtown Knoxville, Tennessee, between Wall and Union avenues

WHY: Eat your fill along "BiscuitBoulevard," with a floury array of samples for sale. On Saturday, start with a biscuit breakfast at 9 a.m. or a brunch hosted by luxury resort Blackberry Farm at 10:30 a.m. The bake-off heats up at 1 p.m.

DON'T MISS: Watching locals compete for the title of Miss or Mr. Biscuit.

Peanut Butter Spread

quick prep

MAKES: ½ cup
HANDS-ON TIME: 5 min.
TOTAL TIME: 5 min.

1. Stir together ⅓ cup creamy peanut butter, ¼ cup powdered sugar, 1 Tbsp. fat-free milk, and ¼ tsp. vanilla extract in a microwave-safe bowl. Microwave at HIGH at 30-second intervals until softened; stir until smooth.
NOTE: We tested with Jif Creamy Peanut Butter.   **RECIPE FROM KIMBERLY PACK**
KNOXVILLE, TENNESSEE

June

The *Ultimate* Backyard Pizza Party

Bubbling farmers' market-inspired pizzas, grown-up frozen pops (dunked in Prosecco), and a brink-of-summer garden in full bloom create an alfresco party where everyone feels at home.

Summer Gathering

SERVES 8

Grilled Tomato Bruschetta

Simple Grilled Asparagus

Dan's Pizza Dough

Fresh Tomato Sauce

Meet the Hostess

Danielle Rollins is an avid gardener and entertainer in Atlanta. She is also the mother of Emerson (14), Carlyle (12), and Preston (8). "My favorite thing about entertaining outdoors is seeing how beautiful everyone looks in candlelight," says Danielle, as she sets up a surprise birthday party for her husband, Glen.

Danielle's Tips for Easy Outdoor Entertaining

{1}

LET THE FOOD SET THE TONE. To play up the pizza parlor theme, Danielle covered one long table with burlap, topped with checkered cloths.

{2}

EMBRACE ORGANIC ELEMENTS. "When it comes to outdoor serving pieces, I prefer wicker and wood," she says. Danielle also topped the tables with pots of lush, fragrant (and affordable) Italian herbs and trellises of heirloom tomatoes.

{3}

WORK WITH WHAT YOU HAVE. Terra-cotta pots (with small wooden stakes for names) create impromptu place cards. "I like to elevate the simple things I have on hand."

{4}

DON'T OVERTHINK IT. "I'm not one to get hung up on things having to match. Entertaining should be about family and friends, not perfection."

Grilled Tomato Bruschetta

quick prep • good for you • party perfect

MAKES: 8 servings
HANDS-ON TIME: 17 min.
TOTAL TIME: 17 min.

- 16 (½-inch thick) French bread baguette slices
- 3 Tbsp. extra virgin olive oil
- 4 ripe tomatoes, seeded and chopped
- ½ small sweet onion, thinly sliced
- ½ cup torn fresh basil
- 1 garlic clove, minced
- ½ tsp. kosher salt
- ¼ tsp. freshly ground pepper

1. Preheat grill to 350° to 400° (medium-high) heat. Brush both sides of bread with oil. Grill 1 to 1½ minutes per side or until toasted.

2. Toss together tomatoes and next 5 ingredients; serve over bread slices.

Simple Grilled Asparagus

quick prep • good for you • party perfect

MAKES: 8 servings
HANDS-ON TIME: 14 min.
TOTAL TIME: 14 min.

- Vegetable cooking spray
- 1½ lb. fresh asparagus
- 1 Tbsp. extra virgin olive oil
- ½ tsp. kosher salt, divided
- ¼ tsp. freshly ground pepper
- ½ lemon
- ¼ cup shaved Parmesan cheese

1. Coat cold cooking grate of grill with cooking spray, and place on grill. Preheat grill to 350° to 400° (medium-high) heat. Snap off and discard tough ends of asparagus.

2. Place asparagus in a shallow dish; add oil and ¼ tsp. salt, and toss well to coat. Grill asparagus 2 minutes on each side or until crisp-tender.

3. Add pepper and remaining salt. Squeeze juice from lemon over asparagus; sprinkle with cheese.

Party at a Glance

Chef-catered pizza and checkered tablecloths help bring Danielle's vision of pizza parlor chic to life. "Nothing delights me more than seeing people having a good time," says the seasoned hostess. "It makes the effort so worthwhile."

THE STARTER
Offer an antipasto platter: Grilled Tomato Bruschetta and Simple Grilled Asparagus (see recipes at left).

THE MAIN
Serve made-to-order gourmet pizzas. (See "Party-Worthy Pizza in 5 Steps" on page 121.)

THE TABLE
Let place cards double as favors for guests.

THE DESSERT
Fancy up frozen fruit pops with a splash of Prosecco.

Meet the Chef

Dan Latham is a James Beard winner who previously owned L & M's Kitchen and Salumeria in Oxford, Mississippi. Now as a partner with Fresh Hospitality, he operates a mobile wood-fired oven under the name Moto Bene. Danielle and Dan met at Atlanta's Peachtree Road Farmers' Market, and it was love at first whiff. "You have to get this guy for Dad's birthday," her daughter said. Danielle booked him on the spot. You can track Dan's crew on Twitter (twitter.com/motobene).

Dan's Pizza Dough

good for you • make-ahead • party perfect

MAKES: 4 dough portions
HANDS-ON TIME: 30 min.
TOTAL TIME: 3 hr.

Italian 00 flour is a very fine soft flour that offers a balanced, crisp but delicate texture. Find it at large supermarkets or kingarthurflour.com.

- **4 cups Italian 00 soft wheat or all-purpose flour**
- **1½ tsp. active dry yeast**
- **1½ tsp. kosher salt**
- **1½ cups ice-cold water**
- **2 Tbsp. extra virgin olive oil**

1. Place first 3 ingredients in bowl of a heavy-duty electric stand mixer; beat at low speed (using a dough hook attachment) until blended. Gradually add water and oil in a slow, steady stream, and beat at low speed 3 minutes. Beat at high speed 5 minutes.

2. Cover dough with plastic wrap; let rise in a warm place (85°), free from drafts, 1½ to 2 hours or until almost doubled in bulk and dough is springy when lightly touched. Punch dough down, and shape into a large ball; cut dough into 4 equal pieces.

3. Roll each piece of dough into a ball. Stretch top of dough around outside of ball, and pinch the edges together, forming a smooth ball.

4. Place dough balls on a lightly greased baking sheet, and dust with flour. Cover with a damp towel. Let stand in a cool place 1 hour.

Fresh Tomato Sauce

quick prep • good for you • party perfect

1. Stir together 1 (28-oz.) can whole peeled tomatoes with basil, 1½ Tbsp. extra virgin olive oil, and 1 tsp. kosher salt. Process with a hand-held blender until smooth. Makes: 3 cups

Party-Worthy Pizza in 5 Steps

{1}

Start with Dan's Pizza Dough (see recipe at left). Place a pizza stone or baking sheet in oven. Preheat oven to 500° for 30 minutes. Stretch dough into a 10- to 12-inch circle on a separate lightly floured baking sheet. (No need to perfect the round shape.)

NOTE: To make ahead, prepare dough as directed; after dough stands 1 hour, place each dough ball in a separate zip-top plastic freezer bag, and chill up to 24 hours or freeze up to 1 month.

{2}

Spread ½ cup Fresh Tomato Sauce (see recipe at left) on each dough circle.

{3}

Top with 4 oz. of shredded, sliced, or crumbled cheese. Some of Dan's favorites include Decimal Place Farm goat cheese, Atlanta Fresh Artisan Creamery's Fresh Mozzarella, and Sweet Grass Dairy's Thomasville tomme (a mild and creamy French-style cheese).

{4}

Choose the toppings. Try these straight-from-the-farmers' market suggestions. Get creative by mixing and matching your favorites here.

- Sliced roasted turnips
- Assorted olives
- Fresh basil pesto
- Thinly sliced radishes
- Assorted greens
- Fresh herbs
- Fresh peas and pea shoots
- Fresh garlic
- Sliced fennel
- Spring onions
- Cooked and crumbled local pork sausage or ground beef

{5}

Season pizza with desired amount of salt and pepper. Slide pizza from baking sheet onto hot pizza stone or baking sheet in oven. Bake at 500° for 9 to 11 minutes or until edges are golden.

Try These Combos!

Chef Dan Latham offers his personal favorites inspired by the farmers' market.

THE CLASSIC
Fresh Tomato Sauce
+ fresh mozzarella
+ torn basil

KALE & BEEF
Crumbled beef
+ sliced green onions
+ torn kale

GO GREEN
Pesto
+ peas
+ goat cheese
+ pea shoots

SAUSAGE LOVER'S
Crumbled sausage
+ sliced fennel
+ sliced garlic
+ green onion

GOLDEN ONION
Caramelized onions
+ goat cheese
+ olives
+ arugula

MARKET VEGGIES
Turnips
+ tomme cheese
+ shaved garlic
+ green onions
+ olives
+ oregano

The Easy, Breezy Summer Party

We love the no-fuss vibe of a wine and cheese party, but something about a big block of Cheddar feels too hearty for 90-degree days. Consider this our just-as-relaxed summer alternative: an appetizer-driven menu that pairs well with crisp summer whites (linens and wine). Cheers!

Outdoor Party

SERVES 12

Green Goddess Dip

Asiago-Pecan Shortbread

Bacon-Parmesan Tassies

Shrimp Salad-Stuffed Endive

Kentucky Benedictine
Tea Sandwiches

Summer Fruit Salad

Chicken-and-Tortellini Salad

Sweet Pea Crostini

Gorgonzola-Grilled
Pear Crostini

Green Goddess Dip

make-ahead • party perfect

MAKES: about 1⅔ cups
HANDS-ON TIME: 15 min.
TOTAL TIME: 2 hr., 15 min.

Serve with: blanched green or white asparagus spears, sliced cauliflower florets, halved baby zucchini, blanched sugar snap peas, blanched haricots verts (tiny green beans).

- ¾ **cup mayonnaise**
- ¾ **cup sour cream**
- ½ **cup loosely packed fresh flat-leaf parsley leaves**
- 1 **Tbsp. chopped fresh tarragon**
- 2 **tsp. white wine vinegar**
- 1 **tsp. anchovy paste**
- 1 **tsp. lemon zest**
- 1 **Tbsp. fresh lemon juice**
- 2 **garlic cloves, minced**
- ⅓ **cup chopped fresh chives**
  Salt and freshly ground pepper to taste

1. Process first 9 ingredients in a food processor until smooth, stopping to scrape down sides if needed. Stir in chives; season with salt and pepper to taste. Cover and chill 2 to 24 hours. Serve with assorted vegetables.

PAIR WITH: *Bründlmayer, Grüner Veltliner 2009 or Chilean Sauvignon Blanc*

Asiago-Pecan Shortbread

make-ahead • party perfect

MAKES: about 8 dozen
HANDS-ON TIME: 30 min.
TOTAL TIME: 9 hr., 40 min.

- 2 **cups (8 oz.) shredded Asiago cheese**
- 1 **cup butter, softened**
- ¼ **tsp. ground red pepper**
- 2 **cups all-purpose flour**
- 1 **cup finely chopped pecans**
  Parchment paper
  Kosher salt

1. Beat first 3 ingredients at medium speed with a heavy-duty electric stand mixer (using the paddle attachment) until blended. Gradually add flour, beating at low speed just until blended. Add pecans, beating at low speed just until blended. Shape dough into 4 (6-inch-long) logs. Wrap each log in plastic wrap; chill 8 hours.

2. Preheat oven to 350°. Cut logs into ⅓-inch-thick rounds, and place on parchment paper-lined baking sheets.

3. Bake at 350° for 10 to 12 minutes or until lightly browned. Remove from oven, and sprinkle tops of hot shortbread lightly with kosher salt. Transfer to wire racks, and let cool completely (about 30 minutes).

PAIR WITH: *Champagne or Gruet Demi Sec Sparkling Wine*

Test Kitchen Tip

The unbaked dough can be frozen up to 2 months when wrapped securely with wax paper or plastic wrap and sealed in a zip-top plastic freezer bag. Thaw overnight in refrigerator before baking.

Set a Pretty Table

Here, tips from *Southern Living* stylist Buffy Hargett:

{1}

START SIMPLE: Echo the natural beauty of a garden setting with a neutral color scheme of cool leafy greens and crisp white linens. (Our menu was even inspired by the color palette!)

{2}

MIX AND MATCH: Skip the formal centerpiece and fill glass decanters and carafes with fresh-cut ferns and flowers such as Queen Anne's lace or oakleaf hydrangeas.

{3}

ADD A TOUCH OF GLAM: Tuck unexpected touches of silver in with serving pieces—julep cups are a standout on the vegetable tray.

Bacon-Parmesan Tassies

make-ahead • party perfect

MAKES: 2 dozen
HANDS-ON TIME: 30 min.
TOTAL TIME: 2 hr.
(Pictured on page 13)

- ½ cup butter, softened
- ½ (8-oz.) package cream cheese, softened
- 1¼ cups all-purpose flour
- ½ cup half-and-half
- 1 large egg
- ⅛ tsp. salt
- 4 bacon slices, cooked and crumbled
- ½ cup grated Parmesan cheese
- ¼ cup chopped fresh chives

1. Beat butter and cream cheese at medium speed with an electric mixer until creamy. Gradually add flour to butter mixture, beating at low speed until blended. Shape mixture into 24 balls, and place on a baking sheet; cover and chill 1 hour.

2. Place dough balls into cups of a lightly greased 24-cup miniature muffin pan; press dough, forming a shell.

3. Preheat oven to 375°. Whisk together half-and-half and next 2 ingredients. Sprinkle bacon into pastry shells; top each with 1 tsp. cheese. Drizzle half-and-half mixture over cheese. Sprinkle chives over half-and-half mixture.

4. Bake at 375° for 25 to 30 minutes or until puffed and golden brown. Remove from pan to a wire rack, and cool 5 minutes. Serve warm.

PAIR WITH: *Sauternes, or Muscat de Beaumes-de-Venise, or German Riesling*

Shrimp Salad-Stuffed Endive

Shrimp Salad-Stuffed Endive

MAKES: 24 appetizer servings
HANDS-ON TIME: 20 min.
TOTAL TIME: 20 min.

- ¼ cup mayonnaise
- ¼ cup cream cheese, softened
- 2 Tbsp. finely chopped green onions
- 1 Tbsp. finely chopped fresh parsley
- 1 tsp. lemon zest
- 1 Tbsp. fresh lemon juice
- 1 garlic clove, pressed
- ¼ tsp. salt
- ¼ tsp. ground red pepper
- 2½ cups finely chopped, peeled and deveined, cooked shrimp (about 1 lb. of any size)
- ½ cup finely diced celery
- 24 Belgian endive leaves (about 2 heads)

1. Stir together first 9 ingredients in a large bowl; stir in shrimp and celery. Spoon shrimp mixture onto bottom half of endive leaves.

PAIR WITH: *Sancerre Sauvignon Blanc or Vermentino*

Kentucky Benedictine Tea Sandwiches

MAKES: 8 dozen
HANDS-ON TIME: 15 min.
TOTAL TIME: 15 min.
(Pictured on page 12)

- 2 (8-oz.) packages cream cheese, softened
- 1 cup peeled, seeded, and finely chopped cucumber
- ½ cup minced green onions
- ¼ cup chopped fresh dill
- 2 Tbsp. mayonnaise
- ½ tsp. salt
- ½ tsp. freshly ground pepper
- 48 white bread slices

1. Stir together first 7 ingredients. Spread mixture on 1 side of 24 bread slices; top with remaining 24 bread slices. Trim crusts from sandwiches; cut each sandwich into 4 triangles with a serrated knife.

PAIR WITH: *Baumard Savennières or Oregon Pinot Gris*

Summer Fruit Salad

quick prep • good for you • party perfect

MAKES: 8 to 10 appetizer servings
HANDS-ON TIME: 20 min.
TOTAL TIME: 20 min.

- ½ cup bottled poppy seed dressing
- 2 tsp. grated fresh ginger
- 2 avocados, thinly sliced
- 4 cups loosely packed arugula
- 2 cups halved seedless green grapes
- 1 mango, julienned
- 1 cup diced fresh strawberries
- ¼ cup thinly sliced green onions
- ¼ cup chopped fresh cilantro

1. Whisk together dressing and grated ginger in a large bowl. Cut avocado slices in half crosswise; gently toss with dressing mixture. Add arugula and remaining ingredients; gently toss to coat. Serve immediately.

PAIR WITH: *Tramin Gewürztraminer, Italy, or Vouvray*

Refresher Course

A FEW TIPS WHEN IT COMES TO THE WINE:

- Play up the setting by chilling bottles in a garden urn filled with ice.
- Remember that I (750-milliliter) bottle of wine holds about 5 (5-oz.) glasses.
- Estimate 2 glasses of wine per guest for the first hour of a party plus I glass per guest for each additional hour.
- For a wine tasting, choose 5 to 6 different wines and plan on I bottle of each for every 6 to 8 people.

Chicken-and-Tortellini Salad

quick prep • party perfect

MAKES: I2 to I5 appetizer servings
HANDS-ON TIME: 20 min.
TOTAL TIME: 30 min.
(Pictured on page I2)

2 (9-oz.) packages refrigerated cheese-filled tortellini
½ cup olive oil
½ cup grated Parmesan cheese
¼ cup fresh lemon juice
2 garlic cloves
I tsp. Worcestershire sauce
2 cups chopped cooked chicken
I cup frozen sweet peas, thawed
½ cup thinly sliced green onions
½ cup chopped fresh flat-leaf parsley
   Salt and pepper to taste

1. Prepare tortellini according to package directions.
2. Process olive oil and next 4 ingredients in a blender until smooth. Toss olive oil mixture with tortellini, chicken, and next 3 ingredients. Add salt and pepper to taste.

PAIR WITH: *La Torrazza Erbaluce di Caluso, Italy, or Chablis, or an unoaked Chardonnay*

Sweet Pea Crostini

good for you • make-ahead • party perfect

MAKES: 20 appetizer servings
HANDS-ON TIME: I5 min.
TOTAL TIME: 2 hr., I5 min.

2 (9-oz.) packages frozen sweet peas, thawed
3 garlic cloves, chopped
3 Tbsp. extra virgin olive oil
2 Tbsp. fresh lemon juice
   Salt and freshly ground pepper to taste
40 French bread baguette slices, toasted
½ cup (2 oz.) crumbled blue cheese or goat cheese

1. Place peas and garlic in a food processor; with processor running, pour oil through food chute in a slow, steady stream, processing until smooth. Stir in lemon juice; season with salt and pepper to taste. Cover and chill 2 hours.
2. Spoon pea mixture onto toasted baguette slices; sprinkle with cheese.

PAIR WITH: *Vincent Delaporte, Sancerre 2009, or Vinho Verde, or a New Zealand Sauvignon Blanc*

Gorgonzola-Grilled Pear Crostini

quick prep • party perfect

MAKES: 36 crostini
HANDS-ON TIME: 22 min.
TOTAL TIME: 22 min.
(Pictured on page I3)

3 firm ripe Bartlett pears, cut into ¼-inch-thick wedges
½ (8-oz.) package cream cheese, softened
4 oz. Gorgonzola cheese, crumbled
¼ cup butter, softened
2 Tbsp. dry sherry
36 French bread baguette slices, toasted
½ cup finely chopped, lightly salted roasted pecans
2 Tbsp. finely chopped fresh rosemary
¼ cup honey

1. Preheat grill to 350° to 400° (medium-high) heat. Grill pear wedges, covered with grill lid, I to 2 minutes on each side or until golden.
2. Stir together cream cheese and next 3 ingredients; spread about ½ Tbsp. on each baguette slice. Top with grilled pears; sprinkle with pecans and rosemary, and drizzle with honey.

PAIR WITH: *Château de Malle, Sauternes 2004 or Chenin Blanc*

Toasted Baguette Slices:

1. Preheat oven to 375°. Cut I (8.5-oz.) French bread baguette into ⅓-inch-thick slices. Lightly brush slices with olive oil or melted butter; arrange in a single layer on baking sheets. Bake 8 to I0 minutes or until golden brown, turning once. Makes: about 52 slices. Hands-on time: I0 min. Total time: I8 min.

Raising the Bar

Maraschino cherries? So 1982. The farm-to-table phenomenon has inspired a similar grass-to-glass trend, and event planners are garnishing drinks with sprigs from our own backyards. Here, an herb tower, dreamed up by the women behind Ritzy Bee Events in D.C.

Kelly Seizert, Maria Cooke

COCKTAIL RECIPES
quick prep • party perfect

Gin & Tonic
Pour 2 Tbsp. gin and 6 Tbsp. chilled tonic water over ice in a cocktail glass. Serve with a wedge of lime.

Margarita
Rub rim of a chilled margarita glass with a lime wedge, and dip rim in margarita salt. Fill a cocktail shaker half full with ice. Add ⅓ cup powdered sugar, ⅓ cup fresh lime juice, 3 Tbsp. orange liqueur, and 2 Tbsp. tequila. Cover with lid; shake until thoroughly chilled. Strain into prepared glass.

Bellini
Fill a Champagne flute with ¼ cup chilled peach nectar and ½ cup chilled sparkling wine.

Arnold Palmer
Serve equal parts iced tea and lemonade over ice. Add a splash of vodka, if desired.

Sazerac
Stir together ¼ cup rye whiskey, 1 tsp. simple syrup, ¼ tsp. Peychaud's Bitters, and 1 cup ice in a cocktail shaker until chilled. Coat inside of a chilled 3½-oz. glass with ¼ tsp. anise liqueur; pour out excess. Rub a lemon zest strip over rim, and place in glass. Strain whiskey mixture into prepared glass.

Build Your Own Herb Tour

Ours is from **Leaf & Petal** ($39), 205/877-3030.

Our Five Favorite Ways to Add an Herbaceous Kick to Summer Sips

{1}
GIN & TONIC

Drop In: Rosemary. This herb brings out gin's woodsy notes. Opt for lemon verbena to enhance the spirit's citrus side.

{2}
MARGARITA

Drop In: Cilantro. A staple of Mexican cuisine, this herb complements the often peppery flavor of tequila. Or give basil a try instead.

{3}
BELLINI

Drop In: Basil. This cupboard essential pairs well with fruits, making it a natural complement to the peach puree in this celebratory brunch beverage.

{4}
ARNOLD PALMER

Drop In: Lavender. Its soft, floral flavor contrasts with the sharpness of the lemonade found in this classic iced tea "mocktail."

{5}
SAZERAC

Drop In: Tarragon. The dainty, aromatic plant and Herbsaint—a key ingredient in this Southern concoction—share sweet licorice undertones.

"How can I bring beach flavor to the dinner table?"

RACHEL REHWINKEL AUSTIN, TEXAS

Step away from the store-bought fish sticks, and try one of these speedy seafood suppers, all sure to please guests to the gills.

Introducing the New and Improved Quick-Fix Suppers—Online!

What's for supper? Get quick and easy solutions from *Southern Plate* author and blogger Christy Jordan in our NEW how-to video series.

🖱 *southernliving.com/quickfix*

HERE'S WHAT YOU'LL FIND:

EVERY DAY
• Daily time-saving tips

EVERY WEEK
• Meal ideas with Christy Jordan

ANYTIME!
• Hundreds of recipes, ideas, and tips for family suppers
• Quick fixes for chicken, beef, pasta, and more

{1}
FRY UP SOME CRABMEAT

Crunchy Crab Cakes
quick prep • party perfect

MAKES: 8 servings
HANDS-ON TIME: 23 min.
TOTAL TIME: 25 min.

Try this side: *Toss together 1 (5-oz.) package arugula; 1 pt. grape tomatoes, halved; 2 Tbsp. fresh lemon juice; 2 Tbsp. olive oil; and ½ tsp. salt. Serve immediately.*

- 1 (16-oz.) package fresh lump crabmeat, drained
- 4 large lemons, divided
- 1 (4-oz.) jar diced pimiento, well drained
- 2 green onions, chopped
- 1 large egg, lightly beaten
- 2 Tbsp. mayonnaise
- 1 tsp. Old Bay seasoning
- 2 tsp. Dijon mustard
- 1 cup panko (Japanese breadcrumbs), divided
- ¼ cup canola oil

1. Pick crabmeat, removing any bits of shell.
2. Grate zest from 2 lemons to equal 2 tsp.; cut lemons in half, and squeeze juice into a measuring cup to equal ¼ cup. Stir together lemon zest and juice, pimiento, and next 5 ingredients until well blended. Gently fold in crabmeat and ½ cup breadcrumbs.
3. Shape mixture into 8 patties. Dredge patties in remaining ½ cup breadcrumbs.
4. Cook half of patties, in 2 Tbsp. hot oil in a large nonstick skillet over medium heat, 2 minutes on each side or until golden brown; drain on a wire rack. Repeat procedure with remaining oil and patties.
5. Cut remaining 2 lemons into wedges. Serve crab cakes with lemon wedges.

{2}
TURN ON THE OVEN

Barbecue Shrimp
quick prep • party perfect

MAKES: 6 servings
HANDS-ON TIME: 10 min.
TOTAL TIME: 35 min.

In New Orleans, this dish is a staple on restaurant menus.

Try this side: *While the shrimp are baking to perfection, you can add some frozen Texas toast to the oven. Bake 6 slices according to package directions, and use the bread to sop up the rich buttery sauce.*

1½ **lb. unpeeled jumbo raw shrimp (21/25 count)**
1 **large lemon, cut into wedges**
1 **(0.7-oz.) envelope Italian dressing mix**
½ **cup melted butter**
½ **cup loosely packed fresh flat-leaf parsley**

1. Preheat oven to 425°. Place shrimp and lemon in a 13- x 9-inch baking dish. Stir together dressing mix and butter. Pour butter mixture over shrimp, stirring to coat.
2. Bake, covered, at 425° for 25 to 30 minutes or just until shrimp turn pink, stirring once.
3. Remove shrimp mixture from oven, and sprinkle with parsley.

Test Kitchen Notebook

VANESSA'S SEAFOOD TIPS:
Test Kitchen Specialist Vanessa Rocchio, who created these easy, delicious meals, shares some pointers.

• Avoid fish that smells fishy. Fresh fish should not have an odor.
• Choose shrimp that are firm in texture, and avoid any that have dark spots.
• If purchasing shrimp with shells, make sure the shells are tightly intact.
• Fresh seafood is best stored packed in ice.

{3}
WRAP IT IN A TORTILLA

Poblano Fish Tacos
quick prep • good for you • party perfect

MAKES: 6 servings
HANDS-ON TIME: 22 min.
TOTAL TIME: 40 min.

Try this Twist: *Top with crumbled queso fresco (fresh Mexican cheese) for a tasty variation.*

1 **large poblano pepper**
½ **English cucumber, coarsely chopped**
1 **cup grape tomatoes, quartered**
2 **Tbsp. chopped red onion**
1 **garlic clove, minced**
½ **tsp. salt**
3 **Tbsp. fresh lime juice, divided**
4 **Tbsp. olive oil, divided**
1 **Tbsp. mango-lime seafood seasoning**
1½ **lb. grouper or other firm white fish fillets**
12 **(6-inch) fajita-size corn tortillas, warmed**
   Lime wedges

1. Preheat grill to 350° to 400° (medium-high) heat. Grill pepper, covered with grill lid, 3 to 4 minutes or until pepper looks blistered, turning once. Place pepper in a large zip-top plastic freezer bag; seal and let stand 10 minutes to loosen skins. Peel pepper; remove and discard seeds. Coarsely chop.
2. Combine pepper, cucumber, next 4 ingredients, 2 Tbsp. lime juice, and 2 Tbsp. olive oil in a bowl.
3. Whisk together seafood seasoning and remaining 1 Tbsp. lime juice, and 2 Tbsp. olive oil in a large shallow dish or zip-top plastic freezer bag; add fish, turning to coat. Cover or seal, and chill 5 minutes, turning once. Remove fish from marinade, discarding marinade.
4. Grill fish, covered with grill lid, 3 to 4 minutes on each side or just until fish begins to flake when poked with the tip of a sharp knife and is opaque in center. Cool 5 minutes. Flake fish into bite-size pieces.
5. Serve fish and salsa in warm tortillas with lime wedges.
NOTE: We tested with Weber Mango-Lime Seafood Seasoning.

{4}
FIRE UP THE GRILL

Grilled Grouper with Watermelon Salsa
quick prep • good for you • party perfect

MAKES: 4 servings
HANDS-ON TIME: 21 min.
TOTAL TIME: 21 min.

Try this Twist: For a sandwich option, serve fish and salsa in pita pockets.

- 4 (4-oz.) grouper fillets
- 1 tsp. freshly ground pepper
- 1 tsp. salt, divided
- 3 Tbsp. olive oil, divided
- 2 cups chopped seedless watermelon
- ¼ cup chopped pitted kalamata olives
- ½ English cucumber, chopped
- 1 small jalapeño pepper, seeded and minced
- 2 Tbsp. minced red onion
- 2 Tbsp. white balsamic vinegar

1. Preheat grill to 350° to 400° (medium-high) heat. Sprinkle grouper with pepper and ½ tsp. salt. Drizzle with 2 Tbsp. olive oil.
2. Grill fish, covered with grill lid, 3 to 4 minutes on each side or just until fish begins to flake when poked with the tip of a sharp knife and is opaque in center.
3. Combine chopped watermelon, next 5 ingredients, and remaining ½ tsp. salt and 1 Tbsp. olive oil. Serve with grilled fish.

{5}
BOWL 'EM OVER

Spicy Shrimp Noodle Bowl
quick prep • good for you

MAKES: 4 servings
HANDS-ON TIME: 15 min.
TOTAL TIME: 20 min.

Try this Twist: Add additional fresh cilantro and a squeeze of lime juice for extra flavor.

- 1 (8.2-oz.) package teriyaki-flavored Asian-style noodles
- 2 (14.5-oz.) cans chicken broth
- 1 lb. peeled and deveined, medium-size raw shrimp (31/40 count)
- ¼ cup spicy Szechuan sauce
- 2 cups shredded napa cabbage
- 1 cup fresh snow peas, trimmed and cut into 1-inch pieces
- ¾ cup shredded carrots
- ¼ cup loosely packed fresh cilantro leaves
- 3 green onions, thinly sliced

1. Cook noodles according to package directions; drain.
2. Stir together flavor packet from noodles and chicken broth in a 3-qt. saucepan. Bring to a boil; add shrimp, and cook 3 minutes. Stir in Szechuan sauce and next 3 ingredients. Cook 2 minutes. Stir in noodles, cilantro, and green onions.
NOTE: We tested with Annie Chun's All Natural Asian Cuisine Teriyaki Meal Starter and House of Tsang Szechuan Spicy Stir Fry Sauce.

QUICK & EASY

Perfect Pesto

Break out the food processor (chop, chop!) and enjoy these fresh summer flavors.

Cilantro Pesto
quick prep • good for you • make-ahead

MAKES: 2 cups
HANDS-ON TIME: 15 min.
TOTAL TIME: 25 min.

We suggest: Spread it over grilled corn, or toss with chopped grilled veggies for extra flavor.

- ½ cup chopped pecans
- 1 tsp. cumin seeds
- 2 cups loosely packed fresh cilantro leaves
- ½ cup grated Parmesan cheese
- ⅓ cup olive oil
- ¼ cup cold water
- 2 garlic cloves
- 1 Tbsp. lemon juice
- ½ tsp. salt

1. Preheat oven to 350°. Bake pecans in a single layer in a shallow pan 5 to 6 minutes or until toasted and fragrant, stirring halfway through. Cool 10 minutes.
2. Meanwhile, place a small skillet over medium-high heat until hot; add cumin seeds, and cook, stirring constantly, 1 to 2 minutes or until toasted. Cool 10 minutes.
3. Process pecans, cumin seeds, and next 7 ingredients in a food processor until smooth, stopping to scrape down sides as needed.

Olive Pesto

quick prep • good for you • make-ahead

MAKES: about 2 cups
HANDS-ON TIME: 10 min.
TOTAL TIME: 10 min.

We suggest: Spoon it over goat cheese or warm brie for an easy party appetizer.

- 1 (7-oz.) jar pitted kalamata olives, drained
- 1 (7-oz.) jar pimiento-stuffed Spanish olives, drained
- ¼ cup grated Parmesan cheese
- 3 Tbsp. olive oil
- 2 Tbsp. balsamic vinegar
- 3 to 4 garlic cloves
- 1 tsp. pepper
- 1 tsp. smoked paprika

1. Process all ingredients in a food processor until smooth, stopping to scrape down sides as needed.

Sun-Dried Tomato Pesto

quick prep • good for you • make-ahead

MAKES: 1½ cups
HANDS-ON TIME: 10 min.
TOTAL TIME: 10 min.

We suggest: Use this zesty mixture as a tasty substitute for pizza sauce.

- 2 (3-oz.) packages sun-dried tomato halves
- ½ cup grated Parmesan cheese
- ½ cup loosely packed fresh flat-leaf parsley
- ½ cup olive oil
- ¼ cup pine nuts
- 3 garlic cloves
- 3 Tbsp. cold water
- 1 Tbsp. lemon juice

1. Process all ingredients in a food processor until smooth, stopping to scrape down sides as needed.

Herb Pesto

quick prep • good for you • make-ahead

MAKES: 1 cup
HANDS-ON TIME: 10 min.
TOTAL TIME: 10 min.

We suggest: Stir a spoonful or two into lightly beaten eggs to make a seasoned omelet or scrambled eggs.

- ⅔ cup olive oil
- ½ cup loosely packed fresh basil leaves
- ½ cup loosely packed fresh flat-leaf parsley leaves
- ½ cup grated Parmesan cheese
- ¼ cup pine nuts
- ¼ cup cold water
- 1 to 2 garlic cloves
- 2 Tbsp. fresh oregano leaves
- 1 Tbsp. fresh rosemary leaves
- 1 Tbsp. lemon juice
- ½ tsp. salt
- ½ tsp. pepper

1. Process all ingredients in a food processor until smooth, stopping to scrape down sides as needed.

Mint Pesto

quick prep • good for you • make-ahead

MAKES: 1 cup
HANDS-ON TIME: 10 min.
TOTAL TIME: 10 min.

We suggest: Add a pop of color and garden-fresh flavor to any main-dish meat. It's great over steak, chicken, lamb, pork, and fish. Simply top the meat after grilling, or just serve the pesto on the side.

- 2 cups loosely packed fresh mint leaves
- ½ cup grated Parmesan cheese
- ⅓ cup olive oil
- ¼ cup pine nuts
- ¼ cup cold water
- 2 garlic cloves
- 1 Tbsp. lemon juice

1. Process all ingredients in a food processor until smooth, stopping to scrape down sides as needed.

Basil Pesto

quick prep • good for you • make-ahead

MAKES: 2 cups
HANDS-ON TIME: 10 min.
TOTAL TIME: 10 min.

We suggest: Stir some summertime goodness into hot cooked pasta, rice, or grits for a tasty side dish to your meal. You can also use it as a dipping sauce for French fries.

- 2 cups loosely packed fresh basil leaves
- 1 cup grated Parmesan cheese
- ⅔ cup olive oil
- ¼ cup pine nuts
- 2 garlic cloves
- 3 Tbsp. cold water
- 1 Tbsp. lemon juice
- ½ tsp. salt

1. Process all ingredients in a food processor until smooth, stopping to scrape down sides as needed.

8 Ways with Green Tomatoes

Crisp, golden-crusted, and hot-off-the-skillet. Could it get any better? Best make that call after you try these favorites.

Fried Green Tomatoes

Fried Green Tomatoes

quick prep

MAKES: 6 servings
HANDS-ON TIME: 30 min.
TOTAL TIME: 30 min.

- 1 large egg, lightly beaten
- ½ cup buttermilk
- ½ cup self-rising cornmeal mix
- ½ tsp. salt
- ½ tsp. pepper
- ½ cup all-purpose flour
- 3 medium-size, firm green tomatoes, cut into ⅓-inch-thick slices (about 1 ¼ lb.)
  Vegetable oil

1. Whisk together egg and buttermilk. Combine cornmeal mix, salt, pepper, and ¼ cup flour in a shallow dish. Dredge tomato slices in remaining ¼ cup flour; dip in egg mixture, and dredge in cornmeal mixture.
2. Pour oil to a depth of ½ inch in a large cast-iron skillet; heat to 375° over medium-high heat. Drop tomatoes, in batches, into hot oil, and cook 2 minutes on each side or until golden. Drain on paper towels. Sprinkle hot tomatoes with salt to taste.

Fried Green Tomato Po'boys

(Pictured on page 182)

1. Cut French bread baguettes into 6-inch lengths. Split each lengthwise, cutting to but not through the other side; spread with Rémoulade Sauce (recipe below). Layer with shredded lettuce, Fried Green Tomatoes, cooked bacon, and avocado slices.

Green Tomato Salsa

good for you • make-ahead • party perfect

The tangy-sweet taste of this quick, colorful salsa pairs perfectly with grilled chicken, pork, or crisp-fried catfish.

1. Stir together 2 large green tomatoes, diced; 1 large fresh peach, diced; 3 green onions, sliced; ¼ cup olive oil; 1 Tbsp. minced fresh cilantro; 2 Tbsp. white wine vinegar; 1 Tbsp. honey; ½ tsp. salt; and ¼ tsp. ground red pepper. Cover and chill 1 hour before serving. Makes: about 4 cups

Fried Green Tomatoes with Shrimp Rémoulade

quick prep • party perfect

Ice-cold shrimp top sizzling-hot fried green tomatoes in this easy at-home spin on the classic recipe created by New Orleans' Upperline Restaurant.

1. Place 2 to 3 Fried Green Tomatoes on individual serving plates, and top each with 1½ Tbsp. Rémoulade Sauce and 3 medium-size, peeled, cooked shrimp. Garnish with fresh pea shoots or arugula, if desired.

Rémoulade Sauce

1. Stir together 1 cup mayonnaise, ¼ cup sliced green onions, 2 Tbsp. Creole mustard, 1 Tbsp. chopped fresh parsley, 1 Tbsp. minced fresh garlic, and 1 tsp. horseradish; cover and chill until ready to serve. Makes: 1¼ cups

Grilled Green Tomatoes Caprese

Fried Green Tomato-and-Bacon Biscuits

quick prep • party perfect

1. Split hot buttermilk or sweet potato biscuits; spread with pear preserves. Fill with Fried Green Tomatoes and cooked bacon.

Sweet Green Tomato Cornmeal Muffins

quick prep • party perfect

MAKES: about 2 dozen
HANDS-ON TIME: 30 min.
TOTAL TIME: 45 min.

Serve with fresh basil butter: Stir together ½ cup softened butter and 2 Tbsp. finely chopped fresh basil.

- 2 cups seeded, diced green tomatoes (about ¾ lb.)
- ½ cup sugar, divided
- ½ cup butter, melted and divided
- 2 cups self-rising white cornmeal mix
- 2 tsp. lemon zest
- 5 large eggs
- 1 (16-oz.) container sour cream
  Vegetable cooking spray

1. Preheat oven to 450°. Sauté tomatoes and 2 Tbsp. sugar in 2 Tbsp. melted butter in a large skillet over medium-high heat 10 to 12 minutes or until tomatoes begin to caramelize and turn light brown.
2. Stir together cornmeal mix, lemon zest, and remaining 6 Tbsp. sugar in a large bowl; make a well in center of mixture. Whisk together eggs, sour cream, and remaining 6 Tbsp. butter; add to cornmeal mixture, stirring just until dry ingredients are moistened. Fold in tomatoes.
3. Generously coat small (¼ cup) brioche molds or muffin pans with vegetable cooking spray; spoon batter into molds, filling two-thirds full. Bake at 450° for 15 to 17 minutes or until a wooden pick inserted in center comes out clean.

Grilled Green Tomatoes Caprese

MAKES: 8 to 10 servings
HANDS-ON TIME: 21 min.
TOTAL TIME: 1 hr., 21 min.

Ciao, y'all! Green tomatoes go from the frying pan into the fire with a Southern-Italian twist. Using white (rather than brown) balsamic vinegar in the marinade brightens the color of the grilled tomatoes, but the salad's flavor is extraordinary with either. (Pictured on page 183)

- ½ cup olive oil
- ¼ cup white balsamic vinegar
- 2 garlic cloves, minced
- 1 Tbsp. brown sugar
- ⅛ tsp. salt
- 4 medium-size green tomatoes, cut into ¼-inch-thick slices (about 2 lb.)
- 1 (16-oz.) package sliced fresh mozzarella cheese
  Kosher salt and freshly ground pepper to taste
- ⅓ cup thinly sliced fresh basil

1. Combine first 5 ingredients in a large zip-top plastic freezer bag; add tomatoes, seal, and shake gently to coat. Chill 1 hour.
2. Preheat grill to 350° to 400° (medium-high) heat. Remove tomatoes from marinade, reserving marinade. Grill tomatoes, covered with grill lid, 3 to 4 minutes on each side or until tender and grill marks appear.
3. Arrange alternating slices of warm grilled tomatoes and mozzarella cheese on a large, shallow platter. Drizzle with reserved marinade; season with salt and pepper to taste. Sprinkle with basil.

Green Tomato Garden Party Salad

good for you • make-ahead • party perfect

1. Toss together gourmet mixed salad greens, sliced nectarines, sliced fresh strawberries, diced green tomato (trust us, it adds a delicious, citrus-like crunch!), crumbled feta cheese, chopped fresh basil, glazed pecans, and poppy seed dressing.

Field Peas

Southern peas and butter beans, popped fresh from the pod and simmered in pork-laced potlikker, signal the start of summer. And there are dozens of types—each with a subtle difference in taste and texture. We like to combine different kinds of beans and peas and use a light hand with the seasoning (a whisper of garlic, a sprinkling of salt and pepper, and bacon drippings) to bring out their delicate flavors. Be sure to snap up these favorites!

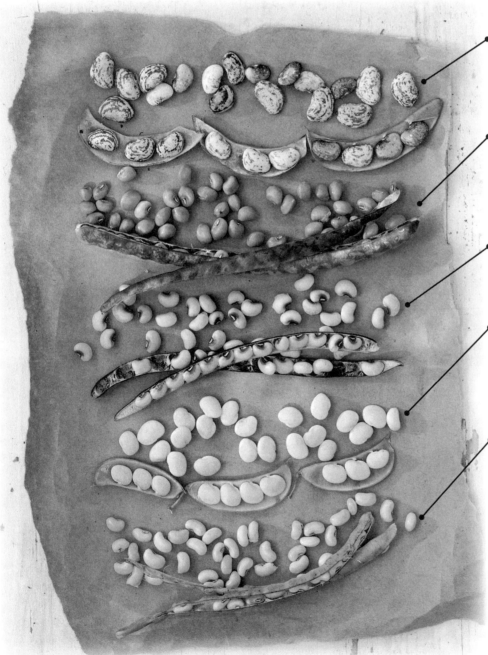

SPECKLED BUTTER BEANS have a rich, creamy texture and earthy, nut-like flavor. When cooked, they lose their variegated color and turn a pinkish brown.

CROWDERS nestle so closely inside the pod that the ends of the peas begin to square off. Brown crowders are favored by many for their hearty flavor and rich, dark potlikker.

PINK-EYED PEAS have a colorful purple hull and a lighter, less earthy taste than their black-eyed pea cousins.

BUTTER BEANS, the colloquial name for baby green limas, are highly prized in the South. When perfectly cooked, the inside of the bean becomes creamy and takes on a rich, buttery texture.

LADY CREAM PEAS are smaller and sweeter in flavor than other field peas. Considered the doyenne of cream selections, they remain pale green or white when cooked and yield a bright, clear potlikker.

Hearty, Not Heavy

This family reunion favorite is rich with creamy goodness but easy on the fat and calories.

Five Reasons to Indulge!

Get a colorful mix of benefits from these nutritious ingredients.

{1}

RED POTATOES:

Leave the skins on! The red color indicates the presence of important nutrients that promote heart health and lower the risk of cancer.

{2}

CARROTS:

High in vitamin A, a key nutrient for healthy eyes and skin, carrots are also a good source of vitamin K and potassium. And they add a flavorful crunch.

{3}

CELERY AND RADISHES:

Need to add more fiber to your diet? Celery and radishes are fiber-rich foods that keep you satisfied longer between meals.

{4}

FRESH GREEN BEANS:

They are packed with vitamin C, which helps the body fight infections. Steaming them keeps the nutrients, color, and flavor at their peak.

{5}

OLIVE OIL MAYO:

This new and improved pantry staple has almost half the fat and calories of regular mayonnaise and makes a delicious substitute in salads.

Veggie Potato Salad

good for you • make-ahead • party perfect

MAKES: 7½ cups
HANDS-ON TIME: 25 min.
TOTAL TIME: 2 hr., 30 min.

- 2½ lb. baby red potatoes, cut into 1-inch cubes
- 2 Tbsp. apple cider vinegar
- 1 Tbsp. olive oil
- ½ cup whole buttermilk
- ¼ cup reduced-fat sour cream
- ¼ cup reduced-fat mayonnaise with olive oil
- 1 Tbsp. Dijon mustard
- 2 carrots, grated
- ½ cup chopped celery
- ½ cup sliced radishes
- ½ cup steamed, cut fresh green beans
- ¼ cup finely chopped fresh parsley
- 1 Tbsp. lemon zest
- 1 garlic clove, minced
  Sea salt and freshly ground pepper to taste

1. Bring potatoes and salted water to cover to a boil in a large saucepan; reduce heat, and simmer 7 to 10 minutes or until tender. Drain. Place potatoes in a large bowl; sprinkle with vinegar and oil, and toss gently. Cool completely (about 1 hour).
2. Whisk together buttermilk and next 3 ingredients. Stir in carrots and next 6 ingredients; season with salt and pepper to taste. Spoon buttermilk mixture over potato mixture; toss gently to coat. Cover and chill 1 to 24 hours before serving.
NOTE: We tested with Kraft Reduced-Fat Mayonnaise with Olive Oil.

PER ¾ CUP: **CALORIES** 176; **FAT** 6G (SAT 1G, MONO 3G, POLY 1G); **PROTEIN** 4G; **CARB** 28G; **FIBER** 4G; **CHOL** 9MG; **IRON** 1MG; **SODIUM** 158MG; **CALC** 44MG

Ice Cream

Our Test Kitchen couldn't get enough of this ridiculously low-calorie concoction, which is why we proceeded to try out every flavor imaginable.

Lightened Vanilla Bean Ice Cream

good for you • make-ahead • party perfect

MAKES: about I qt.
HANDS-ON TIME: 20 min.
TOTAL TIME: 9 hr., 20 min., not including freezing

- ½ cup granular sweetener for ice cream*
- 2 Tbsp. cornstarch
- ⅛ tsp. salt
- 2 cups 2% reduced-fat milk
- I cup half-and-half
- I egg yolk
- 1½ tsp. vanilla bean paste or extract

1. Whisk together first 3 ingredients in a large heavy saucepan. Gradually whisk in milk and half-and-half. Cook over medium heat, stirring constantly, 8 to 10 minutes or until mixture thickens slightly. Remove from heat.

2. Whisk egg yolk until slightly thickened. Gradually whisk about I cup hot cream mixture into yolk. Add yolk mixture to remaining cream mixture, whisking constantly. Whisk in vanilla.

3. Pour mixture through a fine wire-mesh strainer into a bowl, discarding solids. Cool I hour, stirring occasionally. Place plastic wrap directly on cream mixture; chill 8 to 24 hours.

4. Pour mixture into freezer container of a 1½-qt. electric ice-cream maker, and freeze according to manufacturer's instructions. Let stand at room temperature 5 to 10 minutes before serving.

*Granulated sugar may be substituted.

NOTE: We tested with Whey Low 100% All Natural Granular Sweetener for Ice Cream.

PER ½ CUP: CALORIES 92; FAT 5G (SAT 3G, MONO 2G, POLY OG); PROTEIN 3G; CARB 18G; FIBER OG; CHOL 42MG; IRON OMG; SODIUM 76MG; CALC 106MG

Test Kitchen Notebook

ICE CREAM IDEAS:

- Before you begin, get acquainted with your ice-cream freezer. Read the manufacturer's instructions carefully.
- Freeze ice cream 8 hours or longer after churning for the best texture. Allow to stand at room temperature 5 to 10 minutes for best serving.

Try These Twists!

CHERRY-BOURBON ICE CREAM: Stir in ½ cup drained and coarsely chopped canned, pitted cherries in heavy syrup and 3 Tbsp. bourbon halfway through freezing.

PER ½ CUP: CALORIES 110; FAT 5G (SAT 3G, MONO 2G, POLY OG); PROTEIN 3G; CARB 20G; FIBER OG; CHOL 42MG; IRON OMG; SODIUM 76MG; CALC 108MG

COFFEE-CHOCOLATE ICE CREAM: Substitute 2 Tbsp. instant espresso for 1½ tsp. vanilla bean paste. Stir in ¼ cup shaved semisweet chocolate baking bar halfway through freezing.

PER ½ CUP: CALORIES 103; FAT 6G (SAT 4G, MONO 2G, POLY OG); PROTEIN 4G; CARB 21G; FIBER OG; CHOL 42MG; IRON OMG; SODIUM 76MG; CALC 107MG

KEY LIME PIE ICE CREAM: Omit vanilla bean paste. Stir in I tsp. Key lime zest, ⅓ cup Key lime juice, and ½ cup coarsely crushed graham crackers halfway through freezing.

PER ½ CUP: CALORIES 104; FAT 6G (SAT 3G, MONO 2G, POLY OG); PROTEIN 4G; CARB 21G; FIBER OG; CHOL 42MG; IRON OMG; SODIUM 102MG; CALC 106MG

BANANA PUDDING ICE CREAM: Preheat oven to 400°. Peel 3 medium-size ripe bananas, and cut into ½-inch slices. Place in a 2-qt. baking dish, and sprinkle with 2 Tbsp. light brown sugar and I Tbsp. butter, cut up. Bake 20 minutes, stirring halfway through. Let cool 30 minutes. Gently mash into chunks. Prepare ice cream as directed, stirring in bananas and ½ cup coarsely crushed vanilla wafers halfway through freezing.

PER ½ CUP: CALORIES 172; FAT 7G (SAT 4G, MONO 2G, POLY OG); PROTEIN 4G; CARB 36G; FIBER 1G; CHOL 47MG; IRON OMG; SODIUM 100MG; CALC 112MG

July

Peaches: A Love Story

An unabashedly affectionate, gloriously sticky, dripping with nostalgia, so gushing we're blushing, ode to the peach.

As summer rites of passage go, there is perhaps nothing more quintessentially Southern than pulling over at a roadside stand, handing over a few crinkled bills for a basket of farm-fresh peaches, and proceeding to take one big, satisfying bite of summer as juice trickles down your chin. In fact, we'll go out on a limb and declare the peach the unofficial fruit of the region. Sure, these juicy bombshells are embraced elsewhere, but where else do you hear people use phrases like "She's a real peach"? Where else do you pass water towers shaped like giant peaches (we're lookin' at you Gaffney, South Carolina, and Clanton, Alabama)? Where else can you find a reigning Peach Queen? Here, a no-holds-barred celebration of the beloved Southern staple.

AT FIRST BLUSH

Peaches originally hail from China, but they've been grown in the South since 1857, when the first trees were planted by Samuel H. Rumph at his orchard near Marshallville, Georgia. The 'Chinese Cling' variety bore an exceptional yellow freestone peach and was eventually renamed the 'Elberta' peach after Rumph's wife, Clara Elberta Moore. The 'Elberta' peach was so firm that it made its trial journey to New York City uniced in a railroad car. (It arrived in good condition and demanded a "fancy" price of $15 per bushel.) Suddenly, the Southern peach industry was born.

The business has changed dramatically since then, and yet many things remain the same. Peaches are still primarily handpicked straight into bushel baskets, and many of today's growers have roots back to those early orchards. For example, the Pearsons, owners of Pearson Farm in Fort Valley, Georgia, have been growing peaches since the 1880s. Today Al Pearson, 61, farms with son Lawton, 35, a fifth-generation farmer. "Farming peaches is something I've done since I was old enough to work, which at that time was 6 years old," Al says. "I have 55 years of experience contributing to my family's operation. We own a lot of the same land that we did back then. It's hard to think about not doing it."

And it's equally tough to imagine a summer without the beloved fruit. On the following pages, you'll find some of the people, the places, and the recipes that help bring the peach to the table—that is, if you can resist eating it on the car ride home.

Meet the Growers

Al and Lawton Pearson of Pearson Farm in Fort Valley, Georgia

KELLY ALEXANDER
My Fuzzy Memory

The assumption about women from Georgia is not just that we enjoy our celebrated native stone fruit—it's that we embody it. "Georgia peaches" means us girls born in the thirteenth of the original 13 New World colonies, us girls who've rafted the Chattahoochee River, witnessed the Pink Floyd laser light show projected onto Stone Mountain, drunk Coca-Cola out of bottles with boiled peanuts on the side. That's a Georgia peach for you.

I was born in Georgia, and so was my mother (my grandmother was born in the Bronx, but that's another story), and being a girl from Georgia is a big part of who I am: It's why I'm soft on the outside but tough on the inside, rather like that peach for which the state is so well-known. The only problem was that for a long time I carried a secret inside my summer tan (which was never protected well enough by sunscreen from that Georgia heat—another trait of the Georgia woman, I'm afraid, is sun addiction): For most of my early life, I didn't much care about peaches. It wasn't that I didn't appreciate their essence—sweet, floral, fragrant, summer in a fruit and all the rest. It was that they were so ubiquitous. There was fresh peach ice cream at every Fourth of July barbecue; there were peaches at every roadside stand when we drove to Florida; my grandfather ate a bowl of peaches and sour cream every day for breakfast.

You see, I may love being from Georgia, but I didn't always love being in Georgia. Growing up, I longed for the big city, the bustle and traffic and different sorts of people and different sorts of music. And when I got there, I immediately noticed that New York girls all ate cut-up fruit that they bought on the corner on the refrigerated shelves of bodegas. A fresh peach was so rural, so rustic—a plastic container of perfectly diced pineapple was much more sophisticated. The peaches were in your muffin or in the chutney at the Indian restaurant, never in the palm of your hand.

And a funny thing happened to me, that kind of thing that happens when you're far away from home and kind of blue, and you go to a party and the song "Melissa" by the Allman Brothers Band is playing, and you remember that the Allman Brothers lived in Macon, Georgia, and that the album is called "Eat a Peach." And then you want a peach more than you've ever wanted anything. You want to push your lips against that fuzzy skin, let your jaws go to work feasting on the flesh as the juice pours down your throat, let your teeth scrape the red pit to get every last bite. You realize that a peach is Georgia, and that Georgia is you, and that the things that seem so common, so humble, are the things that make up your life. That's a Georgia peach.

KELLY ALEXANDER IS AN AWARD-WINNING FOOD WRITER BASED IN CHAPEL HILL, NC.

THE PEOPLE

Well before the first fragrant, pink buds bloom in spring and begin their journey toward fruit, passionate growers are hard at work making our peach dreams come true. "I was born with a love of growing anything, and I've been growing peaches since 1954," says John Neighbors of Neighbors Farm and Nursery in Alexander City, Alabama. John specializes in white-flesh 'Peento,' or 'Saturn,' peaches. "I started growing 'Saturn' peaches about 10 years ago, and there's an unbelievable demand for them," he says. "To know that you're growing something that people are that fond of is a great feeling."

Ben Smith, the 78-year-old owner of The Peach Tree Orchards in York, South Carolina, was born on a peach farm. "I got out of the Army in 1958 and have been back here ever since," he says. "We have a roadside market, and I like meeting and talking with people. Eighty-five percent of our sales are repeat customers, folks that come down for a peck of peaches a week."

Because peaches are such a demanding crop, orchards are often a family business of multigenerational farmers, and an all-hands-on-deck affair during harvest. Kathy Cooper, of Cooper Farms in Fairfield, Texas, met her husband, Tim, when they were both working at a Texas peach orchard in 1978. They got married in 1983 and have been farming together ever since. "Our family is totally occupied with harvest from the time school lets out until it starts up again," says Kathy. "Our kids don't get summer off; we all work on the farm. The upside is it's a great place to raise a family."

At many orchards the "family" extends to the migrant workers who arrive each year (with seasonal federal work permits) to usher in the harvest. Al Pearson and family say they have a real connection to their employees and have even visited them in Mexico. "It's a joy to have experienced labor coming back again," he says.

THE PROCESS

The business of growing such a fragile crop is not for the faint of heart. Even before the buds break into blooms, peaches have their demands. The fruit requires a certain number of "cold hours" (below 45 degrees) during the winter to produce a flower. Without sufficient cold days, the season's production will be low.

Once the blooms arrive in spring there's the matter of a late frost—the heart-wrenching possibility that can kill blossoms and any chance for fruit that season. "Because we grow peaches in a temperate area, there's a month or so in the spring after the bloom with the chance of a killing frost," Al says. "There have been three times in my lifetime that we've lost all of them."

Peach Cred

A look at recent peach production numbers in four key states

ALABAMA
Bragging rights:
4,500-5,000 acres and production valued at $10-$15 million

GEORGIA
Bragging rights:
10,800 acres and production valued at $31.5 million

SOUTH CAROLINA
Bragging rights:
15,500 acres and production valued at $55 million

TEXAS
Bragging rights:
5,400 acres and production valued at $27.3 million

Finally, when farmers are past the risk of freezing temperatures, they shift their worries to new culprits—hail and high winds—which can destroy a crop in a matter of minutes. If peaches survive these early months, farmers breathe a (cautiously optimistic) sigh of relief and the fruit is able to mature. As the heat intensifies throughout the summer, so does the sweetness of the peach. To ensure a safe journey to market, peaches are picked when they are ripe but still firm. "I ride peaches on the seat of my truck for a few days," says Al. "Then I perform a taste test and eat them, and when the peach is ready, I know the fruit from the harvest on will be a good piece of fruit."

When the peaches are ripe, most everything else stops. "The harvest time for peaches is very narrow," says Arlie Powell, who grows heirloom roses and an abundance of fruit with son Jason at Petals from the Past Nursery and Farm in Jemison, Alabama. "Unlike oranges, which can hang ripe on a tree for months, a peach must get picked on time or it will fall to the ground or rot."

"We actually don't eat many peaches, or much of anything, during harvest," says Andy Kemp, owner of A & P Farms in Gallant, Alabama. "We're at it daylight to dark. We have supper at 9 p.m. and then we're back at it in the morning."

In the packing houses of some farms, peaches are showered with cold water in a hydro cooler to take the "field heat" out of them. (This slows down ripening.) Coolers hold the peaches between 34 to 38 degrees for 24 hours, which continues to slow down ripening. Then they're graded, sized, inspected, and packed into shipping containers. When peaches finally arrive at market, they have a definite shelf life—between two to four weeks for optimum flavor.

THE REWARD

For most of us, the moment that a peach is selected at the market is where the story begins. To make the most of this year's bounty, we've gathered recipes from orchards, peach contest winners, and some of the most inspired chefs in the South. A perfectly ripe peach, however, needs no adornment. "My favorite way to eat a peach," says Kathy Cooper of Cooper Farms in Fairfield, Texas, "is right over the sink because it's so juicy."

 READER RECIPE

Caramelized Peach Soup

good for you • make-ahead • party perfect

MAKES: 3½ cups
HANDS-ON TIME: 15 min.
TOTAL TIME: 5 hr., 10 min.

- 3 large fresh, ripe peaches, peeled and halved
- 2 Tbsp. light brown sugar
- 1½ Tbsp. honey
  Parchment paper
- 1½ cups fresh orange juice
- ½ tsp. ground cinnamon
- ¼ tsp. salt
- 1 tsp. fresh lemon juice
- ¼ cup crème fraîche
- ½ tsp. vanilla bean paste

1. Preheat oven to 350°. Toss together first 3 ingredients. Place peaches, cut sides down, on a parchment paper-lined jelly-roll pan. Bake 25 minutes or until juices begin to caramelize, turning after 15 minutes.

2. Transfer peaches and juices to a food processor; cool completely (about 30 minutes). Add orange juice, cinnamon, and salt; process until smooth. Stir in lemon juice. Cover and chill 4 hours.

3. Combine crème fraîche and vanilla bean paste. Ladle soup into bowls; dollop with crème fraîche mixture.

EXECUTIVE CHEF JAMES R. PATTERSON, III
MUSGROVE MILL GOLF CLUB
CLINTON, SOUTH CAROLINA

Meet the Growers

Family-run Cooper Farms in Fairfield, Texas, includes Tim, Ben, Elizabeth, and Kathy. Dogs Sweetie and Precious also enjoy picking peaches but, warns Kathy, "they do not like to share!"

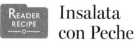 Insalata con Peche

quick prep • good for you • party perfect

MAKES: 4 servings
HANDS-ON TIME: 15 min.
TOTAL TIME: 15 min.

- 1 (6-oz.) package spring greens mix
- 2 (8-oz.) packages fresh mozzarella cheese, sliced
- 2 large fresh, ripe peaches, peeled and thinly sliced
- 4 oz. thinly sliced prosciutto
- ½ Tbsp. fresh thyme leaves
- ½ cup extra virgin olive oil
- ¼ cup fresh lemon juice
  Salt and freshly ground pepper

1. Place greens on 4 serving plates. Top with mozzarella, peaches, and prosciutto; sprinkle with thyme. Whisk oil into lemon juice in a slow stream until blended; whisk in salt and pepper to taste. Drizzle over salads.

CHEF TRACY LAMOTHE, RIVA'S TRATTORIA
GREENSBORO, NORTH CAROLINA

Summer Grilled Peach Salad

MAKES: 4 servings
HANDS-ON TIME: 20 min.
TOTAL TIME: 30 min.
(Pictured on page 185)

- 1 cup pecans
- 4 large fresh, ripe peaches, halved
- 3 Tbsp. extra virgin olive oil, divided
  Salt and freshly ground pepper
- 1 (4-oz.) wedge Gorgonzola cheese, broken into 8 pieces
- 2 cups arugula
- ¼ cup honey*
- 2 Tbsp. finely chopped chives

1. Preheat oven to 350°. Bake pecans in a single layer in a shallow pan 10 to 12 minutes or until toasted and fragrant, stirring halfway through.

2. Preheat grill to 350° to 400° (medium-high) heat. Gently toss peach halves in 1 Tbsp. olive oil; sprinkle with salt and pepper to taste. Grill peaches, cut sides down, covered with grill lid, 2 to 3 minutes or until golden. Turn peaches, and place 1 cheese piece in center of each peach; grill, covered with grill lid, 2 to 3 minutes or until cheese begins to melt.

3. Toss arugula with remaining 2 Tbsp. olive oil and salt and pepper to taste. Arrange arugula on a serving platter; sprinkle with toasted pecans, and top with grilled peach halves. Drizzle peaches with honey, and sprinkle with chives.

*Aged balsamic vinegar may be substituted.

EXECUTIVE CHEF HALLER MAGEE
SATTERFIELD'S RESTAURANT
BIRMINGHAM, ALABAMA

"To me, there's nothing better than a hot summer day with peaches and ice cream, sweet and smooth with a bit of tart—like a lot of Southern women, come to think of it! Sweet with a little sassiness."

COURTNEY WALKER
MISS GEORGIA PEACH, 2011

Grilled Pork Porterhouse with Peach Agrodolce

good for you • party perfect

MAKES: 4 servings
HANDS-ON TIME: 15 min.
TOTAL TIME: 1 hr., 25 min., including agrodolce

Agrodolce (agro: sour; dolce: sweet), a traditional Italian sweet-and-sour sauce made with vinegar and sugar (or sweet ingredients such as fresh peaches and raisins), adds fresh summer flavor to the granddaddy of all pork chops. Thick-cut pork porterhouse includes a juicy portion of the tenderloin on one side and a large cut of the loin on the other. (Pictured on page 184)

- 4 (1½-inch-thick) pork porterhouse chops (about 2½ lb.)
- 1 Tbsp. olive oil
- ¾ tsp. kosher salt
- ½ tsp. freshly ground pepper
  Peach Agrodolce

1. Let pork stand at room temperature 30 minutes. Light one side of grill, heating to 350° to 400° (medium-high) heat; leave other side unlit. Brush pork with olive oil, and sprinkle with salt and pepper.
2. Grill pork over lit side of grill, covered with grill lid, 4 minutes on each side; transfer pork to unlit side, and grill, covered with grill lid, 10 minutes on each side or until a meat thermometer registers 150°. Let stand 5 minutes. Arrange pork on a serving platter, and top with Peach Agrodolce.

Peach Agrodolce

quick prep • good for you • party perfect

MAKES: 1½ cups
HANDS-ON TIME: 15 min.
TOTAL TIME: 15 min.

- 2 Tbsp. raisins
- 2 Tbsp. tawny port wine
- 1 Tbsp. chopped fresh parsley
- 1 Tbsp. balsamic vinegar
- 1 Tbsp. olive oil
- 2 large fresh, ripe peaches, peeled and diced into 1-inch pieces
  Salt and freshly ground pepper

1. Cook raisins, port, and 2 Tbsp. water in a small saucepan over medium heat, stirring occasionally, 5 minutes. Remove from heat; whisk in parsley, vinegar, and oil. Stir in peaches and salt and pepper to taste.

CHEF HUGH ACHESON, FIVE & TEN
ATHENS, GEORGIA

Peach Enchiladas

party perfect

MAKES: 16 servings
HANDS-ON TIME: 20 min.
TOTAL TIME: 1 hr., 5 min.

This quick and easy recipe won first place at the 2004 South Carolina State Cook-Off in Columbia.

- 2 (8-oz.) cans refrigerated crescent rolls
- 2 lb. fresh, firm, ripe peaches, peeled and quartered (4 large)
- 1½ cups sugar
- 1 cup butter, melted
- 1 tsp. ground cinnamon
- 1 (12-oz.) can citrus-flavored soft drink

1. Preheat oven to 350°. Unroll crescent rolls; separate into triangles. Place 1 peach quarter on wide end of each triangle; roll up triangles around peaches, starting at wide end. Place, point sides down, in a lightly greased 13- x 9-inch pan.
2. Stir together sugar, butter, and cinnamon, and drizzle over rolls; pour soft drink over rolls.
3. Bake at 350° for 45 minutes or until golden brown and bubbly.
NOTE: For citrus-flavored soft drink, we tested with Mountain Dew.

HETTIE WILKERSON
MCBEE, SOUTH CAROLINA

JULIANNA BAGGOTT
My Fuzzy Memory

I never knew my grandfather. He died when my mother was only 23. Raised in North Carolina, a pool hall hustler and eventual bar owner, he'd lived a hard life and was a difficult man. As a result, my mother doesn't have a stockpile of sweet memories of him—just a handful, but she holds them dear.

One of her fondest memories was that he had an ice-cream maker. It was a hand-turn thing. It involved rock salt on the outer circumference of an inner cylinder where you put the good stuff. He was a firm believer in the natural goodness and sweetness of peaches, so the only ingredients my mother remembers were very ripe peaches and heavy cream. Knowing my grandmother, she probably put some sugar in when he wasn't looking.

My mother still remembers the taste. And I remember the story. So when we were in France a few years ago doing research for one of my books—living there for six weeks with five kids on a shoestring budget—we bought heavy cream and fresh, roadside peaches, and my oldest daughter and my niece made peach ice cream, the hard way, and I told them the sweet story of my grandfather. Food works that way. It helps us hand down our most treasured memories of sweetness.

JULIANNA BAGGOTT IS A NOVELIST AND ASSOCIATE PROFESSOR AT FLORIDA STATE.

Peach Brûlée with
Honey Crème Anglaise

Peach Brûlée with Honey Crème Anglaise

party perfect

MAKES: 4 servings
HANDS-ON TIME: 10 min.
TOTAL TIME: 30 min., including crème anglaise

1. Preheat broiler with oven rack 5 inches from heat. Arrange 4 large fresh, ripe peaches, halved, cut sides up in a broiler pan. Brush cut sides with 1½ Tbsp. melted butter, and sprinkle each with ½ Tbsp. sugar. Broil 10 to 11 minutes or until sugar is caramelized. Serve immediately with Honey Crème Anglaise.

Honey Crème Anglaise

quick prep • party perfect

MAKES: about 2⅓ cups
HANDS-ON TIME: 10 min.
TOTAL TIME: 10 min.

1. Whisk together 2 cups half-and-half, ¼ cup sugar, 1 Tbsp. cornstarch, 2 Tbsp. honey, ⅛ tsp. salt, and 3 egg yolks in a heavy 3-qt. saucepan. Bring to a boil over medium heat, whisking constantly. Boil, whisking constantly, 1 minute. Remove from heat. Serve warm or cold.

Spiced Peach-Carrot Bread

quick prep • make-ahead • party perfect

MAKES: 1 loaf
HANDS-ON TIME: 15 min.
TOTAL TIME: 2 hr., 50 min.

This recipe won first place in the side-dish category in South Carolina's 2009 Annual Peach-Off contest.

- ¾ cup chopped pecans
- 2½ cups all-purpose flour
- 1 cup sugar
- 1 tsp. ground cinnamon
- ¾ tsp. baking soda
- ½ tsp. baking powder
- ½ tsp. salt
- ¼ tsp. ground nutmeg
- 1½ cups peeled and chopped fresh, ripe peaches
- ¾ cup freshly grated carrots
- ⅔ cup vegetable oil
- ½ cup milk
- 2 large eggs, lightly beaten

1. Preheat oven to 350°. Bake pecans in a single layer in a shallow pan 8 to 10 minutes or until toasted and fragrant, stirring halfway through. Cool 15 minutes.
2. Stir together flour and next 6 ingredients in a large bowl; add peaches, next 4 ingredients, and toasted pecans, stirring just until dry ingredients are moistened. Spoon batter into a lightly greased 9- x 5-inch loaf pan.
3. Bake at 350° for 1 hour and 5 minutes to 1 hour and 10 minutes or until a long wooden pick inserted in center comes out clean. Cool in pan on a wire rack 5 minutes. Remove from pan to wire rack, and cool completely (about 1 hour).

ELLEN J. COOK
MCCORMICK, SOUTH CAROLINA

Peach Melba Shortcakes

quick prep • party perfect

MAKES: 8 servings
HANDS-ON TIME: 20 min.
TOTAL TIME: 45 min., including whipped cream

- 2½ cups all-purpose flour
- 1 Tbsp. plus 1 tsp. baking powder
- 1 tsp. salt
- 7 Tbsp. sugar, divided
- ¼ cup cold butter, cut into small cubes
- 1 large egg
- ½ tsp. vanilla extract
- ¾ cup half-and-half
- Parchment paper
- 1 Tbsp. half-and-half
- 6 large fresh, ripe peaches, peeled and sliced
- 1 Tbsp. fresh lemon juice
- 1½ tsp. vanilla bean paste
- 2 pt. fresh raspberries
- ¼ cup honey
- Sorghum Whipped Cream

1. Preheat oven to 425°. Combine first 3 ingredients and 1 Tbsp. sugar in a large bowl; cut in butter with a pastry blender or 2 forks until crumbly. Whisk together egg, vanilla, and ¾ cup half-and-half; add to dry ingredients, stirring just until dry ingredients are moistened and dough comes together.

2. Turn dough out onto a lightly floured surface; roll or pat dough into a 7-inch circle (about 1 inch thick). Cut into 8 wedges; place on a parchment paper-lined baking sheet. Brush tops with 1 Tbsp. half-and-half; sprinkle with 2 Tbsp. sugar.

3. Bake at 425° for 15 to 20 minutes or until golden.

4. Meanwhile, stir together peaches, next 2 ingredients, and remaining 4 Tbsp. sugar in a bowl.

5. Cook raspberries and honey in a medium saucepan over medium-low heat 3 minutes, stirring with a fork to lightly crush berries. Spoon raspberry mixture onto 8 individual serving plates.

6. Split warm shortcakes in half horizontally. Place shortcake bottoms on top of raspberry mixture, and top with peaches and shortcake tops. Serve immediately with Sorghum Whipped Cream.

Sorghum Whipped Cream

quick prep • party perfect

MAKES: about 2 cups
HANDS-ON TIME: 5 min.
TOTAL TIME: 5 min.

1. Beat 1 cup whipping cream at high speed with an electric mixer until foamy; add 2 Tbsp. sorghum syrup, and beat until soft peaks form.

PASTRY CHEF SHAE REHMEL, FIVE & TEN
ATHENS, GEORGIA

Brown Sugar-Cinnamon Peach Pie

make-ahead • party perfect

MAKES: 8 servings
HANDS-ON TIME: 30 min.
TOTAL TIME: 4 hr., 50 min.

Serve with vanilla ice cream sprinkled with candied or toasted pecans. (Pictured on page 184)

- 1⅓ cups cold butter
- 4¼ cups all-purpose flour, divided
- 1½ tsp. salt
- ½ to ¾ cup ice-cold water
- 8 large fresh, firm, ripe peaches (about 4 lb.)
- ½ cup firmly packed light brown sugar
- ⅓ cup granulated sugar
- 1 tsp. ground cinnamon
- ⅛ tsp. salt
- 1½ Tbsp. butter, cut into pieces
- 1 large egg, beaten
- 1½ Tbsp. granulated sugar

1. Cut 1⅓ cups butter into small cubes, and chill 15 minutes. Stir together 4 cups flour and 1½ tsp. salt. Cut butter into flour mixture with a pastry blender until mixture resembles small peas. Gradually stir in

½ cup ice water with a fork, stirring until dry ingredients are moistened and dough begins to form a ball and leaves sides of bowl, adding more ice water, I Tbsp. at a time, if necessary. Turn dough out onto a piece of plastic wrap; press and shape dough into 2 flat disks. Wrap each disk in plastic wrap, and chill 30 minutes to 24 hours.

2. Preheat oven to 425°. Place I dough disk on a lightly floured surface; sprinkle dough lightly with flour. Roll dough to about ¼-inch thickness. Starting at I edge of dough, wrap dough around a rolling pin. Place rolling pin over a 9-inch pie plate, and unroll dough over pie plate. Press dough into pie plate.

3. Roll remaining dough disk to about ¼-inch thickness on a lightly floured surface.

4. Peel peaches, and cut into ½-inch-thick slices; cut slices in half. Stir together brown sugar, next 3 ingredients, and remaining ¼ cup flour in a bowl; add peaches, stirring to coat. Immediately spoon peach mixture into piecrust in pie plate, and dot with I½ Tbsp. butter. (Do not make mixture ahead or it will become too juicy.)

5. Carefully place remaining piecrust over filling; press edges of crusts together to seal. Cut off excess crust, and reserve. Crimp edges of pie. If desired, reroll excess crust to ¼-inch thickness. Cut into 3-inch leaves using a knife. Brush top of pie with beaten egg; top with leaves. Brush leaves with egg; sprinkle with I½ Tbsp. granulated sugar. Cut 4 to 5 slits in top of pie for steam to escape.

6. Freeze pie I5 minutes. Meanwhile, heat a jelly-roll pan in oven I0 minutes. Place pie on hot jelly-roll pan.

7. Bake at 425° on lower oven rack I5 minutes. Reduce oven temperature to 375°; bake 40 minutes. Cover loosely with aluminum foil to prevent excessive browning, and bake 25 more minutes or until juices are thick and bubbly (juices will bubble through top). Transfer to a wire rack; cool 2 hours before serving.

PASTRY CHEF SHAE REHMEL, FIVE & TEN
ATHENS, GEORGIA

Lovely Lattice

For an equally impressive top crust, cut remaining dough disk in Step 3 into 3 (I½-inch-wide) strips and 8 (¼-inch-wide) strips using a fluted pastry wheel. Proceed as directed through Step 4. In Step 5, replace whole crust with dough strips, making a lattice design. Omit pastry leaves. Brush lattice with beaten egg, and sprinkle with sugar. Omit slits in crust. Proceed as directed in Steps 6 and 7, shielding just the edges with foil.

Brown Sugar-Cinnamon Peach Pie

"Life is better than death, I believe, if only because it is less boring, and because it has fresh peaches in it."

ALICE WALKER
IN SEARCH OF OUR MOTHERS' GARDENS

Burgers You Won't Believe

We could describe, in delicious detail, how we took this backyard basic to new heights by stacking beef (and turkey) patties with irresistible toppings, make-your-own condiments, and better-than-store-bought buns. Or we could just let you feast your eyes on photo at right.

Best Turkey Burgers

good for you • party perfect

MAKES: 6 servings
HANDS-ON TIME: 32 min.
TOTAL TIME: 3 hr., including buns

- 2 lb. lean ground turkey breast
- 1 tsp. salt
- 1 tsp. lemon zest
- ½ cup mayonnaise
- ¼ cup chopped fresh parsley
  Homemade Hamburger Buns (next page)

1. Preheat grill to 350° to 400° (medium-high) heat. Combine first 5 ingredients gently. Shape mixture into 6 (5-inch) patties.

2. Grill, covered with grill lid, 6 to 7 minutes on each side or until a meat thermometer inserted into thickest portion registers 170°. Serve on Home-made Hamburger Buns.

Try These Twists!

MUFFULETTA BURGERS: Stir ½ cup chopped pimiento-stuffed Spanish olives into meat mixture. Proceed as directed. Pulse ½ (16-oz.) jar mixed pickled vegetables, drained, and 2 Tbsp. Italian dressing in a food processor until coarsely chopped. Top each burger with vegetable mixture and salami, ham, and provolone cheese slices.
NOTE: We tested with Mezzetta Italian Mix Giardiniera pickled vegetables.

GREEN TOMATO-FETA BURGERS: Stir 1 (4-oz.) container crumbled feta cheese, 1 Tbsp. finely minced red onion, and 1 tsp. minced oregano into meat mixture. Proceed as directed. Top each burger with sliced pickled green tomatoes, lettuce, thinly sliced cucumber, a pinch of dried crushed red pepper, and a fresh dill sprig.

PICKLED ONION-CHUTNEY BURGERS: Stir 2 Tbsp. finely chopped red onion and ⅓ cup mango chutney into meat mixture. Proceed as directed. Top each burger with a small wedge of blue cheese, arugula, whole grain Dijon mustard, and Red Onion Relish (at right).

Make Your Own Condiments!

Red Onion Relish

good for you • make-ahead • party perfect

MAKES: 1½ cups
HANDS-ON TIME: 10 min.
TOTAL TIME: 1 hr., 10 min.

- ½ medium-size red onion
- 2 tsp. cumin seeds
- 3 Tbsp. fresh lemon juice
- 2 Tbsp. cider vinegar
- 1 Tbsp. dark brown sugar
- ½ tsp. kosher salt

1. Thinly slice onion, and place in a 2-qt. glass bowl.
2. Heat a medium skillet over medium-high heat until hot; add cumin seeds, and cook, stirring constantly, 1 to 2 minutes or until toasted. Slowly stir in ½ cup water, lemon juice, and next 3 ingredients. Stir until brown sugar is melted and mixture comes to a boil.
3. Pour over red onion slices, and let stand 1 hour. Store in an airtight container in refrigerator up to 1 week.

Cilantro-Jalapeño Cream

make-ahead • party perfect

MAKES: ¾ cup
HANDS-ON TIME: 10 min.
TOTAL TIME: 40 min.

- ½ cup sour cream
- ¼ cup chopped fresh cilantro
- 1 medium-size jalapeño pepper, seeded and minced
- 2 Tbsp. fresh lime juice

1. Combine all ingredients, and let stand at room temperature 30 minutes. To make ahead, store mixture in an airtight container in refrigerator up to 2 days.

Pimiento Cheese-Bacon Burgers

Best Beef Burgers

party perfect

MAKES: 6 servings
HANDS-ON TIME: 28 min.
TOTAL TIME: 3 hr., including buns

Let ground beef stand at room temperature for 10 minutes before grilling.

- 1 **lb. ground sirloin**
- 1 **lb. ground chuck**
- 1 **tsp. salt**
- ½ **tsp. freshly ground pepper**
  Homemade Hamburger Buns (at right)

1. Preheat grill to 350° to 400° (medium-high) heat. Combine first 4 ingredients gently. Shape mixture into 6 (5-inch) patties.
2. Grill, covered with grill lid, 4 to 5 minutes on each side or until beef is no longer pink in center. Serve on Homemade Hamburger Buns.

Try These Twists!

PIMIENTO CHEESE-BACON BURGERS: Stir ¼ cup mixed chopped fresh herbs (such as basil, mint, and oregano) into meat mixture. Proceed as directed. Top each burger with pimiento cheese, cooked bacon slices, lettuce, and tomato slices.

SUN-DRIED TOMATO-PESTO BURGERS: Stir 1 (3-oz.) package sun-dried tomato halves, chopped, and 1 garlic clove, pressed, into meat mixture. Proceed as directed. Top each burger with refrigerated pesto, sliced goat cheese, and sliced pepperoncini salad peppers.

PINEAPPLE-JALAPEÑO BURGERS: Stir ⅓ cup pickled sliced jalapeño peppers, minced, into meat mixture. Proceed as directed. Grill 6 (¼-inch-thick) pineapple slices over medium-high heat 1 to 2 minutes on each side. Top each burger with Cilantro-Jalapeño Cream(at left), grilled pineapple, avocado slices, and a fresh cilantro sprig.

Dress Up Your Fries!

MANGO KETCHUP: Combine ½ cup ketchup and ¼ cup mango chutney, and let stand 5 minutes. Fig preserves may be substituted for mango chutney. Makes: ¾ cup.

Homemade Hamburger Buns

make-ahead • party perfect

MAKES: 12 buns
HANDS-ON TIME: 15 min.
TOTAL TIME: 2 hr., 35 min.

- 1 **(48-oz.) package frozen white bread dough loaves**
- 1 **large egg**
- 2 **Tbsp. sesame seeds or poppy seeds (optional)**

1. Let dough stand at room temperature for 15 minutes. Cut dough into 12 equal portions. Place dough portions on a lightly greased 15- x 10-inch jelly-roll pan. Let rise in a warm place (85°), free from drafts, 30 minutes or until doubled in bulk.
2. Shape each dough portion into a 5-inch circle, and place on lightly greased jelly-roll pan. Whisk together egg and 2 Tbsp. water. Brush dough lightly with egg mixture; sprinkle with sesame seeds, if desired.
3. Let rise in a warm place (85°), free from drafts, 1 hour or until doubled in bulk.
4. Preheat oven to 400°. Bake rolls 20 to 22 minutes or until browned. Let stand 15 minutes. Cut rolls in half crosswise; toast, if desired.
NOTE: We tested with Bridgford Frozen White Ready-Dough loaves.

Fourth of July Feast

Seeking freedom from party stress? Pledge allegiance to this no-fail festive menu, with liberty and potato salad for all.

Set the Scene

Small bursts of Queen Anne's lace echo the sparklers.

Patriotic Picnic

SERVES 8

Smoky Chicken or Steak Barbecue Kabobs with White Barbecue Sauce

Deviled Eggs with Assorted Toppings

Hot Bacon Potato Salad with Green Beans

Grilled Jalapeño-Lime Corn on the Cob

Fizzy, Fruity Ice-Cream Floats

Plan Ahead

Test Kitchen Director Rebecca Kracke Gordon suggests devoting just 30 minutes a day for three days to pull off this great menu.

2 DAYS BEFORE:
- Prepare barbecue sauce, rub, and butter mixture for corn.

I DAY BEFORE:
- Fill eggs; chop toppings, and place in bowls.
- Thread kabob skewers.

30 MINUTES BEFORE GUESTS ARRIVE:
- Prepare potato salad.
- Ice down eggs and drinks

I5 MINUTES AFTER GUESTS ARRIVE:
- Grill kabobs and corn.

Party Improv
Party Improv Pick up hard-cooked eggs in your grocer's deli section.

Smoky Chicken Barbecue Kabobs

quick prep • good for you • party perfect

MAKES: 8 servings
HANDS-ON TIME: 20 min.
TOTAL TIME: 30 min., including rub and sauce

- 2 lb. skinned and boned chicken breasts
- ½ large red onion, cut into fourths and separated into pieces
- 1 pt. cherry tomatoes
- 8 (8-inch) metal skewers
  Smoky Barbecue Rub
  White Barbecue Sauce

1. Preheat grill to 350° to 400° (medium-high) heat. Cut chicken into 1-inch cubes. Thread chicken, onion, and tomatoes alternately onto skewers, leaving a ¼-inch space between pieces. Sprinkle kabobs with Smoky Barbecue Rub.
2. Grill kabobs, covered with grill lid, 4 to 5 minutes on each side. Serve with White Barbecue Sauce.

Smoky Steak Barbecue Kabobs: Substitute 2 lb. top sirloin steak, trimmed, for chicken. Proceed with recipe as directed.

Smoky Barbecue Rub

quick prep • make-ahead

MAKES: about ¼ cup
HANDS-ON TIME: 5 min.
TOTAL TIME: 5 min.

1. Stir together 2 Tbsp. firmly packed dark brown sugar, 2 tsp. garlic salt, 1 tsp. ground chipotle chile powder, ½ tsp. ground cumin, and ¼ tsp. dried oregano.

White Barbecue Sauce

quick prep • party perfect

MAKES: about 1 ¾ cups
HANDS-ON TIME: 5 min.
TOTAL TIME: 5 min.

1. Stir together 1½ cups mayonnaise, ⅓ cup white vinegar, 1 tsp. pepper, ½ tsp. salt, ½ tsp. sugar, and 1 pressed garlic clove.

Deviled Eggs with Assorted Toppings

quick prep • make-ahead • party perfect

MAKES: 8 servings
HANDS-ON TIME: 15 min.
TOTAL TIME: 15 min.

- 1 dozen hard-cooked eggs, peeled
- ½ cup mayonnaise
- 1 green onion, finely chopped
- 2 tsp. hot sauce
  Salt and freshly ground pepper
  Toppings: chopped cooked bacon, smoked salmon, chopped black olives, chopped Spanish olives, sour cream, chopped sun-dried tomatoes, and chopped fresh herbs (dill, parsley, chives)

1. Slice eggs in half lengthwise, and carefully remove yolks. Reserve egg whites.
2. Mash yolks with mayonnaise, onion, and hot sauce until well blended. Add salt and pepper to taste. Spoon or pipe yolk mixture into reserved egg whites; cover loosely with plastic wrap. Serve immediately, or cover and chill up to 1 day. Serve with desired toppings.

Set the Scene

String lights attach easily to bamboo poles anchored with sand in buckets.

Hot Bacon Potato Salad with Green Beans

quick prep • make-ahead • party perfect

MAKES: 8 servings
HANDS-ON TIME: 30 min.
TOTAL TIME: 30 min.

- 3 lb. fingerling potatoes, cut in half
- 1 (8-oz.) package haricots verts (tiny green beans)
- ½ cup white wine vinegar
- 1 shallot, minced
- 3 Tbsp. honey
- 1 Tbsp. Dijon mustard
- 1½ tsp. salt
- 1 tsp. pepper
- ½ cup olive oil
- 2 Tbsp. chopped fresh dill
- ¼ cup coarsely chopped fresh parsley
- 4 fully cooked bacon slices, chopped

1. Bring potatoes and water to cover to a boil in a large Dutch oven over medium-high heat, and cook 20 minutes or until tender. Drain.

2. Meanwhile, cook green beans in boiling water to cover in a medium saucepan 3 to 4 minutes or until crisp-tender. Plunge in ice water to stop the cooking process; drain.

3. Whisk together vinegar and next 5 ingredients in a medium bowl. Add oil in a slow, steady stream, whisking constantly, until smooth.

4. Pour vinegar mixture over potatoes. Just before serving, add green beans, dill, and parsley, and toss gently until blended. Sprinkle with bacon. Serve immediately, or cover and chill until ready to serve.

Grilled Jalapeño-Lime Corn on the Cob

quick prep • party perfect

MAKES: 8 servings
HANDS-ON TIME: 30 min.
TOTAL TIME: 30 min.

- 8 ears fresh corn, husks removed
- Vegetable cooking spray
- Salt and freshly ground pepper
- ½ cup butter, softened
- 1 jalapeño pepper, seeded and minced
- 1 small garlic clove, pressed
- 1 Tbsp. lime zest
- 1 Tbsp. fresh lime juice
- 2 tsp. chopped fresh cilantro
- Garnish: lime zest

1. Preheat grill to 350° to 400° (medium-high) heat. Coat corn lightly with cooking spray. Sprinkle with desired amount of salt and pepper. Grill corn, covered with grill lid, 15 minutes or until golden brown, turning occasionally.

2. Meanwhile, stir together butter and next 5 ingredients. Remove corn from grill, and cut into thirds. Serve corn with butter mixture. Garnish, if desired.

Fizzy, Fruity

ICE-CREAM FLOATS: Let guests pour their favorite fruit-flavored soft drinks (such as grape, lime, or black cherry) over scoops of vanilla ice cream. Striped straws add a retro touch (greenpartygoods.com or jackandlulu.com).

"How can I put my farmers' market finds to use?"

JENNIFER TAIT ATLANTA, GEORGIA

{1}

SLICE UP FRESH PEPPERS FOR FLAVORFUL, NUTRITIOUS "CHIPS"

Pepper and Chicken Nachos

quick prep • party perfect

MAKES: 4 servings
HANDS-ON TIME: 18 min.
TOTAL TIME: 37 min.

- 4 **garlic cloves, pressed**
- ¼ **cup cider vinegar**
- ⅓ **cup olive oil**
- ½ **tsp. ground cumin**
- ½ **tsp. salt**
- ½ **tsp. freshly ground pepper**
- 4 **medium-size bell peppers, cut into 2-inch pieces**
- 2 **cups chopped deli-roasted chicken**
- 1 **(15½-oz.) can black-eyed peas, drained and rinsed**
- 1 **(7.5-oz.) package sliced sharp Cheddar cheese**
- ⅓ **cup loosely packed fresh cilantro leaves**

1. Preheat grill to 350° to 400° (medium-high) heat. Combine garlic and next 5 ingredients. Reserve 3 Tbsp. garlic mixture. Pour remaining garlic mixture into a large shallow dish; add peppers, turning to coat. Cover and chill 15 minutes, turning once. Remove peppers from marinade, reserving marinade for basting.

2. Grill peppers, covered with grill lid, 8 to 10 minutes or until peppers blister and are tender, turning occasionally and basting with marinade.

3. Preheat broiler with oven rack 4 inches from heat. Combine chicken and peas with reserved 3 Tbsp. garlic mixture. Place peppers in a single layer on a lightly greased rack in an aluminum foil-lined broiler pan. Quarter cheese slices. Top each pepper with chicken mixture and one cheese quarter.

4. Broil 4 to 5 minutes or until cheese is melted. Remove from oven, sprinkle with cilantro, and serve immediately.

Farmers' Market Tips

Test Kitchen Specialist Vanessa McNeil Rocchio shares some pointers.

{1}

Visit *localharvest.org* to find markets in your area.

{2}

Stop by near the day's end. Vendors are packing up and more willing to cut you a deal.

{3}

Replace plastic produce bags with green bags (*evertfresh.com*), which keep food fresh up to a month.

{4}

Stash a cooler in your trunk. Produce will stay fresh even if you have to run a few errands before heading home.

Test Kitchen Tip

QUICK-FIX SUPPERS ONLINE: Find quick and easy meal ideas and daily time-saving tips at *southernliving.com/quickfix*

{2}
PULL OUT THE GRIDDLE

Grilled Chicken with Fresh Corn Cakes

quick prep • party perfect

MAKES: 4 servings
HANDS-ON TIME: 15 min.
TOTAL TIME: 56 min.

- 3 lemons
- 2 garlic cloves, pressed
- ⅓ cup olive oil
- 1 tsp. Dijon mustard
- ¼ tsp. pepper
- 1½ tsp. salt, divided
- 3 skinned and boned chicken breasts
- 3 ears fresh corn, husks removed
- 1 Tbsp. olive oil
- 1 (6-oz.) package buttermilk cornbread mix
- ¼ cup chopped fresh basil
- 8 cooked thick hickory-smoked bacon slices
- 2 cups loosely packed arugula

1. Preheat grill to 350° to 400° (medium-high) heat. Grate zest from lemons to equal 1 Tbsp. Cut lemons in half; squeeze juice from lemons into a measuring cup to equal ¼ cup.
2. Whisk together lemon zest, lemon juice, garlic, next 3 ingredients, and 1 tsp. salt. Reserve ¼ cup lemon mixture. Pour remaining lemon mixture in a large zip-top plastic freezer bag; add chicken. Seal and chill 15 minutes, turning once. Remove chicken from marinade, discarding marinade.
3. Brush corn with 1 Tbsp. olive oil; sprinkle with remaining ½ tsp. salt.
4. Grill chicken and corn at the same time, covered with grill lid, 20 minutes, turning chicken once and turning corn every 4 to 5 minutes. Remove chicken, and cover. Hold each grilled cob upright on a cutting board, and carefully cut downward, cutting kernels from cob.
5. Stir together cornbread mix and ⅔ cup water in a small bowl until smooth. Stir in basil and 1 cup grilled corn kernels. Pour about ¼ cup batter for each corn cake onto a hot, lightly greased griddle. Cook cakes 3 to 4 minutes or until tops are covered with bubbles and edges look dry and cooked; turn and cook other side.
6. Thinly slice chicken. To serve, place 2 corn cakes on each plate, top with chicken and 2 bacon slices. Toss arugula with reserved lemon mixture. Place arugula on bacon, and sprinkle with corn kernels.

{3}
COLOR UP A SALAD WITH FRESH CORN

Grilled Steak-Corn-Spinach Salad

quick prep • party perfect

MAKES: 6 servings
HANDS-ON TIME: 30 min.
TOTAL TIME: 30 min.

- 2 lb. rib-eye steak
- 4 Tbsp. olive oil
- 4 garlic cloves, pressed
- 1¼ tsp. salt
- ½ tsp. freshly ground pepper
- 4 ears fresh corn, husks removed
- 1 (5-oz.) package fresh baby spinach
- 2 ripe avocados, thinly sliced
- 1 red grapefruit, sectioned
  Bottled peppercorn Ranch dressing

1. Preheat grill to 350° to 400° (medium-high) heat. Rub steak with 2 Tbsp. olive oil and next 3 ingredients. Brush corn with remaining 2 Tbsp. olive oil.
2. Grill steaks and corn at the same time, covered with grill lid, 7 to 8 minutes, turning steak once and turning corn every 4 to 5 minutes. Let steak stand 10 minutes.
3. Meanwhile, hold each grilled cob upright on a cutting board, and carefully cut downward, cutting kernels from cob. Discard cobs. Thinly slice steak.
4. Layer spinach, grilled corn kernels, steak, avocados, and grapefruit on serving plates. Serve with bottled Ranch dressing.

{4}
COMPLEMENT A TENDERLOIN

Caribbean Pork with Butter Pea Toss

quick prep • good for you • party perfect

MAKES: 4 servings
HANDS-ON TIME: 15 min.
TOTAL TIME: 45 min.

Try this side: *Combine 3 Tbsp. fresh lime juice, 2 tsp. olive oil, ¼ cup each chopped fresh mint and cilantro, and ½ tsp. salt. Cut 3 large carrots and 1 English cucumber into strips, using a julienne vegetable peeler. Toss with lime mixture; serve immediately.*

- 1 lb. pork tenderloin
- 3 Tbsp. olive oil, divided
- 1½ tsp. salt, divided
- 1 Tbsp. Caribbean jerk seasoning
- 3 cups fresh or frozen butter peas
- ¼ cup chopped fresh parsley
- 1 tsp. fresh thyme leaves
- ¼ cup fresh lemon juice
- 1 Tbsp. sugar
- ½ tsp. dried crushed red pepper
- ¼ tsp. ground black pepper

1. Preheat grill to 350° to 400° (medium-high) heat. Remove silver skin from tenderloin, leaving a thin layer of fat. Rub 1 Tbsp. olive oil, ½ tsp. salt, and 1 Tbsp. Caribbean seasoning over tenderloin.
2. Grill tenderloin, covered with grill lid, 10 to 12 minutes on each side or until a meat thermometer inserted into thickest portion registers 155°. Remove from grill, and let stand 5 minutes before slicing.
3. Meanwhile, bring butter peas and water to cover to a boil in a 3-qt. saucepan over high heat; reduce heat to medium, and simmer 25 minutes; drain. Combine peas, next 6 ingredients, and remaining 2 Tbsp. olive oil and 1 tsp. salt. Serve with sliced pork.

Grilled Peppers and Sausage with Cheese Grits

quick prep • party perfect

MAKES: 6 servings
HANDS-ON TIME: 32 min.
TOTAL TIME: 37 min.

- 2 medium-size red bell peppers, cut into quarters
- 2 medium-size sweet onions, cut into quarters
- 2 Tbsp. olive oil
- 1 tsp. fresh thyme leaves
- 1 tsp. salt, divided
- 1 (19.76-oz.) package garlic pork sausage links
- 2 (14.5-oz.) cans chicken broth
- 1 cup uncooked quick-cooking grits
- 2 Tbsp. butter
- 1 cup grated Parmesan cheese
- ⅓ cup chopped fresh basil
- ½ tsp. freshly ground pepper

1. Preheat grill to 350° to 400° (medium-high) heat. Toss peppers and onions with olive oil, thyme, and ½ tsp. salt.

2. Grill pepper mixture and sausage at the same time, covered with grill lid. Grill pepper mixture, turning occasionally, 8 to 10 minutes or until wilted. Grill sausage 5 minutes on each side or until done.

3. Bring remaining ½ tsp. salt, chicken broth, and ½ cup water to a boil in a 3-qt. saucepan; slowly stir in grits, reduce heat, and simmer 12 minutes or until thickened and creamy, stirring often. Remove from heat, and stir in butter and next 3 ingredients.

4. Coarsely chop peppers and onions, and slice sausage into 1-inch pieces. Serve sausage-and-pepper mixture over hot cooked grits.

NOTE: We tested with Johnsonville Irish O'Garlic Sausage.

IN SEASON

5 Ways with Tomatoes & Basil

Think outside the mozz! Here, fresh summer pairing ideas.

{1}

MAKE IT A MEAL

Texas Toast Tomato Sandwiches

quick prep • party perfect

MAKES: 6 servings
HANDS-ON TIME: 15 min.
TOTAL TIME: 15 min.

- 1 (9.5-oz.) package five-cheese Texas toast
- 2 lb. assorted heirloom tomatoes
- ¼ cup bottled blue cheese vinaigrette
- 6 Tbsp. torn fresh basil
  Salt and pepper
  Garnishes: crumbled blue cheese, fresh basil leaves

1. Prepare Texas toast according to package directions.

2. Meanwhile, halve larger tomatoes and cut into ¼-inch-thick slices; halve or quarter smaller tomatoes. Gently toss tomatoes with vinaigrette, basil, and salt and pepper to taste. Serve immediately over hot Texas toast. Garnish, if desired.

NOTE: We tested with Pepperidge Farm Five Cheese Texas Toast.

{2}
REINVENT FRUIT COCKTAIL

Watermelon-Peach Salsa and Tomatoes

quick prep • good for you • party perfect

MAKES: 6 servings
HANDS-ON TIME: 20 min.
TOTAL TIME: 20 min.

- ½ cup hot pepper jelly
- 1 Tbsp. lime zest
- ¼ cup fresh lime juice
- 2 cups seeded and diced fresh watermelon
- 1 cup peeled and diced fresh peaches
- ⅓ cup chopped fresh basil
- ⅓ cup chopped fresh chives
- 3 cups baby heirloom tomatoes, halved
  Salt and freshly ground pepper
  Garnish: fresh basil sprigs

1. Whisk together pepper jelly, lime zest, and lime juice in a bowl; stir in watermelon and next 3 ingredients.
2. Season halved baby tomatoes with salt and freshly ground pepper to taste; spoon into cocktail glasses. Top with salsa. Garnish, if desired.

Grow 'em Together!

Tomatoes and basil also make excellent companions in the garden—and you can still set out plants. For how-to tips on growing these two Southern favorites, visit *southernliving.com/gardens.*

{3}
BRIGHTEN A PASTA SALAD

Tortellini-and-Tomato Salad

quick prep • good for you • party perfect

MAKES: 6 servings
HANDS-ON TIME: 20 min.
TOTAL TIME: 20 min.

- 2 (9-oz.) packages refrigerated cheese-filled tortellini
- ½ cup olive oil
- ½ cup freshly grated Parmesan cheese
- 3 Tbsp. fresh lemon juice
- 2 garlic cloves
- 1 tsp. Worcestershire sauce
- ½ tsp. salt
- 2 cups baby heirloom tomatoes, halved
- 1 cup fresh corn kernels
- ½ cup thinly sliced green onions
- ½ cup coarsely chopped fresh basil
  Salt and pepper

1. Prepare tortellini according to package directions.
2. Meanwhile, process olive oil and next 5 ingredients in a blender until smooth. Toss olive oil mixture with hot cooked tortellini, tomatoes, and next 3 ingredients. Season with salt and pepper to taste.

Take It Up a Notch

{4}
BASIL AÏOLI : Whisk together 1 cup mayonnaise; ¼ cup minced fresh basil; 1 garlic clove, pressed; 1 tsp. lemon zest; 2 Tbsp. fresh lemon juice; and 1 tsp. Dijon mustard. Cover and chill 1 hour. Spread on tomato sandwiches, drizzle over sliced tomatoes, or toss with chopped cooked chicken and diced celery, and spoon into tomato shells.

{5}
BALSAMIC GLAZE: Bring 1 cup balsamic vinegar to a boil in a large heavy saucepan over medium heat. Cook, stirring occasionally, 10 to 15 minutes or until reduced to ½ cup and a syrup-like consistency. Remove from heat; cool completely. Drizzle over broiled tomato halves topped with crumbled goat cheese and torn fresh basil leaves.

Squash Casserole

This summer veggie is overflowing at farm stands and ready for some golden bubbly goodness in the oven.

Lightened Squash Casserole

good for you • party perfect

MAKES: 10 to 12 servings
HANDS-ON TIME: 25 min.
TOTAL TIME: 1 hr., 10 min.

A combo of cornflakes and French fried onions adds an irresistible crunch.

- **3 lb. yellow squash**
- **½ cup chopped sweet onion**
- **1½ tsp. salt, divided**
- **1 cup grated carrots**
- **1 (10¾-oz.) can reduced-fat cream of chicken soup**
- **1 (8-oz.) container light sour cream**
- **¼ cup chopped fresh chives**
- **½ cup crushed cornflakes cereal**
- **½ cup crushed French fried onions**
- **2 Tbsp. melted butter**
- **¼ tsp. freshly ground pepper**

1. Preheat oven to 350°. Cut squash into ¼-inch-thick slices; place in a Dutch oven. Add onion, 1 tsp. salt, and water to cover. Bring to a boil over medium-high heat, and cook 5 minutes; drain well, and pat squash dry with paper towels.

2. Stir together grated carrots, next 3 ingredients, and remaining ½ tsp. salt in a large bowl; fold in squash mixture. Spoon into a lightly greased 2-qt. oval baking dish.

3. Stir together cornflakes and next 3 ingredients in a small bowl. Sprinkle over squash mixture.

4. Bake at 350° for 30 to 35 minutes or until bubbly and golden brown, shielding with aluminum foil after 20 to 25 minutes to prevent excessive browning, if necessary. Let stand 10 minutes before serving.

PER SERVING: CALORIES 139; FAT 7G (SAT 4G, MONO 1G, POLY 0G); PROTEIN 4G; CARB 15G; FIBER 4G; CHOL 9MG; IRON 1MG; SODIUM 586MG; CALC 38MG

TRY THIS TWIST!

Parmesan Squash Casserole: Omit cornflakes and butter. Substitute 1½ lb. zucchini for 1½ lb. yellow squash. Prepare recipe as directed through Step 2, stirring in 1 (4-oz.) jar diced pimientos, drained, into carrot mixture in Step 2. Stir together French fried onions, ground pepper, and ¼ cup grated Parmesan cheese. Sprinkle over squash mixture. Proceed as directed in Step 4.

PER SERVING: CALORIES 112; FAT 5G (SAT 2G, MONO 0G, POLY 0G); PROTEIN 4G; CARB 132G; FIBER 3G; CHOL 2MG; IRON 1MG; SODIUM 564MG; CALC 34MG

More Great Uses for Yellow Squash

YELLOW SQUASH SALAD: Combine 3 medium-size yellow squash, thinly sliced; ½ cup frozen green peas, blanched; 2 Tbsp. chopped fresh basil, and ¼ cup crumbled feta cheese; drizzle with your favorite vinaigrette.

FRESH SQUASH CHIPS: *We "ruffled" these chips using a crinkle cutter, available for about $8 at kitchen or homes stores or online. For smooth slices, use a chef's knife.*

Cut 2 yellow squash and 2 zucchini into ¼-inch-thick rounds. Combine squash, zucchini, 4 cups cold water, and ¼ tsp. salt in a large bowl. Cover and chill 30 minutes; drain and pat dry with paper towels. Serve with your favorite dip as an alternative to potato chips.

Great on the Grill

Grilled Summer Vegetables

MAKES: 4 servings
HANDS-ON TIME: 30 min.
TOTAL TIME: 30 min.

1. Preheat grill to 350° to 400° (medium-high) heat. Cut 6 medium-size yellow squash (about 1½ lb.) lengthwise into ½-inch slices, 2 red bell peppers into 1-inch strips, and 1 bunch green onions into 3-inch pieces. Toss vegetables with 2 Tbsp. olive oil, ½ tsp. salt, and ½ tsp. pepper. Grill half of vegetables, covered with grill lid, in a grill wok or metal basket, 7 minutes or until lightly charred and tender, stirring halfway through. Repeat with remaining vegetables. Toss vegetables with 1 Tbsp. each fresh lemon juice and chopped fresh parsley. Season with salt and pepper to taste.

August

Supper at Sundown

Chef Shawn Cirkiel's Texas Hill Country get-together is the party equivalent of a pair of old blue jeans— relaxed, comfortable, and tailor-made for a low-key, corral-the-friends weekend. Pass the Shiner Bock!

Shawn's Hill Country Menu

SERVES 8 TO 10

Grilled Tri-Tip with Citrus-Chile Butter

Garlic Shrimp

Lemon-Herb Potatoes

Sautéed Squash and Tomatoes

Southwest Watermelon Salad

Easy Mocha Mousse

It's hot in Texas. But not too hot for Austin chef Shawn Cirkiel. He thinks August is the perfect opportunity to embrace the heat and sneak out to the Hill Country for gorgeous vistas and wide-open spaces. Shawn and his family often escape to Willow City, about 90 minutes due west of town, to hang out with friends Heather Keating and Griffin Davis at their sprawling, longhorn-studded ranch.

"Being out here in the summer has its own rhythm. You focus more on the morning and late afternoon. It's actually a great way to slow down and reconnect with folks over food," Shawn says while crumbling Cotija cheese over a refreshing, vibrant Southwest Watermelon Salad (page 160). "We love a siesta, which gets us through the steamiest part of the day. Then we're ready for these wonderful sundown suppers."

Once the heat breaks and the sun heads for the horizon, the kids make a beeline for the grand oak trees and rope swing. The adults mosey out from underneath the ranch's wide porch and onto a large stone patio for ice-cold cans of Lone Star or glasses of limeade.

Shawn's wife, Bria, chops juicy tomatoes and firm yellow squash, while friend Rashelle McKim creates soft peaks on sweetened whipped cream, the latter to be used on the evening's dessert—a rich yet light Easy Mocha Mousse (page 160). Rashelle and her husband, Mike, own

Meet the Chef

After cooking in some of America's toniest restaurants, Shawn moved back to Austin in 2002, where he became the city's youngest ever five-star chef. Wanting to shift gears to a more laid-back setting and approachable menu, he opened Parkside in 2009 on bustling Sixth Street. Find out more about Shawn and his restaurant at *parkside-austin.com.*

Cuvée Coffee (cuveecoffee.com), which specializes in premium, micro-roasted coffee from all over the world. Their Meritage Espresso is the inspiration for Rashelle's creamy mousse.

"I love cooking out here," Shawn says while firing up the mesquite-fueled grill. "The timing's not the same. No one gets mad if the food's a few minutes late. It's very low-key." As he watches the charcoal chunks smolder, he adds, "Out here the only reservation I take is 'a table for everyone.'"

Grilled Tri-Tip with Citrus-Chile Butter

quick prep • party perfect

MAKES: 8 to 10 servings
HANDS-ON TIME: 30 min.
TOTAL TIME: 40 min., including butter
(Pictured on page 186)

2 (2-lb.) tri-tip steaks*
2 tsp. salt, divided
1¼ tsp. pepper, divided
   Citrus-Chile Butter
3 bunches baby Vidalia or green onions, trimmed
3 Tbsp. olive oil

1. Preheat grill to 350° to 400° (medium-high) heat. Sprinkle steaks with 1½ tsp. salt and 1 tsp. pepper. Grill steaks, covered with grill lid, 9 to 12 minutes on each side or to desired degree of doneness.
2. Remove from grill, and rub 3 Tbsp. Citrus-Chile Butter onto steaks. Cover steaks with aluminum foil; let stand 5 minutes.
3. Meanwhile, toss onions with olive oil; season with remaining ½ tsp. salt and ¼ tsp. pepper. Grill onions, without grill lid, 2 minutes; turn and grill 1 more minute.
4. Uncover steaks, and cut diagonally across the grain into thin slices. Serve with grilled onions and remaining Citrus-Chile Butter.
*Beef strip steaks (about 2 inches thick) may be substituted.

Citrus-Chile Butter

quick prep • make-ahead • party perfect

MAKES: 1 cup
HANDS-ON TIME: 10 min.
TOTAL TIME: 10 min.

1. Stir together 1 cup softened butter, 2 Tbsp. lime zest, 2 Tbsp. lemon zest, 3 minced garlic cloves, 1 Tbsp. seeded and minced jalapeño pepper, and 1 tsp. chopped fresh thyme. Season with salt and freshly ground pepper to taste. Cover and chill until ready to serve, or shape into a log with plastic wrap, and freeze up to 1 month.

Test Kitchen Tip

Tri-tip steak, perfect for grilling, is our new favorite! It's leaner than most cuts and so flavorful. Keep it tender by not overcooking it. If you don't see it at the meat counter, be sure to ask your butcher.

Garlic Shrimp

quick prep • party perfect

MAKES: 10 servings
HANDS-ON TIME: 30 min.
TOTAL TIME: 30 min.

8 fresh Texas toast bread slices
5 Tbsp. olive oil, divided
1½ lb. peeled, large raw shrimp (20/25 count)
½ tsp. salt
¼ tsp. pepper
¼ cup butter
4 fresh thyme sprigs
2 Tbsp. jarred minced garlic
2 Tbsp. minced shallots or sweet onion
⅓ cup fresh lemon juice
2 Tbsp. chopped fresh parsley
   Garnish: lemon zest

1. Preheat grill to 300° to 350° (medium) heat. Drizzle 1 side of bread slices with 3 Tbsp. olive oil. Grill bread slices 1 to 2 minutes or until toasted. Cut bread slices into triangles. Place on a serving platter.
2. Devein shrimp, if desired. Season shrimp with salt and pepper. Melt butter with remaining 2 Tbsp. olive oil in a large skillet over medium-high heat; add shrimp, thyme, and next 2 ingredients, and sauté 2 to 3 minutes or just until shrimp turn pink. Add lemon juice and parsley. Serve immediately over grilled bread. Garnish, if desired.

Lemon-Herb Potatoes

quick prep • good for you • party perfect

MAKES: 8 to 10 servings
HANDS-ON TIME: 20 min.
TOTAL TIME: 25 min.

This zippy dish is great served warm, chilled, or at room temperature. (Pictured on page 186)

1. Bring 3 lb. assorted small potatoes, halved, and salted water to cover to a boil in a large saucepan. Cook 10 to 15 minutes or until tender; drain. Toss potatoes with ¾ cup assorted chopped fresh herbs, ¼ cup olive oil, 3 Tbsp. fresh lemon juice, and 1 minced garlic clove.

Sautéed Squash and Tomatoes

MAKES: 8 to 10 servings
HANDS-ON TIME: 47 min.
TOTAL TIME: 47 min.
(Pictured on page 186)

3 thick hickory-smoked bacon slices
1 cup chopped sweet onion
3 garlic cloves, minced
1 Tbsp. chopped fresh thyme
1 tsp. chopped fresh oregano
1 bay leaf
4 cups sliced zucchini
4 cups sliced yellow or zephyr squash
2 cups cherry tomatoes, halved
2 Tbsp. butter
1 Tbsp. red wine vinegar
   Salt and freshly ground pepper
   Garnish: bay leaf

1. Sauté bacon in a large skillet over medium-high heat 8 minutes or until crisp; remove bacon, and drain on paper towels, reserving 2 Tbsp. drippings in skillet.
2. Sauté onion and next 4 ingredients in hot drippings 4 minutes or until onion is tender. Add zucchini and yellow squash; cook, stirring often, 10 minutes. Stir in tomatoes, and cook, stirring occasionally, 10 minutes. Remove from heat, and stir in butter and vinegar. Season with salt and pepper to taste. Discard bay leaf. Garnish, if desired.

Southwest Watermelon Salad

good for you • make-ahead • party perfect

MAKES: 8 to 10 servings
HANDS-ON TIME: 30 min.
TOTAL TIME: 3 hr., 5 min., plus 2 days for chilling rind

The reserved watermelon flesh from the Pickled Watermelon Rind is perfect for this recipe.

- 4 cups seeded and cubed red watermelon
- 4 cups seeded and cubed yellow watermelon
- 2 Tbsp. sugar
- 1 Tbsp. lime zest
- 2 Tbsp. fresh lime juice
- ½ cup Pickled Watermelon Rind
- ¼ cup coarsely chopped fresh cilantro
- ¼ cup coarsely chopped fresh basil
- 1 Tbsp. chopped fresh chives
- 1 Tbsp. seeded and thinly sliced jalapeño pepper
- 1 Tbsp. thinly sliced shallots
- 1 tsp. minced garlic
- 2 Tbsp. olive oil
- ½ cup crumbled Cotija cheese*

1. Combine first 5 ingredients in a large glass bowl. Stir in Pickled Watermelon Rind and next 6 ingredients. Drizzle with oil; sprinkle with cheese. Serve immediately, or cover and chill up to 2 hours.
*Feta cheese may be substituted.

Soda Ice Pops

Turn your favorite drinks into frozen pops for an easy, heat-busting treat. Sipper-style molds keep chins and shirts clean, while looped handles are perfect for tiny hands. Acme Sipper Ice Pop Maker and Prepara Volcano Fillable Ice Pops are available at *amazon.com*. Let the little ones enjoy after-supper Soda Ice Pops.

Pickled Watermelon Rind

make-ahead • party perfect

MAKES: 1 qt.
HANDS-ON TIME: 30 min.
TOTAL TIME: 1 hr., 35 min., plus 2 days for chilling

- ½ small watermelon (about 5 lb.)
- 3 Tbsp. salt
- ¾ cup sugar
- ¾ cup vinegar
- 2 star anise

1. Remove rind from watermelon, leaving a small amount of red flesh attached to rind. Reserve watermelon flesh for another use. Peel rind, and cut into 1-inch cubes (about 5 cups cubed). Place in a large bowl.
2. Stir together salt and 3 cups water. Pour over rind. Cover and chill 24 hours. Drain; rinse well.
3. Combine rind, sugar, next 2 ingredients, and ¾ cup water in a large Dutch oven. Bring to a boil; remove from heat. Cool completely (about 1 hour), stirring occasionally. Cover and chill 24 hours before serving. Store in refrigerator up to 1 week.

Easy Mocha Mousse

make-ahead • party perfect

MAKES: 12 servings
HANDS-ON TIME: 10 min.
TOTAL TIME: 4 hr., 10 min.
(Pictured on page 187)

- 1⅓ cups milk
- 1 (12-oz.) package semisweet chocolate morsels
- ½ cup egg substitute
- ¼ cup brewed espresso
- 4 Tbsp. sugar
- ⅛ tsp. salt
  Sweetened whipped cream
  Garnish: fresh berries

1. Cook milk in a heavy nonaluminum saucepan over medium-high heat 2 to 3 minutes or until tiny bubbles begin to appear around edges of pan. Remove from heat.
2. Combine chocolate morsels and next 4 ingredients in a blender. Process mixture on low speed 20 seconds or until smooth. With blender running on low, add milk in a slow, steady stream, processing 1 minute or until smooth.
3. Pour ⅓ cup chocolate mixture into each of 12 (5-oz.) glasses. Cover and chill 4 to 24 hours. Top with whipped cream, and garnish, if desired.

Mama's Double-Crust
Chicken Pot Pie *(page 54)*

Baked Tex-Mex Pimiento Cheese Dip *(page 39)*

Southwest Salsa *(page 39)*

Blue Cheese "Hot Wing" Dip *(page 38)*

Big-Batch Veggie Chili *(page 34)*

"Big Easy" Gumbo
(page 36)

Bourbon-Brown Sugar Pork Tenderloin *(page 49)*
with Garlic-Chive Mashed Potatoes *(page 50)*
and steamed green beans

**Panzanella Salad with
Cornbread Croutons** (page 51)

**Spicy Mango Shrimp pairs with
Coconut-Lime Rice** (page 51)

Fresh Vegetable Lasagna *(page 59)*

Cheesy Chili Hash Brown Bake *(page 52)*

Chicken Cutlets with Pecan Sauce *(page 53)*

**BLT Benedict with Avocado-
Tomato Relish** *(page 62)*

(top) **Mango-Spinach Salad with Warm Bacon Vinaigrette**
and (bottom) **Springtime Pasta with Bacon** (page 63)

Buttermilk Pound Cake with Custard Sauce *(page 72)*

Strawberry Swirl Cream Cheese Pound Cake *(page 76)*

Lemon-Coconut Pound Cake Loaf *(page 74)*

Sauvignon Blanc Pound Cake *(page 73)*

Fruit Salad with Yogurt *(page 85)*

Tomato-Herb Mini Frittatas, *(page 84)*

Quick Buttermilk Biscuits *(page 86)*

Fried Chicken Bites
(page 104)

**Strawberry-Rhubarb
Hand Pies** *(page 105)*

Sweet Tea Icebox Tart *(page 102)*

Kentucky Hot Browns
(page 109)

Kentucky Hot Brown Tart *(page 109)*

Iced Mexican Chocolate Sippers and Oven-Baked Churros *(page 108)*

**Beer 'Garitas, Spicy Queso Dip,
and Fresh Salsa** *(page 107)*

Fried Green Tomato Po'boys *(page 132)*

**Grilled Green Tomatoes
Caprese** (page 133)

Grilled Pork Porterhouse with Peach Agrodolce *(page 142)*

Brown Sugar-Cinnamon Peach Pie *(page 144)*

**Summer Grilled
Peach Salad** *(page 141)*

Sautéed Squash and Tomatoes, Grilled Tri-Tip with Citrus-Chile Butter, Lemon-Herb Potatoes
(page 159)

Easy Mocha Mousse (page 160)

Broccoli, Grape, and Pasta Salad *(page 222)*

Grilled Sweet Potato-Poblano Salad *(page 222)*

Mango Salad *(page 222)*

Smoked Paprika Pork Roast with Sticky Stout Barbecue Sauce, Grilled Peppers and Mushrooms *(page 235)*

**Butternut Squash
Spoon Bread** *(page 236)*

**Caramelized Pear
Cannoli with Praline
Sauce** *(page 236)*

**Mint Chocolate Chip
Ice-Cream Cake** *(page 193)*

Our Best Ice-Cream Treats

Have your cake (or pie)—and ice cream too!—with these parlor-perfect recipes.

Mint Chocolate Chip Ice-Cream Cake

make-ahead • party perfect

MAKES: 10 to 12 servings
HANDS-ON TIME: 30 min.
TOTAL TIME: 10 hr., 30 min., including batter and ganache

This crowd-pleasing cake is topped with whipped cream, crème de menthe chocolates, and, yes, chocolate ganache. (pictured on opposite page)

Parchment paper
Devil's Food Cake Batter
½ gal. mint chocolate chip ice cream, softened
10 chocolate wafers, coarsely crushed
Chocolate Ganache
Garnishes: sweetened whipped cream, thin crème de menthe chocolate mints

1. Preheat oven to 350°. Grease and flour 3 (8-inch) round cake pans. Line with parchment paper. Prepare Devil's Food Cake Batter, and spoon into pans.
2. Bake at 350° for 12 to 14 minutes or until a wooden pick inserted in center comes out clean. Cool in pans on a wire rack 10 minutes. Remove from pans to wire racks, peel off parchment paper, and cool completely (about 1 hour).
3. Place 1 cake layer in a 9-inch springform pan. Top with one-third of ice cream (about 2⅓ cups); sprinkle with half of crushed wafers. Repeat layers once. Top with remaining cake layer and ice cream. Freeze 8 to 12 hours.

4. Remove cake from springform pan, and place on a cake stand or plate. Prepare Chocolate Ganache, and spread over top of ice-cream cake. Let stand 15 minutes before serving. Garnish, if desired.

Devil's Food Cake Batter

MAKES: 3 cups
HANDS-ON TIME: 20 min.
TOTAL TIME: 20 min.

½ cup butter, softened
¾ cup sugar
1 large egg
1 tsp. vanilla extract
1 cup all-purpose flour
⅓ cup unsweetened cocoa
1 tsp. baking soda
¾ cup hot strong brewed coffee
1 tsp. white vinegar

1. Beat butter and sugar at medium speed with a heavy-duty electric stand mixer until creamy. Add egg, beating just until blended. Beat in vanilla. Combine flour, cocoa, and baking soda. Add to butter mixture alternately with coffee, beating until blended. Stir in vinegar. Bake batter immediately.

Chocolate Ganache

1. Microwave 1 (4-oz.) semisweet chocolate baking bar, chopped, and 4 Tbsp. whipping cream in a microwave-safe bowl at HIGH 1 minute or until melted, stirring at 30-second intervals. Stir in up to 4 Tbsp. additional cream for desired consistency. Use immediately.

Easy Mocha Chip Ice-Cream Cake

make-ahead • party perfect

MAKES: 8 to 10 servings
HANDS-ON TIME: 20 min.
TOTAL TIME: 5 hr., 15 min., including ganache

Get your chocolate fix here—chocolate-covered coffee beans add a finishing touch.

1 pt. premium dark chocolate chunk-coffee ice cream, softened
3 sugar cones, crushed
⅓ cup chocolate fudge shell topping
1 (14-oz.) container premium chocolate-chocolate chip ice cream, softened
6 cream-filled chocolate sandwich cookies, finely crushed
Mocha Ganache
Garnish: chocolate-covered coffee beans

1. Line an 8- x 5-inch loaf pan with plastic wrap, allowing 3 inches to extend over sides. Spread chocolate chunk-coffee ice cream in pan. Sprinkle with cones, and drizzle with shell topping. Freeze 30 minutes.
2. Spread chocolate-chocolate chip ice cream over topping. Top with crushed cookies, pressing into ice cream. Freeze 4 hours or until firm.
3. Lift ice-cream loaf from pan, using plastic wrap as handles; invert onto a serving plate. Discard plastic wrap. Prepare Mocha Ganache, and slowly pour over ice-cream loaf, allowing ganache to drip down sides. Freeze 10 minutes. Let stand at room temperature 10 minutes before serving. Garnish, if desired.

Mocha Ganache

1. Microwave 1 (4-oz.) semisweet chocolate baking bar, chopped; 1 tsp. instant espresso; and 3 Tbsp. whipping cream in a microwave-safe bowl at HIGH 1 minute or until melted and smooth, stirring at 30-second intervals. Whisk in an additional 1 Tbsp. cream until smooth. Use immediately.

Lemon Meringue Ice-Cream Pie

make-ahead • party perfect

MAKES: 8 servings
HANDS-ON TIME: 15 min.
TOTAL TIME: 11 hr., 25 min., including crust, curd, and topping

Homemade Lemon Curd delivers a burst of bright citrus flavor to this simple-to-fix pie, and—sweeter still—it can be made up to 2 weeks ahead!

2 pt. vanilla ice cream
   Vanilla Wafer Crust
1½ cups Homemade Lemon Curd
16 vanilla wafers
   Meringue Topping

1. Let ice cream stand at room temperature 5 minutes or just until soft enough to spread. Spoon 1 pt. ice cream into Vanilla Wafer Crust. Top with ¾ cup lemon curd; repeat with remaining ice cream and lemon curd. Gently swirl ice cream and curd with a knife or small spatula. Insert vanilla wafers around edge of pie. Cover and freeze 8 hours.

2. Spread Meringue Topping over pie. If desired, brown meringue using a kitchen torch, holding torch 1 to 2 inches from pie and moving torch back and forth. (If you do not have a torch, preheat broiler with oven rack 8 inches from heat; broil 30 to 45 seconds or until golden.) Serve immediately, or cover loosely with plastic wrap, and freeze 4 hours or up to 1 week.

Vanilla Wafer Crust

1. Preheat oven to 350°. Stir together 2½ cups coarsely crushed vanilla wafers, ¼ cup powdered sugar, and ½ cup melted butter; firmly press on bottom, up sides, and onto lip of a lightly greased 9-inch pie plate. Bake 10 to 12 minutes or until golden brown. Remove from oven, and cool completely (about 1 hour). Makes: 1 (9-inch) crust. Hands-on time: 10 min.; Total time: 1 hr., 20 min.

Lemon Meringue Ice-Cream Pie

Homemade Lemon Curd

MAKES: 2 cups
HANDS-ON TIME: 30 min.
TOTAL TIME: 1 hr., 30 min.

You'll have about ½ cup lemon curd left after making the pie. Serve it alongside the pie, drizzle over fresh fruit, or spread on hot biscuits.

2 cups sugar
½ cup butter, coarsely chopped
2 Tbsp. lemon zest
1 cup fresh lemon juice (about 6 lemons)
4 large eggs, lightly beaten

1. Stir together first 4 ingredients in a large heavy saucepan over medium heat, and cook, stirring constantly, 3 to 4 minutes or until sugar dissolves and butter melts.

2. Whisk about one-fourth of hot sugar mixture gradually into eggs; add egg mixture to remaining hot sugar mixture, whisking constantly. Cook over medium-low heat, whisking constantly, 15 minutes or until mixture thickens and coats back of a spoon. Remove from heat; cool completely (about 1 hour), stirring occasionally. Store in an airtight container in refrigerator up to 2 weeks.

PRETTY IN PINK!
Marshmallow crème stirred into Strawberry Semifreddo Shortcake eliminates the traditional use of raw eggs.

Meringue Topping

MAKES: about 4 cups
HANDS-ON TIME: 17 min.
TOTAL TIME: 20 min.

- 2 **egg whites**
- 1¼ **cups sugar**
- 1 **Tbsp. light corn syrup**
- 1 **tsp. vanilla extract**

1. Pour water to depth of 1½ inches into a 3½-qt. saucepan; bring to a boil over medium-high heat. Reduce heat to medium, and let simmer.
2. Meanwhile, combine egg whites, next 3 ingredients, and ¼ cup water in a 2½-qt. glass bowl; beat mixture at high speed with an electric mixer until blended. Place bowl over simmering water, and beat at high speed 5 to 7 minutes or until soft peaks form; remove from heat. Beat to spreading consistency (about 2 to 3 minutes). Use immediately.

Strawberry Semifreddo Shortcake

make-ahead • party perfect

MAKES: 16 servings
HANDS-ON TIME: 30 min.
TOTAL TIME: 5 hr., 45 min.

Look for soft ladyfingers in the bakery section of the grocery store.

- 2 **(3-oz.) packages soft ladyfingers**
- 2 **pt. strawberry ice cream, softened**
- 1 **pt. strawberry sorbet, softened**
- 1 **pt. fresh strawberries, hulled**
- 2 **Tbsp. powdered sugar**
- ½ **(7-oz.) jar marshmallow crème**
- 1 **cup heavy cream**

1. Arrange ladyfingers around sides and on bottom of a 9-inch springform pan. (Reserve any remaining ladyfingers for another use.) Spread strawberry ice cream over ladyfingers, and freeze 30 minutes.
2. Spread softened strawberry sorbet over ice cream. Freeze 30 minutes.
3. Process strawberries and powdered sugar in a food processor 1 minute or until pureed. Reserve ¼ cup mixture. Whisk remaining strawberry mixture into marshmallow crème until well blended.
4. Beat cream at high speed with an electric mixer until stiff peaks form. Fold into marshmallow mixture. Pour over sorbet in pan. Drizzle reserved strawberry mixture over top, and gently swirl with a paring knife. Freeze 4 hours or until firm. Let ice-cream cake stand at room temperature 15 minutes before serving.
NOTE: We tested with Blue Bell Strawberry Ice Cream and Häagen-Dazs Strawberry Sorbet.

"I'm looking to go meatless one night a week— any suggestions?"

KATHLEEN WIDENER, BIRMINGHAM, ALABAMA

{1}

RETHINK TACO NIGHT

Mexicali Meatless Tostadas

quick prep • good for you

MAKES: 6 servings
HANDS-ON TIME: 10 min.
TOTAL TIME: 15 min.

Try this side: Coarsely chop 2 ripe avocados. Toss with ¼ cup chopped red onion, 1 minced garlic clove, 3 Tbsp. fresh cilantro leaves, 2 Tbsp. fresh lime juice, and ½ tsp. salt.

- 1 (12-oz.) package frozen meatless burger crumbles
- 3 tsp. taco seasoning
- 12 tostada shells
- 1 (8.5-oz.) pouch ready-to-serve whole-grain Santa Fe rice
- 1 (16-oz.) can refried beans
- 1 (8-oz.) package shredded Mexican four-cheese blend
  Topping: pico de gallo

1. Preheat oven to 425°. Prepare crumbles according to package directions. Stir taco seasoning into hot crumble mixture. Prepare tostada shells and rice according to package directions.
2. Layer refried beans, crumble mixture, and rice on tostada shells. Sprinkle with cheese. Bake at 425° for 5 to 6 minutes or until cheese is melted. Serve with topping.
NOTE: We tested with MorningStar Farms Meal Starters Grillers Recipe Crumbles.

{2}

TRY A SUMMERY TWIST ON TOMATO SOUP

Pepper Gazpacho

quick prep • good for you • make-ahead

MAKES: 8¾ cups
HAND-ON TIME: 15 min.
TOTAL TIME: 15 min.

Try this side: Brush softened butter on 1 side of 12 whole grain bread slices. Place 6 bread slices, buttered sides down, on a griddle. Top each with 1 Havarti cheese slice, 1 Swiss cheese slice, and remaining bread slices, buttered sides up. Cook over medium heat 1 to 2 minutes on each side or until golden and cheese is melted.

- 1 (46-oz.) bottle vegetable juice
- 1 (12-oz.) jar roasted red bell peppers, drained
- 1 cup loosely packed fresh parsley leaves
- ½ cup chopped fresh basil leaves
- 1 cup chopped cucumber
- ½ cup banana pepper rings
- 2 garlic cloves
- 3 Tbsp. lemon juice
- 2 Tbsp. extra virgin olive oil
  Toppings: sliced cucumber, fresh basil leaves

1. Process half of vegetable juice and next 7 ingredients in a blender until smooth. Transfer to a large bowl. Stir in remaining vegetable juice and olive oil. Serve immediately with toppings, or cover and chill until ready to serve.

{3}

BAKE A CASSEROLE WITH FARMERS' MARKET FAVORITES

Zucchini-and-Spinach Lasagna

quick prep

MAKES: 4 servings
HANDS-ON TIME: 15 min.
TOTAL TIME: 55 min.

- 1 (8-oz.) container whipped chive-and-onion cream cheese
- 1 (15-oz.) container ricotta cheese
- ⅓ cup chopped fresh basil
- 1 tsp. salt
- 5 medium zucchini, thinly sliced (about 2½ lb.)
- 2 Tbsp. olive oil
- 1 (10-oz.) package fresh spinach
- 2 garlic cloves, pressed
- 6 no-boil lasagna noodles
- 1 (7-oz.) package shredded mozzarella cheese
  Garnish: fresh basil leaves

1. Preheat oven to 425°. Stir together first 4 ingredients in a bowl.
2. Sauté zucchini in hot oil in a large skillet over medium-high heat 3 to 4 minutes or until lightly browned. Add spinach; gently toss until wilted. Add garlic; cook 1 minute.
3. Spoon one-third of vegetables into a lightly greased 9-inch square baking dish; top with 2 noodles and one-third of ricotta mixture. Repeat twice. Sprinkle with mozzarella.
4. Bake, covered with lightly greased aluminum foil, at 425° for 25 to 30 minutes or until bubbly and noodles are tender. Uncover and bake 5 to 10 minutes or until golden. Let stand 10 minutes. Garnish, if desired.

{4}
PICK A HEARTY PASTA SO YOU WON'T MISS THE MEAT

Fresh Tomato-and-Asparagus Gnocchi

quick prep • good for you

MAKES: 4 servings
HANDS-ON TIME: 25 min.
TOTAL TIME: 30 min.

Gnocchi, small, Italian dense and fluffy dumplings made with potatoes, are a hearty alternative to pasta.

- I lb. fresh asparagus
- I (16-oz.) package gnocchi
- ½ cup chopped sweet onion
- 2 Tbsp. olive oil
- 4 garlic cloves, pressed
- 4 large tomatoes, seeded and chopped
- ½ cup chopped fresh basil
- I tsp. salt
- ½ tsp. freshly ground pepper
  Grated Parmesan cheese

1. Snap off and discard tough ends of asparagus. Cut asparagus into 2-inch pieces. Fill a 3-qt. saucepan three-fourths full with salted water. Bring to a boil; add asparagus and gnocchi, and cook 2 to 4 minutes or until tender. Drain.
2. Sauté onion in hot oil in a medium skillet over medium-high heat 5 to 6 minutes or until tender; add garlic, and cook I minute. Add tomatoes, and cook 3 to 5 minutes. Stir in basil, salt, pepper, and asparagus mixture.
3. Sprinkle each serving with Parmesan cheese; serve immediately.

{5}
START WITH GOOD PROTEIN FROM A CAN

Black-eyed Pea Cakes with Heirloom Tomatoes and Slaw

quick prep

MAKES: 6 servings
HANDS-ON TIME: 20 min.
TOTAL TIME: 20 min.

- I (15-oz.) can seasoned black-eyed peas, undrained
- 2 garlic cloves, pressed
- I (6-oz.) package buttermilk cornbread mix
- I large egg, lightly beaten
- ¼ cup sour cream
- 1½ tsp. Southwest chipotle salt-free seasoning blend
- I tsp. salt, divided
- ⅓ cup sour cream
- I tsp. lime zest
- I Tbsp. fresh lime juice
- 2 tsp. sugar
- I (12-oz.) package fresh broccoli slaw
- 2 large beefsteak tomatoes, cut into ¼-inch-thick slices

1. Coarsely mash peas with fork. Stir in garlic, next 4 ingredients, and ½ tsp. salt. Stir until blended.
2. Spoon about ⅓ cup batter for each cake onto a hot, lightly greased griddle. Cook cakes 2 minutes or until edges look dry and cooked; turn and cook 2 more minutes.
3. Stir together ⅓ cup sour cream, next 3 ingredients, and remaining ½ tsp. salt in a large bowl. Stir in slaw.
4. Place each cooked cake on a serving plate; top each with 2 tomato slices. Add salt and pepper to taste. Top with slaw; serve immediately.

Summer in a Salad

All burgered out? These satisfying salads, featuring late-summer vegetables and fruits, are fresh and fancy enough for company. Lettuce be thankful!

Grilled Steak-and-Ratatouille Salad with Basil-Garlic Vinaigrette

good for you • party perfect

MAKES: 4 servings
HANDS-ON TIME: 40 min.
TOTAL TIME: 1 hr., 30 min., including vinaigrette

- 2 (8-oz.) beef tenderloin fillets
- 1 tsp. freshly cracked pepper
- ½ tsp. kosher salt
- 2 small yellow squash, cut in half lengthwise
- 2 small zucchini, cut in half lengthwise
- 2 small eggplants, cut in half lengthwise
   Basil-Garlic Vinaigrette
- 3 plum tomatoes, cut in half lengthwise
- 1 (8-oz.) package romaine lettuce heart leaves

1. Preheat grill to 350° to 400° (medium-high) heat. Sprinkle fillets with pepper and salt, and let stand 15 minutes. Toss squash, zucchini, and eggplant with 3 Tbsp. Basil-Garlic Vinaigrette.

2. Grill steaks, covered with grill lid, 5 to 6 minutes on each side or to desired degree of doneness. Remove steaks, and cover with aluminum foil. Let stand 10 minutes.

3. Meanwhile, grill vegetable mixture, covered with grill lid, 5 to 6 minutes on each side or until tender. Add tomato halves during last 6 minutes of grilling time, and grill 3 minutes on each side or until softened and warm.

4. Coarsely chop grilled vegetables, and toss together. Cut steak into thin slices. Fan romaine leaves onto a serving platter. Top with grilled vegetables and steak slices; drizzle with desired amount of vinaigrette.

NOTE: We tested with Organic Girl Romaine Heart Leaves.

Basil-Garlic Vinaigrette

MAKES: about ¾ cup
HANDS-ON TIME: 5 min.
TOTAL TIME: 35 min.

- ¼ cup red wine vinegar
- 1 garlic clove, minced
- ½ tsp. kosher salt
- ¼ tsp. coarsely ground pepper
- ½ cup olive oil
- 3 Tbsp. chopped fresh basil

1. Whisk together first 4 ingredients until blended. Gradually add oil in a slow, steady stream, whisking constantly until smooth. Stir in basil. Cover vinaigrette, and chill 30 minutes. Store in refrigerator up to 24 hours.

RECIPE INSPIRED BY STACEY BOYD
SPRINGFIELD, VIRGINIA

Tropical Salad with Pork Kabobs and Citrus-Chimichurri Vinaigrette

good for you • party perfect

MAKES: 6 servings
HANDS-ON TIME: 50 min.
TOTAL TIME: 1 hr., 40 min., including vinaigrette

Look for sweet mini bell peppers in the produce section.

- 6 (12-inch) wooden skewers
- 1 (1½-lb.) package pork tenderloins
   Citrus-Chimichurri Vinaigrette
- 1 pt. sweet mini bell peppers
   Salt and pepper
- 1 (5-oz.) package spring greens mix
- 2 mangoes, peeled and sliced
- ½ cup golden raisins
- ½ cup roasted, salted cashews, chopped

1. Soak wooden skewers in hot water to cover 30 minutes.

2. Meanwhile, remove silver skin from tenderloin, leaving a thin layer of fat; cut pork into 2-inch pieces. Pour ¼ cup Citrus-Chimichurri Vinaigrette into a large shallow dish; add pork pieces, turning to coat. Cover and chill 30 minutes.

3. Preheat grill to 350° to 400° (medium-high) heat. Remove pork from marinade, discarding marinade. Thread pork and sweet peppers alternately onto skewers, leaving a ¼-inch space between pieces. Let stand 15 minutes. Grill kabobs, covered with grill lid, 5 to 7 minutes or until done. Sprinkle with salt and pepper to taste. Let stand 5 minutes.

4. Divide salad greens among 6 salad plates. Top with sliced mango and kabobs. Drizzle with desired amount of remaining vinaigrette, and sprinkle with raisins and cashews.

Tropical Salad with Pork Kabobs and Citrus-Chimichurri Vinaigrette

Citrus-Chimichurri Vinaigrette

MAKES: about 1 cup
HANDS-ON TIME: 10 min.
TOTAL TIME: 10 min.

Orange and lime juice take the place of vinegar in this dressing for some fresh-squeezed flavor.

- ½ **cup loosely packed fresh flat-leaf parsley**
- ¼ **cup loosely packed fresh cilantro**
- 1 **garlic clove, coarsely chopped**
- 1 **tsp. kosher salt**
- ½ **tsp. coarsely ground pepper**
- 3 **Tbsp. fresh orange juice**
- 2 **Tbsp. fresh lime juice**
- ¼ **tsp. ground red pepper**
- ⅓ **cup olive oil**

1. Process first 8 ingredients in a blender or food processor until smooth, stopping to scrape down sides as needed. Turn blender on high; gradually add oil in a slow, steady stream. Cover and chill 30 minutes. Store in refrigerator up to 24 hours.

Test Kitchen Tip

Use wide flat or two-prong bamboo skewers to hold food in place while turning on the grill. Find them at your grocer or at kitchen and grill shops.

More Ways to Get Your Greens

In addition to the inspired salads on these pages, here are four more creative combos from our Test Kitchen. Just drizzle with a favorite vinaigrette and you're ready to serve.

{1}
Grilled pork cutlets
+ grilled peach halves
+ grilled onion slices
+ fresh cherries
+ goat cheese

{2}
Grilled flank steak
+ tomato and avocado slices
+ blue cheese
+ torn basil leaves

{3}
Blackened shrimp
+ cannellini beans
+ grilled peppers
+ orange sections

{4}
Smoked pulled chicken
+ grilled figs
+ cooked and crumbled bacon
+ shaved manchego cheese
+ toasted walnuts

Grilled Chicken Salad with Raspberry-Tarragon Dressing

quick prep • make-ahead • party perfect

MAKES: 4 servings
HANDS-ON TIME: 30 min.
TOTAL TIME: 1 hr.

Raspberry-Tarragon Dressing
4 skinned and boned chicken breasts
     (about 1¼ lb.)
     Vegetable cooking spray
1 fennel bulb, cut in half
2 heads Bibb lettuce, torn
½ English cucumber, thinly sliced
½ cantaloupe, peeled and sliced
¼ cup chopped green onions
1 cup fresh blackberries
4 oz. Gorgonzola cheese, crumbled
½ cup honey-roasted sliced almonds

1. Pour ½ cup Raspberry-Tarragon Dressing into a large zip-top plastic freezer bag. Cover and refrigerate remaining dressing.
2. Add chicken to ½ cup dressing in bag. Seal and chill 30 minutes to 2 hours. Coat cold cooking grate of grill with cooking spray, and place on grill. Preheat grill to 350° to 400° (medium-high) heat. Remove chicken from marinade, discarding marinade. Grill chicken and fennel bulb halves, covered with grill lid, 8 to 10 minutes on each side or until chicken is done and fennel is tender. Let chicken stand 5 to 10 minutes.

Bread, Please!

While the grill is still warm, throw on some garlic-buttered French bread slices. Add freshly grated Parmesan cheese and chopped fresh herbs for even more flavor.

3. Meanwhile, divide lettuce and next 3 ingredients among 4 plates. Thinly slice chicken and fennel; place on salads. Drizzle with remaining dressing; top with berries, cheese, and almonds. Serve immediately.

RECIPE INSPIRED BY DIANE SPARROW
OSAGE, IOWA

Raspberry-Tarragon Dressing

1. Whisk together 1 (12-oz.) bottle raspberry vinaigrette, ¼ cup chopped green onions, and 2 tsp. chopped fresh tarragon in a bowl. Makes: about 2 cups.
NOTE: We tested with Maple Grove Farms of Vermont Fat Free Raspberry Vinaigrette.

Shrimp Po'boy Salad with Rémoulade Dressing

good for you • party perfect

MAKES: 6 servings
HANDS-ON TIME: 38 min.
TOTAL TIME: 1 hr., 19 min., including dressing

You can swap steamed or fried shrimp, fried chicken tenders, or fried oysters for grilled shrimp.

2 lb. unpeeled, extra-large raw
     shrimp (16/20 count)
2½ Tbsp. olive oil, divided
6 (12-inch) metal skewers
2 tsp. Cajun seasoning
1 (12-oz.) package romaine
     lettuce hearts
1 (12-oz.) French bread baguette
3 Tbsp. butter, melted
1 garlic clove, minced
3 tomatoes, cored and cut into
     wedges
⅓ small red onion, thinly sliced
     Rémoulade Dressing

1. Peel shrimp; devein, if desired. Toss shrimp with 1 Tbsp. olive oil in a medium bowl. Thread shrimp on skewers, and sprinkle both sides with Cajun seasoning.

2. Cut romaine lettuce hearts in half lengthwise. Brush cut sides of hearts with remaining 1½ Tbsp. olive oil.
3. Preheat oven to 375°. Cut baguette into 18 (½-inch-thick) slices; place on a baking sheet. Stir together butter and garlic. Brush 1 side of bread with butter mixture. Bake 8 to 10 minutes or until golden.
4. Meanwhile, preheat grill to 350° to 400° (medium-high) heat. Grill shrimp, covered with grill lid, 3 to 4 minutes on each side or just until shrimp turn pink. Remove shrimp, and cover with aluminum foil to keep warm. Place romaine, cut sides down, on cooking grate of grill. Grill, covered with grill lid, 2 to 3 minutes or until just wilted and grill marks appear.
5. Place 1 grilled romaine heart half on each of 6 plates. Top with tomato wedges, onion, and shrimp. Drizzle with Rémoulade Dressing. Serve with toasted French bread slices.
NOTE: We tested with Walker & Sons "Slap Ya Mama" Cajun Seasoning.

Rémoulade Dressing

MAKES: 1½ cups
HANDS-ON TIME: 5 min.
TOTAL TIME: 35 min.

1 cup mayonnaise
⅓ cup milk
¼ cup sliced green onions
2 Tbsp. Creole mustard
2 tsp. lemon zest
2 tsp. lemon juice
½ tsp. ground red pepper

1. Whisk together all ingredients. Cover and chill 30 minutes before serving. Store in an airtight container in refrigerator up to 3 days.

Lightly Southern Fried

How do you get crispy crab cakes minus all the grease? Follow this irresistible recipe and you're golden!

Cornbread Crab Cakes

good for you

MAKES: 16 cakes
HANDS-ON TIME: 45 min.
TOTAL TIME: 2 hr., 40 min., including cornbread

Only 224 calories! Enjoy a guilt-free serving of these hearty cakes and a rich dollop of sauce. Add fresh greens to your plate for extra goodness.

- 1 (8-oz.) container reduced-fat sour cream
- 2 Tbsp. chopped pickled jalapeño pepper slices
- 2 Tbsp. chopped fresh cilantro
- ⅔ cup finely diced red bell pepper
- ½ cup sliced green onions
- 2 tsp. olive oil
- 1 garlic clove, minced
- ⅓ cup reduced-fat mayonnaise
- ¼ cup chopped fresh parsley
- 2 large eggs, lightly beaten
- 1 tsp. hot sauce
- 1 tsp. Old Bay seasoning
- 1 tsp. lemon zest
- 2 cups Light Cornbread crumbs
- 1 lb. fresh lump crabmeat
  Vegetable cooking spray

1. Stir together first 3 ingredients. Cover and chill up to 3 days.
2. Sauté bell pepper and onions in hot oil in a small nonstick skillet over medium-high heat 1 minute; add garlic, and sauté 1 minute. Remove from heat; cool 15 minutes.

Cornbread Crab Cakes

3. Combine bell pepper mixture, mayonnaise, and next 5 ingredients in a large bowl. Fold in cornbread and crabmeat. Shape mixture into 16 (2½-inch) cakes (about ¼ cup each); place on a lightly greased baking sheet. Cover loosely with plastic wrap, and chill 1 hour.
4. Lightly coat cakes with cooking spray. Cook crab cakes, in batches, in a large nonstick skillet or on a griddle over medium heat 3 to 4 minutes on each side or until lightly browned. Serve immediately with cilantro-jalapeño sour cream.

PER CAKE (INCLUDING 1 TBSP. CILANTRO-JALAPEÑO SOUR CREAM): CALORIES 112; FAT 6.1G (SAT 1.8G, MONO 1.2G, POLY 1.3G); PROTEIN 6.8G; CARB 8.1G; FIBER 0.7G; CHOL 64MG; IRON 0.8MG; SODIUM 357MG; CALC 78MG

3 Reasons To Indulge!

{1}

FRESH CRABMEAT
offers high-quality protein with minimal saturated fat. It's also a good source of calcium and other minerals.

{2}

OIL-FREE FRYING
still leads to a crispy golden texture. All you need? Vegetable cooking spray and a nonstick skillet.

{3}

REDUCED-FAT MAYO
adds just enough heart-healthy fat, leaving a moist bite on the inside.

Light Cornbread

quick prep • good for you • party perfect

MAKES: 10 servings
HANDS-ON TIME: 10 min.
TOTAL TIME: 35 min.

1. Preheat oven to 425°. Add 2 tsp. vegetable oil to a 10-inch cast-iron skillet; heat in oven 5 minutes. Stir together 2 cups self-rising white cornmeal mix and 2 Tbsp. sugar in a large bowl. Add 2 cups nonfat buttermilk; 1 large egg, lightly beaten; and ¼ cup vegetable oil, stirring just until blended. Pour batter into hot skillet. Bake 20 to 22 minutes or until golden and cornbread pulls away from sides.

PER SERVING: CALORIES 172; FAT 7.9G (SAT 1.2G, MONO 1.8G, POLY 4.7G); PROTEIN 4.5G; CARB 22.5G; FIBER 1.6G; CHOL 22MG; IRON 1.5MG; SODIUM 359MG; CALC 151MG

Recipe for Refreshment

Huntsville chef Jimmy Boyce shares deliciously quenching new riffs on iced teas and lemonades.

August in Alabama is hot as the hinges of you-know-where, and about all you can do to beat the scorching heat is either (a) stay inside and blast the air-conditioning or (b) sip on something refreshing. Chef James "Jimmy" Boyce delivers on the latter thanks to a tasty selection of inspired iced tea-and-lemonade concoctions at his Cotton Row Restaurant (one of four Boyce-owned restaurants in the area, including Commerce Kitchen, Pane e Vino Pizzeria, and the newly opened James Steakhouse). But sipper beware: This isn't your mama's lemonade. In addition to ingredients such as house-made peach syrup and fresh watermelon, you'll find pomegranate vodka, peach schnapps, and bourbon.

The drinks are so delicious that parched Huntsvillians have been lining up for them ever since the James Beard Award-nominated chef opened Cotton Row Restaurant three years ago. He dreams up the cool concoctions, and bartender Chase Shelton muddles, layers, and mixes the ingredients until they meet Jimmy's standards. "It's an adventurous menu, and you have to work hard to implement it," Jimmy says. Here's a sample of a lemonade concoction, as well as a recipe inspired by Jimmy's creations to enjoy, just in case you can't make it to Huntsville.

Meet the Chef

Chef Jimmy Boyce at the bar at Cotton Row

TRY THIS AT HOME!

Blueberry Lemonade

MAKES: 1 serving
HANDS-ON TIME: 15 min.
TOTAL TIME: 45 min.

1. Cook ½ cup sugar and ½ cup water in a small saucepan over medium heat, stirring occasionally, 5 minutes or until sugar is melted. Cool 30 minutes. Stir together 2 Tbsp. cooled syrup, 2 Tbsp. fresh lemon juice, and 2 Tbsp. water in a 12-oz. glass. Add ice to fill. Add ¼ cup blueberry vodka. Smash 1 Tbsp. fresh blueberries and 1 tsp. syrup together in a small bowl. Press mixture through a fine wire-mesh strainer into a bowl, using back of a spoon to squeeze out juice. Discard pulp. Spoon blueberry mixture into glass. Garnish with fresh blueberries and lemon zest, if desired.
NOTE: We tested with Stolichnaya Stoli Blueberi vodka.

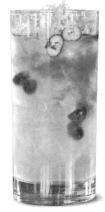

IN SEASON

Okra

Southerners' devotion to okra—whether it's pickled, fried, or stewed with homegrown tomatoes—runs deep. Delta State University in Cleveland, Mississippi, has even dubbed "The Fighting Okra" the unofficial mascot. Here are two of our favorite ways to enjoy this end-of-summer favorite—they're anything but medi-okra!

MAKE IT!

Nutty Okra

quick prep

MAKES: 4 servings
HANDS-ON TIME: 22min.
TOTAL TIME: 42 min.

Pulse the peanuts in a food processor for easy chopping.

- 1 lb. fresh okra, cut into ½-inch pieces*
- 1 tsp. salt
- 1 egg white, lightly beaten
- 1 cup all-purpose baking mix
- ½ cup finely chopped salted dry-roasted peanuts
- ½ tsp. pepper
  Peanut oil

1. Toss okra with salt, and let stand 20 minutes. Add egg white, stirring to coat. Stir together baking mix and next 2 ingredients in a large bowl. Add okra, tossing to coat; gently press peanut mixture onto okra, shaking off excess.
2. Pour oil to a depth of 2 inches into a Dutch oven or cast-iron skillet; heat to 375°. Fry okra, in batches, 2 to 4 minutes or until golden; drain on paper towels.
*1 (16-oz.) package frozen cut okra, thawed, may be substituted.

GIVE IT!

Wickles Wicked Okra

Pick up a jar of Wickles Wicked Okra (made in Dadeville, Alabama) for the picnic-loving pal. This sweet-and-spicy pickled okra is just right next to a plate of barbecue or on the rim of a Bloody Mary; $5. *simsfoods.com*

Find 10 of our best okra recipes: *southernliving.com/okra*

Tomato Pie

From the kitchens of
Libbo McCollum and
Elizabeth Goodwyn. See
this month's adorable duo's
takes on a summer favorite.

Tomato Pie

party perfect

MAKES: 6 servings
HANDS-ON TIME: 15 min.
TOTAL TIME: 2 hr., 15 min., including pastry

   Sour Cream Pastry
 4 **medium tomatoes, peeled and
   cut into ½-inch-thick slices
   (about 1½ lb.)**
 ½ **tsp. salt**
 ½ **cup mayonnaise**
 3 **green onions, chopped**
 2 **Tbsp. chopped fresh basil**
 1 **cup (4 oz.) shredded
   Parmesan cheese, divided
   Garnish: fresh basil**

1. Preheat oven to 350°. Prepare Sour
Cream Pastry.
2. Meanwhile, place tomatoes in a single
layer on paper towels; sprinkle with salt.
Let stand 30 minutes. Pat dry with paper
towels. Stir together next 3 ingredients
and ¾ cup cheese.
3. Roll Sour Cream Pastry into a 13-inch
circle on a lightly floured surface. Fit
into a 9-inch pie plate; fold edges under,
and crimp.
4. Bake at 350° for 10 to 12 minutes or
until lightly brown. Remove from oven,
and sprinkle remaining ¼ cup cheese over
bottom of crust. Arrange tomato slices
over cheese in crust; spread mayonnaise
mixture over tomatoes.
5. Bake at 350° for 34 to 37 minutes.
Let cool 5 minutes before serving. Garnish,
if desired.

Tomato Pie

Meet Mom!

Lives in Jasper, AL; loves golf, fishing,
happy hour, and Led Zeppelin; is
part of a Hamburger Club that rates
local burgers; thinks Apalachicola is
one of the loveliest places on Earth.

Herbed Tomato Tart

Herbed Tomato Tart

party perfect

MAKES: 6 servings
HANDS-ON TIME: 25 min.
TOTAL TIME: 1 hr., 10 min.

We used basil, dill, thyme, and parsley, but just about any combination of herbs that pair well with tomatoes—such as oregano and tarragon—would work.

- **2 medium tomatoes, thinly sliced (about ¾ lb.)**
- **½ pt. assorted small tomatoes, halved**
- **¾ tsp. salt, divided**
- **1 (17.3-oz.) package frozen puff pastry sheets, thawed**
- **1 (8-oz.) package shredded mozzarella cheese**
- **1 (4-oz.) package crumbled feta cheese**
- **¼ cup finely chopped chives**
- **1 garlic clove, minced**
- **¼ cup finely chopped assorted fresh herbs**
- **1 Tbsp. olive oil**

1. Preheat oven to 400°. Place tomatoes in a single layer on paper towels; sprinkle with ½ tsp. salt. Let stand 30 minutes. Pat dry with paper towels.

2. Meanwhile, roll 1 pastry sheet into a 14-inch square on a lightly floured surface; place on an ungreased baking sheet. Cut 4 (12- x 1-inch) strips from remaining pastry sheet, and place strips along outer edges of pastry square, forming a border. Reserve remaining pastry for another use.

3. Bake at 400° for 14 minutes or until browned.

4. Sprinkle pastry with mozzarella cheese and next 3 ingredients. Top with tomatoes in a single layer. Sprinkle tomatoes with herbs and remaining ¼ tsp. salt; drizzle with oil.

5. Bake at 400° for 14 to 15 minutes or until cheese melts. Serve immediately.

Sour Cream Pastry

MAKES: enough dough for 1 (9-inch) piecrust
HANDS-ON TIME: 10 min.
TOTAL TIME: 1 hr., 10 min.

- **1¼ cups all-purpose flour**
- **2 tsp. baking powder**
- **½ tsp. salt**
- **½ cup shortening**
- **½ cup sour cream**

1. Stir together first 3 ingredients in a bowl. Cut shortening into flour mixture with a pastry blender until mixture resembles small peas. Add sour cream; stir with a fork until combined. Gently gather dough into a flat disk; wrap in plastic wrap, and chill 1 to 24 hours.

Meet Daughter!

A Birmingham newlywed who loves English period pieces, frozen (!) boiled peanuts, and Bama sports; was once attacked by a mockingbird while carrying a tomato pie (really!)

Easy Preserves

Spread the word: This fruity goodness cooks in minutes in the microwave. (We'll toast to that!)

Stone Fruit Preserves

make-ahead

MAKES: about 3 cups
HANDS-ON TIME: 10 min.
TOTAL TIME: 2 hr., 26 min.

4½ cups peeled and diced peaches
    (about 2½ lb.)*
1½ cups sugar
3   Tbsp. fresh lemon juice
1   (1.75-oz.) package powdered
    fruit pectin

1. Stir together all ingredients in a 4-qt. microwave-safe glass bowl.
2. Microwave at HIGH 8 minutes (mixture will boil). Stir mixture, and microwave at HIGH 8 to 10 minutes or until thickened. (You're going for the viscosity of pancake syrup here. The mixture will thicken to soft-set preserves after it cools and chills.) Cool mixture completely (about 2 hours). Serve immediately, or cover and chill preserves in an airtight container until ready to serve. Store in refrigerator up to 3 weeks.
*Unpeeled plums or nectarines may be substituted.

Make It Snappy

Kilner wire-bale canning jars are ideal for storing small-batch refrigerator preserves ($2.79-$3.99; canningpantry.com). Or you can simply recycle empty condiment and jelly jars—one quick run through the dishwasher and they're ready to fill and chill.

Test Kitchen Notebook

SET FOR SUCCESS

Sugar and lemon juice combine with fruit pectin to thicken Stone Fruit Preserves as they cook. When the fruit is overly ripe and juicy, or you add a different type of fruit (as we did in the Tomato-Peach Preserves), the mixture may take longer to thicken to a syrup-like consistency. Simply continue to cook at HIGH power, and check the consistency at 1-minute intervals.

Signature Creations

Spiked with fiery-hot jalapeño peppers, plum tomatoes and rosemary, or a splash of balsamic vinegar and basil, the basic recipe for Stone Fruit Preserves takes on a whole new dimension of sweet and spicy summer flavors.

BALSAMIC-PLUM PRESERVES: Substitute balsamic vinegar for lemon juice and unpeeled plums for peaches. Stir 1 Tbsp. chopped fresh basil into warm preserves. **TRY IT WITH:** Smoked turkey, pulled pork, fried green tomatoes, or warm baked brie.

NECTARINE-GINGER PRESERVES: Substitute unpeeled nectarines for peaches. Stir ⅓ cup minced crystallized ginger into nectarine mixture in Step 1. **TRY IT WITH:** Sweet potato biscuits, blueberry pancakes, or praline ice cream.

PEACH-PEPPER PRESERVES: Substitute fresh lime juice for lemon juice. Stir 1 minced jalapeño pepper and ½ red bell pepper, finely chopped, into peach mixture in Step 1. **TRY IT WITH:** Coconut fried shrimp, chicken quesadillas, or ham and fontina panini.

TOMATO-PEACH PRESERVES: Reduce peaches to 2¼ cups. Stir 2¼ cups seeded and diced plum tomatoes into peach mixture in Step 1. Increase second microwave time to 12 to 16 minutes or until thickened. Stir 1½ tsp. minced fresh rosemary and ½ tsp. freshly ground pepper into warm preserves. **TRY IT WITH:** Goat cheese crostini, grilled flank steak, or turkey burgers.

September

CHEF SHOWDOWN

Lowcountry Style

Three chefs. Five key ingredients. One killer location. We took the South's culinary superstars and challenged each to create a three-course harvest feast at the oh-so-Southern Inn at Palmetto Bluff. The result? Nothing short of spectacular.

Food lovers love Charleston. The persistent reliance on local farmers and fishermen, a profound respect for seasonality, and an ingenious appreciation for tradition make for showstopping meals. Recently, this honest, homespun approach to great food has garnered national attention. The James Beard Foundation Awards (the Oscars of the food world) named Charleston chefs the top toques in the Southeast three

years in a row: Robert Stehling of Hominy Grill (2008), Mike Lata of FIG (2009), and Sean Brock of McCrady's (2010; he has since opened Husk, a semifinalist for Best New Restaurant 2011). We took them out of their kitchens to the Inn at Palmetto Bluff, gave them five key ingredients—peaches, rice, pork belly, okra, and shrimp—and challenged them to go head-to-head and celebrate the bounty with a harvest feast. It's clear that we're the winners here.

Roasted Pork Belly with Late-Harvest Peaches and Arugula

party perfect

MAKES: 8 servings
HANDS-ON TIME: 30 min.
TOTAL TIME: 4 hr., 10 min.

- 1 (3 ½- to 4-lb.) pork belly*
- 1 Tbsp. kosher salt
- 2 tsp. freshly ground pepper
- 1 large sweet onion, chopped
- 2 celery ribs, chopped
- 5 garlic cloves, crushed
- 6 fresh thyme sprigs
- 1 Tbsp. extra virgin olive oil
- 4 to 6 peaches, peeled and cut into 6 wedges each
- 2 Tbsp. sherry vinegar
- 2 Tbsp. honey
- 1 tsp. chopped fresh thyme
- 4 cups loosely packed arugula

1. Preheat oven to 300°. Make ¼-inch-deep cuts in fattiest side of pork. Rub pork with kosher salt and freshly ground pepper. Arrange onion and next 3 ingredients in a large roasting pan; drizzle with oil, stirring to coat. Place pork, fattiest side up, on vegetables in pan.
2. Bake at 300° for 3½ to 4 hours or until tender. Let stand 10 minutes. Remove pork from pan, reserving 1 Tbsp. drippings. Discard remaining drippings and vegetables.
3. Cook pork in a 12-inch cast-iron skillet over medium heat 3 to 5 minutes on each side or until browned and crisp.
4. Stir together peaches and next 3 ingredients. Heat reserved 1 Tbsp. drippings in a large skillet over medium heat. Cook peach mixture in hot drippings, stirring often, 3 to 5 minutes or until thoroughly heated. Season with additional salt and pepper to taste. Slice pork, and serve with warm peaches and arugula.
*See "Pantry Key" throughout for unfamiliar ingredients.

Mike Lata, FIG

A soulful chef who treats "seasonal" as a mandate and makes "simple" an art form; James Beard Foundation Award Winner, 2009

Skillet-Roasted Okra and Shrimp

Lemony Rice Pudding with Figs and Saba

make-ahead • party perfect

MAKES: 10 servings
HANDS-ON TIME: 10 min.
TOTAL TIME: 10 hr., 10 min.

- 1 cup uncooked long-grain rice
- 1 Tbsp. powdered sugar
- 7 cups milk
- ¾ cup granulated sugar
- 1 Tbsp. lemon zest
- ½ tsp. salt
- 1 vanilla bean, split
- 1 pt. fresh figs, quartered
  Saba

1. Bring 4 cups water to a boil in a large saucepan. Stir in first 2 ingredients, and cook, stirring occasionally, 5 minutes; drain.
2. Return rice to saucepan; stir in milk and next 4 ingredients. Bring to a boil over medium-high heat; reduce heat to low, and simmer, stirring occasionally, 45 minutes or until thick. Remove vanilla bean. Remove from heat, and transfer to a glass bowl. Let stand 1 hour, stirring occasionally. Cover and chill 8 hours.
3. Spoon into serving dishes; top each with figs and a drizzle of saba.
NOTE: We tested with Carolina Plantation Rice (carolinaplantation rice.com) and Zingerman's Saba Balsamic Syrup (zingermans.com).

Skillet-Roasted Okra and Shrimp

quick prep • party perfect

MAKES: 6 servings
HANDS-ON TIME: 30 min.
TOTAL TIME: 30 min.

- 1 lb. unpeeled, large raw shrimp (31/35 count)
- 3 cups (about 8 oz.) fresh okra, cut in half lengthwise
- 3 Tbsp. olive oil, divided
- 1 pt. heirloom cherry tomatoes
- 3 large garlic cloves, thinly sliced
- ½ tsp. dried crushed red pepper
  Garnish: thinly sliced okra blossoms

1. Peel shrimp; devein, if desired.
2. Sauté okra in 1 Tbsp. hot oil in a large cast-iron skillet over medium-high heat 4 to 5 minutes or until browned. Transfer to a bowl.
3. Cook tomatoes in 1 Tbsp. hot oil in skillet over medium-high heat, stirring occasionally, 2 to 3 minutes or until skins are charred. Place in bowl with okra.
4. Sauté shrimp, garlic, and dried crushed red pepper in remaining 1 Tbsp. hot oil in skillet over medium-high heat 2 to 3 minutes or just until shrimp turn pink. Stir in okra and tomatoes. Add salt and pepper to taste; cook 1 to 2 minutes or until thoroughly heated. Garnish, if desired.

Pantry Key

PORK BELLY: This new chef fave has nothing to do with the digestive tract—it's uncured bacon. Order it from your butcher or cawcawcreek.com.

SABA: An ancient sweetener traditionally made from grape juice.

Sean Brock, McCrady's and Husk

The reigning king of "local," with an affinity for pork and heirloom crops (benne seed, farro); James Beard Foundation Award Winner, 2010

Caw Caw Creek Pork Belly

make-ahead • party perfect

MAKES: 6 to 8 servings
HANDS-ON TIME: 1 hr.
TOTAL TIME: 8 hr., 45 min., including farro and chanterelles, plus 36 hr., 30 min. for chilling

- 5 Tbsp. kosher salt
- 1 Tbsp. dark brown sugar
- 1 (3 ½-lb.) pork belly
- 1 tsp. table salt
- ¼ tsp. pepper
- 1 Tbsp. canola oil
  Parchment paper
  Herbed Farro
  Sautéed Chanterelles

1. Combine first 2 ingredients in a Dutch oven; add 2 cups water. Cook over medium heat, stirring occasionally, 2 minutes or until salt and sugar are dissolved. Add 1 cup water, and pour mixture into a 13- x 9-inch baking dish; cover and chill 30 minutes. Add pork belly, fat side up; cover and chill 24 hours.
2. Remove pork from salt-water mixture; discard salt-water mixture, and rinse pork under cold water. Pat dry with paper towels. Sprinkle with 1 tsp. table salt and ¼ tsp. pepper.

Pantry Key

FARRO: A deliciously chewy whole grain that's high in protein and has a bold, nutty flavor; a great alternate for anyone who loves barley.

3. Preheat oven to 275°. Cook pork in hot oil in a large ovenproof skillet over medium-high heat 5 minutes on each side or until browned. Remove from heat, and cover.
4. Bake at 275° for 6 hours or until fork-tender. Remove from oven, and cool completely (about 45 minutes). Place parchment paper over pork; top with a large heavy skillet, and press down on pork. Chill 12 hours (with skillet on top).
5. Cut pork into ½-inch slices. Cook pork in a large cast-iron skillet over medium-high heat 3 to 5 minutes on each side or until crisp.
6. Serve over Herbed Farro with Sautéed Chanterelles.

Herbed Farro

quick prep • party perfect

MAKES: 4 to 6 servings
HANDS-ON TIME: 40 min.
TOTAL TIME: 40 min.

- 1 (1-oz.) package fresh chervil*
- 2 cups loosely packed fresh flat-leaf parsley leaves
- 2 Tbsp. salt
- 4 cups chicken broth
- 1 cup finely chopped onion
- 1 Tbsp. canola oil
- 1 garlic clove, minced
- 1½ cups uncooked farro

1. Remove leaves from chervil. Cook chervil, parsley, and salt in boiling water to cover in a small saucepan 45 seconds; drain. Plunge into ice water to stop the cooking process; drain. Process herbs and 1 cup water in a blender until smooth. Pour through a fine wire-mesh strainer into a bowl. Discard liquid.
2. Microwave chicken broth in a microwave-safe bowl at HIGH 5 minutes or until warm.
3. Meanwhile, sauté onion in hot oil in a Dutch oven over medium-high heat 5 to 6 minutes or until softened. Add garlic, and cook 1 minute. Add farro, and sauté 1 minute. Reduce heat to medium; add ½ cup hot broth, and cook, stirring constantly, until liquid is absorbed. Repeat procedure with remaining broth, ½ cup at a time, stirring constantly, until liquid is absorbed. Stir in ¼ cup herb puree; reserve remaining puree for another use. Season with pepper to taste.
*1 (1-oz.) package fresh tarragon may be substituted.

Sautéed Chanterelles

Sautéed Chanterelles

quick prep • party perfect

1. Melt 1 Tbsp. butter in a large skillet; add 2 cups fresh chanterelle mushrooms*; sauté over medium-high heat 15 minutes or until lightly browned. Stir in 1 tsp. red wine vinegar. Season with salt and pepper to taste.
*Baby portobello mushrooms may be substituted.

Lowcountry Shrimp-and-Okra Pilau

party perfect

MAKES: 4 servings
HANDS-ON TIME: 50 min.
TOTAL TIME: I hr., 25 min.

Sean serves this stew over buttered Carolina Gold Rice cooked in stock made from leftover shrimp shells. (Pictured on page 14)

- I **lb. unpeeled, large raw shrimp (31/35 count)**
- I **cup diced smoked sausage**
- 2 **Tbsp. butter**
- I **cup diced sweet onion**
- I **garlic clove, chopped**
- ½ **cup diced celery**
- 4 **large plum tomatoes, peeled, seeded, and chopped (about 1¼ lb.)**
- 2 **cups chicken or shrimp broth**
- I **cup sliced fresh okra**
- 3 **Tbsp. chopped fresh parsley**
- I **Tbsp. fresh lemon juice**
- I **tsp. dried crushed red pepper**
- 2 **tsp. hot sauce**
- I **tsp. Worcestershire sauce**
  Hot cooked rice
- 3 **green onions, thinly sliced**
  Garnish: grilled halved okra

1. Peel shrimp; devein, if desired.
2. Cook sausage in a large Dutch oven over medium-low heat, stirring often, 5 minutes or until golden brown. Remove sausage, reserving drippings in Dutch oven. Melt butter in drippings. Stir in onion and garlic, and sauté 3 minutes or until tender. Add celery, and cook 2 minutes. Stir in tomatoes and chicken broth; bring to a boil. Reduce heat to low, and simmer 30 minutes.
3. Stir in shrimp, sausage, and okra; cook 5 minutes. Stir in parsley and next 4 ingredients. Season with salt and pepper to taste. Serve over hot cooked rice; top with green onions. Garnish, if desired.
NOTE: We tested with Conecuh Hickory Smoked Sausage.

Lowcountry Shrimp-and-Okra Pilau

Pantry Key

BENNE SEED: The Lowcountry cousin to the sesame seed, brought to the South from West Africa; used throughout the Sea Islands in desserts and breads.

BENNECAKE FLOUR: Benne seeds stone-milled into flour. Order from Anson Mills (ansonmills.com), which specializes in heirloom grains.

Benne Seed-Topped Peach Tart

party perfect

MAKES: 10 to 12 servings
HANDS-ON TIME: 45 min.
TOTAL TIME: 2 hr., 20 min.

Sean loves pairing this tart with a buttermilk custard.

- ½ **cup butter, softened**
- 1⅓ **cups sugar**
- 3 **large eggs**
- I **cup all-purpose flour**
- ½ **cup bennecake flour**
- ½ **tsp. salt**
- ⅛ **tsp. baking soda**
- ½ **cup sour cream**
- ½ **tsp. vanilla extract**
- 5½ **to 6 lb. fresh peaches, peeled and sliced (12 cups)**
- 2 **tsp. benne (sesame) seeds**

1. Preheat oven to 350°. Beat butter at medium speed with an electric mixer until creamy. Gradually add sugar, beating well. Add eggs, I at a time, beating until blended after each addition.
2. Sift together flours, salt, and baking soda. Add flour mixture to butter mixture alternately with sour cream, beginning and ending with flour mixture. Beat at low speed until blended after each addition. Stir in vanilla.
3. Place peach slices in a lightly greased 12-inch cast-iron skillet; pour batter over peaches. Sprinkle with benne seeds.
4. Bake at 350° for I hour and 25 minutes to I hour and 35 minutes or until a wooden pick inserted in center comes out clean; let stand 10 minutes before serving.

Okra-Shrimp Beignets

quick prep • party perfect

MAKES: about 30
HANDS-ON TIME: 27 min.
TOTAL TIME: 47 min., including salsa and sour cream
(Pictured page 15)

    Peanut oil
2 **cups sliced fresh okra**
½ **green bell pepper, diced**
½ **medium onion, diced**
1 **large egg**
½ **cup all-purpose flour**
¼ **cup heavy cream**
1 **jalapeño pepper, finely chopped**
¾ **tsp. salt**
¼ **tsp. freshly ground pepper**
¼ **lb. unpeeled, medium-size raw shrimp (31/35 count), peeled and coarsely chopped**
    Fresh Tomato Salsa
    Cilantro Sour Cream

1. Pour oil to depth of 3 inches into a Dutch oven; heat to 350°.
2. Stir together okra and next 8 ingredients in a large bowl until well blended; stir in shrimp.

3. Drop batter by rounded tablespoonfuls into hot oil, and fry, in batches, 2 to 3 minutes on each side or until golden brown. Drain on a wire rack over paper towels. Serve with salsa and sour cream.

Fresh Tomato Salsa

1. Stir together 4 large plum tomatoes, seeded and chopped (about 2 cups); ¼ cup chopped fresh cilantro; 1 jalapeño pepper, seeded and finely diced; 3 Tbsp. finely diced red onion; 2½ Tbsp. fresh lime juice; 1 Tbsp. extra virgin olive oil; and salt and pepper to taste.

Cilantro Sour Cream

1. Stir together 1 (8-oz.) container sour cream, ¼ cup finely chopped fresh cilantro, 1 tsp. lime zest, 1 tsp. fresh lime juice, and salt and pepper to taste.

Robert Stehling, Hominy Grill

The trailblazer who re-imagined Lowcountry fare and put it on the national map; James Beard Foundation Award Winner, 2008

Red Rice

party perfect

MAKES: 8 servings
HANDS-ON TIME: 45 min.
TOTAL TIME: 1 hr., 45 min.

3 **bacon slices, diced**
1 **cup cubed, cooked ham**
½ **lb. smoked sausage, sliced**
¼ **lb. ground Italian sausage**
2 **cups diced onion**
1 **cup diced celery**
1 **cup diced green bell pepper**
1 **cup diced red bell pepper**
1½ **tsp. salt, divided**
1 **Tbsp. minced garlic**
1 **cup peeled and diced eggplant**
2 **cups uncooked long-grain rice**
2 **Tbsp. peanut oil, divided**
2 **cups sliced fresh okra**
½ **cup dry red wine**
2 **cups chicken broth**
1 **(14.5-oz.) can tomato puree**
2 **bay leaves**
½ **tsp. dried basil**
½ **tsp. dried thyme**
½ **tsp. freshly ground black pepper**
    Hot sauce

1. Preheat oven to 375°. Cook bacon in a large skillet over medium-high heat 8 minutes or until crisp. Remove bacon, and drain on paper towels, reserving 1 Tbsp. drippings in skillet.
2. Sauté ham and next 2 ingredients in hot drippings until well browned. Remove ham mixture, reserving 1 Tbsp. drippings in skillet. Sauté onion, next 3 ingredients, and ½ tsp. salt in drippings 5 to 8 minutes or until tender. Stir in garlic. Cook 2 minutes; stir in eggplant. Cook 5 minutes or until tender. Spoon mixture into a 13- x 9-inch baking dish.

Okra-Shrimp Beignets

3. Cook rice in 1 Tbsp. hot oil in skillet, stirring often, 2 to 3 minutes or until fragrant and golden. Spoon rice over onion mixture in dish; top with ham mixture and bacon.

4. Sauté okra in remaining 1 Tbsp. hot oil in skillet over medium-high heat 5 minutes or until lightly browned. Add wine, and cook 3 to 4 minutes or until liquid evaporates. Stir in broth, next 5 ingredients, and remaining 1 tsp. salt; bring to a boil. Pour okra mixture over meat, and cover dish tightly with aluminum foil.

5. Bake at 375° for 1 hour or until rice is tender. Remove and discard bay leaves. Serve with hot sauce.

Crispy Roasted Pork Belly

party perfect

MAKES: 4 servings
HANDS-ON TIME: 31 min.
TOTAL TIME: 3 hr., 46 min.

- 1 (1¾-lb.) pork belly
- 1 tsp. salt
- ½ tsp. pepper
- 1 large onion, cut into wedges
- 2 celery ribs, coarsely chopped
- 2 carrots, coarsely chopped
- 4 garlic cloves, crushed
- 6 fresh thyme sprigs
- 2 bay leaves
- ½ cup chicken broth

1. Preheat oven to 325°. Make ¼-inch-deep cuts in fattiest side of pork. Sprinkle pork with salt and pepper. Place in a large roasting pan. Place onion and next 5 ingredients around pork. Pour broth in pan, and cover tightly with aluminum foil.

2. Bake at 325° for 3 to 3½ hours or until fork-tender. Remove pork from pan, and let stand 15 minutes. Discard vegetables and liquid in pan.

3. Cook pork in a large cast-iron skillet over medium-low heat 8 to 10 minutes on each side or until browned and crisp.

Buttermilk Peach Pudding

Buttermilk Peach Pudding

party perfect

MAKES: 8 to 10 servings
HANDS-ON TIME: 15 min.
TOTAL TIME: 1 hr., 5 min.

- 1½ cups all-purpose flour
- 1 tsp. baking soda
- 1 tsp. baking powder
- 1 tsp. ground cinnamon
- ½ tsp. salt
- ½ tsp. freshly grated nutmeg
- ½ tsp. ground ginger
- 3½ peaches, peeled and coarsely chopped (about 1½ lb.)
- 1 cup buttermilk
- ½ cup butter, softened
- 1½ cups sugar
- 3 large eggs
- 2 ripe peaches, peeled and sliced (about 1 lb.)
  Vanilla ice cream

1. Preheat oven to 350°. Sift together first 7 ingredients; sift again.

2. Process chopped peaches in a food processor or blender until smooth. (Yield should be 2 cups puree.) Stir in buttermilk.

3. Beat butter and sugar at high speed with a heavy-duty electric stand mixer until fluffy. Add eggs, 1 at a time, beating until blended after each addition. Add peach mixture, and beat until well blended.

4. Layer sliced peaches in a greased 13- x 9-inch pan.

5. Fold flour mixture into butter mixture. Pour batter over sliced peaches in pan. Place pan in a large roasting pan, and add boiling water to roasting pan to a depth of 1 inch.

6. Bake at 350° for 50 minutes or until set. (Pudding will still be moist.) Serve warm or cold with ice cream.

Sweet Temptations

Sinfully delicious? Nah. These fresh apple desserts are good to the core. No repentance required.

Apple-Cream Cheese Bundt Cake

make-ahead • party perfect

MAKES: 12 servings
HANDS-ON TIME: 40 min.
TOTAL TIME: 4 hr., 10 min.

Garnish the frosting with extra toasted pecans. (Pictured on page 16)

CREAM CHEESE FILLING:

- 1 (8-oz.) package cream cheese, softened
- ¼ cup butter, softened
- ½ cup granulated sugar
- 1 large egg
- 2 Tbsp. all-purpose flour
- 1 tsp. vanilla extract

APPLE CAKE BATTER:

- 1 cup finely chopped pecans
- 3 cups all-purpose flour
- 1 cup granulated sugar
- 1 cup firmly packed light brown sugar
- 2 tsp. ground cinnamon
- 1 tsp. salt
- 1 tsp. baking soda
- 1 tsp. ground nutmeg
- ½ tsp. ground allspice
- 3 large eggs, lightly beaten
- ¾ cup canola oil
- ¾ cup applesauce
- 1 tsp. vanilla extract
- 3 cups peeled and finely chopped Gala apples (about 1½ lb.)

PRALINE FROSTING:

- ½ cup firmly packed light brown sugar
- ¼ cup butter
- 3 Tbsp. milk
- 1 tsp. vanilla extract
- 1 cup powdered sugar

1. Prepare Filling: Beat first 3 ingredients at medium speed with an electric mixer until blended and smooth. Add egg, flour, and vanilla; beat just until blended.

2. Prepare Batter: Preheat oven to 350°. Bake pecans in a shallow pan 8 to 10 minutes or until toasted and fragrant, stirring halfway through. Stir together 3 cups flour and next 7 ingredients in a large bowl; stir in eggs and next 3 ingredients, stirring just until dry ingredients are moistened. Stir in apples and pecans.

3. Spoon two-thirds of apple mixture into a greased and floured 14-cup Bundt pan. Spoon Cream Cheese Filling over apple mixture, leaving a 1-inch border around edges of pan. Swirl filling through apple mixture using a paring knife. Spoon remaining apple mixture over Cream Cheese Filling.

4. Bake at 350° for 1 hour to 1 hour and 15 minutes or until a long wooden pick inserted in center comes out clean. Cool cake in pan on a wire rack 15 minutes; remove from pan to wire rack, and cool completely (about 2 hours).

5. Prepare Frosting: Bring ½ cup brown sugar, ¼ cup butter, and 3 Tbsp. milk to a boil in a 2-qt. saucepan over medium heat, whisking constantly; boil 1 minute, whisking constantly. Remove from heat; stir in vanilla. Gradually whisk in powdered sugar until smooth; stir gently 3 to 5 minutes or until mixture begins to cool and thickens slightly. Pour immediately over cooled cake.

ROBERT KINDRED
SEAGOVILLE, TEXAS

Easy Skillet Apple Pie

make-ahead • party perfect

MAKES: 8 to 10 servings
HANDS-ON TIME: 20 min.
TOTAL TIME: 1 hr., 50 min.

- 2 lb. Granny Smith apples
- 2 lb. Braeburn apples
- 1 tsp. ground cinnamon
- ¾ cup granulated sugar
- ½ cup butter
- 1 cup firmly packed light brown sugar
- 1 (14.1-oz.) package refrigerated piecrusts
- 1 egg white
- 2 Tbsp. granulated sugar
  Butter-pecan ice cream

1. Preheat oven to 350°. Peel apples, and cut into ½-inch-thick wedges. Toss apples with cinnamon and ¾ cup granulated sugar.

2. Melt butter in a 10-inch cast-iron skillet over medium heat; add brown sugar, and cook, stirring constantly, 1 to 2 minutes or until sugar is dissolved. Remove from heat, and place 1 piecrust in skillet over brown sugar mixture. Spoon apple mixture over piecrust, and top with remaining piecrust. Whisk egg white until foamy. Brush top of piecrust with egg white; sprinkle with 2 Tbsp. granulated sugar. Cut 4 or 5 slits in top for steam to escape.

3. Bake at 350° for 1 hour to 1 hour and 10 minutes or until golden brown and bubbly, shielding with aluminum foil during last 10 minutes to prevent excessive browning, if necessary. Cool on a wire rack 30 minutes before serving. Serve with butter-pecan ice cream.

MRS. JAMES WRIGHT
CHATTANOOGA, TENNESSEE

Apple Brown Betty

make-ahead • party perfect

MAKES: 6 to 8 servings
HANDS-ON TIME: 20 min.
TOTAL TIME: I hr., 25 min.

    4 cups soft, fresh breadcrumbs
    ⅓ cup butter, melted
    I cup firmly packed brown sugar
   1½ tsp. ground cinnamon
    4 large Granny Smith apples, peeled
       and cut into ¼-inch-thick wedges
    I cup apple cider

1. Preheat oven to 350°. Stir together breadcrumbs and melted butter. Stir together brown sugar and cinnamon.
2. Place half of apple wedges in a lightly greased II- x 7-inch baking dish; sprinkle apples with half of brown sugar mixture and half of breadcrumb mixture. Repeat procedure with remaining apples, brown sugar mixture, and breadcrumb mixture. Pour apple cider over top.
3. Bake at 350° for 55 minutes to I hour or until browned and bubbly. Let stand IO minutes before serving.

Apple Butter-Pecan Ice Cream

MAKES: 8 servings
HANDS-ON TIME: I5 min.
TOTAL TIME: 2 hr., 55 min.

    ½ cup chopped pecans
    I Tbsp. butter
    2 pt. vanilla ice cream, softened
    ½ cup apple butter

1. Heat pecans and butter in a small nonstick skillet over medium-low heat, stirring often, 4 to 5 minutes or until toasted and fragrant. Cool completely (about 40 minutes).
2. Stir pecans into ice cream; swirl apple butter through ice cream using a mixer set on low speed. Freeze until firm (about 2 hours).
NOTE: We tested with Bama Apple Butter and Blue Bell Homemade Vanilla Ice Cream.

Caramel-Apple Cheesecake

Caramel-Apple Cheesecake

make-ahead • party perfect

MAKES: I2 servings
HANDS-ON TIME: 30 min.
TOTAL TIME: I2 hr., 5 min.

   2¾ lb. large Granny Smith apples
       (about 6 apples)
   1⅔ cups firmly packed light brown
       sugar, divided
    I Tbsp. butter
    2 cups cinnamon graham cracker
       crumbs (about I5 whole crackers)
    ½ cup melted butter
    ½ cup finely chopped pecans
    3 (8-oz.) packages cream cheese,
       softened
    2 tsp. vanilla extract
    3 large eggs
    ¼ cup apple jelly
       Sweetened whipped cream

1. Peel apples, and cut into ½-inch-thick wedges. Toss together apples and ⅓ cup brown sugar. Melt I Tbsp. butter in a large skillet over medium-high heat; add apple mixture, and sauté 5 to 6 minutes or until crisp-tender and golden. Cool completely (about 30 minutes).
2. Meanwhile, preheat oven to 350°. Stir together cinnamon graham cracker crumbs and next 2 ingredients in a medium bowl until well blended. Press mixture on bottom and 1½ inches up sides of a 9-inch springform pan. Bake at 350° for IO to I2 minutes or until lightly browned. Remove to a wire rack, and cool crust completely before filling (about 30 minutes).
3. Beat cream cheese, vanilla, and remaining 1⅓ cups brown sugar at medium speed with a heavy-duty electric stand mixer until blended and smooth. Add eggs, I at a time, beating just until blended after each addition. Pour batter into prepared crust. Arrange apples over cream cheese mixture.
4. Bake at 350° for 55 minutes to I hour and 5 minutes or until set. Remove from oven, and gently run a knife around outer edge of cheesecake to loosen from sides of pan. (Do not remove sides of pan.) Cool completely on a wire rack (about 2 hours). Cover and chill 8 to 24 hours.
5. Cook apple jelly and I tsp. water in a small saucepan over medium heat, stirring constantly, 2 to 3 minutes or until jelly is melted; brush over apples on top of cheesecake. Serve with whipped cream.

Mocha-Apple Cake
with Browned
Butter Frosting

From Caramel Apple Muffins to Pecan Pie Cobbler, find 25 more irresistible apple recipes at *southernliving.com/apples*

Mocha-Apple Bundt Cake: Omit Browned Butter Frosting. Prepare batter as directed; spoon into a greased and floured 12-cup Bundt pan. Bake at 350° for 1 hour to 1 hour and 10 minutes or until a long wooden pick inserted in center comes out clean. Cool in pan on a wire rack 15 minutes; remove from pan to wire rack, and cool completely (about 2 hours).

MILLIE SOUZA
FALL RIVER, MASSACHUSETTS

Browned Butter Frosting

make-ahead • party perfect

MAKES: about 3½ cups
HANDS-ON TIME: 15 min.
TOTAL TIME: 1 hr., 15 min.

  1 cup butter
  1 (16-oz.) package powdered sugar
  ¼ cup milk
  1 tsp. vanilla extract

1. Cook butter in a small heavy saucepan over medium heat, stirring constantly, 6 to 8 minutes or until butter begins to turn golden brown. Remove pan immediately from heat. Pour butter into a bowl. Cover and chill 1 hour or until butter is cool and begins to solidify.
2. Beat butter at medium speed with an electric mixer until fluffy; gradually add powdered sugar alternately with milk, beginning and ending with sugar. Beat at low speed until well blended after each addition. Stir in vanilla.

READER RECIPE

Mocha-Apple Cake with Browned Butter Frosting

make-ahead • party perfect

MAKES: 12 servings
HANDS-ON TIME: 25 min.
TOTAL TIME: 3 hr., 30 min., including frosting

  1 cup chopped pecans
  1 cup sugar
  1 cup canola oil
  2 large eggs
  1 Tbsp. instant coffee granules
  1 tsp. vanilla extract
  3 cups all-purpose flour
  2 tsp. baking powder
  1 tsp. ground cinnamon
  1 tsp. ground nutmeg
  ½ tsp. salt
  4 cups peeled and diced **Granny Smith** apples (about 2 lb.)
  2 (2.6-oz.) milk chocolate candy bars, chopped
     Browned Butter Frosting

1. Preheat oven to 350°. Bake pecans in a single layer in a shallow pan 8 to 10 minutes or until toasted and fragrant, stirring halfway through.
2. Beat sugar and next 4 ingredients at high speed with a heavy-duty electric stand mixer 5 minutes. Stir together flour and next 4 ingredients; gradually add flour mixture to sugar mixture, beating at low speed just until blended. Add apples, chocolate, and pecans; beat just until blended. Spoon into 2 greased and floured 9-inch round cake pans.
3. Bake at 350° for 28 to 32 minutes or until a wooden pick inserted in center comes out clean. Cool in pans on a wire rack 10 minutes; remove from pans to wire rack, and cool completely (about 1 hour). Spread Browned Butter Frosting between layers and on top and sides of cake.

Fresh Applesauce

good for you • make-ahead

MAKES: 10 to 12 servings
HANDS-ON TIME: 45 min.
TOTAL TIME: 50 min.

For the best taste and texture, use a variety of apples.

- 12 large apples, peeled and coarsely chopped (6½ lb.)
- 1 cup sugar
- ½ lemon, sliced

1. Bring all ingredients to a light boil in a Dutch oven over medium-high heat. Reduce heat to medium-low, and simmer, stirring often, 25 to 30 minutes or until apples are tender and juices thicken. Remove and discard lemon slices. Serve warm, or let cool to room temperature (about 2 hours). Store in an airtight container in refrigerator up to 2 weeks.

Apple-Butterscotch Brownies

make-ahead • party perfect

MAKES: about 2 dozen
HANDS-ON TIME: 15 min.
TOTAL TIME: 2 hr.

- 1 cup chopped pecans
- 2 cups firmly packed dark brown sugar
- 1 cup butter, melted
- 2 large eggs, lightly beaten
- 2 tsp. vanilla extract
- 2 cups all-purpose flour
- 2 tsp. baking powder
- ½ tsp. salt
- 3 cups peeled and diced Granny Smith apples (about 1½ lb.)

1. Preheat oven to 350°. Bake pecans in a single layer in a shallow pan 8 to 10 minutes or until toasted and fragrant, stirring halfway through.

2. Stir together brown sugar and next 3 ingredients.

3. Stir together flour and next 2 ingredients; add to brown sugar mixture, and stir until blended. Stir in apples and pecans. Pour mixture into a greased and floured 13- x 9-inch pan; spread in an even layer.

4. Bake at 350° for 35 to 45 minutes or until a wooden pick inserted in center comes out clean. Cool completely (about 1 hour). Cut into bars.

Apple Hello Dolly Bars

make-ahead • party perfect

MAKES: about 2 dozen
HANDS-ON TIME: 15 min.
TOTAL TIME: 2 hr.

- 2 cups graham cracker crumbs
- ½ cup butter, melted
- ½ (12-oz.) package semisweet chocolate morsels
- ½ (12-oz.) package butterscotch morsels
- 1 cup sweetened flaked coconut
- 2 cups peeled and finely chopped Granny Smith apples (about 1 lb.)
- 1½ cups coarsely chopped pecans
- 1 (14-oz.) can sweetened condensed milk

1. Preheat oven to 350°. Stir together graham cracker crumbs and butter; press onto bottom of a lightly greased 13- x 9-inch pan. Layer semisweet chocolate and next 4 ingredients (in order of ingredient list) in prepared pan; drizzle with sweetened condensed milk.

2. Bake at 350° for 40 to 45 minutes or until deep golden brown. Cool completely on a wire rack (about 1 hour). Cut into bars.
NOTE: We tested with Keebler Graham Cracker Crumbs.

Fresh Applesauce

LIGHTENED-UP
Southern Favorites

September's full of fresh starts: School's back in session, your team has a chance at football glory, and optimism is in the air. In honor of the unofficial new year, enjoy these healthier twists on beloved dishes in case "eat better" tops your list of resolutions.

If you love FRIED PORK CHOPS...

TRY: Sage-and-Pecan Pork Tenderloin Cutlets

quick prep • good for you

WHY IT'S BETTER FOR YOU: *Tenderloin is low in fat, and this recipe is "fried" with just enough heart-healthy oil for the crispy crunch you crave!*

MAKES: 4 servings
HANDS-ON TIME: 35 min.
TOTAL TIME: 51 min.

It's important to turn the cutlets every 2 minutes for even browning.

- 1 cup red wine vinegar
- 5 Tbsp. seedless blackberry preserves
- ½ tsp. salt
- 1 lb. pork tenderloin
- ¾ cup fine, dry breadcrumbs
- ½ cup finely chopped pecans
- 2 tsp. rubbed sage
- 2 large eggs, beaten
- 4 tsp. olive oil
  Garnishes: fresh blackberries, fresh sage leaves

1. Bring vinegar to a boil in a small saucepan over medium-high heat. Reduce heat to medium, and cook 6 minutes or until reduced by half. Stir in preserves, and cook 5 minutes. Stir in salt.

2. Remove silver skin from tenderloin, leaving a thin layer of fat covering meat. Cut pork into 8 slices. Place pork between 2 sheets of plastic wrap, and flatten to ¼-inch thickness, using a rolling pin or flat side of a meat mallet.
3. Stir together breadcrumbs, pecans, and sage in a shallow bowl.
4. Dredge pork in breadcrumb mixture, dip in beaten eggs, and dredge again in breadcrumb mixture.

5. Cook 4 pork slices in 2 tsp. hot oil in a large nonstick skillet over medium heat 8 minutes or until done, turning every 2 minutes. Repeat procedure with remaining pork and oil. Serve with vinegar mixture, and garnish, if desired.

PER SERVING (NOT INCLUDING GARNISH): **CALORIES** 479; **FAT** 23.2G (**SAT** 4.5G, **MONO** 12.2G, **POLY** 4.2G); **PROTEIN** 31.8G; **CARB** 33.7G; **FIBER** 2.2G; **CHOL** 181MG; **IRON** 2.3MG; **SODIUM** 532MG; **CALC** 36MG

Sage-and-Pecan Pork Tenderloin Cutlets

Southern Favorites

If you love GREENS WITH HAM HOCK...

TRY: Turnip Greens Stew
quick prep • good for you • make-ahead

WHY IT'S BETTER FOR YOU: *Lean ham and fat-free broth offer the good flavor of the original dish minus the added saturated fat. Beans add extra fiber too!*

MAKES: about 10 cups
HANDS-ON TIME: 10 min.
TOTAL TIME: 40 min.

- 2 cups chopped cooked ham
- 1 Tbsp. vegetable oil
- 3 cups chicken broth
- 2 (16-oz.) packages frozen chopped turnip greens
- 2 (15.5-oz.) cans cannellini beans, drained and rinsed
- 4 cups frozen diced onion, red and green bell peppers, and celery
- 1 tsp. sugar
- 1 tsp. seasoned pepper

Turnip Greens Stew and
Lightened Buttermilk Biscuits

1. Sauté ham in hot oil in a Dutch oven over medium-high heat 5 minutes or until lightly browned. Add broth and remaining ingredients; bring to a boil. Cover, reduce heat to low, and simmer, stirring occasionally, 25 minutes.

PER CUP: **CALORIES** 176; **FAT** 4.3G (**SAT** 1.1G, **MONO** 1.5G, **POLY** 1.3G); **PROTEIN** 16G; **CARB** 18.5G; **FIBER** 5.3G; **CHOL** 26MG; **IRON** 3.0MG; **SODIUM** 927MG; **CALC** 141MG

Find lightened Squash Casserole, Mac and Cheese, Slightly Sweet Tea, and 18 more recipes at *southernliving.com/light*

If you love BUTTERY BISCUITS...

TRY: Lightened Buttermilk Biscuits

WHY IT'S BETTER FOR YOU: *We used half the butter typically used in traditional biscuits, and they're just as flaky!*

MAKES: 1½ dozen
HANDS-ON TIME: 20 min.
TOTAL TIME: 45 min.

- 2 cups all-purpose flour
- 2½ tsp. baking powder
- ½ tsp. salt
- ¼ cup cold butter, cut into pieces
- 1¼ cups nonfat buttermilk
   Parchment paper

1. Preheat oven to 400°. Combine first 3 ingredients in a large bowl; cut in butter with a pastry blender until mixture resembles coarse meal. Chill 10 minutes.

2. Add buttermilk to flour mixture, stirring just until moistened. Turn dough out onto a lightly floured surface; knead lightly 3 or 4 times.

3. With floured hands, pat dough into a ½-inch-thick rectangle (about 9 x 5 inches); dust top with flour. Fold dough over itself in 3 sections, starting with short end (as if folding a letter-size piece of paper). Repeat once, beginning with patting dough into a rectangle.

4. Pat dough to ¾-inch thickness. Cut dough with a 2-inch round cutter, and place 1 inch apart on a parchment paper-lined baking sheet.

5. Bake at 400° for 13 to 15 minutes or until golden brown. Remove from baking sheets to wire racks; cool 2 minutes. Serve warm.

PER BISCUIT: **CALORIES** 79; **FAT** 2.7G (**SAT** 1.6G, **MONO** 0.7G, **POLY** 0.2G); **PROTEIN** 2.1G; **CARB** 11.6G; **FIBER** 0.4G; **CHOL** 7MG; **IRON** 0.7MG; **SODIUM** 155MG **CALC** 57MG

Roasted
Vegetable Pizza

If you love a LOADED-OUT PIZZA...

TRY: Roasted Vegetable Pizza

good for you • party perfect

WHY IT'S BETTER FOR YOU: *Whole wheat crust topped with roasted sweet potatoes and other colorful veggies ups the good-for-you factor!*

MAKES: 4 servings
HANDS-ON TIME: 25 min.
TOTAL TIME: 1 hr., 40 min.

- 1 medium eggplant, peeled and cubed
- ¼ tsp. salt
- 2 medium zucchini, sliced
- 1 large sweet potato, peeled and cut into ½-inch cubes
- 1 onion, peeled and cut into eighths
- 1 red bell pepper, cut into 1-inch pieces
- ¼ cup olive oil
- 1 Tbsp. chopped fresh rosemary
- ¼ tsp. pepper
- ½ (16-oz.) package whole wheat prebaked pizza crusts
- 1 tsp. olive oil
- ⅓ cup shaved Asiago cheese

1. Sprinkle eggplant with salt, and let stand 30 minutes. Pat dry.
2. Preheat oven to 400°. Toss together eggplant, zucchini, and next 6 ingredients, and arrange in a single layer in 2 aluminum foil-lined 15- x 10-inch jelly-roll pans.
3. Bake at 400° for 45 minutes or until vegetables are tender and golden brown. Season with salt to taste.
4. Place crust on a baking sheet. Brush crust with 1 tsp. olive oil. Top with 2 cups roasted vegetables; reserve remaining vegetables for another use. Sprinkle with cheese. Bake at 400° for 15 minutes or until crust is crisp and cheese is melted.

PER SERVING: CALORIES 401; **FAT** 20.6G (**SAT** 5G, **MONO** 10.9G, **POLY** 1.5G); **PROTEIN** 11.5G; **CARB** 48.0G; **FIBER** 12.1G; **CHOL** 8MG; **IRON** 1.1MG; **SODIUM** 538MG; **CALC** 113MG

If you love FRIED CHICKEN...

TRY: Oven-Fried Chicken

quick prep • good for you

WHY IT'S BETTER FOR YOU: *One bite into these chicken breasts with a crunch courtesy of cornflakes and you won't even miss the grease!*

MAKES: 4 servings
HANDS-ON TIME: 20 min.
TOTAL TIME: 45 min.

- 4 skinned and boned chicken breasts (1 lb.)
- ½ tsp. salt
- ¼ tsp. pepper
- 2 egg whites
  Vegetable cooking spray
- ¾ cup crushed cornflakes cereal
- ½ cup freshly grated Parmesan cheese
- 1 tsp. dried Italian seasoning
- ½ cup all-purpose flour

1. Preheat oven to 425°. Sprinkle chicken with salt and pepper. Whisk egg whites just until foamy.
2. Place a wire rack coated with cooking spray in a 15- x 10-inch jelly-roll pan. Stir together cornflakes, Parmesan cheese, and Italian seasoning.
3. Dredge chicken in flour, shaking off excess. Dip chicken in egg white, and dredge in cornflake mixture. Lightly coat chicken on each side with cooking spray; arrange chicken on wire rack.
4. Bake at 425° for 25 to 30 minutes or until golden brown and done.

PER SERVING: CALORIES 313; **FAT** 4.4G (**SAT** 2.1G, **MONO** 0.1G, **POLY** 0.1G); **PROTEIN** 27.3G; **CARB** 39.7G; **FIBER** 3.5G; **CHOL** 50MG; **IRON** 3.2MG; **SODIUM** 275MG; **CALC** 208MG

TRY THIS TWIST!

Chicken Parmigiana: Top each chicken breast with your favorite pasta sauce and shredded reduced-fat cheese. Bake 5 more minutes or until cheese is melted.

LIGHTENED-UP
Southern Favorites

If you love DECADENT CHOCOLATE...

TRY: Chocolate Pudding

good for you • make-ahead • party perfect

WHY IT'S BETTER FOR YOU: *This pudding is everything you dream of—chocolaty rich, silky smooth, and light on calories! We love this mixture so much that we would use it as a pie filling!*

MAKES: 5 servings
HANDS-ON TIME: 15 min.
TOTAL TIME: 2 hr., 15 min.

- 2 **cups fat-free milk**
- ⅔ **cup sugar**
- ⅓ **cup unsweetened cocoa**
- 3 **Tbsp. cornstarch**
- ⅛ **tsp. salt**
- 1 **large egg, lightly beaten**
- ½ **(4-oz.) semisweet chocolate baking bar, chopped**
- 1 **tsp. vanilla extract**
- ⅓ **cup thawed reduced-fat frozen whipped topping**
  Garnishes: toasted sliced almonds, chocolate shavings

1. Whisk together milk, sugar, cocoa, cornstarch, and salt in a medium-size heavy saucepan over medium-high heat, and cook, whisking constantly, 5 minutes or until mixture is hot. Gradually whisk ⅓ cup hot milk mixture into egg. Whisk egg mixture into remaining hot milk mixture.

2. Cook, whisking constantly, 3 minutes or until mixture thickens. Remove from heat, and add chopped chocolate, stirring until chocolate melts and mixture is smooth. Stir in vanilla. Pour mixture into a glass bowl. Place heavy-duty plastic wrap directly on warm mixture (to prevent a film from forming), and chill 2 hours or until pudding is completely cool.

3. Spoon ½ cup pudding into each of 5 individual serving dishes, and top each with 1 Tbsp. whipped topping. Garnish, if desired.

PER ½ CUP: **CALORIES** 259; **FAT** 5.3G (**SAT** 2.8G, **MONO** 0.4G, **POLY** 0.1G); **PROTEIN** 6.3G; **CARB** 48.2G; **FIBER** 1.7G; **CHOL** 44MG; **IRON** 1MG; **SODIUM** 123MG; **CALC** 206MG

If you love KEY LIME PIE...

TRY: Key "Light" Pie

good for you • make-ahead • party perfect

WHY IT'S BETTER FOR YOU: *You'll hear angels sing (Jimmy Buffet tunes) when you taste how rich this version is without all the fat!*

MAKES: 8 servings
HANDS-ON TIME: 10 min.
TOTAL TIME: 1 hr., 20 min.

Bake the pie on a baking sheet for easier removal from the oven.

- 1 **(14-oz.) can fat-free sweetened condensed milk**
- ¾ **cup egg substitute**
- 2 **tsp. lime zest (about 2 limes)**
- ½ **cup fresh lime juice**
- 1 **(6-oz.) reduced-fat ready-made graham cracker piecrust**
  Garnishes: thawed fat-free frozen whipped topping, lime wedges, lime zest curls

1. Preheat oven to 350°. Process first 4 ingredients in a blender until smooth. Pour mixture into piecrust.

2. Bake at 350° for 10 to 12 minutes or until pie is set. Let pie cool completely on a wire rack (about 1 hour). Garnish, if desired.

PER SLICE: **CALORIES** 246; **FAT** 3.6G (**SAT** 0.5G, **MONO** 0G, **POLY** 0G); **PROTEIN** 7.1G; **CARB** 46.4G; **FIBER** 0.1G; **CHOL** 6MG; **IRON** 0.8MG; **SODIUM** 184MG; **CALC** 137MG

Try These Twists!

CHOCOLATE-ESPRESSO PUDDING: Whisk together milk, sugar, cocoa, cornstarch, and salt, adding 1 Tbsp. instant espresso to milk mixture. Proceed with recipe as directed.

PER ½ CUP: **CALORIES** 260; **FAT** 5.3G (**SAT** 2.8G, **MONO** 0.4G, **POLY** 0.1G); **PROTEIN** 6.4G; **CARB** 48.5G; **FIBER** 1.7G; **CHOL** 44MG; **IRON** 1MG; **SODIUM** 123MG; **CALC** 207MG

RASPBERRY-CHOCOLATE PUDDING: Prepare pudding as directed through Step 2. Microwave ⅓ cup raspberry jam in a small microwave-safe bowl at HIGH 30 seconds or until melted. Spoon 1 Tbsp. melted jam into bottom of each individual serving dish, and top each with ½ cup pudding and 1 Tbsp. whipped topping. Stir 1 tsp. water into remaining melted jam, and drizzle ½ tsp. jam mixture on top of whipped topping on each pudding. Garnish with fresh raspberries, if desired.

PER ½ CUP: **CALORIES** 312; **FAT** 5.3G (**SAT** 2.8G, **MONO** 0.4G, **POLY** 0.1G); **PROTEIN** 6.3G; **CARB** 62.1G; **FIBER** 1.7G; **CHOL** 44MG; **IRON** 1MG; **SODIUM** 123MG; **CALC** 206MG

Harvest Salads

Turn over a new leaf! Tender greens and bold dressings pair the best of summer with the first crisp tastes of fall for a colorful collection of all-in-one sides.

Broccoli, Grape, and Pasta Salad

make-ahead • party perfect

MAKES: 6 to 8 servings
HANDS-ON TIME: 25 min.
TOTAL TIME: 3 hr., 30 min.

If you're a broccoli salad fan, you'll love the combination of these colorful ingredients. Cook the pasta al dente so it's firm enough to hold its own when tossed with the tangy-sweet salad dressing. (Pictured on page 188)

- 1 cup chopped pecans
- ½ (16-oz.) package farfalle (bow-tie) pasta
- 1 lb. fresh broccoli
- 1 cup mayonnaise
- ⅓ cup sugar
- ⅓ cup diced red onion
- ⅓ cup red wine vinegar
- 1 tsp. salt
- 2 cups seedless red grapes, halved
- 8 cooked bacon slices, crumbled

1. Preheat oven to 350°. Bake pecans in a single layer in a shallow pan 5 to 7 minutes or until lightly toasted and fragrant, stirring halfway through.
2. Prepare pasta according to package directions.
3. Meanwhile, cut broccoli florets from stems, and separate florets into small pieces using tip of a paring knife. Peel away tough outer layer of stems, and finely chop stems.
4. Whisk together mayonnaise and next 4 ingredients in a large bowl; add broccoli, hot cooked pasta, and grapes, and stir to coat. Cover and chill 3 hours. Stir bacon and pecans into salad just before serving.

Mango Salad

good for you • make-ahead • party perfect

MAKES: 6 to 8 servings
HANDS-ON TIME: 25 min.
TOTAL TIME: 2 hr., 25 min., including vinaigrette
(Pictured on page 189)

- 2 mangoes, peeled and cut into thin slices
- 1½ cups halved, seeded, and sliced English cucumber
- 1½ cups halved baby heirloom tomatoes
- 1½ cups fresh corn kernels
- ½ cup diced red onion
- ½ cup chopped fresh basil
  Fresh Lime Vinaigrette
- 4 cups fresh arugula

1. Toss together first 7 ingredients in a large bowl; cover and chill 2 hours. Toss with arugula just before serving.

Fresh Lime Vinaigrette

quick prep • party perfect

MAKES: ¾ cup
HANDS-ON TIME: 10 min.
TOTAL TIME: 10 min.

1. Whisk together ¼ cup rice vinegar; 2 Tbsp. sugar; 3 Tbsp. fresh lime juice; 1 garlic clove, minced; and ½ tsp. each salt and freshly ground pepper. Gradually whisk in ½ cup canola oil until smooth.

Grilled Sweet Potato-Poblano Salad

quick prep • good for you • party perfect

MAKES: 6 to 8 servings
HANDS-ON TIME: 20 min.
TOTAL TIME: 40 min., including vinaigrette
(Pictured on page 189)

  Vegetable cooking spray
- 2½ lb. small sweet potatoes
- 1 poblano pepper, seeded and diced
  Cilantro Vinaigrette
- 1 (5-oz.) package fresh mâche
- 1 cup crumbled queso fresco (fresh Mexican cheese)
- ½ cup sweetened dried cranberries
- ½ cup shelled roasted pumpkin seeds

1. Coat cold cooking grate of grill with cooking spray, and place on grill. Preheat grill to 350° to 400° (medium-high) heat.
2. Peel sweet potatoes, and cut into ½-inch-thick rounds. Bring potatoes and water to cover to a boil in a large Dutch oven over medium-high heat; cook 5 to 6 minutes or until crisp-tender. Drain. Coat potatoes with cooking spray.
3. Grill potatoes, covered with grill lid, 8 to 10 minutes or until tender, turning occasionally. Gently toss warm potatoes with poblano and Cilantro Vinaigrette. Arrange mâche on a serving platter, and sprinkle with queso fresco and cranberries. Top with sweet potato mixture, and sprinkle with pumpkin seeds.

Cilantro Vinaigrette

quick prep • party perfect

MAKES: 1 cup
HANDS-ON TIME: 10 min.
TOTAL TIME: 10 min.

1. Whisk together ¼ cup red wine vinegar, 2 Tbsp. chopped fresh cilantro, 2 Tbsp. minced sweet onion, 1 Tbsp. grated fresh ginger, 2 Tbsp. honey, 2 tsp. orange zest, 2 tsp. Dijon mustard, and ½ tsp. salt; add ½ cup canola oil in a slow, steady stream, whisking constantly until smooth.

Melon and Plum Salad

Melon and Plum Salad

quick prep • good for you • party perfect

MAKES: 6 servings
HANDS-ON TIME: 20 min.
TOTAL TIME: 30 min., including vinaigrette

- 4 cups seeded and cubed watermelon
- 4 cups honeydew melon balls
- 3 red plums, sliced
- 2 cups torn watercress
- I cup crumbled feta cheese
  Pepper Jelly Vinaigrette

1. Gently toss together first 5 ingredients, and place on a serving platter. Drizzle with vinaigrette, and season with salt and pepper to taste.

Pepper Jelly Vinaigrette

quick prep • party perfect

MAKES: ¾ cup
HANDS-ON TIME: 10 min.
TOTAL TIME: 10 min.

1. Whisk together ¼ cup rice wine vinegar, ¼ cup hot jalapeño pepper jelly, I Tbsp. chopped fresh mint, I Tbsp. grated onion, and I Tbsp. fresh lime juice. Gradually add ¼ cup canola oil in a slow, steady stream, whisking until smooth.

Garden Variety

Dozens of lettuces are available in stores—from watercress and arugula to mâche, a tender heirloom lettuce with a slightly sweet, nutty flavor. But it's also super easy to plant and harvest a bountiful fall crop just outside your back door.

Grilled Pear Salad

good for you • quick prep • party perfect

MAKES: 6 to 8 servings
HANDS-ON TIME: 25 min.
TOTAL TIME: 25 min.

- 3 firm ripe Bartlett pears, cut into ½-inch-thick wedges
- ¼ cup red wine vinegar
- ½ (10-oz.) jar seedless raspberry preserves
- 2 Tbsp. chopped fresh basil
- I garlic clove, pressed
- ½ tsp. salt
- ½ tsp. seasoned pepper
- ⅓ cup canola oil
- I (5-oz.) package gourmet mixed salad greens
- ½ small red onion, thinly sliced
- 2 cups fresh raspberries
- ¾ cup honey-roasted cashews
- 4 oz. crumbled goat cheese

1. Preheat grill to 350° to 400° (medium-high) heat. Grill pear wedges, covered with grill lid, I to 2 minutes on each side or until golden.
2. Whisk together red wine vinegar and next 5 ingredients in a small bowl; add canola oil in a slow, steady stream, whisking constantly until smooth.
3. Combine salad greens, next 4 ingredients, and pears in a large bowl. Drizzle with desired amount of vinaigrette, and toss to combine. Serve immediately with remaining vinaigrette.

Cobb Potato Salad

party perfect

MAKES: 6 to 8 servings
HANDS-ON TIME: 20 min.
TOTAL TIME: 2 hr., 35 min.

- I lb. baby red potatoes, quartered
- ⅓ cup sliced green onions
- I (11.5-oz.) bottle refrigerated blue cheese vinaigrette, divided
- 2 large avocados
- I Tbsp. fresh lemon juice
- 6 cups shredded romaine lettuce
- I pt. grape tomatoes, halved
- I cup (4 oz.) shredded white Cheddar cheese
- 2 oz. blue cheese, crumbled
- 6 cooked bacon slices, crumbled

1. Cook potatoes in boiling salted water to cover 15 to 20 minutes or until tender; drain. Toss potatoes with green onions and ⅓ cup vinaigrette; season with salt and pepper to taste. Cover and chill 2 to 24 hours.
2. Peel and chop avocados; toss with lemon juice. Toss lettuce with avocado mixture, tomatoes, and next 2 ingredients. Arrange lettuce mixture on a large serving platter; top with potato mixture, and sprinkle with bacon. Serve with remaining vinaigrette.
NOTE: We tested with Marie's Blue Cheese Vinaigrette.

Our Easiest Fan Fare

Follow this game plan for delicious pregame grub, and watch guests huddle up near the food, whether you're at home or on campus (it's easily transportable!).

Store-bought craft paper and simple twine make clever, team-inspired sandwich wrappers

Mini Muffulettas

Game Day Celebration

SERVES 8

Mini Muffulettas

Apple Coleslaw, Pear Coleslaw, or Cranberry-Almond Coleslaw

Deli-fried chicken tenders

Jalapeño-Mustard Dipping Sauce

Blue Moon Inn Cheese Spread

Cajun Lemonade

Graham Nut Clusters

Mini Muffulettas

quick prep • make-ahead • party perfect

MAKES: 12 appetizer servings
HANDS-ON TIME: 25 min.
TOTAL TIME: 25 min.

Tailgate tip: *Prepare sandwiches the day before the game. Place in zip-top plastic freezer bags, and refrigerate overnight.*

- 2 (16-oz.) jars mixed pickled vegetables
- ¾ cup pimiento-stuffed Spanish olives, chopped
- 2 Tbsp. bottled olive oil-and-vinegar dressing
- 12 small dinner rolls, cut in half
- 6 Swiss cheese slices, cut in half
- 12 thin deli ham slices
- 12 Genoa salami slices
- 6 provolone cheese slices, cut in half

1. Pulse pickled vegetables in food processor 8 to 10 times or until finely chopped. Stir in olives and dressing.
2. Spread 1 heaping tablespoonful pickled vegetable mixture over cut side of each roll bottom. Top each with 1 Swiss cheese slice half, 1 ham slice, 1 salami slice, 1 provolone cheese slice half, and roll tops. Cover with plastic wrap. Serve immediately, or chill until ready to serve.
NOTE: We tested with Mezzetta Italian Mix Giardiniera pickled vegetables and Newman's Own Olive Oil & Vinegar dressing.

> *"Don't forget a cleverly titled dish that lets you 'devour' your opponent: Not-So-Hot Dawgs, Gator Bites, Blue Deviled Eggs."*
>
> **REBECCA KRACKE GORDON**
> TEST KITCHEN DIRECTOR

Apple Coleslaw

quick prep • make-ahead • good for you • party perfect

MAKES: 8 servings
HANDS-ON TIME: 15 min.
TOTAL TIME: 15 min.

Tailgate tip: You can prepare slaw up to a day ahead, omitting apples. Chop the apples. Combine 2 cups water and 3 Tbsp. lemon juice, and pour over apples. Cover and chill apples and slaw in two separate containers overnight. Drain apples, and stir apples into slaw just before serving.

- ¼ cup apple cider vinegar
- 2 Tbsp. Dijon mustard
- 2 Tbsp. honey
- ¾ tsp. salt
- ¼ tsp. freshly ground pepper
- ¼ cup canola oil
- 2 (10-oz.) packages shredded coleslaw mix
- 4 green onions, sliced
- 2 celery ribs, sliced
- 2 small Honeycrisp, Gala, or Pink Lady apples, chopped

1. Whisk together first 5 ingredients. Gradually add oil in a slow, steady stream, whisking constantly until blended. Stir together coleslaw mix and next 3 ingredients in a large bowl; add vinegar mixture, tossing to coat.

TRY THESE TWISTS!
Pear Coleslaw: Prepare recipe as directed, substituting Bosc pears for apples.

Cranberry-Almond Coleslaw: Omit apples. Prepare recipe as directed, stirring in 1 cup chopped, smoked almonds and ¾ cup sweetened dried cranberries.

 Fast Flourish

Team spirit skewers are a fun addition to chicken tenders. Simply cut flags from scrapbook paper in the shape of pennants, and tape to wooden skewers.

Jalapeño-Mustard Dipping Sauce

quick prep • make-ahead • party perfect

MAKES: about 1 cup
HANDS-ON TIME: 5 min.
TOTAL TIME: 5 min.

Tailgate tip: Just before parking on campus, stop by a grocer's deli counter or the drive-through window of your favorite restaurant for fresh, hot chicken tenders.

- ¾ cup mayonnaise
- 2 Tbsp. jalapeño pepper jelly
- ¼ cup Creole mustard

1. Stir together all ingredients until blended.

Blue Moon Inn Cheese Spread

quick prep • make-ahead • party perfect

MAKES: 8 servings
HANDS-ON TIME: 15 min.
TOTAL TIME: 20 min.

Tailgate tip: Store in airtight container in refrigerator up to 4 days ahead.

- ½ cup pecans
- ¾ cup mayonnaise
- ½ cup pimiento-stuffed Spanish olives, chopped
- ⅓ cup bottled chili sauce
- 1 tsp. Worcestershire sauce
- 1 (10-oz.) block sharp Cheddar cheese, finely shredded
  Garnish: sliced pimiento-stuffed Spanish olives
  Assorted vegetables and crackers

1. Preheat oven to 350°. Bake pecans in a single layer in a shallow pan 8 to 10 minutes or until toasted and fragrant. Cool 5 minutes; finely chop pecans.
2. Stir together mayonnaise and next 3 ingredients until well blended. Stir in cheese and pecans. Garnish, if desired. Serve with vegetables and crackers.

 Plan Ahead

"For easy transport, pack food in a wheeled cooler," says Test Kitchen Director Rebecca Kracke Gordon, who spends many of her fall Saturdays in Tuscaloosa. (See her tailgating blog at *tidefanfare.com*.)

Graham Nut Clusters

Tailgate Tips

- Rinse gallon milk jugs and use as a spill-proof way to transport Cajun Lemonade.
- Protect your stash from sneaky tent spectators while you're at the game by putting a padlock on your cooler.
- Freeze water bottles the night before for handy ice packs that later double as drinks.
- For more winning, transportable recipes (Bacon Cheese Dip!), drinks, and menu ideas, go to *southernliving.com/tailgating*.

Plug megaphones with foil to contain snack mix. Look for them at party-supply stores.

Cajun Lemonade

quick prep • make-ahead • party perfect

MAKES: about 8 cups
HANDS-ON TIME: 10 min.
TOTAL TIME: 10 min.

Tailgate tip: Be sure to pack a separate bag of ice for drinks.

- 2 **cups light rum**
- 1 **(12-oz.) can frozen lemonade concentrate, thawed**
- 1 **tsp. hot sauce**
- 1 **(1-liter) bottle club soda, chilled**
  Crushed ice
  Garnishes: sugarcane sticks, lemon slices

1. Stir together first 3 ingredients. Add club soda just before serving. Serve over crushed ice. Garnish, if desired.
NOTE: We tested with Tabasco hot sauce.

Graham Nut Clusters

quick prep • make-ahead • party perfect

MAKES: 12 servings
HANDS-ON TIME: 10 min.
TOTAL TIME: 30 min.

Tailgate tip: Make up to five days ahead and store in an airtight container.

- 6 **cups honey graham cereal**
- 1 **cup honey-roasted peanuts**
- 1 **cup coarsely chopped pecans**
- ½ **cup butter**
- 1 **cup firmly packed light brown sugar**
- ¼ **cup light corn syrup**
  Wax paper
- 2 **cups pretzel sticks**
- 1 **cup candy-coated chocolate pieces**

1. Preheat oven to 350°. Combine cereal and next 2 ingredients in a very large bowl.
2. Melt butter in a 3-qt. saucepan over medium-low heat; stir in sugar and corn syrup. Bring to a boil over medium heat; boil 2 minutes.
3. Pour butter mixture over cereal mixture, and stir quickly to coat. Spread in a single layer on a lightly greased aluminum foil-lined jelly-roll pan.
4. Bake at 350° for 10 minutes. Transfer to wax paper, and cool completely (about 10 minutes). Break into pieces, and toss with pretzel sticks and chocolate pieces.

"My family loves Italian night, but I'm tired of the same old spaghetti. Any inspired ideas?"

KATIE PENLAND, DYERSBURG, TENNESSEE

{1}
HAVE FISH FOR A CHANGE

Crispy Oven-Baked Tilapia with Lemon-Tomato Fettuccine

quick prep

MAKES: 4 servings
HANDS-ON TIME: 33 min.
TOTAL TIME: 33 min.

- 2 **lemons**
- 1 **cup panko (Japanese breadcrumbs)**
- 1 **tsp. paprika**
- 4 **(4-oz.) tilapia fillets**
- 2 **tsp. salt, divided**
- 6 **Tbsp. butter, melted**
- 1 **(16-oz.) package spinach fettuccine**
- 2 **Tbsp. butter**
- 1 **cup chopped sweet onion**
- 4 **garlic cloves, pressed**
- 1 **(14.5-oz.) can petite-diced tomatoes**
- 2 **Tbsp. drained capers**
- ¼ **cup crumbled feta cheese**
- ¼ **cup chopped fresh basil**

1. Preheat oven 425°. Grate zest from lemons to equal 4 tsp. Cut lemons in half; squeeze juice from lemons into a measuring cup to equal 2 Tbsp. Combine panko, paprika, and 2 tsp. lemon zest in a shallow dish. Sprinkle fish with 1 tsp. salt. Dip fish in ¼ cup melted butter; dredge in panko mixture, pressing panko to adhere. Place fish on a lightly greased rack in an aluminum foil-lined broiler pan. Drizzle remaining 2 Tbsp. melted butter over fish. Bake at 425° for 20 to 25 minutes or until fish flakes with a fork.

2. Meanwhile, prepare pasta according to package directions. Melt 2 Tbsp. butter in a large skillet over medium heat; add onion, and sauté 5 to 6 minutes or until golden. Add garlic, and cook 1 minute. Add tomatoes, and cook 5 to 6 minutes or until tomato mixture begins to thicken. Stir in 2 Tbsp. lemon juice, 2 Tbsp. capers, and remaining 2 tsp. lemon zest and 1 tsp. salt; cook 2 to 3 minutes. Remove from heat, and toss with hot cooked pasta, feta cheese, and basil. Serve with fish.

{2}
BEEF UP YOUR RAVIOLI

Grilled Fillets with Pecans and Green Bean Ravioli

quick prep

MAKES: 4 servings
HANDS-ON TIME: 22 min.
TOTAL TIME: 36 min.

- 4 **(4-oz.) beef tenderloin fillets**
- 1 **tsp. salt**
- ½ **tsp. freshly ground pepper**
- 1 **(20-oz.) package refrigerated cheese-filled ravioli**
- 1 **(8-oz.) package fresh small green beans**
- ½ **cup chopped pecans**
- ½ **cup butter**
- 3 **garlic cloves, thinly sliced**
- 1 **Tbsp. chopped fresh sage**
- ½ **cup (2 oz.) shredded Parmesan cheese**

1. Preheat grill to 350° to 400° (medium-high) heat. Sprinkle fillets with salt and pepper. Grill, covered with grill lid, 5 to 8 minutes on each side or until a meat thermometer inserted into thickest portion registers 155°. Let stand 10 minutes.

2. Cook ravioli and green beans in boiling water to cover in a Dutch oven 4 to 5 minutes or until green beans are crisp-tender. Drain.

3. Heat pecans in a large nonstick skillet over medium-low heat, stirring often, 2 to 3 minutes or until toasted and fragrant. Remove from skillet; wipe skillet clean. Melt butter in skillet over medium heat. Add garlic, and sauté 5 to 7 minutes or until garlic is caramel-colored and butter begins to brown. Remove from heat, and stir in sage, hot pasta mixture, and pecans. Sprinkle with cheese. Serve immediately with fillets.

Pesto-Crusted Pork Chops with Sweet-and-Sour Collards

{3}
USE PESTO AS A COATING

Pesto-Crusted Pork Chops with Sweet-and-Sour Collards

quick prep

MAKES: 5 servings
HANDS-ON TIME: 30 min.
TOTAL TIME: 42 min.

- ½ cup golden raisins
- 1 cup hot water
- 6 (1-inch-thick) boneless pork chops (about 2 lb.)
- 1 (7-oz.) container reduced-fat pesto, divided
- 1 cup panko (Japanese breadcrumbs)
- 6 Tbsp. olive oil, divided
- ½ cup chopped sweet onion
- 1 garlic clove, minced
- 1 (16-oz.) package frozen chopped collard greens
- ¼ cup balsamic vinegar
- 1 Tbsp. brown sugar
- 1 tsp. salt
- ½ tsp. dried crushed red pepper
- ⅓ cup pine nuts, toasted

1. Stir together first 2 ingredients. Let stand 12 to 15 minutes; drain.
2. Coat pork chops with half of pesto; dredge in panko, pressing gently to adhere. Cook in ¼ cup hot oil in a large nonstick skillet over medium heat 6 to 7 minutes on each side or until done.
3. Heat remaining 2 Tbsp. olive oil in skillet; add onion and garlic, and sauté 3 to 4 minutes or until tender. Add collards, and cook 3 to 4 minutes or until tender. Stir together vinegar and next 3 ingredients; add to collards, and cook 2 minutes. Remove from heat. Stir in raisins and pine nuts.
4. Serve pork chops with collards and remaining pesto.

{4}
REACH FOR THE RICE

Baked Chicken Risotto

MAKES: 4 servings
HANDS-ON TIME: 20 min.
TOTAL TIME: 1 hr.

- 3 Tbsp. butter
- 1 cup minced sweet onion
- 2 garlic cloves, pressed
- 1 cup Arborio rice (short-grain)
- ¼ cup dry white wine
- 4 cups chicken broth
- 1 (14-oz.) can quartered artichoke hearts, drained
- 3 cups chopped cooked chicken
- 2 medium zucchini, coarsely chopped (about 2 cups)
- ½ tsp. freshly ground pepper
- ½ cup grated Parmesan cheese
- ¼ cup chopped fresh parsley
- 1 tsp. lemon zest

1. Preheat oven to 425°. Melt butter in a Dutch oven over medium-high heat; add onion and garlic, and sauté 5 minutes. Add rice, and cook 2 minutes or until golden brown. Add wine, and cook 2 to 3 minutes or until wine is absorbed. Add chicken broth. Bring to a boil, cover, and transfer to oven. Bake 20 minutes.
2. Remove rice from oven, and stir in artichokes and next 3 ingredients. Cover and bake 10 minutes. Remove from oven, and let stand 5 minutes. Stir in cheese and remaining ingredients. Serve immediately.

Two More Tricks!

{1}
Add a little cream and dried crushed red pepper to a jar of pasta sauce.

{2}
Jazz up frozen lasagna with pizza toppings halfway through baking.

October

Nuts About Pecans

Is it pee-can or peh-kahn? Doesn't matter when your mouth is full. We're officially pronouncing these recipes some of the best we've ever tasted!

Sticky-Bun Pumpkin Muffins

quick prep • party perfect

MAKES: 2 dozen
HANDS-ON TIME: 20 min.
TOTAL TIME: 1 hr.

2 cups pecan halves and pieces
½ cup butter, melted
½ cup firmly packed light brown sugar
2 Tbsp. light corn syrup
3½ cups all-purpose flour
3 cups granulated sugar
1 Tbsp. pumpkin pie spice
1 tsp. baking soda
1 tsp. salt
1 (15-oz.) can pumpkin
1 cup canola oil
4 large eggs

1. Preheat oven to 350°. Bake pecans in a single layer in a shallow pan 8 to 10 minutes or until toasted and fragrant, stirring halfway through.
2. Stir together melted butter and next 2 ingredients. Spoon 1 rounded teaspoonful butter mixture into each cup of 2 lightly greased 12-cup muffin pans, and top each with 1 rounded tablespoonful pecans.

3. Stir together flour and next 4 ingredients in a large bowl, and make a well in center of mixture. Whisk together pumpkin, next 2 ingredients, and ⅔ cup water; add to dry ingredients, stirring just until moistened.
4. Spoon batter into prepared muffin pans, filling three-fourths full.
5. Bake at 350° for 25 to 30 minutes or until a wooden pick inserted in center comes out clean. Invert pan immediately to remove muffins, and arrange muffins on a wire rack. Spoon any topping remaining in muffin cups over muffins. Let cool 5 minutes.

TRY THIS TWIST!
Pecan-Pumpkin Bread: Omit butter, brown sugar, and corn syrup. Substitute 1½ cups chopped pecans for 2 cups pecan halves and pieces; toast as directed in Step 1. Omit Step 2. Prepare batter as directed in Step 3; stir in pecans. Spoon batter into 2 greased and floured 9- x 5-inch loaf pans. Bake at 350° for 1 hour to 1 hour and 10 minutes or until a long wooden pick inserted in center comes out clean. Cool in pans on a wire rack 10 minutes. Remove from pans to wire rack, and cool completely (about 1 hour). Makes: 2 loaves. Hands-on time: 20 min.; Total time: 2 hr., 40 min.

Mama's German Chocolate Cake

make-ahead • party perfect

MAKES: 12 servings
HANDS-ON TIME: 30 min.
TOTAL TIME: 3 hr., 48 min., including frosting

Parchment paper
2 (4-oz.) packages sweet chocolate baking bars
2 cups all-purpose flour
1 tsp. baking soda
¼ tsp. salt
1 cup butter, softened
2 cups sugar
4 large eggs, separated
1 tsp. vanilla extract
1 cup buttermilk
Coconut-Pecan Frosting
Garnish: chocolate-dipped toasted pecan halves

1. Preheat oven to 350°. Lightly grease 3 (9-inch) round cake pans; line bottoms with parchment paper, and lightly grease paper.
2. Microwave chocolate baking bars and ½ cup water in a large microwave-safe bowl at HIGH for 1 to 1½ minutes or until chocolate is melted and smooth, stirring once halfway through.

Food Gift of the Month

PECAN-PUMPKIN BREAD

What would truly horrify your etiquette-minded mama this Halloween season? Showing up to a party empty-handed. For a charming fall gift that's more inspired than a bottle of wine, wrap a loaf of our moist Pecan-Pumpkin Bread (recipe above) in this hand block-printed organic cotton tea towel by Chattanooga's Patch Design Studio (*patchdesignstudio.com*; $12). Tie with raffia, and take heart that a certain someone won't be mortified.

Layered with Tradition

The original recipe for German chocolate cake first appeared in a Dallas, Texas, newspaper in 1957. Sent in by a local homemaker, the cake (gilded with a rich, coconut-pecan frosting that only a Southerner could have dreamed up) was an instant hit.

Here, Executive Editor Jessica Shapard Thuston shares her grandmother Alpha Pool's version of the recipe—one that continues to be the highlight of family holidays and celebrations.

3. Combine flour and next 2 ingredients in a medium bowl.

4. Beat butter and sugar at medium speed with an electric mixer until fluffy. Add egg yolks, 1 at a time, beating just until blended after each addition. Stir in chocolate mixture and vanilla. Add flour mixture alternately with buttermilk, beginning and ending with flour mixture. Beat at low speed just until blended after each addition.

5. Beat egg whites at high speed until stiff peaks form; gently fold into batter. Pour batter into prepared pans.

6. Bake at 350° for 25 to 30 minutes or until a wooden pick inserted in center comes out clean. Remove from oven, and gently run a knife around outer edge of cake layers to loosen from sides of pans. Cool in pans on wire racks 15 minutes. Remove from pans to wire racks; discard parchment paper. Cool completely (about 1 hour). Spread Coconut-Pecan Frosting between layers and on top and sides of cake. Garnish, if desired.

NOTE: We tested with Baker's German's Sweet Chocolate Bar.

Coconut-Pecan Frosting

party perfect

MAKES: about 5 cups
HANDS-ON TIME: 25 min.
TOTAL TIME: 1 hr., 38 min.

- 2 cups chopped pecans
- 1 (12-oz.) can evaporated milk
- 1½ cups sugar
- ¾ cup butter
- 6 egg yolks, lightly beaten
- 2 cups sweetened flaked coconut
- 1½ tsp. vanilla extract

1. Preheat oven to 350°. Bake pecans in a single layer in a shallow pan 8 to 10 minutes or until toasted and fragrant, stirring halfway through. Cool completely (about 20 minutes).

2. Meanwhile, cook evaporated milk, sugar, butter, and egg yolks in a heavy 3-qt. saucepan over medium heat, stirring constantly, 3 to 4 minutes or until butter melts and sugar dissolves. Cook, stirring constantly, 12 to 14 minutes or until mixture becomes a light caramel color, is bubbling, and reaches a pudding-like thickness.

3. Remove pan from heat; stir in coconut, vanilla, and pecans. Transfer mixture to a bowl. Let stand, stirring occasionally, 45 minutes or until cooled and spreading consistency.

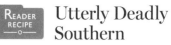

Utterly Deadly Southern Pecan Pie

make-ahead • party perfect

MAKES: 8 to 10 servings
HANDS-ON TIME: 10 min.
TOTAL TIME: 4 hr., 10 min.

- ½ (14.1-oz.) package refrigerated piecrusts
- 1 Tbsp. powdered sugar
- 4 large eggs
- 1½ cups firmly packed light brown sugar
- ½ cup butter, melted and cooled to room temperature
- ½ cup granulated sugar
- ½ cup chopped pecans
- 2 Tbsp. all-purpose flour
- 2 Tbsp. milk
- 1½ tsp. bourbon*
- 1½ cups pecan halves

1. Preheat oven to 325°. Fit piecrust into a 10-inch cast-iron skillet; sprinkle piecrust with powdered sugar.

2. Whisk eggs in a large bowl until foamy; whisk in brown sugar and next 6 ingredients. Pour mixture into piecrust, and top with pecan halves.

3. Bake at 325° for 30 minutes; reduce oven temperature to 300°, and bake 30 more minutes. Turn oven off, and let pie stand in oven, with door closed, 3 hours.

* Vanilla extract may be substituted.

RECIPE FROM SYLVIA SUBIALDEA
HUNGRY TEXAN (HUNGRY-TEXAN.COM)
DALLAS, TEXAS

Nine Quick and Easy Ways with Pecans. Get Crackin'!

PECAN-CHEESE CRISPS

MAKES: about 2½ dozen **HANDS-ON TIME:** 15 min. **TOTAL TIME:** 45 min.

Preheat oven to 400°. Stir together 1½ cups (6 oz.) freshly shredded Parmesan cheese and ¾ cup finely chopped toasted pecans in a small bowl. Spoon cheese mixture by rounded tablespoonfuls 2 inches apart onto parchment paper-lined baking sheets, forming mounds. Flatten each into a 2-inch round, creating an even thickness. Bake 7 to 10 minutes or until golden brown. Transfer to a wire rack, and let cool 15 minutes or until crisp. Store between layers of wax paper in an airtight container up to 3 days.

SPINACH-ARTICHOKE DIP

MAKES: 8 to 10 appetizer servings **HANDS-ON TIME:** 15 min. **TOTAL TIME:** 40 min.

Preheat oven to 375°. Stir together 1 (14-oz.) can artichoke hearts, drained and chopped; 1 (10-oz.) package frozen chopped spinach, thawed and drained; 1 (8-oz.) package cream cheese, softened; 1 cup freshly grated Parmesan cheese; 1 cup chopped toasted pecans; ½ cup each sour cream and mayonnaise; 2 garlic cloves, pressed; and ½ tsp. ground red pepper in a medium bowl. Spoon spinach mixture into a shallow 1½-qt. baking dish; top with an additional ½ cup freshly grated Parmesan cheese. Bake 25 to 30 minutes or until golden. Serve with pita chips.

HONEY-PECAN BUTTERSCOTCH SAUCE

MAKES: 1½ cups **HANDS-ON TIME:** 12 min. **TOTAL TIME:** 42 min.

Bring 1 cup firmly packed light brown sugar, ½ cup butter, ¼ cup milk, and ¼ cup honey to a boil in a medium saucepan over medium-high heat, stirring constantly; boil, stirring constantly, 2 minutes. Remove from heat, and cool 30 minutes. Stir in ¾ cup coarsely chopped toasted pecans. Serve over hot apple pie topped with vanilla ice cream.

JALAPEÑO-PECAN MUSTARD BUTTER

MAKES: 1½ cups **HANDS-ON TIME:** 10 min. **TOTAL TIME:** 10 min.

Stir together 1 cup softened butter; ⅓ cup finely chopped toasted pecans; 2 Tbsp. minced red onion; 3 Tbsp. Creole mustard; 1 jalapeño pepper, seeded and minced; and 1 garlic clove, pressed, in a small bowl. Spread on hot biscuits filled with ham or on a grilled flank steak sandwich, toss with oven-roasted new potatoes, or stir into hot cooked stone-ground grits. Store, covered, in refrigerator up to 1 week.

PECAN QUESADILLA

MAKES: 2 appetizer servings **HANDS-ON TIME:** 10 min. **TOTAL TIME:** 10 min.

Sprinkle 1 side of 1 (8-inch) soft taco-size flour tortilla with ⅓ cup (1½ oz.) shredded Havarti cheese and 2 Tbsp. chopped toasted pecans. Fold in half over filling. Cook quesadilla in a lightly greased skillet over medium-high heat 2 minutes on each side or until cheese melts and tortilla is golden brown. Cut into wedges, and serve with pear preserves.

PECAN-CHUTNEY CHEESE SPREAD

MAKES: 2 (6-inch) logs **HANDS-ON TIME:** 20 min. **TOTAL TIME:** 20 min. plus 1 day for chilling

Process 2 (8-oz.) packages cream cheese, softened; 1 (9-oz.) jar mango chutney; 1 Tbsp. curry powder; and ½ tsp. dry mustard in a food processor until smooth, stopping to scrape down sides as needed. Stir in ¼ cup minced green onions and 1 cup each finely chopped toasted pecans and toasted sweetened flaked coconut. Transfer to a large bowl; cover and chill 24 hours. Shape cheese mixture into 2 (6-inch) logs. Stir together 1 cup chopped toasted pecans and ½ cup chopped fresh parsley in a shallow dish; roll logs in pecan mixture. Serve with gingersnaps, sliced Gala apples and Bartlett pears, and assorted crackers.

PECAN-CRUSTED TILAPIA

MAKES: 4 servings **HANDS-ON TIME:** 16 MIN. **TOTAL TIME:** 16 min.

Process ½ cup pecan halves in a food processor until finely chopped. Sprinkle 4 (6-oz.) tilapia fillets with 1½ tsp. seasoned salt and ½ tsp. freshly ground pepper. Dredge fish in finely chopped pecans. Melt 3 Tbsp. butter in a large nonstick skillet over medium-high heat; add fish, and cook 3 to 4 minutes on each side or until well browned and fish flakes with a fork. Serve with lemon wedges.

PECAN CLUSTERS

MAKES: about 2½ dozen **HANDS-ON TIME:** 20 min. **TOTAL TIME:** 1 hr., 15 min.

Preheat oven to 300°. Toss 3 cups coarsely chopped pecans with 3 Tbsp. melted butter; spread in a 15- x 10-inch jelly-roll pan. Bake 30 minutes, stirring every 10 minutes. Microwave 6 (2-oz.) chocolate candy coating squares in a 1-qt. microwave-safe glass bowl at MEDIUM (50% power) 2 to 3 minutes or until melted. Stir in pecans and 1½ cups chopped chocolate-coated caramels. Drop by tablespoonfuls onto wax paper; let stand 30 minutes or until chocolate hardens. **NOTE:** We tested with Rolo Chewy Caramels in Milk Chocolate.

BACON-WRAPPED FIGS

MAKES: 12 appetizer servings **HANDS-ON TIME:** 15 min. **TOTAL TIME:** 21 min.

Preheat oven to 350°. Stir together 1 (4-oz.) goat cheese log, softened, and 2 Tbsp. chopped fresh basil. Cut 6 large fresh figs in half lengthwise. Place 1 heaping teaspoonful goat cheese mixture and 1 toasted pecan half on cut side of each fig half. Wrap 1 ready-to-serve bacon slice around each fig half, and secure with a wooden pick. Place figs on a wire rack in a 15- x 10-inch jelly-roll pan, and bake 6 to 8 minutes or until bacon is crisp and browned. **NOTE:** We tested with Oscar Mayer Fully Cooked Bacon.

Chicken Marsala

party perfect

MAKES: 4 servings
HANDS-ON TIME: 40 min.
TOTAL TIME: 45 min.

- 3 Tbsp. butter, divided
- 1 cup pecan pieces, divided
- ⅓ cup all-purpose flour
- 4 skinned and boned chicken breasts (about 1½ lb.)
- 1 tsp. salt
- ½ tsp. pepper
- 2 Tbsp. olive oil
- 8 oz. assorted mushrooms, trimmed and sliced
- 2 shallots, sliced
- ¾ cup chicken broth
- ½ cup Marsala
- ¼ cup coarsely chopped fresh flat-leaf parsley

1. Melt 1 Tbsp. butter in a small nonstick skillet over medium-low heat; add ⅔ cup pecans, and cook, stirring often, 4 to 5 minutes or until toasted and fragrant.

2. Process flour and remaining ⅓ cup pecans in a food processor until finely ground; place flour mixture in a large shallow bowl.

3. Place chicken between 2 sheets of heavy-duty plastic wrap; flatten to ¼-inch thickness, using a rolling pin or flat side of a meat mallet. Sprinkle chicken with salt and pepper; lightly dredge in flour mixture.

4. Melt remaining 2 Tbsp. butter with olive oil in a large nonstick skillet over medium-high heat; add chicken, and cook 2 to 3 minutes on each side or until golden brown and done. Remove chicken from skillet.

5. Add mushrooms and shallots to skillet; sauté 3 minutes or until mushrooms are tender. Add broth and Marsala to skillet, stirring to loosen particles from bottom of skillet. Bring mixture to a boil, reduce heat to medium, and cook, stirring occasionally, 5 minutes or until sauce is slightly thickened. Return chicken to skillet, and cook 1 to 2 minutes or until thoroughly heated.

6. Transfer chicken to a serving platter; spoon mushroom-Marsala mixture over chicken, and sprinkle with parsley and toasted pecans.

Apple-Pear Salad with Maple-Pecan Bacon

quick prep • party perfect

MAKES: 8 servings
HANDS-ON TIME: 20 min.
TOTAL TIME: 1 hr., including vinaigrette

- 8 thick bacon slices
- ¼ cup maple syrup
- 1½ cups finely chopped pecans
- 2 (5-oz.) packages gourmet salad greens
- 1 large Bartlett pear
- 1 large Gala apple
- 1 cup halved seedless red grapes
- 4 oz. Gorgonzola cheese, crumbled
  Cranberry Vinaigrette

1. Preheat oven to 400°. Place a lightly greased wire rack in an aluminum foil-lined 15- x 10-inch jelly-roll pan. Dip bacon slices in syrup, allowing excess to drip off; press pecans onto both sides of bacon. Arrange bacon slices in a single layer on rack, and bake 20 minutes; turn bacon slices, and bake 5 to 10 more minutes or until browned and crisp. Remove from oven, and let stand 5 minutes. Cut bacon crosswise into 1-inch pieces.

2. Place salad greens on a serving platter. Cut pear and apple into thin slices; toss with salad greens. Top with grapes, cheese, and bacon.

3. Serve with Cranberry Vinaigrette.

Cranberry Vinaigrette

quick prep • make-ahead • party perfect

MAKES: 2 cups
HANDS-ON TIME: 10 min.
TOTAL TIME: 10 min.

1. Whisk together 1 cup canned whole-berry cranberry sauce, 1 tsp. orange zest, ½ cup fresh orange juice, ¼ cup each balsamic vinegar and olive oil, 1 Tbsp. light brown sugar, 2 tsp. grated fresh ginger, and ½ tsp. salt in a medium bowl until blended and smooth.

Fettuccine with Zucchini and Pecans

quick prep

MAKES: 6 servings
HANDS-ON TIME: 30 min.
TOTAL TIME: 30 min.

The inspiration for this quick-to-fix pasta dish? Italian. The taste? Pure Southern comfort.

- ¾ cup coarsely chopped pecans
- 1 (12-oz.) package fettuccine
- 2 Tbsp. butter
- 2 Tbsp. olive oil
- 1 lb. small zucchini, shredded
- 2 garlic cloves, minced
- 1 cup freshly grated Asiago cheese
- ¼ cup thinly sliced fresh basil

1. Heat pecans in a small nonstick skillet over medium-low heat, stirring often, 6 to 8 minutes or until toasted and fragrant.

2. Prepare fettuccine according to package directions.

3. Meanwhile, melt butter with olive oil in a large nonstick skillet over medium-high heat; add zucchini and garlic, and sauté 3 to 4 minutes or until zucchini is tender. Toss with hot cooked fettuccine, pecans, Asiago cheese, and basil. Season with salt and freshly ground pepper to taste. Serve immediately.

Turkey Burger Patty Melts

quick prep

MAKES: 6 servings
HANDS-ON TIME: 45 min.
TOTAL TIME: 45 min.

- ¾ cup chopped pecans
- 1½ lb. lean ground turkey
- ⅔ cup crumbled Gorgonzola cheese
- 1 tsp. garlic salt
- ¾ tsp. freshly ground pepper
- ½ cup canned whole-berry cranberry sauce
- ⅓ cup Dijon mustard
- 12 sourdough bread slices
- 6 (¾-oz.) Monterey Jack cheese slices
- 3 cups loosely packed fresh arugula

1. Heat pecans in a small nonstick skillet over medium-low heat, stirring often, 8 to 10 minutes or until toasted and fragrant.
2. Combine ground turkey, next 3 ingredients, and pecans in a large bowl. Shape into 6 (½-inch-thick) patties, shaped to fit bread slices.
3. Cook patties in a large lightly greased skillet over medium heat 5 to 6 minutes on each side or until done.
4. Stir together cranberry sauce and Dijon mustard. Spread 1 Tbsp. cranberry mixture on 1 side of each bread slice. Layer 6 sourdough bread slices with Monterey Jack cheese, arugula, and turkey burgers; top with remaining bread slices, cranberry mixture side down.
5. Cook sandwiches, in 2 batches, on a hot griddle or in a lightly greased skillet over medium heat 2 to 3 minutes on each side or until golden brown and cheese melts.

SOUTHERN HOSPITALITY

The Ultimate Fall Party Menu

When you have crowd-pleasing recipes, bold seasonal flavors, and a few make-ahead strategies, your party will simply fall into place.

Menu

SERVES 8

Sparkling Autumn Chianti

Smoked Paprika Pork Roast with Sticky Stout Barbecue Sauce

Grilled Peppers and Mushrooms

Butternut Squash Spoon Bread

Caramelized Pear Cannoli with Praline Sauce

Cheddar-Pecan Shortbread Leaves

Season's Best Appetizer Platter

Sparkling Autumn Chianti

make-ahead • party perfect

MAKES: 7 cups
HANDS-ON TIME: 15 min.
TOTAL TIME: 8 hr., 15 min.

A blanc de noirs, with its fruity, hint of vanilla flavor, is a great sparkling wine choice for this recipe. We also suggest using Lady or Gala apples.

Make-ahead tip: *Prepare and chill up to 24 hours beforehand.*

- 1 Bartlett pear
- 3 small apples
- 3 fresh plums, cut into wedges
- ½ cup cane syrup
- 2 (4-inch) rosemary sprigs
- 1 vanilla bean, split
- 1 (750-milliliter) bottle Chianti
- 1 (750-milliliter) bottle sparkling white wine, chilled
- Garnish: fresh rosemary sprigs

1. Cut pear lengthwise into ¼-inch slices, cutting from stem end through the bottom. Cut apples crosswise into ¼-inch slices.
2. Stir together pear, apples, plums, and next 3 ingredients in a 3-qt. glass container until fruit is coated. Gradually stir in Chianti. Cover and chill 8 to 24 hours.
3. Stir in sparkling white wine just before serving. Serve over ice. Garnish, if desired.

Smoked Paprika Pork Roast with Sticky Stout Barbecue Sauce

MAKES: 8 servings
HANDS-ON TIME: 25 min.
TOTAL TIME: 1 hr., 30 min., including sauce, plus 1 day for chilling

We "dry-brined" the pork before grilling it. This method calls for rubbing a mixture on the pork and chilling it. This allows for salt to pull seasonings into the meat and improve juiciness and flavor. It's unusual, but you do chill uncovered to keep the rub "dry." (Otherwise, the rub dilutes in trapped moisture.) (Pictured on page 190)

Make-ahead tip: Mix together the paprika pork rub a couple hours ahead.

- 2 **Tbsp. smoked paprika**
- 2 **Tbsp. brown sugar**
- 1 **Tbsp. kosher salt**
- 1 **garlic clove, pressed**
- 1 **tsp. coarsely ground pepper**
- 4 **tsp. chopped fresh thyme, divided**
- 1 **(3½- to 4-lb.) boneless pork loin roast**
  Kitchen string
  Sticky Stout Barbecue Sauce

1. Stir together first 5 ingredients and 2 tsp. thyme. Trim pork roast. Rub paprika mixture over pork. Tie roast with kitchen string at 1½-inch intervals, and place in a 13- x 9-inch baking dish. Chill, uncovered, 24 hours.
2. Light one side of grill, heating to 350° to 400° (medium-high) heat; leave other side unlit. Place pork over lit side, and grill, covered with lid, 8 minutes on each side or until browned. Transfer pork to unlit side, and grill, covered with lid, 35 to 45 minutes or until a meat thermometer inserted in thickest portion registers 145°. Let stand 10 minutes. Brush with Sticky Stout Barbecue Sauce. Sprinkle with remaining 2 tsp. thyme. Serve with remaining sauce.

PAIR WITH: Charles Smith Wines Kungfu Girl Riesling (white) or Edmeades Mendocino County Zinfandel (red) or O'Dempsey's Big Red Ale beer (brewed in Atlanta, GA)

Sticky Stout Barbecue Sauce

quick prep • make-ahead • party perfect

MAKES: about 2 cups
HANDS-ON TIME: 25 min.
TOTAL TIME: 25 min.

"Sticky" is a Kansas City barbecue (and Asian) term for thick and sweet sauces.

Make-ahead tip: Prep and cook sauce 3 days ahead. Cover and chill, and reheat when ready.

- 1 **small onion, finely chopped**
- 1 **Tbsp. vegetable oil**
- 2 **garlic cloves, minced**
- 1 **(11.2-oz.) bottle stout beer**
- 1 **cup spicy barbecue sauce**
- ¼ **cup fig preserves**
- 2 **Tbsp. apple cider vinegar**

1. Sauté onion in hot oil in a large saucepan over medium-high heat 4 to 5 minutes or until tender. Add garlic; sauté 1 minute. Gradually stir in beer. Cook 8 to 10 minutes or until mixture is reduced by half. Reduce heat to medium.
2. Stir in barbecue sauce and next 2 ingredients, and cook 4 to 5 minutes or until thoroughly heated.
NOTE: We tested with Guinness Extra Stout beer and Sweet Baby Ray's Sweet 'n Spicy Barbecue Sauce.

Grilled Peppers and Mushrooms

quick prep • make-ahead • party perfect

MAKES: 8 servings
HANDS-ON TIME: 20 min.
TOTAL TIME: 50 min.

Make-ahead tip: Prep the vinaigrette 3 days early, and wash and cut peppers 1 day ahead.

- ¼ **cup white balsamic vinegar***
- 2 **Tbsp. coarse-grained Dijon mustard**
- 1 **Tbsp. honey**
- ½ **tsp. salt**
- ¼ **tsp. coarsely ground pepper**
- ½ **cup olive oil**
- 4 **large, assorted bell peppers, cut into 2-inch-wide strips**
- 1 **large red onion, thickly sliced**
- 1 **(8-oz.) package baby portobello mushrooms**

1. Whisk together first 5 ingredients. Gradually add oil in a slow, steady stream, whisking constantly until blended. Reserve 2 Tbsp. mixture; cover and chill. Stir bell peppers and next 2 ingredients into remaining vinegar mixture. Cover and chill 30 minutes.
2. Preheat grill to 350° to 400° (medium-high) heat. Remove vegetables from vinegar mixture; discard mixture. Grill vegetables at the same time, placing peppers skin side down on cooking grate. Grill vegetables, covered with grill lid, 6 minutes or until peppers look blistered and grill marks appear. Turn all vegetables, and grill about 2 more minutes or until crisp-tender.
3. Arrange vegetables in a single layer on a serving platter. Drizzle with reserved 2 Tbsp. vinegar mixture just before serving. Season with salt and pepper to taste.
*White wine vinegar may be substituted.

Butternut Squash Spoon Bread

party perfect

MAKES: 8 servings
HANDS-ON TIME: 25 min.
TOTAL TIME: I hr., I0 min.

For the ideal texture, we recommend serving this immediately once baked. (Pictured on page I91)

- 2 cups buttermilk
- 4 large eggs, separated
- 2 cups thawed, frozen unseasoned, pureed butternut squash
- ⅓ cup freshly grated Parmesan cheese
- I cup stone-ground white cornmeal
- I tsp. baking powder
- I tsp. chopped fresh rosemary
- ½ tsp. baking soda
- ½ tsp. salt
- ¼ cup butter, melted

1. Preheat oven to 350°. Cook buttermilk in a heavy saucepan over medium-high heat, stirring often, 4 to 6 minutes or until bubbles appear around edges (do not boil); remove from heat. (Mixture may curdle.)
2. Lightly beat egg yolks in a large bowl; stir in squash and cheese. Combine cornmeal and next 4 ingredients in a small bowl. Stir cornmeal mixture into squash mixture. Pour warm buttermilk over squash mixture; whisk until smooth. Let stand I5 minutes or until lukewarm.
3. Brush a 2½- to 3-qt. baking dish or I2-inch cast-iron skillet with I Tbsp. melted butter; stir remaining melted butter into squash mixture.
4. Beat egg whites at high speed with an electric mixer until stiff peaks form. Carefully fold into squash mixture. Pour mixture into prepared baking dish.
5. Bake at 350° for 30 to 35 minutes or until top is golden and a wooden pick inserted in center comes out clean.
NOTE: We tested with Birds Eye Frozen Butternut Squash. Buy 2 (I2-oz.) packages to measure 2 cups.

Caramelized Pear Cannoli with Praline Sauce

make-ahead • party perfect

MAKES: 8 servings
HANDS-ON TIME: 25 min.
TOTAL TIME: 8 hr., I0 min., including sauce and garnish

Change up this dessert by layering pear filling between purchased pizzelles (Italian waffle-style cookies) and then topping with Praline Sauce and toasted pecans. (Pictured on page I91)

Make-ahead tip: *Get Caramelized Pear Cannoli made, stuffed, and in the fridge 2 days ahead.*

- 3 firm ripe pears, cut into I-inch cubes
- 2 Tbsp. granulated sugar
- I Tbsp. butter, melted
  Parchment paper
- ½ cup chopped pecans
- I (8-oz.) package mascarpone cheese
- I tsp. lemon zest
- ½ cup heavy cream
- 2 Tbsp. powdered sugar
- 8 (5-inch-long) cannoli shells
  Praline Sauce
  Garnish: Paper-Thin Pears

1. Preheat oven to 400°. Toss together first 3 ingredients. Spread in a single layer on a parchment paper-lined I5- x I0-inch jelly-roll pan. Bake 30 to 35 minutes or until lightly browned and tender. Reduce oven temperature to 350°. Let pears cool 20 minutes.
2. Meanwhile, bake pecans at 350° in a single layer in a shallow pan 6 to 8 minutes or until toasted and fragrant, stirring halfway through.
3. Stir together pears, mascarpone, and lemon zest. Beat cream and powdered sugar at high speed with an electric mixer until soft peaks form. Fold whipped cream mixture into pear mixture.
4. Spoon pear mixture into a zip-top plastic freezer bag; snip I corner of bag to make a I-inch hole. Pipe pear mixture into

cannoli shells. Place in a I3- x 9-inch pan. Cover and chill 2 hours before serving. Serve cannoli with warm Praline Sauce, and sprinkle with toasted pecans. Garnish, if desired.
NOTE: We tested with cannoli shells purchased from our grocer's bakery. Ask the bakery clerk if you don't see them.

PAIR WITH:
Saracco Moscato d'Asti

Praline Sauce

quick prep • make-ahead • party perfect

MAKES: about 2 cups
HANDS-ON TIME: I0 min.
TOTAL TIME: 20 min.

This is so good you'll want to make a second batch to try over brownie ice-cream sundaes!

Make-ahead tip: *Make 3 days ahead; cover, chill, then reheat over low heat.*

- I cup firmly packed brown sugar
- ½ cup half-and-half
- ½ cup butter
- ½ tsp. vanilla extract

1. Bring first 3 ingredients to a boil in a small saucepan over medium heat, stirring constantly. Cook, stirring constantly, I minute. Remove from heat, and stir in vanilla; cool slightly (about I0 minutes). Serve warm.

Paper-Thin Pears

make-ahead • party perfect

MAKES: about 24
HANDS-ON TIME: I0 min.
TOTAL TIME: 4 hr., 30 min.

Make-ahead tip: *Make these up to 4 days ahead.*

1. Preheat oven to 200°. Thinly slice I pear lengthwise using a mandoline; reserve first and last slices (with outer skin) for another use. Place pear slices in a single layer on a parchment paper-lined baking sheet. Bake 4 to 5 hours or until crisp. Let cool 20 minutes.

Test Kitchen Tip

Position cookie cutters close together when cutting shapes; dough will be tough if rerolled.

Cheddar-Pecan Shortbread Leaves

make-ahead • party perfect

MAKES: about 2½ dozen
HANDS-ON TIME: 20 min.
TOTAL TIME: 2 hr., 15 min.

Make-ahead tip: Bake shortbread 3 days ahead and store in airtight containers, or make dough, chill up to 3 days, and bake right before your party.

- ⅓ **cup chopped pecans**
- 1 **cup (4 oz.) freshly shredded sharp Cheddar cheese**
- 3 **Tbsp. butter, softened**
- ½ **cup all-purpose flour**
- ¼ **cup cornstarch**
- ½ **tsp. coarsely ground pepper**
- ¼ **tsp. salt**
- 1 **Tbsp. half-and-half**
  Parchment paper

1. Preheat oven to 350°. Bake pecans in a single layer in a shallow pan 8 to 10 minutes or until toasted and fragrant, stirring halfway through. Cool completely (about 20 minutes). Reduce oven temperature to 325°.

2. Process cheese and butter in a food processor 10 to 15 seconds or until creamy, stopping to scrape down sides as needed. Add flour and next 3 ingredients; pulse 9 to 10 times or until mixture is crumbly. Add toasted pecans; pulse 4 to 5 times or until combined. Add half-and-half, and process 10 to 15 seconds or until mixture forms moist clumps.

3. Transfer mixture onto plastic wrap on a flat surface; gather dough into a ball, and flatten into a 1-inch-thick disk. Wrap in plastic wrap, and chill 1 hour until firm, or seal wrapped dough in a zip-top plastic freezer bag, and chill up to 3 days.

4. Turn dough out onto a floured surface. Roll to ⅛- to ¼-inch thickness. Cut with 1½- and 2-inch leaf-shaped cutters. Place on parchment paper-lined baking sheets.

5. Bake at 325° for 16 to 18 minutes or until golden brown. Transfer to a wire rack; let cool 15 minutes.

NOTE: You can also freeze thoroughly cooled, baked shortbread leaves in an airtight container. Store in freezer up to 2 weeks.

TRY THIS TWIST!
Blue Cheese-Pecan Shortbread Leaves: Omit half-and-half. Substitute 1 (4-oz.) container crumbled blue cheese for Cheddar cheese. Prepare recipe as directed, pulsing 9 to 10 times after adding pecans in Step 2.

Season's Best Appetizer Platter

Put together a "Season's Best Appetizer Platter" with Dante goat cheese (sweetgrassdairy.com), spicy aged salami, figs, muscadine grapes, and pecans.

MAMA'S WAY OR YOUR WAY?

Grilled Chicken

Monica McSwain and Megan McSwain get fired up about the juicy, flavorful results of outdoor cooking.

MAMA'S WAY

Chicken Under a Skillet

party perfect

MAKES: 4 servings
HANDS-ON TIME: 25 min.
TOTAL TIME: 2 hr., 15 min.

  1 **(3- to 4-lb.) whole chicken**
  3 **garlic cloves, peeled and quartered**
  1 **cup loosely packed fresh flat-leaf parsley leaves**
  ¼ **cup extra virgin olive oil**
  1 **Tbsp. fresh rosemary leaves**
  1 **Tbsp. lemon zest**
  2 **Tbsp. fresh lemon juice**
1½ **tsp. kosher salt**
1½ **tsp. herbes de Provence**
  1 **tsp. freshly ground pepper**

Meet Mom!

Lives in Winston-Salem, NC; roots for the Tar Heels; has visited 42 of the 58 national parks; likes playing the card game canasta with friends; enjoys visiting Blowing Rock, NC; has hiked the Grand Canyon rim to rim.

1. Remove and discard giblets and neck from chicken. Rinse chicken, and pat dry. Place chicken, breast side down, on a cutting board. Cut chicken, using kitchen shears, along both sides of backbone, separating backbone from chicken; discard backbone. Open chicken as you would a book. Turn chicken, breast side up, and press firmly against breastbone with the heel of your hand until bone cracks. Tuck wing tips under. Place chicken in a baking dish or pan.
2. Pulse garlic and next 8 ingredients in a food processor until mixture forms a thick paste. Reserve half of paste. Rub remaining half of paste on both sides of chicken. Cover chicken with plastic wrap, and chill 1 hour.
3. Heat one side of grill to 300° to 350° (medium) heat; leave other side unlit. Place chicken, breast side down, over lit side of grill; top with a piece of aluminum foil. Place a cast-iron skillet on foil-topped chicken to flatten. Grill, covered with grill lid, 10 to 15 minutes or until chicken is browned. Remove skillet and foil. Turn chicken over, and transfer to unlit side of grill. Grill, covered with grill lid, 45 minutes or until a meat thermometer inserted into thickest portion of breast registers 165°. Remove chicken from grill, and let stand 5 minutes. Brush with reserved paste, if desired.

MEGAN'S WAY

Spicy Honey-Lime Grilled Drumsticks

party perfect

MAKES: 4 servings
HANDS-ON TIME: 30 min.
TOTAL TIME: 1 hr., 20 min., including sauce

  8 **chicken drumsticks**
  1 **tsp. salt**
  ½ **tsp. pepper**
      Vegetable cooking spray
      Spicy Honey-Lime Barbecue Sauce
      Garnishes: fresh cilantro leaves, lime wedges

1. Sprinkle chicken with salt and pepper. Let stand, covered, 30 minutes.
2. Coat cold cooking grate of grill with cooking spray, and place on grill. Preheat grill to 350° to 400° (medium-high) heat. Grill chicken, covered with grill lid, 5 to 10 minutes on each side or until browned. Reduce grill temperature to 250° to 300° (low) heat; grill chicken, covered with grill lid, 20 to 30 minutes.
3. Meanwhile, prepare Spicy Honey-Lime Barbecue Sauce. Reserve 1 cup sauce.
4. Brush chicken with remaining barbecue sauce. Cover with grill lid, and grill 10 more minutes or until done. Serve chicken with reserved 1 cup barbecue sauce. Garnish, if desired.

Meet Daughter!

Southern Living Photo Coordinator; dances in the car; favorite cookbook is her recipe binder; wishes she still had her pink Barbie Corvette; can't live without comfy slippers; once had a bag of cake mix explode all over her.

Spicy Honey–Lime Barbecue Sauce

quick prep • good for you

MAKES: about 2 cups
HANDS-ON TIME: 10 min.
TOTAL TIME: 20 min.

- ¼ cup butter
- 1 medium onion, diced (about 1 cup)
- 1 (12-oz.) bottle chili sauce
- ¼ cup honey
- 2 Tbsp. lime juice
- ¼ tsp. pepper

1. Melt butter in a small saucepan over medium heat; add onion, and sauté 4 to 5 minutes or until tender. Stir in chili sauce, next 3 ingredients, and ⅓ cup water; bring to a boil. Reduce heat to low, and simmer 5 minutes. Store in refrigerator up to 1 week.

HEALTHY INDULGENCE

Shrimp and Grits

Enjoy a hearty bowl of pure comfort. It's fast (ready in 30 minutes!) and free of guilt.

Shrimp and Grits

quick prep • make-ahead • party perfect

MAKES: 6 servings
HANDS-ON TIME: 25 min.
TOTAL TIME: 30 min.

PARMESAN GRITS

- ½ tsp. salt
- 1 cup uncooked quick-cooking grits
- ½ cup freshly grated Parmesan cheese
- ½ tsp. freshly ground pepper

CREAMY SHRIMP SAUCE

- 1 lb. unpeeled, medium-size raw shrimp (41/50 count)
- ¼ tsp. freshly ground pepper
- ⅛ tsp. salt
  Vegetable cooking spray
- 1 Tbsp. olive oil
- 1 Tbsp. all-purpose flour
- 1¼ cups low-sodium fat-free chicken broth
- ½ cup chopped green onions
- 2 garlic cloves, minced
- 1 Tbsp. fresh lemon juice
- ¼ tsp. salt
- ¼ tsp. hot sauce
- 2 cups firmly packed fresh baby spinach

1. Prepare Parmesan Grits: Bring ½ tsp. salt and 4 cups water to a boil in a medium saucepan; gradually whisk in grits. Cook over medium heat, stirring occasionally, 8 minutes or until thickened. Whisk in cheese and pepper. Keep warm.
2. Prepare Creamy Shrimp Sauce: Peel shrimp; devein, if desired. Sprinkle shrimp with pepper and ⅛ tsp. salt. Cook in a large nonstick skillet coated with cooking spray over medium-high heat 1 to 2 minutes on each side or just until shrimp turn pink. Remove from skillet.

3. Reduce heat to medium. Add oil; heat 30 seconds. Whisk in flour; cook 30 seconds to 1 minute. Whisk in broth and next 5 ingredients; cook 2 to 3 minutes or until thickened. Stir in shrimp and spinach; cook 1 minute or until spinach is slightly wilted. Serve immediately over grits.

PER SERVING (INCLUDING ⅓ CUP GRITS AND ABOUT ⅓ CUP SAUCE): **CALORIES** 235; **FAT** 6.1G (SAT 1.9G, MONO 2G, POLY 0.6G); **PROTEIN** 19.1G; **CARB** 25.2G; **FIBER** 1.4G; **CHOL** 118.7MG; **IRON** 3.3MG; **SODIUM** 749MG; **CALC** 177MG

3 Reasons to Indulge!

Smart choices equal delicious results.

{1}
FRESH SHRIMP
High in cholesterol, yes. But this fine protein is low in saturated fat (the true culprit of our bad cholesterol levels).

{2}
GRITS
Even the quick kind are enriched with nutrients such as iron and folate, two must-haves in pregnancy.

{3}
SPINACH
Quick sautéeing significantly increases the antioxidant capacity in spinach, making it a "super" superfood.

The Bounty of Glen Leven

The Hermitage Hotel is serving up farm-fresh sustainability on every plate.

Chef Tyler Brown wants you to eat your veggies. And not just because they're good for you. Through his work with Nashville's Glen Leven, a 66-acre urban farmstead owned by the Land Trust for Tennessee, he's proving they're good for the land too. The Hermitage Hotel, where Tyler works as executive chef of the Capitol Grille, has a unique relationship with the Land Trust. Through donations, the hotel helps fund land conservation.

And in exchange, chef Tyler and his kitchen staff are allowed to cultivate the garden at Glen Leven—trading in chefs' whites for overalls—and bring the harvest right back to the dining room, where his guests enjoy the bounty.

In July 2008, the 122-room Hermitage Hotel (thehermitagehotel.com or 888/888-9414) initiated a line-item charge on guests' room bills: a $2 per night donation to the Land Trust. People can remove the charge, but very few do (about 0.1%). To date, hotel guests have donated $189,000, which the Land Trust has used to purchase property (roughly 1,849 acres) to put into conservation easements and protect against future development. That means virgin forests and lands can stay that way.

Meet the Chefs

Chef Tyler Brown (left) and chef de cuisine Cole Ellis of the Hermitage Hotel's Capitol Grille tend the garden at Glen Leven, a conservation project of the Land Trust for Tennessee.

Orange-Cranberry Braised Cabbage

quick prep

MAKES: 6 servings
HANDS-ON TIME: 30 min.
TOTAL TIME: 30 min.

- 1 medium cabbage, shredded (10 cups)
- 3 Tbsp. olive oil
- 1 (6-oz.) package sweetened dried cranberries
- 1 tsp. orange zest
- ¾ cup fresh orange juice (about 2 oranges)
- ½ cup rice wine vinegar
- 1 Tbsp. honey
- 1 tsp. salt
- ½ tsp. pepper
- ½ tsp. freshly grated nutmeg
- 3 Tbsp. butter

1. Cook cabbage in hot oil in a Dutch oven over medium-high heat, stirring constantly, 5 minutes or until tender. Stir in cranberries and next 7 ingredients. Cook, stirring often, 6 to 7 minutes or until liquid is reduced by half. Remove from heat, and stir in butter.

Sorghum-Glazed Turnips

quick prep

MAKES: 4 servings
HANDS-ON TIME: 40 min.
TOTAL TIME: 50 min.

- 2 lb. small turnips (about 2 inches long)
- 2 Tbsp. butter
- 1 Tbsp. lemon juice
- 1½ tsp. sugar
- ½ tsp. salt
- 2 tsp. sorghum
  Garnish: fresh thyme sprigs

1. Peel turnips, and cut in half.
2. Place turnips in a single layer in a 12-inch heavy skillet; add water to reach halfway up turnips (about 1½ cups). Add butter

and next 3 ingredients. Cover and bring to a boil over high heat; reduce heat to medium-high, and cook, stirring occasionally, 10 minutes. Uncover and cook, stirring often, 8 minutes or until turnips are tender and water has evaporated. Cook, stirring often, 5 more minutes or until turnips are golden. Stir in sorghum and 3 Tbsp. water; toss turnips to coat. Serve immediately. Garnish, if desired.

Roasted Baby Beets

party perfect

MAKES: 4 to 6 servings
HANDS-ON TIME: 25 min.
TOTAL TIME: I hr., 55 min.

- **2 lb. baby beets**
- **4 Tbsp. butter, cut into pieces**
- **I cup vegetable broth**
- **¼ cup honey**
- **2 Tbsp. cider vinegar**
- **3 fresh thyme sprigs**
- **3 fresh parsley sprigs**
- **⅛ tsp. salt**
- **⅛ tsp. pepper**
- **I Tbsp. olive oil**
- **Toppings: chopped hazelnuts, coarsely chopped fresh parsley, crumbled ricotta salata cheese**

1. Preheat oven to 350°. Remove tops and ends of beets; wash beets, and place in an II- x 7-inch baking dish. Dot with butter. Stir together broth and next 6 ingredients; pour over beets. Cover tightly with aluminum foil. Bake I hour and 15 minutes or until tender. Remove beets, reserving ¼ cup pan juices. Cool beets 15 minutes; peel and quarter.

2. Cook beets in hot oil in a large skillet over medium heat, stirring often, 3 to 4 minutes or until lightly browned. Pour reserved pan juices over beets; increase heat to medium-high. Cook 2 to 3 minutes or until liquid is reduced to about I Tbsp. Serve with desired toppings.

Roasted Apples and Parsnips

quick prep • good for you

MAKES: 8 servings
HANDS-ON TIME: 20 min.
TOTAL TIME: 50 min.

- **2 lb. parsnips, peeled and cut lengthwise into quarters**
- **2 lb. Fuji apples, peeled and cut into quarters**
- **1½ to 2 Tbsp. coarsely chopped fresh sage**
- **3 Tbsp. extra virgin olive oil**
- **I tsp. salt**
- **½ to I tsp. pepper**
- **Pinch of ground nutmeg**
- **Pinch of ground allspice**
- **Garnish: fresh sage leaves**

1. Preheat oven to 475°. Toss together all ingredients. Arrange in a single layer in a lightly greased 17- x 12-inch jelly-roll pan.

2. Bake at 475° on an oven rack one-third down from top of oven, stirring occasionally, 30 minutes or until tender and browned. Garnish, if desired.

Bacon-and-Bourbon Collards

party perfect

MAKES: 10 servings
HANDS-ON TIME: 40 min.
TOTAL TIME: I hr., 40 min.

- **4 thick bacon slices**
- **3 Tbsp. butter**
- **I large sweet onion, diced**
- **I (12-oz.) bottle ale beer**
- **½ cup firmly packed brown sugar**
- **½ cup bourbon**
- **I tsp. dried crushed red pepper**
- **6 lb. fresh collard greens, trimmed and chopped**
- **½ cup apple cider vinegar**
- **I tsp. salt**
- **½ tsp. pepper**

1. Cut bacon crosswise into ¼-inch strips. Melt butter in a large Dutch oven over medium heat; add bacon, and cook, stirring often, 8 minutes or until crisp. Drain bacon on paper towels, reserving drippings in skillet. Sauté onion in hot drippings 3 minutes or until onion is tender. Stir in bacon, ale, and next 3 ingredients; cook 3 minutes or until mixture is reduced by one-fourth.

2. Add collards, in batches, and cook, stirring occasionally, 5 minutes or until wilted. Reduce heat to medium-low; cover and cook I hour or to desired degree of doneness. Stir in vinegar, salt, and pepper.

Buttermilk Cornbread

quick prep

MAKES: 8 servings
HANDS-ON TIME: 5 min.
TOTAL TIME: 35 min.

- **1¼ cups all-purpose flour**
- **I cup plus 3 Tbsp. plain white cornmeal**
- **¼ cup sugar**
- **I Tbsp. baking powder**
- **I tsp. salt**
- **¼ cup butter, melted**
- **2 large eggs**
- **I cup buttermilk**

1. Preheat oven to 400°. Lightly grease an 8-inch cast-iron skillet, and heat in oven 5 minutes.

2. Meanwhile, whisk together first 5 ingredients in a bowl; whisk in melted butter. Add eggs and buttermilk, whisking just until smooth.

3. Pour batter into hot skillet. Bake at 400° for 30 to 33 minutes or until golden brown.

Fix-and-Freeze Soups

Warm up and fill up with our big-batch chowders and stews.

Queso Potato Chowder

make-ahead • party perfect

MAKES: 9 cups
HANDS-ON TIME: 40 min.
TOTAL TIME: 1 hr., 10 min.

- ¼ cup butter
- 1 cup finely chopped red bell pepper
- 1 cup finely chopped onion
- 3 poblano peppers, seeded and finely chopped
- 2 garlic cloves, minced
- ½ (20-oz.) package refrigerated Southwestern-style hash brown potatoes
- ¼ tsp. ground cumin
- 2 (14-oz.) cans low-sodium fat-free chicken broth
- ⅓ cup all-purpose flour
- 1½ cups milk
- 1 cup half-and-half
- 1 cup (4 oz.) freshly shredded asadero cheese*
- 1 cup (4 oz.) freshly shredded sharp Cheddar cheese
  Toppings: fried corn tortilla chips, coarsely chopped deli-fried chicken tenders, finely chopped red onion, sliced jalapeño peppers, fresh cilantro sprigs

1. Melt butter in a Dutch oven over medium-high heat; add bell pepper and next 3 ingredients, and sauté 4 to 5 minutes or until tender. Add potatoes and cumin, and sauté 5 minutes or until browned and tender. Gradually stir in broth, stirring to loosen particles from bottom of Dutch oven. Bring to a boil; cover, reduce heat to low, and simmer 25 minutes.

2. Whisk together flour and next 2 ingredients. Stir into potato mixture, and cook over medium heat, stirring constantly, 5 minutes or until thickened. Reduce heat to low.

3. Add cheeses, and cook, stirring constantly, until cheeses melt and mixture is thoroughly heated. Serve with desired toppings.

*Monterey Jack cheese may be substituted.

NOTE: We tested with Simply Potatoes Southwest Style Hash Browns.

Try These Twists!

QUESO-BROCCOLI POTATO CHOWDER: Prepare recipe as directed. Place 1 (12-oz.) package fresh broccoli florets in a 1-qt. microwave-safe glass bowl. Cover tightly with plastic wrap; fold back a small edge to allow steam to escape. Microwave at HIGH 3 to 4½ minutes or until broccoli is crisp-tender, stirring after 2 minutes. Drain and pat dry. Stir hot broccoli into chowder. Top each serving with sautéed chopped ham. Makes: 12 cups. Hands-on time: 40 min.; Total time: 1 hr., 15 min.

CORN-AND-ZUCCHINI QUESO CHOWDER: Omit hash browns. Prepare recipe as directed in Step 1, adding 2 cups frozen whole kernel corn, thawed, and 2 cups chopped zucchini with cumin, and decreasing simmering time to 15 minutes. Proceed as directed, stirring in ½ tsp. kosher salt with cheese in Step 3. Top each serving with chopped cooked bacon, shredded Cheddar cheese, and diced red onion. Makes: 11 cups. Hands-on time: 40 min.; Total time: 1 hr.

Chicken-and-Brisket Brunswick Stew

make-ahead • party perfect

MAKES: 16 cups
HANDS-ON TIME: 25 min.
TOTAL TIME: 2 hr., 40 min.

- 2 large onions, chopped
- 2 garlic cloves, minced
- 1 Tbsp. vegetable oil
- 1½ Tbsp. jarred beef soup base
- 2 lb. skinned and boned chicken breasts
- 1 (28-oz.) can fire-roasted crushed tomatoes
- 1 (12-oz.) package frozen white shoepeg or whole kernel corn
- 1 (10-oz.) package frozen cream-style corn, thawed
- 1 (9-oz.) package frozen baby lima beans
- 1 (12-oz.) bottle chili sauce
- 1 Tbsp. brown sugar
- 1 Tbsp. yellow mustard
- 1 Tbsp. Worcestershire sauce
- ½ tsp. coarsely ground pepper
- 1 lb. chopped barbecued beef brisket (without sauce)
- 1 Tbsp. fresh lemon juice
  Hot sauce (optional)

1. Sauté onions and garlic in hot oil in a 7.5-qt. Dutch oven over medium-high heat 3 to 5 minutes or until tender.

2. Stir together beef soup base and 2 cups water, and add to Dutch oven. Stir in chicken and next 9 ingredients. Bring to a boil. Cover, reduce heat to low, and cook, stirring occasionally, 2 hours.

3. Uncover and shred chicken into large pieces using 2 forks. Stir in brisket and lemon juice. Cover and cook 10 minutes. Serve with hot sauce, if desired.

NOTE: We tested with Superior Touch Better Than Bouillon Beef Base and Muir Glen Organic Fire Roasted Crushed Tomatoes.

Hearty Italian Soup with Parmesan-Pepper Cornbread Biscotti

make-ahead • party perfect

MAKES: 12 cups
HANDS-ON TIME: 40 min.
TOTAL TIME: 2 hr., 40 min., including biscotti

- 1 (16-oz.) package mild Italian sausage
- 2 tsp. olive oil
- 1 large onion, diced
- 2 garlic cloves, minced
- 1 (48-oz.) container chicken broth
- 2 (15-oz.) cans cannellini beans, drained and rinsed
- 2 (14.5-oz.) cans diced tomatoes
- 1 tsp. dried Italian seasoning
- 1 (5-oz.) package baby spinach
- ¼ cup chopped fresh parsley
- ¼ cup chopped fresh basil
   Freshly shaved Parmesan cheese
   Parmesan-Pepper Cornbread Biscotti

1. Cook sausage in hot oil in a Dutch oven over medium heat 7 to 8 minutes on each side or until browned. Remove sausage from Dutch oven, reserving drippings in Dutch oven. Sauté onion in hot drippings 3 minutes or until tender. Add garlic, and sauté 1 minute. Cut sausage into ¼-inch-thick slices, and return to Dutch oven.

2. Stir chicken broth and next 3 ingredients into sausage mixture; bring to a boil over medium-high heat. Reduce heat to medium-low, and simmer 25 minutes.

3. Stir in spinach and next 2 ingredients; cook, stirring occasionally, 5 to 6 minutes or until spinach is wilted. Top each serving with Parmesan cheese. Serve with Parmesan-Pepper Cornbread Biscotti.

Try These Twists!

JALAPEÑO-PEPPER JACK CORNBREAD BISCOTTI: Omit pepper and rosemary. Substitute 1 cup (4 oz.) shredded pepper Jack cheese for Parmesan cheese. Add 1 jalapeño pepper, seeded and finely chopped, to food processor in Step 1. Proceed as directed.

BACON-CHEDDAR-CHIVE CORNBREAD BISCOTTI: Omit pepper and rosemary. Substitute 1 cup (4 oz.) shredded sharp Cheddar cheese for Parmesan cheese. Add 1 Tbsp. chopped fresh chives and 4 cooked bacon slices, crumbled, to food processor in Step 1. Proceed as directed.

PARMESAN-GARLIC CORNBREAD BISCOTTI: Omit pepper and rosemary. Reduce eggs to 2. Add 1 large garlic clove, minced, and ¼ tsp. salt to food processor in Step 1. Brush 2 Tbsp. melted butter on top of dough rectangle before baking. Proceed as directed.

Parmesan-Pepper Cornbread Biscotti

make-ahead • party perfect

MAKES: about 1½ dozen
HANDS-ON TIME: 15 min.
TOTAL TIME: 1 hr., 30 min.

- 2 (6-oz.) packages buttermilk cornbread-and-muffin mix
- 1 cup freshly grated Parmesan cheese, divided
- 2 tsp. freshly ground pepper
- ¾ tsp. chopped fresh rosemary
- ¼ cup cold butter, cut into pieces
- 3 large eggs, divided
- ¼ cup buttermilk
   Parchment paper

1. Preheat oven to 350°. Combine cornbread mix, ¾ cup grated Parmesan cheese, and next 2 ingredients in a food processor bowl. Add butter, and pulse 5 to 6 times or until crumbly.

2. Whisk together 2 eggs and buttermilk. With processor running, gradually add egg mixture through food chute, and process just until well moistened. (Batter will be thick.)

3. Spread dough into a 12- x 4-inch rectangle on a parchment paper-lined baking sheet using lightly greased hands. Lightly beat remaining egg; brush over dough. Sprinkle with remaining cheese.

4. Bake at 350° for 20 minutes or until pale golden brown and firm. Let cool on baking sheet on a wire rack 10 minutes. Reduce oven temperature to 300°.

5. Gently slide loaf (on parchment paper) onto a cutting board, and cut loaf diagonally into ½-inch-thick slices using a serrated knife. Place slices, cut sides down, on a baking sheet lined with a new sheet of parchment paper.

6. Bake at 300° for 15 to 20 minutes on each side or until golden and crisp. Let cool on baking sheet on wire rack 15 minutes. Serve warm. Store in an airtight container up to 3 days, or freeze up to 2 weeks.

NOTE: We tested with Martha White Buttermilk Cornbread & Muffin Mix.

RECIPE INSPIRED BY KELLY MAPES
FORT COLLINS, COLORADO

Chicken-Andouille Gumbo with Roasted Potatoes

make-ahead • party perfect

MAKES: 10 cups
HANDS-ON TIME: 45 min.
TOTAL TIME: 3 hr., 10 min., including potatoes

- 1 lb. andouille sausage, cut into ¼-inch-thick slices
- ½ cup peanut oil
- ¾ cup all-purpose flour
- 1 large onion, coarsely chopped
- 1 red bell pepper, coarsely chopped
- 1 cup thinly sliced celery
- 2 garlic cloves, minced
- 2 tsp. Cajun seasoning
- ⅛ tsp. ground red pepper (optional)
- 1 (48-oz.) container chicken broth
- 2 lb. skinned and boned chicken breasts
  Roasted Potatoes
  Toppings: chopped fresh parsley, cooked and crumbled bacon, hot sauce

1. Cook sausage in a large skillet over medium heat, stirring often, 7 minutes or until browned. Remove sausage; drain and pat dry with paper towels.
2. Heat oil in a stainless-steel Dutch oven over medium heat; gradually whisk in flour, and cook, whisking constantly, 18 to 20 minutes or until flour is caramel-colored. (Do not burn mixture.) Reduce heat to low, and cook, whisking constantly, until mixture is milk chocolate-colored and texture is smooth (about 2 minutes).
3. Increase heat to medium. Stir in onion, next 4 ingredients, and, if desired, ground red pepper. Cook, stirring constantly, 3 minutes. Gradually stir in chicken broth; add chicken and sausage. Increase heat to medium-high, and bring to a boil. Reduce heat to low, and simmer, stirring occasionally, 1 hour and 30 minutes to 1 hour and 40 minutes or until chicken is done. Shred chicken into large pieces using 2 forks.

4. Place Roasted Potatoes in serving bowls. Spoon gumbo over potatoes. Serve immediately with desired toppings.

TRY THIS TWIST!
Chicken-and-Shrimp Gumbo:
Prepare recipe as directed through Step 3. Stir in ½ to ¾ lb. peeled and deveined, medium-size raw shrimp (31/40 count). Cook 5 minutes or just until shrimp turn pink. Serve with Roasted Potatoes and desired toppings.

Roasted Potatoes

quick prep • party perfect

MAKES: 6 to 8 servings
HANDS-ON TIME: 10 min.
TOTAL TIME: 50 min.

- 3 lb. baby red potatoes, quartered
- 1 Tbsp. peanut oil
- 1 tsp. kosher salt

1. Preheat oven to 450°. Stir together all ingredients in a large bowl. Place potatoes in a single layer in a lightly greased 15- x 10-inch jelly-roll pan. Bake 40 to 45 minutes or until tender and browned, stirring twice.

RECIPE INSPIRED BY TRAVIS DARCY
FAIRFAX, CALIFORNIA

Pumpkin Cornbread Muffins

MAKES: 2 dozen
HANDS-ON-TIME: 10 min.
TOTAL TIME: 30 min.

- 2 cups self-rising white cornmeal
- ⅓ cup sugar
- ½ tsp. pumpkin pie spice
- 5 large eggs
- 1 (15-oz.) can pumpkin
- 1 (8-oz.) container sour cream
- ½ cup butter, melted

1. Preheat oven to 450°. Stir together first 3 ingredients in a large bowl; make a well in center of mixture. Whisk together eggs and next 3 ingredients; add to cornmeal mixture, stirring just until dry ingredients are moistened. Spoon batter into 2 lightly greased 12-cup Bundt brownie muffin pans or regular muffin pans, filling three-fourths full.
2. Bake at 450° for 13 to 15 minutes or until tops are golden brown. Cool in pan on a wire rack 5 minutes. Remove from pan to wire rack.

NOTE: We tested with Nordic Ware Pro Cast Bundt Brownie Pan.

Soup Anytime!

Leftovers from these recipes (if you have any!) will last up to 3 days in the fridge or up to 1 month in the freezer. Follow these steps for easy storage.

{1}
COOL. Refrigerators and freezers cannot cool soups quickly enough to be food safe. Speed up the cooling process by placing the pot of soup in a bath of ice water in the sink. Stir soup often to help release the heat.

{2}
PACKAGE. Label and date gallon- or quart-size zip-top plastic freezer bags, place in a bowl, and cuff the bag over the edge. Ladle soup into each bag, then let out any excess air and seal.

{3}
FREEZE. Lay bags flat in a single layer in the freezer; when frozen, stack bags to save space.

{4}
REHEAT. Thaw overnight in fridge. Reheat chowders over low heat; gumbo, stew, and Hearty Italian Soup over medium-low. Stir occasionally.

"I'm looking for a few new go-to casseroles. Any suggestions?"

MELODY LEE, DOTHAN, ALABAMA

{1}
REINVENT "BREAKFAST FOR SUPPER"

Ham-Hash Brown Casserole

quick prep

MAKES: 8 servings
HANDS-ON TIME: 10 min.
TOTAL TIME: 55 min.

- 1 (30-oz.) package frozen shredded country-style hash browns, thawed
- 1 (10-oz.) package frozen diced onion, red and green bell pepper, and celery, thawed
- 1 (10¾-oz.) can cream of potato soup
- 1 (10-oz.) container refrigerated Alfredo sauce
- 3 cups chopped cooked ham
- 2 cups (8 oz.) shredded sharp Cheddar cheese
- 1 cup grated fresh zucchini
- 1 cup milk
- 2 cups crushed round buttery crackers
- 3 Tbsp. melted butter

1. Preheat oven to 400°. Combine first 8 ingredients. Spoon mixture into a lightly greased 13- x 9-inch baking dish.
2. Combine crushed crackers and butter. Top casserole with cracker mixture.
3. Bake at 400° for 30 to 35 minutes or until bubbly and cracker mixture is browned. Let stand 15 minutes.

{2}
TAKE A SHORTCUT THROUGH THE FREEZER SECTION

Chicken-and-Rice Bake

quick prep

MAKES: 6 servings
HANDS-ON TIME: 15 min.
TOTAL TIME: 55 min.

- 2 Tbsp. butter
- 1 (10-oz.) package frozen chopped onions
- 2 (10-oz.) packages frozen steam-in-bag brown-and-wild rice with broccoli and carrots
- 3 cups chopped cooked chicken
- 1 (14-oz.) can chicken broth
- 1 (10¾-oz.) can cream of chicken soup with herbs
- 1 (8-oz.) container sour cream
- 1 (8-oz.) can diced water chestnuts, drained
- ¼ tsp. pepper
- ¾ cup sliced almonds

1. Preheat oven to 400°. Melt butter in a large skillet over medium heat; add onions, and sauté 6 to 8 minutes or until tender.
2. Stir together frozen rice packages and next 6 ingredients; stir in onions. Spoon mixture into a lightly greased 13- x 9-inch baking dish. Top with sliced almonds.
3. Bake at 400° for 30 to 35 minutes or until bubbly and almonds are lightly browned. Let stand 10 minutes.
NOTE: We tested with Birds Eye Steamfresh Brown & Wild Rice With Broccoli & Carrots.

{3}
MAKE A COOKTOP CASSEROLE

One-Dish Chicken Pasta

quick prep

MAKES: 6 servings
HANDS-ON TIME: 30 min.
TOTAL TIME: 30 min.

- 1 (12-oz.) package farfalle (bow-tie) pasta
- 5 Tbsp. butter, divided
- 1 medium onion, chopped
- 1 medium-size red bell pepper, chopped
- 1 (8-oz.) package fresh mushrooms, quartered
- ⅓ cup all-purpose flour
- 3 cups chicken broth
- 2 cups milk
- 3 cups chopped cooked chicken
- 1 cup (4 oz.) shredded Parmesan cheese
- 1 tsp. pepper
- ½ tsp. salt
  Toppings: toasted sliced almonds, chopped fresh flat-leaf parsley, shredded Parmesan cheese

1. Prepare pasta according to package directions. Meanwhile, melt 2 Tbsp. butter in a Dutch oven over medium heat. Add onion and bell pepper; sauté 5 minutes or until tender. Add mushrooms; sauté 4 minutes. Remove from Dutch oven.
2. Melt remaining 3 Tbsp. butter in Dutch oven over low heat; whisk in flour until smooth. Cook, whisking constantly, 1 minute. Gradually whisk in chicken broth and milk; cook over medium heat, whisking constantly, 5 to 7 minutes or until thickened and bubbly.
3. Stir chicken, sautéed vegetables, and hot cooked pasta into sauce. Add cheese, pepper, and salt. Serve with desired toppings.

{4}
SERVE A SOUTHWEST FAVE

Chicken Enchiladas

quick prep

MAKES: 4 servings
HANDS-ON TIME: 35 min.
TOTAL TIME: 55 min.

- 5 Tbsp. butter, divided
- 1 medium onion, chopped
- 1 medium-size red bell pepper, chopped
- 2 cups chopped cooked chicken
- 3 (4-oz.) cans diced green chiles, divided
- 3 cups (12 oz.) shredded colby-Jack cheese blend, divided
- 8 (8-inch) soft taco-size flour tortillas
- 2 Tbsp. all-purpose flour
- ¾ cup chicken broth
- ½ cup milk
   Toppings: fresh cilantro leaves, chopped tomato, shredded lettuce

1. Preheat oven to 350°. Melt 2 Tbsp. butter in a large skillet over medium heat; add onion and bell pepper, and sauté 5 minutes or until tender.
2. Stir together onion mixture, chicken, 1 can diced green chiles, and 2 cups shredded cheese. Spoon a heaping ⅓ cupful chicken mixture on 1 end of each tortilla, and roll up. Arrange enchiladas, seam sides down, in a lightly greased 13- x 9-inch baking dish.
3. Bake at 350° for 10 minutes.
4. Meanwhile, melt remaining 3 Tbsp. butter in a heavy saucepan over low heat; whisk in flour until smooth. Cook, whisking constantly, 1 minute. Gradually whisk in chicken broth and milk; cook over medium heat, whisking constantly, 3 to 4 minutes or until thickened and bubbly. Remove from heat, and stir in remaining 2 cans green chiles.
5. Remove enchiladas from oven. Pour green chile mixture over enchiladas. Sprinkle with remaining 1 cup cheese.
6. Bake at 350° for 20 to 25 minutes or until bubbly. Serve with desired toppings.

{5}
FANCY IT UP WITH SEAFOOD

Shrimp Casserole

quick prep

MAKES: 6 servings
HANDS-ON TIME: 15 min.
TOTAL TIME: 1 hr.

- 1 cup uncooked long-grain rice
- ¼ cup butter
- 2 lb. peeled and deveined, medium-size raw shrimp (21/25 count)
- 1 (10-oz.) package frozen diced onion, red and green bell pepper, and celery
- 4 garlic cloves, minced
- 1 (10¾-oz.) can cream of shrimp soup
- 1 (10-oz.) container refrigerated Alfredo sauce
- ⅓ cup dry white wine or chicken broth
- ½ tsp. Cajun seasoning
- ¼ tsp. ground red pepper
- ¾ cup grated Parmesan cheese

1. Preheat oven to 400°. Bring 2 cups water to a boil; stir in rice, and cover. Reduce heat, and simmer 20 minutes or until water is absorbed and rice is tender.
2. Meanwhile, melt butter in a large skillet over medium-high heat. Add shrimp and next 2 ingredients; sauté 4 to 5 minutes or just until shrimp turn pink. Stir in soup, next 4 ingredients, hot cooked rice, and ½ cup Parmesan cheese. Spoon into a lightly greased 11- x 7-inch baking dish. Sprinkle with remaining ¼ cup Parmesan cheese.
3. Bake at 400° for 25 to 30 minutes or until bubbly. Let stand 5 minutes.
NOTE: We tested with Pictsweet Seasoning Blend for frozen diced vegetables.

November

THE ULTIMATE SOUTHERN
Thanksgiving Cookbook

As Southerners, we can't take credit for Thanksgiving.* But we sure know how to feast, so it's no surprise that dishes like sweet potato casserole and cornbread dressing have become part of the national holiday menu. Here, we offer ways to feed guests from Thursday through Sunday—so you can obsess less about the menu and devote more time to what matters.

Thanksgiving. The very name of this holiday implies action: giving thanks. So it's no surprise that the day itself is full of activity—setting the table, folding the napkins, rearranging the chairs, roasting the turkey, and so on. But at some point during this whirlwind, there's usually a moment when you, the here-and-there hostess, get to pause and enjoy, say, the subtle squeeze of your mother's hand as you bow your heads to bless the meal. And that's when, instead of doing the moving and shuffling around, you are moved. By the fact that everyone you love is assembled under one roof. By the fact that, despite her passing, Grandma is present through her famous green bean casserole. By the fact that your children's children are now at the kids' table. And by the fact that the recipes you have lovingly prepared could very well become one of their most cherished memories of you. Now that's something to savor.

The Turkey

Roasted, deep-fried, or grilled, one of these stunning centerpieces is sure to please.

Creole Deep-Fried Turkey
make-ahead • party perfect

MAKES: 8 servings
HANDS-ON TIME: 20 min.
TOTAL TIME: 2 hr., 10 min.

  Peanut oil (about 3 gal.)
1 (12- to 14-lb.) whole fresh turkey*
4 Tbsp. Creole seasoning

1. Pour oil into a deep propane turkey fryer 10 to 12 inches from top; heat to 350° over a medium-low flame according to manufacturer's instructions (about 45 minutes).
2. Meanwhile, remove giblets and neck from turkey, and rinse turkey with cold water. Drain cavity well; pat dry. Loosen and lift skin from turkey with fingers, without totally detaching skin; spread 1 Tbsp. Creole seasoning under skin. Carefully replace skin. Sprinkle 1 Tbsp. Creole seasoning inside cavity; rub into cavity. Sprinkle outside of turkey with remaining 2 Tbsp. Creole seasoning; rub into skin. Let turkey stand at room temperature 30 minutes.
3. Place turkey on fryer rod. Carefully lower turkey into hot oil with rod attachment.
4. Fry 35 to 45 minutes or until a meat thermometer inserted in thickest portion of thigh registers 165° (about 3 minutes per pound plus an additional 5 minutes. Keep oil temperature between 300° and 325°). Remove turkey from oil; drain and let stand 30 minutes before slicing.
*Frozen whole turkey, thawed, may be substituted.

*Actually, some claim that the earliest Thanksgiving celebration took place in St. Augustine, Florida, while others point to Virginia, but in the spirit of harmony during this holiday season, we won't argue with the Plymouth contingency.

Citrus-Grilled Turkey Breast

make-ahead • party perfect

MAKES: 6 servings
HANDS-ON TIME: 40 min.
TOTAL TIME: 3 hr., 40 min.

To prevent a top-heavy turkey breast from tipping over onto its side, use kitchen shears to trim the bony lower portion of the rib cage—just enough to level the underside of the breast so it rests securely in the pan or on the grill.

- 1 (5- to 6-lb.) skin-on, bone-in turkey breast
- ¼ cup chopped fresh flat-leaf parsley
- 2 garlic cloves, minced
- 1 Tbsp. lemon zest
- 2 Tbsp. olive oil
- 1 tsp. freshly ground pepper
- 2 tsp. salt

1. Let turkey breast stand at room temperature 30 minutes; rinse with cold water, and pat turkey dry.
2. Stir together parsley, next 4 ingredients, and 1 tsp. salt. Loosen and lift skin from turkey without totally detaching skin, and rub parsley mixture under skin. Replace skin. Sprinkle cavity with ½ tsp. salt; rub into cavity. Sprinkle remaining ½ tsp. salt on skin; rub into skin.
3. Light 1 side of grill, heating to 350° to 400° (medium-high) heat; leave other side unlit. Place turkey over lit side, and grill, without grill lid, 4 minutes on each side or until golden brown. Transfer turkey to unlit side, and grill, covered with grill lid, 2 to 2½ hours or until a meat thermometer inserted into thickest portion registers 165°. Remove from heat, and let stand 30 minutes before slicing.

Test Kitchen Tip

Cranberry Salsa (page 255) spiked with crystallized ginger and jalapeños is the perfect match for Citrus-Grilled Turkey Breast. Garnish with fresh cranberries, lemon leaves, and grilled citrus slices.

Apple-Bourbon Turkey and Gravy

make-ahead • party perfect

MAKES: 8 servings
HANDS-ON TIME: 55 min.
TOTAL TIME: 4 hr., 40 min., plus 12 hr. for chilling

Apple slices and aromatic vegetables line the roasting pan, creating a colorful rack that adds terrific flavor to both the turkey and pan juices.

- 4 cups apple juice
- 1 cup bourbon
- ½ cup firmly packed light brown sugar
- 1 (12- to 15-lb.) whole fresh turkey*
  Cheesecloth
  Kitchen string
- 4 celery ribs
- 4 large carrots
- 3 small apples, quartered or halved
- 1 large onion, sliced
- ¼ cup butter
- ¼ cup all-purpose flour
- ½ cup chicken broth (optional)

1. Stir together apple juice and next 2 ingredients, stirring until sugar dissolves.
2. Remove giblets and neck from turkey, and rinse turkey with cold water. Drain cavity well; pat dry. Place turkey in a large roasting pan. Dip cheesecloth in apple juice mixture. Wring dry. Cover turkey with cheesecloth; pour apple juice mixture over cheesecloth, coating completely. Cover and chill 12 to 24 hours, basting occasionally with marinade.
3. Preheat oven to 325°. Remove turkey from pan, discarding cheesecloth and reserving 3 cups marinade. Sprinkle cavity with desired amount of salt; rub into cavity. Sprinkle desired amount of salt and freshly ground pepper on skin; rub into skin. Tie ends of legs together with string; tuck wingtips under.
4. Arrange celery and next 3 ingredients in a single layer in bottom of roasting pan. Place turkey, breast side up, on celery mixture; pour reserved marinade over turkey in pan.
5. Bake at 325° for 3 hours and 15 minutes to 4 hours or until a meat thermometer inserted into thickest portion of thigh registers 165°, basting every 30 minutes with pan juices and shielding with aluminum foil after 2 hours and 30 minutes to prevent excessive browning, if necessary. Remove from oven, and let stand 30 minutes.
6. Transfer turkey to a serving platter, reserving 2½ cups pan drippings. Pour reserved drippings through a fine wire-mesh strainer into a large measuring cup, discarding solids.
7. Melt butter in a saucepan over medium heat; whisk in flour, and cook, whisking constantly, 1 to 2 minutes or until smooth. Gradually add drippings to pan, and bring to a boil. Reduce heat to medium, and simmer, stirring mixture occasionally, 5 minutes or until gravy thickens. Add up to ½ cup chicken broth for desired consistency. Stir in salt and freshly ground pepper to taste. Serve turkey with warm gravy.

*Frozen whole turkey, thawed, may be substituted.

Roasted Turkey with Béarnaise Butter

party perfect

MAKES: 8 servings
HANDS-ON TIME: 40 min.
TOTAL TIME: 4 hr., 50 min., including Béarnaise Butter

1	(12- to 15-lb.) whole fresh turkey*
	Béarnaise Butter, divided
	Kitchen string
2	cups dry white wine
2½	cups chicken broth, divided
¼	cup all-purpose flour
	Garnishes: Roasted Onions (page 254), fresh herb sprigs, grapes

1. Preheat oven to 325°. Remove giblets and neck from turkey, and rinse turkey with cold water. Drain cavity well; pat dry. Loosen and lift skin from turkey breast without totally detaching skin. Rub ¼ cup Béarnaise Butter under skin; replace skin. Sprinkle cavity and outside of turkey with desired amount of salt and freshly ground pepper.
2. Place turkey, breast side up, on a lightly greased roasting rack in a large roasting pan. Tie ends of legs together with string; tuck wingtips under. Rub entire turkey with ¼ cup Béarnaise Butter. Pour wine and 2 cups chicken broth into roasting pan.
3. Bake at 325° for 3 hours and 15 minutes to 4 hours or until a meat thermometer inserted into thickest portion of thigh registers 165°, basting every 30 minutes with pan juices. Shield with aluminum foil after 1½ hours to prevent excessive browning, if necessary. Remove from oven, and let stand 30 minutes.
4. Transfer turkey to a serving platter, reserving 2½ cups pan drippings. Pour reserved drippings through a fine wire-mesh strainer into a bowl, discarding solids.

5. Melt remaining Béarnaise Butter in a saucepan over medium heat; whisk in flour, and cook, whisking constantly, 1 to 2 minutes or until smooth. Gradually add reserved drippings to saucepan, and bring to a boil, whisking constantly. Reduce heat, and simmer, stirring occasionally, 5 minutes or until thickened. Add up to ½ cup remaining chicken broth for desired consistency. Add salt and pepper to taste. Serve turkey with gravy.
*Frozen whole turkey, thawed, may be substituted.

Béarnaise Butter

quick prep • make-ahead • party perfect

MAKES: about 1 cup
HANDS-ON TIME: 15 min.
TOTAL TIME: 25 min.

Not only does this holiday favorite add rich flavor to roasted turkey, but also it's delicious stirred into hot cooked grits or mashed potatoes, melted over steamed broccoli or grilled asparagus, or spread on warm cocktail buns filled with sliced beef tenderloin.

⅓	cup dry white wine
1	Tbsp. white wine vinegar
2	shallots, minced (about ¼ cup)
¾	cup butter, softened
1	Tbsp. chopped fresh tarragon
1	tsp. lemon zest
⅛	tsp. pepper

1. Cook first 3 ingredients in a small saucepan over medium-high heat 5 minutes or until liquid is reduced to 1 Tbsp. Remove from heat, and cool 10 minutes. Stir in butter and remaining ingredients. Store in an airtight container in refrigerator up to 5 days.

The Dressing

Turkey may be the centerpiece, but cornbread dressing is the heart and soul of a Southern Thanksgiving. We're sharing five favorites, including an irresistible twist with shrimp and grits.

Cornbread Dressing

make-ahead • party perfect

MAKES: 14 to 16 servings
HANDS-ON TIME: 25 min.
TOTAL TIME: 2 hr., 20 min., including Cornbread Crumbles

½	cup butter
3	cups diced celery
2	cups diced sweet onions
½	cup finely chopped fresh sage
	Cornbread Crumbles
3	cups soft, fresh breadcrumbs
4	large eggs, lightly beaten
7	cups chicken broth
1	Tbsp. freshly ground pepper

1. Preheat oven to 400°. Melt butter in a large skillet over medium-high heat; add celery and onions, and sauté 5 to 6 minutes or until onions are tender. Stir in sage, and sauté 1 minute.
2. Stir together Cornbread Crumbles and breadcrumbs in a large bowl. Stir in eggs, next 2 ingredients, and celery mixture, stirring until blended. Divide cornbread mixture between lightly greased 13- x 9-inch baking dish and 1 lightly greased 8-inch square baking dish.
3. Bake at 400° for 45 to 55 minutes or until set and golden brown.

Try These Twists!

CHORIZO-AND-DRIED CHERRY DRESSING: Sauté ¾ lb. diced chorizo sausage in 1 Tbsp. hot oil in a large skillet over medium-high heat 4 to 5 minutes or until browned; drain. Prepare recipe as directed, stirring sausage and 1½ cups coarsely chopped dried cherries into breadcrumbs in Step 2.

FRESH CORN-AND-GREEN CHILE DRESSING: Substitute 3 cups fresh corn kernels for diced celery and ½ cup chopped fresh cilantro for sage. Prepare recipe as directed, stirring in 2 (4-oz.) cans chopped green chiles with cilantro in Step 1.

Cornbread Crumbles

make-ahead • party perfect

MAKES: enough for 1 dressing recipe
HANDS-ON TIME: 10 min.
TOTAL TIME: 1 hr., 10 min.

1. Preheat oven to 425°. Stir together 3 cups self-rising white cornmeal mix, 1 cup all-purpose flour, and 2 Tbsp. sugar in a large bowl; whisk in 3 cups buttermilk; 3 large eggs, lightly beaten; and ½ cup butter, melted. Pour batter into a lightly greased 13- x 9-inch pan. Bake 30 minutes or until golden brown. Remove from oven, invert onto a wire rack, and cool completely (about 30 minutes); crumble cornbread.

Creole Cornbread Dressing

party perfect

MAKES: 14 to 16 servings
HANDS-ON TIME: 55 min.
TOTAL TIME: 2 hr., 55 min.

- 1 (12-oz.) package andouille sausage, chopped
- 8 green onions, thinly sliced
- 3 large celery ribs, diced
- 1 large sweet onion, diced
- 1 medium-size green bell pepper, diced
  Cornbread Crumbles
- ½ cup butter
- 1 (8-oz.) package fresh mushrooms, diced
- 1 cup dry sherry
- ½ cup chopped fresh parsley
- 2 cups chopped toasted pecans
- 2 Tbsp. Creole seasoning
- 2 (14-oz.) cans low-sodium chicken broth
- 2 large eggs

1. Preheat oven to 350°. Sauté andouille sausage in a large skillet over medium-high heat 3 to 4 minutes or until lightly browned. Add green onions and next 3 ingredients, and sauté 5 minutes or until vegetables are tender. Transfer mixture to a large bowl; stir in Cornbread Crumbles.
2. Melt butter in skillet over medium-high heat; add mushrooms, and sauté 3 minutes. Add sherry, and cook, stirring often, 5 to 6 minutes or until liquid is reduced by half; stir in parsley. Stir mushroom mixture, toasted pecans, and Creole seasoning into cornbread mixture.
3. Whisk together chicken broth and eggs; add to cornbread mixture, stirring gently just until moistened. Divide mixture between 1 lightly greased 13- x 9-inch baking dish and 1 lightly greased 8-inch square baking dish.
4. Bake dressing at 350° for 40 to 45 minutes or until golden brown.

Shrimp and Grits Dressing

party perfect

MAKES: 6 to 8 servings
HANDS-ON TIME: 35 min.
TOTAL TIME: 1 hr., 50 min.

- 1 lb. peeled, medium-size raw shrimp (51/60 count)
- 3 cups chicken broth
- ½ tsp. salt
- ¼ tsp. ground red pepper
- 1 cup uncooked regular grits
- ½ cup butter
- 3 large eggs, lightly beaten
- 1 red bell pepper, diced
- 1 cup fine, dry breadcrumbs
- 1 cup chopped green onions
- ½ cup grated Parmesan cheese

1. Preheat oven to 325°. Devein shrimp, if desired.
2. Bring broth and next 2 ingredients to a boil in a large saucepan over medium-high heat. Whisk in grits, and return to a boil; reduce heat to low, and stir in butter. Cover and simmer, stirring occasionally, 10 minutes or until liquid is absorbed. Remove from heat.
3. Stir together eggs and next 4 ingredients in a large bowl. Gradually stir about one-fourth of hot grits mixture into egg mixture; add egg mixture to remaining hot grits mixture, stirring constantly. Stir in shrimp until blended. Pour grits mixture into a lightly greased 11- x 7-inch baking dish.
4. Bake at 325° for 55 minutes to 1 hour or until mixture is set. Let stand 10 minutes.

The Sides

These fresh and easy recipes celebrate Southern bounty.

Sweet Potato-Carrot Casserole

make-ahead • party perfect

MAKES: 8 to 10 servings
HANDS-ON TIME: 40 min.
TOTAL TIME: 3 hr., 40 min., including pecans

Sugared pecans and mini marshmallows add a sweet note to this updated classic.

  6 **large sweet potatoes (about 5 lb.)**
1½ **lb. carrots, sliced**
  ¼ **cup butter**
  1 **cup sour cream**
  2 **Tbsp. sugar**
  1 **tsp. lemon zest**
  ½ **tsp. salt**
  ½ **tsp. ground nutmeg**
  ½ **tsp. freshly ground pepper**
1½ **cups miniature marshmallows**
  1 **cup Sugar-and-Spice Pecans**

1. Preheat oven to 400°. Bake sweet potatoes on an aluminum foil-lined 15- x 10-inch jelly-roll pan 1 hour or until tender. Reduce oven temperature to 350°. Cool potatoes 30 minutes.
2. Meanwhile, cook carrots in boiling water to cover 20 to 25 minutes or until very tender; drain.
3. Process carrots and butter in a food processor until smooth, stopping to scrape down sides as needed. Transfer carrot mixture to a large bowl.
4. Peel and cube sweet potatoes. Process, in batches, in food processor until smooth, stopping to scrape down sides as needed. Add sweet potatoes to carrot mixture.

Stir in sour cream and next 5 ingredients, stirring until blended. Spoon mixture into a lightly greased 13- x 9-inch baking dish.
5. Bake at 350° for 30 minutes or until thoroughly heated. Remove from oven. Sprinkle with marshmallows. Bake 10 more minutes or until marshmallows are golden brown. Remove from oven, and sprinkle with Sugar-and-Spice Pecans.
NOTE: To make ahead, prepare recipe as directed through Step 4; cover and chill up to 24 hours. Remove from refrigerator, and let stand 30 minutes. Proceed with recipe as directed in Step 5.

Sugar-and-Spice Pecans

make-ahead • party perfect

MAKES: 4 cups
HANDS-ON TIME: 15 min.
TOTAL TIME: 1 hr., 10 min.

  1 **egg white**
  4 **cups pecan halves and pieces**
  ½ **cup sugar**
  1 **Tbsp. orange zest**
  1 **tsp. ground cinnamon**
  1 **tsp. ground ginger**

1. Preheat oven to 350°. Whisk egg white in a large bowl until foamy. Add pecans, and stir until evenly coated.
2. Stir together sugar and next 3 ingredients in a small bowl until blended. Sprinkle sugar mixture over pecans; stir gently until pecans are evenly coated. Spread pecans in a single layer in a lightly greased aluminum foil-lined 15- x 10-inch jelly-roll pan.
3. Bake at 350° for 24 to 26 minutes or until pecans are toasted and dry, stirring once after 10 minutes. Remove from oven, and let cool completely (about 30 minutes).
NOTE: To make ahead, prepare pecans as directed. Store in a zip-top plastic freezer bag at room temperature up to 3 days, or freeze up to 3 weeks.

Balsamic-Roasted Carrots and Parsnips

quick prep • party perfect

MAKES: 8 to 10 servings
HANDS-ON TIME: 20 min.
TOTAL TIME: 1 hr.

  1 **(4-oz.) package feta cheese, crumbled**
  ½ **cup chopped dried sweet cherries**
  ¼ **cup chopped fresh flat-leaf parsley**
  1 **tsp. lemon zest**
  ½ **tsp. dried crushed red pepper**
  4 **Tbsp. olive oil, divided**
1½ **lb. carrots**
1½ **lb. parsnips**
  2 **Tbsp. light brown sugar**
  3 **Tbsp. balsamic vinegar**

1. Preheat oven to 400°. Toss together first 5 ingredients and 1 Tbsp. olive oil in a small bowl.
2. Cut carrots and parsnips lengthwise into long, thin strips.
3. Whisk together brown sugar, balsamic vinegar, and remaining 3 Tbsp. olive oil in a large bowl. Toss with carrots and parsnips, and place on a lightly greased 15- x 10-inch jelly-roll pan. Sprinkle with desired amount of salt and freshly ground pepper.
4. Bake at 400° for 40 to 45 minutes or until vegetables are tender and browned, stirring every 15 minutes. Transfer to a serving platter, and gently toss with feta cheese mixture.

New Ambrosia

make-ahead • party perfect

MAKES: 6 servings
HANDS-ON TIME: 40 min.
TOTAL TIME: 1 hr., 40 min., including dressing

This recipe is a fresh way to use holiday citrus. Sprinkle toasted sweetened flaked coconut over each serving, if desired.

- 2 large **Ruby Red grapefruit,** peeled and sectioned
- 2 large **navel oranges,** peeled and sectioned
- 3 **celery ribs,** chopped (about ¾ cup)
- 2 large **avocados,** cut into 1-inch cubes
- 1 large **cucumber,** peeled, seeded, and chopped (about 1½ cups)
- 1 **jalapeño pepper,** seeded and minced
- ½ cup chopped fresh **basil**
  Buttermilk-Coconut Dressing
- 1 (5-oz.) package **arugula**

1. Combine first 7 ingredients in a large bowl. Pour Buttermilk-Coconut Dressing over mixture, and toss to coat. Cover and chill 1 hour.
2. Arrange arugula on 6 salad plates. Toss grapefruit mixture, and season with salt to taste. Spoon mixture over arugula using a slotted spoon.

Buttermilk-Coconut Dressing

MAKES: about 1 cup
HANDS-ON TIME: 10 min.
TOTAL TIME: 10 min.

- 1 **garlic clove**
- 1 tsp. **kosher salt**
- ⅔ cup **buttermilk**
- 1 Tbsp. plus 1 tsp. finely chopped fresh **tarragon**
- 1 Tbsp. plus 1 tsp. sweetened flaked **coconut**
- 2 Tbsp. fresh **lime juice**
- 1 Tbsp. **extra virgin olive oil**
- ½ tsp. freshly ground **pepper**

1. Peel garlic clove. Place garlic clove and salt on a cutting board, and smash garlic and salt together using flat side of a knife to make a paste.
2. Whisk together garlic mixture, buttermilk, tarragon, and remaining ingredients until blended. Cover and chill until ready to use.

MATT AND TED LEE
THE LEE BROS. SOUTHERN COOKBOOK

Wild Rice with Mushrooms

quick prep • make-ahead • party perfect

MAKES: 8 to 10 servings
HANDS-ON TIME: 30 min.
TOTAL TIME: 30 min.

- 2 (6-oz.) packages **long-grain and wild rice mix**
- 3 Tbsp. **butter**
- 1 large **sweet onion,** diced
- 12 oz. assorted fresh **mushrooms,** trimmed and sliced
- ¼ tsp. **salt**
- ½ cup **Marsala**
- ½ cup chopped fresh **flat-leaf parsley**

1. Prepare rice mix according to package directions.
2. Meanwhile, melt butter in a large skillet over medium-high heat; add onion, and sauté 7 minutes or until golden. Add mushrooms and salt; sauté 4 to 5 minutes or until mushrooms are tender. Add Marsala, and sauté 3 minutes or until liquid is absorbed. Stir mushroom mixture and parsley into prepared rice.

Squash Casserole

party perfect

MAKES: 8 to 10 servings
HANDS-ON TIME: 40 min.
TOTAL TIME: 1 hr., 15 min.

- 4 lb. **yellow squash,** sliced
- 1 large **sweet onion,** finely chopped
- 1 cup (4 oz.) freshly shredded **Cheddar cheese**
- 1 cup **mayonnaise**
- 2 Tbsp. chopped fresh **basil**
- 1 tsp. **garlic salt**
- 1 tsp. freshly ground **pepper**
- 2 large **eggs,** lightly beaten
- 2 cups soft, fresh **breadcrumbs,** divided
- 1¼ cups (5 oz.) freshly shredded **Parmesan cheese,** divided
- 2 Tbsp. **butter,** melted
- ½ cup crushed **French fried onions**

1. Preheat oven to 350°. Cook yellow squash and onion in boiling water to cover in a Dutch oven 8 minutes or just until vegetables are tender; drain squash mixture well.
2. Combine squash mixture, freshly shredded Cheddar cheese, next 5 ingredients, 1 cup breadcrumbs, and ¾ cup Parmesan cheese. Spoon into a lightly greased 13- x 9-inch baking dish.
3. Stir together melted butter, French fried onions, and remaining 1 cup breadcrumbs and ½ cup Parmesan cheese. Sprinkle over squash mixture in baking dish.
4. Bake at 350° for 35 to 40 minutes or until set.

Harvest Salad

quick prep • party perfect

MAKES: 6 to 8 servings
HANDS-ON TIME: 20 min.
TOTAL TIME: 50 min.

- 1 large butternut squash
- 2 Tbsp. olive oil
- 2 Tbsp. honey
- 1 tsp. kosher salt
- ½ tsp. freshly ground pepper
- 1 (8-oz.) bottle poppy-seed dressing
- ¼ cup fresh or frozen cranberries
- 2 (4-oz.) packages gourmet mixed salad greens
- 4 oz. goat cheese, crumbled
- ¾ cup lightly salted, roasted pecan halves
- 6 bacon slices, cooked and crumbled

1. Preheat oven to 400°. Peel and seed butternut squash; cut into ¾-inch cubes. Toss together squash, olive oil, and next 3 ingredients in a large bowl; place in a single layer in a lightly greased aluminum foil-lined 15- x 10-inch jelly-roll pan. Bake 20 to 25 minutes or until squash is tender and begins to brown, stirring once after 10 minutes. Remove from oven, and cool in pan 10 minutes.

2. Meanwhile, pulse poppy-seed dressing and cranberries in a blender 3 to 4 times or until cranberries are coarsely chopped.

3. Toss together squash, gourmet salad greens, and next 3 ingredients on a large serving platter. Serve with dressing mixture.

Lemon Broccolini

quick prep • party perfect

MAKES: 6 to 8 servings
HANDS-ON TIME: 20 min.
TOTAL TIME: 20 min.

- 1 cup (½-inch) French bread baguette cubes
- 2 Tbsp. butter
- 1 garlic clove, pressed
- 2 Tbsp. chopped fresh flat-leaf parsley
- 2 tsp. lemon zest
- 1½ lb. fresh broccolini
- 2 Tbsp. fresh lemon juice
- 1 Tbsp. olive oil

1. Process bread in a food processor 30 seconds to 1 minute or until coarsely crumbled.

2. Melt butter with garlic in a large skillet over medium heat; add breadcrumbs, and cook, stirring constantly, 2 to 3 minutes or until golden brown. Remove from heat, and stir in parsley and lemon zest.

3. Cook broccolini in boiling salted water to cover 3 to 4 minutes or until crisp-tender; drain well. Toss broccolini with lemon juice, olive oil, and salt and freshly ground pepper to taste. Transfer to a serving platter, and sprinkle with breadcrumb mixture.

Green Beans with Caramelized Shallots

quick prep • party perfect

MAKES: 8 to 10 servings
HANDS-ON TIME: 30 min.
TOTAL TIME: 30 min.

- 2 lb. haricots verts (tiny green beans), trimmed
- 3 Tbsp. butter
- 1 Tbsp. light brown sugar
- 1 Tbsp. olive oil
- 1 lb. shallots, halved lengthwise and peeled
- 2 Tbsp. red wine vinegar

1. Cook green beans in boiling salted water to cover 3 to 4 minutes or until crisp-tender; drain. Plunge beans into ice water to stop the cooking process; drain.

2. Melt butter and brown sugar with olive oil in a large skillet over medium-high heat; add shallots, and sauté 2 minutes. Reduce heat to medium-low, add vinegar, and sauté 10 minutes or until shallots are golden brown and tender.

3. Increase heat to medium-high; add green beans, and sauté 5 minutes or until thoroughly heated. Season with salt and freshly ground pepper to taste.

Roasted Onions

party perfect

MAKES: 8 to 10 servings
HANDS-ON TIME: 45 min.
TOTAL TIME: 1 hr., 15 min.

- ¼ cup firmly packed light brown sugar
- ¼ cup olive oil
- ¼ cup balsamic vinegar
- ½ tsp. salt
- 4 small red onions, quartered
- 1 lb. pearl onions
- 1 lb. cipollini onions
- 1 lb. shallots

1. Preheat oven to 450°. Whisk together first 4 ingredients in a large bowl.

2. Toss red onions and next 3 ingredients with oil mixture. Arrange in a single layer on a lightly greased 17- x 12-inch jelly-roll pan. Bake at 450° for 30 to 40 minutes or until tender and golden brown, stirring twice.

Fried Confetti Corn

quick prep • party perfect

MAKES: 8 servings
HANDS-ON TIME: 30 min.
TOTAL TIME: 30 min.

- 8 **bacon slices**
- 6 **cups fresh sweet corn kernels (about 8 ears)**
- 1 **cup diced sweet onion**
- ½ **cup chopped red bell pepper**
- ½ **cup chopped green bell pepper**
- 1 **(8-oz.) package cream cheese, cubed**
- ½ **cup half-and-half**
- 1 **tsp. sugar**
- 1 **tsp. salt**
- 1 **tsp. pepper**

1. Cook bacon in a large skillet over medium-high heat 6 to 8 minutes or until crisp. Remove bacon, and drain on paper towels, reserving 2 Tbsp. drippings in skillet. Coarsely crumble bacon.
2. Sauté corn and next 3 ingredients in hot drippings in skillet over medium-high heat 6 minutes or until tender. Add cream cheese and half-and-half, stirring until cream cheese melts. Stir in sugar and next 2 ingredients. Transfer to a serving dish, and top with bacon.

The Trimmings

Add a little sparkle to your holiday table with some of these traditional Thanksgiving recipes.

Cranberry Salsa

make-ahead • party perfect

MAKES: 3 cups
HANDS-ON TIME: 15 min.
TOTAL TIME: 2 hr., 15 min.

- 1 **(12-oz.) package fresh or frozen cranberries**
- 1 **Tbsp. orange zest**
- 1 **navel orange, peeled and coarsely chopped**
- 1 **cup sugar**
- 2 **jalapeño peppers, seeded and coarsely chopped**
- 3 **Tbsp. coarsely chopped crystallized ginger**
- 2 **Tbsp. chopped fresh cilantro**

1. Pulse cranberries in a food processor until coarsely chopped. Transfer to a bowl.
2. Pulse orange zest and next 5 ingredients in food processor 3 to 5 times or until orange, ginger, and pepper are finely chopped. Stir into cranberries; cover and chill 2 to 24 hours.

 READER RECIPE

Grandma Erma's Spirited Cranberry Sauce

make-ahead • party perfect

MAKES: about 3½ cups
HANDS-ON TIME: 20 min.
TOTAL TIME: 8 hr., 35 min.

You can keep this reader recipe on hand up to 3 weeks, so it's great for leftovers. Serve it chilled or at room temperature.

- 2 **cups sugar**
- ½ **cup port**
- 4 **cups fresh cranberries**
- ¼ **cup orange liqueur**

1. Stir together sugar, port, and ¾ cup water in a heavy 3-qt. saucepan until blended. Add cranberries; bring to a boil, and cook over medium-high heat, stirring often, 8 to 10 minutes or until cranberry

skins begin to split. Remove from heat, and let cool 15 minutes.
2. Pulse cranberry mixture in a food processor 3 to 4 times or until cranberries are almost pureed; stir in orange liqueur. Cover and chill 8 hours before serving. Store in refrigerator in an airtight container up to 3 weeks.
NOTE: We tested with Grand Marnier for orange liqueur.

LESLIE SUTHERLAND
FORT WORTH, TEXAS

Hot-and-Spicy Cranberry-Pear Chutney

make-ahead • party perfect

MAKES: 6 cups
HANDS-ON TIME: 30 min.
TOTAL TIME: 2 hr., 30 min.

This versatile, quick, and easy chutney makes a wonderful gift. One recipe yields about 6 cups and will keep up to 1 month in the refrigerator.

- 1½ **cups fresh cranberries**
- 1 **(6-oz.) package sweetened dried cranberries**
- 1 **cup fresh orange juice**
- ⅓ **cup sugar**
- 1 **Tbsp. grated fresh ginger**
- 2 **(10½-oz.) jars pear preserves**
- 1 **(10½-oz.) jar hot jalapeño pepper jelly**
- 1 **(9-oz.) jar mango chutney**
- 1 **Tbsp. orange zest**

1. Bring first 5 ingredients to a boil in a large saucepan over medium-high heat, stirring constantly. Reduce heat to low, and simmer, stirring constantly, 5 minutes or until cranberry skins begin to split.
2. Stir in preserves and remaining ingredients; simmer, stirring constantly, 5 minutes. Remove from heat, and cool chutney completely (about 2 hours).

The Bread Basket

Take two (or three!) and butter 'em while they're hot. Blackberry cornbread, featherlight pocketbook rolls, and pecan pie muffins—quick starts and simple techniques give rise to fabulous homemade breads.

Blackberry Cornbread Muffins

quick prep • party perfect

MAKES: 2 dozen
HANDS-ON TIME: 15 min.
TOTAL TIME: 35 min.

- 2 cups self-rising white cornmeal mix
- ½ cup sugar
- 5 large eggs
- 1 (16-oz.) container sour cream
- ½ cup butter, melted
- 2 cups frozen blackberries

1. Preheat oven to 450°. Stir together cornmeal and sugar in a large bowl; make a well in center of mixture. Whisk together eggs, sour cream, and butter; add to cornmeal, stirring just until dry ingredients are moistened. Fold in blackberries. Spoon batter into 2 lightly greased 12-cup muffin pans, filling three-fourths full.
2. Bake at 450° for 15 to 17 minutes or until tops are golden brown. Cool in pan on a wire rack 5 minutes.

Pecan Pie Muffins

quick prep • party perfect

MAKES: 2 dozen
HANDS-ON TIME: 15 min.
TOTAL TIME: 27 min.

- 1 cup firmly packed light brown sugar
- 1 cup chopped pecans
- ½ cup all-purpose flour
- ½ tsp. baking powder
- ¼ tsp. salt
- ½ cup butter, melted
- 2 large eggs, lightly beaten
- 1 tsp. vanilla extract
  Vegetable cooking spray
- ½ cup finely chopped pecans

1. Preheat oven to 425°. Combine first 5 ingredients in a large bowl; make a well in center of mixture. Stir together butter and next 2 ingredients; add to brown sugar mixture, and stir just until moistened. Coat 2 (12-cup) miniature muffin pans well with cooking spray. Place 1 tsp. finely chopped pecans in each muffin cup; spoon batter over pecans, filling almost to top. Place muffin pans on an aluminum foil-lined jelly-roll pan.
2. Bake at 425° for 10 to 12 minutes or until a wooden pick inserted in center comes out clean. Cool on a wire rack 2 minutes. Run a knife around edge of each cup to loosen muffins, and remove from pans.

Sour Cream Pocketbook Rolls

make-ahead • party perfect

MAKES: about 4½ dozen
HANDS-ON TIME: 30 min.
TOTAL TIME: 9 hr., 32 min.

- 1 (8-oz.) container sour cream
- ½ cup butter
- ½ cup sugar
- 1¼ tsp. salt
- 2 (¼-oz.) envelopes active dry yeast
- ½ cup warm water (105° to 110°)
- 2 large eggs, lightly beaten
- 4 cups all-purpose flour
- ¼ cup butter, melted and divided

1. Cook first 4 ingredients in a saucepan over medium-low heat, stirring occasionally, 3 to 4 minutes or until butter melts. Let cool to 115°.
2. Combine yeast and warm water in a liquid measuring cup; let stand 5 minutes. Stir together eggs, flour, yeast mixture, and sour cream mixture in a large bowl until well blended. Cover and chill 8 to 24 hours.
3. Divide dough into fourths, and shape each portion into a ball. Roll each ball to ¼-inch thickness on a floured surface; cut dough into rounds with a 2½-inch round cutter.
4. Brush rounds with 2 Tbsp. melted butter. Make a crease across each round with a knife, and fold in half; gently press edges to seal. Place rolls, with sides touching, in a lightly greased 15- x 10-inch jelly-roll pan. Place any remaining rolls on a lightly greased baking sheet. Cover and let rise in a warm place (85°), free from drafts, 45 minutes or until doubled in bulk.
5. Preheat oven to 375°, and bake rolls 12 to 15 minutes or until golden brown. Brush rolls with remaining 2 Tbsp. melted butter.

ELEANOR HELMS
GRANNY'S DRAWERS COOKBOOK
CHARLOTTE, NORTH CAROLINA

Lemon-Orange Rolls

quick prep • party perfect

MAKES: 4 dozen
HANDS-ON TIME: 30 min.
TOTAL TIME: 1 hr.

If needed, you can bake these miniature rolls in batches—just refrigerate any extra dough while you wait to refill the pans.

- 1 (16-oz.) package hot roll mix
- ¼ cup butter, softened
- ⅔ cup granulated sugar
- 2 Tbsp. orange zest
- 1 Tbsp. lemon zest
- 2 cups powdered sugar
- ¼ cup orange juice

1. Prepare roll mix according to package directions. Divide dough into 2 equal portions. Roll 1 portion of dough into a 12- x 8-inch rectangle on a lightly floured surface. Spread with 2 Tbsp. butter.
2. Stir together granulated sugar and next 2 ingredients; sprinkle half of sugar mixture over butter on dough rectangle. Roll up rectangle, jelly-roll fashion, starting at 1 long side. Repeat procedure with remaining dough, butter, and sugar mixture.
3. Cut each roll into ½-inch slices, and place slices in cups of 4 lightly greased 12-cup miniature muffin pans. Cover and let rise in a warm place (85°), free from drafts, 20 minutes.
4. Preheat oven to 375°. Bake rolls 10 to 12 minutes or until golden. Remove from pans to wire racks, and let cool 5 minutes.
5. Stir together powdered sugar and orange juice until smooth; drizzle over tops of rolls.
NOTE: We tested with Pillsbury Specialty Mix Hot Roll Mix.

Butter Muffins

quick prep • party perfect

MAKES: 2 dozen
HANDS-ON TIME: 15 min.
TOTAL TIME: 40 min.

For pretty, rounded muffin tops, use a small ice-cream scoop to fill the muffin cups.

- 2 cups self-rising flour
- 1 (8-oz.) container sour cream
- ½ cup butter, melted

1. Preheat oven to 350°. Stir together flour and next 2 ingredients in a large bowl just until blended. Spoon batter into 2 lightly greased 12-cup miniature muffin pans, filling completely full. Bake 25 to 28 minutes or until muffins are golden brown.

The Desserts

Lawd have mercy. These desserts are brilliant hybrids of our favorite holiday flavors: Pumpkin-Pecan Cheesecake, Eggnog Pound Cake, Chocolate-Pecan Chess Pie. And how darling are those Pear Dumplings? Run, don't walk, to the buffet.

Chocolate-Pecan Chess Pie

make-ahead • party perfect

MAKES: 8 servings
HANDS-ON TIME: 15 min.
TOTAL TIME: 2 hr., 5 min.

Dark, rich, and intensely chocolaty, this is our favorite new twist on pecan pie.

- ½ (14.1-oz.) package refrigerated piecrusts
- ½ cup butter
- 2 (1-oz.) unsweetened chocolate baking squares
- 1 (5-oz.) can evaporated milk (⅔ cup)
- 2 large eggs
- 2 tsp. vanilla extract, divided
- 1½ cups granulated sugar
- 3 Tbsp. unsweetened cocoa
- 2 Tbsp. all-purpose flour
- ⅛ tsp. salt
- 1½ cups pecan halves and pieces
- ⅔ cup firmly packed light brown sugar
- 1 Tbsp. light corn syrup

1. Preheat oven to 350°. Roll piecrust into a 13-inch circle on a lightly floured surface. Fit into a 9-inch pie plate; fold edges under, and crimp.
2. Microwave butter and chocolate squares in a large microwave-safe bowl at MEDIUM (50% power) 1½ minutes or until melted and smooth, stirring at 30-second intervals. Whisk in evaporated milk, eggs, and 1 tsp. vanilla.
3. Stir together granulated sugar and next 3 ingredients. Add sugar mixture to chocolate mixture, whisking until smooth. Pour mixture into prepared crust.
4. Bake pie at 350° for 40 minutes. Stir together pecans, next 2 ingredients, and remaining 1 tsp. vanilla; sprinkle over pie. Bake 10 minutes or until set. Remove from oven to a wire rack, and cool completely (about 1 hour).

Pumpkin-Pecan Cheesecake

make-ahead • party perfect

MAKES: 12 servings
HANDS-ON TIME: 25 min.
TOTAL TIME: 11 hr., 32 min., including topping and pecans

Test Kitchen Professional Pam Lolley combined the flavors of three holiday favorites to create this luscious dessert. (Pictured on page 1)

- 2 cups graham cracker crumbs
- ⅓ cup finely chopped pecans
- 5 Tbsp. butter, melted
- 3 Tbsp. light brown sugar
- 4 (8-oz.) packages cream cheese, softened
- 1 cup granulated sugar
- 1 tsp. vanilla extract
- 4 large eggs
- 1½ cups canned pumpkin
- 1½ Tbsp. lemon juice
  Praline Topping
  Garnishes: coarsely chopped Pecan Pie-Glazed Pecans, fresh sage leaves

1. Preheat oven to 325°. Stir together first 4 ingredients in a bowl until well blended. Press mixture on bottom and 1½ inches up sides of a 9-inch springform pan. Bake 8 to 10 minutes or until lightly browned.
2. Beat cream cheese and next 2 ingredients at medium speed with a heavy-duty electric stand mixer until blended and smooth. Add eggs, 1 at a time, beating just until blended after each addition. Add pumpkin and lemon juice, beating until

blended. Pour batter into prepared crust. (Pan will be very full.)
3. Bake at 325° for 1 hour to 1 hour and 10 minutes or until almost set. Turn oven off. Let cheesecake stand in oven, with door closed, 15 minutes. Remove cheesecake from oven, and gently run a knife around outer edge of cheesecake to loosen from sides of pan. (Do not remove sides of pan.) Cool completely on a wire rack (about 1 hour). Cover and chill 8 to 24 hours.
4. Remove sides and bottom of pan, and transfer cheesecake to a serving plate. Prepare Praline Topping; immediately pour slowly over top of cheesecake, spreading to within ¼-inch of edge. Garnish, if desired.

TRY THIS TWIST!
Sweet Potato-Pecan Cheesecake: Substitute 1½ cups mashed, cooked sweet potatoes for canned pumpkin. Proceed with recipe as directed, baking 1 hour or until almost set.

Praline Topping

quick prep • party perfect

MAKES: 1⅓ cups
HANDS-ON TIME: 15 min.
TOTAL TIME: 20 min.

- 1 cup firmly packed brown sugar
- ⅓ cup whipping cream
- ¼ cup butter
- 1 cup powdered sugar, sifted
- 1 tsp. vanilla extract

1. Bring first 3 ingredients to a boil in a 1-qt. saucepan over medium heat, stirring

often. Boil, stirring occasionally, 1 minute; remove from heat. Gradually whisk in powdered sugar and vanilla until smooth. Let stand 5 minutes, whisking occasionally. Use immediately.

Pecan Pie-Glazed Pecans

1. Stir together ¼ cup dark corn syrup and 2 Tbsp. sugar. Add 2 cups pecan halves; stir until pecans are coated. Line a jelly-roll pan with parchment paper; coat parchment paper with vegetable cooking spray. Spread pecans in a single layer in prepared pan. Bake at 350° for 15 minutes or until glaze bubbles slowly and thickens, stirring every 3 minutes. Transfer pan to a wire rack. Spread pecans in a single layer, separating individual pecans; cool completely. Cooled pecans should be crisp; if not, bake 5 more minutes.

Blackberry-Apple Pie

make-ahead • party perfect

MAKES: 8 to 10 servings
HANDS-ON TIME: 45 min.
TOTAL TIME: 7 hr., 40 min., including filling

- 2½ cups all-purpose flour
- 1 tsp. salt
- ¾ cup cold butter, cut into pieces
- 1½ cups (6 oz.) shredded white Cheddar cheese
- ½ to ¾ cup ice water
- 1 large egg, lightly beaten
  Blackberry-Apple Pie Filling (next page)
- 1 Tbsp. sparkling sugar

1. Stir together flour and salt in a large bowl. Cut butter into flour mixture with a pastry blender until mixture resembles small peas. Stir in cheese. Drizzle ½ cup ice water over flour mixture, stirring with a fork until dry ingredients are moistened and dough is crumbly but forms a ball when pressed together, adding more ice water, 1 Tbsp. at a time, if necessary

---

Fast Flourish!

PRALINE APPLE PIE: Bake and cool your favorite double-crust apple pie according to the package directions (or pick one up from the local bakery!). Prepare Praline Topping, and immediately pour slowly over top of pie, spreading to within ½ inch of sides of pie. Garnish with coarsely chopped Pecan Pie-Glazed Pecans.

(up to ¼ cup). Divide dough in half. Place each half on a large piece of plastic wrap. Shape each dough half into a flat disk. Wrap each disk in plastic wrap, and chill 2 to 24 hours.

2. Preheat oven to 400°. Place I dough disk on a lightly floured surface; sprinkle dough lightly with flour. Roll dough to about ¼-inch thickness. Starting at I edge of dough, wrap dough around rolling pin. Place rolling pin over a 9-inch pie plate, and unroll dough over pie plate. Press dough into pie plate; trim off excess crust along edges. Brush edges of crust lightly with egg; reserve remaining egg. Spoon Blackberry-Apple Pie Filling into crust, mounding filling slightly in center.

3. Roll remaining dough disk to about ¼-inch thickness on a lightly floured surface. Cut dough into 9 (I-inch-wide) strips. Arrange strips in a lattice design over filling; gently press ends of strips into bottom crust; crimp edge of crust. Brush lattice with reserved egg; sprinkle with sparkling sugar. Place on a baking sheet.

4. Bake at 400° on lower oven rack 45 to 50 minutes. Cover loosely with foil to prevent excessive browning, and bake 25 minutes or until juices are thick and bubbly. Cool on a wire rack 2 hours.

TRY THIS TWIST!
Cranberry-Apple Pie: Substitute Cranberry-Apple Pie Filling for Blackberry-Apple Pie Filling. Prepare as directed.

Blackberry-Apple Pie Filling
MAKES: enough for I (9-inch) pie
HANDS-ON TIME: 45 min.
TOTAL TIME: I hr., 45 min.

Make ahead: Prepare through Step 2. Chill up to I week. Stir in berries before spooning into crust.

- 3 lb. Granny Smith apples
- 3 lb. Braeburn apples
- 1½ cups sugar

- ½ cup all-purpose flour
- ½ cup butter
- I (12-oz.) package frozen blackberries (2 cups)
- I Tbsp. all-purpose flour

1. Peel apples, and cut into ½-inch-thick wedges; toss with sugar and ½ cup flour.

2. Melt butter in a large skillet over medium-high heat; add apple mixture, and sauté 15 to 20 minutes or until apples are tender. Remove from heat. Cool completely (about I hour).

3. Toss frozen blackberries with I Tbsp. flour, and stir into apple mixture. Use immediately.

TRY THIS TWIST!
Cranberry-Apple Pie Filling: Omit blackberries and I Tbsp. flour. Reduce remaining flour from ½ cup to ⅓ cup. Stir in I cup sweetened dried cranberries just before removing apples from heat in Step 2.

Pear Dumplings
party perfect

MAKES: 6 servings
HANDS-ON TIME: 40 min.
TOTAL TIME: I hr., 20 min.
(Pictured on page I)

- 3 cups all-purpose flour
- 2 tsp. baking powder
- I tsp. salt
- I cup shortening
- ¾ cup milk
- 6 ripe Bosc pears
- ¼ cup firmly packed light brown sugar
- ½ cup chopped macadamia nuts
- I tsp. ground cinnamon
- ¼ cup butter, softened
- 1½ cups granulated sugar
  Zest of I medium orange, cut into strips
- I (3-inch) piece fresh ginger
- I Tbsp. butter

1. Preheat oven to 375°. Stir together first 3 ingredients; cut shortening into flour mixture with a pastry blender until crumbly. Gradually add milk, stirring just until dry ingredients are moistened.

2. Turn dough out onto a lightly floured surface, and knead lightly 4 to 5 times. Shape into a 12-inch log. Cut log into 6 (2-inch) pieces. Shape each into a disk, and roll each into an 8-inch circle on a lightly floured surface.

3. Peel pears, reserving peels. Core each pear from bottom, leaving top 2 inches and stems intact.

4. Stir together brown sugar and next 2 ingredients; spoon about I½ Tbsp. brown sugar mixture into each pear cavity, pressing firmly. Sprinkle remaining sugar mixture in center of pastry circles (about I½ Tbsp. each). Place I pear in center of each pastry circle. Dot pears with ¼ cup softened butter. Press dough around pears with palms of hands, sealing around stem. Place in a lightly greased 13- x 9-inch baking dish.

5. Bake at 375° for 40 to 50 minutes, shielding with aluminum foil after 30 minutes to prevent excessive browning, if necessary.

6. Bring granulated sugar, next 3 ingredients, reserved pear peels, and 1½ cups water to a boil over medium-high heat, stirring constantly. Boil, stirring constantly, I minute or until sugar is dissolved. Reduce heat to low. Cook, stirring occasionally, 5 minutes. Pour through a wire-mesh strainer into a bowl; discard solids. Pour syrup over dumplings. Serve immediately.

Peppermint Brownie Tarts

quick prep • make-ahead • party perfect

MAKES: 2 (9-inch) tarts
HANDS-ON TIME: 30 min.
TOTAL TIME: 2 hr., 55 min., including ganache

Crushed candy canes and a rich Chocolate Ganache hide a sweet layer of peppermint buttercream inside these tarts. One recipe makes 2 (9-inch) tarts—just right for entertaining or holiday gift giving.

- 4 (1-oz.) unsweetened chocolate baking squares
- 1 cup butter, softened
- 2 cups granulated sugar
- 4 large eggs
- 1 cup all-purpose flour
- 1 tsp. vanilla extract
- 1 cup semisweet chocolate morsels
- ½ cup butter, softened
- 1 (16-oz.) package powdered sugar
- ⅓ cup milk
- ¼ tsp. peppermint oil
   Chocolate Ganache
- ½ cup crushed peppermint candy canes

1. Preheat oven to 350°. Microwave chocolate squares in a microwave-safe bowl at MEDIUM (50% power) 1½ minutes or until melted, stirring at 30-second intervals. Stir until smooth.
2. Beat 1 cup butter and granulated sugar at medium speed with an electric mixer until light and fluffy. Add eggs, 1 at a time, beating just until blended after each addition. Add melted chocolate, beating just until blended.
3. Add flour, beating at low speed just until blended. Stir in vanilla and chocolate morsels. Spread batter into 2 greased and floured 9-inch tart pans with removable bottoms.

4. Bake at 350° for 20 minutes or until center is set. Cool in pans completely on wire racks (about 1 hour).
5. Beat ½ cup butter at medium speed with an electric mixer until creamy; gradually add powdered sugar alternately with milk, beating at low speed after each addition. Stir in peppermint oil.
6. Spread butter mixture over cooled tarts; cover and chill 1 hour or until firm.
7. Spread Chocolate Ganache over each tart. Sprinkle crushed peppermint candies around edges of tarts. Remove tarts from pans before serving, if desired.

Chocolate Ganache

party perfect

MAKES: about 2 cups
HANDS-ON TIME: 5 min.
TOTAL TIME: 5 min.

- 1 (12-oz.) package semisweet chocolate morsels
- ½ cup whipping cream

1. Microwave chocolate morsels and whipping cream in a 2-qt. microwave-safe bowl at MEDIUM (50% power) 2½ to 3 minutes or until chocolate begins to melt. Whisk until chocolate melts and mixture is smooth.

Lemon Curd Pound Cake

make-ahead • party perfect

MAKES: 12 servings
HANDS-ON TIME: 20 min.
TOTAL TIME: 2 hr., 45 min., including glaze

Wait to prepare the Lemon Curd Glaze until the cake comes out of the oven so it will still be warm when spread over the cake.

- 1 cup butter, softened
- ½ cup shortening
- 3 cups sugar
- 6 large eggs
- 3 cups all-purpose flour
- ½ tsp. baking powder
- ⅛ tsp. salt
- 1 cup milk
- 1 Tbsp. lemon zest
- 1 tsp. vanilla extract
- 1 tsp. lemon extract
   Lemon Curd Glaze
   Garnishes: candied lemon slices, sugared cranberries, fresh thyme sprigs

1. Preheat oven to 325°. Beat first 2 ingredients at medium speed with a heavy-duty electric stand mixer until creamy. Gradually add sugar, beating at medium speed until light and fluffy. Add eggs, 1 at a time, beating just until yellow disappears.
2. Sift together flour and next 2 ingredients; add to butter mixture alternately with milk, beginning and ending with flour mixture. Beat at low speed just until blended after each addition. Stir in lemon zest and next 2 ingredients.
3. Pour batter into a greased and floured 10-inch (16-cup) tube pan.
4. Bake at 325° for 1 hour and 15 minutes to 1 hour and 30 minutes or until a long wooden pick inserted in center of cake comes out clean. Cool cake in pan on wire rack 15 minutes.

5. Meanwhile, prepare Lemon Curd Glaze. Remove cake from pan to wire rack; gently brush warm glaze over top and sides of cake. Cool completely on a wire rack (about 1 hour). Garnish, if desired.

TRY THIS TWIST!

Lime Curd Pound Cake: Omit lemon extract. Substitute lime zest for lemon zest and Lime Curd Glaze for Lemon Curd Glaze. Proceed with recipe as directed.

Lemon Curd Glaze

quick prep • party perfect

MAKES: about ¾ cup
HANDS-ON TIME: 15 min.
TOTAL TIME: 15 min.

⅔ cup sugar
1½ Tbsp. butter, melted
2 tsp. lemon zest
2 Tbsp. fresh lemon juice
1 large egg, lightly beaten

1. Stir together first 4 ingredients in a small heavy saucepan; add egg, and stir until blended. Cook over low heat, stirring constantly, 10 to 12 minutes or until mixture thickens slightly and begins to bubble around the edges (cooked mixture will have a thickness similar to heavy cream). Use immediately.

TRY THIS TWIST!

Lime Curd Glaze: Substitute lime zest for lemon zest and lime juice for lemon juice.

Eggnog Pound Cake

quick prep • make-ahead • party perfect

MAKES: 12 servings
HANDS-ON TIME: 15 min.
TOTAL TIME: 2 hr., 25 min.

1 (16-oz.) package pound cake mix
1¼ cups eggnog
2 large eggs
½ tsp. freshly grated nutmeg
½ tsp. vanilla extract

1. Preheat oven to 350°. Beat all ingredients together at low speed with an electric mixer until blended. Increase speed to medium, and beat 2 minutes. Pour into a lightly greased 9- x 5-inch loaf pan.
2. Bake at 350° for 1 hour to 1 hour and 5 minutes or until a long wooden pick inserted in center comes out clean. Cool in pan on a wire rack 10 minutes. Remove from pan to wire rack, and cool completely (about 1 hour).

Bananas Foster Upside-Down Cake

party perfect

MAKES: 8 servings
HANDS-ON TIME: 20 min.
TOTAL TIME: 1 hr., 18 min.

One quick flip and Bananas Foster Upside-Down Cake tumbles from the skillet perfectly golden and party ready.

½ cup chopped pecans
½ cup butter, softened and divided
1 cup firmly packed light brown sugar
2 Tbsp. rum
2 ripe bananas
¾ cup granulated sugar
2 large eggs
¾ cup milk
½ cup sour cream
1 tsp. vanilla extract
2 cups all-purpose baking mix
¼ tsp. ground cinnamon

1. Preheat oven to 350°. Bake pecans in a single layer 8 to 10 minutes or until toasted and fragrant, stirring once.
2. Melt ¼ cup butter in a lightly greased 10-inch cast-iron skillet or 9-inch round cake pan (with sides that are at least 2 inches high) over low heat. Remove from heat; stir in brown sugar and rum.
3. Cut bananas diagonally into ¼-inch-thick slices; arrange in concentric circles over brown sugar mixture. Sprinkle pecans over bananas.
4. Beat granulated sugar and remaining ¼ cup butter at medium speed with an electric mixer until blended. Add eggs, 1 at a time, beating just until blended after each addition. Add milk and next 2 ingredients; beat just until blended. Beat in baking mix and cinnamon until blended. (Batter will be slightly lumpy.) Pour batter over mixture in skillet. Place skillet on a foil-lined jelly-roll pan.
5. Bake at 350° for 40 to 45 minutes or until a wooden pick inserted in center comes out clean. Cool in skillet on a wire rack 10 minutes. Run a knife around edge to loosen. Invert onto a serving plate, spooning any topping in skillet over cake.

Fast Flourish!

BALSAMIC STRAWBERRIES: Stir together 2 cups sliced fresh strawberries, ¼ cup sugar, and 4 tsp. balsamic vinegar; let stand 1 hour. Top round shortbread cookies with vanilla ice cream; spoon strawberry mixture over ice cream. Garnish with chocolate curls and fresh basil.

Creole Bread Pudding with Bourbon Sauce

make-ahead • party perfect

MAKES: 10 to 12 servings
HANDS-ON TIME: 20 min.
TOTAL TIME: 1 hr., 15 min., including sauce

- 2 (12-oz.) cans evaporated milk
- 6 large eggs, lightly beaten
- 1 (16-oz.) day-old **French bread loaf,** cubed
- 1 (8-oz.) can crushed pineapple, drained
- 1 large **Red Delicious apple,** unpeeled and grated
- 1½ cups sugar
- 1 cup raisins
- 5 Tbsp. vanilla extract
- ¼ cup butter, cut into ½-inch cubes and softened
  Bourbon Sauce

1. Preheat oven to 350°. Whisk together evaporated milk, eggs, and 1 cup water in a large bowl until well blended. Add bread cubes, stirring to thoroughly coat. Stir in crushed pineapple and next 4 ingredients. Stir in butter, blending well. Pour into a greased 13- x 9-inch baking dish.
2. Bake at 350° for 35 to 45 minutes or until set and crust is golden. Remove from oven, and let stand 2 minutes. Serve with Bourbon Sauce.

Bourbon Sauce

MAKES: 1½ cups
HANDS-ON TIME: 18 min.
TOTAL TIME: 18 min.

- 3 Tbsp. butter
- 1 Tbsp. all-purpose flour
- 1 cup whipping cream
- ½ cup sugar
- 2 Tbsp. bourbon
- 1 Tbsp. vanilla extract
- 1 tsp. ground nutmeg

1. Melt butter in a small saucepan over medium-low heat; whisk in flour, and cook, whisking constantly, 5 minutes. Stir in cream and sugar; cook, whisking constantly, 3 minutes or until thickened. Stir in bourbon, vanilla, and nutmeg; cook, whisking constantly, 5 minutes or until thoroughly heated.

CHEF LEAH CHASE
DOOKY CHASE'S RESTAURANT
NEW ORLEANS, LOUISIANA

MAMA'S WAY OR YOUR WAY?

The Appetizers

Caterer Ashley McMakin shares her family's menu of small bites. Serve these as heavy hors d'oeuvres or as a light holiday supper all season long.

MAMA'S (AND GRANDMAMA'S!) WAY

Marinated Shrimp-and-Artichokes

make-ahead • party perfect

MAKES: 8 servings
HANDS-ON TIME: 15 min.
TOTAL TIME: 15 min., plus 8 hr. for chilling

"My grandmother, mom, and mother-in-law have made so many versions of this, we forgot who started it!" says Ashley.

- ¼ cup white balsamic vinegar
- 2 Tbsp. finely chopped fresh parsley
- 2 Tbsp. finely chopped green onion
- 3 Tbsp. olive oil
- 1 (0.75-oz.) envelope garlic-and-herb dressing mix
- 1 lb. peeled and deveined, large cooked shrimp (21/30 count)
- 1 (14-oz.) can artichoke hearts, drained and cut in half
- 1 (6-oz.) can large black olives, drained
- 1 cup halved grape tomatoes
- 1 (4-oz.) package feta cheese, cut into ½-inch cubes
  Small fresh basil leaves

1. Whisk together first 5 ingredients in a bowl. Stir in shrimp and next 4 ingredients. Cover and chill 8 to 24 hours.

2. Stir in desired amount of basil just before serving. Serve with a slotted spoon.

NOTE: We tested with Good Seasons Garlic & Herb Salad Dressing & Recipe Mix.

ASHLEY'S WAY

Cheese Ring with Strawberry Preserves

make-ahead • party perfect

MAKES: 8 to 10 servings
HANDS-ON TIME: 20 min.
TOTAL TIME: 2 hr., 45 min.

"My go-to crowd-pleaser is a cheese ring," says Ashley. *"There's just something so charmingly retro about it!"*

- 1 **cup finely chopped pecans**
- ¾ **cup mayonnaise**
- ½ **tsp. hot sauce**
- 1 **garlic clove, minced**
- 2 **(8-oz.) blocks sharp Cheddar cheese, finely grated***
- ½ **cup strawberry preserves**
  Assorted crackers
  Garnishes: chopped toasted pecans, fresh strawberries, strawberry flowers

1. Preheat oven to 350°. Bake pecans in a single layer in a shallow pan 8 to 10 minutes or until toasted and fragrant, stirring halfway through. Cool 15 minutes.

2. Stir together mayonnaise and next 2 ingredients. Stir in pecans and cheese.

3. Spoon mixture into a plastic wrap-lined 4-cup ring mold with a 2½-inch center. Cover and chill 2 hours.

4. Unmold cheese ring onto a serving platter. Discard plastic wrap. Fill center of ring with preserves. Serve with crackers. Garnish, if desired.

***Sharp white Cheddar cheese may be substituted.

Meet the Family

Owner of Ashley Mac's cafe and catering *(ashleymacs.com)* in Birmingham, Ashley grew up in a family that adores food and celebrating. She learned cooking basics from her mom, Sandy King Deaton (right), and inherited the crowd-pleasing gene from grandma Ethel King (left), who can be found entertaining one of 18 grandkids at any given time! Here Ashley shares her family favorites.

4 Swaps for Strawberry Preserves

Serve any one of these fruit-and-herb mixtures with Ashley's Cheese Ring for a delicious new take on a classic.

{1}

MINT-PEPPER JELLY: Stir together ½ cup pepper jelly and 1½ tsp. chopped fresh mint in a small bowl.

{2}

BASIL-BLACKBERRY PRESERVES: Stir together ½ cup blackberry preserves and 1½ to 2 tsp. chopped fresh basil.

{3}

ROSEMARY-PEAR PRESERVES: Stir together ½ cup pear preserves and ½ tsp. chopped fresh rosemary.

{4}

BALSAMIC-STRAWBERRY PRESERVES: Bring ¾ cup balsamic vinegar to a boil over medium-high heat. Reduce heat to medium-low, and simmer, stirring occasionally, 18 to 20 minutes or until reduced to about 2 Tbsp. Let cool 10 minutes. Stir in 1 cup strawberry preserves.

Mushroom Puffs
make-ahead • party perfect

MAKES: about 3 dozen
HANDS-ON TIME: 30 min.
TOTAL TIME: 1 hr., 50 min.

- 1 (8-oz.) package cream cheese, softened*
- 1 (8-oz.) can mushroom pieces and stems, drained and chopped
- ¼ cup finely chopped onion
- ¼ cup grated Parmesan cheese
- 1 Tbsp. finely chopped green onion
- ¼ tsp. hot sauce
- 1 large egg
- 1 (17.3-oz.) package frozen puff pastry sheets, thawed
  Parchment paper
- 2 tsp. freshly ground pepper

1. Beat cream cheese at medium speed with a heavy-duty electric stand mixer until smooth. Stir in mushrooms and next 4 ingredients. Cover and chill 1 to 24 hours.

2. Preheat oven to 400°. Whisk together egg and 1 Tbsp. water in a small bowl. Roll 1 puff pastry sheet into a 16- x 10-inch rectangle on a lightly floured surface. Cut pastry in half lengthwise. Spread ½ cup cream cheese mixture lengthwise down center of each rectangle; brush edges with egg mixture. Fold pastry in half lengthwise over filling, pinching edges to seal. Cut each into 10 pieces, and place on a parchment paper-lined baking sheet. Repeat procedure with remaining puff pastry sheet, egg mixture, and cream cheese mixture.

3. Brush remaining egg mixture over tops of pastry pieces; sprinkle with pepper.

4. Bake at 400° for 20 to 25 minutes or until browned. Serve immediately.

*2 (5.2-oz.) packages buttery garlic-and-herb spreadable cheese may be substituted.

NOTE: To make ahead, prepare recipe as directed through Step 3. Freeze pieces on baking sheet until firm (about 1 hour), and transfer to zip-top plastic freezer bags. Freeze up to 1 month. To bake, place frozen puffs on parchment paper-lined baking sheets, and proceed as directed in Step 4.

Tuna-Apple Mini Melts
party perfect

MAKES: 45 tartlets
HANDS-ON TIME: 30 min.
TOTAL TIME: 1 hr., 30 min.

- 1 cup mayonnaise
- ½ cup diced Pink Lady apple*
- ⅓ cup finely chopped celery
- 2 Tbsp. minced red onion
- 1 hard-cooked egg, peeled and chopped
- 1 tsp. fresh lemon juice
- ¼ tsp. kosher salt
- ¼ tsp. freshly cracked pepper
- 2 (12-oz.) cans solid white tuna in spring water, drained and flaked
- 3 (1.9-oz.) packages frozen mini-phyllo pastry shells, thawed
- 12 deli Havarti cheese slices, cut into 4 pieces each
  Garnish: thin Pink Lady apple slices

1. Stir together first 8 ingredients in a medium bowl. Stir in tuna. Cover and chill 1 hour.

2. Divide mixture among phyllo shells (about 1 Tbsp. each), and place on a 15- x 10-inch jelly-roll pan. Top with cheese pieces.

3. Preheat broiler with oven rack 5½ inches from heat. Broil 1 to 2 minutes or until cheese is melted. Serve immediately. Garnish, if desired.

*Gala apple may be substituted.

Tiny Tomato Tarts
quick prep • make-ahead • party perfect

MAKES: 24 tartlets
HANDS-ON TIME: 30 min.
TOTAL TIME: 50 min.

- ½ (14.1-oz.) package refrigerated piecrusts
- 1 (14.5-oz.) can petite diced tomatoes
- 1 Tbsp. chopped fresh basil
- ⅔ cup mayonnaise
- ½ cup grated Parmesan cheese
- ¼ cup (1 oz.) freshly shredded Cheddar cheese
- ¼ cup (1 oz.) freshly shredded mozzarella cheese
  Garnish: fresh basil leaves

1. Preheat oven to 425°. Unroll piecrust on a lightly floured surface; roll into a 12-inch circle. Cut into 24 rounds using a 2-inch scalloped-edge round cutter. Press rounds into bottoms of ungreased miniature muffin cups (dough will come slightly up sides, forming a cup). Prick bottom of dough once with a fork.

2. Bake at 425° for 4 to 5 minutes or until set. Cool in pans on a wire rack 15 minutes. Reduce oven temperature to 350°.

3. Meanwhile, drain tomatoes well, pressing between paper towels. Combine tomatoes and chopped basil in a small bowl; season with desired amount of salt and pepper. Stir together mayonnaise and next 3 ingredients in a medium bowl. Divide tomato mixture among pastry shells, and top with mayonnaise mixture.

4. Bake at 350° for 18 to 20 minutes. Serve immediately. Garnish, if desired.

NOTE: To make ahead, bake and cool pastry shells as directed in Steps 1 and 2. Remove from muffin pans, and store in an airtight container up to 3 days. Return pastry shells to muffin pans, and fill and bake as directed.

The Biscuit Brunch

As the holiday weekend comes to an end, this laid-back, build-your-own biscuit buffet gives you and your guests one more chance to break (buttery, flaky) bread together. Start with one or all three of our home-cooked biscuits, add a big platter of thick-cut bacon, sliced country ham, piled-high sausage patties, or our crispy chicken cutlets. Then round out the selection with our flavorful toppings or a few of your own.

Holiday Brunch

SERVES 10 TO 12

Angel Biscuits

Sweet Potato Biscuits

Cornbread Biscuits

Crispy Chicken Cutlets

Up-a-Notch Sausage
and Gravy

Sweet Tomato Chutney

Mustard-Peach Preserves

Thyme-Scented
Fried Apples

Angel Biscuits

quick prep • make-ahead • party perfect

MAKES: about 2 dozen
HANDS-ON TIME: 20 min.
TOTAL TIME: 32 min.

The addition of yeast will guarantee fluffy biscuits every time.

1 (¼-oz.) envelope active dry yeast
¼ cup warm water (105° to 115°)
5 cups all-purpose flour
2 Tbsp. sugar
1 Tbsp. baking powder
1 tsp. baking soda
1 tsp. salt
½ cup shortening, cut into pieces
½ cup cold butter, cut into pieces
1½ cups buttermilk

1. Preheat oven to 400°. Combine yeast and warm water in a 1-cup glass measuring cup; let stand 5 minutes.
2. Meanwhile, whisk together flour and next 4 ingredients in a large bowl; cut in shortening and butter with a pastry blender until crumbly.
3. Combine yeast mixture and buttermilk, and add to flour mixture, stirring just until dry ingredients are moistened. Turn dough out onto a lightly floured surface, and knead about 1 minute.
4. Roll dough to ½-inch thickness. Cut with a 2-inch round cutter or into 2-inch squares. Place on 2 ungreased baking sheets.
5. Bake at 400° for 12 to 15 minutes or until golden.

TRY THIS TWIST!
Cinnamon-Raisin Angel Biscuits:
Substitute ¼ cup firmly packed brown sugar for 2 Tbsp. sugar. Stir 1 cup baking raisins, 2 tsp. lemon zest, and 1 tsp. ground cinnamon into flour mixture in Step 2. Proceed with recipe as directed.
NOTE: We tested with Sun-Maid Baking Raisins.

5 Flavored Butters

Stir these ingredients into a softened stick of butter.

BOURBON-PECAN BUTTER:
⅓ cup toasted chopped pecans, 1 Tbsp. bourbon, and 2 Tbsp. cane syrup

CHOCOLATE-CHERRY BUTTER: ¼ cup finely grated semi-sweet chocolate baking bar, 1 Tbsp. cherry jam, and ¼ tsp. almond extract

HONEY-GINGER BUTTER:
3 Tbsp. chopped fresh chives, 1 Tbsp. honey, and 2 tsp. finely chopped crystallized ginger

ORANGE-MANGO BUTTER:
2 Tbsp. mango chutney, 1 Tbsp. orange zest, and ¾ tsp. freshly ground peppercorn medley

MUSTARD-POPPY SEED BUTTER: 1 Tbsp. minced green onions, 1 Tbsp. Dijon mustard, and 1 tsp. poppy seeds

Sweet Potato Biscuits

quick prep • party perfect

MAKES: about I dozen
HANDS-ON TIME: 20 min.
TOTAL TIME: 40 min.

These slightly sweet and oh-so-tender biscuits pair nicely with ham, sausage, or bacon.

2   cups all-purpose flour
¼   cup firmly packed brown sugar
I   Tbsp. baking powder
½   tsp. salt
¾   tsp. ground cinnamon, divided
½   cup cold butter, cut into pieces
½   cup cooked, mashed sweet potatoes
½   cup cold whipping cream
    Parchment paper
    Vegetable cooking spray
2   Tbsp. whipping cream
2   tsp. granulated sugar

1. Preheat oven to 450°. Stir together first 4 ingredients and ½ tsp. cinnamon in a large bowl; cut in butter with a pastry blender until mixture resembles small peas and dough is crumbly. Freeze 5 minutes.
2. Stir together sweet potatoes and ½ cup whipping cream. Add to flour mixture, stirring just until dry ingredients are moistened.
3. Turn dough out onto a lightly floured surface (mixture will be crumbly); knead I minute. Pat dough into a ¾-inch-thick circle. Cut dough with a well-floured 2½-inch round cutter, rerolling scraps as needed.
4. Line baking sheets with parchment paper; lightly grease paper with cooking spray. Place biscuits 2 inches apart on prepared baking sheets. Brush tops of biscuits with 2 Tbsp. whipping cream.
5. Stir together granulated sugar and remaining ¼ tsp. cinnamon. Sprinkle dough rounds with sugar mixture.
6. Bake at 450° for I3 to I5 minutes or until golden brown.

Cornbread Biscuits

quick prep • party perfect

MAKES: about I5 biscuits
HANDS-ON TIME: 30 min.
TOTAL TIME: 53 min.

Add your own signature spin with a few teaspoons of your favorite herb, such as thyme or rosemary.

3   cups self-rising soft-wheat flour
½   cup yellow self-rising cornmeal mix
¼   cup cold butter, cut into pieces
¼   cup shortening, cut into pieces
I½   cups buttermilk
I   tsp. yellow cornmeal
2   Tbsp. butter, melted

1. Preheat oven to 500°. Whisk together first 2 ingredients in a large bowl. Cut in cold butter and shortening with a pastry blender until mixture resembles small peas and dough is crumbly. Cover and chill I0 minutes. Add buttermilk, stirring just until dry ingredients are moistened.
2. Turn dough out onto a heavily floured surface; knead 3 or 4 times. Pat dough into a ¾-inch-thick circle.
3. Cut dough with a well-floured 2½-inch round cutter, rerolling scraps as needed. Sprinkle cornmeal on ungreased baking sheets; place biscuits on baking sheets. Lightly brush tops with 2 Tbsp. melted butter.
4. Bake at 500° for I3 to I5 minutes or until golden brown.
NOTE: We tested with White Lily Bleached Self-Rising Flour.

Test Kitchen Tip

Set out mix-and-match vintage jars with these purchased condiments and delicious fillers:

• Pimiento cheese
• Local honey
• Pepper jelly

• Sweetened whipped cream
• Fig preserves

• Pulled pork
• Fresh mixed berries
• Hazelnut spread

Crispy Chicken Cutlets

make-ahead • party perfect

MAKES: about 16 servings
HANDS-ON TIME: 30 min.
TOTAL TIME: 8 hr., 30 min.

These taste similar to the chicken from a certain closed-on-Sundays fast-food chain that folks love. The secret? Dill pickle juice! If your cutlets are thick, put between sheets of plastic wrap, and flatten to ½ inch thick using a rolling pin.

- 8 (4-oz.) chicken breast cutlets, cut in half crosswise
- 2 cups dill pickle juice from jar
- 2 large eggs
- ¾ cup self-rising cornmeal mix
- ¾ cup fine, dry breadcrumbs
- ¼ cup finely chopped fresh parsley
- 1 tsp. pepper
- ½ tsp. salt
- 1 cup peanut oil

1. Combine first 2 ingredients in a 1-gal. zip-top plastic freezer bag. Seal bag, pressing out most of air, and chill 8 hours.
2. Whisk together eggs and 3 Tbsp. water in a shallow bowl. Combine cornmeal mix and next 3 ingredients in a second shallow bowl. Remove chicken from marinade, discarding marinade; sprinkle chicken with salt. Dip chicken in egg mixture, and dredge in cornmeal mixture, pressing firmly to adhere.
3. Heat oil in a large nonstick skillet over medium-high heat. Add chicken, and cook, in batches, 2 to 3 minutes on each side or until done.

Up-a-Notch Sausage and Gravy

quick prep • party perfect

MAKES: 3 cups
HANDS-ON TIME: 30 min.
TOTAL TIME: 30 min.

- ½ (1-lb.) package mild ground pork sausage
  Butter (optional)
- 1 (4-oz.) package fresh shiitake mushrooms, stemmed and sliced
- 2 shallots, minced
- ¼ cup all-purpose flour
- ½ cup chicken broth
- ¼ cup dry sherry or white wine
- 2 cups half-and-half
- 2 Tbsp. chopped fresh parsley
- 1 Tbsp. chopped fresh sage
- 1 tsp. Worcestershire sauce
- ½ tsp. salt
- ½ tsp. freshly ground pepper

1. Cook sausage in a large heavy skillet over medium-high heat, stirring often, 3 to 5 minutes or until sausage crumbles and is no longer pink; drain, reserving ¼ cup drippings in skillet. (If necessary, add melted butter to drippings to equal ¼ cup.)
2. Sauté mushrooms and shallots in hot drippings over medium-high heat 4 to 5 minutes or until golden. Whisk flour into mushroom mixture, and cook over medium-high heat, whisking constantly, 1 minute or until lightly browned. Add chicken broth and sherry, and cook 2 minutes, stirring to loosen particles from bottom of skillet. Stir in sausage.
3. Gradually add half-and-half, and cook over medium heat, stirring constantly, 2 to 3 minutes or until thickened and bubbly. Stir in parsley and next 4 ingredients. Reduce heat to low, and cook, stirring occasionally, 5 minutes. Serve warm.

Try these Combos!

{1}
CHICKEN BISCUIT: A Crispy Chicken Cutlet, Mustard-Peach Preserves, and pickled okra on a Cornbread Biscuit

{2}
FRIED APPLE BISCUIT: Thyme-Scented Fried Apples and pancetta on a Sweet Potato Biscuit

{3}
TOMATO-PROSCIUTTO BISCUIT: Sweet Tomato Chutney, prosciutto, and pepper on a Sweet Potato Biscuit

{4}
SALTY-SWEET BANANA BISCUIT: Hazelnut spread, bananas, and bacon on an Angel Biscuit

{5}
SAUSAGE-CRANBERRY BISCUIT: Sausage patty, cranberry sauce, and fresh sage on an Angel Biscuit

{6}
PIMIENTO CHEESE BISCUIT: Pimiento cheese, bacon, and pickled jalapeños on a Cornbread Biscuit

Sweet Tomato Chutney

quick prep • party perfect

MAKES: about 2 cups
HANDS-ON TIME: 30 min.
TOTAL TIME: 50 min.

½ sweet onion, finely chopped
I garlic clove, minced
I Tbsp. olive oil
I (14.5-oz.) can diced tomatoes
3 Tbsp. light brown sugar
I Tbsp. finely grated fresh ginger
I Tbsp. fresh lime juice
2 tsp. apple cider vinegar
¼ tsp. salt
¼ tsp. dried crushed red pepper
I mango, peeled and finely diced
I Tbsp. finely chopped fresh cilantro

1. Sauté onion and garlic in hot oil in a medium saucepan over medium heat 4 minutes or until onion is tender. Add tomatoes and next 6 ingredients. Cook, stirring occasionally, 10 minutes or until almost all liquid evaporates. Stir in mango, and cook I minute. Let cool 20 minutes. Stir in cilantro. Serve warm, or cover and chill until ready to serve.

Mustard-Peach Preserves

quick prep • party perfect

MAKES: 1¾ cups
HANDS-ON TIME: 15 min.
TOTAL TIME: 15 min.

I Tbsp. olive oil
½ medium-size sweet onion, finely chopped
I cup peach preserves
¾ cup chopped dried peaches
¼ cup coarse-grained Dijon mustard
¼ tsp. salt
¼ tsp. pepper

1. Heat oil in a large nonstick skillet over medium heat. Add onion, and cook, stirring often, 5 to 6 minutes or until onions are golden brown. Remove from heat, and stir in preserves and next 4 ingredients. Cover and chill I hour or up to I week.

Thyme-Scented Fried Apples

quick prep • party perfect

MAKES: 4 to 6 servings
HANDS-ON TIME: 32 min.
TOTAL TIME: 32 min.

3 Tbsp. butter
2 shallots, minced
3 large Granny Smith apples, peeled and sliced (about 1¾ lb.)
½ cup firmly packed light brown sugar
2 Tbsp. apple cider vinegar
½ tsp. minced fresh thyme
¼ tsp. salt
⅛ tsp. pepper

1. Melt butter in a 12-inch skillet over medium-high heat; add shallots, and sauté 2 minutes. Stir in apples, and sauté 5 minutes. Add brown sugar and remaining ingredients; sauté 15 to 18 minutes or until apples are tender. Serve warm.

TRY THIS TWIST!
Rosemary-Scented Fried Apples:
Substitute rosemary for thyme and balsamic vinegar for apple cider vinegar.

The Movable Feast

Too many houseguests can lead to cabin fever. Get outside with this perfectly portable menu.

Fall Picnic

SERVES 6

Persimmon-Pear Salad

Smoky Red Pepper Soup

Collard Green Pistou

Pancetta-Arugula-Turkey Sandwiches

Sweet Potato Pound Cake

Decadent Chai Latte

Persimmon-Pear Salad

quick prep • make-ahead • party perfect

MAKES: 6 to 8 servings
HANDS-ON TIME: 10 min.
TOTAL TIME: 35 min., including vinaigrette

- ½ cup walnut halves
- 3 heads butter or Bibb lettuce, torn (about 8 cups)
- 2 ripe Bosc pears, sliced
- 2 Fuyu persimmons, sliced
- 12 pitted dates, coarsely chopped
  Honey-Cider Vinaigrette

1. Preheat oven to 350°. Bake walnuts in a single layer in a shallow pan 6 to 8 minutes or until toasted and fragrant, stirring halfway through. Cool 10 minutes.

2. Layer lettuce, pears, and next 2 ingredients in a container or on a serving platter. Sprinkle with toasted walnuts. Drizzle with Honey-Cider Vinaigrette just before serving. Sprinkle with salt and pepper to taste.

TRY THIS TWIST!
Orange-Pear Salad: Substitute 2 oranges, peeled and sectioned, for persimmons. Proceed as directed.

Honey-Cider Vinaigrette

MAKES: 1¼ cups
HANDS-ON TIME: 5 min.
TOTAL TIME: 10 min.

- ⅓ cup cider vinegar
- 1 shallot, minced
- 2 Tbsp. honey
- 1 Tbsp. whole grain Dijon mustard
- ½ tsp. kosher salt
- ¼ tsp. pepper
- ⅔ cup olive oil

1. Combine first 2 ingredients in a small bowl, and let stand 5 minutes. Whisk honey and next 3 ingredients into vinegar mixture. Add oil in a slow, steady stream, whisking constantly until well blended.

Smoky Red Pepper Soup

make-ahead • party perfect

MAKES: 8 cups
HANDS-ON TIME: 30 min.
TOTAL TIME: 1 hr., 25 min., including pistou

- 3 Tbsp. butter
- 6 large red bell peppers, chopped
- 3 medium carrots, chopped
- 1 large sweet onion, diced
- 2 garlic cloves, minced
- 3 Tbsp. tomato paste
- 1 Tbsp. finely grated fresh ginger
- 2 tsp. smoked paprika
- 1 tsp. ground coriander
- 5 cups vegetable broth
- 2 bay leaves
- ¼ cup whipping cream
  Collard Green Pistou

1. Melt butter in a large Dutch oven over medium-high heat; add bell peppers and next 2 ingredients. Sauté 12 to 15 minutes or until onion is golden. Stir in garlic and next 4 ingredients. Cook, stirring constantly, 2 minutes.

2. Add broth and bay leaves; bring to a boil. Reduce heat to medium-low, and simmer, stirring often, 25 minutes or until vegetables are tender. Discard bay leaves.

3. Process soup with a handheld blender until smooth. Stir in cream, and season with salt and pepper to taste. Cook over medium heat 10 minutes or until thoroughly heated. Serve with Collard Green Pistou.

NOTE: If you don't have a handheld blender, let mixture cool slightly after Step 2; process mixture, in batches, in a regular blender until smooth. Return mixture to Dutch oven, and proceed with recipe as directed in Step 3.

Collard Green Pistou

MAKES: 1 cup
HANDS-ON TIME: 15 min.
TOTAL TIME: 15 min.

This pesto partners well with ciabatta or sourdough. Turnip, kale, or mustard greens may be substituted for collard greens.

- 2 cups firmly packed chopped fresh collard greens
- 2 garlic cloves
- ⅔ cup extra virgin olive oil
- ¼ tsp. dried crushed red pepper
- 2 tsp. lemon zest
- 1 Tbsp. fresh lemon juice
- ¾ tsp. salt
- ¼ tsp. pepper

1. Cook collard greens in boiling salted water to cover 4 to 6 minutes or until tender; drain. Plunge into ice water to stop the cooking process; drain well. Process garlic in a food processor until finely ground. Add greens, olive oil, and red pepper; process 2 to 3 seconds or until finely chopped. Stir in remaining ingredients.

Pancetta-Arugula-Turkey Sandwiches

quick prep • make-ahead • party perfect

MAKES: 6 servings
HANDS-ON TIME: 15 min.
TOTAL TIME: 15 min.

Not a fan of blue cheese? Try soft Brie instead.

- 12 multigrain sourdough bakery bread slices
- 5 oz. soft ripened blue cheese
- 1½ lb. sliced roasted turkey
- ½ cup whole-berry cranberry sauce
- 12 cooked pancetta slices
- 2 cups loosely packed arugula
- ¼ cup whole grain Dijon mustard

1. Spread 1 side of 6 bread slices with blue cheese. Layer with turkey, cranberry sauce, pancetta, and arugula. Spread 1 side of remaining 6 bread slices with mustard, and place, mustard sides down, on arugula.
NOTE: We tested with Saga Classic Soft-Ripened Blue-Veined Cheese.

TRY THIS TWIST!
Bacon-Horseradish-Turkey Sandwiches: Substitute 6 split croissants for bread, 6 Havarti cheese slices for blue cheese, 6 cooked bacon slices for pancetta, and peach preserves for cranberry sauce. Stir 1 Tbsp. refrigerated horseradish into peach preserves. Proceed as directed.

Try 3 More Picnic-Perfect Side Dishes.

Simply toss and season with salt and pepper.

{1}

SWEET FETA COUSCOUS: Start with cooked Israeli couscous. Then add chopped sun-dried tomatoes, golden raisins, chopped fresh mint, red wine vinegar, and olive oil. Sprinkle with crumbled feta cheese.

{2}

CRANBERRY-APPLE RICE: Cook and cool long-grain and wild rice mix. Combine rice, fresh baby spinach, diced Gala apple, sweetened dried cranberries, chopped celery, sliced green onions, and Honey-Cider Vinaigrette (page 269).

{3}

TWO-BEAN TOSS: Steam cut fresh green beans. Drain and rinse a can of chickpeas. Toss beans and chickpeas with thinly sliced red onion, whole grain mustard, sherry vinegar, and olive oil. Sprinkle with toasted sliced almonds.

Sweet Potato Pound Cake

make-ahead • party perfect

MAKES: 10 to 12 servings
HANDS-ON TIME: 25 min.
TOTAL TIME: 2 hr., 40 min.

- 1 (8-oz.) package cream cheese, softened
- ½ cup butter, softened
- 2 cups sugar
- 4 large eggs
- 2½ cups cooked, mashed sweet potatoes
- 3 cups all-purpose flour
- 2 tsp. baking powder
- 1 tsp. baking soda
- ¼ tsp. salt
- 1 tsp. ground cinnamon or nutmeg (optional)
- 1 tsp. vanilla extract

1. Preheat oven to 350°. Beat cream cheese and butter at medium speed with a heavy-duty electric stand mixer until creamy. Gradually add sugar, beating until light and fluffy. Add eggs, 1 at a time, beating just until yellow disappears. Add sweet potatoes, and beat well.
2. Stir together flour, next 3 ingredients, and, if desired, cinnamon in a medium bowl. Gradually add flour mixture to butter mixture, beating at low speed just until blended after each addition. Stir in vanilla. Spoon batter into a greased and floured 10-inch (12-cup) tube pan.
3. Bake at 350° for 1 hour and 5 minutes to 1 hour and 10 minutes or until a long wooden pick inserted in center comes out clean. Cool in pan on a wire rack 10 minutes. Remove from pan to wire rack, and cool completely (about 1 hour).

TRY THIS TWIST!
Sweet Potato Pound Cake Loaves:
Prepare batter as directed; pour into 2 greased and floured 8½- x 4½-inch loaf-pans. Bake and cool as directed.

Decadent Chai Latte

quick prep • make-ahead • party perfect

MAKES: 7 cups
HANDS-ON TIME: 15 min.
TOTAL TIME: 25 min.

Chai is an Indian spiced tea. This rich version is a wonderful complement to a thick slice of Sweet Potato Pound Cake (recipe at left).

- 4 **cups milk**
- 1 **cup whipping cream**
- ½ **cup firmly packed light brown sugar**
- 1 **(1-inch) piece fresh ginger, sliced**
- 6 **cardamom pods**
- 1 **star anise**
- ¼ **tsp. whole cloves**
- ¼ **tsp. black peppercorns**
- 4 **regular-size black tea bags**

1. Bring first 8 ingredients and 2 cups water to a boil in a large saucepan over medium-high heat, stirring occasionally. Add tea bags; cover, reduce heat to low, and simmer 10 minutes. Pour mixture through a fine wire-mesh strainer into a heatproof pitcher, discarding solids. Serve warm or chilled over ice.

TRY THIS TWIST!

Dark Chocolate Chai Latte: Stir 4 oz. chopped dark chocolate and ¼ tsp. ground cinnamon in with first 8 ingredients, stirring until chocolate is melted. Proceed with recipe as directed.

The Leftovers

We're not saying you have to give up the beloved leftover sandwich (we wouldn't dare!), but why not explore a few new ways to enjoy turkey, cranberry sauce, and all of your favorite fixin's after the big feast? Once you try these inspired, crowd-pleasing recipes—pizza! cobbler!—that poor loaf of Wonder bread could face a very lonely, thankless weekend.

USE IT UP: HAM, VEGGIES, CRACKERS

Dinner Mac and Cheese

quick prep

MAKES: 8 servings
HANDS-ON TIME: 30 min.
TOTAL TIME: 1 hr.

- 1 **(16-oz.) package uncooked cellentani (corkscrew) pasta**
- 3 **Tbsp. butter**
- ¼ **cup all-purpose flour**
- 4 **cups milk**
- 1 **cup (4 oz.) shredded sharp Cheddar cheese**
- 1 **(10-oz.) block sharp white Cheddar cheese, shredded**
- 1 **(3-oz.) package cream cheese, softened**
- ½ **tsp. salt**
- 2 **cups chopped cooked ham**
- 2 **cups coarsely chopped assorted roasted vegetables**
- 1¼ **cups crushed round buttery crackers**
- 2 **Tbsp. butter, melted**

1. Preheat oven to 400°. Prepare cellentani pasta according to package directions.
2. Meanwhile, melt 3 Tbsp. butter in a Dutch oven over medium heat. Gradually whisk in flour; cook, whisking constantly, 1 minute. Gradually whisk in milk until smooth; cook, whisking constantly, 8 to 10 minutes or until slightly thickened. Whisk in 1 cup sharp Cheddar cheese and next 3 ingredients until smooth. Remove from heat, and stir in ham, vegetables, and hot cooked pasta.
3. Spoon pasta mixture into a lightly greased 13- x 9-inch baking dish. Stir together crushed cracker crumbs and 2 Tbsp. melted butter; sprinkle over pasta mixture.
4. Bake at 400° for 25 to 30 minutes or until golden and bubbly. Let stand 5 minutes before serving.

Turn 3 Leftover Holiday Sides into Something New.

{1}

SWEET POTATO CASSEROLE: Add a hearty spoonful (or more) to waffle or pancake batter for a sweet breakfast.

{2}

CORNBREAD DRESSING: Use pan-fried slices of dressing as a base for Southern-style eggs Benedict.

{3}

CRANBERRY SAUCE: Stir some into mayonnaise or chicken salad for extra sweetness.

USE IT UP: TURKEY, SAUSAGE, SHRIMP, VEGGIES, CHEESES

After-Thanksgiving Pizza

quick prep

MAKES: 6 servings
HANDS-ON TIME: 20 min.
TOTAL TIME: 40 min.

1 (11-oz.) can refrigerated thin pizza crust dough
  Desired toppings

1. Preheat oven to 450°. Unroll dough; pat to an even thickness on a lightly greased baking sheet. Bake 10 to 12 minutes or until lightly browned. Top and bake as directed in recipes at right.

Try These Twists!

We used leftovers and extra ingredients from the recipes on pages 248-270 for these pizzas.

TURKEY CLUB PIZZA: Stir together ¼ cup mayonnaise and 3 Tbsp. refrigerated reduced-fat pesto sauce; spread over crust. Top with 2 cups cubed cooked turkey, 2 thinly sliced plum tomatoes, and ¼ cup thinly sliced red onion. Bake at 450° for 6 to 8 minutes. Sprinkle with 1½ cups (6 oz.) shredded colby Jack cheese and 4 cooked and crumbled bacon slices. Bake until cheese melts. Top with chopped fresh avocado.

MEXICAN PIZZA: Sauté ½ lb. sliced smoked chorizo sausage and ½ cup thinly sliced sweet onion in 2 tsp. hot olive oil until onion is tender; drain. Combine 4 oz. softened cream cheese, 1 cup (4 oz.) shredded Monterey Jack cheese, ¼ cup chopped fresh cilantro, ½ tsp. lime zest, and 1 Tbsp. lime juice; spread over crust. Top with sausage mixture and 1½ cups fresh corn kernels. Bake at 450° for 8 to 10 minutes. Sprinkle with fresh cilantro leaves.

APPLE-GOAT CHEESE PIZZA: Sauté 1 thinly sliced Granny Smith apple and ½ cup thinly sliced red onion in 2 tsp. hot olive oil in a nonstick skillet until tender. Spread ⅓ cup fig preserves over crust. Top with apple mixture and 4 oz. crumbled goat cheese. Bake at 450° for 8 to 10 minutes or until cheese is slightly melted. Top with 1 cup arugula and ½ cup chopped toasted pecans.

SHRIMP-PESTO PIZZA: Spread 3 Tbsp. refrigerated pesto sauce over crust. Top crust with ½ lb. peeled and cooked, medium-size shrimp (41/50 count) and 1 cup halved grape tomatoes. Bake pizza at 450° for 8 to 10 minutes. Sprinkle pizza with ⅓ cup freshly grated Parmesan cheese and ¼ cup chopped fresh basil.

USE IT UP: ROLLS, TURKEY OR HAM, CRANBERRY SAUCE

Turkey Salad with Cranberry Dressing

quick prep

MAKES: 8 servings
HANDS-ON TIME: 20 min.
TOTAL TIME: 35 min.

2 Tbsp. butter, melted
½ tsp. dried Italian seasoning
4 medium-size dinner rolls, cut into 2-inch cubes (about 2 cups)
1 (5.5-oz.) package spring greens mix
1 small head romaine lettuce, chopped
2 cups coarsely chopped turkey or ham
½ English cucumber, thinly sliced
½ cup balsamic vinegar
½ cup canola oil
¼ cup whole-berry cranberry sauce
2 Tbsp. Dijon mustard
2 garlic cloves, minced
¼ tsp. salt
¼ tsp. pepper

1. Preheat oven to 425°. Stir together first 2 ingredients in a bowl. Add bread cubes; toss to coat. Bake cubes in a single layer in a jelly-roll pan 3 to 5 minutes or until golden, stirring once. Cool completely on a wire rack (about 15 minutes).
2. Combine spring greens, next 3 ingredients, and toasted bread cubes in a serving bowl. Process vinegar and next 6 ingredients in a blender until smooth. Serve with salad.

USE IT UP: TURKEY

Tortilla Turkey Soup

quick prep

MAKES: 8 cups
HANDS-ON TIME: 30 min.
TOTAL TIME: 40 min.

10 (6-inch) fajita-size corn tortillas, cut into ½-inch-wide strips
    Vegetable cooking spray
1 small onion, chopped
2 garlic cloves, chopped
1 small jalapeño pepper, seeded and minced
1 Tbsp. olive oil
1 (32-oz.) container chicken broth
1 (10-oz.) can medium enchilada sauce
2 cups chopped cooked turkey
1 tsp. ground cumin
   Toppings: chopped avocado, shredded sharp Cheddar cheese, chopped fresh cilantro, chopped tomatoes

1. Preheat oven to 450°. Place half of tortilla strips in a single layer on a baking sheet. Coat strips with cooking spray; bake 10 minutes or until browned and crisp, stirring once.
2. Sauté onion and next 2 ingredients in hot olive oil in a Dutch oven over medium-high heat 5 to 6 minutes or until browned.
3. Add chicken broth and remaining unbaked tortilla strips to onion mixture. Cook broth mixture over medium heat 3 to 5 minutes or until tortilla strips soften and broth mixture thickens slightly.
4. Stir in enchilada sauce and next 2 ingredients, and cook 6 to 8 minutes or until mixture is thoroughly heated. (Do not boil.) Serve with baked tortilla strips and desired toppings.

USE IT UP: HAM

Ham-and-Vegetable Cobbler

quick prep

MAKES: 6 servings
HANDS-ON TIME: 30 min.
TOTAL TIME: 50 min.

¼ cup butter
¼ cup all-purpose flour
3½ cups milk
½ tsp. dried thyme
1 tsp. chicken bouillon granules
2 cups diced cooked ham
1 (10-oz.) package frozen sweet peas and mushrooms
1 cup frozen crinkle-cut carrots
1 (14.1-oz.) package refrigerated piecrusts

1. Preheat oven to 450°. Melt butter in a large saucepan over medium heat. Gradually whisk in flour, and cook, whisking constantly, 1 minute. Add milk and next 2 ingredients; cook, stirring constantly, 6 to 8 minutes or until thickened and bubbly. Stir in ham and next 2 ingredients; cook 4 to 5 minutes or until mixture is thoroughly heated. Spoon into a lightly greased 11- x 7-inch baking dish.
2. Unroll each piecrust on a lightly floured surface. Cut piecrusts into 1¼-inch-wide strips. Arrange strips in a lattice design over ham mixture.
3. Bake at 450° for 40 minutes or until crust is browned and filling is bubbly.

Company-Ready Cider

Greet guests with a welcoming beverage this holiday season.

CREAMY

HOT CIDER NOG: Whisk together 2 cups half-and-half, 1 cup each milk and apple cider, 2 large eggs, ½ cup sugar, ¼ tsp. ground cinnamon, and ⅛ tsp. each salt and ground nutmeg in a heavy saucepan. Cook over medium-low heat, whisking occasionally, 15 to 20 minutes or until mixture thickens and coats a spoon. Remove from heat, and stir in ½ cup bourbon, if desired. Top each serving with sweetened whipped cream. Garnish with cinnamon sticks, if desired. Makes: 5½ cups

MULLED

CIDER TEA: Place 6 regular-size hibiscus tea bags and 2½ cups water in a medium saucepan; bring to a boil. Boil, uncovered, until liquid is reduced to 2 cups. Remove tea bags, and stir in 4 each whole allspice and cloves and 2 (3-inch) cinnamon sticks. Let cool about 1 hour; chill 1 hour. Discard solids. Cook tea mixture and 6 cups apple cider in a large saucepan over medium heat until thoroughly heated.
NOTE: We tested with Celestial Seasonings Red Zinger Herbal Tea. Makes: 8 cups

SPIKED

RUM CIDER TEA: Prepare Cider Tea as directed, stirring 1 cup spiced rum into cider mixture in saucepan. Makes: 9 cups

BOURBON CIDER SOUR: Stir together ¾ cup each bourbon and apple cider, ½ cup orange juice, and ¼ cup sugar. Serve over finely crushed ice. Makes: 2⅓ cups

PARTY APPLE PUNCH: Stir together 2 cups chilled pear nectar, ¼ cup honey, and, if desired, 1 cup brandy in a large punch bowl. Stir in 2 (750-milliliter) bottles chilled sparkling apple cider and 1 liter chilled club soda just before serving. Makes: 13 cups

Irresistible Side

This holiday essential gets a much-needed makeover from fresh veggies and a lightened (but super-rich!) homemade sauce.

Home-style Green Bean Casserole

good for you • party perfect

MAKES: 8 servings
HANDS-ON TIME: 25 min.
TOTAL TIME: 55 min.

Only 168 calories! And not just for a spoonful but a whole Thanksgiving-size serving of this hearty yet wholesome dish.

- 1½ **lb. fresh green beans, trimmed**
- 2 **Tbsp. butter**
- ¼ **cup all-purpose flour**
- 1½ **cups 2% reduced-fat milk**
- ½ **cup nonfat buttermilk**
- 1 **Tbsp. Ranch dressing mix**
- 2 **tsp. chopped fresh thyme**
- ¼ **tsp. salt**
- ¼ **tsp. pepper**
- 1 **tsp. butter**
- 1 **(8-oz.) package sliced fresh mushrooms**
  Vegetable cooking spray
- 1 **cup French fried onions, crushed**
- ½ **cup panko (Japanese breadcrumbs)**
- 2 **plum tomatoes, seeded and chopped**

3 Reasons to Indulge!

Smart choices equal delicious results.

- **Fresh green beans** offer better texture, less sodium, and more available nutrients than the usual canned green beans.
- **White sauce,** made with sautéed mushrooms, reduced-fat dairy, and a touch of butter, replaces canned cream of mushroom soup.
- **A traditional topping** of fried onions mixed with breadcrumbs adds guilt-free crunch.

1. Preheat oven to 350°. Cook green beans in boiling salted water to cover in a Dutch oven 4 to 6 minutes or to desired degree of doneness; drain. Plunge into ice water to stop the cooking process; drain and pat dry.
2. Melt 2 Tbsp. butter in Dutch oven over medium heat; whisk in flour until smooth. Cook, whisking constantly, 1 minute. Gradually whisk in 1½ cups milk; cook, whisking constantly, 3 to 4 minutes or until sauce is thickened and bubbly. Remove from heat, and whisk in buttermilk and next 4 ingredients.
3. Melt 1 tsp. butter in a medium skillet over medium-high heat; add mushrooms, and sauté 6 to 8 minutes or until lightly browned. Remove from heat; let stand 5 minutes. Gently toss mushrooms and green beans in buttermilk sauce. Place in a 13- x 9-inch or 3-qt. baking dish coated with cooking spray.
4. Combine French fried onions and next 2 ingredients; sprinkle over green bean mixture.
5. Bake at 350° for 25 to 30 minutes or until golden brown and bubbly. Serve immediately.

PER SERVING: CALORIES 168; FAT 8.4G (SAT 3.9G, MONO 1.1G, POLY 0.2G); PROTEIN 5.7G; CARB 18.5G; FIBER 3.9G; CHOL 15MG; IRON 0.9MG; SODIUM 296MG; CALC 104MG

December

Our Best Hanukkah Recipes

From traditional brisket to updated warm frisée salad, these dishes are some of our favorites for celebrating the Festival of Light. Just add candlelight and smiling faces for a memorable holiday meal.

Hanukkah Celebration

SERVES 6 TO 8

Caramelized Maple-and-Garlic-Glazed Salmon

Roasted Paprika Chicken

Southern Baked Brisket

Asparagus Sauté

Pepper Jelly-Glazed Carrots

Sweet Potato Latkes

Warm Frisée Salad with Crispy Kosher Salami

Spiced Thyme Applesauce

Peach-Pecan Rugelach

Hanukkah Doughnuts with Strawberry Preserves

Caramelized Maple-and-Garlic-Glazed Salmon

MAKES: 8 servings
HANDS-ON TIME: 20 min.
TOTAL TIME: 20 min.

- 8 (2-inch-thick) salmon fillets (about 2½ lb.)
- ¾ tsp. salt
- ¾ tsp. garlic powder
- 2 Tbsp. butter or margarine
- ⅓ cup maple syrup, divided
- 1 Tbsp. chopped fresh chives

1. Preheat broiler with oven rack 5½ inches from heat. Sprinkle salmon with salt and garlic powder.
2. Melt butter in a large skillet over medium heat. Add salmon, skin side up; cook 2 minutes. Place salmon, skin side down, on a lightly greased rack in a broiler pan; brush with half of syrup.
3. Broil salmon 5 to 7 minutes or until fish is cooked to desired degree of doneness and syrup caramelizes. Brush with remaining syrup; sprinkle with chives.

Roasted Paprika Chicken

MAKES: 6 to 8 servings
HANDS-ON TIME: 20 min.
TOTAL TIME: 1 hr.

- ¼ cup smoked paprika
- 2 Tbsp. chopped fresh thyme
- 3 Tbsp. extra virgin olive oil
- 2 tsp. kosher salt
- 1 tsp. coarsely ground pepper
- 5 lb. skin-on, bone-in chicken thighs and breasts
- 2 lemons, thinly sliced
  Garnishes: lemon slices, fresh thyme sprigs

1. Preheat oven to 425°. Stir together first 5 ingredients, forming a paste.
2. Loosen and lift skin from chicken pieces with fingers (do not totally detach skin). Spread half of paprika mixture underneath skin. Place 1 to 2 lemon slices on paprika mixture under skin; carefully replace skin. Rub remaining paprika mixture over outside of skin. Arrange chicken pieces in a single layer on a lightly greased wire rack in an aluminum foil-lined 17- x 12-inch jelly-roll pan.
3. Bake at 425° for 35 to 40 minutes or until a meat thermometer inserted into thickest portion of each piece registers 165°. Let chicken stand 5 minutes; lightly brush with pan juices just before serving. Garnish, if desired.

Southern Baked Brisket

MAKES: 8 to 10 servings
HANDS-ON TIME: 10 min.
TOTAL TIME: 4 hr., 30 min.

- 1 (12-oz.) bottle chili sauce
- 2 cups ketchup
- 1¼ cups cola soft drink
- 1 (1.9-oz.) envelope French onion recipe mix
- 1 (3- to 4-lb.) beef brisket flat, trimmed

1. Preheat oven to 350°. Stir together first 3 ingredients and both envelopes from soup mix packages in a large bowl.
2. Place brisket, fat side up, in an aluminum foil-lined roasting pan. Pour chili sauce mixture over brisket.
3. Bake, tightly covered, at 350° for 4 to 4½ hours or until fork-tender. Remove from oven; let stand 20 minutes. Cut brisket across the grain into thin slices using a sharp knife, and pour pan juices over slices.
NOTE: We tested with Lipton Kosher Recipe Secrets Onion Recipe Soup & Dip Mix.

Asparagus Sauté

MAKES: 6 servings
HANDS-ON TIME: 15 min.
TOTAL TIME: 15 min.

- 2 lb. fresh asparagus
- ¼ cup butter or margarine
- 1 large red bell pepper, diced
- ½ tsp. salt
- ½ tsp. pepper

1. Snap off and discard tough ends of asparagus.
2. Melt butter in a large skillet over medium heat. Add asparagus, bell pepper, and remaining ingredients, and sauté 4 to 5 minutes or until crisp-tender. Serve immediately.

Pepper Jelly-Glazed Carrots

MAKES: 6 servings
HANDS-ON TIME: 20 min.
TOTAL TIME: 25 min.

Find rainbow baby carrots at some large supermarkets and specialty stores.

- 4 (7-oz.) packages assorted colors baby carrots, halved*
- 1 (10½-oz.) can condensed chicken broth, undiluted
- 2 Tbsp. butter or margarine
- 1 (10½-oz.) jar red pepper jelly**

1. Combine carrots and chicken broth in a skillet over medium-high heat. Bring to a boil, and cook, stirring often, 6 to 8 minutes or until carrots are crisp-tender and broth is reduced to ¼ cup.
2. Stir in butter and pepper jelly, and cook, stirring constantly, 5 minutes or until mixture thickens and carrots are glazed. Transfer to a serving dish, using a slotted spoon. Pour half of pan juices over carrots.

*1 (2-lb.) package baby carrots may be substituted.
**1 (10½-oz.) jar hot jalapeño pepper jelly may be substituted.

Sweet Potato Latkes

MAKES: about 2 dozen
HANDS-ON TIME: 40 min.
TOTAL TIME: 40 min., not including cream sauce and applesauce

- 2½ lb. sweet potatoes, peeled
- 6 Tbsp. all-purpose flour
- 4 large eggs, lightly beaten
- 4 green onions, sliced
- ½ tsp. salt
  Vegetable oil
  Horseradish Cream Sauce (optional)
  Spiced Thyme Applesauce (next page) (optional)

1. Grate potatoes through large holes of a box grater. Stir together potatoes and flour. Stir in eggs and next 2 ingredients until blended.
2. Pour oil to depth of ½ inch into a large heavy skillet; heat to 350°.
3. Gently press 1 rounded tablespoon potato mixture to form a patty. Repeat to make about 2 dozen patties. Fry, in batches, 2 to 3 minutes on each side or until golden. Drain on paper towels. Serve immediately with Horseradish Cream Sauce and Spiced Thyme Applesauce, if desired.

Horseradish Cream Sauce

MAKES: 1 cup
HANDS-ON TIME: 10 min.
TOTAL TIME: 40 min.

- 1 (8-oz.) container sour cream
- 2 Tbsp. thinly sliced fresh chives
- 4 tsp. refrigerated horseradish
- 1 tsp. lemon zest
- ½ tsp. coarsely ground pepper
- ¼ tsp. salt
  Garnish: sliced fresh chives

1. Stir together first 6 ingredients in a small bowl. Cover and chill 30 minutes. Garnish, if desired. Store in an airtight container in refrigerator up to 2 days.

Warm Frisée Salad with Crispy Kosher Salami

MAKES: 8 servings
HANDS-ON TIME: 30 min.
TOTAL TIME: 30 min.

- ½ (12-oz.) package kosher beef salami slices
- ¼ cup extra virgin olive oil
- ½ medium-size red onion, sliced
- 1 garlic clove, minced
- ⅓ cup plus 1 Tbsp. sherry vinegar
- 2 tsp. whole grain mustard
- ½ tsp. kosher salt
- ¼ tsp. coarsely ground pepper
- 4 bunches frisée, torn
- 1 pt. grape tomatoes, halved

1. Cut kosher beef salami slices into ¼-inch-wide strips.
2. Cook salami strips in hot oil in a medium skillet over medium heat 5 to 10 minutes or until crisp. Remove salami from skillet using a slotted spoon; reserve drippings in skillet. Drain salami strips on paper towels.
3. Sauté onion and garlic in reserved drippings 2 minutes. Stir in vinegar and next 3 ingredients; cook, stirring constantly, 1 minute.
4. Place frisée and tomato halves in a large bowl, and drizzle with vinegar mixture; toss to coat. Sprinkle with crisp salami strips, and serve immediately.
NOTE: We tested with Hebrew National Kosher Beef Salami.

Spiced Thyme Applesauce

MAKES: 1¾ cups
HANDS-ON TIME: 20 min.
TOTAL TIME: 20 min.

- 1 cup chunky applesauce
- 1 large ripe pear, peeled and finely chopped
- 1 Tbsp. butter or margarine
- 1 tsp. fresh lemon juice
- 1 tsp. finely grated fresh ginger
- ¾ tsp. finely chopped fresh thyme
- ⅛ tsp. ground cloves
- ⅛ tsp. kosher salt

1. Stir together all ingredients in a medium saucepan. Bring to a boil, stirring often, over medium-high heat. Reduce heat to low, and simmer, stirring occasionally, 5 to 7 minutes or until pear is tender.
NOTE: We tested with Musselman's Chunky Apple Sauce. To make ahead, prepare recipe as directed. Cool completely (about 45 minutes). Store in an airtight container in refrigerator up to 2 days. Microwave in a microwave-safe glass bowl at HIGH 1 to 2 minutes or until thoroughly heated, stirring at 30-second intervals.

Peach-Pecan Rugelach

MAKES: about 5 dozen
HANDS-ON TIME: 1 hr., 15 min.
TOTAL TIME: 3 hr.

- 1 cup chopped pecans
- 2¼ cups all-purpose flour
- 1 cup butter, cut into pieces
- 1 (8-oz.) package cream cheese, cut into pieces
- ½ tsp. salt
- 1 (12-oz.) jar peach preserves
- Parchment paper
- 3 Tbsp. sugar
- 2 tsp. ground cinnamon

1. Preheat oven to 350°. Bake pecans in a single layer in a shallow pan 10 to 12 minutes or until toasted and fragrant, stirring halfway through. Increase oven temperature to 375°.

2. Pulse flour and next 3 ingredients in a food processor 3 or 4 times until dough forms a small ball and leaves sides of bowl. Divide dough into 8 portions, shaping each portion into a ball. Wrap each ball separately in plastic wrap, and chill 1 to 24 hours.
3. Heat preserves in a small saucepan over medium heat, stirring often, 2 to 3 minutes or until warm. Roll 1 dough ball into an 8-inch circle on a lightly floured surface. Brush dough with 1 to 2 Tbsp. warm preserves. Sprinkle 2 Tbsp. toasted pecans over preserves on dough. Cut circle into 8 wedges, and roll up wedges, starting at wide end, to form a crescent shape. Place, point side down, on a lightly greased parchment paper-lined baking sheet. Repeat procedure with remaining dough balls, preserves, and pecans.
4. Combine sugar and cinnamon; sprinkle over crescents.
5. Bake at 375° for 15 to 20 minutes or until golden. Remove from baking sheets, and transfer to wire racks to cool completely (about 20 minutes).

TRY THIS TWIST!
Apricot-Almond Rugelach: Substitute apricot preserves for peach preserves and almonds for pecans. Prepare recipe as directed, decreasing toasting time in Step 1 to 8 to 10 minutes.

Hanukkah Doughnuts with Strawberry Preserves

MAKES: about 2½ dozen
HANDS-ON TIME: 40 min.
TOTAL TIME: 9 hr., including Crème Fraîche

- ½ cup butter or margarine
- 1 Tbsp. sugar
- 1 cup all-purpose flour
- 2 large eggs
- Vegetable oil
- Powdered sugar
- ¾ cup strawberry preserves
- Crème Fraîche

1. Bring butter, sugar, and 1 cup water to a boil in a heavy saucepan over medium-high heat, stirring occasionally. Immediately remove saucepan from heat, and quickly whisk in flour. Return saucepan to heat, and cook, whisking constantly, 2 to 3 minutes or until mixture thickens. Remove saucepan from heat; let mixture cool 10 minutes.
2. Transfer mixture to a large bowl. Beat in eggs, 1 at a time, beating at medium speed with an electric mixer until blended after each addition.
3. Turn dough out onto a lightly floured surface. Pat or roll dough to ⅛-inch thickness, and cut with star- or dreidel-shaped cutters, rerolling scraps as needed.
4. Pour oil to depth of ½ inch into a large cast-iron skillet; heat to 375°. Fry doughnuts, in batches, 1 to 2 minutes on each side or until golden. Drain on paper towels. Sprinkle immediately with powdered sugar.
5. Microwave preserves in a microwave-safe glass bowl at HIGH 1 to 2 minutes or until thoroughly heated, stirring once. Serve doughnuts with melted preserves and Crème Fraîche.

Crème Fraîche

1. Heat 1 cup whipping cream and 1 tsp. buttermilk in a small saucepan over low heat 3 to 5 minutes or until lukewarm. Pour mixture into a glass jar, and loosely cover with lid. Let stand, free from drafts, 8 to 24 hours or until thickened. Store, tightly covered, in refrigerator up to 10 days. Makes: about 1 cup. Hands-on time: 5 min.; Total time: 8 hr., 5 min.

Sweet Christmas Breakfasts

Baked Toasted-Pecan Pancake with Caramel-Apple Topping

MAKES: 6 to 8 servings
HANDS-ON TIME: 15 min.
TOTAL TIME: 56 min., including topping

Use a light hand when stirring the batter; overmixing will cause a rubbery texture.

- 1 cup chopped pecans
- 1¾ cups all-purpose flour
- 2 tsp. sugar
- 1½ tsp. baking powder
- 1 tsp. baking soda
- ½ tsp. salt
- 2 cups buttermilk
- 2 large eggs
- ¼ cup butter, melted
- Caramel-Apple Topping

1. Preheat oven to 350°. Bake pecans in a single layer in a shallow pan 4 to 5 minutes or until lightly toasted, stirring halfway through. Cool 10 minutes.
2. Meanwhile, combine flour and next 4 ingredients in a large bowl. Whisk together buttermilk and eggs. Gradually stir buttermilk mixture into flour mixture. Gently stir in butter. (Batter will be lumpy.)
3. Pour batter into a lightly greased 15- x 10-inch jelly-roll pan. Sprinkle with pecans.
4. Bake at 350° for 25 to 30 minutes or until golden brown and a wooden pick inserted into center comes out clean. Serve immediately with warm Caramel-Apple Topping.

Caramel-Apple Topping: Stir together 2 (12-oz.) packages frozen spiced apples, thawed; ½ cup firmly packed brown sugar; 2 Tbsp. butter; 1 tsp. vanilla extract; and ¼ tsp. salt in a medium saucepan. Bring to a boil over medium heat, stirring occasionally; reduce heat to low, and simmer, stirring occasionally, 2 to 3 minutes or until thoroughly heated. Makes: about 3 cups. Hands-on time: 15 min., Total time: 15 min.
NOTE: We tested with Stouffer's Harvest Apples.

Giant Sweet Potato Swirls with Caramel Glaze

MAKES: 10 to 12 servings
HANDS-ON TIME: 30 min.
TOTAL TIME: 3 hr., including glaze

- 2 (¼-oz.) envelopes active dry yeast
- ½ cup warm water (105° to 115°)
- 1 tsp . granulated sugar
- 5½ cups bread flour, divided
- 1½ tsp. salt
- 1 tsp. baking soda
- 1 cup cooked mashed sweet potato
- 1 large egg, lightly beaten
- 1 cup buttermilk
- ½ cup granulated sugar
- ¼ cup butter, melted
- 1 Tbsp. orange zest
- ⅔ cup granulated sugar
- ⅔ cup firmly packed brown sugar
- 1 Tbsp. ground cinnamon
- ¼ cup butter, melted
- Caramel Glaze

1. Stir together first 3 ingredients in a 1-cup glass measuring cup; let stand 5 minutes.
2. Stir together 4½ cups bread flour, salt, and baking soda.
3. Beat yeast mixture and ½ cup bread flour at medium speed with a heavy-duty electric stand mixer until well blended. Gradually add sweet potato, next 5 ingredients, and flour mixture, beating until well blended.
4. Turn dough out onto a well-floured surface, and knead until smooth and elastic (about 4 to 5 minutes), gradually adding remaining ½ cup bread flour. Place dough in a lightly greased large bowl, turning to grease top. Cover and let rise in a warm place (85°), free from drafts, 1 to 1½ hours or until doubled in bulk.
5. Stir together ⅔ cup granulated sugar and next 2 ingredients in a small bowl. Punch dough down; turn out onto a well-floured surface. Divide dough in half. Roll one portion into a 16- x 12-inch rectangle. Brush dough with half of ¼ cup melted butter. Sprinkle with half of sugar mixture. Cut dough lengthwise into 6 (2-inch-wide) strips using a pizza cutter or sharp knife. Loosely coil 1 strip, and place in center of a lightly greased 10-inch round pan. Loosely coil remaining dough strips, 1 at a time, around center strip, attaching each to the end of the previous strip, to make a single large spiral. (Sugared sides of dough strips should face center of spiral). Repeat procedure with remaining dough half, butter, and sugar mixture.
7. Cover and let rise in a warm place (85°), free from drafts, 30 minutes or until doubled in bulk.
8. Preheat oven to 350°. Bake 30 minutes or until lightly browned and done. Cool in pans on a wire rack 10 minutes. Remove from pans to serving plates. Prepare Caramel Glaze; brush over swirls.

Caramel Glaze

MAKES: about 1½ cups
HANDS-ON TIME: 15 min.
TOTAL TIME: 15 min.

- 1 cup firmly packed brown sugar
- ½ cup butter
- ¼ cup evaporated milk
- 1 cup powdered sugar, sifted
- 1 tsp. vanilla extract

1. Bring first 3 ingredients to a boil in a 2-qt. saucepan over medium heat, whisking constantly; boil, whisking constantly, 1 minute. Remove from heat; whisk in powdered sugar and vanilla until smooth. Stir gently 3 to 5 minutes or until mixture begins to cool and thickens slightly. Use immediately.

Cinnamon Rolls with Cream Cheese Icing

MAKES: 16 rolls
HANDS-ON TIME: 30 min.
TOTAL TIME: 3 hr., 40 min., including icing

Make sure the butter you spread on the rolled out dough is very soft.

- 1 (¼-oz.) envelope active dry yeast
- ¼ cup warm water (105° to 115°)
- 1 tsp. granulated sugar
- ½ cup butter, softened
- 1 cup granulated sugar, divided
- 1 tsp. salt
- 2 large eggs, lightly beaten
- 1 cup milk
- 1 Tbsp. fresh lemon juice
- 4½ cups bread flour
- ¼ tsp. ground nutmeg
- ¼ to ½ cup bread flour
- 1 cup chopped pecans
- ½ cup very soft butter
- ½ cup firmly packed light brown sugar
- 1 Tbsp. ground cinnamon
  Cream Cheese Icing

1. Combine first 3 ingredients in a 1-cup glass measuring cup; let stand 5 minutes.
2. Beat ½ cup softened butter at medium speed with a heavy-duty electric stand mixer until creamy. Gradually add ½ cup granulated sugar and 1 tsp. salt, beating at medium speed until light and fluffy. Add eggs and next 2 ingredients, beating until blended. Stir in yeast mixture.
3. Combine 4½ cups bread flour and ¼ tsp. nutmeg. Gradually add flour mixture to butter mixture, beating at low speed 1 to 2 minutes or until well blended.
4. Sprinkle about ¼ cup bread flour onto a flat surface; turn dough out, and knead until smooth and elastic (about 5 minutes), adding up to ¼ cup bread flour as needed to prevent dough from sticking to hands and surface. Place dough in a lightly greased large bowl, turning to grease top. Cover and let rise in a warm place (85°), free from drafts, 1½ to 2 hours or until doubled in bulk.
5. Meanwhile, preheat oven to 350°. Bake pecans in a single layer in a shallow pan 8 to 10 minutes or until toasted and fragrant, stirring halfway through.
6. Punch dough down; turn out onto a lightly floured surface. Roll into a 16- x 12-inch rectangle. Spread with ½ cup very soft butter, leaving a 1-inch border around edges. (Butter should be very soft so dough will not tear.) Stir together brown sugar, cinnamon, and remaining ½ cup granulated sugar, and sprinkle sugar mixture over butter. Top with pecans.
7. Roll up dough, jelly-roll fashion, starting at 1 long side; cut into 16 slices (about 1-inch thick). Place rolls, cut sides down, in 2 lightly greased 10-inch round pans.
8. Cover and let rise in a warm place (85°), free from drafts, 1 hour or until doubled in bulk.
9. Bake at 350° for 20 to 22 minutes or until rolls are golden brown. Cool in pans 5 minutes. Brush warm rolls with Cream Cheese Icing. Serve immediately.

Cream Cheese Icing:

MAKES: 1½ cups
HANDS-ON TIME: 10 min.
TOTAL TIME: 10 min.

- 2 Tbsp. butter, softened
- 1 (3-oz.) package cream cheese, softened
- 2¼ cups powdered sugar
- 1 tsp. vanilla extract
- 2 Tbsp. milk, divided

1. Beat butter and cream cheese at medium speed with an electric mixer until creamy. Gradually add powdered sugar, beating at low speed until blended. Stir in vanilla and 1 Tbsp. milk. Add remaining 1 Tbsp. milk, 1 tsp. at a time, as needed, until icing is smooth and creamy.

TRY THIS TWIST!
Almond-Cream Cheese Icing:
Prepare recipe as directed, substituting ¼ tsp. almond extract for 1 tsp. vanilla.

Try These Twists!

APPLE-CINNAMON ROLLS: Prepare recipe as directed through Step 5. Peel and chop 2 Granny Smith apples (about 3 cups chopped). Place apples in a small microwave-safe bowl, and pour 1 cup apple cider or apple juice over apples. Microwave at HIGH 5 minutes or until tender. Drain and cool 15 minutes. Proceed with recipe as directed, sprinkling apples over brown sugar mixture in Step 6 before topping with pecans. Hands-on time: 30 min.; Total time: 4 hr., including icing

CHOCOLATE-CINNAMON ROLLS: Prepare recipe as directed through Step 6 (do not top with pecans). Chop 2 (4-oz.) bittersweet chocolate baking bars. Sprinkle chocolate over brown sugar mixture. Top with pecans. Proceed as directed. Hands-on time: 35 min.; Total time: 3 hr., 45 min., including icing

CRANBERRY-CINNAMON ROLLS: Prepare recipe as directed through Step 5. Pour 1 cup boiling water over 1 cup dried cranberries; let stand 15 minutes. Drain cranberries. Proceed with recipe as directed, sprinkling cranberries over brown sugar mixture in Step 6 before topping with pecans. Hands-on time: 30 min.; Total time: 3 hr., 55 min., including icing

CHERRY-ALMOND-CINNAMON ROLLS: Substitute 1 cup slivered almonds for pecans and Almond-Cream Cheese Icing for Cream Cheese Icing. Prepare recipe as directed through Step 5. Pour 1 cup boiling water over 1 cup coarsely chopped dried cherries; let stand 15 minutes. Drain cherries. Proceed with recipe as directed, sprinkling cherries over brown sugar mixture in Step 6 before topping with toasted almonds. Hands-on time: 30 min.; Total time: 3 hr., 55 min.

Mini Banana-Cranberry-Nut Bread Loaves

MAKES: 5 loaves
HANDS-ON TIME: 20 min.
TOTAL TIME: I hr., 35 min., including glaze

Bananas that appear to be past their prime are perfect for this recipe.

- ¾ cup chopped pecans
- I (8-oz.) package cream cheese, softened
- ¾ cup butter, softened
- 2 cups sugar
- 2 large eggs
- 3 cups all-purpose flour
- ½ tsp. baking powder
- ½ tsp. baking soda
- ½ tsp. salt
- I½ cups mashed ripe bananas
- ¾ cup chopped fresh cranberries
- ½ tsp. vanilla extract
  Orange Glaze

1. Preheat oven to 350°. Bake pecans in a single layer in a shallow pan 8 to 10 minutes or until toasted and fragrant, stirring halfway through.

2. Beat cream cheese and butter at medium speed with an electric mixer until creamy. Gradually add sugar, beating until light and fluffy. Add eggs, I at a time, beating just until blended after each addition.

3. Combine flour and next 3 ingredients; gradually add to butter mixture, beating at low speed just until blended. Stir in bananas, next 2 ingredients, and pecans. Spoon about I½ cups batter into each of 5 greased and floured 5- x 3-inch miniature loaf pans.

4. Bake at 350° for 40 to 44 minutes or until a wooden pick inserted in center comes out clean and sides pull away from pans. Cool in pans 10 minutes. Transfer to wire racks. Prepare Orange Glaze; drizzle over warm bread loaves, and cool 10 minutes.

NOTE: To make ahead, freeze baked, unglazed loaves in zip-top plastic freezer bags. Thaw loaves at room temperature. Reheat loaves at 300° for 10 to 12 minutes; drizzle with Orange Glaze.

Try These Twists!

REGULAR-SIZE BANANA-CRANBERRY-NUT BREAD LOAVES:
Spoon batter into 2 greased and floured 8- x 4-inch loaf pans. Bake at 350° for I hour and 10 minutes. Cool in pans 10 minutes. Transfer to wire racks; drizzle with glaze, and cool 30 minutes. Makes: 2 loaves. Hands-on time: 20 min.; Total time: 2 hr., 25 min., including glaze.

BANANA-CRANBERRY-NUT MUFFINS: Spoon batter into 2 lightly greased (12-cup) muffin pans. Bake at 350° for 23 to 25 minutes. Cool in pans 2 minutes; transfer to wire rack. Cool 5 minutes; dip warm muffins in glaze. Makes: 2 dozen. Hands-on time: 20 min.; Total time: I hr., 5 min., including glaze.

Orange Glaze

MAKES: ½ cup
HANDS-ON TIME: 5 min.
TOTAL TIME: 5 min.

- I cup powdered sugar
- I tsp. orange zest
- 2 to 3 Tbsp. fresh orange juice

1. Stir together all ingredients in a small bowl until blended. Use immediately.

Blueberry Muffins with Lemon-Cream Cheese Glaze

MAKES: I½ dozen
HANDS-ON TIME: 15 min.
TOTAL TIME: 40 min., including glaze

- 3½ cups all-purpose flour
- I cup sugar
- I Tbsp. baking powder
- I½ tsp. salt
- 3 large eggs
- I½ cups milk
- ½ cup butter, melted
- 2 cups frozen blueberries*
- I Tbsp. all-purpose flour
  Lemon-Cream Cheese Glaze

1. Preheat oven to 450°. Stir together first 4 ingredients. Whisk together eggs and next 2 ingredients; add to flour mixture, stirring just until dry ingredients are moistened. Toss blueberries with I Tbsp. flour, and gently fold into batter.

2. Spoon mixture into I½ lightly greased 12-cup muffin pans, filling three-fourths full.

3. Bake at 450° for 14 to 15 minutes or until lightly browned and a wooden pick inserted into center comes out clean. Immediately remove from pans to wire racks, and let cool 10 minutes.

4. Meanwhile, prepare Lemon-Cream Cheese Glaze; drizzle over warm muffins.
*Fresh blueberries may be substituted.

Lemon-Cream Cheese Glaze

MAKES: about ¾ cup
HANDS-ON TIME: 10 min.
TOTAL TIME: 10 min.

- I (3-oz.) package cream cheese, softened
- I tsp. lemon zest
- I Tbsp. fresh lemon juice
- ¼ tsp. vanilla extract
- I½ cups sifted powdered sugar

1. Beat cream cheese at medium speed with an electric mixer until creamy. Add lemon zest and next 2 ingredients; beat until smooth. Gradually add powdered sugar, beating until smooth.

Snickerdoodle Muffins

MAKES: I dozen
HANDS-ON TIME: 20 min.
TOTAL TIME: 45 min.

- 3 cups all-purpose flour
- I cup sugar
- 2½ tsp. baking powder
- ¾ tsp. salt
- ½ tsp. ground nutmeg
- 2 large eggs
- I¼ cups milk
- ⅓ cup butter, melted
- ¼ cup sugar
- ¾ tsp. ground cinnamon
- ¼ cup butter, melted

1. Preheat oven to 350°. Whisk together first 5 ingredients. Make a well in center of mixture. Whisk together eggs and next 2 ingredients. Add egg mixture to flour mixture, stirring just until moistened.
2. Spoon mixture into a lightly greased 12-cup muffin pan, filling three-fourths full.
3. Bake at 350° for 25 to 30 minutes or until muffins are golden.
4. Meanwhile, stir together ¼ cup sugar and ¾ tsp. cinnamon in a small shallow bowl until thoroughly blended. Remove muffins from pan, and immediately dip tops in ¼ cup melted butter, and then into sugar mixture. Serve warm.

Cream Cheese-Filled Wreath with Vanilla Glaze

MAKES: I0 to I2 servings
HANDS-ON TIME: 30 min.
TOTAL TIME: I0 hr., I5 min., including filling and glaze

- I (8-oz.) container sour cream
- ½ cup sugar
- ½ cup butter, cut into pieces
- I tsp. salt
- 2 (¼-oz.) envelopes active dry yeast
- ½ cup warm water (I05° to II5°)
- 2 tsp. sugar
- 2 large eggs, lightly beaten
- 4 cups bread flour
  Cream Cheese Filling
  Vanilla Glaze

1. Cook first 4 ingredients in a small saucepan over medium-low heat, stirring occasionally, 4 to 5 minutes or until butter melts. Cool to I05° to II5° (about I0 minutes).
2. Combine yeast, warm water, and 2 tsp. sugar in a large bowl; let stand 5 minutes. Stir in sour cream mixture and eggs; gradually stir in flour. (Dough will be soft.) Cover and chill 8 to 24 hours.
3. Turn dough out onto a heavily floured surface, and knead 4 or 5 times.
4. Roll dough into a 24- x 8-inch rectangle, and spread with Cream Cheese Filling, leaving a I-inch border around edges. Roll up dough, jelly-roll fashion, starting at I long side; press seam. Place, seam side down, on a lightly greased baking sheet. Bring ends of roll together to form a ring, moistening and pinching edges together to seal. Cover and let rise in a warm place (85°), free from drafts, about I hour or until doubled in bulk.
5. Preheat oven to 375°. Bake 20 to 22 minutes or until browned. Remove from pan to serving dish. Drizzle warm wreath with Vanilla Glaze.

Cream Cheese Filling

MAKES: about 2 cups
HANDS-ON TIME: 5 min.
TOTAL TIME: 5 min.

- 2 (8-oz.) packages cream cheese, softened
- ½ cup sugar
- I large egg
- 2 tsp. vanilla extract

1. Beat all ingredients in a medium bowl at medium speed with an electric mixer until smooth.

Vanilla Glaze

MAKES: about I cup
HANDS-ON TIME: 5 min.
TOTAL TIME: 5 min.

- 2½ cups powdered sugar
- ¼ cup milk
- 2 tsp. vanilla extract

1. Stir together all ingredients in a small bowl until blended.

Overnight Coffee Cake with Cinnamon-Nut Crumble and Sweet Bourbon Drizzle

MAKES: 8 to I0 servings
HANDS-ON TIME: 20 min.
TOTAL TIME: 9 hr., 7 min., including crumble and drizzle

- ¾ cup butter, softened
- I cup sugar
- 2 large eggs
- 2 cups all-purpose flour
- I tsp. baking powder
- I tsp. baking soda
- ½ tsp. salt
- I cup buttermilk
- I tsp. vanilla extract
  Cinnamon-Nut Crumble
  Sweet Bourbon Drizzle

1. Beat butter at medium speed with an electric mixer until creamy; gradually add sugar, beating well. Add eggs, I at a time, beating just until blended after each addition.
2. Combine flour and next 3 ingredients in a medium bowl. Add flour mixture to butter mixture alternately with buttermilk, beginning and ending with flour mixture. Stir in vanilla. Pour batter into a greased and floured I3- x 9-inch pan. Cover tightly, and chill 8 to 24 hours.
3. Preheat oven to 350°. Let cake stand at room temperature 30 minutes. Uncover cake, and sprinkle with Cinnamon-Nut Crumble. Bake 32 to 35 minutes or until a wooden pick inserted in center comes out clean. Prepare Sweet Bourbon Drizzle; drizzle over warm cake.

Cinnamon-Nut Crumble

MAKES: about 2 cups
HANDS-ON TIME: I0 min.
TOTAL TIME: I0 min.

- ½ cup coarsely chopped pecans
- ½ cup coarsely chopped walnuts
- ½ cup slivered almonds
- ½ cup firmly packed brown sugar
- 6 Tbsp. all-purpose flour
- I tsp. ground cinnamon
- 3 Tbsp. butter, melted

1. Stir together all ingredients in a medium bowl.

Sweet Bourbon Drizzle

MAKES: about 1 cup
HANDS-ON TIME: 5 min.
TOTAL TIME: 5 min.

2 cups powdered sugar
1 Tbsp. bourbon
2 to 3 Tbsp. milk

1. Stir together powdered sugar, bourbon, and 2 Tbsp. milk in a small bowl. Add remaining 1 Tbsp. milk, 1 tsp. at a time, as needed for desired consistency. Use immediately.

SOUTHERN HOSPITALITY

Holiday Open House

Christmas Gathering

SERVES 8 TO 10

Baked ham with seeded rolls

Roquefort Cheesecake with Pear Preserves and Walnuts

Spicy Cranberry-Orange Chutney

Brown Sugar-Pecan-Mustard Butter

Tortellini Caprese Bites with Basil Vinaigrette

Hot Spinach-Artichoke Dip

Gingerbread Cocoa

Citrus Sangria

Gingerbread Men Cookies

Party Improv:

Pick up a spiral-sliced honey-glazed ham and several pans of dinner rolls. Bake all according to package directions, and fill biscuits with ham slices for a delicious and easy party offering.

Roquefort Cheesecake with Pear Preserves and Walnuts

MAKES: 12 appetizer servings
HANDS-ON TIME: 15 min.
TOTAL TIME: 9 hr., 55 min.

½ **cup pecan or walnut halves**
2 **(8-oz.) packages cream cheese, softened**
1 **(8-oz.) package Roquefort cheese, chopped**
½ **cup sour cream**
2 **Tbsp. chopped fresh chives**
1 **Tbsp. chopped fresh parsley**
2 **large eggs**
2 **Tbsp. all-purpose flour**
½ **(11.5-oz.) jar pear preserves**
  Garnish: seedless red grapes
  Assorted fresh vegetables and crackers

1. Preheat oven to 350°. Bake nuts in a single layer in a shallow pan 8 to 10 minutes or until lightly toasted and fragrant, stirring halfway through. Reduce oven temperature to 325°.
2. Beat cream cheese and next 4 ingredients at medium speed with an electric mixer until blended. Add eggs, 1 at a time, beating just until yellow disappears after each addition; fold in flour. Spoon cheese mixture into a lightly greased 7-inch springform pan.
3. Bake at 325° for 1 hour or until set. Run a knife around outer edge of cheesecake to loosen from sides of pan. Let cool in pan on a wire rack 30 minutes. Cover and chill 8 hours.

4. Remove sides of pan. Transfer cheesecake to a platter, and spoon pear preserves over the top; sprinkle with walnuts. Garnish, if desired. Serve with assorted fresh vegetables and crackers.

Spicy Cranberry-Orange Chutney

MAKES: 2⅔ cups
HANDS-ON TIME: 20 min.
TOTAL TIME: 25 min.

1 **small onion, finely chopped**
1 **tsp. vegetable oil**
1 **(10-oz.) jar red pepper jelly**
1 **(6-oz.) package sweetened dried cranberries**
1 **cup chunky applesauce**
½ **tsp. orange zest**
¼ **tsp. salt**

1. Sautè onion in hot oil over medium-high heat in a 3-qt. saucepan 5 minutes or until tender.
2. Add pepper jelly and remaining ingredients. Bring mixture to a boil, reduce heat to medium-low, and cook, stirring occasionally, 10 minutes or until thickened.

Plan Ahead

UP TO 1 MONTH AHEAD:
• Bake and freeze Gingerbread Men Cookies.

2 DAYS BEFORE:
• Prepare Spicy Cranberry-Orange Chutney and Brown Sugar-Pecan-Mustard Butter.

1 DAY BEFORE:
• Prepare Tortellini Caprese Bites and Roquefort Cheesecake.
• Remove cookies from freezer.

30 MINUTES BEFORE GUESTS ARRIVE:
• Assemble and bake Hot Spinach-Artichoke Dip.
• Prepare cocoa.

JUST BEFORE GUESTS ARRIVE:
• Heat rolls.
• Prepare frosting and icing for cookies.

Brown Sugar-Pecan-Mustard Butter

MAKES: about ½ cup
HANDS-ON TIME: 10 min.
TOTAL TIME: 26 min.

½ cup pecan halves
½ cup butter, softened
1 Tbsp. brown sugar
3 Tbsp. Dijon mustard

1. Preheat oven to 350°. Bake pecans in a single layer in a shallow pan 6 to 8 minutes or until toasted and fragrant, stirring half-way through. Cool 10 minutes. Pulse in a food processor until finely ground.
2. Stir together butter and next 2 ingredients until sugar dissolves. Stir in ground pecans. Serve immediately, or chill until ready to serve. Let stand at room temperature 20 minutes before serving.

Tortellini Caprese Bites

MAKES: 12 servings
HANDS-ON TIME: 30 min.
TOTAL TIME: 2 hr., 47 min., including vinaigrette

1 (9-oz.) package refrigerated cheese-filled tortellini
3 cups halved grape tomatoes
3 (8-oz.) containers fresh small mozzarella cheese balls
60 (6-inch) wooden skewers
Basil Vinaigrette

1. Prepare tortellini according to package directions. Rinse under cold running water.
2. Thread 1 tomato half, 1 mozzarella ball, another tomato half, and 1 tortellini onto each skewer. Place skewers in a 13-x 9-inch baking dish. Pour Basil Vinaigrette over skewers, turning to coat. Cover and chill 2 hours. Transfer skewers to serving platter, and sprinkle with salt and pepper to taste. Discard any remaining vinaigrette.
NOTE: We tested with Whole Foods Ciliegine Fresh Mozzarella Cheese.

Basil Vinaigrette

MAKES: about 1½ cups
HANDS-ON TIME: 10 min.
TOTAL TIME: 10 min.

½ cup white balsamic vinegar
1 tsp. kosher salt
⅔ cup extra virgin olive oil
6 Tbsp. chopped fresh basil

1. Whisk together vinegar and salt until blended. Gradually add oil in a slow, steady stream, whisking constantly until smooth. Stir in basil and freshly ground pepper to taste.

Hot Spinach-Artichoke Dip

MAKES: 8 servings
HANDS-ON TIME: 15 min.
TOTAL TIME: 45 min.

1 cup freshly grated Parmesan cheese
1 cup reduced-fat sour cream
½ cup mayonnaise
4 green onions, sliced
3 Tbsp. fresh lemon juice
1 garlic clove, pressed
1¼ cups (5 oz.) shredded pepper Jack cheese
1 (10-oz.) package frozen chopped spinach, thawed and well drained
1 (14-oz.) can medium-size artichoke hearts, drained and chopped
Corn chips, assorted fresh vegetables

1. Preheat oven to 350°. Stir together first 6 ingredients and 1 cup pepper Jack cheese. Fold in spinach and artichokes. Spoon into a lightly greased 1-qt. baking dish. Sprinkle with remaining ¼ cup pepper Jack cheese.
2. Bake at 350° for 30 minutes or until center is hot and edges are bubbly. Sprinkle with freshly ground pepper to taste. Serve with corn chips and assorted vegetables.

TRY THIS TWIST!
Hot Spinach-Artichoke Dip with Crab: Increase mayonnaise to 1 cup and Parmesan cheese to 1¼ cups. Prepare recipe as directed in Step 1, folding in 1 lb. fresh jumbo lump crabmeat, drained and picked, with spinach and artichokes and spooning into a 2-qt. baking dish. Bake at 350° for 40 minutes or until center is hot and edges are bubbly. Makes: 10 to 12 servings. Hands-on time: 15 min., Total time: 55 min.

Gingerbread Cocoa

MAKES: about 16 cups
HANDS-ON TIME: 25 min.
TOTAL TIME: 25 min.

- 2 **cups sugar**
- ½ **cup unsweetened cocoa**
- 2 **tsp. apple pie spice**
- 1½ **tsp. ground ginger**
- 1 **gal. milk**
  Garnish: miniature marshmallows

1. Whisk together first 4 ingredients in a 6-qt. Dutch oven until blended; gradually whisk in milk.
2. Cook mixture over medium heat, stirring constantly, 20 minutes or until thoroughly heated. Transfer to a 6-qt. slow cooker, and keep warm on LOW. Garnish, if desired.

Citrus Sangria

MAKES: 14 cups
HANDS-ON TIME: 10 min.
TOTAL TIME: 4 hr., 10 min.

- 2 **(750-milliliter) bottles white Zinfandel**
- 4 **cups white grape juice**
- 1 **orange, sliced**
- 1 **lemon, sliced**
- 1 **lime, sliced**

1. Combine first 2 ingredients; stir in citrus slices. Chill 4 hours. Serve over ice.

Gingerbread Men Cookies

MAKES: 2 dozen (4-inch) cookies
HANDS-ON TIME: 1 hr.
TOTAL TIME: 3 hr., 50 min., including icing and frosting.

- 1 **cup butter, softened**
- 1 **cup sugar**
- 1½ **tsp. baking soda**
- ¼ **cup hot water**
- 1 **cup molasses**
- 5½ **cups all-purpose flour**
- 1½ **Tbsp. ground ginger**
- 1½ **tsp. ground cinnamon**
- ¼ **tsp. salt**
- ¼ **tsp. ground allspice**
  Parchment paper
  Royal Icing and Buttermilk Frosting
  Assorted candies
  Assorted colors decorator sugar crystals

1. Beat butter and sugar at medium speed with a heavy-duty electric stand mixer until fluffy.
2. Stir together baking soda and ¼ cup hot water until dissolved; stir in molasses.
3. Stir together flour and next 4 ingredients. Add to butter mixture alternately with molasses mixture, beginning and ending with flour mixture. Shape mixture into a ball; cover and chill 1 hour.
4. Preheat oven to 350°. Roll dough to ¼-inch thickness on a lightly floured surface. Cut dough with a 4-inch gingerbread man-shaped cookie cutter. Place 2 inches apart on parchment paper-lined baking sheets.
5. Bake at 350° for 15 to 18 minutes. Let cool on baking sheets 2 minutes; transfer to wire racks to cool completely (about 30 minutes).
6. Spoon Royal Icing into a small zip-top plastic freezer bag. Snip 1 corner of bag to make a small hole; pipe faces on cookies, or spread cookies with Buttermilk Frosting. Decorate cookies as desired with candies and sugar crystals.

TRY THIS TWIST!
Gingerbread Snowflake Cookies: Prepare recipe as directed, cutting dough with a 1- to 2½-inch snowflake-shaped cutter. Place 2 inches apart on parchment-lined baking sheets. Bake at 350° for 13 to 17 minutes. Cool and decorate as directed. Makes: about 9 dozen. Hands-on time: 1 hr.; Total time: 4 hr., 50 min.

Royal Icing

MAKES: about 3 cups
HANDS-ON TIME: 10 min.
TOTAL TIME: 10 min.

Use less water for a stiff icing perfect for attaching cookies to cake stands. Use more water for thinner icing suitable for piping delicate designs on cookies.

- 1 **(16-oz.) package powdered sugar**
- 3 **Tbsp. meringue powder**
- 6 **to 8 Tbsp. warm water**

1. Beat first 2 ingredients and 6 Tbsp. water at low speed with an electric mixer until blended. Beat at high speed 4 minutes or until stiff peaks form. Add up to 2 Tbsp. additional water, ¼ tsp. at a time, until desired consistency is reached.
NOTE: Royal Icing dries rapidly. Work quickly, keeping extra icing tightly covered at all times. Place a damp paper towel directly on surface of icing (to prevent a crust from forming) while icing cookies.

Buttermilk Frosting

MAKES: 2 cups
HANDS-ON TIME: 10 min.
TOTAL TIME: 10 min.

- ½ **cup butter, softened**
- 1 **(16-oz.) package powdered sugar**
- 1 **tsp. vanilla extract**
- 4 **to 5 Tbsp. buttermilk**

1. Beat butter at medium speed with an electric mixer until creamy. Gradually add powdered sugar, beating at low speed until blended. Slowly beat in vanilla and 4 Tbsp. buttermilk. Increase speed to medium, and beat until smooth. If desired, beat in remaining 1 Tbsp. buttermilk, 1 tsp. at a time, until desired consistency is reached.

Soup and Sandwich Supper

Keep your family warm and cozy this season with one of these tasty favorites paired with an easy sandwich.

GREAT TO KEEP FROZEN AND CANNED VEGETABLES

Taco Soup

MAKES: 14 cups
HANDS-ON TIME: 20 min.
TOTAL TIME: 55 min.

Easy Sandwich: Sprinkle shredded pepper Jack cheese on 6 (6-inch) fajita-size flour tortillas. Fold tortillas in half, press gently to seal, and spread butter on each. Cook quesadillas in a hot skillet 2 to 3 minutes on each side or until browned. Cut into wedges.

- 1 lb. ground beef
- 2 (16-oz.) cans pinto beans, drained and rinsed
- 1 (16-oz.) package frozen cut green beans
- 1 (15-oz.) can ranch beans, undrained
- 1 (14.5-oz.) can stewed tomatoes
- 1 (14.5-oz.) can petite diced tomatoes, undrained
- 1 (12-oz.) package frozen whole kernel corn
- 1 (12-oz.) bottle beer*
- 1 (1-oz.) envelope taco seasoning mix
- 1 (1-oz.) envelope Ranch dressing mix
  Toppings: corn chips, shredded Cheddar cheese

1. Brown ground beef in a large Dutch oven over medium-high heat, stirring constantly, 5 to 8 minutes or until meat crumbles and is no longer pink; drain. Return beef to Dutch oven.

2. Stir pinto beans, next 8 ingredients, and 2 cups water into beef; bring to a boil. Reduce heat to medium-low, and simmer, stirring occasionally, 30 minutes. Serve with desired toppings.

*1½ cups chicken broth may be substituted.

Cheddar Cheese Soup

MAKES: 8 cups
HANDS-ON TIME: 35 min.
TOTAL TIME: 35 min.

Easy Sandwich: Layer guacamole, bacon slices, tomato slices sprinkled with salt and pepper, and arugula between whole grain bread slices.

- ¼ cup butter
- ½ cup finely chopped carrots
- ½ cup finely chopped celery
- 1 small onion, finely chopped
- ½ small green bell pepper, finely chopped
- 2 garlic cloves, minced
- ⅓ cup all-purpose flour
- 1 extra-large chicken bouillon cube
- 2 cups milk
- 1 (8-oz.) block sharp Cheddar cheese, shredded
- ¼ tsp. ground red pepper

1. Melt butter in a 3-qt. saucepan over medium-high heat; add carrots and next 4 ingredients, and sauté 5 to 7 minutes or until tender. Sprinkle flour over vegetable mixture, and stir until coated. Stir in bouillon cube, milk, and 3 cups water; cook, stirring occasionally, 10 to 11 minutes or until mixture is slightly thickened and bubbly.

2. Add shredded cheese and pepper, stirring until well blended. Serve immediately.

Baked Potato Soup

MAKES: 8 cups
HANDS-ON TIME: 40 min.
TOTAL TIME: 40 min.

Easy Sandwich: Combine ¼ cup mayonnaise; 2 Tbsp. reduced-fat refrigerated pesto sauce; and ⅓ lb. peeled, cooked shrimp, chopped. Spoon onto 6 toasted French bread slices. Sprinkle with grated Parmesan cheese. Bake at 400° for 10 minutes or until browned and bubbly.

- ¼ cup butter
- ½ cup chopped sweet onion
- 1 garlic clove, minced
- ¼ cup all-purpose flour
- 1 extra-large chicken bouillon cube
- 1 (24-oz.) package frozen steam-and-mash potatoes
- 2 cups milk
- ½ tsp. pepper
  Toppings: cooked and crumbled bacon, shredded sharp Cheddar cheese, sliced green onions

1. Melt butter in a Dutch oven over medium heat; add onion and garlic, and cook, stirring often, 5 to 10 minutes or until golden.

2. Sprinkle onion mixture with flour, and stir until coated. Stir in bouillon cube and 3 cups water. Bring to a boil over medium heat, stirring occasionally. Reduce heat to medium-low, and simmer, stirring occasionally, 10 minutes.

3. Meanwhile, microwave potatoes according to package directions. (Do not add butter or milk.) Stir potatoes, milk, and pepper into onion mixture. Cook over medium heat, stirring occasionally, 10 minutes or until thickened. Serve with desired toppings.

Vegetarian Black Bean Chili

MAKES: 10 cups
HANDS-ON TIME: 20 min.
TOTAL TIME: 55 min.

Easy Sandwich: Stir together 2 (6-oz.) packages buttermilk cornbread-and-muffin mix according to package directions, stirring ⅓ cup store-bought pimiento cheese into batter. Spoon batter into a lightly greased 12-cup muffin pan. Bake at 400° for 20 minutes or until done. Split warm muffins, and spread with additional pimiento cheese.

- 3 (15.5-oz.) cans black beans
- 1 large sweet onion, chopped
- 3 garlic cloves, minced
- 2 Tbsp. vegetable oil
- 4 tsp. chili powder
- 1 tsp. ground cumin
- ½ tsp. pepper
- ¼ tsp. salt
- 2 (14.5-oz.) cans petite diced tomatoes with jalapeño peppers
- 1 (12-oz.) package meatless burger crumbles
- 1 extra-large vegetable bouillon cube
  Toppings: sour cream, shredded Cheddar cheese, sliced pickled jalapeño peppers, chopped fresh cilantro

1. Drain and rinse 2 cans black beans. (Do not drain third can.)
2. Sauté onion and garlic in hot oil in a large Dutch oven over medium-high heat 6 to 8 minutes or until tender. Stir in chili powder and next 3 ingredients; sauté 3 minutes. Stir in diced tomatoes, next 2 ingredients, drained and undrained beans, and 2 cups water. Bring to a boil over medium-high heat; reduce heat to medium-low, and simmer, stirring occasionally, 30 minutes. Serve chili with desired toppings.

TRY THIS TWIST!

Meaty Black Bean Chili: Omit vegetable oil. Substitute 1 lb. lean ground beef for meatless burger crumbles. Prepare recipe as directed, sautéing ground beef with onion and garlic in Step 2 and increasing cook time to 10 minutes or until meat crumbles and is no longer pink. Proceed as directed. Makes: 11 cups. Hands-on time: 25 min.; Total time: 1 hr.

Curry Coconut Soup

MAKES: 8 cups
HANDS-ON TIME: 20 min.
TOTAL TIME: 25 min.

Easy Sandwich: Toss together 1 cup chopped fresh snow peas, 2 grated carrots, 1 cup sliced English cucumber, and ¼ cup bottled refrigerated ginger dressing. Spread ¼ cup refrigerated hummus onto 4 large whole wheat wraps. Divide vegetables among wraps, and roll up.

- 1½ lb. peeled, medium-size raw shrimp (21/30 count)
- 1 extra-large vegetable bouillon cube
- 2 tsp. grated fresh ginger
- 1 (8-oz.) package sliced fresh baby portobello mushrooms
- 1 (13.66-oz.) can coconut milk
- 3 tsp. curry powder
- ½ tsp. salt
- ¼ to ½ tsp. ground red pepper
- ¼ cup chopped fresh basil
- ¼ cup chopped fresh cilantro leaves
- 1 Tbsp. fresh lime juice

1. Devein shrimp, if desired.
2. Stir together bouillon cube, ginger, and 3 cups water in a 3-qt. saucepan. Bring to a boil over medium-high heat. Add shrimp, and cook, stirring often, 2 minutes. Add mushrooms and next 4 ingredients, and cook 5 minutes or just until shrimp turn pink. Stir in basil and next 2 ingredients just before serving. Season with salt to taste.

FREEZES NICELY FOR A QUICK SUPPER

Red Lentil Soup

MAKES: 11 cups
HANDS-ON TIME: 25 min.
TOTAL TIME: 55 min.

Quick Sandwich: Layer chutney, Havarti cheese slices, deli pork slices, and Dijon mustard between multigrain bread slices. Spread outside of sandwiches with butter; cook on a hot griddle over medium heat 3 minutes on each side or until lightly browned.

- 2 Tbsp. butter
- 1 sweet onion, diced
- 1 cup chopped carrots
- 1 cup chopped celery
- 4 garlic cloves, minced
- 1 (28-oz.) can diced tomatoes
- 2 cups dried red lentils
- 2 extra-large chicken bouillon cubes
- ½ tsp. ground cumin
- ½ tsp. salt
- ¼ tsp. pepper
- 1 cup chopped fresh basil

1. Melt butter in a Dutch oven over medium-high heat. Add onion and next 3 ingredients, and sauté 5 to 6 minutes or until tender.
2. Add tomatoes, next 5 ingredients, and 5 cups water.
3. Bring to a boil; reduce heat to medium, and cook, stirring occasionally, 30 minutes or until lentils are tender. Stir in basil.

The 12 Cocktails of Christmas

Shake up your parties with fancy, new drinks/libations (with and without alcohol) straight from top bartenders across the South—including Norman King, our very own Test Kitchen mixologist!

{1}
Gingerbread Martini

MAKES: I serving
HANDS-ON TIME: 5 min.
TOTAL TIME: 5 min.

Accent martini glasses by dipping rims in simple syrup and then in gingersnap cookie crumbs and graham cracker crumbs. Store prepared glasses in freezer up to 2 days.

- 2 **Tbsp. ginger liqueur**
- 2 **Tbsp. vanilla-citrus liqueur**
- I½ **Tbsp. coffee-flavored rum**
- I **Tbsp. honey**
- 2 **tsp. whipping cream**
- I **cup ice cubes**
  Garnish: vanilla bean rolled in sugar

1. Stir together first 5 ingredients in a cocktail shaker until thoroughly blended. Add ice cubes; cover with lid and shake vigorously until thoroughly chilled (about 30 seconds). Strain into a chilled martini glass. Serve immediately. Garnish, if desired.
NOTE: We tested with Brinley Gold Coffee Rum, Tuaca Vanilla Citrus Liqueur, and Domaine de Canton ginger liqueur.

RECIPE FROM KEN MACIEJEWSKI, BAR MANAGER
TRISTAN, CHARLESTON, SOUTH CAROLINA

Bar Tip

A GOOD RULE OF THUMB
To mix cocktails, shake until your hand gets really cold and frost forms on the outside of the container.

{2}
Cherry Frost

MAKES: I serving
HANDS-ON TIME: 5 min.
TOTAL TIME: 5 min.

- 3 **Tbsp. black cherry liqueur**
- I **Tbsp. brandy**
- I **cup crushed ice**
- 4 **Tbsp. sparkling white wine**
  Garnish: maraschino cherries

1. Combine first 3 ingredients in a cocktail shaker. Cover with lid, and shake vigorously until thoroughly chilled (about 30 seconds). Strain into a Champagne flute, and top with sparkling white wine. Serve immediately. Garnish, if desired.
NOTE: We tested with Heering Cherry Liqueur and Riondo Prosecco Spago Nero.

{3}
Hot Buttered Rye

MAKES: I serving
HANDS-ON TIME: 5 min.
TOTAL TIME: I hr., 10 min., including Maple Butter

For a unique touch, add a scant pinch of salt to the drink.

- ¼ **cup rye whiskey**
- 6 **Tbsp. hot water**
- 2 **Tbsp. ginger liqueur**
  Maple Butter
  Garnish: freshly grated nutmeg

1. Pour first 3 ingredients into a 6-oz. heatproof coffee cup. Dollop with desired amount of Maple Butter. Garnish, if desired.
NOTE: We tested with Jim Beam Kentucky Straight Rye Whiskey and Domaine de Canton ginger liqueur.

Maple Butter

MAKES: about I½ cups
HANDS-ON TIME: 5 min.
TOTAL TIME: I hr., 5 min.

Makes enough to top six drinks (4 Tbsp. each).

- I **cup heavy cream**
- 2 **Tbsp. pure maple syrup**

1. Beat both ingredients at medium speed with a heavy-duty electric stand mixer 2 minutes or until mixture is the consistency of softened butter. Cover and chill I to 24 hours.

RECIPE FROM STACIE STEWART, BAR MANAGER
HARVEST, LOUISVILLE, KENTUCKY

Southern-Made Spirits

Order cocktails at one of our drink chefs' bars and you'll find they shake up the drinks with crafted spirits/alcohols/liquors produced in their states. Support local and give them a try!

- **SWEET LUCY BOURBON LIQUEUR** (Tennessee, for Capital Eggnog, prichardsdistillery.com)
- **SEA ISLAND JAVA RUM** (South Carolina, for Gingerbread Martini, seaislandrums.com)
- **OLD SOUTH WINERY BAYOU BLUSH MUSCADINE WINE** (Mississippi, for Mississippi Bourbon-Muscadine Punch, oldsouthwinery.com)
- **FIREFLY DISTILLERY STRAIGHT VODKA** (South Carolina, for Sparkling Charleston Cosmopolitan, fireflyvodka.com)
- **MICHTER'S SINGLE BARREL STRAIGHT RYE WHISKEY** (Kentucky, for Hot Buttered Rye, michters.com)

{4}
Apple-Ale Wassail

MAKES: about 7 cups
HANDS-ON TIME: 5 min.
TOTAL TIME: 3 hr., 5 min.

- 2 (12-oz.) bottles ale
- 2 cups apple cider
- 1 cup port
- 1 cup lemonade
- ¾ cup firmly packed light brown sugar
- 1 apple, diced
- 2 (3-inch) cinnamon sticks
- 2 whole allspice
- 6 whole cloves
- ⅛ tsp. ground cardamom
- Garnishes: lemon wedges, cinnamon sticks, apple slices

1. Stir together first 10 ingredients in a 5-qt. slow cooker. Cover and cook on LOW 3 hours or until hot. Remove diced apple, if desired. Ladle into mugs. Garnish, if desired.
NOTE: We tested with Sierra Nevada Tumbler Autumn Brown Ale.

RECIPE FROM LARA CREASY
BEVERAGE DIRECTOR
JCT. KITCHEN & BAR AND NO. 246, ATLANTA, GEORGIA

{5}
Sparkling Charleston Cosmopolitan

MAKES: 1 serving
HANDS-ON TIME: 5 min.
TOTAL TIME: 5 min.

- 1 cup crushed ice
- 3 Tbsp. vodka
- 1½ Tbsp. peach nectar
- 1 Tbsp. orange liqueur
- 1 Tbsp. white cranberry juice
- 2 lemon wedges
- 2 Tbsp. sparkling white wine
- Garnish: orange slice

1. Combine first 5 ingredients in a cocktail shaker. Squeeze juice from lemon wedges over mixture, and place wedges in shaker; cover with lid, and shake vigorously until thoroughly chilled (about 30 seconds). Strain into a 6- to 8-oz. glass; discard lemon wedges and ice. Top with sparkling white wine. Serve immediately. Garnish, if desired.
NOTE: We tested with Absolut Vodka.

RECIPE FROM KEN MACIEJEWSKI, BAR MANAGER
TRISTAN, CHARLESTON, SOUTH CAROLINA

{6}
Mississippi Bourbon-Muscadine Punch

MAKES: about 14 cups
HANDS-ON TIME: 10 min.
TOTAL TIME: 10 min.

- 2 (750-milliliter) bottles dry muscadine wine, chilled*
- 1 (12-oz.) bottle grenadine, chilled
- 1½ cups bourbon, chilled
- 1 cup cranberry juice, chilled
- 1 cup fresh orange juice, chilled
- ⅓ cup fresh lime juice
- 8 cups ice cubes
- 1 (12-oz.) can lemon-lime soft drink, chilled
- 1 cup club soda, chilled
- Garnishes: orange slices, red and green muscadine halves

1. Pour first 6 ingredients into a punch bowl; stir in ice cubes and next 2 ingredients. Serve immediately. Garnish, if desired.
*Chardonnay may be substituted.
NOTE: We tested with Morgan Creek Vineyards Cahaba White Alabama Muscadine wine and Stirrings Authentic Grenadine.

RECIPE FROM DREW STEVENS
GENERAL MANAGER, AND
JAYCE MCCONNEL, HEAD BARTENDER
SNACKBAR, OXFORD, MISSISSIPPI

{7}
Pecan "Milk" Punch

MAKES: about 2 cups
HANDS-ON TIME: 15 min.
TOTAL TIME: 3 hr., 33 min.

This unique version of milk punch doesn't call for dairy milk (except for garnish). Instead, you prepare a liquid from pecans. Serve small portions of this rich drink, or add 1 cup milk with bourbon.

- 1 cup chopped pecans
- ½ cup cane syrup
- 1 Tbsp. cream of coconut
- 1 tsp. ground cinnamon
- ½ tsp. vanilla extract
- ⅛ tsp. kosher salt
- ¼ cup bourbon
  Garnishes: sweetened whipped cream, fresh mint leaves

1. Preheat oven to 350°. Bake pecans in a single layer in a shallow pan 8 to 10 minutes or until toasted and fragrant, stirring halfway through. Let cool 10 minutes.
2. Process pecans, syrup, and next 4 ingredients in a food processor 30 to 60 seconds or until smooth. With processor running, pour 1 cup water through food chute. Press mixture through a fine wire-mesh strainer into a pitcher, using back of spoon to squeeze out liquid. Discard solids. Cover and chill 3 to 24 hours.
3. Stir in bourbon just before serving. Serve over ice. Garnish, if desired.
NOTE: We tested with Steen's 100% Pure Cane Syrup and Old Weller Antique Original 107 Brand Bourbon.

RECIPE FROM DREW STEVENS, GENERAL MANAGER, AND JAYCE MCCONNEL, HEAD BARTENDER
SNACKBAR, OXFORD, MISSISSIPPI

TRY THIS TWIST!
Milky Pecan "Milk" Punch: Prepare recipe as directed, adding 1 cup milk with bourbon. Makes: 3 cups.

{8}
Capital Eggnog
WONDERFUL WITHOUT ALCOHOL!

MAKES: 9 cups
HANDS-ON TIME: 35 min.
TOTAL TIME: 4 hr., 5 min.

This top-rated recipe is well worth the prep time.

- 6 cups milk
- 2 cups heavy cream
- ⅛ tsp. ground nutmeg
- 12 pasteurized egg yolks
- 2 cups granulated sugar
  Bourbon liqueur or praline liqueur (optional)*
  Garnish: freshly ground nutmeg

1. Cook milk, heavy cream, and nutmeg in a large saucepan over medium heat, stirring occasionally, 5 to 7 minutes or until steaming (about 150°). Reduce heat to low, and keep warm.
2. Whisk together egg yolks and granulated sugar in a large saucepan until smooth. Cook over low heat, whisking constantly, until mixture reaches a temperature of at least 160° (about 25 minutes).
3. Whisk milk mixture into egg mixture until thoroughly combined. Let cool 30 minutes, and transfer to a large pitcher. Cover and chill 3 to 24 hours.
4. Pour desired amount of liqueur into each glass, if desired. Top with eggnog. Garnish, if desired.
*Straight bourbon may be substituted.

RECIPE FROM DAVID BURNETTE, BARTENDER
THE CAPITAL HOTEL, LITTLE ROCK, ARKANSAS

{9}
Orange-Cranberry Gin and Tonic

MAKES: 1 serving
HANDS-ON TIME: 5 min.
TOTAL TIME: 5 min.

- 1 (2-inch) orange rind strip
- 1 Tbsp. fresh cranberries*
- 1 tsp. sugar
- 1 cup ice cubes
- 3 Tbsp. gin
- 1 Tbsp. fresh orange juice
- ¼ cup tonic water
  Garnish: orange rind strip

1. Muddle first 3 ingredients in a cocktail shaker. Add ice, gin, and orange juice. Cover with lid, and shake vigorously until thoroughly chilled (about 30 seconds). Pour into an 8-oz. glass; top with tonic water. Serve immediately. Garnish, if desired.
*Frozen cranberries, thawed, may be substituted.

{10}
Pear-Basil Sipper

MAKES: 1 serving
HANDS-ON TIME: 5 min.
TOTAL TIME: 5 min.

- 3 fresh basil leaves
- ½ tsp. sugar
- 1 cup crushed ice
- 4 Tbsp. pear nectar
- 3 Tbsp. pear-flavored vodka
- 3 Tbsp. lemon-lime soft drink
  Garnishes: pear slice, fresh basil leaves

1. Muddle first 2 ingredients in a cocktail shaker. Add ice, nectar, and vodka. Cover with lid, and shake vigorously until thoroughly chilled (about 30 seconds). Pour into a glass, and top with lemon-lime soft drink. Serve immediately. Garnish, if desired.

{11}
Merry Berry Christmas, Sugar!
ALCOHOL FREE!

MAKES: I serving
HANDS-ON TIME: 5 min.
TOTAL TIME: 5 min.

- 5 fresh raspberries
- 4 fresh blueberries
- 2 fresh blackberries
- 1½ Tbsp. light agave nectar
- 5 fresh mint leaves
- 2 Tbsp. fresh lime juice
- I cup crushed ice
- 2 Tbsp. ginger ale
- Garnishes: halved fresh berries

1. Muddle first 6 ingredients in a cocktail shaker. Stir in ice and 6 Tbsp. water. Cover with lid, and shake vigorously until thoroughly chilled (7 to 10 seconds). Pour mixture into a 16-oz. glass, and top with ginger ale. Serve immediately. Garnish, if desired.

RAMSEY PIMENTEL, LEAD MIXOLOGIST
THE RITZ-CARLTON, SOUTH BEACH, MIAMI, FLORIDA

{12}
Vanilla Bean-Rosemary Lemonade
ALCOHOL FREE!

MAKES: 6 cups
HANDS-ON TIME: 40 min.
TOTAL TIME: 4 hr., 10 min.

This is exceptional when made with freshly squeezed lemon juice. Make it quicker with a friend's help or a citrus juicer ($13.99; oxo.com).

- 1½ cups sugar
- I vanilla bean, split
- 3 small fresh rosemary sprigs
- 3 cups fresh lemon juice (about 26 to 30 lemons)*
- Garnishes: fresh rosemary sprigs, lemon slices

1. Combine first 3 ingredients and 3 cups water in a medium saucepan. Bring to a light boil over medium heat, stirring occasionally. Simmer 5 minutes. Remove from heat, and let cool 30 minutes.
2. Pour through a fine wire-mesh strainer into a large pitcher, discarding solids. Stir in lemon juice. Cover and chill 3 to 48 hours. Stir just before serving over ice. Garnish, if desired.
*3 (7.5-oz.) containers frozen lemon juice, thawed, may be substituted.

MAUREEN HOLT, CHEF AND CO-OWNER
LITTLE SAVANNAH RESTAURANT, BIRMINGHAM, ALABAMA

IN SEASON
Satsumas

The season for these petite oranges disappears faster than Santa's sleigh, so eat your fill this month.

Satsuma-cello

MAKES: about 3 quarts
HANDS-ON TIME: 2 hr., 30 min.
TOTAL TIME: 7 hr., plus 8 days for standing and chilling

- 20 satsuma oranges*
- 2 (750-milliliter) bottles vodka
- 4 cups sugar

1. Peel satsuma oranges, using vegetable peeler, reserving flesh for another use. Scrape bitter white pith from orange rind strips, and discard pith. Place orange rind strips in a large glass pitcher or 3-qt. jar; pour vodka over strips. Cover and let stand at room temperature 7 to 10 days.
2. Bring sugar and 5 cups water to a boil in a large saucepan over medium heat. Reduce heat to low, and simmer, stirring occasionally, I minute or until sugar is dissolved. Remove from heat; let stand 30 minutes. Pour syrup into the vodka mixture. Cover and let stand at room temperature 24 hours.
3. Pour mixture through a fine wire-mesh strainer into another pitcher, discarding orange rind strips. Pour into sealable bottles or mason jars. Seal, and chill 4 hours before serving. Store in refrigerator up to I month.
*15 Minneola tangelos may be substituted.

Make a Good Thing Even Better

Try one of these cocktail recipes developed in our Test Kitchen.

SATSUMA OLD FASHIONED: Stir together I cup Satsuma-cello, ½ cup whiskey, 4 dashes angostura bitters, and 4 dashes Peychaud's Bitters in a pitcher. Stir in 2 cups each ice and club soda. Makes: 4 to 6 servings. Hands-on time: 5 min., Total time: 5 min.

ROSEMARY-SATSUMA JULEP: Muddle I Tbsp. fresh rosemary leaves with I cup Satsuma-cello. Let stand 5 minutes. Strain into a pitcher. Stir in 2 cups each ice and club soda. Makes: 4 to 6 servings. Hands-on time: 5 min., Total time: 10 min.

BASIL-SATSUMA JULEP: Muddle ¼ cup fresh basil leaves with I Tbsp. sugar. Add I cup Satsuma-cello. Let stand 5 minutes. Strain into a pitcher. Stir in 2 cups each ice and club soda. Makes: 4 to 6 servings. Hands-on time: 5 min., Total time: 10 min.

Cozy Casseroles

Bake up a relaxing Christmas Eve with one of these family-pleasing recipes. Pair with a simple salad, and dinner is on the table.

Creamy Chicken-and-Wild Rice Casserole ·

MAKES: 10 to 12 servings
HANDS-ON TIME: 30 min.
TOTAL TIME: 1 hr., 15 min.

- 1 (2.25-oz.) package sliced almonds
- 2 (6.2-oz.) boxes fast-cooking long-grain and wild rice mix
- ¼ cup butter
- 4 celery ribs, chopped
- 2 medium onions, chopped
- 5 cups chopped cooked chicken
- 2 (10¾-oz.) cans cream of mushroom soup
- 2 (8-oz.) cans chopped water chestnuts, drained
- 1 (8-oz.) container sour cream
- 1 cup milk
- ½ tsp. salt
- ½ tsp. pepper
- 4 cups (16 oz.) shredded Cheddar cheese, divided
- 2 cups soft fresh breadcrumbs

1. Preheat oven to 350°. Bake almonds in a single layer in a shallow pan 4 to 6 minutes or until toasted and fragrant, stirring halfway through.

2. Prepare rice mixes according to package directions.

3. Meanwhile, melt butter in a large skillet over medium heat; add celery and onions. Sauté 10 minutes or until tender. Stir in chicken, next 6 ingredients, rice, and 3 cups cheese. Spoon mixture into a lightly greased 15- x 10-inch baking dish or 2 (11- x 7-inch) baking dishes. Top with breadcrumbs.

4. Bake at 350° for 35 minutes. Sprinkle with remaining 1 cup cheese; top with toasted almonds. Bake 5 more minutes.

NOTE: To make ahead, prepare recipe as directed through Step 3. Cover with aluminum foil, and freeze up to 1 month. Remove from freezer, and let stand at room temperature 1 hour. Bake, covered, at 350° for 30 minutes. Uncover casserole, and bake 1 hour and 15 minutes. Sprinkle with 1 cup (4 oz.) shredded Cheddar cheese, and top with toasted almonds. Bake 5 more minutes.

Try These Twists!

CAJUN CHICKEN-AND-WILD RICE CASSEROLE: Omit salt and pepper. Reduce chicken to 2½ cups. Prepare recipe as directed, sautéing 1 lb. andouille sausage, chopped, and 1 green bell pepper, diced, with celery and onions in Step 3. Stir 1 (15-oz.) can black-eyed peas, drained, and 1 tsp. Cajun seasoning into rice mixture. Proceed with recipe as directed.

CREAMY SHRIMP-AND-WILD RICE CASSEROLE: Substitute 2 lb. peeled and deveined, medium-size raw shrimp (41/50 count) for chicken; 2 cups (8 oz.) shredded Monterey Jack cheese and 2 cups grated Parmesan cheese for Cheddar cheese; and 1 cup dry white wine for milk. Proceed with recipe as directed.
NOTE: To make ahead, follow the same instructions as Creamy Chicken-and-Wild Rice Casserole (see recipe note).

Chicken Enchiladas
MAKES: 4 to 6 servings
HANDS-ON TIME: 15 min.
TOTAL TIME: 45 min.

- 3 cups chopped cooked chicken
- 2 cups (8 oz.) shredded pepper Jack cheese*
- ½ cup sour cream
- 1 (4.5-oz.) can chopped green chiles, drained
- ⅓ cup chopped fresh cilantro
- 8 (8-inch) soft taco-size flour tortillas
  Vegetable cooking spray
- 1 (8-oz.) bottle green taco sauce
- 1 (8-oz.) container sour cream
  Toppings: diced tomatoes, chopped avocado, chopped green onions, sliced black olives, fresh cilantro

Try These Twists!

PULLED PORK ENCHILADAS: Substitute 3 cups shredded barbecued pork (without sauce) for chicken and 1 (8-oz.) package shredded Mexican four-cheese blend for pepper Jack cheese. Stir together pork and ½ cup barbecue sauce. Proceed as directed.

VEGETABLE ENCHILADAS: Omit chicken, ½ cup sour cream, and chiles. Sauté 1 medium zucchini, chopped; 3 plum tomatoes, chopped; and 1 medium onion, chopped, in 1 Tbsp. hot olive oil 8 minutes or until vegetables are tender and liquid evaporates. Add 2 garlic cloves, minced, and 1 (5-oz.) package fresh baby spinach; sauté 2 minutes or until wilted. Sprinkle with ½ tsp. salt. Remove from heat, and stir in cheese and cilantro. Spoon about ½ cup vegetable mixture down center of each tortilla; roll up tortillas. Proceed with recipe as directed in Step 2. Hands-on time: 25 min., Total time: 55 min.

1. Preheat oven to 350°. Stir together first 5 ingredients. Spoon about ½ cup chicken mixture down center of each tortilla; roll up tortillas.

2. Place, seam sides down, in a lightly greased 13- x 9-inch baking dish. Lightly coat tops of tortillas with cooking spray.

3. Bake at 350° for 30 to 35 minutes or until golden brown.

4. Stir together taco sauce and 1 (8-oz.) container sour cream. Spoon over hot enchiladas, and sprinkle with desired toppings.

*Monterey Jack cheese may be substituted.

Citrus Starters

Citrus-Marinated Feta and Olives

MAKES: 6 to 8 servings
HANDS-ON TIME: 10 min.
TOTAL TIME: 10 min., plus 1 day for chilling

- ¼ cup chopped fresh basil
- ¼ cup olive oil
- 1 Tbsp. orange zest
- 1 tsp. coarsely ground pepper
- 1 garlic clove, minced
- 1 cup pitted kalamata olives
- 1 cup pimiento-stuffed Spanish olives
- 1 (8-oz.) feta cheese block, cubed

1. Whisk together first 5 ingredients in a medium-size glass bowl; gently stir in olives and cheese. Cover and chill 24 hours.

Fresh Orange Guacamole

Serve this versatile dip as an appetizer, or add a gourmet touch to a casual taco bar.

1. Cut 4 medium-size ripe avocados in half. Scoop avocado pulp into a bowl; mash with a fork just until chunky. Stir in 1 large navel orange, peeled, sectioned, and cut into ½-inch pieces; 2 Tbsp. finely chopped red onion; 3 Tbsp. fresh orange juice; 1 jalapeño pepper, seeded and finely chopped; 1 garlic clove, pressed; and ¾ tsp. salt. Cover and chill 1 to 4 hours. Garnish with fresh pomegranate seeds, if desired. Serve with tortilla chips. Makes: 4 servings. Hands-on time: 15 min.; Total time: 1 hr., 15 min.

Shrimp and Citrus Cocktail

MAKES: 4 to 6 servings
HANDS-ON TIME: 15 min.
TOTAL TIME: 3 hr., 15 min.

Martini glasses give this updated classic a fresh new look.

- 1 lb. peeled, large cooked shrimp (31/40 count)
- ⅓ cup olive oil
- ⅓ cup red wine vinegar
- 2 large shallots, minced
- 2 tsp. Dijon mustard
- 2 tsp. orange zest
- ½ tsp. salt
- ½ tsp. dried crushed red pepper
- 2 large navel oranges, peeled and sectioned
- 3 Tbsp. chopped fresh basil

1. Devein shrimp, if desired. Whisk together olive oil and next 6 ingredients in a large bowl. Pour mixture into a large zip-top plastic freezer bag; add shrimp, turning to coat. Seal and chill 3 to 8 hours, turning occasionally. Drain shrimp mixture, and stir in oranges and basil. Spoon into 4 chilled martini glasses or small bowls.

Spiced Orange Salad with Goat Cheese and Glazed Pecans

MAKES: 6 servings
HANDS-ON TIME: 20 min.
TOTAL TIME: 20 min.

- 6 large navel oranges
- 6 cups watercress
- ¼ cup canola oil
- ¼ cup rice wine vinegar
- 2 Tbsp. chopped fresh chives
- 1 Tbsp. light brown sugar
- 1 Tbsp. grated fresh ginger
- ¼ tsp. salt
- ½ cup crumbled goat cheese
- 1 (3.5-oz.) package roasted-and-glazed pecan pieces

1. Peel oranges, and cut into ¼-inch-thick slices. Arrange watercress on a serving platter; top with orange slices. Whisk together canola oil and next 5 ingredients; drizzle over salad. Sprinkle with goat cheese and pecans.

Celebrate the Season

Within these pages, we will share some of our best recipes
to make the holidays even more memorable.

Host a Fancy Dinner Party

Keep the guest list small and the wow factor high with our menu of small portioned dishes to be leisurely served—and enjoyed—throughout the evening.

Dressed Up Holiday Dinner

SERVES 8

Honey-Rosemary Cherries and
Blue Cheese Crostini

Cream of Chestnut Soup

Fig-and-Balsamic Glazed Quail

Herbs-and-Greens Salad

Roasted Green Beans

Butternut Squash Ravioli
with Mushrooms

Layered Peppermint Cheesecake
(see page 304)

Vieux Carré

Honey-Rosemary Cherries and Blue Cheese Crostini

MAKES: 8 appetizer servings
HANDS-ON TIME: 20 min.
TOTAL TIME: 30 min.

Assemble and enjoy this appetizer around the kitchen island to keep it casual. Or make up single-serving plates of the cherry mixture, blue cheese, and crostini and serve first course-style to guests at the dinner table.

- 1 shallot, thinly sliced
- 2 tsp. olive oil
- 1 (12-oz.) package frozen dark, sweet, pitted cherries, thawed
- 2 Tbsp. balsamic vinegar
- 2 Tbsp. honey
- ¼ tsp. chopped fresh rosemary
- ⅛ tsp. salt
- ⅛ tsp. pepper
- 2 cups loosely packed arugula
- 16 (¼-inch-thick) ciabatta bread slices, toasted
- 1 (8-oz.) wedge blue cheese, thinly sliced*
   Garnish: freshly ground pepper

1. Sauté shallot in hot oil in a medium skillet over medium-high heat 2 to 3 minutes or until tender. Add cherries (with any liquid) and next 5 ingredients. Cook, stirring occasionally, 8 to 10 minutes or until thickened. Let stand 10 minutes.
2. Divide arugula among toasted bread slices. Top each with a blue cheese slice and cherry mixture. Garnish, if desired.
*Manchego or goat cheese may be substituted.

Cream of Chestnut Soup

MAKES: 8 cups
HANDS-ON TIME: 30 min.
TOTAL TIME: 1 hr., 5 min.

- 3 Tbsp. butter
- 1 medium-size sweet onion, chopped
- 2 celery ribs, chopped
- 2 carrots, chopped
- ¼ cup Marsala*
- 6 cups vegetable broth
- 1 (14.1-oz.) can steamed, peeled chestnuts**
- 1 fresh thyme sprig
- ⅓ cup half-and-half
   Toppings: cooked, crumbled bacon; dried cherries; crème fraîche; truffle oil

1. Melt butter in a large Dutch oven over medium-high heat. Add onion and next 2 ingredients, and sauté 8 to 10 minutes or until tender.
2. Add Marsala, and cook 2 minutes, stirring to loosen particles from bottom of skillet. Stir in vegetable broth, chestnuts, and thyme. Bring to a boil; reduce heat to low, and simmer 20 to 25 minutes or until chestnuts are tender. Discard thyme. Let cool slightly (about 10 minutes).
3. Process soup, in batches, in a blender

or food processor until smooth. Return to Dutch oven. Stir in half-and-half and salt and pepper to taste. Cook over low heat, stirring often, 5 minutes or until thoroughly heated. Serve with desired toppings.

*¼ cup dry white wine plus I tsp. brandy may be substituted.

**Roasted, peeled, fresh chestnuts may be substituted.

NOTE: We tested with Minerve Whole Chestnuts in Water, found on the baking aisle.

LYDA JONES BURNETTE
BIRMINGHAM, ALABAMA

Fig-and-Balsamic-Glazed Quail

MAKES: 8 servings
HANDS-ON TIME: 20 min.
TOTAL TIME: I hr., 15 min.

Call ahead to be sure your butcher has quail on hand. For a delicious alternative to quail, use cornish hens and follow our directions (at right).

- I (11.5-oz.) jar fig preserves
- ½ cup dry red wine
- 3 Tbsp. balsamic vinegar
- ½ tsp. coarsely ground pepper
- 2 tsp. country-style Dijon mustard
- 8 (3.5-oz.) semiboneless quail
   Kitchen string
- I tsp. kosher salt
- 2 Tbsp. dry red wine

1. Preheat oven to 450°. Bring first 5 ingredients to a boil in a small saucepan over medium-high heat; reduce heat to low, and simmer 8 to 10 minutes or until slightly thickened. Reserve half of fig mixture; cover and chill. Let remaining fig mixture stand at room temperature.
2. Tie ends of quail legs together with string.
3. Place quail on an aluminum foil-lined jelly-roll pan or in a shallow roasting pan, and sprinkle with salt.

4. Bake at 450° for 10 minutes. Brush quail generously with room-temperature fig mixture. Reduce oven temperature to 400°. Bake quail 30 minutes or until leg meat is no longer pink, basting with fig mixture every 10 minutes.
5. Place reserved, chilled fig mixture in a small saucepan; stir in red wine, and cook over low heat, stirring often, 2 minutes or until thoroughly heated. Serve quail with sauce.

NOTE: To make ahead, prepare recipe as directed through Step 3. Cover and chill up to 8 hours. Let stand at room temperature 15 minutes before proceeding with Steps 4 and 5.

TRY THIS TWIST!
Fig-and-Balsamic-Glazed Cornish Hens: Substitute 4 (1¼- to 1½-lb.) Cornish hens for quail. Prepare Step I as directed; omit Step 2. Rinse hens with cold water, and pat dry. Place hens, breast sides down, on a cutting board. Cut hens through backbone using kitchen shears to make 2 halves. Proceed with recipe as directed in Steps 3 through 5, increasing second bake time (at 400°) to 45 minutes. Let stand 10 minutes before serving. Hands-on time: 20 min.; Total time: I hr., 40 min.

Wine Pairings

CHERRIES-AND-BLUE CHEESE CROSTINI: La Marca Prosecco, Italy

CREAM OF CHESTNUT SOUP: Joel Gott Sauvignon Blanc, California

RAVIOLI: Numanthia Termes, Spain

FIG-BALSAMIC- GLAZED QUAIL: Erath Pinot Noir, Oregon

HERBS-AND- GREENS SALAD: Laurenz und Sophie Singing Grüner Veltliner, Austria

---

Herbs-and-Greens Salad

MAKES: 6 to 8 servings
HANDS-ON TIME: 10 min.
TOTAL TIME: 30 min.

Lemony olive bread croutons top this lightly dressed salad. Double the dressing, if desired. Prep, bake, and cool the croutons up to three days ahead, and store in an airtight container.

- ½ tsp. lemon zest
- 4 Tbsp. olive oil, divided
- 3 cups I-inch olive bread cubes*
- 4 cups torn butter lettuce (about I head)
- 2 cups firmly packed fresh baby spinach
- I cup torn escarole
- ½ cup loosely packed fresh parsley leaves
- ¼ cup fresh I-inch chive pieces
- 2 Tbsp. fresh lemon juice

1. Preheat oven to 425°. Stir together lemon zest and I Tbsp. olive oil in a large bowl. Add bread cubes, and toss to coat. Arrange in a single layer on a baking sheet. Bake 5 minutes or until crisp. Let cool completely (about 15 minutes).
2. Meanwhile, combine butter lettuce and next 4 ingredients in a large bowl. Drizzle with lemon juice and remaining 3 Tbsp. olive oil, and toss to coat. Add salt and pepper to taste. Serve immediately with toasted bread cubes.

*Ciabatta, focaccia, or country white bread may be substituted.

Roasted Green Beans

MAKES: 6 to 8 servings
HANDS-ON TIME: 10 min.
TOTAL TIME: 25 min.

Seasoned green beans may be covered and chilled up to 24 hours before baking. Slide into oven to bake about 15 minutes before the quail is done.

- 1 lb. haricots verts (tiny green beans), trimmed
- 1 Tbsp. olive oil
- 1 Tbsp. butter, melted
- 1 tsp. kosher salt
- 1 tsp. country-style Dijon mustard

1. Preheat oven to 400°. Toss together all ingredients. Spread in a single layer on a 15- x 10-inch jelly-roll pan. Bake 15 to 18 minutes or to desired degree of doneness, stirring twice.

Butternut Squash Ravioli with Mushrooms

MAKES: 8 servings
HANDS-ON TIME: 25 min.
TOTAL TIME: 25 min.

- 2 (8-oz.) packages refrigerated butternut squash-filled ravioli
- 6 Tbsp. butter, divided
- 1 (8-oz.) package sliced baby portobello mushrooms
- 4 garlic cloves, thinly sliced
- 3 Tbsp. sliced fresh shallots
- 2 Tbsp. chopped fresh flat-leaf parsley
- 1 Tbsp. thinly sliced fresh sage
- 1 tsp. kosher salt
- ¼ tsp. freshly ground pepper
  Toppings: freshly shaved Parmesan cheese, freshly ground pepper, chopped fresh parsley

1. Prepare ravioli according to package directions. Keep warm.

2. Melt 2 Tbsp. butter in a large skillet over medium-high heat. Add mushrooms, and sauté 3 to 5 minutes or until lightly browned. Add garlic and shallots; cook, stirring often, 2 minutes or until tender. Remove from skillet. Wipe skillet clean.

3. Melt remaining 4 Tbsp. butter in skillet over medium-high heat; cook 2 to 3 minutes or until lightly browned. Stir in parsley, sage, and mushroom mixture. Add hot cooked ravioli, and toss gently. Stir in salt and pepper. Serve immediately with desired toppings.

NOTE: We tested with Whole Foods 365 Everyday Value Butternut Squash-Filled Ravioli.

TRY THESE TWISTS!

Cheese Ravioli with Mushrooms: Substitute 2 (8-oz.) packages three cheese-filled ravioli for butternut squash ravioli.

Sweet Potato Gnocchi with Mushrooms: Substitute 1 (16-oz.) package sweet potato gnocchi for ravioli.

Vieux Carré

MAKES: 1 serving
HANDS-ON TIME: 5 min.
TOTAL TIME: 5 min.

We suggest serving this stiff sipping cocktail after dinner. It was created in 1938 by Walter Bergeron, head bartender at the Monteleone Hotel in New Orleans. Vieux Carré (voo cah-RAY) means "old square," referring to the French Quarter.

- Crushed ice
- 2 Tbsp. rye whiskey
- 2 Tbsp. cognac
- 2 Tbsp. sweet vermouth
- 1 tsp. Bénédictine liqueur
- 2 dashes Peychaud's Bitters
- 2 dashes Angostura bitters

1. Fill 1 (8-oz.) glass with crushed ice. Pour remaining ingredients into glass; stir and serve immediately.

Party-Worthy Roasts and Potatoes

Treat guests to the simple pleasure of perfectly cooked, seasoned, and garnished prime cuts of meat. Round out the meal with one of these pretty potato side dishes.

Spicy Fruit-Stuffed Pork Loin with Roasted Pears and Onions

MAKES: 8 to 10 servings
HANDS-ON TIME: 1 hr.
TOTAL TIME: 2 hr., 20 min.

Adding dried crushed red pepper to the stuffing keeps this fruity dish savory and creates a fun flavor surprise for guests. Ask your butcher to butterfly the roast for stuffing and rolling. Once the pork is done, increase oven temp to 425°, and bake pears and onions while the pork roast stands.

PORK LOIN

- 2 (7-oz.) packages mixed dried fruit bits
- 2 Tbsp. dark brown sugar
- 1 Tbsp. chopped fresh sage
- ¼ tsp. dried crushed red pepper
- 1 (4-lb.) boneless pork loin
- 1½ tsp. kosher salt, divided
- 1½ tsp. coarsely ground pepper, divided
  Kitchen string
- 2 Tbsp. olive oil

ROASTED PEARS AND ONIONS

6 firm, ripe Seckel pears*
2 Tbsp. butter, melted
2 tsp. fresh lemon juice
2 tsp. honey**
¼ tsp. finely chopped fresh rosemary
¼ tsp. kosher salt
¼ tsp. freshly ground pepper
2 (10-oz.) packages cipollini onions, peeled

GLAZE

½ cup pear preserves

1. Prepare Pork Loin: Bring first 4 ingredients and 1 cup water to a boil in a small saucepan over medium-high heat. Cook 2 minutes, stirring once. Remove from heat, and cool completely (about 40 minutes).

2. Meanwhile, butterfly pork by making a lengthwise cut down center of 1 flat side, cutting to within ½ inch of other side. (Do not cut all the way through pork.) Open pork, forming a rectangle, and place between 2 sheets of heavy-duty plastic wrap. Flatten to ½-inch thickness using a meat mallet or rolling pin. Sprinkle with ½ tsp. each salt and pepper.

3. Spoon fruit mixture over pork, leaving a ½-inch border around edges. Roll up pork, jelly-roll fashion, starting at 1 long side. Tie with string at 1½-inch intervals. Sprinkle with remaining 1 tsp. salt and 1 tsp. pepper.

4. Preheat oven to 375°. Brown pork in hot oil in a large roasting pan over medium-high heat until browned on all sides (about 2 to 3 minutes per side). Place pork seam side down.

5. Prepare Roasted Pears and Onions: Cut pears in half lengthwise, and remove core. Stir together butter and next 5 ingredients. Stir in onions; gently stir in pear halves. Spoon mixture around roast in roasting pan.

6. Bake pork-and-pear mixture at 375° for 1 hour to 1 hour and 5 minutes or until a meat thermometer inserted into thickest portion of stuffing registers 135°, stirring pear mixture halfway through. Cover with aluminum foil, and let stand 15 minutes.

7. Prepare Glaze: Microwave preserves in a microwave-safe bowl at HIGH 1 minute or until thoroughly heated. Pour warm preserves over pork. Slice pork, and serve with Roasted Pears and Onions and pan juices.

*3 firm, ripe Bartlett pears may be substituted. Core pears and cut into 4 wedges each.

**Sugar may be substituted.

NOTE: To make ahead, prepare recipe as directed in Step 1, chilling fruit mixture 30 minutes after cooling. Proceed with recipe as directed in Steps 2 and 3. Cover stuffed pork tightly, and chill up to 4 hours. Let roast stand at room temperature 30 minutes before proceeding with Steps 4 through 7.

Honey-Curry Glazed Lamb with Roasted Grapes and Cranberries

MAKES: 6 servings
HANDS-ON TIME: 15 min.
TOTAL TIME: 1 hr., 30 min., including Roasted Grapes and Cranberries

Consider ordering lamb from your butcher a few days ahead.

2 (8-rib) lamb rib roasts (2½ lb. each), trimmed
1 Tbsp. red curry powder
1½ tsp. kosher salt
1½ tsp. freshly ground pepper
   Roasted Grapes and Cranberries
5 Tbsp. olive oil
2 Tbsp. honey
   Garnish: fresh rosemary sprigs

1. Preheat oven to 425°. Sprinkle lamb on all sides with curry powder, salt, and pepper. Let stand 30 minutes.

2. Meanwhile, prepare Roasted Grapes and Cranberries as directed.

3. Cook lamb in 1 Tbsp. hot oil in a 12-inch cast-iron skillet over medium heat 6 to 7 minutes, turning often to brown tops and sides. Place lamb, meat side up, in skillet. Stir together honey and remaining 4 Tbsp. olive oil; brush mixture on tops and sides of lamb.

4. Bake at 425° for 15 to 18 minutes or until a meat thermometer inserted into thickest portion registers 130°. Remove lamb from oven; let stand 10 minutes. Cut into chops, and serve with Roasted Grapes and Cranberries. Garnish, if desired.

Roasted Grapes and Cranberries

MAKES: 6 servings
HANDS-ON TIME: 5 min.
TOTAL TIME: 20 min.

Pair this accompaniment with grilled pork tenderloin, or add to a cheese tray for a unique touch.

6 to 8 seedless red grape clusters (about 1 lb.)
1 cup fresh cranberries
1 Tbsp. olive oil
1 tsp. chopped fresh rosemary

1. Preheat oven to 400°. Place grape clusters on a 15- x 10-inch jelly-roll pan. Stir together cranberries and next 2 ingredients. Spoon mixture over grape clusters.

2. Bake at 400° for 15 to 18 minutes or until grapes begin to blister and cranberries start to pop, shaking pan occasionally. Serve immediately, or let stand up to 4 hours.

Herb-and-Potato Chip-Crusted Beef Tenderloin

MAKES: 6 to 8 servings
HANDS-ON TIME: 40 min.
TOTAL TIME: 2 hr., 20 min.

Let your guests in on the secret to this beef tenderloin's crispy herb coating and rich salty seasoning—potato chips! Great with our Saucy Pairings for Beef (at right).

- 1 (4- to 5-lb.) beef tenderloin, trimmed
- 3 tsp. kosher salt, divided
- ¾ cup panko (Japanese bread-crumbs)
- 3 garlic cloves, pressed
- 2 tsp. coarsely ground pepper, divided
- 3 Tbsp. olive oil, divided
- 1¼ cups crushed, plain kettle-cooked potato chips
- ¼ cup finely chopped fresh parsley
- 1 Tbsp. finely chopped fresh thyme
- 1 bay leaf, crushed
- 1 egg white, lightly beaten
- 1 Tbsp. Dijon mustard
- Garnish: fresh herbs

1. Preheat oven to 400°. Sprinkle tenderloin with 2 tsp. salt. Let stand 30 to 45 minutes.

2. Meanwhile, sauté panko, garlic, 1 tsp. pepper, and remaining 1 tsp. salt in 1 Tbsp. hot oil in a skillet over medium heat 2 to 3 minutes or until deep golden brown. Let cool completely (about 10 minutes). Stir in potato chips and next 4 ingredients.

3. Pat tenderloin dry with paper towels, and sprinkle with remaining 1 tsp. pepper. Brown beef in remaining 2 Tbsp. hot oil in a roasting pan over medium-high heat until browned on all sides (about 2 to 3 minutes per side). Transfer tenderloin to a wire rack in an aluminum foil-lined jelly-roll pan. Let stand 10 minutes.

4. Spread mustard over tenderloin. Press panko mixture onto top and sides of tenderloin.

5. Bake at 400° for 40 to 45 minutes or until coating is crisp and a meat thermometer inserted into thickest portion of tenderloin registers 130° (rare). Let stand 10 minutes. Garnish, if desired.

NOTE: We tested with Lay's Kettle Cooked Original Potato Chips. For medium-rare, cook tenderloin to 135°; for medium, cook to 150°.

Saucy Pairings for Beef

Each of these sauces is a perfect complement to tenderloin at a dinner party. At an open house, they make praise-worthy condiments for sandwiches of carved beef tenderloin and cocktail buns. Make each sauce up to three days ahead, and store in an airtight container in the refrigerator.

HORSERADISH-PEPPER AÏOLI: Beat ½ cup heavy cream at medium-high speed with an electric mixer until stiff peaks form. Beat in 1 cup mayonnaise, 3 Tbsp. olive oil, 1 Tbsp. refrigerated horseradish, 1½ tsp. freshly ground pepper, 1 tsp. lemon zest, and ¼ tsp. salt at medium speed until blended. Cover and chill 2 hours. Makes: 2 cups. Hands-on time: 10 min.; Total time: 2 hr., 10 min.

RED PEPPER-CHERRY CHUTNEY: Melt 2 Tbsp. butter in a large skillet over medium heat. Stir in 1½ cups diced red bell pepper and ¼ cup thinly sliced green onions; cook, stirring occasionally, 12 to 15 minutes or until browned and tender. Stir in ½ cup coarsely chopped dried cherries, 3 Tbsp. balsamic vinegar, 2 tsp. brown sugar, and 1 tsp. finely chopped fresh thyme; cook, stirring occasionally, 2 to 5 minutes or until slightly thickened. Add salt and pepper to taste. Serve warm over tenderloin slices, and top with desired amount of crumbled blue cheese. Makes: 1 cup. Hands-on time: 20 min.; Total time: 20 min.
NOTE: Reheat chutney that has been made ahead and chilled in small saucepan over low heat, stirring occasionally, until warm.

CHIVE-MUSTARD SAUCE: Stir together 1 (8-oz.) container crème fraîche, ¼ cup whole grain Dijon mustard, 2 Tbsp. chopped fresh chives, 1 Tbsp. fresh lemon juice, and ¼ tsp. hot sauce. Cover and chill 1 hour. Makes: 1¼ cups. Hands-on time: 5 min.; Total time: 1 hr., 5 min.

Kitchen Express

You can never go wrong serving beef tenderloin. For a basic version, you'll need only the following ingredients: 1 (4- to 5-lb.) beef tenderloin, trimmed; 2 tsp. kosher salt; 1 tsp. coarsely ground pepper; and 2 Tbsp. olive oil. Prepare as directed in Steps 1, 3, and 5.

Celebrate the Season

Buttermilk Mashed Potatoes

MAKES: 6 to 8 servings
HANDS-ON TIME: 25 min.
TOTAL TIME: 50 min.

Microwave buttermilk and milk at HIGH 1 minute to warm.

- 4 lb. baking potatoes, peeled and cut into 2-inch pieces
- 1 Tbsp. salt, divided
- ¾ cup buttermilk, warmed
- ½ cup milk, warmed
- ¼ cup butter, melted
- ½ tsp. pepper

1. Bring potatoes, 2 tsp. salt, and water to cover to a boil in a large Dutch oven over medium-high heat; boil 20 minutes or until tender. Drain. Reduce heat to low. Return potatoes to Dutch oven, and cook, stirring occasionally, 3 to 5 minutes or until potatoes are dry.

2. Mash potatoes with a potato masher to desired consistency. Stir in buttermilk, next 3 ingredients, and remaining 1 tsp. salt, stirring just until blended.

TRY THIS TWIST!
Double Baked Potato Casserole:
Increase buttermilk to 1¼ cups. Prepare recipe as directed. Spoon mixture into a lightly greased 2½-qt. baking dish. Stir together 1 cup mashed baked sweet potatoes and 1½ Tbsp. chopped canned chipotle peppers in adobo sauce. Swirl sweet potato mixture into potato mixture in baking dish. Bake at 350° for 35 minutes.

Fennel-and-Potato Gratin

MAKES: 8 servings
HANDS-ON TIME: 30 min.
TOTAL TIME: 1 hr., 22 min.

Be sure to use a ceramic dish (not glass) when broiling the gratin.

- 3 Tbsp. butter
- 1 shallot, sliced
- 1 garlic clove, minced
- 2 Tbsp. all-purpose flour
- 1¼ cups half-and-half
- ½ (10-oz.) block sharp white Cheddar cheese, shredded
- ½ tsp. salt
- ¼ tsp. freshly ground pepper
- ⅛ tsp. ground nutmeg
- 2 large baking potatoes (about 2 lb.), peeled and thinly sliced
- 1 small fennel bulb, thinly sliced

1. Preheat oven to 400°. Melt butter in a heavy saucepan over medium heat. Add shallot, and sauté 2 to 3 minutes or until tender. Add garlic, and sauté 1 minute.

2. Whisk in flour; cook, whisking constantly, 1 minute. Gradually whisk in half-and-half; cook, whisking constantly, 3 to 4 minutes or until thickened and bubbly. Remove from heat. Whisk in cheese until melted and smooth. Stir in salt and next 2 ingredients.

3. Layer potato and fennel slices alternately in a lightly greased, broiler-safe ceramic 2-qt. casserole dish. Spread cheese sauce over layers. Cover with aluminum foil.

4. Bake at 400° for 50 minutes or until potatoes are tender. Remove casserole dish from oven. Increase oven temperature to broil with oven rack 5 inches from heat. Uncover casserole dish, and broil 2 to 4 minutes or until golden brown.

Stuffed-and-Baked Mashed Potatoes

Preheat oven to 350°. Prepare Buttermilk Mashed Potatoes as directed, increasing buttermilk to 1¼ cups. Stir in one of the tasty combos below. Spoon mixture into a lightly greased 2½-qt. baking dish or 8 (10-oz.) ramekins. Bake 35 minutes.

GARLIC LOVER'S: 8 roasted garlic cloves, chopped; 2 Tbsp. chopped fresh chives; and ½ tsp. smoked paprika.

ONION LOVER'S: 1¼ cups freshly grated Gruyère cheese, 1 cup chopped caramelized onions, and 2 Tbsp. chopped fresh parsley.

ROSEMARY-CHEDDAR: 1¼ cups (5 oz.) shredded sharp white Cheddar cheese, 1 tsp. chopped fresh rosemary, and 1 tsp. hot sauce.

CREAMY SPINACH: 1 (5-oz.) package fresh baby spinach, wilted; 1 (5½-oz.) package buttery garlic-and-herb spreadable cheese; and ¼ cup chopped toasted pecans.

SQUASH LOVER'S: 1 cup mashed roasted butternut squash, ½ cup freshly grated Parmesan cheese, and 1 to 2 Tbsp. chopped fresh sage.

BACON AND BLUE: 1 (4-oz.) wedge blue cheese, crumbled, and 8 cooked and crumbled bacon slices.

SMOKY SAUSAGE: 1 cup (4 oz.) shredded smoked Gouda cheese and 1 cup finely chopped cooked smoked sausage.

TASTY TEX-MEX: 1 (4.5-oz.) can chopped green chiles, 1¼ cups (5 oz.) shredded pepper Jack cheese, and ½ cup finely chopped cooked chorizo sausage.

Parmesan-Roasted Potato Salad with Roasted Garlic Vinaigrette

MAKES: 6 to 8 servings
HANDS-ON TIME: 15 min.
TOTAL TIME: 1 hr., 5 min.

4 large garlic cloves, unpeeled
1 tsp. olive oil
1½ lb. small or baby Yukon gold potatoes, halved
1 cup freshly grated Parmesan cheese
2 Tbsp. olive oil
2 tsp. kosher salt, divided
½ tsp. freshly ground pepper, divided
½ lb. haricots verts (tiny green beans), trimmed
2 Tbsp. red wine vinegar
1 Tbsp. fresh lemon juice
1 tsp. Dijon mustard
⅓ cup olive oil
1 (5-oz.) package baby spinach and arugula mix
½ small red onion, thinly sliced

1. Preheat oven to 425°. Place garlic on a piece of aluminum foil, and drizzle with 1 tsp. olive oil; fold to seal. Toss together potatoes, cheese, 2 Tbsp. olive oil, 1½ tsp. salt, and ¼ tsp. pepper. Spread mixture in a single layer in a 15- x 10-inch jelly-roll pan.
2. Bake potato mixture and foil-wrapped garlic at 425° for 35 minutes. Remove garlic from oven. Stir potato mixture, and bake 15 more minutes or until golden.
3. Meanwhile, cook haricots verts in boiling salted water to cover 3 to 4 minutes or until crisp-tender. Plunge into ice water to stop the cooking process; drain.
4. Peel garlic cloves. Process garlic, vinegar, next 2 ingredients, and remaining ½ tsp. salt and ¼ tsp. pepper in a blender or food processor until blended. With blender running, add ⅓ cup olive oil in slow, steady stream, processing until smooth.
5. Place spinach mix in a large bowl; top with onion, haricots verts, and roasted potatoes. Drizzle with vinaigrette, and serve immediately.
NOTE: We tested with Organic Girl Baby Spinach & Arugula.

Christmas Cocktails

Spiced Eggnog

MAKES: about 3¼ cups
HANDS-ON TIME: 30 min.
TOTAL TIME: 2 hr., 30 min.

4 egg yolks
½ cup sugar
2 cups milk
2 whole cloves
Pinch of ground cinnamon
1 cup heavy cream
1 tsp. freshly grated nutmeg
1 tsp. vanilla extract
2 Tbsp. bourbon

1. Beat egg yolks in a large bowl until thick and pale. Gradually beat in sugar until blended.
2. Stir together milk and next 2 ingredients in a 4-qt. saucepan. Cook mixture over medium heat, stirring constantly, 8 to 10 minutes or just until mixture begins to bubble around edges of pan. (Do not boil.)
3. Gradually stir half of hot milk mixture into egg mixture. Stir egg mixture into remaining hot milk mixture in pan.
4. Cook mixture over medium heat, stirring constantly, 7 to 8 minutes or until mixture thickens and coats the back of a spoon and a candy thermometer registers 160°;. (Do not boil.) Remove from heat, and stir in cream. Pour mixture through a fine wire-mesh strainer.
6. Let cool 1 hour. Stir in nutmeg, vanilla, and bourbon. Chill 1 hour.

Candy Cane Gimlet

MAKES: 1 serving
HANDS-ON TIME: 5 min.
TOTAL TIME: 5 min.

2 Tbsp. gin
1½ tsp. peppermint schnapps
1 tsp. fresh lime juice
½ cup lemon-lime soft drink, chilled
Garnish: peppermint sticks

1. Pour first 3 ingredients over ice in a 10-oz. glass. Top with lemon-lime soft drink. Garnish, if desired. Serve beverage immediately.

Kir Royale

MAKES: 5 servings
HANDS-ON TIME: 5 min.
TOTAL TIME: 5 min.

5 Tbsp. black raspberry liqueur
1 (750-milliliter) bottle Champagne
Fresh raspberries (optional)

1. Pour liqueur into a pitcher; add Champagne. Serve with raspberries, if desired.

Make It, Give It

Pecan-Toffee Shortbread

MAKES: about 2 dozen
HANDS-ON TIME: 15 min.
TOTAL TIME: 2 hr., 5 min.

2 cups coarsely chopped pecans
1 cup butter, softened
⅔ cup firmly packed light brown sugar
⅓ cup cornstarch
2 cups all-purpose flour
¼ tsp. salt
2 tsp. vanilla extract
1 (12-oz. package) semisweet chocolate morsels

Celebrate the Season

1. Preheat oven to 350°. Bake pecans in a single layer in a shallow pan 8 to 10 minutes or until toasted and fragrant, stirring halfway through. Cool completely (about 15 minutes).

2. Beat butter at medium speed with an electric mixer until creamy. Stir together brown sugar and cornstarch; gradually add to butter, beating at low speed until well blended. Stir together flour and salt; gradually add flour mixture to butter mixture, beating at low speed just until blended. Add vanilla and 1 cup pecans, beating at low speed just until blended.

3. Turn dough out onto a lightly greased baking sheet; pat or roll dough into an 11- x 14-inch rectangle, leaving at least a 1-inch border on all sides of baking sheet.

4. Bake at 350° for 20 minutes or until golden brown. Remove from baking sheet to a wire rack; sprinkle shortbread with chocolate morsels. Let stand 5 minutes; gently spread melted morsels over shortbread. Sprinkle with remaining 1 cup pecans, and let cool completely (about 1 hour). Cut or break shortbread into 2- to 3-inch pieces.

Bourbon Balls

MAKES: about 5 dozen
HANDS-ON TIME: 30 min.
TOTAL TIME: 53 min.

- 1 **cup chopped pecans**
- 1 **(12-oz.) package vanilla wafers, finely crushed**
- ¾ **cup powdered sugar**
- 2 **Tbsp. unsweetened cocoa**
- ½ **cup bourbon**
- 2½ **Tbsp. light corn syrup**
   Powdered sugar

1. Preheat oven to 350°. Bake pecans in a single layer in a shallow pan 8 to 10 minutes or until toasted and fragrant, stirring halfway through. Cool completely (about 15 minutes).

2. Stir together vanilla wafers, next 2 ingredients, and toased pecans in a large bowl until well blended.

3. Stir together corn syrup and bourbon in a small bowl until well blended. Pour bourbon mixture over wafer mixture; stir until blended. Shape into 1-inch balls; roll in powdered sugar. Store in an airtight container up to 2 weeks.

Pecan Pralines

MAKES: 2 dozen
HANDS-ON TIME: 30 min.
TOTAL TIME: 1 hr., 8 min.

Be sure to use a heavy Dutch oven (and a candy thermometer!), and make pralines on a day when the weather is dry—humidity tends to make them grainy.

- 2 **cups pecan halves and pieces**
- 3 **cups firmly packed brown sugar**
- 1 **cup whipping cream**
- ¼ **cup butter**
- 2 **Tbsp. light corn syrup**
- 1 **tsp. vanilla extract**
   Wax or parchment paper

1. Preheat oven to 350°. Bake pecans in a single layer in a shallow pan 8 to 10 minutes or until toasted and fragrant, stirring halfway through. Cool completely (about 15 minutes).

2. Meanwhile, bring brown sugar and next 3 ingredients to a boil in a heavy Dutch oven over medium heat, stirring constantly. Boil, stirring occasionally, 6 to 8 minutes or until a candy thermometer registers 236° (soft ball stage). Remove sugar mixture from heat.

3. Let sugar mixture stand until candy thermometer reaches 150° (about 20 to 25 minutes). Stir in vanilla and pecans using a wooden spoon; stir constantly 1 to 2 minutes or just until mixture begins to lose its gloss. Quickly drop by heaping tablespoonfuls onto wax paper or parchment paper; let stand until firm (about 10 to 15 minutes).

Try These Twists!

CHOCOLATE-PECAN PRALINES: Prepare as directed through Step 2. Add 2 (1-oz.) unsweetened chocolate baking squares to sugar. (Do not stir.) Proceed as directed in Step 3.

CAFÉ AU LAIT PECAN PRALINES: Add 2 Tbsp. instant coffee granules with brown sugar in Step 2.

BOURBON-PECAN PRALINES: Add ¼ cup bourbon with brown sugar in Step 2.

Butter-Pecan Granola

MAKES: about 8 cups
HANDS-ON TIME: 15 min.
TOTAL TIME: 1 hr., 10 min.

1. Preheat oven to 325°. Stir together ½ cup melted butter, ¼ cup honey, 2 Tbsp. light brown sugar, 1 tsp. vanilla extract, and ⅛ tsp. salt in a large bowl. Add 3 cups uncooked regular oats, 1½ cups coarsely chopped pecans, ½ cup toasted wheat germ, and 2 Tbsp. sesame seeds, and stir until oat mixture is evenly coated. Spread oat mixture on a lightly greased 15- x 10-inch jelly-roll pan. Bake 25 to 30 minutes or until toasted, stirring every 10 minutes. Spread granola onto wax paper, and cool completely (about 30 minutes). Stir in 1 (8-oz.) package chopped dates. Store in an airtight container at room temperature up to 3 days, or freeze up to 6 months.

Celebrate the Season

Bourbon-Cream Cheese Brownies

MAKES: 16 brownies
HANDS-ON TIME: 30 min.
TOTAL TIME: 2 hr., 10 min.

- 4 (1-oz.) unsweetened chocolate baking squares
- ¾ cup butter
- ½ cup firmly packed light brown sugar
- 1¾ cups granulated sugar, divided
- 4 large eggs, divided
- 1 tsp. vanilla extract
- ⅛ tsp. salt
- 1 cup all-purpose flour
- 1 (8-oz.) package cream cheese, softened
- 2 Tbsp. all-purpose flour
- ¼ cup bourbon

1. Preheat oven to 350°. Line bottom and sides of a 9-inch square pan with aluminum foil, allowing 2 to 3 inches to extend over sides; lightly grease foil.
2. Microwave chocolate squares and butter in a large microwave-safe bowl at HIGH 1½ to 2 minutes or until melted and smooth, stirring at 30-second intervals. Whisk in brown sugar and 1½ cups granulated sugar. Add 3 eggs, 1 at a time, whisking just until blended after each addition. Whisk in vanilla, salt, and 1 cup flour. Spread half of batter in prepared pan.
3. Beat cream cheese at medium speed with an electric mixer until smooth; add 2 Tbsp. flour and remaining ¼ cup granulated sugar, beating until blended. Add bourbon and remaining 1 egg, beating until blended.
4. Slowly pour cream cheese mixture over brownie batter in pan. Slowly pour remaining brownie batter over cream cheese mixture, and swirl together using a paring knife.

5. Bake at 350° for 40 to 45 minutes or until a wooden pick inserted in center comes out with a few moist crumbs. Cool completely in pan on a wire rack (about 1 hour). Lift brownies from pan, using foil sides as handles. Gently remove foil, and cut brownies into 16 squares.

Bourbon Ganache–Filled Chocolate Chip Cookies

MAKES: about 2½ dozen
HANDS-ON TIME: 45 min.
TOTAL TIME: 5 hr., 48 min., including ganache

- ¾ cup butter, softened
- ¾ cup granulated sugar
- ¾ cup firmly packed dark brown sugar
- 2 large eggs
- 1½ tsp. vanilla extract
- 2½ cups all-purpose flour
- 1 tsp. baking soda
- ¾ tsp. salt
- 1 (12-oz.) package semisweet chocolate morsels
  Parchment paper
  Bourbon Ganache

1. Preheat oven to 350°. Beat butter and sugars at medium speed with a heavy-duty electric stand mixer until creamy. Add eggs, 1 at a time, beating just until blended after each addition. Add vanilla, beating until blended.
2. Combine flour and next 2 ingredients in a small bowl; gradually add to butter mixture, beating at low speed just until blended. Stir in morsels just until combined. Drop by level spoonfuls onto parchment paper-lined baking sheets, using a small cookie scoop (about 1⅛ inches).
3. Bake at 350° for 12 minutes or until golden brown. Remove from baking sheets to wire racks; cool completely (about 30 minutes).
4. Spread Bourbon Ganache on flat side of half of cookies (about 1 level table-

spoonful per cookie); top with remaining cookies. Cover and chill cookies 2 hours or until ganache is firm.

Bourbon Ganache

MAKES: about 2 cups
HANDS-ON TIME: 15 min.
TOTAL TIME: 1 hr., 45 min.

- 1 (12-oz.) package semisweet chocolate morsels
- ½ cup whipping cream
- 3 Tbsp. bourbon
- ½ tsp. vanilla extract
- 3 Tbsp. butter, softened

1. Microwave chocolate morsels and whipping cream in a 2-qt. microwave-safe bowl at MEDIUM (50% power) 2½ to 3 minutes or until chocolate begins to melt, stirring after 1 minute and then at 30-second intervals. Whisk until chocolate melts and mixture is smooth. Whisk in bourbon and next 2 ingredients, whisking until smooth. Cover and chill, stirring occasionally, 1 hour and 30 minutes or until thickened to a spreadable consistency.

Herb Cheese Spread

MAKES: about 2½ cups
HANDS-ON TIME: 15 min.
TOTAL TIME: 15 min., plus 24 hr. for chilling

- 1 (8-oz.) package cream cheese, softened
- 1 (8-oz.) package feta cheese, softened
- ½ cup butter, softened
- 3 Tbsp. chopped fresh flat-leaf parsley
- 2 Tbsp. chopped fresh chives
- 1 Tbsp. chopped fresh tarragon
- 2 tsp. lemon zest
- 1 tsp. freshly ground pepper
- 1 garlic clove, pressed
  Garnishes: fresh herbs
  Biscuit Crostini or assorted crackers

Celebrate the Season

1. Beat first 9 ingredients at medium speed with an electric mixer 2 to 3 minutes or until smooth. Add salt and freshly ground pepper to taste.

2. Line 2 (10-oz.) ramekins with plastic wrap, allowing 3 inches to extend over sides; spoon cheese mixture into ramekins. Cover and chill 24 hours.

3. Invert chilled cheeses onto small serving dishes; discard plastic wrap. Garnish, if desired. Serve with Biscuit Crostini or assorted crackers.

Biscuit Crostini

MAKES: 4 dozen
HANDS-ON TIME: 10 min.
TOTAL TIME: 55 min.

Mary B's Tea Biscuits (found in the freezer section) make a quick and easy start for these Southern-style crostini, but feel free to substitute your favorite made-from-scratch biscuits (use a 2-inch cutter for appetizer-size portions).

1. Preheat oven to 350°. Bake 1 (24-oz.) package frozen tea biscuits according to package directions. Cool biscuits completely on a wire rack (about 10 minutes).

2. Cut biscuits in half, and brush cut sides lightly with 2 Tbsp. olive oil. Arrange biscuits, cut sides up, on baking sheets, and bake 20 minutes or until crisp, turning biscuits after 15 minutes.

Cranberry-Pecan Cheese Wafers

MAKES: about 18 dozen
HANDS-ON TIME: 30 min.
TOTAL TIME: 3 hr., 15 min., plus 8 hr. for chilling

1½ cups coarsely chopped sweetened dried cranberries
1½ cups chopped pecans
2 cups butter, softened
4 cups (16 oz.) freshly shredded extra-sharp Cheddar cheese
1½ tsp. salt
1½ tsp. ground red pepper
4 cups all-purpose flour
Parchment paper

1. Preheat oven to 350°. Bake pecans in a single layer in a shallow pan 8 to 10 minutes or until toasted and fragrant, stirring halfway through. Cool completely (about 15 minutes).

2. Meanwhile, soak cranberries in boiling water to cover 15 minutes; drain and pat dry with paper towels.

3. Beat butter and next 3 ingredients at medium speed with a heavy-duty electric stand mixer until blended. Gradually add flour, beating just until combined. Stir in cranberries and pecans. Shape dough into 4 (12-inch-long) logs; wrap each log in plastic wrap. Chill 8 hours to 3 days.

4. Preheat oven to 350°. Cut each log into ¼-inch-thick slices; place on parchment paper-lined baking sheets. Bake 13 to 15 minutes or until lightly browned. Remove from baking sheets to wire racks, and cool completely (about 20 minutes). Store in an airtight container up to 1 week.

NOTE: To freeze dough, place wrapped logs in zip-top plastic freezer bags, and freeze up to 1 month. Thaw dough in refrigerator overnight, and bake as directed.

Caramelized Ginger Pears

MAKES: 8 (4-oz.) jars
HANDS-ON TIME: 40 min.
TOTAL TIME: 4 hr., 25 min.

Pair a 4-oz. jar of these homemade pear preserves with a small (8-oz.) round of Brie (we tested with Ile de France), and include instructions for serving (see below). One recipe makes enough to package with about eight brie rounds.

4 lb. firm, ripe Anjou pears, peeled and chopped
2 cups granulated sugar
1 cup firmly packed light brown sugar
½ cup finely chopped crystallized ginger
2 Tbsp. fresh lemon juice

1. Stir together all ingredients in a large Dutch oven, and let stand at room temperature, stirring occasionally, 2 hours.

2. Bring pear mixture to a boil over medium-high heat, stirring constantly. Reduce heat to low, and cook, stirring often, 1 hour or until thickened and golden. Cool completely (about 45 minutes).

3. Spoon into 8 (4-oz.) jars or airtight containers. Store in refrigerator up to 2 weeks.

TRY THIS TWIST!
Caramelized Ginger Pears and Baked Brie: Preheat oven to 350°. Trim rind from top of 1 (8-oz.) Brie round, leaving a ½-inch border on top. Place Brie round in a 9-inch pie plate or on an ovenproof plate. Spoon 1 (4-oz.) jar Caramelized Ginger Pears over Brie round. Bake 15 minutes or until cheese begins to melt. Serve immediately with gingersnaps and assorted crackers. Makes: 6 to 8 servings. Hands-on time: 5 min., Total time: 20 min.

Dreamy Desserts

 Layered Peppermint Cheesecake

MAKES: 10 to 12 servings
HANDS-ON TIME: 1 hr., 10 min.
TOTAL TIME: 8 hr., 30 min.

PEPPERMINT CHEESECAKE LAYERS

- 3 (8-oz.) packages cream cheese, softened
- ½ cup sugar
- 2 Tbsp. unsalted butter, softened
- 3 large eggs
- 1 Tbsp. all-purpose flour
- 1½ cups sour cream
- 2 tsp. vanilla extract
- ¼ tsp. peppermint extract
- ⅔ cup crushed hard peppermint candies

SOUR CREAM CAKE LAYERS

- 1 (18.25-oz.) package white cake mix
- 2 large eggs
- 1 (8-oz.) container sour cream
- ⅓ cup vegetable oil

WHITE CHOCOLATE MOUSSE FROSTING

- ⅔ cup sugar
- 1 cup white chocolate morsels
- 2 cups whipping cream
- 2 tsp. vanilla extract
  Peppermint Candy Plate (optional)

GARNISHES

white chocolate curls, peppermint candies

1. Prepare Peppermint Cheesecake Layers: Preheat oven to 325°. Line bottom and sides of 2 (8-inch) round cake pans with aluminum foil, allowing 2 to 3 inches to extend over sides; lightly grease foil. Beat cream cheese, ½ cup sugar, and butter at medium speed with an electric mixer 1 to 2 minutes or until creamy and smooth. Add 3 eggs, 1 at a time, beating until blended after each addition. Add flour and next 3 ingredients, beating until blended. Fold in crushed candies. Pour batter into prepared pans. Place cake pans in a large baking pan; add water to baking pan to depth of 1 inch.

2. Bake cheesecakes at 325° for 25 minutes or until set. Remove from oven to wire racks; cool completely in pans (about 1 hour). Cover cheesecakes (do not remove from pans), and freeze 4 to 6 hours or until frozen solid. Lift frozen cheesecakes from pans, using foil sides as handles. Gently remove foil from cheesecakes. Rewrap cheesecakes, and return to freezer until ready to assemble cake.

3. Prepare Sour Cream Cake Layers: Preheat oven to 350°. Beat cake mix, next 3 ingredients, and ½ cup water at low speed with an electric mixer 30 seconds or just until moistened; beat at medium speed 2 minutes. Spoon batter into 3 greased and floured 8-inch round cake pans.

4. Bake at 350° for 15 to 20 minutes or until a wooden pick inserted in center comes out clean. Cool in pans on wire racks 10 minutes; remove from pans to wire racks, and cool completely (about 1 hour).

5. Prepare White Chocolate Mousse Frosting: Cook ⅔ cup sugar and ¼ cup water in a small saucepan over medium-low heat, stirring often, 3 to 4 minutes or until sugar is dissolved. Add morsels; cook, stirring constantly, 2 to 3 minutes or until white chocolate is melted and smooth. Remove from heat. Cool to room temperature (about 30 minutes), whisking occasionally. Beat cream and 2 tsp. vanilla at high speed with an electric mixer 1 to 2 minutes or until soft peaks form. Gradually fold white chocolate mixture into whipped cream mixture, folding until mixture reaches spreading consistency.

6. Assemble Cake: Place 1 Sour Cream Cake Layer on Peppermint Candy Plate or a cake stand or plate. Top with 1 frozen Peppermint Cheesecake Layer. Top with second Sour Cream Cake Layer and remaining Peppermint Cheesecake Layer. Top with remaining Sour Cream Cake Layer, Spread top and sides of cake with White Chocolate Mousse Frosting. Chill until ready to serve. Garnish, if desired.

MELODIE BELCHER
LAGRANGE, GEORGIA

Peppermint Candy Plate

MAKES: 1 (5- to 6-inch) plate
HANDS-ON TIME: 10 min.
TOTAL TIME: 46 min.

Add a festive touch to everyday dessert plates with easy-to-make candy liners.

**25 to 26 hard peppermint candies
Parchment paper**

1. Preheat oven to 350°. Trace a 5- to 6-inch circle on parchment paper, and place parchment paper on a baking sheet. Arrange peppermint candies inside circle on paper, leaving about 1/16-inch space between candies. (Candies should be as close as possible to each other without touching.) Bake 6 to 7 minutes or until candies begin to melt and touch. Remove from oven, and cool completely on pan on a wire rack (about 30 minutes).

TRY THESE TWISTS!
Peppermint Candy Ring: Decrease candies to 14 to 15. Prepare recipe as directed, placing candies around only outer edge of circle on paper. Remove from oven, and cool completely on a wire rack (about 10 minutes).

Peppermint Candy Cake Plate: Increase peppermints to 60. Prepare recipe as directed, tracing a 10-inch circle on parchment paper and increasing bake time to 9 to 10 minutes. Remove from oven, and cool completely on a wire rack (about 10 minutes).

Tiramisù Layer Cake

MAKES: 10 to 12 servings
HANDS-ON TIME: 45 min.
TOTAL TIME: 6 hr., 40 min., including syrup and frosting

- ½ cup butter, softened
- ½ cup shortening
- 2 cups sugar
- ⅔ cup milk
- 3 cups all-purpose flour
- 1 Tbsp. baking powder
- 1 tsp. salt
- 1 Tbsp. vanilla bean paste*
- 1 tsp. almond extract
- 6 egg whites
  Wooden picks
  Coffee Syrup
  Mascarpone Frosting
  Garnishes: raspberries, strawberries, red currants, fresh mint

1. Preheat oven to 350°. Beat butter and shortening at medium speed with an electric mixer until fluffy; gradually add sugar, beating well.

2. Stir together milk and ⅔ cup water. Combine flour and next 2 ingredients; add to butter mixture alternately with milk mixture, beginning and ending with flour mixture. Beat at low speed just until blended after each addition. Stir in vanilla bean paste and almond extract.

3. Beat egg whites at high speed until stiff peaks form, and fold into batter. Spoon batter into 3 greased and floured 8-inch round cake pans.

4. Bake at 350° for 25 to 30 minutes or until a wooden pick inserted in center comes out clean. Cool in pans on wire racks 10 minutes; remove from pans to wire racks, and cool completely (about 1 hour).

5. Meanwhile, prepare Coffee Syrup.

6. Prepare Mascarpone Frosting. Pierce each cake layer with a wooden pick, making holes about 1 inch apart. Brush or spoon Coffee Syrup over layers.

7. Place 1 cake layer, brushed side up, on a cake stand or serving plate. Spread top with 1⅓ cups Mascarpone Frosting. Top with second cake layer, brushed side up, and spread with 1⅓ cups Mascarpone Frosting. Top with remaining cake layer, brushed side up. Spread top and sides of cake with remaining Mascarpone Frosting. Chill 4 hours before serving. Garnish, if desired.

*Vanilla extract may be substituted.

Coffee Syrup

MAKES: about 1½ cups
HANDS-ON TIME: 5 min.
TOTAL TIME: 1 hr., 5 min.

- ½ cup sugar
- ⅔ cup strong brewed coffee
- ¼ cup brandy

1. Combine sugar and ⅓ cup water in a microwave-safe bowl. Microwave at HIGH 1½ minutes or until sugar is dissolved, stirring at 30-second intervals. Stir in coffee and brandy. Let cool 1 hour.

Mascarpone Frosting

MAKES: about 8 cups
HANDS-ON TIME: 20 min.
TOTAL TIME: 20 min.

- 2 (8-oz.) packages mascarpone cheese
- 3 cups heavy cream
- 1 Tbsp. vanilla extract
- ⅔ cup sugar

1. Stir mascarpone cheese in a large bowl just until blended. Beat cream and vanilla at low speed with an electric mixer until foamy; increase speed to medium-high, and gradually add sugar, beating until stiff peaks form. (Do not overbeat, or cream will be grainy.) Gently fold whipped cream mixture into mascarpone cheese. Use immediately.

MICHELLE MATILE
CRANSTON, RHODE ISLAND

Brown Sugar Pound Cake

MAKES: 12 servings
HANDS-ON TIME: 28 min.
TOTAL TIME: 2 hr., 38 min.

Don't preheat the oven for this scrumptious pound cake—it gets its start in a cold oven.

- 2 cups chopped pecans
- 1 cup butter, softened
- ½ cup shortening
- 2 cups firmly packed light brown sugar
- 1 cup granulated sugar
- 6 large eggs
- 3 cups cake flour
- 1 tsp. baking powder
- 1 cup evaporated milk
- 2 tsp. vanilla extract

1. Heat nuts in a large nonstick skillet over medium-low heat, stirring often, 8 to 10 minutes or until lightly toasted and fragrant. Remove from heat and cool completely (about 30 minutes).

2. Beat butter and shortening at medium speed with an electric mixer until creamy. Gradually add sugars, until light and fluffy. Add eggs, 1 at a time, beating just until the yellow yolk disappears.

3. Sift together flour and baking powder; add to butter mixture alternately with milk, beginning and ending with flour mixture. Beat batter at low speed just until blended after each addition. Stir in vanilla and pecans. Pour batter into a greased and floured 12-cup tube pan. Place pan in a cold oven; set oven temperature at 300°.

4. Bake at 300° for 1 hour and 30 minutes to 1 hour and 45 minutes or until a long wooden pick inserted in center of cake comes out clean. Cool in pan on a wire rack 10 to 15 minutes. Remove from pan; cool completely on wire rack.

Chocolate Cinnamon Pound Cake

MAKES: 12 servings
HANDS-ON TIME: 16 min.
TOTAL TIME: 3 hr., 14 min.

    1 (8-oz.) package semisweet
       chocolate baking squares, chopped
    1 cup butter, softened
 1½ cups sugar
    4 large eggs
  ½ cup chocolate syrup
    2 tsp. vanilla extract
 2½ cups all-purpose flour
    1 tsp. ground cinnamon
  ¼ tsp. baking soda
  ⅛ tsp. salt
    1 cup buttermilk
       Garnish: powdered sugar

1. Microwave chocolate baking squares in a microwave-safe bowl at HIGH 1 minute and 15 seconds or until chocolate is melted and smooth, stirring every 15 seconds.
2. Preheat oven to 325°. Beat butter at medium speed with an electric mixer 2 minutes or until creamy. Gradually add sugar, beating 5 to 7 minutes or until light and fluffy. Add eggs, 1 at a time, beating just until yellow disappears after each addition. Stir in melted chocolate, chocolate syrup, and vanilla until smooth.
3. Combine flour and next 3 ingredients; add to butter mixture alternately with buttermilk, beginning and ending with flour mixture. Beat at low speed just until blended after each addition. Pour batter into a greased and floured 10-inch tube pan or a 12-cup Bundt pan.
4. Bake at 325° for 1 hour and 10 minutes or until a long wooden pick inserted in center of cake comes out clean. Cool in pan on a wire rack 10 to 15 minutes; remove from pan to a wire rack, and let cool 1½ hours or until completely cool. Garnish, if desired.

Perfect Pound Cakes

Here are some tips for getting great results every time.

- Use name-brand ingredients. Store brands of sugar are often more finely ground than name brands, yielding more sugar per cup, which can cause the cake to fall. Store brands of butter may contain more liquid fat or flours more hard wheat, making the cake heavy.

- Measure accurately. Extra sugar or leavening causes a cake to fall; extra flour makes it dry.

- For maximum volume, have ingredients at room temperature. We like to pre-measure our ingredients and assemble them in the order listed. That way, if interrupted, we're less likely to make a mistake.

- Beat softened butter (and cream cheese or vegetable shortening) at medium speed with an electric mixer until creamy. This can take from 1 to 7 minutes, depending on the power of your mixer. Gradually add sugar, continuing to beat until light and fluffy. These steps are so important because they whip air into the cake batter so it will rise during baking.

- Add the eggs, one at a time, beating just until the yellow disappears. Overbeating the eggs may cause the batter to overflow the sides of the pan when baked or create a fragile crust that crumbles and separates from the cake as it cools.

- Grease cake pans with solid vegetable shortening, such as Crisco, and always dust with flour.

- Use an oven thermometer to check your oven's temperature for accuracy.

- Place the cake pan in the center of the oven, and keep the door closed until the minimum baking time has elapsed. If the cake requires more baking, gently close the oven door as soon as possible after testing to prevent jarring and loss of heat—both can cause a cake to fall if it's not completely done.

- Test for doneness by inserting a long wooden pick into the center of the cake. It should come out clean, with no batter clinging to it.

- Be sure to use the correct type of cake pan. Pound cakes bake differently in each pan. When unsure of size, use a cup measure to fill the cake pan with water.

Brandy Alexander Cheesecake

MAKES: 10 to 12 servings
HANDS-ON TIME: 20 min.
TOTAL TIME: 11 hr., 8 min.

Allowing chill time for a cheesecake is important for developing texture and flavor. To freeze up to one month, wrap springform pan tightly with aluminum foil, and slide into a zip-top plastic freezer bag.

- 1 **(10-oz.) box chocolate-flavored bear-shaped graham crackers, crushed (about 2¼ cups)**
- 6 **Tbsp. butter, melted**
- 2 **Tbsp. sugar, divided**
- 4 **(8-oz.) packages cream cheese, softened**
- 1¼ **cups sugar**
- 3 **Tbsp. cornstarch**
- 4 **large eggs, at room temperature**
- 4 **Tbsp. brandy, divided**
- 4 **Tbsp. crème de cacao, divided***
- 1 **(16-oz.) container sour cream**
  Garnishes: blackberries, currants, raspberries, strawberries

1. Preheat oven to 325°. Stir together crushed graham crackers, melted butter, and 1 Tbsp. sugar. Press mixture on bottom and halfway up sides of a 9-inch springform pan. Freeze 10 minutes.
2. Beat cream cheese, 1¼ cups sugar, and cornstarch at medium speed with an electric mixer 2 to 3 minutes or until smooth. Add eggs, 1 at a time, beating at low speed just until yellow disappears after each addition. Add 3 Tbsp. brandy and 3 Tbsp. crème de cacao, and beat just until blended. Pour into prepared crust.
3. Bake at 325° for 1 hour or just until center is almost set.
4. During last 2 minutes of baking, stir together sour cream and remaining 1 Tbsp. sugar, 1 Tbsp. brandy, and 1 Tbsp. crème de cacao.

5. Spread sour cream mixture over cheesecake. Bake at 325° for 8 more minutes. Remove cheesecake from oven; gently run a knife along outer edge of cheesecake, and cool completely in pan on a wire rack (about 1½ hours). Cover and chill 8 to 24 hours.
6. Remove sides of springform pan, and place cheesecake on a serving plate. Garnish, if desired.
*Coffee liqueur may be substituted. We tested with Kahlúa.
NOTE: We tested with Nabisco Teddy Grahams chocolate graham snacks.

Lightened Hummingbird Cake

MAKES: 20 servings
HANDS-ON TIME: 20 min.
TOTAL TIME: 2 hr., 13 min., including frosting

We lowered the fat and calories by substituting applesauce for some of the oil, using less butter and sugar, fewer eggs, and substituting light for regular cream cheese.

- **Vegetable cooking spray**
- 3 **cups plus 2 tsp. all-purpose flour, divided**
- 1 **tsp. baking soda**
- ½ **tsp. salt**
- 1¾ **cups sugar**
- 1 **tsp. ground cinnamon**
- 2 **large eggs**
- ½ **cup unsweetened applesauce**
- 3 **Tbsp. vegetable oil**
- 5 **to 6 bananas, mashed (1¾ cups)**
- 1½ **tsp. vanilla extract**
- 1 **(8-oz.) can crushed pineapple in juice, undrained**
  Lightened Cream Cheese Frosting
  Garnishes: orange rind curls, pecan halves

1. Preheat oven to 350°. Coat 3 (9-inch) round cake pans with cooking spray; sprinkle 2 tsp. flour into pans, shaking to coat.

2. Combine remaining 3 cups flour and next 4 ingredients in a large bowl. Stir together eggs and next 2 ingredients; add to flour mixture, stirring just until dry ingredients are moistened. (Do not beat.) Stir in banana and next 2 ingredients. Pour batter into prepared pans.
3. Bake at 350° for 23 to 25 minutes or until a wooden pick inserted in center of cake comes out clean. Cool layers in pans on wire racks 10 minutes; remove layers to wire racks, and cool completely (about 1 hour).
4. Meanwhile, prepare Lightened Cream Cheese Frosting. Spread frosting between layers and on top and sides of cake. Garnish, if desired.

Lightened Cream Cheese Frosting

MAKES: 3½ cups
HANDS-ON TIME: 10 min.
TOTAL TIME: 20 min.

- ¾ **cup chopped pecans**
- 1 **(8-oz.) package reduced-fat cream cheese (unsoftened)**
- 1 **(3-oz.) package cream cheese, softened**
- 1 **Tbsp. light butter (unsoftened)**
- 6 **cups powdered sugar**
- 1 **tsp. vanilla extract**

1. Preheat oven to 350°. Bake pecans in a single layer in a shallow pan 10 to 12 minutes or until lightly toasted and fragrant, stirring halfway through. Let cool.
2. Beat cream cheeses and butter at high speed with an electric mixer until creamy. Gradually add powdered sugar, beating at low speed just until smooth. Stir in vanilla and pecans.

Chocolate-Ginger-bread-Toffee Cake

MAKES: 10 to 12 servings
HANDS-ON TIME: 45 min.
TOTAL TIME: 10 hr., 5 min., including ganache and whipped cream (not including cookie garnish)

The addition of hot water at the end of this recipe makes for an exceptionally moist cake.

Ginger Whipped Cream
1½ cups semisweet chocolate morsels
1 (16-oz.) package light brown sugar
½ cup butter, softened
3 large eggs
2 cups all-purpose flour
¾ tsp. ground ginger
¾ tsp. ground cinnamon
½ tsp. salt
½ tsp. ground allspice
¼ tsp. freshly ground nutmeg
1 (8-oz.) container sour cream
1 cup hot water
½ cup molasses
1 tsp. baking soda
2 tsp. vanilla extract
Silky Ganache
1 cup toffee bits
Garnishes: Gingerbread Snowflake Cookies (page 285), chocolate curls, fresh cranberries, fresh mint

1. Preheat oven to 350°. Prepare Ginger Whipped Cream as directed in Step 1 of recipe (through chilling).

2. Microwave chocolate morsels in a microwave-safe bowl at HIGH 1 to 1½ minutes or until melted and smooth, stirring at 30-second intervals.

3. Beat sugar and butter at medium speed with an electric mixer until well blended (about 5 minutes). Add eggs, 1 at a time, beating just until blended after each addition. Add melted chocolate, beating just until blended.

4. Sift together flour and next 5 ingredients. Gradually add to chocolate mixture alternately with sour cream, beginning and ending with flour mixture. Beat at low speed just until blended after each addition. Stir together hot water and next 2 ingredients. (Mixture will foam.) Gradually stir molasses mixture and vanilla into chocolate mixture just until blended. Spoon batter into 3 greased and floured 8-inch round cake pans.

5. Bake at 350° for 25 to 30 minutes or until a wooden pick inserted in center comes out clean. Cool in pans on wire racks 10 minutes; remove from pans to wire racks, and cool completely (about 1 hour).

6. Prepare Silky Ganache. Place 1 cake layer on a cake stand or serving plate. Spread with half of ganache; sprinkle with ½ cup toffee bits. Top with second cake layer; spread with remaining ganache, and sprinkle with remaining ½ cup toffee bits. Top with remaining cake layer. Cover and chill 2 to 8 hours.

7. Finish preparing Ginger Whipped Cream as directed in Step 2 of recipe. Spread top and sides of cake with whipped cream just before serving. Garnish, if desired.

Silky Ganache

MAKES: 2¾ cups
HANDS-ON TIME: 20 min.
TOTAL TIME: 1 hr., 10 min.

For best results, use premium chocolate morsels.

1 (12-oz.) package semisweet chocolate morsels
¼ tsp. salt
1 (14-oz.) can sweetened condensed milk
2 Tbsp. butter
1 tsp. vanilla extract
2 Tbsp. heavy cream

1. Pour water to a depth of 1 inch into bottom of a double boiler over medium-high heat; bring to a boil. Reduce heat to medium-low, and simmer; place chocolate and salt in top of double boiler over simmering water. Cook, stirring constantly, 2 to 3 minutes or until melted. Add sweetened condensed milk; cook, stirring constantly, 1 to 2 minutes or until blended and smooth. Remove from heat; add butter and vanilla, and stir 4 to 5 minutes or until smooth. Let cool to room temperature (about 45 minutes). Transfer to a bowl. Gradually add cream to chocolate mixture, and beat with an electric mixer at high speed 2 to 3 minutes or until smooth and the consistency of a thick, spreadable buttercream frosting. Use immediately.
NOTE: We tested with Ghirardelli Chocolate Premium Semi-Sweet Baking Chips.

Celebrate the Season

Ginger Whipped Cream

MAKES: 4 cups
HANDS-ON TIME: 15 min.
TOTAL TIME: 4 hr., 35 min.

2 cups heavy cream
5 (⅛-inch-thick) slices peeled fresh ginger
6 Tbsp. powdered sugar

1. Cook cream and ginger in a heavy nonaluminum saucepan over medium-high heat, stirring often, 3 to 5 minutes or just until bubbles appear (do not boil); remove from heat, and let cool completely (about 20 minutes). Chill 4 to 12 hours. (Cream needs to be ice cold before beating.)
2. Pour cream mixture through a fine, wire-mesh strainer into a bowl, discarding ginger. Beat cream at medium-high speed with an electric mixer 1 minute or until foamy; increase speed to high, and gradually add powdered sugar, beating 2 to 3 minutes or just until stiff peaks form. (Do not overbeat or cream will be grainy.) Use immediately.

LYNN BROWN
CENTENNIAL, COLORADO

Red Velvet Cupcakes with White Chocolate-Amaretto Frosting

MAKES: 2 dozen
HANDS-ON TIME: 25 min.
TOTAL TIME: 2 hr., 18 min., including frosting

¾ cup butter, softened
1½ cups sugar
3 large eggs
1 (1-oz.) bottle red liquid food coloring
1 tsp. vanilla extract
2½ cups all-purpose flour
3 Tbsp. unsweetened cocoa
½ tsp. salt
1 cup buttermilk
1 Tbsp. white vinegar
1 tsp. baking soda
24 paper baking cups
White Chocolate-Amaretto Frosting
Garnish: white chocolate snowflakes, red candy sprinkles

1. Preheat oven to 350°. Beat butter at medium speed with an electric mixer until fluffy; gradually add sugar, beating well. Add eggs, 1 at a time, beating until blended after each addition. Stir in food coloring and vanilla, blending well.
2. Combine flour, cocoa, and salt. Stir together buttermilk, vinegar, and baking soda in a 4-cup liquid measuring cup. (Mixture will bubble.) Add flour mixture to butter mixture alternately with buttermilk mixture, beginning and ending with flour mixture. Beat at low speed until blended after each addition. Place paper baking cups in 2 (12-cup) muffin pans; spoon batter into cups, filling three-fourths full.

3. Bake at 350° for 18 to 20 minutes or until wooden pick inserted in centers comes out clean. Remove cupcakes from pan to wire racks, and let cool completely (about 45 minutes).
4. Pipe or spread cupcakes with White Chocolate-Amaretto Frosting. Garnish, if desired.

White Chocolate-Amaretto Frosting

MAKES: 4 cups
HANDS-ON TIME: 20 min.
TOTAL TIME: 50 min.

2 (4-oz.) white chocolate baking bars, broken into pieces
⅓ cup heavy cream
1 cup butter, softened
6 cups sifted powdered sugar
¼ cup almond liqueur

1. Microwave white chocolate pieces and cream in a microwave-safe bowl at MEDIUM (50% power) 1 minute or until melted and smooth, stirring at 30-second intervals. (Do not overheat mixture.) Let cool to room temperature (about 30 minutes).
2. Beat butter and 1 cup powdered sugar at low speed with an electric mixer until blended. Add remaining 5 cups powdered sugar alternately with almond liqueur, beating at low speed until blended after each addition. Add white chocolate mixture; beat at medium speed until spreading consistency.

Celebrate the Season

Chocolate Velvet Cupcakes with Browned Butter-Cinnamon-Cream Cheese Frosting

MAKES: 3 dozen
HANDS-ON TIME: 20 min.
TOTAL TIME: 2 hr., 38 min., including frosting

- 1½ cups semisweet chocolate morsels
- ½ cup butter, softened
- 1 (16-oz.) package light brown sugar
- 3 large eggs
- 2 cups all-purpose flour
- 1 tsp. baking soda
- ½ tsp. salt
- 1 (8-oz.) container sour cream
- 1 cup hot water
- 2 tsp. vanilla extract
- 36 paper baking cups
  Browned Butter-Cinnamon-Cream Cheese Frosting
  Garnishes: chocolate curls, white candy sprinkles

1. Preheat oven to 350°. Microwave chocolate morsels in a microwave-safe bowl at HIGH 1 to 1½ minutes or until melted and smooth, stirring at 30-second intervals.
2. Beat butter and sugar at medium speed with an electric mixer until well blended (about 5 minutes). Add eggs, 1 at a time, beating just until blended after each addition. Add melted chocolate, beating just until blended.
3. Sift together flour, baking soda, and salt. Gradually add to chocolate mixture alternately with sour cream, beginning and ending with flour mixture. Beat at low speed just until blended after each addition. Gradually add hot water in a slow, steady stream, beating at low speed just until blended. Stir in vanilla.
4. Place paper baking cups in 3 (12-cup) muffin pans; spoon batter into cups, filling three-fourths full.
5. Bake at 350° for 18 to 20 minutes or until wooden pick inserted in centers comes out clean. Remove cupcakes from pans to wire racks, and let cool completely (about 45 minutes). Pipe or spread cupcakes with frosting.

Browned Butter-Cinnamon-Cream Cheese Frosting

MAKES: 5 cups
HANDS-ON TIME: 15 min.
TOTAL TIME: 1 hr., 15 min.

- ½ cup butter
- 2 (8-oz.) packages cream cheese, softened
- 2 (16-oz.) packages powdered sugar
- 1 tsp. ground cinnamon
- 2 tsp. vanilla extract

1. Cook butter in a small heavy saucepan over medium heat, stirring constantly, 6 to 8 minutes or until butter begins to turn golden brown. Remove from heat immediately. Pour butter into a bowl. Cover and chill 1 hour or until butter is cool and begins to solidify.
2. Beat butter and cream cheese at medium speed with an electric mixer until creamy; gradually add powdered sugar, beating until light and fluffy. Stir in cinnamon and vanilla.

Coconut-Pecan Cupcakes

MAKES: 3 dozen
HANDS-ON TIME: 20 min.
TOTAL TIME: 2 hr., 15 min., including frosting

- 1 cup finely chopped pecans
- ½ cup butter, softened
- ½ cup shortening
- 2 cups sugar
- 5 large eggs, separated
- 1 Tbsp. vanilla extract
- 2 cups all-purpose flour
- 1 tsp. baking soda
- 1 cup buttermilk
- 1 cup sweetened flaked coconut
- 36 paper baking cups
  Caramel Frosting
  Garnish: chopped roasted salted pecans

1. Preheat oven to 350°. Bake pecans in a single layer in a shallow pan 8 to 10 minutes or until toasted and fragrant, stirring halfway through.
2. Beat butter and shortening at medium speed with an electric mixer until fluffy; gradually add sugar, beating well. Add egg yolks, 1 at a time, beating until blended after each addition. Add vanilla, beating until blended.
3. Combine flour and baking soda; add to butter mixture alternately with buttermilk, beginning and ending with flour mixture. Beat at low speed just until blended after each addition. Stir in coconut and pecans.
4. Beat egg whites at high speed until stiff peaks form, and fold into batter. Place paper baking cups in 3 (12-cup) muffin pans; spoon batter into cups, filling half full.
5. Bake at 350° for 18 to 20 minutes or until a wooden pick inserted in centers comes out clean. Remove from pans to wire racks and let cool completely (about 45 minutes).
6. Spread cupcakes with Caramel Frosting. Garnish, if desired.

Caramel Frosting

MAKES: 4½ cups
HANDS-ON TIME: 15 min.
TOTAL TIME: 45 min.

- 1 (14-oz.) package caramels
- ½ cup heavy cream
- 1 cup butter, softened
- 5 cups powdered sugar
- 2 tsp. vanilla extract

1. Microwave caramels and cream in a medium-size microwave-safe bowl at HIGH 1 to 2 minutes or until smooth, stirring at 30-second intervals. Let cool until lukewarm (about 30 minutes).
2. Beat butter at medium speed with an electric mixer until creamy. Gradually add powdered sugar alternately with caramel mixture, beating at low speed until blended and smooth after each addition. Stir in vanilla.

Quick Slow-Cooker Favorites

Meaty Suppers

The slow cooker serves up these favorites the way that they are meant to be—juicy, tender, full-flavored, and cooked to perfection.

Grillades and Cheese Grits

MAKES: 6 servings
HANDS-ON TIME: 15 min.
TOTAL TIME: 6 hr., 30 min.

- 2 **lb. top round steak (about ½ inch thick)**
- 1 **tsp. salt, divided**
- ¼ **tsp. pepper**
- ¼ **cup all-purpose flour, divided**
- 2 **Tbsp. vegetable oil**
- 2 **(8-oz.) containers refrigerated prechopped celery, onion, and bell pepper mix**
- 3 **garlic cloves, minced**
- 1 **(14-oz.) can beef broth**
- 1 **tsp. dried Italian seasoning**
- ½ **tsp. ground red pepper**
- 2 **(14.5-oz.) cans diced tomatoes with basil, garlic, and oregano**
- 2 **cups uncooked quick-cooking grits**
- 2 **cups (8 oz.) Gruyère cheese, shredded**
  Garnish: chopped fresh parsley

1. Sprinkle steak with ½ tsp. salt and pepper. Set aside 1 Tbsp. flour. Cut steak into 2-inch pieces; dredge in remaining flour.
2. Heat oil in a large nonstick skillet over medium-high heat; add steak, and cook 3 minutes on each side or until browned. Transfer to a 5-qt. slow cooker. Add celery mix and garlic to skillet; sauté 3 minutes. Add beef broth, stirring to loosen particles from bottom. Stir in Italian seasoning and red pepper. Pour mixture over steak. Drain 1 can tomatoes. Add drained tomatoes and remaining can tomatoes to steak mixture. Cover and cook on LOW 6 hours or until steak is very tender.
3. Increase heat to HIGH. Stir together reserved flour and 2 Tbsp. water until smooth; gently stir into steak mixture. Cover and cook 15 minutes or until mixture is slightly thickened.
4. Meanwhile, bring 8 cups water and remaining ½ tsp. salt to a boil in a 4-qt. saucepan; gradually whisk in grits. Reduce heat, and simmer, whisking often, 5 minutes or until thickened; stir in cheese. Serve grillades over grits. Garnish, if desired.

Pepper Steak with Mushrooms

MAKES: 6 servings
HANDS-ON TIME: 15 min.
TOTAL TIME: 8 hr., 25 min.

Some stores carry a "fajita mix" of precut vegetables that includes peppers and onions.

- 1½ **lb. top round steak**
- 1 **tsp. salt, divided**
- ½ **tsp. pepper, divided**
- 1 **Tbsp. vegetable oil**
- 3 **cups presliced green, yellow, and red bell pepper mix**
- 2 **garlic cloves, minced**
- 1 **medium onion, vertically sliced**
- 1 **(14½-oz.) can diced tomatoes with basil, garlic, and oregano**
- 1 **(8-oz.) package sliced baby portobello mushrooms**
- 1 **(10½-oz.) can beef consommé**
- 2 **Tbsp. soy sauce**
- 2 **Tbsp. tomato paste**
- 2 **Tbsp. cornstarch**

1. Cut beef diagonally across the grain into thin slices. Sprinkle beef with ¾ tsp. salt and ¼ tsp. pepper. Heat oil in a large nonstick skillet over medium-high heat. Cook beef in hot oil, stirring frequently, 6 to 8 minutes or until browned; drain. Place beef in a 5-qt. slow cooker. Add bell peppers and next 4 ingredients to slow cooker. Toss gently.
2. Whisk together consommé, soy sauce, tomato paste, and remaining ¼ tsp. each salt and pepper; stir into beef mixture. Cover and cook on LOW 8 hours or until beef is very tender.
3. Whisk together cornstarch and 2 Tbsp. water; gradually stir into liquid in slow cooker. Cover and cook on HIGH 10 minutes or until thickened. Serve over mashed potatoes.

Beef with Olives

MAKES: 8 to 10 servings
HANDS-ON TIME: 15 min.
TOTAL TIME: 5 hr., 15 min.

Roast some new potatoes instead of serving yellow rice.

- ¼ cup butter, melted
- 3 lb. boneless top sirloin steak, cut into 1½-inch pieces
- ¼ tsp. salt
- ½ tsp. pepper
- 1 Tbsp. olive oil
- 3 large garlic cloves, sliced
- 2 shallots, vertically sliced
- 2 cups pimiento-stuffed Spanish olives
- 2 Tbsp. olive juice from jar
- 1 (12-oz.) jar roasted red bell peppers, drained and cut into thick strips

1. Pour melted butter into a 4- or 5-qt. slow cooker.
2. Sprinkle beef with salt and pepper. Heat oil in a large skillet over medium-high heat. Cook beef, in 2 batches, 2 minutes on each side. Place beef in slow cooker. Add garlic and shallots to skillet; sauté 1 minute over medium-high heat. Spoon over beef in slow cooker. Coarsely chop 1 cup olives. Sprinkle chopped and whole olives and olive juice over beef.
3. Cover and cook on LOW 5 hours or until beef is tender. Stir in roasted bell peppers just before serving.

Spicy Shredded Beef Sandwiches

MAKES: 6 to 8 servings
HANDS-ON TIME: 5 min.
TOTAL TIME: 9 hr., 5 min.

Save extra sauce to top Mexican rice or cooked pinto beans.

- 1 (2½ lb.) boneless chuck roast, trimmed
- 1 (14½-oz.) can diced tomatoes, undrained
- 1 (7-oz.) can adobo sauce or 1 (7-oz.) jar spicy salsa
- 1 (4-oz.) can jalapeño peppers, drained
- 1 (8-oz.) container refrigerated prechopped onion (about 1¾ cups)
- 1½ tsp. jarred minced garlic
- 2 Tbsp. chili powder
- 1 Tbsp. honey
- 2½ tsp. kosher salt
- 1 tsp. ground cumin
- 2 cups beef broth
   Crusty French rolls
   Toppings: shredded cabbage, sliced red onion, sliced tomato, sour cream, chopped cilantro

1. Place beef in a 5-qt. slow cooker. Add tomatoes, adobo sauce, jalapeños, onion, garlic, chili powder, honey, salt, and cumin; pour broth over the top.
2. Cover and cook on HIGH 1 hour; reduce heat to LOW, and cook 8 hours. If desired, remove lid during last 30 minutes to allow sauce to reduce and thicken.
3. With a heavy fork, transfer meat to a rimmed board or plate. Shred with two forks. Ladle out half the sauce, and reserve. Return shredded beef to the remaining sauce in slow cooker; cover and keep warm. Serve on rolls. Add desired toppings.

Beef Stroganoff

MAKES: 6 to 8 servings
HANDS-ON TIME: 15 min.
TOTAL TIME: 3 hr., 15 min.

Look for beef sirloin tips as a time-saver. Or purchase top sirloin, and cut it into thin slices.

- ¼ cup all-purpose flour
- 2 lb. beef sirloin tips
- ½ tsp. salt
- ½ tsp. freshly ground pepper
- 2 Tbsp. olive oil
- 2 medium onions, chopped
- 2 (8-oz.) packages sliced fresh mushrooms
- 1½ cups beef broth
- 2 Tbsp. tomato paste
- 1 Tbsp. Dijon mustard
- 1½ cups sour cream
- ¼ cup dry sherry (optional)
   Hot cooked egg noodles
   Chopped fresh parsley (optional)

1. Place flour in a shallow dish. Sprinkle beef with salt and pepper; dredge in flour, shaking off excess. Heat a large skillet over medium-high heat; add oil. Add beef; cook 7 minutes or until browned, stirring occasionally; reserve drippings in skillet. Transfer to a greased 5-qt. slow cooker. Add onion and mushrooms to drippings in skillet; cook, stirring often, 3 minutes or until tender.
2. Meanwhile, combine broth, tomato paste, and mustard. Add broth mixture to skillet, stirring to loosen particles from bottom of skillet. Pour over beef in slow cooker.
3. Cover and cook on LOW 3 hours or until beef is tender. Just before serving, stir in sour cream and, if desired, sherry. Serve over noodles. Sprinkle with parsley, if desired.

Quick Slow-Cooker Favorites

Home-style Meatloaf

MAKES: 8 servings
HANDS-ON TIME: 11 min.
TOTAL TIME: 4 hr., 36 min.

Using an oval slow cooker helps maintain the traditional meatloaf shape.

- 2 Tbsp. butter
- 1 (8-oz.) container refrigerated prechopped celery, onion, and bell pepper mix
- 2 garlic cloves, minced
- 2 lb. ground round
- ¾ cup uncooked quick-cooking oats
- 1 cup ketchup, divided
- ¾ tsp. salt
- ½ tsp. freshly ground pepper
- 2 large eggs, lightly beaten
- 2 Tbsp. brown sugar
- 1 Tbsp. yellow mustard

1. Melt butter in a large skillet over medium-high heat. Add celery mixture and garlic; sauté 3 minutes or until tender. Combine sautéed mixture, ground round, oats, ½ cup ketchup, salt, pepper, and eggs in a large bowl.
2. Shape mixture into a 9- x 4-inch loaf; place in a lightly greased 5- or 6-qt. oval slow cooker.
3. Cover and cook on HIGH 1 hour. Reduce heat to LOW, and cook 3 more hours. Remove slow cooker insert, and carefully pour off excess fat. Return insert to cooker.
4. Stir together remaining ½ cup ketchup, brown sugar, and mustard. Spread over meatloaf. Cover and cook on LOW 15 minutes or until no longer pink in center. Remove meatloaf from insert, and let stand 10 minutes before serving.

Swedish Meatballs

MAKES: 6 servings
HANDS-ON TIME: 14 min.
TOTAL TIME: 3 hr., 14 min.

- 1 (32-oz.) package frozen fully cooked meatballs
- 2 Tbsp. vegetable oil
- ¼ cup all-purpose flour
- ½ tsp. salt
- ¼ tsp. garlic powder
- ¼ tsp. freshly ground pepper
- ⅛ tsp. ground nutmeg
- 2 cups chicken broth
- ½ cup white wine
- ½ cup sour cream
- 2 Tbsp. chopped fresh parsley
- ½ cup red currant jelly (optional)
  Hot cooked noodles
  Garnish: chopped fresh parsley

1. Cook meatballs in a large skillet over medium-high heat 5 minutes, turning occasionally until browned on all sides.
2. Place meatballs in a 4-qt. slow cooker, reserving drippings in skillet. Reduce heat to low; add oil to skillet. Whisk in flour and next 4 ingredients until smooth. Increase heat to medium; cook, whisking constantly, 1 minute. Gradually whisk in chicken broth and wine. Cook, whisking frequently, 4 minutes or until slightly thickened. Pour gravy over meatballs. Cover and cook 3 hours on LOW.
3. Remove meatballs from slow cooker with a slotted spoon, and place in a serving bowl. Add sour cream, parsley, and, if desired, jelly to gravy, whisking until blended. Pour over meatballs. Serve over hot cooked noodles; garnish, if desired.

Baked Four-Cheese Spaghetti with Italian Sausage

MAKES: 8 to 10 servings
HANDS-ON TIME: 15 min.
TOTAL TIME: 3 hr., 25 min.

Open sausage casings using kitchen shears; then just squeeze the sausage into the pan for browning.

- 8 oz. uncooked spaghetti
- 1 lb. Italian sausage (about 4 links)
- 1 (8-oz.) container refrigerated prechopped bell pepper-and-onion mix
- 2 tsp. jarred minced garlic
- 1 Tbsp. vegetable oil
- 1 (24-oz.) jar fire-roasted tomato and garlic pasta sauce
- 1 (16-oz.) package shredded sharp Cheddar cheese
- 1 (8-oz.) package shredded mozzarella cheese, divided
- 4 oz. fontina cheese, shredded
- ½ cup (2 oz.) shredded Parmesan cheese

1. Cook pasta in boiling salted water in a large Dutch oven according to package directions. Drain and return to pan.
2. Meanwhile, brown sausage, bell pepper mix, and garlic in oil in a large nonstick skillet over medium-high heat, stirring often, 8 to 10 minutes or until meat crumbles and is no longer pink. Drain. Stir meat mixture, pasta sauce, and Cheddar cheese into pasta. Spoon half of pasta mixture into a lightly greased 5-qt. slow cooker coated with cooking spray.
3. Combine mozzarella cheese and fontina cheese. Sprinkle half of mozzarella mixture over pasta mixture in slow cooker. Top with remaining pasta mixture, remaining mozzarella mixture, and Parmesan cheese. Cover and cook on LOW 3 hours. Let stand, covered, 10 minutes before serving.

Veal Chops with Figs

MAKES: 4 servings
HANDS-ON TIME: 15 min.
TOTAL TIME: 6 hr., 15 min.

We tested this recipe using veal rib chops, but loin chops would work as well. The thicker the better here, since the meat simmers low and slow to melt-in-your-mouth tenderness.

- 1 cup pomegranate juice
- ¾ cup sugar
- 6 garlic cloves, minced
- 1 Tbsp. chopped fresh thyme
- 1 tsp. coarsely ground or freshly ground pepper
- 4 (1- to 1½-inch-thick) veal rib chops
- 1 Tbsp. olive oil
- 2 shallots, vertically sliced
- 1 (8-oz.) package dried figs, coarsely chopped (1 cup)
- 1 Tbsp. balsamic vinegar
  Garnish: fresh thyme

1. Combine pomegranate juice, sugar, and ¾ cup water in a saucepan. Bring to a boil over high heat. Boil 12 to 15 minutes or until syrupy. Set aside.
2. Meanwhile, combine garlic, thyme, and pepper; rub over veal. Heat oil in a large skillet over medium-high heat. Brown veal 2 minutes on each side.
3. Arrange veal in a lightly greased 6-qt. oval slow cooker. Add shallots to skillet; toss gently. Spoon shallots and figs over veal. Pour reserved pomegranate syrup over figs. Drizzle with vinegar. Cover and cook on LOW 6 hours or until tender. Garnish, if desired.

Mediterranean Stuffed Pork Tenderloin

MAKES: 6 servings
HANDS-ON TIME: 15 min.
TOTAL TIME: 3 hr., 27 min.

- ⅓ cup drained sun-dried tomatoes in oil, chopped
- 3½ Tbsp. oil from sun-dried tomatoes in oil, divided
- 1¼ tsp. salt, divided
- ¾ tsp. pepper, divided
- 1 Tbsp. dried Italian seasoning
- 2 Tbsp. chopped pitted kalamata olives
- ¾ tsp. lemon zest
- 2 garlic cloves, pressed
- 2 (1-lb.) pork tenderloins
- ½ cup (2 oz.) crumbled feta cheese
- 1 (14.5-oz.) can diced tomatoes with basil, garlic, and oregano, undrained
- 1 Tbsp. cornstarch

1. Place sun-dried tomatoes in a small bowl. Stir in 2 Tbsp. sun-dried tomato oil, 1 tsp. salt, ½ tsp. pepper, and next 4 ingredients. Butterfly pork by making a lengthwise cut down center of 1 side of each tenderloin, cutting to within ½ inch of other side. Unfold, forming 2 rectangles. Sprinkle with ⅛ tsp. salt and ⅛ tsp. pepper. Spread half of sun-dried tomato mixture over each tenderloin, leaving a ½-inch border; sprinkle with cheese. Fold long sides of tenderloins together to enclose filling; secure with wooden picks. Heat remaining 1½ Tbsp. sun-dried tomato oil in a skillet; add stuffed tenderloins. Cook 4 minutes, turning occasionally until browned on all sides. Place tenderloins, seam side up, in a 5-qt. slow cooker; add diced tomatoes. Cover; cook on LOW 3 hours.

2. Remove tenderloins to a platter, reserving tomato mixture in slow cooker; cover and let stand 10 to 15 minutes.
3. Meanwhile, stir together cornstarch and 2 Tbsp. water until smooth; stir into tomato mixture. Increase heat to HIGH; cook 10 minutes or until slightly thickened. Remove wooden picks; cut tenderloins into slices. Spoon tomato gravy over pork slices.

Cheesy Ham and Noodles

MAKES: 6 servings
HANDS-ON TIME: 9 min.
TOTAL TIME: 3 hr., 9 min.

This family-friendly pasta dish is adaptable. Use your favorite type of frozen peas, and substitute whipping cream and Gruyère cheese for easy alternatives to the half-and-half and Swiss cheese.

- 12 oz. uncooked linguine
- 3 cups half-and-half
- 2 cups (8 oz.) shredded Swiss cheese
- 1 cup frozen peas
- 1 Tbsp. Dijon mustard
- 1 (12-oz.) lean ham steak, chopped
- 1 (10-oz.) package refrigerated Alfredo sauce

1. Bring water to a boil in a 4-qt. saucepan. Cook linguine 5 minutes; drain. Transfer pasta to a lightly greased 4-qt. slow cooker. Add half-and-half, 1 cup cheese, and remaining 4 ingredients, stirring gently to blend. Sprinkle with remaining 1 cup cheese. Cover and cook on LOW 3 hours or until pasta is tender.

Poultry Pleasers

Chicken Enchilada Dip

MAKES: 8 servings
HANDS-ON TIME: 10 min.
TOTAL TIME: 4 hr., 10 min.

The corn tortillas cook into this dish and thicken it—you won't see them after they're cooked, but you will still taste their authentic Mexican flavor.

2 (10-oz.) cans mild green chile enchilada sauce
10 (6-inch) corn tortillas, torn into 3-inch pieces
4 cups pulled cooked chicken breasts
1½ cups sour cream
1 (12-oz.) package shredded colby-Jack cheese blend, divided
1 (10¾-oz.) can cream of mushroom soup
8 cups shredded iceberg lettuce
1 (15-oz.) can black beans
3 tomatoes, diced

1. Spoon ½ cup enchilada sauce over bottom of a greased 4-qt. slow cooker. Add enough tortilla pieces to cover sauce.
2. Stir together chicken, sour cream, 2 cups cheese, and soup. Spread 2 cups chicken mixture over tortilla pieces. Top with tortilla pieces to cover. Drizzle with ½ cup enchilada sauce. Repeat layers twice, ending with tortilla pieces and remaining enchilada sauce. Sprinkle with remaining 1 cup cheese.
3. Cover and cook on LOW 4 hours. Place lettuce on plates; top with chicken, beans, and tomatoes. Serve hot.

Chicken and Dumplings

MAKES: 8 servings
HANDS-ON TIME: 15 min.
TOTAL TIME: 8 hr., 38 min.

5 large carrots, cut into 2-inch pieces
3 small Yukon gold potatoes, unpeeled and cut into chunks
6 skinned and boned chicken breasts
1 tsp. salt
1 tsp. freshly ground pepper
1 cup chicken broth or water
2 (10¾-oz.) cans cream of chicken soup
   Freshly ground pepper
1 cup frozen peas
2 hard-cooked eggs, chopped
2 cups all-purpose baking mix
⅔ cup half-and-half or milk
2 Tbsp. chopped fresh herbs such as flat-leaf parsley, thyme, and rosemary
   Garnishes: chopped fresh herbs, freshly ground pepper

1. Place carrot and potato in a lightly greased 6-qt. slow cooker.
2. Sprinkle chicken with 1 tsp. each of salt and pepper. Heat a large nonstick skillet over medium-high heat. Coat with cooking spray. Sauté chicken, in 2 batches, 2 minutes on each side or until browned. Place chicken over vegetables in slow cooker. Stir together broth and soup; pour over chicken. Sprinkle with freshly ground pepper.
3. Cover and cook on LOW 7 hours. Add peas and egg, stirring gently to break up chicken into bite-size pieces.
4. Combine baking mix, half-and-half, and herbs; stir with a fork until blended. Drop by 8 spoonfuls onto chicken mixture. Cover and cook on HIGH 1 hour and 15 minutes or until dumplings are done. Garnish, if desired.

Chicken Parmesan

MAKES: 6 servings
HANDS-ON TIME: 12 min.
TOTAL TIME: 3 hr., 47 min.

Shop for the "value size" jar of pasta sauce. It's the ideal amount for this recipe, especially if chicken breasts are on the large size. Otherwise, pick up 2 (24-oz.) jars and enjoy about ½ cup leftover sauce on a small pizza.

2 cups Italian-seasoned Japanese breadcrumbs (panko)
6 skinned and boned chicken breasts
2 large eggs, lightly beaten
4 Tbsp. olive oil, divided
1 (44-oz.) jar tomato-basil pasta sauce
¾ tsp. salt
½ tsp. pepper
1 (8-oz.) package shredded mozzarella cheese
¾ cup (3 oz.) shredded Parmesan cheese
   Garnish: fresh oregano

1. Spread breadcrumbs on a large plate. Dip chicken in beaten egg, 1 breast at a time. Dredge chicken in breadcrumbs, pressing gently for crumbs to adhere.
2. Heat 2 Tbsp. oil in a large nonstick skillet over medium-high heat. Cook chicken, in 2 batches, 2 minutes on each side or until browned, adding remaining 2 Tbsp. oil with second batch.
3. Pour sauce into a lightly greased 6- or 7-qt. oval slow cooker. Arrange chicken in slow cooker over sauce. Sprinkle with salt and pepper. Cover and cook on HIGH 3½ hours. Add cheeses; cover and cook on HIGH 5 more minutes or until cheese melts. Garnish, if desired.

Quick Slow-Cooker Favorites

Sesame Chicken

MAKES: 4 to 6 servings
HANDS-ON TIME: 7 min.
TOTAL TIME: 2 hr., 37 min.

All the flavor of traditional sesame chicken is in this recipe, but without the work of breading and frying the chicken pieces.

- 1¼ cups chicken broth
- ½ cup firmly packed brown sugar
- ¼ cup cornstarch
- 2 Tbsp. rice vinegar
- 2 Tbsp. soy sauce
- 2 Tbsp. sweet chili sauce
- 2 Tbsp. honey
- 2 tsp. dark sesame oil
- 1½ lb. skinned and boned chicken breasts, cut into 1-inch pieces
- 2 cups sugar snap peas
- 2 cups crinkle-cut carrots
- 1½ Tbsp. sesame seeds, toasted
- Hot cooked rice
- Garnish: chopped green onions

1. Whisk together first 8 ingredients in a 4-qt. slow cooker. Stir in chicken. Cover and cook on HIGH 2½ hours or until chicken is done, stirring after 1½ hours.
2. Steam sugar snap peas and carrots. Stir vegetable mixture and sesame seeds into slow cooker. Serve over hot cooked rice. Garnish, if desired.

Creamy Mustard Chicken with Leeks

MAKES: 6 servings
HANDS-ON TIME: 5 min.
TOTAL TIME: 3 hr., 13 min.

- 2 medium leeks, sliced
- 2 Tbsp. olive oil
- 6 skinned and boned chicken breasts
- ¾ tsp. salt, divided
- ¾ tsp. freshly ground pepper, divided
- ¼ cup whipping cream
- 3 Tbsp. coarse-grained mustard
- 5 garlic cloves, minced
- 1 (10¾-oz.) can cream of chicken soup
- Hot cooked rice

1. Place leeks in a lightly greased 5-qt. slow cooker.
2. Heat oil in a large nonstick skillet over medium-high heat. Sprinkle chicken with ½ tsp. each salt and pepper. Sauté chicken, in 2 batches, 2 minutes on each side or until browned. Place chicken in slow cooker.
3. Combine remaining ¼ tsp. each of salt and pepper, whipping cream, and next 3 ingredients; pour over chicken in slow cooker. Cover and cook on LOW 3 hours. Serve over hot cooked rice.

Chicken with Wine-Mushroom Gravy

MAKES: 6 servings
HANDS-ON TIME: 15 min.
TOTAL TIME: 3 hr., 15 min.

Searing chicken breasts briefly in a hot skillet gets a jump start on cooking and developing rich flavor.

- 6 skinned and boned chicken breasts
- ¼ tsp. salt
- ¼ tsp. pepper
- 1 Tbsp. olive oil
- 1 (8-oz.) package sliced fresh mushrooms
- 1 large shallot, minced
- 1 cup dry white wine
- 1 (10¾-oz.) can cream of mushroom soup
- 2 cups sour cream
- 2 Tbsp. chopped fresh parsley

1. Sprinkle chicken with salt and pepper. Heat oil in a large skillet over medium-high heat. Add chicken to skillet; cook 3 minutes on each side or until browned. Place chicken in a lightly greased 5-qt. slow cooker.
2. Add mushrooms to skillet; sauté on high heat 4 minutes or until browned. Add shallot; cook 1 more minute. Whisk in wine and soup until blended. Pour mushroom mixture over chicken.
3. Cover and cook on LOW 3 hours or until chicken is done. Remove chicken to a serving platter. Stir sour cream into juices in slow cooker; spoon over chicken. Sprinkle with parsley.

Spicy Asian Barbecued Drummettes

MAKES: 2 to 4 servings
HANDS-ON TIME: 8 min.
TOTAL TIME: 3 hr., 8 min.

Look for sriracha hot chili sauce with Asian foods on the grocery shelves. It's a staple on the kitchen table in parts of Asia—much like ketchup is in the states. The blend of chilies, garlic, sugar, salt, and vinegar is very spicy.

- 3 lb. chicken drummettes (about 20)
- ½ tsp. salt
- ¼ tsp. pepper
- 1 cup honey-barbecue sauce
- 1 Tbsp. Asian sriracha hot chili sauce
- 1 Tbsp. soy sauce
- 3 garlic cloves, pressed
  Toasted sesame seeds, sliced green onions (optional)

1. Preheat broiler.
2. Sprinkle drummettes with salt and pepper. Place on a lightly greased rack in a broiler pan. Broil 3 inches from heat 8 minutes or until browned. Place drummettes in a 4-qt. slow cooker.
3. Combine barbecue sauce and next 3 ingredients; pour over drummettes. Cover and cook on LOW 3 hours. Sprinkle with sesame seeds and sliced green onions, if desired. Serve with sauce for dipping.

Open-Faced Sloppy Toms

MAKES: 6 to 8 servings
HANDS-ON TIME: 12 min.
TOTAL TIME: 6 hr., 12 min.

Worcestershire sauce adds a rich, beefy flavor to turkey, so you won't miss the red meat. There are several brands of frozen Texas toast available, and some supermarkets prepare their own versions (ready to toast). The choice is yours.

- 2 lb. ground turkey
- 2 (8-oz.) packages frozen chopped celery, onion, and bell pepper mix
- 1 Tbsp. jarred minced garlic
- 1 (15-oz.) can tomato sauce
- 1 (6-oz.) can tomato paste
- ⅓ cup firmly packed light brown sugar
- ¼ cup cider vinegar
- 2 Tbsp. Worcestershire sauce
- 2 tsp. paprika
- ½ tsp. chili powder
- ½ tsp. salt
- ½ tsp. freshly ground pepper
- 6 to 8 slices Texas toast
  Garnishes: finely chopped red onion, dill pickle slices

1. Brown first 3 ingredients in a large skillet over medium-high heat, stirring often, 10 minutes or until turkey crumbles and is no longer pink.
2. Meanwhile, combine tomato sauce and next 8 ingredients in a 5-qt. slow cooker. Stir turkey mixture into tomato sauce mixture. Cover and cook on LOW 6 hours.
3. Prepare Texas toast according to package directions. To serve, spoon turkey mixture over toast. Garnish, if desired.

Catch of the Day

With flavors that are hard to beat, fish and shellfish offer a healthy option for weeknight fare.

Orange-Rosemary Poached Salmon

MAKES: 4 servings
HANDS-ON TIME: 9 min.
TOTAL TIME: 2 hr., 39 min.

Select fillets from the ends of the salmon. These are thinner and not as wide as those cut from the center of the fish.

- 1 cup orange juice
- 1 cup vegetable broth
- ½ cup fresh parsley leaves
- 3 Tbsp. butter
- 6 garlic cloves, pressed
- 2 (5-inch) sprigs fresh rosemary
- 1 navel orange, sliced
- 4 (6-oz.) skinless salmon fillets (½ to ¾ inch thick)
- 1 tsp. salt
- 2 tsp. orange zest
- ½ tsp. freshly ground black pepper
- ¼ tsp. ground red pepper

1. Place first 7 ingredients in a 5-qt. oval slow cooker. Cover and cook on HIGH 2 hours.
2. Meanwhile, sprinkle salmon with salt, orange zest, and peppers. Cover and chill.
3. Place salmon in liquid in slow cooker. Cover and cook 30 more minutes or until desired degree of doneness. Carefully transfer salmon to a serving platter using a large spatula. Discard cooking liquid.

Quick Slow-Cooker Favorites

Greek Snapper

MAKES: 4 servings
HANDS-ON TIME: 9 min.
TOTAL TIME: 3 hr., 9 min.

Heating the poaching liquid on HIGH for 1 hour brings it to the perfect temperature to poach the fish in 2 hours. For best results, use an oval slow cooker because that size provides more surface area to arrange the fish in a single layer.

- 1½ cups dry white wine
- 1 cup thinly sliced onion
- 3 garlic cloves, minced
- 2 bay leaves
- 4 (6-oz.) red snapper fillets (1 inch thick)
- 4 plum tomatoes, chopped
- 1 tsp. dried oregano
- ½ tsp. salt
- ½ tsp. freshly ground pepper
- 1 Tbsp. olive oil
  Hot cooked rice
- 1 oz. crumbled feta cheese
  Lemon wedges
  Garnish: fresh oregano

1. Combine first 4 ingredients in a 6-qt. oval slow cooker. Cover and cook on HIGH 1 hour.
2. Add fish to slow cooker in a single layer. Combine tomato and next 3 ingredients in a bowl; spoon over fish. Drizzle olive oil over fish. Cover and cook on LOW 2 hours.
3. Carefully remove fish from cooking liquid. Serve fish over rice. Spoon tomato mixture over fish. Sprinkle with feta cheese, and serve with lemon wedges. Garnish, if desired.

Seafood Pot Pie

MAKES: 6 servings
HANDS-ON TIME: 15 min.
TOTAL TIME: 3 hr., 15 min.

  Parchment paper
- ¼ cup butter
- 1 cup chopped onion or 1 leek, thinly sliced
- 2 tsp. jarred minced garlic
- 1 (8-oz.) package sliced baby portobello mushrooms
- ¼ cup all-purpose flour
- 1 cup half-and-half
- 1 cup chicken broth
- 1 (11-oz.) package frozen baby broccoli blend
- 1 (1-lb.) cod fillet, cut into 2-inch pieces
- ½ lb. fresh lump crabmeat, drained and picked free of shell
- ½ tsp. each salt and freshly ground pepper
- ½ (17.3-oz.) package frozen puff pastry sheets, thawed
- 1 egg yolk, beaten
- ¼ cup dry sherry

1. To make a template for pastry lid, place a 3½-qt. slow cooker lid on parchment; trace lid shape. Remove lid. Cut out parchment shape, and set aside.
2. Melt butter in a large skillet over medium-high heat. Add onion, garlic, and mushrooms; sauté 5 minutes. Whisk in flour until smooth. Cook 1 minute, whisking constantly. Gradually whisk in half-and-half and broth; cook over medium heat, whisking constantly, until thickened and bubbly. Transfer to a slow cooker. Stir in vegetables. Cover and cook on LOW 2 hours. Uncover and stir in cod, crabmeat, salt, and pepper (cooker will be almost full). Cover and cook on HIGH 1 hour or until cod flakes with a fork.
3. Preheat oven to 400°. Roll out 1 pastry sheet on a lightly floured surface until smooth. Place parchment template on pastry, and cut out pastry using a paring knife. Place pastry on a parchment paper-lined baking sheet. Brush with egg yolk. Bake at 400° for 14 to 15 minutes. Stir sherry into pot pie mixture. Top pot pie mixture with pastry lid just before serving. Serve hot.

Lowcountry Boil

MAKES: 6 servings
HANDS-ON TIME: 4 min.
TOTAL TIME: 5 hr., 34 min.

To make this South Carolina classic work in the slow cooker, you'll need the largest one available—a 7-qt. one. This is an easy dump-and-go recipe. Just pay attention to the times for adding the different ingredients.

- 12 small new potatoes (1¼ lb.)
- 1 (12-oz.) can beer
- 4 to 5 Tbsp. Old Bay seasoning
- 2 celery ribs, cut into 4-inch pieces
- 1 onion, quartered
- 2 lemons, halved
- 1 lb. kielbasa sausage, cut into 1-inch pieces
- ½ (12-ct.) package frozen corn on the cob (do not thaw)
- 2 lb. unpeeled, large raw shrimp
  Cocktail sauce

1. Place potatoes in a 7-qt. slow cooker. Add 10 cups water, beer, and next 3 ingredients. Squeeze juice from lemon halves into mixture in slow cooker; add lemon halves to slow cooker. Cover and cook on LOW 3 hours.
2. Add sausage and corn. Cover and cook on LOW 2 hours. Add shrimp; stir gently. Cover and cook on HIGH 15 minutes or until shrimp turn pink. Turn off cooker; let stand 15 minutes. Drain. Serve with cocktail sauce.

Meatless Mains

Enjoy a delicious vegetarian home-style meal at the end of the day with one of these quick-and-easy favorites.

Slow-Cooker Cajun Succotash

MAKES: 8 servings
HANDS-ON TIME: 6 min.
TOTAL TIME: 4 hr., 6 min.

If you don't want to go meatless with this recipe, stir in leftover ham.

- 2 cups frozen whole kernel corn
- 1 (14-oz.) can low-sodium fat-free vegetable broth
- 1½ tsp. Cajun seasoning
- 3 garlic cloves, minced
- 2 (16-oz.) cans red beans, drained and rinsed
- 1 (28-oz.) can diced tomatoes, undrained
- 1 (16-oz.) package frozen cut okra
- 1 large onion, chopped
  Hot cooked brown rice

1. Combine all ingredients, except rice, in a 5-qt. slow cooker. Cover and cook on LOW 4 hours. Serve over hot cooked brown rice.

Vegetable Moussaka

MAKES: 8 to 10 servings
HANDS-ON TIME: 15 min.
TOTAL TIME: 8 hr., 15 min.

- ¼ cup butter
- ¼ cup all-purpose flour
- 3 cups milk
- 1½ cups (6 oz.) shredded Parmesan cheese, divided
- 2 large eggs
- 2 egg yolks
- ½ tsp. salt
- ½ tsp. freshly ground pepper
- 1 (1½-lb.) eggplant, peeled and cubed
- 1½ cups refrigerated presliced onion
- 1 (8-oz.) package sliced baby portobello mushrooms
- 1 (20-oz.) package refrigerated sliced potatoes
- 4 cups chunky spaghetti sauce
  Garnish: fresh chopped parsley

1. Melt butter in a heavy saucepan over low heat; whisk in flour until smooth. Cook 2 minutes, whisking constantly. Gradually whisk in milk; cook over medium heat 3 to 4 minutes, whisking constantly, until mixture is thickened and bubbly. Stir in ½ cup Parmesan cheese. Gradually whisk together eggs, egg yolks, salt, and pepper in a medium bowl. Gradually stir about one-fourth of hot cheese mixture into egg mixture; add egg mixture to remaining hot cheese mixture, whisking constantly.
2. Arrange eggplant in bottom of a 7-qt. slow cooker. Layer onion, mushrooms, and potatoes over eggplant; pour spaghetti sauce over vegetables. Top with cheese sauce and remaining 1 cup cheese. Cover and cook on LOW 8 hours or until vegetables are tender. Garnish, if desired.

Savory Italian Vegetable Bread Pudding

MAKES: 6 servings
HANDS-ON TIME: 8 min.
TOTAL TIME: 3 hr., 23 min.

If you're a fan of sweet bread pudding for dessert, try this savory version. It has a similar texture, but it's cheesy and loaded with flavor.

- 1 Tbsp. olive oil
- 1 large zucchini, cubed
- 1 red bell pepper, chopped
- 1 small onion, chopped
- 6 large eggs
- 1 cup half-and-half
- 1½ tsp. Dijon mustard
- 1 tsp. dried Italian seasoning
- ½ tsp. salt
- ¼ tsp. pepper
- 1 (9.5-oz.) package frozen mozzarella and Monterey Jack cheese Texas toast, cut into 1-inch cubes
- 1 cup (4 oz.) shredded Italian six-cheese blend

1. Heat a large skillet over medium-high heat. Add oil. Sauté zucchini and next 2 ingredients in hot oil 5 minutes or until crisp-tender.
2. Whisk together eggs and next 5 ingredients.
3. Layer half of Texas toast in a lightly greased 5-qt. slow cooker; top with half of zucchini mixture and ½ cup cheese. Repeat layers. Pour egg mixture over all ingredients. Cover and cook on LOW 3 hours and 15 minutes or until set.

Mexican Beans and Vegetables with Rice

MAKES: 6 servings
HANDS-ON TIME: 9 min.
TOTAL TIME: 8 hr., 9 min.

Picante sauce is a spicy sauce that's similar to salsa. It contributes a great deal of flavor in this veggie-laden dish.

⅔ cup picante sauce
1 Tbsp. vegetable oil
1½ tsp. ground cumin
1 tsp. salt
½ tsp. dried oregano
1 (28-oz.) can diced tomatoes, undrained
1 (16-oz.) can red beans
1 (15-oz.) can black beans, drained and rinsed
1 large onion, chopped
1 large yellow squash or zucchini, cut into ½-inch pieces
1 green bell pepper, cut into ¾-inch pieces
1 red bell pepper, cut into ¾-inch pieces
Hot cooked rice
Garnishes: shredded Cheddar cheese, sour cream, chopped fresh cilantro

1. Stir together first 12 ingredients in a 4-qt. slow cooker. Cover and cook on LOW 8 hours or until vegetables are tender. Serve over hot cooked rice. Garnish, if desired.

Enchilada Casserole

MAKES: 6 servings
HANDS-ON TIME: 14 min.
TOTAL TIME: 4 hr., 19 min.

This recipe is relatively mild as is but could be spiced up with hot salsa and hot enchilada sauce. Try substituting chopped pickled jalapeños for the roasted red bell peppers for a jalapeño cornbread topping.

3 Tbsp. diced green chiles, divided
½ cup mild salsa
¼ cup chopped green onions
¼ cup chopped fresh cilantro
1 (15-oz.) can black beans, drained
1 (11-oz.) can yellow corn with red and green bell peppers, drained
1 (10-oz.) can enchilada sauce
2 large eggs
2 Tbsp. chopped jarred roasted red bell peppers
1 (8.5-oz.) package corn muffin mix
1½ cups (6 oz.) shredded Mexican four-cheese blend
Garnishes: sour cream, chopped fresh cilantro

1. Stir together 2 Tbsp. green chiles and next 6 ingredients in a lightly greased 4-qt. slow cooker. Cover and cook on LOW 3 hours.
2. Whisk eggs in a medium bowl; stir in remaining 1 Tbsp. green chiles, roasted bell peppers, and muffin mix. Spoon batter over bean mixture in slow cooker. Cover and cook on LOW 1 hour or until cornbread is done.
3. Sprinkle cheese over cornbread. Increase heat to HIGH; cover and cook 5 minutes or until cheese melts. Spoon into shallow bowls. Garnish, if desired.

Mushroom-Stuffed Red Peppers

MAKES: 6 servings
HANDS-ON TIME: 15 min.
TOTAL TIME: 4 hr., 15 min.

An oval 6- or 7-qt. slow cooker works best for this recipe to ensure that all the peppers can be set in a single layer in the cooker. Place raw peppers in the insert before beginning the recipe to make sure there's enough room for all to stand upright. Serve a little of the leftover pasta sauce for dipping the breadsticks.

1 cup fire-roasted tomato and garlic pasta sauce
6 medium-size red bell peppers
4 cups coarsely chopped baby portobello mushrooms
½ cup (2 oz.) shredded Parmesan cheese, divided
⅓ cup finely chopped sweet onion
⅓ cup soft, fresh breadcrumbs
1 tsp. chopped fresh thyme
½ tsp. salt
¼ tsp. freshly ground pepper
1 (16-oz.) can navy beans, drained
1 (8.8-oz.) package precooked brown rice
Garnish: fresh thyme

1. Pour pasta sauce into bottom of a 7-qt. oval slow cooker.
2. Cut ½ inch from stem end of each bell pepper. Remove and discard seeds and membranes.
3. Combine mushrooms, ¼ cup cheese, and next 7 ingredients in a large bowl, stirring well. Spoon mushroom mixture into bell peppers. Place peppers in a single layer in slow cooker. Top with remaining ¼ cup cheese. Cover and cook on LOW 4 hours or until peppers are tender. Garnish, if desired.

Soups and Stews

Always satisfying, these hearty recipes simmer all day and have been perfected for fast preparation and incredible flavor.

Corn and Potato Chowder

MAKES: 4 to 6 servings
HANDS-ON TIME: 15 min.
TOTAL TIME: 8 hr., 15 min.

Cook bacon in the microwave, or substitute packaged fully cooked bacon, prepared according to package directions.

- 1 lb. baking potatoes, peeled and cut into ¼-inch cubes (about 2 cups)
- 1 (14.75-oz.) can cream-style corn
- 1 (14.5-oz.) can diced tomatoes
- 1 (14-oz.) can chicken broth
- ½ cup chopped onion
- ½ cup coarsely chopped celery
- ¾ tsp. dried basil
- ½ tsp. salt
- ¼ tsp. pepper
- 1 bay leaf
- 1 cup whipping cream
- ¼ cup butter
- 4 bacon slices, cooked and crumbled
  Chopped green onions

1. Stir together first 10 ingredients in a 5-qt. slow cooker. Cover and cook on LOW 8 hours or until potato is tender. Add whipping cream and butter, stirring until butter melts. Discard bay leaf. Ladle into bowls; sprinkle each serving with bacon and chopped green onions.

Parsnip and Pear Soup

MAKES: 6 to 8 servings
HANDS-ON TIME: 15 min.
TOTAL TIME: 7 hr., 15 min.

A parsnip is a creamy-white, carrot-shaped root vegetable with a unique piquant, yet sweet, flavor. Avoid parsnips that are limp or have brown spots.

- 1 Tbsp. olive oil
- ½ cup refrigerated prechopped onion
- 4 garlic cloves, minced
- 5 cups chicken broth
- 2 tsp. chopped fresh rosemary
- ½ tsp. salt
- ½ tsp. freshly ground pepper
- 2 lb. parsnips, peeled and chopped
- 2 ripe pears, peeled and chopped
- ½ cup half-and-half
  Garnishes: cooked and crumbled bacon, fresh rosemary

1. Heat oil in a large skillet over medium-high heat. Add onion and garlic; sauté 3 minutes or until tender.
2. Combine onion mixture, broth, and next 5 ingredients in a 4-qt. slow cooker. Cover and cook on HIGH for 7 hours.
3. Stir half-and-half into soup. Process soup, in batches, in a blender until smooth, stopping to scrape down sides as necessary. Pour soup into bowls. Garnish, if desired.

Three-Cheese Broccoli Soup

MAKES: 8 servings
HANDS-ON TIME: 15 min.
TOTAL TIME: 4 hr., 15 min.

Stirring the cheese cubes into the soup first helps the other cheeses melt smoother when they're added.

- ¼ cup butter
- 1 large onion, chopped
- ¼ cup all-purpose flour
- 1 (12-oz.) can evaporated milk
- 1 (32-oz.) container chicken broth
- ¼ tsp. salt
- ½ tsp. freshly ground pepper
- 1 (14-oz.) package frozen baby broccoli florets
- 1 (8-oz.) package pasteurized prepared cheese product, cubed
- 1½ cups (6 oz.) shredded extra-sharp Cheddar cheese
- 1 cup shredded Parmesan cheese
  Garnish: shredded extra-sharp Cheddar cheese

1. Melt butter in a large skillet over medium-high heat. Add onion. Sauté 4 minutes or until tender. Stir in flour. Cook, stirring constantly, 1 minute. Gradually stir in milk until smooth. Pour milk mixture into a lightly greased 4-qt. slow cooker. Stir in broth and next 3 ingredients. Cover and cook on LOW 4 hours or until bubbly.
2. Add cheese cubes, stirring until cubes melt. Add Cheddar cheese and Parmesan cheese, stirring until cheeses melt. Garnish, if desired. Serve immediately.

Quick Slow-Cooker Favorites

French Onion Soup

MAKES: 8 to 10 servings
HANDS-ON TIME: 8 min.
TOTAL TIME: 8 hr., 23 min.

This soup makes a large volume and freezes well if not eaten all at once.

- 6 large sweet onions, thinly sliced
- ¼ cup butter, melted
- ½ tsp. salt
- ½ tsp. freshly ground pepper
- 1 (32-oz.) container beef broth
- 2 (10½-oz.) cans beef consommé
- ¼ cup dry white wine
- 1 tsp. fresh thyme leaves
- 8 to 10 (½-inch-thick) French bread baguette slices
- ½ cup (2 ounces) shredded Gruyère cheese
- Garnish: fresh thyme

1. Combine first 4 ingredients in a lightly greased 5- to 6-qt. slow cooker. Cover and cook on LOW 8 hours.
2. Stir broth and next 3 ingredients into onion mixture. Cover and cook 15 more minutes or until hot.
3. Meanwhile, preheat broiler with oven rack 3 inches from heat. Sprinkle baguette slices with shredded cheese; place on a lightly greased baking sheet. Broil 1 to 2 minutes or until cheese melts. Serve soup with cheese toasts. Garnish, if desired.

Roasted Mushroom Soup with Sourdough Croutons

MAKES: 6 to 8 servings
HANDS-ON TIME: 15 min.
TOTAL TIME: 3 hr., 30 min.

- 4 (4-oz.) packages sliced fresh gourmet mushroom blend
- 2 (8-oz.) packages sliced fresh mushrooms
- 4 Tbsp. olive oil, divided
- 1 tsp. kosher salt
- ½ tsp. freshly ground pepper
- 2 (8-oz.) containers refrigerated prechopped celery, onion, and bell pepper mix
- 1 Tbsp. jarred minced garlic
- 1 cup dry white wine
- 2 cups vegetable broth
- ½ tsp. ground sage
- ¼ tsp. ground nutmeg
- 1 cup heavy cream
- ¼ cup all-purpose flour
- 4 (1-inch-thick) sourdough bread slices, cut into 1-inch cubes
- Garnish: chopped fresh chives

1. Preheat broiler with oven rack 5½ inches from heat. Spread mushrooms in a single layer on an aluminum foil-lined rimmed baking sheet. Drizzle with 2 Tbsp. olive oil; sprinkle with salt and pepper. Broil 12 minutes or until browned. Heat 1 Tbsp. oil in a skillet over medium-high heat. Add celery mixture and garlic; sauté 3 minutes. Stir in wine, and cook 5 minutes or until reduced by half.
2. Combine mushrooms and juices, onion mixture, broth, and next 2 ingredients in a 5-qt. slow cooker. Cover and cook on HIGH 3 hours. Stir cream into soup. Stir together flour and ¼ cup water until smooth. Stir into soup.
3. Cover and cook 15 more minutes or until thickened. During last 30 minutes of cook time, preheat oven to 350°. Toss bread cubes with remaining 1 Tbsp. oil. Place on a baking sheet. Bake at 350° for 10 minutes. Garnish, if desired.

Smokehouse Chicken and Vegetable Stew

MAKES: 8 servings
HANDS-ON TIME: 5 min.
TOTAL TIME: 8 hr., 5 min.

Don't be tempted to add more liquid because as the vegetables cook, they release enough liquid to make this thick stew the right consistency.

- 1 cup chicken broth
- ½ cup sweet and spicy barbecue sauce
- 1¼ cups refrigerated prechopped tricolor bell pepper
- 1 cup frozen baby lima beans
- 2 Tbsp. Worcestershire sauce
- ½ tsp. salt
- ½ tsp. pepper
- 2 lb. pulled smoked chicken
- 1 (26-oz.) jar fire-roasted tomato and garlic pasta sauce
- 1 (16-oz.) package frozen mixed vegetables
- 1 (8-oz.) container refrigerated prechopped onion

1. Combine all ingredients in a 5-qt. slow cooker. Cover and cook on HIGH 8 hours.

Quick Slow-Cooker Favorites

Black-eyed Pea Soup

MAKES: 6 to 8 servings
HANDS-ON TIME: 11 min.
TOTAL TIME: 20 hr., 9 min.

If you have the up-front time, you can use the following method to soak the peas for this soup. Place peas in a Dutch oven; add water 2 inches above peas. Bring to a boil. Boil 1 minute; cover, remove from heat, and let stand 1 hour. Drain. Proceed as directed in recipe.

- 1 (16-oz.) package dried black-eyed peas
- 6 bacon slices
- 1 (8-oz.) container refrigerated prechopped onion
- 1 medium-size red bell pepper, chopped
- 1 (48-oz.) container chicken broth
- 1 Tbsp. jarred minced garlic
- 1 (14.5-oz.) can diced tomatoes and zesty mild green chiles, undrained
  Garnish: chopped green onions

1. Rinse and sort peas according to package directions. Place peas in a Dutch oven. Cover with water 2 inches above peas; let soak 8 hours. Drain. Place peas in a 6-qt. slow cooker.
2. Cook bacon in a large skillet over medium-high heat 5 to 7 minutes or until crisp; remove bacon, and drain on paper towels, reserving drippings in skillet. Coarsely crumble bacon.
3. Add onion to drippings in skillet; cook, stirring constantly, 4 minutes or until tender. Stir bacon, onion, bell pepper, and next 3 ingredients into peas in slow cooker. Cover and cook on LOW 12 hours or until peas are tender. Garnish, if desired.

Spicy Chicken Chili Verde

MAKES: 6 servings
HANDS-ON TIME: 8 min.
TOTAL TIME: 10 hr., 8 min.

Crushing some of the beans at the end of cooking slightly thickens the chili and gives it more body and a creamy texture.

- 1 lb. skinned and boned chicken thighs, cut into 1-inch pieces
- 1 Tbsp. vegetable oil
- 1 (8-oz.) container refrigerated prechopped onion
- 1 Tbsp. jarred minced garlic
- 2 cups chicken broth
- 1 cup salsa verde
- 1 cup frozen whole kernel corn
- 1 tsp. ground cumin
- 1 tsp. hot sauce
- ½ tsp. pepper
- 1 (15.5-oz.) can cannellini beans, drained

1. Cook chicken in hot oil in a medium skillet over medium-high heat 4 minutes or until browned, stirring often. Transfer chicken to a 4-qt. slow cooker. Add onion and garlic to drippings in skillet; sauté until vegetables are tender. Add broth, stirring to loosen particles from bottom of skillet. Add broth mixture to chicken in slow cooker. Stir in salsa and next 4 ingredients. Cover and cook on LOW 10 hours.
2. Add beans. Mash beans in soup with a potato masher or back of a spoon until desired consistency.

Tomatillo-Mushroom Chili

MAKES: 8 servings
HANDS-ON TIME: 10 min.
TOTAL TIME: 3 hr., 17 min.

Store tomatillos in a paper bag in the refrigerator for up to one month.

- 1 Tbsp. extra virgin olive oil
- 6 tomatillos, husks removed and coarsely chopped
- 2 onions, coarsely chopped
- 2 garlic cloves, minced
- 1 lb. shiitake mushrooms, stems removed and coarsely chopped
- 2 Tbsp. chili powder
- 1 tsp. ground cumin
- 3 cups organic vegetable broth
- 2 (15-oz.) cans black beans, drained
- 1 (14.5-oz.) can fire-roasted diced tomatoes
  Garnishes: shredded Cheddar cheese, chopped green onions

1. Heat a large skillet over medium-high heat; add oil. Sauté tomatillos, onion, and garlic in hot oil 7 minutes or until tender. Add mushrooms, chili powder, and cumin; sauté 3 minutes.
2. Transfer vegetable mixture to a 5-qt. slow cooker; stir in broth and next 2 ingredients. Cover and cook on LOW 3 hours. Garnish, if desired.

Holiday Favorites

Make-Ahead Progressive Dinner

A progressive dinner lets hosts divide and conquer. Setting the scene and mastering a single dish is all that's required before the party moves to the next home on the menu.

Game Plan

UP TO I WEEK AHEAD:
- Prepare Molasses Vinaigrette; cover and chill.
- Chop vegetables for Roasted Root Vegetables with Praline Crunch, and store in a large airtight container.
- Prepare Praline Crunch; store in an airtight container.

2 DAYS AHEAD:
- Prepare Mint-Garlic Mayonnaise, cover, and chill.
- Cook and mash red potatoes; cover and chill.
- Prepare poached pears; cover and chill.

I DAY AHEAD:
- Combine and chill ingredients for Sweet Tea and Limoncello Martinis.
- Prepare and brine game hens.
- Prepare patties for Lamb Sliders; cover and chill.
- Prepare Parmesan-Pancetta Crisps; store in an airtight container.
- Prepare trifle; cover and chill.

4 HOURS AHEAD:
- Remove hens from brine. Tie with strings and arrange on baking sheets; chill.

2 HOURS AHEAD:
- Prepare Roasted Meyer Lemon-Peppercorn Game Hens. Cover and keep warm.
- Stuff pork loin chops.

I HOUR AHEAD:
- Prepare Lamb Sliders.
- Prepare Roasted Root Vegetables.

30 MINUTES AHEAD:
- Fry sage and garlic for Crispy Sage and Garlic Smashed Baby Red Potatoes.

10 MINUTES AHEAD:
- Arrange salads on serving plates.
- Reheat potatoes in microwave.

WHEN GUESTS ARRIVE:
- Finish Sun-dried Tomato and Goat Cheese-Stuffed Pork Loin Chops.

Menu

SERVES 12

Sweet Tea and Limoncello Martinis

Lamb Sliders with Mint-Garlic Mayonnaise

Hearts of Romaine with Molasses Vinaigrette and Parmesan-Pancetta Crisps

Roasted Meyer Lemon-Peppercorn Game Hens

Sun-Dried Tomato and Goat Cheese-Stuffed Pork Loin Chops

Crispy Sage and Garlic Smashed Baby Red Potatoes

Roasted Root Vegetables with Praline Crunch

Gingersnap and Poached Pear Trifle

Chocolate Velvet Cake with Cream Cheese Frosting

Sweet Tea and Limoncello Martinis

MAKES: 12 servings
HANDS-ON TIME: 4 min.
TOTAL TIME: 2 hr., 4 min.

- 6 cups cold sweetened tea
- 3 cups vodka
- 1½ cups limoncello
- Garnish: lemon twists

1. Combine first 3 ingredients in a large pitcher. Cover and chill thoroughly. Serve in chilled martini glasses. Garnish, if desired.
2. For each serving, fill a martini shaker half full of crushed ice. Add ¾ cup tea mixture. Cover with lid, and shake until thoroughly chilled. Remove lid, and strain into a chilled martini glass. Garnish, if desired, and serve immediately.

Lamb Sliders

MAKES: 2 dozen
HANDS-ON TIME: 23 min.
TOTAL TIME: 27 min.

Regular slider buns were too big for these tiny sandwiches, so we used dinner rolls instead.

- 1 large egg
- 1 lb. ground lamb
- ½ cup soft, fresh white-wheat breadcrumbs (1 slice)
- 3 Tbsp. chopped fresh flat-leaf parsley
- ½ tsp. kosher salt
- ½ tsp. freshly ground pepper
- 2 garlic cloves, minced
- 2 shallots, minced
- 1 English cucumber
- 24 (2½-inch) dinner rolls, halved and toasted
- Mint-Garlic Mayonnaise

1. Preheat broiler with oven rack 3 inches from heat. Whisk egg in a medium bowl. Add lamb and next 6 ingredients; combine, using hands. Shape mixture into 24 (2-inch) patties. Place patties on a lightly greased jelly-roll pan. Broil 3 to 4 minutes or until done.
2. Meanwhile, cut 24 thin slices from cucumber, reserving remaining cucumber for another use.
3. Spread cut sides of rolls with Mint-Garlic Mayonnaise. Place patties on bottoms of rolls; top with cucumber slices and roll tops.

Mint-Garlic Mayonnaise

MAKES: about ½ cup
HANDS-ON TIME: 5 min.
TOTAL TIME: 5 min.

- ½ cup mayonnaise
- 1½ Tbsp. minced fresh mint
- 1½ tsp. fresh lemon juice
- ½ tsp. lemon zest
- ¼ tsp. kosher salt
- ⅛ tsp. ground red pepper
- 2 garlic cloves, minced

1. Stir together all ingredients in a small bowl. Cover and chill until ready to use.
NOTE: Cover and chill patties up to 24 hours ahead. Prepare, cover, and chill Mint-Garlic Mayonnaise up to 2 days ahead.

Hearts of Romaine with Molasses Vinaigrette and Parmesan-Pancetta Crisps

MAKES: 12 servings
HANDS-ON TIME: 18 minutes
TOTAL TIME: 1 hr., 14 min.

- 6 romaine lettuce hearts
- Ice water
- Molasses Vinaigrette
- Parmesan-Pancetta Crisps

1. Cut lettuce hearts in half lengthwise, leaving stem intact. Plunge into ice water to cover; let stand 30 minutes. Drain well, and pat dry with paper towels. Cover and chill until ready to serve.
2. Trim 3 inches from stem end of each lettuce heart half, and arrange on each of 12 serving plates. Drizzle with desired amount of Molasses Vinaigrette, and serve immediately with Parmesan-Pancetta Crisps.

Molasses Vinaigrette

MAKES: 2½ cups
HANDS-ON TIME: 5 min.
TOTAL TIME: 5 min.

- ½ cup sherry vinegar
- ½ cup chopped fresh flat-leaf parsley
- ¼ cup light molasses
- 2 tsp. salt
- 1 tsp. freshly ground pepper
- 3 shallots, minced
- 1 cup extra virgin olive oil

1. Combine first 6 ingredients in a medium bowl; gradually whisk in olive oil. Cover and chill up to 1 week.

Parmesan-Pancetta Crisps

MAKES: 28
HANDS-ON TIME: 14 min.
TOTAL TIME: 30 min.

- 2 oz. (⅛-inch-thick) slices pancetta, minced (about 6 Tbsp.)
- 4 oz. Parmesan cheese, grated
- Parchment paper

1. Preheat oven to 400°. Cook pancetta in a large nonstick skillet over medium-high heat 7 minutes or until crisp, stirring occasionally; remove pancetta, and drain on paper towels.
2. Spoon cheese by about 1 Tbsp. into 28 portions 2 inches apart on large baking sheets lined with parchment paper; flatten each portion slightly, and sprinkle with pancetta. Bake at 400° for 5 to 8 minutes or until lightly browned and crisp. Immediately transfer crisps to a wire rack, using a spatula; let cool completely.

Roasted Meyer Lemon-Peppercorn Game Hens

MAKES: 12 servings
HANDS-ON TIME: 1 hr., 5 min.
TOTAL TIME: 9 hr., 55 min.

These succulent little birds are worth the wait; the overnight brining makes them tender and juicy.

- 1 cup kosher salt
- 1 cup sugar
- 2 Meyer lemons, thinly sliced
- 2 tsp. freshly ground mixed peppercorns*
- 4 bay leaves
- 3 qt. ice water
- 12 (1½-lb.) Cornish hens
- 2 Tbsp. Meyer lemon zest
- 2 Tbsp. freshly ground mixed peppercorns
- ¼ cup butter, melted

1. Bring 1 qt. water, kosher salt, and next 4 ingredients to a boil in a large stockpot over medium-high heat. Reduce heat, and simmer 30 minutes. Stir in 3 qt. ice water. Rinse hens; pat dry, and add to brine. Cover and chill 8 hours or overnight.
2. Preheat oven to 425°. Remove hens from brine; pat dry. Tuck wing tips under. Tie legs together with string. Stir together lemon zest and 2 Tbsp. mixed peppercorns; rub spice mixture on all sides of hens. Arrange hens on racks in 2 large foil-lined rimmed baking sheets. Brush with melted butter.
3. Bake at 425° for 50 minutes or until hens are done. Cover and let stand 15 minutes before serving.
*We tested with Alessi Tip N' Grind Whole Mixed Peppercorns.

MAKE-AHEAD: Brine hens up to 2 days ahead. Remove from brine; pat dry, and prepare for baking. Cover and chill until ready to bake.

Sun-Dried Tomato and Goat Cheese-Stuffed Pork Loin Chops

MAKES: 8 servings
HANDS-ON TIME: 31 min.
TOTAL TIME: 1 hr., 56 min.

- 1 Tbsp. oil from sun-dried tomatoes
- 8 sun-dried tomatoes in oil, drained and minced
- 2 garlic cloves, minced
- 1 tsp. salt, divided
- 1 tsp. freshly ground pepper, divided
- 2 tsp. minced fresh thyme, divided
- ½ cup Japanese breadcrumbs (panko)
- ½ cup (4 oz.) crumbled goat cheese
- 2 Tbsp. shredded Parmesan cheese
- 8 (1-inch-thick) boneless pork loin chops
- 2 Tbsp. olive oil, divided
- 2 cups chicken broth
- 2 tsp. lemon zest
- 4 tsp. Dijon mustard
- 2 Tbsp. fresh lemon juice
- 2 Tbsp. butter

1. Heat sun-dried tomato oil in a large nonstick skillet; add tomatoes, garlic, ½ tsp. salt, ½ tsp. pepper, and 1 tsp. thyme. Sauté 2 minutes; transfer tomato mixture to a bowl. Stir in breadcrumbs and cheeses.
2. Cut a slit (about 2 inches deep and 3 inches long; do not cut in half) in thick side of each pork chop to form a pocket. Spoon 2 Tbsp. goat cheese mixture into each pocket. Pinch edges to seal. Sprinkle pork with remaining ½ tsp. salt and ½ tsp. pepper. Cover and chill 1 hour.
3. Preheat oven to 450°. Heat 1 Tbsp. olive oil in a large nonstick skillet over medium-high heat. Add half of pork; cook 2 minutes on each side. Place pork on a cooling rack in a rimmed baking sheet. Repeat procedure with remaining oil and pork. Bake at 450° for 25 minutes or until

a meat thermometer inserted in center registers 155°.
4. Meanwhile, stir together remaining 1 tsp. thyme, 2 cups chicken broth, and next 3 ingredients in a small bowl; add to pan, stirring to loosen browned bits. Bring to a boil; reduce heat, and simmer 7 minutes or until slightly thickened. Stir in butter. Serve pork with sauce.

MAKE-AHEAD: Prepare and chill pork chops as directed, setting drippings aside. When guests arrive, place pork in oven to bake. Reheat drippings while pork bakes; finish sauce.

Crispy Sage and Garlic Smashed Baby Red Potatoes

MAKES: 12 servings
HANDS-ON TIME: 10 min.
TOTAL TIME: 54 min.

- 6 lb. small red potatoes, halved (about 40 potatoes)
- 2 cups milk
- ⅓ cup butter, melted
- 2 tsp. kosher salt
- 1½ tsp. freshly ground pepper
- 4 garlic cloves, minced
- ½ cup extra virgin olive oil
- 12 large garlic cloves, thinly sliced
- 20 large fresh sage leaves

1. Cook potatoes in boiling salted water to cover in a large Dutch oven 20 minutes or until potato is tender. Drain; return potatoes to pan.
2. Combine milk and next 4 ingredients in a 4-cup glass measuring cup. Microwave at HIGH 2 to 3 minutes or until butter melts. Add milk mixture to potato; mash with a potato masher to desired consistency. Cover and keep warm.

3. Heat oil in a small skillet over medium-low heat; add garlic slices, and fry 2 to 3 minutes or until lightly browned. Remove garlic from oil, using a slotted spoon; drain on paper towels.

4. Increase heat to medium; add half of sage leaves. Fry 45 seconds or until crisp and browned. Remove sage leaves from oil, using a slotted spoon. Drain on paper towels. Repeat procedure with remaining half of sage leaves. Remove pan from heat; let oil cool 10 minutes.

5. Crumble sage leaves slightly. Before serving, drizzle oil over potatoes; sprinkle with sage leaves and garlic slices.

MAKE-AHEAD: Cook and mash potato as directed up to 2 days ahead. Cover and chill. Just before serving, reheat potato in microwave, and fry garlic slices and sage leaves to complete recipe as directed.

Roasted Root Vegetables with Praline Crunch

MAKES: 12 servings
HANDS-ON TIME: 5 min.
TOTAL TIME: 1 hr., 33 min.

- 2 **lb. carrots, peeled, halved lengthwise, and cut into 2-inch pieces**
- 2 **lb. parsnips, peeled, halved lengthwise, and cut into 2-inch pieces**
- 2 **large red onions, halved lengthwise and cut into 1-inch wedges**
- ½ **cup extra virgin olive oil**
- 1 **Tbsp. kosher salt**
- ½ **tsp. freshly ground pepper**
  Praline Crunch

1. Preheat oven to 425°. Combine first 6 ingredients in a large bowl, tossing to coat vegetables. Arrange in a single layer on 2 foil-lined rimmed baking sheets. Bake at 425° for 30 minutes. Stir and bake for 10 more minutes. Remove from oven. Sprinkle with Praline Crunch.

Praline Crunch

MAKES: about 2 cups
HANDS-ON TIME: 5 min.
TOTAL TIME: 45 min.

- 1 **cup sugar**
- ¾ **cup chopped pecans**
- 1 **tsp. kosher salt**

1. Lightly grease a large baking sheet. Combine sugar and ¼ cup water in a medium skillet; cook over medium-high heat 8 minutes or until sugar caramelizes, tipping pan to incorporate mixture.

2. Stir in pecans and salt; remove from heat. Quickly spread mixture onto prepared pan. Cool completely. Peel Praline Crunch off baking sheet, break into large pieces, and chop. Store in an airtight container for up to 1 week.

MAKE-AHEAD: Chop vegetables and store in a large airtight container in the refrigerator up to 3 days ahead. Prepare and store Praline Crunch.

Gingersnap and Poached Pear Trifle

MAKES: 10 servings
HANDS-ON TIME: 32 min.
TOTAL TIME: 8 hr., 32 min.

- 6 **large ripe pears, peeled, cored, and cut into 1-inch cubes**
- 2 **cups Chardonnay or other dry white wine**
- ½ **cup sugar**
- 1 **(3-inch) cinnamon stick**
- 1 **vanilla bean, split lengthwise**
- 1 **whole clove**
- 1 **(4.6-oz) package vanilla-flavored cook-and-serve pudding mix**
- 3 **cups milk**
- 1½ **cups heavy cream**
- 3 **Tbsp. sugar**
- 1 **(1-lb.) package gingersnaps**

1. Bring pears and next 5 ingredients to a boil in a large saucepan over medium heat; reduce heat, and simmer 14 minutes or until pears are tender, stirring occasionally. Remove from heat. Transfer pears to a medium bowl, using a slotted spoon. Reserve pear syrup, discarding cinnamon stick and clove. Cover and chill syrup and pears 8 hours.

2. Prepare pudding mix according to package directions, using 3 cups milk. Place plastic wrap directly onto warm pudding (to prevent a film from forming), and chill thoroughly.

3. Scrape vanilla bean seeds into chilled pears, discarding vanilla bean.

4. Beat cream and 3 Tbsp. sugar at high speed with an electric mixer until stiff peaks form.

5. Arrange one-fourth of gingersnaps in a 3-qt. trifle bowl, dipping each cookie quickly into pear syrup. Sprinkle with one-third of pears. Top with one-third of vanilla pudding and ½ cup sweetened whipped cream. Repeat layers twice, ending with gingersnaps and remaining sweetened whipped cream. Cover and chill 3 to 8 hours.

NOTE: We tested with Murray Gingersnaps.

Chocolate Velvet Cake with Cream Cheese Frosting

MAKES: 10 to 12 servings
HANDS-ON TIME: 40 min.
TOTAL TIME: 3 hr., 2 min., including frosting

To make chocolate curls, microwave a large block of premium chocolate (we used Callebaut) on MEDIUM (50% power) for 30 seconds or until slightly warm. Pull a vegetable peeler along the block, making curls. (pictued on cover)

1½ **cups semisweet chocolate morsels**
½ **cup butter, softened**
1 **(16-oz.) package light brown sugar**
3 **large eggs**
2 **cups all-purpose flour**
1 **tsp. baking soda**
½ **tsp. salt**
1 **(8-oz.) container sour cream**
1 **cup hot water**
2 **tsp. vanilla extract**
    Cream Cheese Frosting
    Garnishes: chocolate curls, fresh raspberries

1. Preheat oven to 350°. Microwave chocolate morsels in a microwave-safe bowl at HIGH 1 to 1½ minutes or until melted and smooth, stirring at 30-second intervals.
2. Beat butter and sugar at medium speed with an electric mixer until creamy, beating about 5 minutes or until well blended. Add eggs, 1 at a time, beating just until blended after each addition. Add melted chocolate, beating just until blended.
3. Sift together flour, baking soda, and salt. Gradually add to chocolate mixture alternately with sour cream, beginning and ending with flour mixture. Beat at low speed just until blended after each addition. Gradually add 1 cup hot water in a slow, steady stream, beating at low speed just until blended. Stir in vanilla.

4. Spoon batter into 3 greased and floured 8-inch round cake pans. Bake at 350° for 32 to 34 minutes or until a wooden pick inserted in center comes out clean. Cool in pans on wire racks 10 minutes; remove from pans to wire racks, and cool completely (about 1 hour). Wrap each cooled cake layer in plastic wrap, and freeze 30 minutes.
5. Spread 1 cup Cream Cheese Frosting on 1 cake layer. Top with a second cake layer; spread with 1 cup frosting. Top with third cake layer. Spread remaining frosting on top and sides of cake. Garnish, if desired.

Cream Cheese Frosting

MAKES: 5½ cups
HANDS-ON TIME: 10 minutes
TOTAL TIME: 10 minutes

2 **(8-oz.) packages cream cheese, softened**
¾ **cup butter, softened**
¼ **tsp. salt**
2 **tsp. vanilla extract**
2 **(16-oz.) packages powdered sugar**

1. Beat first 4 ingredients at medium speed with an electric mixer until creamy. Gradually add sugar, beating until blended.

Christmas Tree-Cutting Party

Let the tree trimming begin! Make a tradition of this simple menu of soul-satisfying comforts to be enjoyed while you select the pick of the forest.

Menu

SERVES 8 TO 10

Chunky Cowboy Chili

Cornmeal Cheddar Scones

Cinnamon-Pecan Cookie S'mores

Hot Mocha

Game Plan

1 DAY AHEAD:
- Prepare Chunky Cowboy Chili. Cover and chill in an airtight container.
- Bake cookies for Cinnamon-Pecan Cookie S'mores.
- Organize marshmallows, chocolate bars, and roasting sticks for s'mores.

2 HOURS AHEAD:
- Prepare Cornmeal Cheddar Scones; wrap tightly in plastic wrap.

1 HOUR AHEAD:
- Prepare Hot Mocha and pour into a thermos.
- Reheat chili and pour into a thermos.
- Pack in a picnic basket.

Chunky Cowboy Chili

editor's favorite • make-ahead

MAKES: about 14 cups
HANDS-ON TIME: 52 min.
TOTAL TIME: 2 hr., 22 min.

The flavor of this chili, like many soups and stews, is better the next day.

- 2 **Tbsp. canola oil, divided**
- 4 **lb. boneless chuck roast, cut into ½-inch pieces**
- 1 **large onion, chopped**
- 1 **green bell pepper, chopped**
- 2 **garlic cloves, minced**
- 1 **Tbsp. Worcestershire sauce**
- 2 **Tbsp. tomato paste**
- 2 **tsp. chili powder**
- ¼ **tsp. ground cumin**
- 2 **(14.5-oz.) cans petite diced tomatoes with jalapeños, undrained**
- 2 **(8-oz.) cans tomato sauce**
- 1 **(16-oz.) can red beans**
- 1 **(15-oz.) can whole kernel corn, drained**
- 1 **(12-oz.) bottle dark beer**

1. Heat 1 Tbsp. oil in a large Dutch oven over medium-high heat; add half of beef. Cook 12 minutes or until dark brown, turning after 5 minutes. Remove beef from pan, and keep warm. Repeat procedure with remaining half of beef.
2. Add remaining 1 Tbsp. oil to pan. Add onion, bell pepper, and garlic to pan. Sauté 5 minutes or until tender. Return beef and accumulated juices to pan. Stir in 1 cup water, Worcestershire sauce, and remaining ingredients. Bring to a boil; cover, reduce heat, and simmer 1 hour and 30 minutes or until beef is tender and chili is thick.
NOTE: We tested with AmberBock Dark Beer.

Cornmeal Cheddar Scones

MAKES: 15 scones
HANDS-ON TIME: 20 min.
TOTAL TIME: 40 min.

Cornmeal provides a little crunch to these tender, cheesy brunch favorites. They also pair well with soups, stews, chili, and fried chicken.

- 2 **cups all-purpose flour**
- ¾ **cup stone-ground cornmeal**
- 1 **Tbsp. sugar**
- 1 **Tbsp. baking powder**
- ½ **tsp. baking soda**
- ½ **tsp. salt**
- ⅛ **tsp. ground red pepper**
- ¾ **cup unsalted butter, cut into chunks**
- 1 **cup (4 oz.) shredded extra-sharp Cheddar cheese**
- 1 **large egg**
- ¾ **cup buttermilk**
  Parchment paper
  Unsalted butter, melted
  Sea salt

1. Preheat oven to 425°. Place first 7 ingredients in a food processor. Add ¾ cup butter; pulse 3 or 4 times or until mixture resembles coarse meal. Place flour mixture in a large bowl; stir in cheese. Whisk together egg and buttermilk until blended. Make a well in center of dry ingredients; add egg mixture, stirring just until dry ingredients are moistened.
2. Turn dough out onto a floured surface; knead lightly 3 or 4 times. Pat dough into a 10- x 7-inch rectangle. Cut into 15 squares. Place squares on a parchment paper-lined baking sheet. Brush tops with melted unsalted butter, and sprinkle with sea salt. Bake at 425° for 20 minutes or until golden.

Cinnamon-Pecan Cookie S'mores

MAKES: 8 servings
HANDS-ON TIME: 14 min.
TOTAL TIME: 33 min.

This variation on the campfire staple is over the top, thanks to the nutty homemade cookies that replace the graham crackers.

- ½ cup butter, softened
- ½ cup firmly packed dark brown sugar
- ¼ cup granulated sugar
- 1 large egg
- 1½ tsp. vanilla extract
- 1¼ cups all-purpose flour
- 1 tsp. baking powder
- 1 tsp. ground cinnamon
- ¼ tsp. salt
- 1 cup coarsely chopped pecans, toasted
- 1 (4-oz.) bittersweet chocolate baking bar
- 8 large marshmallows

1. Preheat oven to 350°. Beat butter at medium speed with an electric mixer until creamy; gradually add sugars, beating well. Add egg and vanilla, beating well.
2. Combine flour and next 3 ingredients; add to butter mixture. Beat at low speed until blended. Stir in pecans.
3. Divide dough into 16 equal portions; roll each portion into a ball. Place balls 1 inch apart on lightly greased baking sheets; flatten slightly.
4. Bake at 350° for 16 minutes or until lightly browned. Cool cookies on pans 1 minute. Transfer cookies to wire racks. Cool completely.
5. Preheat broiler. Separate chocolate bar into 8 squares. Place a chocolate square on flat side of each of 8 cookies.

6. Place marshmallows on a baking sheet. Broil 3 minutes or until puffed and toasted. Immediately transfer marshmallows to tops of chocolate squares, using a small spatula. Top marshmallows with remaining cookies, flat sides down; press down gently.
NOTE: We tested with Ghirardelli Bittersweet Chocolate Baking Bar.

Hot Mocha

MAKES: about 10 cups
HANDS-ON TIME: 12 min.
TOTAL TIME: 12 min.

Whether the Hot Mudslide version or the nonalcoholic one, this comforting drink will warm you down to your toes.

- 1 cup unsweetened cocoa
- 1 cup sugar
- ¼ cup instant espresso*
- 2 cups half-and-half
- 6 cups milk
- 4 tsp. vanilla extract
  Sweetened whipped cream
  Chocolate syrup

1. Whisk together first 4 ingredients in a large saucepan. Cook, whisking constantly, over medium heat until sugar dissolves. Whisk in milk; cook over medium-high heat, whisking constantly, 5 minutes or until very hot. (Do not boil.) Whisk in vanilla.
2. Pour chocolate mixture into mugs; top with whipped cream, and drizzle with chocolate syrup.
*Omit or substitute decaffeinated espresso for the youngsters.
NOTE: To make a Hot Mudslide, omit espresso. Stir ½ cup Kahlúa, ½ cup Baileys Irish Crème, and, if desired, ¼ cup vodka into the hot milk mixture along with the vanilla. Proceed as directed. Keep cocoa hot in a thermos while you search for a tree. Add whipped cream and syrup before serving.

Big Fat Cookies

Cookies are quite possibly the premier food of the holiday season. This selection is no less than stellar, both in ultimate flavor and awesome appearance.

Red Velvet Cookies with Cream Cheese Frosting

MAKES: 20 cookies
HANDS-ON TIME: 35 min.
TOTAL TIME: 1 hr., 34 min., including frosting

Red Velvet is a tradition in the South, and these cookies are every bit as good as the time-honored cake.

- 2¾ cups all-purpose flour
- ⅓ cup unsweetened cocoa
- 1½ tsp. baking powder
- ½ tsp. baking soda
- ¼ tsp. salt
- 1 cup butter, softened
- 1¼ cups sugar
- 2 large eggs
- 2 Tbsp. red liquid food coloring
- 1 Tbsp. vanilla extract
- ¾ cup buttermilk
  Parchment paper
  Cream Cheese Frosting

1. Preheat oven to 350°. Combine first 5 ingredients in a medium bowl.

2. Beat butter at medium speed with an electric mixer 2 minutes or until creamy. Gradually add sugar, beating well. Add eggs, 1 at a time, beating until blended after each addition. Beat in food coloring and vanilla.

3. Add flour mixture alternately with buttermilk, beginning and ending with flour mixture. Beat at low speed until blended after each addition, stopping to scrape bowl as needed.

4. Drop dough by ¼ cupfuls 3 inches apart onto parchment paper-lined baking sheets. Spread dough to 3-inch rounds.

5. Bake at 350° for 15 minutes or until tops are set. Cool on baking sheets 5 minutes. Remove to wire racks, and cool completely (about 20 minutes). Crumble 1 cookie into fine crumbs to use as garnish. Spread about 2½ Tbsp. Cream Cheese Frosting onto each cookie; sprinkle with crumbs. Store cookies in refrigerator up to 5 days.

Cream Cheese Frosting

MAKES: 3 cups
HANDS-ON TIME: 4 min.
TOTAL TIME: 4 min.

- 1 (8-oz.) package cream cheese, softened
- ½ cup butter, softened
- ½ tsp. vanilla extract
- Dash of salt
- 1 (1-lb.) package powdered sugar

1. Beat cream cheese, butter, vanilla, and salt at medium speed with an electric mixer 1 minute or until creamy. Gradually add powered sugar, beating at low speed 2 minutes or until smooth.

Chunky Chocolate-White Chocolate-Espresso Cookies

MAKES: 15 cookies
HANDS-ON TIME: 14 min.
TOTAL TIME: 1 hr.

If you crave an amazingly good drop cookie, these thick cookies with soft white chocolate and a hint of coffee really hit the spot.

- ¾ cup butter, softened
- 1½ cups sugar
- 2 large eggs
- 1 tsp. vanilla extract
- 2 (3.5-oz.) dark chocolate bars with finely ground espresso beans, divided and chopped
- 2¼ cups all-purpose flour
- ¼ cup unsweetened cocoa
- ½ tsp. baking soda
- ¼ tsp. salt
- 2 (4-oz.) white chocolate bars, chopped
- 1 cup coarsely chopped pecan halves, toasted

1. Preheat oven to 350°. Beat butter and sugar at medium speed with an electric mixer until blended. Add eggs and vanilla, beating just until blended. Microwave half of dark chocolate in a small microwave-safe bowl at HIGH 50 seconds to 1 minute or until melted, stirring after 30 seconds. Add melted chocolate to butter mixture, beating just until blended.

2. Combine flour and next 3 ingredients; gradually add to butter mixture, beating just until blended after each addition. Stir in remaining dark chocolate, white chocolate, and pecans.

3. Drop dough by ⅓ cupfuls 2 inches apart onto lightly greased baking sheets.

4. Bake at 350° for 21 minutes. Cool on baking sheets 5 minutes. Remove to wire racks, and cool completely.

NOTE: We tested with Ghirardelli Espresso Escape Dark Chocolate Bars and Ghirardelli White Chocolate Bars.

Ginger Giants

MAKES: 1 dozen
HANDS-ON TIME: 15 min.
TOTAL TIME: 2 hr., 57 min.

These puffy, sugar-crusted cookies have crunchy edges and soft centers.

- ¾ cup butter, softened
- 1 cup firmly packed light brown sugar
- 1 large egg
- ⅓ cup molasses
- 1 tsp. vanilla extract
- 2¼ cups all-purpose flour
- 2 Tbsp. ground ginger
- 2 tsp. baking soda
- 1½ tsp. ground cinnamon
- 1 tsp. ground cloves
- ½ tsp. salt
- ½ cup turbinado sugar
- Parchment paper

1. Beat butter at medium speed with an electric mixer until creamy. Gradually add brown sugar, beating until fluffy. Add egg, molasses, and vanilla, beating until blended.

2. Combine flour and next 5 ingredients; gradually add to butter mixture, beating just until blended after each addition. Cover and chill dough 2 hours or overnight.

3. Preheat oven to 350°. Divide dough into 12 (¼-cup) portions; shape each portion into a ball. Place turbinado sugar in a small bowl; roll each dough ball in sugar. Place balls 2 inches apart on parchment paper-lined baking sheets. Chill 10 to 15 minutes.

4. Bake at 350° for 14 to 16 minutes or until edges are lightly browned; cool on baking sheets 5 minutes. Remove to wire racks, and cool completely.

NOTE: If you chill dough overnight, let it stand at room temperature about 15 minutes or until it becomes pliable.

Cornmeal-Almond Cookies

MAKES: 13 cookies
HANDS-ON TIME: 39 min.
TOTAL TIME: 3 hr., 20 min.

This unique cookie earned our Test Kitchen's highest rating for its texture: a chewiness from the almond paste and a delicate crunch from the cornmeal.

- 1 **cup all-purpose flour**
- 1 **cup yellow cornmeal**
- 1½ **tsp. baking powder**
- ¼ **tsp. salt**
- ¾ **cup butter, softened**
- 1 **(7-oz.) package almond paste, crumbled**
- 1 **cup sugar**
- 2 **egg whites**
- 1 **Tbsp. orange zest**
- 1 **tsp. vanilla extract**
- 1 **cup sliced almonds, coarsely chopped**
   Parchment paper

1. Combine flour and next 3 ingredients in a medium bowl.
2. Beat butter at medium speed with an electric mixer until creamy. Gradually add almond paste; beat until smooth. Gradually add sugar, beating until combined. Add egg whites, orange zest, and vanilla; beat until blended. Gradually add flour mixture; beat at low speed just until blended after each addition. Shape dough into a ball, wrap in plastic wrap, and chill 2 hours or until firm.
3. Preheat oven to 350°. Place almonds in a shallow bowl. Shape dough by ¼ cupfuls into balls; roll each ball in almonds to coat. Place balls 3 inches apart on parchment paper-lined baking sheets.
4. Bake at 350° for 18 minutes or until edges are lightly browned. Cool on baking sheets 5 minutes. Remove to wire racks, and cool completely.

Orange-Frosted Cornmeal Stars

MAKES: 20 cookies
HANDS-ON TIME: 29 min.
TOTAL TIME: 1 hr., 52 min.

- 1 **cup butter, softened**
- 1 **cup granulated sugar**
- 2 **egg whites**
- 1 **egg yolk**
- 2 **Tbsp. orange zest, divided**
- 5 **Tbsp. fresh orange juice, divided**
- 1½ **tsp. vanilla extract**
- 2¾ **cups all-purpose flour**
- ⅔ **cup yellow cornmeal**
- 1½ **tsp. baking powder**
- ½ **tsp. salt**
   Parchment paper
- 2 **cups powdered sugar**

1. Beat butter and granulated sugar at medium speed with an electric mixer until fluffy. In a separate bowl, beat egg whites at high speed until stiff peaks form; add to butter mixture, beating just until blended. Add egg yolk, 1½ Tbsp. orange zest, 2 Tbsp. orange juice, and vanilla, beating just until blended.
2. Combine flour and next 3 ingredients; gradually add to butter mixture, beating just until blended after each addition.
3. Shape dough into a ball, and divide in half. Flatten each half into a 5-inch disk; wrap each disk in plastic wrap. Freeze dough 30 minutes, or chill 8 hours.
4. Preheat oven to 350°. Roll out dough, 1 portion at a time, to ¼-inch thickness on a floured surface; cut into star shapes using a 4- or 5-inch star-shaped cutter. Reroll trimmings to make additional cookies. Place cutouts 1 inch apart on parchment paper-lined baking sheets.
5. Bake at 350° for 14 minutes or until golden. Cool 5 minutes on baking sheets; remove to wire racks, and cool completely (about 20 minutes).

6. Combine remaining ½ Tbsp. orange zest, remaining 3 Tbsp. orange juice, and powdered sugar in a medium bowl, stirring with a whisk until smooth. Spread frosting on stars. Place cookies on wire racks until frosting is set.

Walnut Scotchies

MAKES: 16 cookies
HANDS-ON TIME: 20 min.
TOTAL TIME: 1 hr., 13 min.

Gobble up these crisp, butterscotch-flavored cookies plain, or slather ice cream between pairs of them to make irresistible mega sandwich cookies.

- 1½ **cups coarsely chopped walnuts**
- 2 **cups all-purpose flour**
- 1 **tsp. baking soda**
- ¼ **tsp. salt**
- ½ **cup butter, softened**
- ¾ **cup granulated sugar**
- ½ **cup firmly packed light brown sugar**
- 2 **large eggs**
- 1 **tsp. vanilla extract**
- 1 **cup butterscotch morsels**
   Parchment paper

1. Preheat oven to 350°. Place walnuts in a single layer in a shallow pan. Bake at 350° for 6 to 8 minutes until toasted and fragrant. Cool.
2. Process ½ cup toasted walnuts in a food processor until finely ground; place in a medium bowl. Add flour, baking soda, and salt to ground nuts, stirring well with a whisk.
3. Beat butter at medium speed with an electric mixer until creamy. Gradually add sugars, beating until light and fluffy; beat in eggs and vanilla. Gradually add flour mixture, beating at low speed until blended after each addition. Stir in butterscotch morsels and remaining 1 cup toasted walnuts.

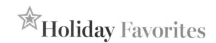

4. Drop dough by level ¼ cupfuls onto parchment paper-lined baking sheets. (Do not flatten.)

5. Bake at 350° for 16 minutes or until edges are lightly browned. Cool on baking sheets 5 minutes. Remove to wire racks, and cool completely.

TRY THIS TWIST!
Walnut Scotchie Ice Cream Sandwiches: Spread about ⅓ cup slightly softened premium vanilla ice cream onto flat side of 1 cookie. Top with another cookie, flat side down; press down gently. Wrap in plastic wrap and freeze, or enjoy right away. Repeat with remaining cookies and additional ice cream. Makes: 8 sandwiches.

Toffee-Pecan Cookies

MAKES: 16 cookies
HANDS-ON TIME: 27 min.
TOTAL TIME: 1 hr., 3 min.

For maximum chunkiness in your cookies, break toffee bars and pecan halves by hand to get big pieces.

 1 **cup pecan halves, broken in half**
 2 **cups all-purpose flour**
 1 **tsp. baking soda**
 ¼ **tsp. salt**
 6 **Tbsp. butter, softened**
 6 **Tbsp. shortening**
 ¾ **cup granulated sugar**
 ½ **cup firmly packed brown sugar**
 1 **large egg**
 1 **tsp. vanilla extract**
 6 **(1.4-oz.) chocolate-covered toffee candy bars, coarsely broken**
    Parchment paper

1. Preheat oven to 350°. Place pecans in a single layer in a shallow pan. Bake at 350° for 7 minutes or until toasted and fragrant; cool.

2. Stir together flour, baking soda, and salt in a medium bowl.

3. Beat butter and shortening at medium speed with an electric mixer until creamy. Gradually add sugars, beating until smooth. Add egg and vanilla, beating until blended. Gradually add flour mixture, beating just until blended after each addition. Stir in pecans and toffee bars.

4. Drop dough by ¼ cupfuls 2 to 3 inches apart onto parchment paper-lined baking sheets.

5. Bake at 350° for 17 minutes or until edges are lightly browned. Cool on baking sheets 2 minutes. Remove to wire racks, and cool completely.

NOTE: We tested with SKOR Chocolate-Covered Toffee Candy Bars.

Oatmeal Cookie Sandwiches with Rum-Raisin Filling

MAKES: 15 sandwiches
HANDS-ON TIME: 50 min.
TOTAL TIME: 1 hr., 47 min., including filling

A creamy rum-flavored filling glues these oversized oatmeal cookies together.

 ½ **cup butter, softened**
 ½ **cup shortening**
 ¼ **cup light corn syrup**
 1¼ **cups firmly packed light brown sugar**
 1 **large egg**
 1½ **tsp. almond extract**
 1½ **cups all-purpose flour**
 1 **tsp. baking soda**
 1 **tsp. ground cinnamon**
 ½ **tsp. salt**
 ½ **tsp. ground cloves**
 2 **cups uncooked regular oats**
 ¾ **cup chopped pecans**
    Parchment paper
    Rum-Raisin Filling

1. Preheat oven to 375°. Beat first 4 ingredients at medium speed with an electric mixer until fluffy. Add egg and almond extract, beating until blended.

2. Whisk together flour, baking soda, and next 3 ingredients in a medium bowl; gradually add to butter mixture, beating at low speed until blended after each addition. Stir in oats and pecans.

3. Shape dough into 1½ inch balls. Place balls 2 inches apart on large parchment paper-lined baking sheets.

4. Bake at 375° for 10 to 12 minutes or until golden. Cool on baking sheets 3 minutes. Remove to wire racks, and cool completely (about 20 minutes). Spread about 3 Tbsp. Rum-Raisin Filling onto each of half the cookies; top with remaining cookies, flat side down, and press down gently.

Rum-Raisin Filling

MAKES: 2½ cups
HANDS-ON TIME: 10 min.
TOTAL TIME: 10 min.

 1 **(3-oz.) package cream cheese, softened**
 3 **Tbsp. milk**
 1 **Tbsp. dark rum***
 ¾ **tsp. vanilla extract**
 ⅛ **tsp. salt**
 1 **(1-lb.) package powdered sugar**
 1½ **cups raisins**

1. Beat cream cheese at medium speed with an electric mixer until creamy. Add milk and next 3 ingredients, beating until blended. Gradually add powdered sugar, beating at low speed until smooth. Stir in raisins.

***Omit rum, if desired.**

German Chocolate Cake Cookies

MAKES: 15 cookies
HANDS-ON TIME: 14 min.
TOTAL TIME: 1 hr., 15 min.

The flavor of these cookies is reminiscent of the classic German chocolate layer cake.

- ¾ cup unsalted butter, softened
- ¾ cup granulated sugar
- ¼ cup firmly packed light brown sugar
- 1 large egg
- 2 tsp. light corn syrup
- 2 tsp. vanilla extract
- ¼ tsp. coconut extract
- 2 cups all-purpose flour
- 1 tsp. baking powder
- ¼ tsp. salt
- 3 (1-oz.) German chocolate baking squares, melted
- 1 cup chopped pecans, toasted
- ½ cup semisweet chocolate chunks
- ½ cup unsweetened organic coconut flakes or sweetened flaked coconut
- 1½ cups powdered sugar
- 2 Tbsp. milk
- ¼ tsp. vanilla extract
- 1 cup sweetened flaked coconut

1. Preheat oven to 350°. Beat butter and sugars at medium speed with an electric mixer until blended. Add egg, corn syrup, 2 tsp. vanilla extract, and coconut extract, beating until blended.
2. Combine flour, baking powder, and salt; gradually add to butter mixture, beating just until blended after each addition. Stir in melted chocolate and next 3 ingredients.
3. Drop dough by ¼ cupfuls 2 inches apart onto lightly greased baking sheets.
4. Bake at 350° for 16 to 18 minutes. Cool 5 minutes on baking sheets; remove to wire racks, and cool completely (about 20 minutes).
5. Whisk together powdered sugar, milk, and ¼ tsp. vanilla in a small bowl until smooth. Spoon icing over cookies; immediately sprinkle with sweetened flaked coconut.
NOTE: We tested with Mounds sweetened flaked coconut. Find unsweetened organic coconut flakes in your local specialty food market.

Chocolate Chip Brownie Pillows

MAKES: 11 cookies
HANDS-ON TIME: 32 min.
TOTAL TIME: 3 hr., 15 min.

These are gargantuan cookies, each with a fudgy brownie "pillow" in the middle. You'll have extra brownies leftover to enjoy right away or to freeze.

- 1 (20-oz.) package double chocolate brownie mix
- ½ cup unsalted butter, softened
- ½ cup butter-flavored shortening
- 1½ cups firmly packed brown sugar
- 2 large eggs
- 1 egg yolk
- 1 Tbsp. vanilla extract
- 2½ cups unbleached all-purpose flour
- 2 tsp. baking powder
- ½ tsp. baking soda
- ½ tsp. salt
- 3 cups semisweet chocolate morsels
  Parchment paper

1. Preheat oven to 325°. Prepare and bake brownie mix according to package directions in an 8-inch square pan. Let cool completely in pan on a wire rack. Cut brownies into 3 dozen squares.
2. Beat butter and shortening at medium speed with an electric mixer until creamy. Add brown sugar, beating until smooth. Add eggs, egg yolk, and vanilla, beating until blended.
3. Combine flour and next 3 ingredients; gradually add to butter mixture, beating just until blended after each addition. Stir in chocolate morsels. Cover and chill dough 1 hour.
4. Increase oven temperature to 350°. For each cookie, scoop a level ½ cup dough onto parchment paper-lined baking sheets; place cookies 3 inches apart. Using your fingers, make an indentation in mound of dough; place 1 brownie square in center. Press chocolate chip dough around brownie, reshaping dough to form a ball. Repeat procedure with remaining dough and 10 brownie squares, placing no more than 6 cookies on a baking sheet. Chill 15 minutes.
5. Bake at 350° for 18 to 20 minutes or until lightly browned and cookies look set. Cool 2 minutes on baking sheets; remove to wire racks, and cool completely.
NOTE: We tested with Ghirardelli Double Chocolate Brownie Mix.

METRIC EQUIVILANTS

The recipes that appear in this cookbook use the standard United States method for measuring liquid and dry or solid ingredients (teaspoons, tablespoons, and cups). The information on this chart is provided to help cooks outside the U.S. successfully use these recipes. All equivalents are approximate.

METRIC EQUIVALENTS FOR DIFFERENT TYPES OF INGREDIENTS

A standard cup measure of a dry or solid ingredient will vary in weight depending on the type of ingredient. A standard cup of liquid is the same volume for any type of liquid. Use the following chart when converting standard cup measures to grams (weight) or milliliters (volume).

Standard Cup	Fine Powder (ex. flour)	Grain (ex. rice)	Granular (ex. sugar)	Liquid Solids (ex. butter)	Liquid (ex. milk)
1	140 g	150 g	190 g	200 g	240 ml
¾	105 g	113 g	143 g	150 g	180 ml
⅔	93 g	100 g	125 g	133 g	160 ml
½	70 g	75 g	95 g	100 g	120 ml
⅓	47 g	50 g	63 g	67 g	80 ml
¼	35 g	38 g	48 g	50 g	60 ml
⅛	18 g	19 g	24 g	25 g	30 ml

USEFUL EQUIVALENTS FOR DRY INGREDIENTS BY WEIGHT

(To convert ounces to grams, multiply the number of ounces by 30.)

1 oz	=	1/16 lb	=	30 g
4 oz	=	¼ lb	=	120 g
8 oz	=	½ lb	=	240 g
12 oz	=	¾ lb	=	360 g
16 oz	=	1 lb	=	480 g

USEFUL EQUIVALENTS FOR LENGTH

(To convert inches to centimeters, multiply the number of inches by 2.5.)

1 in				=	2.5 cm		
6 in	=	½ ft	=	=	15 cm		
12 in	=	1 ft		=	30 cm		
36 in	=	3 ft	=	1 yd =	90 cm		
40 in				=	100 cm	=	1 m

USEFUL EQUIVALENTS FOR LIQUID INGREDIENTS BY VOLUME

¼ tsp	=							1 ml	
½ tsp	=							2 ml	
1 tsp	=							5 ml	
3 tsp	=	1 tbls			=	½ fl oz	=	15 ml	
	=	2 tbls	=	⅛ cup	=	1 fl oz	=	30 ml	
	=	4 tbls	=	¼ cup	=	2 fl oz	=	60 ml	
	=	5⅓ tbls	=	⅓ cup	=	3 fl oz	=	80 ml	
	=	8 tbls	=	½ cup	=	4 fl oz	=	120 ml	
	=	10⅔ tbls	=	⅔ cup	=	5 fl oz	=	160 ml	
	=	12 tbls	=	¾ cup	=	6 fl oz	=	180 ml	
	=	16 tbls	=	1 cup	=	8 fl oz	=	240 ml	
	=	1 pt	=	2 cups	=	16 fl oz	=	480 ml	
	=	1 qt	=	4 cups	=	32 fl oz	=	960 ml	
						33 fl oz	=	1000 ml	= 1 l

USEFUL EQUIVALENTS FOR COOKING/OVEN TEMPERATURES

	Fahrenheit	Celsius	Gas Mark
Freeze Water	32° F	0° C	
Room Temperature	68° F	20° C	
Boil Water	212° F	100° C	
Bake	325° F	160° C	3
	350° F	180° C	4
	375° F	190° C	5
	400° F	200° C	6
	425° F	220° C	7
	450° F	230° C	8
Broil			Grill

Menu Index

This index lists every menu by suggested occasion. Recipes in bold type are provided with the menu and accompaniments are in regular type.

Menus for Special Occasions

Hanukkah Celebration

SERVES 6 TO 8

(page 276)

**Caramelized Maple-and-Garlic-
 Glazed Salmon**
Roasted Paprika Chicken
Southern Baked Brisket
Asparagus Sauté
Pepper Jelly-Glazed Carrots
Sweet Potato Latkes
**Warm Frisée Salad with Crispy
 Kosher Salami**
Spiced Thyme Applesauce
Peach-Pecan Rugelach
**Hanukkah Doughnuts with
 Strawberry Preserves**

Christmas Gathering

SERVES 8 TO 10

(page 283)

Baked ham with seeded rolls
**Roquefort Cheesecake with Pear
 Preserves and Walnuts**
Spicy Cranberry-Orange Chutney
Brown Sugar-Pecan-Mustard Butter
**Tortellini Caprese Bites with Basil
 Vinaigrette**
Hot Spinach-Artichoke Dip
Gingerbread Cocoa
Citrus Sangria
Gingerbread Men Cookies

Dressed Up Holiday Dinner

SERVES 8

(page 294)

**Honey-Rosemary Cherries and
 Blue Cheese Crostini**
Cream of Chestnut Soup
**Fig-and-Balsamic-Glazed Quail and
 Roasted Green Beans**
Herbs-and-Greens Salad
**Butternut Squash Ravioli
 with Mushrooms**
Chocolate Roulade *(see page 307)*
Vieux Carré

Progressive Dinner

SERVES 12

(page 326)

Sweet Tea and Limoncello Martinis
**Lamb Sliders with Mint-Garlic
 Mayonnaise**
**Hearts of Romaine with Molasses
 Vinaigrette and Parmesan-
 Pancetta Crisps**
**Roasted Meyer Lemon-Peppercorn
 Game Hens**
**Sun-Dried Tomato and Goat
 Cheese-Stuffed Pork Loin Chops**
**Crispy Sage and Garlic Smashed
 Baby Red Potatoes**
**Roasted Root Vegetables
 with Praline Crunch**
Gingersnap and Poached Pear Trifle
**Chocolate Velvet Cake with Cream
 Cheese Frosting**

Tree-Cutting Party

SERVES 8 TO 10

(page 330)

Chunky Cowboy Chili
Cornmeal Cheddar Scones
Cinnamon-Pecan Cookie S'mores
Hot Mocha

Lucky New Year's Lunch

SERVES 4

Brown Sugar-Bourbon-Glazed Ham
 (page 96)
**Black-eyed Pea Cakes with Heirloom
 Tomatoes and Slaw** *(page 197)*
Cutting-Edge Collards *(page 52)*
Elegant Citrus Tart *(page 28)*

Menus for Company

Oyster Roast

SERVES 5

(page 46)

Oysters
Mike's Cocktail Sauce
Lemon Aïoli
Shoo-fly Punch

Ladylike Luncheon

SERVES 8

**Cheese Ring with Strawberry
    Preserves** *(page 263)*
**Grilled Chicken Salad with
    Raspberry-Tarragon Dressing**
    (double recipe) *(page 200)*
Sweet Tea Icebox Tart *(page 102)*

Cinco de Mayo Celebration

SERVES 10

(page 106)
Easy Barbecue Tostadas
Spicy Queso Dip
Fresh Salsa
Strawberry-Margarita Spritzers
Beer 'Garitas
Iced Mexican Chocolate Sipper
Oven-Baked Churros

Outdoor Party

SERVES 12

(page 122)
Green Goddess Dip
Asiago-Pecan Shortbread
Bacon-Parmesan Tassies
Shrimp Salad-Stuffed Endive
**Kentucky Benedictine
    Tea Sandwiches**
Summer Fruit Salad
Chicken-and-Tortellini Salad
Sweet Pea Crostini
Gorgonzola-Grilled Pear Crostini

Shawn's Hill Country Menu

SERVES 8 TO 10

(page 158)
**Grilled Tri-Tip with Citrus-
    Chile Butter**
Garlic Shrimp
Lemon-Herb Potatoes
Sautéed Squash and Tomatoes
Southwest Watermelon Salad
Easy Mocha Mousse

Lowcountry Style

SERVES 6 TO 8

(page 208)
MIKE LATA'S MENU
**Roasted Pork Belly with Late-
    Harvest Peaches and Arugula**
Skillet-Roasted Okra and Shrimp
**Lemony Rice Pudding with Figs
    and Saba**

SEAN BROCK'S MENU
**Caw Caw Creek Pork Belly with
    Herbed Farrow and Sautéed
    Chanterelles**
Lowcountry Shrimp-and-Okra Pilau
Benne Seed-Topped Peach Tart

ROBERT STEHLING'S MENU
Okra-Shrimp Beignets
Red Rice
Crispy Roasted Pork Belly
Buttermilk Peach Pudding

Spring Celebration

(page 84)
SERVES 8
Tomato-Herb Mini Frittatas
Fruit Salad with Yogurt
Gouda Grits
**Quick Buttermilk Biscuits with
    Lemon-Herb, Blackberry, or
    Walnut-Honey Butter**
**Sparkling Ginger-Orange Cocktails
    or Mocktails**
Iced sugar cookies

Patriotic Picnic

SERVES 8

(page 148)

Smoky Chicken or Steak Barbecue
  Kabobs with White
  Barbecue Sauce
Deviled Eggs with Assorted Toppings
Hot Bacon Potato Salad with
  Green Beans
Grilled Jalapeño-Lime Corn on
  the Cob
Ice Cream Floats

Summer Gathering

SERVES 8

(page 118)

Grilled Tomato Bruschetta
Simple Grilled Asparagus
Dan's Pizza Dough
Fresh Tomato Sauce

Game-Day Celebration

SERVES 8

(page 224)

Mini Muffulettas
Apple Coleslaw, Pear Coleslaw, or
  Cranberry-Almond Coleslaw
Deli-fried chicken tenders
Jalapeño-Mustard Dipping Sauce
Blue Moon Inn Cheese Spread
Cajun Lemonade
Graham Nut Clusters

Ultimate Fall Party Menu

SERVES 8

(page 234)

Sparkling Autumn Chianti
Smoked Paprika Pork Roast with
  Sticky Stout Barbecue Sauce
Grilled Peppers and Mushrooms
Butternut Squash Spoon Bread
Caramelized Pear Cannoli with
  Praline Sauce
Cheddar-Pecan Shortbread Leaves
Season's Best Appetizer Platter

Elegant Brunch

SERVES 6

Green Tomato Bloody Mary *(page 44)*
Mom-mosa *(page 114)*
Lemon-Poppyseed Belgian Waffles
  with Blackberry Maple Syrup
  (page 31)
BLT Benedict with Avocado-Tomato
  Relish *(page 62)*

Derby Day Delights

SERVES 6

Bacon-Infused Bourbon *(page 63)*
Mint Julep Sweet Tea *(page 99)*
Kentucky Hot Brown Tart *(page 109)*
Green salad
Bacon-Peanut Truffles *(page 64)*

Sweet Fruit-Lover's Social

SERVES AT LEAST 12

Lime-Cornmeal Cookies *(page 31)*
Indulgent Cherries *(page 56)*
Strawberry Swirl Cream Cheese
  Pound Cake *(page 76)*
Ginger-Lemon Bars with Almond
  Streusel *(page 82)*
Brown Sugar-Cinnamon Peach Pie
  (page 144)

Perfect Casserole Potluck

SERVES 6 TO 8

Home-style Green Bean Casserole
  (page 274)
Lightened Squash Casserole *(page 156)*
Chicken-and-Rice Bake *(page 245)*
Blackberry-Apple Pie *(page 258)*

Menus for Family

Spring Picnic

SERVES 4 TO 6

(page 103)
Lime Fizz
Fried Chicken Bites
Fruit, Cheese, and Herb Skewers
Spring Salsa
Strawberry-Rhubarb Hand Pies

Cookout on the Coast

SERVES 4

Grilled Grouper with Watermelon Salsa *(page 130)*
Veggie Potato Salad *(page 135)*
Green Tomato Garden Party Salad *(page 133)*
Lemon Meringue Ice-Cream Pie *(page 194)*

Italiano, Y'all

SERVES 6 TO 8

Hearty Italian Soup with Parmesan-Pepper Cornbread Biscotti *(page 243)*
Panzanella Salad with Cornbread Croutons *(page 51)*
Tortellini-and-Tomato Salad *(page 155)*
Sweet Tea Tiramisù *(page 102)*

Spicy Spread

SERVES 6

Cajun Lemonade *(page 226)*
Hot Spiced Boiled Peanuts *(page 43)*
Spicy Mango Shrimp *(page 51)*
Coconut-Lime Rice *(page 51)*
Peach Enchiladas *(page 142)*

Healthier Homestyle Dinner

SERVES 8

Oven-Fried Chicken (double recipe) *(page 220)*
Creamy Macaroni and Cheese *(page 32)*
Lightened Buttermilk Biscuits *(page 219)*
Sliced tomatoes
Layered Carrot Cake *(page 87)*
Lightened Vanilla Bean Ice Cream *(page 136)*

Kid-Friendly Fare

SERVES 6 TO 8

Stovetop Chicken Pie *(page 55)*
Glazed Baby Carrots *(page 65)*
Easy Skillet Apple Pie *(page 214)*

Snowed-in Supper

SERVES 8

Game Day Chili *(page 34)*
Sautéed Baby Beet Greens (double recipe) *(page 66)*
Skillet Cornbread *(page 50)*
Apple Brown Betty *(page 215)*

Zesty Steak and Potatoes

SERVES 6 TO 8

Pepper Gazpacho *(page 196)*
Cilantro Flank Steak *(page 110)*
Grilled Sweet Potato-Poblano Salad *(page 222)*
Key Lime Pound Cake *(page 75)*

Leftover Makeover

SERVES 4 TO 6

After-Thanksgiving Pizza *(page 272)*
Mixed salad greens

Easy Southwestern Style

SERVES 4 TO 6

Green Tomato Salsa *(page 132)*
Tortilla chips
Mexicali Meatless Tostadas *(page 196)*
Chicken Enchiladas *(page 246)*
Margaritas

Meatless Monday

SERVES 4 TO 6

Herbed Tomato Tart *(page 205)*
Assorted fruit

Cozy Brunswick Dinner

SERVES 8

Blueberry Lemonade *(page 202)*
Chicken and Brisket Brunswick Stew *(page 242)*
Cornmeal Cheddar Scones *(page 331)*

Fall Picnic

SERVES 6

(page 268)
Persimmon-Pear Salad
Smoky Red Pepper Soup
Collard Green Pistou
Pancetta-Arugula-Turkey Sandwiches
Sweet Potato Pound Cake
Decadent Chai Latte

Recipe Title Index

This index alphabetically lists every recipe by exact title.

Ginger-Orange Mocktails, 85
Gingersnap and Poached Pear Trifle, 329
Gingersnap Crust, 102
Ginger Whipped Cream, 309
Glazed Baby Carrots, 65
Goat Cheese and Strawberry Grilled Cheese, 71
Gorgonzola-Grilled Pear Crostini, 125
Gouda Grits, 85
Governor's Mansion Summer Peach Tea Punch, 98
Graham Nut Clusters, 226
Grandma Erma's Spirited Cranberry Sauce, 255
Grape Crostini, 71
Greek Snapper, 319
Green Beans with Caramelized Shallots, 254
Green Goddess Dip, 122
Green Tomato Bloody Mary, 44
Green Tomato-Feta Burgers, 146
Green Tomato Garden Party Salad, 133
Green Tomato Salsa, 132
Grillades and Cheese Grits, 312
Grilled Cheesy Corn, 88
Grilled Chicken Salad with Raspberry-Tarragon
    Dressing, 200
Grilled Chicken Tacos, 95
Grilled Chicken with Fresh Corn Cakes, 153
Grilled Fillets with Pecans and Green Bean
    Ravioli, 227
Grilled Green Tomatoes Caprese, 133
Grilled Grouper with Watermelon Salsa, 130
Grilled Jalapeño-Lime Corn on the Cob, 151
Grilled Onion Crostini, 64
Grilled Pear Salad, 223
Grilled Peppers and Mushrooms, 235
Grilled Peppers and Sausage with Cheese
    Grits, 154
Grilled Pork Porterhouse with Peach Agrodolce, 142
Grilled Pork Tenderloin with Squash Medley, 93
Grilled Shrimp Salad with Sweet Tea Vinaigrette, 100
Grilled Steak-and-Ratatouille Salad with Basil-Garlic
    Vinaigrette, 198
Grilled Steak and Vegetable Kabobs, 67
Grilled Steak-Corn-Spinach Salad, 153
Grilled Summer Vegetables, 156
Grilled Sweet Potato-Poblano Salad, 222
Grilled Tomato Bruschetta, 119
Grilled Tri-Tip with Citrus-Chile Butter, 159
Grits and Grillades, 50
Gruyère Scalloped Potatoes, 92

Ham-and-Broccoli Macaroni and Cheese, 33
Ham-and-Vegetable Cobbler, 273
Ham-Hash Brown Casserole, 245
Hanukkah Doughnuts with Strawberry
    Preserves, 278
Harvest Salad, 254
Hearts of Romaine with Molasses Vinaigrette and
    Parmesan-Pancetta Crisps, 327
Hearty Italian Soup with Parmesan-Pepper Corn-
    bread Biscotti, 243
Hello Dolly Bars, 83
Herb-and-Potato Chip-Crusted Beef Tenderloin, 298
Herb Cheese Spread, 302

Herb Dip, 71
Herbed Farro, 210
Herbed Tomato Tart, 205
Herb Pesto, 131
Herbs-and-Greens Salad, 295
High Society Deviled Eggs, 91
Homemade Chocolate-Dipped Caramels, 57
Homemade Hamburger Buns, 147
Homemade Lemon Curd, 194
Home-style Green Bean Casserole, 274
Home-style Meatloaf, 314
Honey-Cider Vinaigrette, 269
Honey Crème Anglaise, 143
Honey-Curry Glazed Lamb with Roasted Grapes and
    Cranberries, 297
Honey-Ginger Butter, 265
Honey-Pecan Butterscotch Sauce, 232
Honey-Rosemary Cherries and Blue Cheese
    Crostini, 294
Hoppin' John, 36
Horseradish Cream Sauce, 277
Horseradish-Pepper Aïoli, 298
Hot-and-Spicy Cranberry-Pear Chutney, 255
Hot Bacon Potato Salad with Green Beans, 151
Hot Buttered Rye, 288
Hot Cider Nog, 274
Hot Cooked Pasta, 55
Hot Mocha, 332
Hot Spiced Boiled Peanuts, 43
Hot Spinach-Artichoke Dip, 284
Hot Spinach-Artichoke Dip with Crab, 284

Ice-Cream Floats, 151
Iced Mexican Chocolate Sipper, 108
Indulgent Cherries, 56
Insalata con Peche, 141
Italian Bean Salad, 64

Jalapeño-Mustard Dipping Sauce, 225
Jalapeño-Pecan Mustard Butter, 232
Jalapeño-Pepper Jack Cornbread Biscotti, 243
Jicama Slaw, 106

Kentucky Benedictine Tea Sandwiches, 124
Kentucky Hot Browns, 109
Kentucky Hot Brown Tart, 109
Key "Light" Pie, 221
Key Lime Glaze, 75
Key Lime Pie Ice Cream, 136
Key Lime Pound Cake, 75
Kir Royale, 300

Lamb Burgers, 111
Lamb Sliders, 327
Layered Carrot Cake, 87
Layered Guacamole, 64
Layered Peppermint Cheesecake, 304

Lemonade Sweet Tea, 99
Lemon Aïoli, 46
Lemon-Blueberry Sweet Tea, 99
Lemon Broccolini, 254
Lemon-Coconut Pound Cake Loaf, 74
Lemon-Cream Cheese Glaze, 281
Lemon Curd Glaze, 261
Lemon Curd Pound Cake, 260
Lemon Glaze, 74
Lemon-Herb Butter, 86
Lemon-Herb Potatoes, 159
Lemon Meringue Ice-Cream Pie, 194
Lemon-Orange Rolls, 257
Lemon-Poppy Seed Belgian Waffles with Blackberry
    Maple Syrup, 31
Lemon-Poppy Seed Pancakes, 31
Lemony Rice Pudding with Figs and Saba, 209
Light Cornbread, 201
Lightened Buttermilk Biscuits, 219
Lightened Hummingbird Cake, 307
Lightened Squash Casserole, 156
Lightened Vanilla Bean Ice Cream, 136
Lime Chicken Tenders and Orzo Salad, 66
Lime-Cornmeal Cookies, 31
Lime Curd Glaze, 261
Lime Curd Pound Cake, 261
Lime Fizz, 103
Lime Simple Syrup, 103
Loaded Baked Potato Dip, 40
Lovely Lattice, 145
Lowcountry Boil, 319
Lowcountry Shrimp-and-Okra Pilau, 211
Lucky Black-eyed Pea Salad, 37
Luscious Orange Panna Cotta, 28

Mama's German Chocolate Cake, 230
Mango Ketchup, 147
Mango Salad, 222
Mango-Spinach Salad with Warm Bacon
    Vinaigrette, 63
Maple Butter, 288
Marbled Brownies, 83
Margarita, 126
Marinated Shrimp-and-Artichokes, 262
Mascarpone Frosting, 305
Meaty Black Bean Chili, 287
Mediterranean Chicken Salad, 53
Mediterranean Chicken Salad with Rice, 53
Mediterranean Stuffed Pork Tenderloin, 315
Melon and Plum Salad, 223
Meringue Topping, 195
Merry Berry Christmas, Sugar!, 291
Mexicali Meatless Tostadas, 196
Mexican Beans and Vegetables with Rice, 321
Mexican Pizza, 272
Mike's Cocktail Sauce, 46
Milky Pecan "Milk" Punch, 290
Mini Banana-Cranberry-Nut Bread Loaves, 281
Mini Muffulettas, 224
Mint Chocolate Chip Ice-Cream Cake, 193
Mint-Garlic Mayonnaise, 327
Mint Julep Sweet Tea, 99
Mint Pesto, 131

Month-by-Month Index

This index alphabetically lists every food article and accompanying recipes by month.

General Recipe Index

This index lists every recipe by food category and/or major ingredient.

Favorite Recipes Journal

Jot down your family's and your favorite recipes for quick and handy reference. And don't forget to include the dishes that drew rave reviews when company came for dinner.

Recipe	Source/Page	Remarks

Warm Artichoke-Shrimp Dip

Muffuletta Dip

quick prep • make-ahead • party perfect

MAKES: about 4 cups
HANDS-ON TIME: 10 min.
TOTAL TIME: 1 hr., 10 min.

We could call this Saints Dip for the 2010 Super Bowl winners! Parmesan cheese helps hold ingredients together. You can also serve this versatile recipe with crackers over a block of cream cheese or toss leftovers in a Caesar salad. (Pictured on page 2)

Serve with: *French bread crostini*

- 1 cup Italian olive salad, drained
- 1 cup diced salami (about 4 oz.)
- ¼ cup grated Parmesan cheese
- ¼ cup chopped pepperoncini salad peppers
- 1 (2¼-oz.) can sliced black olives, drained
- 4 oz. provolone cheese, diced
- 1 celery rib, finely chopped
- ½ red bell pepper, chopped
- 1 Tbsp. olive oil
- ¼ cup chopped fresh parsley

1. Stir together first 9 ingredients. Cover and chill 1 to 24 hours before serving. Stir in parsley just before serving. Serve with French bread crostini. Store leftovers in refrigerator up to 5 days.

NOTE: We tested with Boscoli Italian Olive Salad.

RECIPE INSPIRED BY KELLI TUTTLE
DRUMMOND, WISCONSIN

Warm Artichoke-Shrimp Dip

quick prep • party perfect

MAKES: about 4 cups
HANDS-ON TIME: 15 min.
TOTAL TIME: 15 min.

Serve half of dip first, keeping remaining half warm in saucepan.

Serve with: *pita crackers, breadsticks*

- 2 (14-oz.) cans artichoke hearts, drained and chopped
- 1 cup freshly grated Parmesan cheese
- ¾ cup mayonnaise
- ½ cup fine, dry breadcrumbs
- 2 garlic cloves, minced
- 2 Tbsp. lemon juice
- ½ lb. peeled, cooked shrimp, chopped
  Garnishes: lemon zest; peeled, cooked shrimp

1. Combine artichoke hearts and next 5 ingredients in a large saucepan. Cook over medium heat, stirring often, 4 to 5 minutes or until thoroughly heated. Stir in shrimp. Transfer to a serving bowl. Garnish, if desired. Serve with pita crackers and breadsticks.

Loaded Baked Potato Dip

quick prep • make-ahead • party perfect

MAKES: about 4 cups
HANDS-ON TIME: 15 min.
TOTAL TIME: 1 hr., 25 min.

We baked frozen waffle fries extra-crispy for our dippers.

Serve with: *waffle fries*

- 1 (2.1-oz.) package fully cooked bacon slices
- 1 (16-oz.) container sour cream
- 2 cups (8 oz.) freshly shredded sharp Cheddar cheese
- ⅓ cup sliced fresh chives
- 2 tsp. hot sauce
  Garnishes: cooked, crumbled bacon; sliced fresh chives; freshly cracked pepper

1. Microwave bacon according to package directions until crisp; drain on paper towels. Cool 10 minutes; crumble. Stir together bacon and next 4 ingredients. Cover and chill 1 to 24 hours before serving. Garnish, if desired. Serve with crispy, warm waffle fries. Store leftovers in refrigerator up to 7 days.

NOTE: We tested with Oscar Mayer Fully Cooked Bacon.

Southwest Salsa

quick prep • make-ahead • party perfect

MAKES: about 2 cups
HANDS-ON TIME: 10 min.
TOTAL TIME: 1 hr., 10 min.

Double the jalapeños and red pepper, if desired. (Pictured on page 162)

Serve with: *tortilla chips*

- 1 (14½-oz.) can diced tomatoes and zesty green chiles
- 5 pickled jalapeño pepper slices
- ¼ cup firmly packed fresh cilantro leaves
- ¼ cup chopped red onion
- 1 Tbsp. fresh lime juice
- ¼ tsp. ground cumin
- ¼ tsp. garlic powder
- ¼ tsp. dried crushed red pepper
- ¼ tsp. salt
- Garnishes: fresh cilantro sprigs, pickled jalapeño pepper slices

1. Drain liquid from tomatoes, reserving 1 Tbsp. liquid; discard remaining liquid. Place reserved liquid, tomatoes, and next 8 ingredients in a food processor or blender. Pulse 5 to 6 times or until finely chopped. Cover and chill 1 to 24 hours before serving. Garnish, if desired. Serve with tortilla chips. Store leftovers in refrigerator up to 7 days.

NOTE: We tested with DelMonte Diced Tomatoes with Zesty Mild Green Chilies.

RECIPE FROM ROXIE HARRIS
SCOTTSDALE, ARIZONA

Sausage, Bean, and Spinach Dip

party perfect

MAKES: about 6 cups
HANDS-ON TIME: 25 min.
TOTAL TIME: 45 min.

Serve with: *Corn chip scoops, red bell pepper strips, pretzel rods*

- 1 sweet onion, diced
- 1 red bell pepper, diced
- 1 (1-lb.) package hot ground pork sausage
- 2 garlic cloves, minced
- 1 tsp. chopped fresh thyme
- ½ cup dry white wine
- 1 (8-oz.) package cream cheese, softened
- 1 (6-oz.) package fresh baby spinach, coarsely chopped
- ¼ tsp. salt
- 1 (15-oz.) can pinto beans, drained and rinsed
- ½ cup (2 oz.) shredded Parmesan cheese

1. Preheat oven to 375°. Cook diced onion and next 2 ingredients in a large skillet over medium-high heat, stirring often, 8 to 10 minutes or until meat crumbles and is no longer pink. Drain. Stir in garlic and thyme; cook 1 minute. Stir in wine; cook 2 minutes or until liquid has almost completely evaporated.
2. Add cream cheese, and cook, stirring constantly, 2 minutes or until cream cheese is melted. Stir in spinach and salt, and cook, stirring constantly, 2 minutes or until spinach is wilted. Gently stir in beans. Pour mixture into a 2-qt. baking dish; sprinkle with Parmesan cheese.
3. Bake at 375° for 18 to 20 minutes or until golden brown. Serve with corn chip scoops, bell pepper strips, and pretzel rods.

RECIPE FROM BRENT GRAINGER
BIRMINGHAM, ALABAMA

Baked Tex-Mex Pimiento Cheese Dip

quick prep • party perfect

MAKES: about 4 cups
HANDS-ON TIME: 15 min.
TOTAL TIME: 35 min.

You can also bake the mixture in two (1-qt.) baking dishes. (Pictured on page 162)

Serve with: *French bread cubes*

- 1½ cups mayonnaise
- ½ (12-oz.) jar roasted red bell peppers, drained and chopped
- ¼ cup chopped green onions
- 1 jalapeño pepper, seeded and minced
- 1 (8-oz.) block extra-sharp Cheddar cheese, shredded
- 1 (8-oz.) block pepper Jack cheese, shredded
- Garnish: fresh cilantro leaves

1. Preheat oven to 350°. Stir together first 4 ingredients in a large bowl; stir in cheeses. Spoon mixture into a lightly greased 2-qt. baking dish.
2. Bake at 350° for 20 to 25 minutes or until dip is golden and bubbly. Garnish, if desired. Serve with French bread cubes.